HER MOTHER'S FAMILY

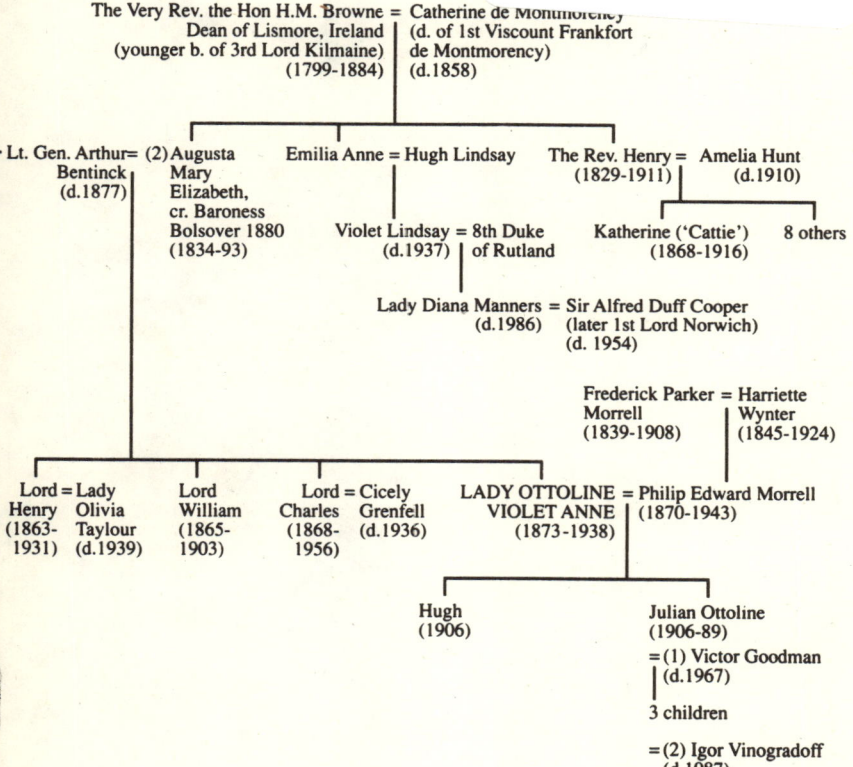

THE FOREBEARS OF LADY OTTOLINE MORRELL

It is indeed a damnably difficult thing to live fully, richly, gorgeously and yet courageously. To live on the grand scale.
OM, Journal, *March 1927*

HER FATHER'S FAMILY

Sir Charles Cavendish = (2) Katherine, Baroness Ogle
(3rd son of Sir William Cavendish and Elizabeth,
'Bess of Hardwick'; granted Welbeck 1597,
granted Bolsover 1608, both by his stepbrother,
Gilbert Earl of Shrewsbury)
(1553-1617)

William Cavendish = (1) Elizabeth Basset (d.1643)
1st Duke of Newcastle
(1593-1676) | (2) Margaret Lucas (d.1673)

Frances Pierrepont = Henry Cavendish
2nd Duke of Newcastle (1631-91)

John Holles, Earl of Clare = Lady Margaret Cavendish
(cr. Duke of Newcastle 1694) | (1661-1716)
(1662-1711)

Lady Henrietta Cavendish-Holles = Edward Harley, 2nd Earl of Oxford
(1694-1755) | (d. 1741)

Lady Margaret = William Bentinck,
Cavendish-Holles-Harley (d.1785) | 2nd Duke of Portland (1708-62)

William Henry Cavendish-Bentinck = Lady Dorothy
3rd Duke of Portland; Prime Minister 1783; 1807-9 | Cavendish
(1738-1809) (d.1794)

William = Henrietta | Lord William | Lord Charles = (1) Georgiana | Lady Charlotte = Charles
4th Duke of | Scott | Gov.-Gen. of | (1780-1826) | Seymour | (1793-1862) | Greville
Portland | (d.1844) | India | | (d.1813) | | (d.1865)
(1768-1854) | | (1774-1839) | = (2) Anne
| | | (Wellesley)
| | | Lady Abdy
| | | (d.1875)

Marquess | Lord George | Lady Lucy | 5 others
of Titchfield | (1802-48) | (d.1899)
(1798-1824) | | = 6th Lord Howard
| | de Walden

John Bentinck,
5th Duke of Portland
(1800-79)

Charles (Rev.) = Louise Burnaby | Elizabeth St Vincent (1) = Lt. Gen Arthur
(1817-65) | (later Mrs Harry | Hawkins Whitshed | Bentinck
| Warren Scott) | (d.1857) | (1818-77)
| (d.1918)

| | | William Arthur Bentinck = Winifred
| | | 6th Duke of | Dallas-Yorke
| | | Portland | (d.1954)
| | | (1857-1943)

Cecilia | Violet (Vava) | Hyacinth
(1862-1938) | (1864-1932) | (1864-1916)
= Earl of
Strathmore

Elizabeth (HM Queen | Lady Victoria | William Arthur Bentinck | Lord Francis
Elizabeth the Queen Mother) | (b. 1890) | 7th Duke of Portland | Morven
(b. 1900) | | (1893-1977) | (1900-50)
| | = Ivy Gordon-Lennox
| | | (d.1982)
| | 2 children

OTTOLINE MORRELL

Life on the Grand Scale

Introduction

Let me start with two images. One is of the ageing Queen Elizabeth I in a little room at Hampton Court, dancing the Spanish Panic by herself to the music of a whistle and tabor. The other is of Ottoline at sixty, doing a music-hall turn with old Walter Sickert for the benefit of their young host, William Plomer. Strikingly dressed as always, trailing orange chiffon and jangling with jewellery, she performed an impromptu cancan, raising and extending a stork-like leg while Sickert did a series of high kicks. And, while they danced, they sang:

> I throw my affection
> In your direction
> You're just my size and style!

D. H. Lawrence was the first to notice that there was something Elizabethan about Ottoline. The resemblance embodied in these cameos of two spirited elderly ladies lies in their splendid dauntlessness and love of life. That is the quality which I have tried to convey in this book and to indicate in its title. A life on the grand scale does not mean that Ottoline ever chose to live grandly, but that she was never afraid to live life to the full, to learn from her failures and to embrace every experience, however hurtful, as a new adventure. Her courage, I now think, was quite remarkable.

The commonly held opinion of Lady Ottoline Morrell (a name which the family pronounce to rhyme with Durrell) is that she was a bizarre and overbearing aristocrat who tried to get into intellectual society. She may be described as a Bloomsbury hostess and as the mistress of Augustus John and Bertrand Russell. Hovering above her head are the words 'pretentious', 'hypochondriac' and even, from readers of Michael Holroyd's biography of Lytton Strachey, 'daemonic'. Formidable is a word men often use to describe her: when questioned, they appear to mean that she had a strong character.

We can look at Ottoline from a different angle if we consider, for a start, some of the tributes paid to her just after her death. 'She gave me a complete mental reorientation' (Aldous Huxley). 'A most noble and generous soul . . . there is no one to be compared with her'

(Augustus John). 'A princess of the Renaissance risen to shame our drab age . . . the impact of such a personality on her circle was tremendous' (David Cecil). 'Her courage was of all the qualities the one I most admired, moral and physical courage' (Duncan Grant). 'It is very difficult to think of things *without* anyone who meant so much to me' (T. S. Eliot). '[She] was so truly a great soul, and the finest character I know' (Julian Huxley). 'No one can ever know the immeasurable good she did' (Henry Green). Trying to describe the impact Ottoline made on the drab world of pre-war Bloomsbury, Virginia Woolf compared her to Helen of Troy; on another occasion, she told Vanessa Bell that, visiting Ottoline in 1917, she had been 'so much overcome by her beauty that I really felt as if I'd suddenly got into the sea, and heard the mermaids fluting on their rocks'. Would any of these writers recognise the woman they so admired in the travesty we have been taught to accept? I doubt it.

The main responsibility for Ottoline's spectacularly bad press lies with the Bloomsbury Group. Its members did not, as this biography will show, play a large part in her life, but it is the Bloomsbury annals which have effectively controlled our image of her since her death in 1938. One major reason for this has been a paucity of source material. The vital information contained in Ottoline's journals, the original memoirs, her letters to her family, her mother's diaries, her husband's unfinished memoirs, her letters to Lytton Strachey, the revelation of her hitherto unknown young lover at Garsington: all this has only now been made available for the first time and it enables us to see Ottoline in a completely different light. Biographers cannot be blamed for having wanted to make the most of such a colourful figure, but even the most eminent of them have succumbed to the pleasure of selective quotation and unverified anecdotage. They have enlivened their books, but the price has been Ottoline's reputation. Of all the relevant biographies I have read, only Robert Skidelsky's study of Maynard Keynes and Claire Tomalin's of Katherine Mansfield have been perceptive enough to question Bloomsbury's image of Ottoline.

Bloomsbury thrived on correspondence. The things that were written about Ottoline were affected by a love of language and of gossip; sincerity was sacrificed to a lively turn of phrase. If we take the example of Virginia Woolf, her letters and diaries can easily be invoked to show that she despised Ottoline. The quotations are there to prove it: they have often been used to do so. She described her as a liar, a spiteful bitch, a mouldy rat-eaten ship, garish as a strumpet, slippery-souled, nefarious and abandoned. But the quotations are also there to prove that Virginia thought of Ottoline as heroic, fascinating, sweet, pure and wonderful. She even praised her – high commendation indeed from Bloomsbury – for 'her fundamental integrity'. It was not hard for Virginia or Lytton Strachey to distinguish between their inventive elaboration and the woman they knew. But the biographers and literary historians who have been forced to rely on the quicksilver brilliance of the Bloomsbury letter-writers for their portraits of Ottoline have not until now been in a position to separate the fantasy from the facts.

What was it about Ottoline that inspired her friends – and enemies – to write about her as they did? It always comes back to her appearance. 'Conventionality is deadness,' Ottoline once wrote, and nobody could have looked less conventional than this six-foot-tall woman with her blazing copper-coloured hair, unbelievably long legs and turquoise eyes that looked like ice-chips in sunlight when she was enraged. Instead of playing down her remarkable looks, she went to great trouble to exaggerate them with huge hats, high-heeled scarlet shoes and dresses which were copied from the Russian Ballet and portraits she had seen on her travels in Europe.

Like the splendid ancestress whom she seems to have taken for her model, the Restoration play-writing Duchess of Newcastle, Ottoline was never afraid of looking extraordinary. Like the duchess, she was damned for it. It is a curious fact that, while a man may look as strange as he likes and still be taken seriously, the woman who does so is ridiculed. Once she has broken the rule of how a woman should wish to be perceived, her presence breeds discomfort. Her refusal to conform makes her into a threat. The simplest way to dismiss her is by mockery, the most insidious form of diminishment.

It was not only for her appearance that Ottoline was mocked and parodied. Appendix III summarises the novels in which she was caricatured during her lifetime: the best known of them, *Women in Love*, is discussed in chapter 16. In it, Lawrence shows us how Ottoline appeared to a hostile observer; Lady Hermione Roddice is Ottoline as seen by his wife, Frieda. Hermione, with her passion for helping people, her singsong voice, her vague platitudes about the wonders of nature, her need to control the lives of her friends and her religious faith, is Ottoline seen in a distorting mirror. There are elements of truth in the portrait, but they are very faint. Fact and fiction have, nevertheless, become so thoroughly confused that it is not uncommon for people to talk about the occasion on which Ottoline threw a paperweight at somebody, as Hermione did in her most famous scene. Ottoline, who prided herself on her self-control, would never have done such a thing.

Ottoline's connection with Bloomsbury would barely fill a chapter; her relationship with Bertrand Russell, on the other hand, is rich enough to make a book by itself. Among famous love-affairs of the twentieth century, this was one of the most passionate, and of more importance than any other single relationship in Ottoline's life. My access to her private papers has enabled me to show that the published memoirs deliberately mislead the reader about her feelings for Russell, and to give a clearer picture of the vital role she played in his life. The two thousand and more letters to her are among the most winning and fascinating things Russell ever wrote; they represent the only time in his long life when, under Ottoline's powerful influence, he tried to engage both the intellectual and the emotional side of his nature. It was heroically attempted, and the letters on both sides blaze with an overwhelming intensity of feeling, on the sexual and the spiritual planes. 'We know each other's souls,' he told her, while she, four years before her death, still thought of him as the only person with whom she had absolute mental rapport. Sexually, they were incompatible – Ottoline sublimated her feelings for her lovers in a sense of mystic communion and Russell had an earthy urgency which she often found hard to deal with – but sex and religion are a famously heady brew. The importance of what they did have to give each other has never been fully recognised. Russell scholars have been understandably reluctant to stress the influence of a woman who is usually seen as a figure of fun. Ottoline's previous biographer, Sandra Jobson Darroch, had already completed her book when the Russell archive of Ottoline's letters was opened: she was given the unenviable task of trying to read all 1,500 letters, in manuscript, on the day they were released.

In December 1932, Russell told Ottoline that all of his later life had been affected by her influence; he described it in his memoirs as having been 'almost wholly beneficial'. That qualifying 'almost' is a reference to Ottoline's religious convictions. These are fully discussed within the book, but I still wonder if I have laid sufficient stress on Ottoline's undogmatic belief in the importance of a religious attitude. Russell quarrelled with her refusal to accept the non-existence of God; he admired and understood her need for a religious stance. Her creed of active benevolence influenced everything she did and thought. It was from her unswerving belief in the power of good that she drew her uncommon courage, and it was her faith in human nature which made her so attractive to creative personalities. She was, as she once ruefully remarked, a magnet for egotists.

There are many other instances where the definitive story can now be presented. Rather than interrupt the narrative with portentous announcements, I will cite some of the most striking examples here.

Ottoline was always assumed to be a very rich woman. We know

INTRODUCTION

now that her late inheritance was much smaller than had been anticipated; from 1912 onwards, she and Philip Morrell had a hard struggle to keep up appearances. She was said to be highly promiscuous, but, while reckless in the bestowing of her affection, she preferred her love-affairs to be platonic; her only happy sexual relationship – it took place in the 1920s and may have contributed to Lawrence's presentation of Lady Chatterley – ended with a horrible tragedy after two years. Philip has been cast in the role of the tolerant, slightly dull husband. Ottoline did impose her friends on him and push him into a political career to which he was not well-suited, but there was another side to the story. It is now possible for the first time to discuss his many affairs, his absolute dependence on his wife's discretion and support, and his precarious mental state. (It was Ottoline's determination, as she told Russell, to rescue Philip 'for all reasons' which saved him from being institutionalised in 1917.) We are told that she was mean, that she never forgave the friends who parodied her in fiction, and that she had the personality of a tyrant. The new material shows her to have been almost obsessively generous, naïvely assuming that friendship could be guaranteed by gifts. There was only one case (Walter Turner's novella, *The Aesthetes*) in which a parody of Ottoline resulted in a lasting estrangement. It is impossible to find any hard evidence for her characterisation as a tyrant. Certainly, Ottoline had a steely will which at times caused even Russell to cower, but I find it rather admirable that she, whose greatest dread was that her friends would turn against her, was never afraid of being bluntly critical when she felt it would be of value to them. 'I hate the safe and coward way,' she wrote, and, on another occasion: 'Self-satisfaction is death.' There is nothing sadder to my mind than that this brave honesty should have become so degraded by posterity that it can only be seen as arrogance.

Before turning again to the subject of source material, let me touch on the three aspects of Ottoline's life which are most often the cause of misunderstanding.

The first is health. I have had no better luck than Ottoline's many doctors in identifying her intermittent illness under any one heading: Appendix I shows three of the scores of diagnoses which were made. Her mother, Lady Bolsover, who died at the age of fifty-nine, was a semi-invalid for the last ten years of her life. Her diaries show that she, like Ottoline, suffered from unusually acute migraine headaches, chronic fatigue, and what the doctors described as an intensely nervous temperament. Ottoline's ill-health began in her late teens; from then until her death, she was hardly ever free of pain. It seemed better to spare the reader a faithful narrative of her sufferings, which were extreme; it is easier to state here that this was the everyday battle of her adult life. Her journals show that she took considerable pride in hiding her illness from her friends. It was only when she almost died of a form of bone cancer in 1928 that they were shocked into realising what she had endured.

The second responds to a question which is frequently posed with a sceptical look: what was it, exactly, that Ottoline did? The most important thing she did was to influence people, to encourage them to question their motives and ideals and to teach them, above all, to believe in their ability. What she did in a more conventional sense was to become an active founder-member of the Contemporary Art Society; to help select the paintings which Roger Fry brought to England for the first Post-Impressionist exhibition in 1910; and to provide her creative contemporaries with what they wanted, the equivalent of a French eighteenth-century salon. She enabled the young writers of the twenties and thirties to meet their literary heroes and heroines in an informal way and to learn from them. She raised funds for poets; she sheltered and defended the pacifists; she used her remarkable sense of colour ('you beat us all at colour', the artist Henry Lamb told her) to create rooms of as unconventional a beauty as her own. At Garsington, she designed one of the most perfect Italianate gardens in England. Above all, I think, she taught people by her own example that nothing new can come about unless rules are broken, and that cautious success is worth less than adventurous failure.

The third question is the most difficult to answer: why, if Ottoline was such a splendid woman, did she provoke so much hostility? It is a familiar truth that friendship cannot be bought: Ottoline, who had been unusually friendless in her early life, had a craving for affection which was as strong as a drug. Her need for it drove her to lavish gifts and hospitality on those she loved in such a way as to put them uncomfortably in her debt. Their protests went unheeded; what she wanted in return was emotional reassurance. But it is notoriously harder to receive than to give, and all that Ottoline conveyed by her largesse was a false impression of her wealth and a faint, off-putting scent of desperation. Lytton Strachey, to take one example, was ready to adore her when she wrote him witty letters to ask if her padre was ready to hear confession since 'sins are heaped high on my soul', or to suggest that they ought to give Henry Lamb as a present to Diaghilev so that Nijinsky would be left free for Lytton. Ottoline as a gossip and fellow conspirator was one of Lytton's favourite women, but he hated it when she begged for friendship, as Ottoline's letters often indirectly – and sometimes directly – did. It was the very sense of her need which provoked resentment in the people she most wanted to love her.

INTRODUCTION

I continue to wonder how different the attitude to Ottoline might have been if she had allowed her friends to know more of the truth about her life. 'I have a horror of opening myself to the world,' she wrote; the original version of her memoirs, only seen by a select group of friends, told just enough to make them unpublishable, and not enough to show her – or her husband – in a new light. The secrets of her marriage remained hidden.

Ottoline did not want the memoirs to be printed during her lifetime. The first person Philip Morrell approached after her death was G. E. Moore's brother, Thomas, who had always expressed a warm admiration for Ottoline's writings; when he declined the job of editor, Philip turned to one of Ottoline's literary executors, Robert Gathorne-Hardy.* After expressing strong reservations about the wisdom of publishing the less discreet parts of the memoirs, Gathorne-Hardy agreed to take on the job, principally because he had been asked to act as sole editor by Ottoline herself in 1933. In 1946, he was at work on two typescripts, one corrected by Ottoline, the other 'mucked about by Philip', who had attempted to impose his own slightly leaden style on Ottoline's prose. During the editing period, Ottoline's original was mislaid and Gathorne-Hardy was left to rely on Philip's version.

The flawed results were eventually published in two volumes: *The Early Memoirs of Ottoline Morrell 1873–1915* in 1963 and *Ottoline at Garsington 1915–18* in 1974. They contain much of Philip's stylistic revision, and many glaring omissions, among them Ottoline's difficult relationship with her daughter, Philip Morrell's infidelities and mental problems, the nature of Ottoline's relationship with Henry Lamb and Augustus John, and no clear chronological account of her affair with Russell. Chunks of information were misplaced and misdated; extracts from the journals were misquoted. A valiant attempt to compress all references to Bertrand Russell into an appendix to the second volume also resulted in a number of errors. I have silently corrected these in all my quotations from the memoirs, substituting the original passages from Ottoline's own typescript. But, while this is a step in the right direction, what is still badly needed is a new edition of the memoirs, free of Philip's 'improvements' to Ottoline's fresh originality.

A biographer must try to remain objective and I have done my best to present the evidence for and against Ottoline without becoming too much of a partisan. It was, however, impossible to keep my admiration for her entirely out of this book.

* The other literary executors were Hope Mirrlees and Francis Hackett.

PART ONE

A Victorian Life

'*All that I remember is a feeling of utter desolation, shyness and loneliness, for I felt myself quite apart from the smart world, and conscious of being out of it ... The lovely scent of gardenias and stephanotis and white lilies is the only happy memory I have left.*'

OM, *The Early Memoirs of Ottoline Morrell 1873–1915*

I

A PROTECTED GIRLHOOD
1873–92

'Is there any intimacy so full and so warm and so abandoned as those early ones before experience has taught one the hundred subtle dangers of telling too much?'

OM, *Early Memoirs*

If an unborn child can be affected by its mother's state of mind, then Ottoline's first lesson was to embrace pain with resignation. Her beautiful Irish mother was thirty-nine when, towards the end of her fourth and most difficult pregnancy, she wrote to warn her eldest son that the doctors did not expect her to survive it. It would, she told him, be God's will if she died.

She survived. The child was born on 16 June 1873, and Augusta Bentinck was soon well enough to start searching through the names in her soldier-husband's distinguished family for one which would do sufficient honour to their only, much-longed-for daughter. It was among Arthur Bentinck's tribe of distant Dutch relations that she found one or two called Ottoline. She liked the name. It might, she thought, be a graceful tribute of the kind to catch the fancy of the reclusive Fifth Duke of Portland whose title her husband, his second cousin, was due to inherit one day along with his vast estates. The duke had never shown any interest in his heir, but Augusta came from a family of determined women and she did not accept defeat easily. On 7 July 1873, she wrote to suggest that he might want to stand as godfather to their little girl. 'I wish to call her Ottoline, after some of her Bentinck ancestors, if you approve of the name,' she added, 'but if not she shall have any other name that you wish.'[1] The duke, while commending the choice of name, refused the invitation:

Ottoline Violet Anne Cavendish Bentinck's London christening was forced to take place without him.*

Ottoline was the only daughter of her father's second marriage. His first wife, Elizabeth St Vincent Hawkins-Whitshed, had died in childbirth only ten months after their wedding. Five years later, in 1862, Lieutenant-General Bentinck married again. Perhaps he was attracted to names with a good roll to them, for Augusta Browne's mother had been a Miss Catherine de Montmorency; her father, the saintly Dean of Lismore, was a son of Lord Kilmaine. Augusta, who was twenty-eight at the time of her marriage, had inherited her mother's beauty and strong character and her father's religious zeal. Ottoline, who was brought up to take great pride in her Irish blood, was told when she was still a small child that the good priests of Ireland punished naughty girls by flaying their naked arms with whips. It was, in her mother's view, important to instil the idea of religious obedience at an early age. Stern in her piety, Augusta was not unworldly. She loved singing and pretty clothes; she looked forward to the time when they would exchange their quiet life in a village on the borders of Hampshire and Berkshire for the splendour of Welbeck Abbey, the Duke of Portland's Nottinghamshire home; she delighted in showing off her pretty little daughter. As soon as Ottoline could walk, she was dressed in fantastically elaborate clothes.

Clothes were a lifelong passion for Ottoline. Her first clear memory was of bursting into tears at the age of three because her brothers had said that she looked fat in her new white party dress. When she was in her fifties, a German doctor told her that all her emotional problems stemmed from her relationship with the four boys who had dominated her early life. She noted that he was probably right.

Ottoline was the Bentincks' youngest child by five years. Henry was born in 1863, William (Bill) in 1865, and Charles (Charlie) in 1868. Arthur, her half-brother, was a glamorous stranger, seventeen years older than herself; to the little girl, he seemed like a god. Arthur had been with their father in Dublin; he had been to balls and boar hunts, to chateaux in France and to the moated castles of their Bentinck cousins in Holland. She longed for him to notice and admire her, but it was hard to know how to make an impression on such a grand person. She was in awe, although to a lesser degree, of Henry and Bill; for company, she turned to Charlie, tall, olive-skinned and

---

* Ottoline's great-grandfather, the Third Duke of Portland, added the name of Cavendish to his own surname of Bentinck, by Royal Licence, in 1801. The prefix was dropped by his children.

supercilious. But Charlie was a reluctant playmate who resented being obliged to stay in the nursery and amuse a babyish girl when he could have been playing with his brothers. He took it out on her in small ways which were not forgotten. When Ottoline showed him her first garden, Charlie laughed and told her not to be so stupid: she had planted it with weeds. Whatever she did, he said, she need not worry, it was sure to fail.

The person who loomed largest in Ottoline's early memories was her father, a big gentle man with smiling blue-grey eyes and a melodious voice more suited to the reciting of poetry than to giving orders. His daughter was his most lovingly-indulged child. On visits to London, she was allowed to sit on his knee when he drove his four-in-hand carriage in Hyde Park. In the country, when the family gathered in the big drawing-room or in the conservatory leading out to the garden, Ottoline only had to scramble on to his lap to keep him all to herself. She was four years old when he came back from London with a special present for her, a pair of black dogskin gloves, slippery as silk. She kept them with her until her death. Ottoline spent twenty years searching for a man to replace her father.

All of the children loved East Court, a red-brick Georgian manor house which the Bentincks rented from the local Walter family, who owned *The Times*. Modernised in the mid-nineteenth century, East Court had a billiard-room, stained-glass representations of Tudor monarchs, a heated conservatory and a white stucco front partly hidden behind a giant wisteria. Its views were magnificent. Some windows looked towards the nearby Norman church over a sea of firs and some down the hill through a frame of cedar branches, while others looked across the garden lawn to a landscape of undulating Berkshire meadowland.

Life was quiet. The childhood treats that Ottoline remembered were being taken to see a parade at nearby Aldershot and being driven through the woods with Henry and Bill trotting beside the carriage on their ponies. Although they were on friendly terms with their landlords the Walters, the Bentincks, as newcomers, were not invited to Bramshill, the magnificent Jacobean home of the Cope family, although it was only three miles away. Its owner was not known for his hospitality and, while Ottoline described Bramshill as the first beautiful house that she saw, she also remembered how Sir William had come out to chase them away when they tried to picnic in the park, and how his butler had consoled her with the present of a pet canary.

Dominating Ottoline's memories of East Court was the figure of

Charles Kingsley. 'I used to admire him so much and loved his books,' she wrote in later life, 'and my mother was so fond of him.' (22 July 1935) Kingsley had been on holiday in Scotland when he first met Ottoline's parents; it was he and his wife, Fanny Grenfell, who persuaded them to settle at East Court, less than two miles from Kingsley's own parish at Eversley. Visits between Eversley Rectory and East Court took place every week and the Canon's blend of candour, kindness and sportsmanship endeared him to the young Bentincks as much as to their parents.

Charles Kingsley was largely responsible for the passion for helping people which Ottoline formed as a young girl and which she never lost. Although she was only two when he died, his influence made itself powerfully felt. Ottoline's mother had read all Kingsley's works. She talked with him about his beliefs and she watched him working night and day among his sick parishioners in the bitter winter before his death in 1875. She was unaware of his passionate sexual nature, on which Kingsley's recent biographers have concentrated. What she saw and admired was a man who practised what he preached.

Kingsley's brand of Christian socialism had considerable appeal for a woman of philanthropic inclinations. The landowning class were born to rule, in his view, but they should learn to do so with kindness and benevolence. A Dickens or a Mrs Gaskell could be relied on to make a villain of a lord: Kingsley was concerned only that the lord should not exploit his privileged position. It was an attitude which the Bentincks of East Court warmly endorsed.

Kingsley's famous children's story, *The Water Babies*, taught Ottoline the simple lesson of good behaviour through the example of the witch-fairy, Mrs Doasyouwouldbedoneby and Mrs Bedonebyasyoudid. In her first form, the fairy is a generous benefactor and guardian; in her second, she punishes those who behave selfishly. Grimes, the wicked master who is wedged into a chimney in an arctic wasteland as a punishment for his cruelty, is only released when he acknowledges his guilt; Tom, the little sweep, can only become happy when he learns to respect the fairy's two forms. Kingsley's message to children was to forgive their enemies, as Tom forgives Mr Grimes, and to seek happiness through acts of kindness. This pattern of active benevolence had been initiated in the nursery at East Court, and Ottoline, a highly impressionable child, absorbed the book's message years before she discovered the writings of Thomas à Kempis, her acknowledged source of inspiration. *The Water Babies* had the added attraction of being set against a familiar background: Tom's adventures take place in the glistening water meadows a few miles from East Court and Ottoline had no difficulty in identifying the wild beauty of Cordery's Moor, or the sleepy backwaters into which Tom slips to join the river children.

A PROTECTED GIRLHOOD

General Bentinck's health was already failing when Ottoline was born. In the summer of 1877, he went to London with Augusta and his oldest son, Arthur, to consult a heart specialist. The diagnosis was reassuring, but he complained of feeling dizzy when they returned to their hotel and he died that evening. The following day, the Duke of Portland received the news in a letter, written in a shaky hand, from Arthur who was only twenty and now his heir. He added, rather touchingly, that he thought the duke would like to know that he had just been accepted by his father's regiment (First Battalion, Coldstream Guards).[2]

Ottoline had been left behind at East Court with Nanny Powell and Charlie.

> When the news came to us we stood side by side at the nursery window and looked out down to the stable yard, feeling sad and solemn. 'Papa is dead. That means he will never come back again,' and suddenly for the first time I became aware of my own existence – realising perhaps that I should also one day die and go out into the unknown.[3]

The sudden death of General Bentinck brought about a shift in family relationships. There had been every reason to suppose that he would outlive the Fifth Duke, who was twenty years his senior. Now, by his premature death, he left his widow and children entirely dependent on Arthur. But there was no cause for alarm. The young man was devoted to his stepmother and to his siblings: his own sincere hope was only that the Fifth Duke would spare him the troubles of inheritance for as long as possible.

For Ottoline, her father's death marked the beginning of her mother's reliance on her. 'Small as I was, I began even then to be her constant companion . . . At night, I always slept in her room, my hard little bed at the side of hers.'[4] A photograph of her at this time, aged four, clasping a book and standing beside a wooden toy wheelbarrow, shows a worried expression which suggests that she was already conscious of her mother's need and ill-health. Diabetes had not been identified as a disease in the 1870s and Mrs Bentinck's fainting fits, headaches and days of crippling fatigue were even more disturbing because of the lack of any convincing explanation of their cause.

Augusta had no widow's army pension, but the Fifth Duke, who had supplemented his cousin's income with a modest allowance, provided enough money for her to rent a London home in Grosvenor Crescent: East Court was to be abandoned as soon as the Walters could find new tenants. In 1878, when Arthur came of age, the duke increased the allowance and subsidised the purchase of a much larger house at 13 Grosvenor Place. Neither Arthur nor his stepmother were surprised that these arrangements were made through the family lawyers rather than by direct communication. Indeed, they had given up hope of any friendly contact. In London, they could stare up at the high screens of glass and wrought iron which defended the duke's privacy at Harcourt House in Cavendish Square. A stroll down Oxford Street led them to his second home at 13 Hyde Park Gardens, a warehouse of porcelain, books and papers – the duke spent over a thousand pounds a year on newspapers and journals which were then filed away – with its queer glass structure projecting from the roof. (This, fondly supposed by the public to be a mausoleum, had recently been inspected by suspicious officials and was revealed to be nothing more sinister than an observatory.) They could look at the duke's London homes, and they could wonder what they would find at Welbeck, about which every kind of strange story was circulated, even that their cousin practised satanic rites in an underground church. Speculation was all that was possible.

The duke's health began to weaken in July 1879 and, on 5 December, he died at Harcourt House. Arthur, sighing over the loss of the month's hunting he had happily anticipated, said goodbye to his friends in the regiment and returned to London, where Augusta was anxiously waiting to discuss the future. The family marked their change of fortune by spending two nights in suites at Claridge's, where the young duke fortified himself with brandy and soda while his stepmother drowned her apprehension in tea.* Grapes and peaches, wrapped in pink tissue, were delivered from the Welbeck hothouses. Mr Horsman Bailey, their lawyer, arrived with documents and formidable lists of estate employees and house servants, together with details of the shipyard, colliery, railway, shooting estates and houses which comprised the inheritance. It was a magnificent legacy; with it, the twenty-two-year-old duke became the most eligible young bachelor in England.

While Arthur and Augusta pored over the documents, young Nanny Powell ('Powie') took Charlie and Ottoline off to London's best toy shop with orders to buy whatever they liked. Ottoline chose a doll in a blue satin dress, but neither this nor the luxuries of the hotel gave her much pleasure. The memory of her father's death was still sharp and it was distressing to be humbly addressed as Lady Ottoline and to hear Arthur called His Grace while their mother remained plain Mrs Bentinck, as if she had no part in their new life. Arthur was equally conscious of the difficulty of his stepmother's position among this sudden flurry of titles. A delicately worded letter to the Prime Minister was despatched and cordially received by Dis-

---

* The hotel only offered suites in those days.

raeli, whose own promotion to landowning rank had been facilitated by a loan from two of the Fifth Duke's brothers.* A reminder was dropped to the Queen, Arthur was invited to Hughenden Manor to renew the link with Lord Beaconsfield[5] and Augusta was created Baroness Bolsover for the castle of that name which formed part of the Portland inheritance.†

They had begun to dread the move to Welbeck. A hint of what was in store came from the Clerk of the Works who, having already told them not to think of driving a carriage between the piles of builder's rubble which littered the park roads, tried to comfort the Bentincks with the news that a plank bridge was being laid to allow them to cross the entrance hall. There was not, he added, so much as a bed to offer them: the main rooms were unfurnished. Their worries increased when Charlie collapsed with peritonitis, but Lady Bolsover decided that there was nothing to be gained by postponement. Welbeck, in however ruinous a state, was now their home. The furniture from their London house was sent on ahead and, shortly before Christmas, they set off from King's Cross Station on the long journey to the north end of Nottinghamshire, where it meets the Yorkshire border.

News had travelled ahead of them. As they climbed down at Worksop station, a crowd of people gathered round to peer at the family on whose goodwill they were now dependent. A glimpse of a brave and beautiful dark-haired woman, a pink young man with sleepy heavy-lidded eyes, two tall schoolboys, a bright-haired girl and, being helped out by the porters and Nurse Powell, an invalid cocooned in rugs against the driving wind – that was all they could discern by lamplight before the family climbed into the two waiting carriages and set off on the last stage of their journey.

Forewarned, the travellers braced themselves for two jolting miles along dark avenues of oaks and past the piles of bricks and debris marking the final stages of the gigantic quarrying schemes which had earned their predecessor the nickname of 'the burrowing duke'. When they arrived at last, they were ushered in and greeted by a row of head employees before being escorted to the few small rooms in the Oxford Wing which had been made habitable. There, the family fell into exhausted sleep.

---

* The Fifth Duke of Portland was predeceased both by his older brother William, Marquess of Titchfield, who died in 1824, unmarried, and by his younger brother, Lord George Bentinck, who died, also unmarried, in 1848.

† Bolsover, long uninhabited when Ottoline and her family arrived at Welbeck, was a twelfth-century keep allegedly built by the third Peverel of the Peak. Less than half an hour's riding distance from Welbeck, it came into the estate when Bess of Hardwick's stepson and son-in-law, Gilbert Earl of Shrewsbury, transferred it to his adored half-brother, Charles Cavendish, Bess's younger son.

Welbeck Abbey was vast, intimidating and, as far as the young duke could see, beyond redemption. Looking from the huge empty rooms on to a devastated garden from which all flowers had been banished and glimpsing in the distance the looming walls of vegetable gardens, each the size of a football ground, Arthur lost his courage. He loved the idea of his new shooting and stalking estates in Northumberland and Scotland, but his instinct now was to order the house to be closed up and to abandon it. Augusta urged him to think again. A born organiser, she offered to shoulder the burden of restoration. Everything was there, stacked away by an owner indifferent rather than careless. She would sort through the paintings, the furniture and tapestries. All she asked in return was to be allowed to create a household chapel and a library and to be given a room of her own to furnish as she pleased. Arthur thankfully agreed.

Ottoline, eager to explore her new home, was up early on the first morning. Charlie was still too weak to leave his bed, but Bill was ready to join her. The first features to catch Ottoline's attention were the double letter-boxes in their own rooms. These had been the late duke's chief means of communication. His letters of instruction were passed out and a bell rung to summon a servant whose response was then passed in by the other box. It was an ideal arrangement for a man who did not relish sociability. The main bedrooms on the second floor – those on the first had been demolished to heighten the ceilings of the state rooms – were empty. Each was painted a light salmon-pink and each had a lavatory sitting exposed to public view in the corner. A narrow staircase brought the explorers down into the Gothic Hall where the furniture was stacked against the walls under a sugar-icing ceiling of elaborate basketwork. Here, as everywhere else at Welbeck, there was a peculiar blend of neglect and care. Nothing was dusty. The floors were polished and the empty bookcases shone, but it was apparent that the room had been used only as a storehouse.

Stranger sights lay ahead. Steps from the Gothic Hall led them down into a maze of underground tunnels and up, through a trapdoor, into a room larger than any they had yet seen. It was flanked by walls of mirrors and hung with rows of chandeliers from a ceiling painted to imitate a brilliant sunset. At the far end, carefully stacked against trestles, were Welbeck's finest pictures. This room, 180 foot long and 50 foot in height, later converted by Lady Bolsover into a library and chapel, had been the riding school of that famous equestrian, the First Duke of Newcastle.

Descending through the trapdoor, the children walked along another tunnel, past three large rooms lying parallel, underground, with the riding school, and into the gigantic room which the Fifth Duke had intended should become the house chapel. It was 160 foot long and 63 foot wide, and lit by twenty-seven large octagonal skylights set into the ceiling at ground level. To Bill's eyes, it was the perfect place for bicycle races. Ottoline envisaged the ballroom it later became, after it served as a picture gallery. What she could not understand was why their strange relation should have wanted to build such rooms underground. (One possible explanation for the Fifth Duke's subterranean creations, although it did not satisfy Ottoline, was that he was anxious to preserve Welbeck's exterior appearance.)

It took more than a day to explore what a contemporary guide-book respectfully described as 'The Wonders of Welbeck'. An unfinished room beyond the underground chapel had been planned as a residence for a hundred local bachelors – this was later converted into a sunken garden – while above-ground the new riding school, roofed in glass and iron like the Crystal Palace, was the second largest in the world. Beyond it, the late duke had built a mile-long roofed tunnel for exercising his horses in bad weather. Yet another tunnel, wide enough for two carriages to pass each other, ran under the lake to the edge of the park; another had been constructed simply for the use of the duke's workmen, as a way of ensuring his privacy.

Perhaps if Ottoline had had brothers and sisters nearer her own age, she might have relished the possibilities offered for games by this extraordinary underground kingdom. She was an isolated child, and the duke's strange buildings served only to frighten her. Nothing that the old servants could tell her about their former employer shook her from the view that he had been as cold and grim as the home which she never learned to love.

Ottoline did have one valuable lesson to learn from the Fifth Duke, although it was an indirect one: that unconventional behaviour in the aristocracy invariably attracts malicious speculation, and that the only way to survive gossip with dignity is to ignore it. She learned it in the 1890s when the Druce–Portland case thrust her family into a glare of publicity which lasted for almost a decade. The case, launched by the Australian relations of a Baker Street shopkeeper, Thomas Druce, sought to prove that Druce and the late duke had been one and the same man and that the Druces were entitled to the dukedom. A secret liaison, a brother's murder, a funeral for a man who had not died, the mysterious burial of an empty coffin weighted with lead – these were the details with which the Druce family hit the headlines. The Fifth Duke was reconstructed in the guise of a monster of duplicity who had plotted to deprive his second family of their legacy. The gutter press took up the tale with enthusiasm, and heart-rending pictures of Welbeck and the Bentincks appeared alongside the mud hut in which the Druces were imagined to have lived in wretched exile. It was not until 1907 that the coffin of the supposedly nonexistent Thomas Druce was opened and found to contain him, bringing a halcyon period of speculative gossip to an end. Discretion would never be Ottoline's strong point, but the Druce case made her aware that the best response to gossip was silence. Only her closest friends ever knew how hurt she was by the unkind slanders of which she, too, became the victim in later life.

Ottoline was to spend much of her adult life trying to make up for her poor schooling, a good education not being high on the list of priorities for the sisters of dukes in the late nineteenth century. Ottoline's governess, 'a really holy woman' called Miss Craig with whom her pupil kept in touch for the rest of her life, was picked by Lady Bolsover more for the soundness of her religious convictions than for anything so showy as erudition. Ottoline learned less in the schoolroom than she did when she and her mother sat sorting through the treasures of Welbeck's history. These were the lessons which she remembered, romantic journeys into the past for which the props were real. A jewelled dagger which had belonged to Henry VIII turned up in a cabinet drawer; in another, they found the pearl earring which Charles I had worn for his execution, together with a rosary of carved cherry and plum stones which had belonged to his queen. Ottoline's own favourite discoveries were a picture of Mary Queen of Scots in an elegant gold cap and another of little Arabella Stuart who had once been shut up as a prisoner at Hardwick, a few miles away from their own castle of Bolsover.

Rebuilt in the finest spirit of Elizabethan fantasy, by Welbeck's second owner, Sir Charles Cavendish, and his son the Duke of Newcastle, the Derbyshire castle of Bolsover was captivating to Ottoline in a way that Welbeck could never be and close enough for many visits. Its rooms were small and easy for a child to feel at home in. A few were gaily painted with mythical and divine figures: the stone walls of one were hidden by a particularly beautiful sea-green panelling edged in gold which Ottoline later copied for one of the rooms at Garsington. The rooms at the top of the castle commanded a magnificent view, while fruit trees in the grass courts behind the ramparts provided cool resting-places for Lady Bolsover to sit and tell her daughter the stories of the past she always wanted to hear.

No place in Ottoline's life ever meant so much to her as Bolsover. When Bertrand Russell took her back to see the castle in 1915 on the eve of her move to Garsington, he was prompted by a desire to see her in the setting she had always said she loved best. Describing the occasion in her memoirs, Ottoline wrote of the terror she had felt at confronting what might have been only the romantic idealisation of a child, and of the relief of finding that nothing had changed when 'I could see my darling Castle face to face . . . High, tall, fair and proud it stood . . .'[6] Her identification with its proud isolation was strong.

Ottoline's passion for Bolsover was closely linked to her enduring interest in the woman who had once lived there, the pretty and eccentric wife of the First Duke of Newcastle, the great equestrian who had been ennobled by Charles II. Ottoline's mother had told her all she knew about Margaret Lucas, the playwright, poet and would-be philosopher whose appearance had fascinated the Restoration court. Lady Bolsover was enchanted by her. Ottoline seems to have used her as a model for her own appearance. It was she who persuaded Virginia Woolf to include a portrait of the duchess in *The Common Reader* (but Virginia seems also to have been describing Ottoline when she wrote of Margaret Lucas's impetuous generosity, her love of extraordinary clothes, her thirst for ideas and her longing to help her friends).

The points of similarity between Ottoline and her distant ancestress are many and striking, but it is in their penchant for unconventional clothes that the resemblance becomes most marked. Ottoline, as is well known, dressed in an eccentric style, achieving an appearance which was romantic or grotesque, depending on the observer's current state of affection for her. 'I have had a passion for clothes,' Ottoline admitted in her diary. And here is the duchess, defending her right to wear unusual clothes in a book which Ottoline often read as a young girl at Welbeck:

I took great delight in attiring, fine dress and fashions, especially such fashions as I did invent myself, not taking that pleasure in such fashions as were invented by others: also I did dislike that any should follow my fashion, for I always took great delight in a singularity, even in accoutrements.[7]

Ottoline resembled Margaret Lucas in one other respect: she suffered from crippling shyness. Like her ancestress, she learned to make a clear division between that private self, nervous, timid and unworldly, and the picture which was created for view. Details were irrelevant: the duchess's clothes were often remarked to be a little soiled and threadbare; it was with supreme detachment that Ottoline glided towards a visitor to Garsington in a flowing skirt of net, between the transparent layers of which flies swarmed as if on a larder door. The visitor was horrified: Ottoline, if she noticed the flies at all, ignored them.

By the summer of 1881, Welbeck was ready to receive visitors and, since Arthur was unmarried, Lady Bolsover was the hostess of the house parties which now became a way of life. Ottoline, a plump-cheeked child dressed like a little princess, peeped around the curtained doorways and lurked bashfully on the fringes of the conversations, ready to be pushed into a chair for a quick pencil sketch by her mother's favourite and most beautiful niece, Violet Lindsay,* or to drop a curtsey to the Prince of Wales and ask him, after a stage-prompt from her governess, for a contribution to her children's hospital fund. The prince obliged with a ten-shilling piece and Ottoline was discreetly removed while the Gothic Hall was set up with tables for whist or planchette, the game of spirit-summoning which was then much in favour with the prince's friends. Lying in bed, Ottoline could hear the lilt of a piano and a lady – it could have been her mother – singing Italian love-songs.

A new era had begun and there was no place in it for Ottoline. Even when the young duke was away, the house was full of new friends of her mother's. Augusta had come into her own. Her stepson could not do enough to thank her for the effort she had put into making Welbeck beautiful. Her room was hung with some of the finest paintings in the collection and the family jewels were hers for the wearing. Young Lady Galway, a neighbour who had been charmed by the modest woman who brought 'her dear little girl' to lunch, was flabbergasted at their next encounter. 'Lady Bolsover was there,' she wrote, 'ablaze with diamonds.'[8]

It was, in Ottoline's recollection, an unhappy time during which she took refuge in a world of private fantasy. She made a secret corner in the schoolroom and furnished it with childish treasures. Twice a week, she looked forward to being taught to ride and drive a little carriage, either by her mother or by Ellis, the young coachman who had come with them from East Court. Sometimes she went to the new chapel to watch her mother rehearsing the choir, or into the park to see the racehorses being exercised. Twice, when her mother visited Paris, Ottoline and her governess went, too, and there were evenings at the theatre and days at Versailles. But for the most part, her memory was of being alone, not because she craved solitude, but because she had no choice. Sitting in her favourite room in the Oxford Wing, she scratched her name on the window-pane and stared at the clock.

'I have suffered very much from not having made friends in my youth,' Ottoline later wrote in the 'Thought-Book' with which she intended to equip her daughter for life. 'It is much more difficult later.' Someone – it might have been the kind-hearted Miss Craig –

---

* Later the Duchess of Rutland and mother of Lady Diana Cooper.

must have drawn Lady Bolsover's attention to the lonely life her daughter was leading, for an arrangement was made whereby Ottoline's Irish cousin Cattie (Katherine) Browne, a rector's daughter, should come and spend a few months at Welbeck before being chaperoned through her London season by Lady Bolsover. Initially alarmed by the prospect of trying to play with a girl five years older than herself, Ottoline was relieved to find that Cattie, who had also led a secluded life, was still delighted to play at being a child. Together, they explored the attics and dressed up in old coronation robes which they found hidden in a chest. Swathed in red velvet and ermine, Ottoline sat at her cousin's feet, listening to stories of growing up in Ireland in a house full of ghosts. When Cattie grew tired of talk, Ottoline practised her carriage-driving skills by taking them on tours of Sherwood Forest in her own miniature phaeton. Subdued though the colours were in which she was to paint her later memories of her Welbeck childhood, she evidently spent some happy months there in the company of her new friend.

Lady Bolsover kept her promise to give her niece a London season and Ottoline went with them. Too young to see how Cattie fared at her balls, she was enrolled in that most exquisite of purgatories for shy children, the dancing class. Dismally aware that she was expected to start making friends of her own age, she endured her lessons in a state of miserable self-consciousness. The pleasure of wearing unconventional clothes came later; at the age of eleven, she was mortified by her mother's insistence on dressing her in a way that made her look different from the rest. Wrongly or rightly, she sensed that the other girls were laughing and making fun of her for looking odd, but there were compensations. She was introduced to Oscar Wilde. She saw Henry Irving in *The Corsican Brothers* and Sarah Bernhardt in *Phèdre*. If the dancing classes were hell, this was a glimpse into heaven. She was happy, too, when her half-brother sent word that she was to put on her riding-habit and come for a midday amble in Rotten Row. Riding always gave her pleasure and she liked it when she saw people looking admiringly at her and asking Arthur questions about her. Clearly, they made a handsome couple.

Lady Bolsover's reign at Welbeck had lasted for almost a decade when her stepson broke the news that he had chosen a wife. The fact that he had conducted the courtship in secrecy indicates the nervousness he felt about her reaction. Lady Bolsover was astonished to discover that her own beloved niece Violet had been busily playing Cupid and arranging house parties at which the young couple could meet. When she heard that the proposal had been accepted at Belvoir

Castle, Violet's home since her marriage to the Duke of Rutland's son, Lady Bolsover told Ottoline that she never wished to see her niece again. Nor did she.

Winifred Dallas-Yorke made her first visit to Welbeck as the duke's fiancée, in March 1889. She was tall, slender, dark and very beautiful; her social skills were impeccable; she was full of enthusiasm for everything and everybody. Her zest for good works appeared to be boundless; her health was magnificent. Nobody could doubt that the duke adored her and that she was entirely capable of managing both him and the house. Ottoline, a gauche fifteen-year-old, thought her a splendid creature.

Lady Bolsover was too dignified to do anything so vulgar as making a scene. Instead, she grew suddenly ill: declining health provided a graceful exit. She asked permission to have the use of the London house in Grosvenor Place and to look for a country home near London; the duke, feeling that he was getting off lightly, agreed at once. The house in Belgravia was made over to Lady Bolsover and a suitable country home was found at St Anne's Hill, Chertsey. By the time the young duke and duchess returned from their honeymoon, Lady Bolsover had left Welbeck for good. She took Ottoline with her.

Ottoline often said that the next three years of her life were the happiest, shadowed only by her mother's illness. Memory was being kind, but it is true that she was glad to escape from the grandeur of Welbeck and to have her mother all to herself.

The house at St Anne's Hill, to which they moved in the summer of 1889, had once been the country home of the great Irish politician Charles James Fox, a fact which gave Lady Bolsover particular pleasure as her mind returned increasingly to her Irish girlhood. Of approximately the same size as East Court, St Anne's Hill was equally charming and it is easy to understand why Fox had been in the habit of strolling out to salute the landscape as the dawn mists uncurled. To the south, it overlooked the downs, while the east front faced a distant panorama of London. Fox's tea-house, a chinoiserie pavilion decorated with coloured pebbles and strung with shells, stood at the far end of a formal garden of rose-beds, low box hedges and sandy paths; leading towards the Home Farm, a rhododendron walk turned aside into a classical temple. Mellow walls of red brick enclosed a broad expanse of lawn shaded at intervals by redwoods and Lebanon cedars.

Lady Bolsover's health had never been strong; deprived of the energy required to restore and govern Welbeck, the will to live abandoned her. Always prone to depression, she grew fretful, nervous and terrified of being alone. Ottoline was required not only to sleep in the same room but to be with her mother every moment that she was awake, to be on hand to take her out in the carriage on a fine day or to push her up and down the garden paths in a wheelchair. On two or three evenings a week, she was permitted to hold Bible classes for the local stablemen and gardeners, and to teach reading to a little gypsy girl she had befriended; for the rest of her nights, she sat and sewed in a window-seat while Lady Bolsover reminisced about her Irish youth.

Ottoline inherited two things from her mother, her appalling health and her religious fervour; like her mother, she depended on the one to help her to endure the other. A staunch believer, it was at St Anne's Hill that she began to see religion as an exercise in asceticism. The sudden change in her family's fortunes with the move to Welbeck had instilled in her a sense of guilt which was now augmented by the despair she felt at being unable to restore her mother's health or good spirits. It was, of course, an impossible task for a young girl to set herself – her governess was horrified to see how exhausted Ottoline looked when she visited St Anne's Hill in the summer of 1890 – but that did not soften the sense of failure. Religion, which had been a solace, was transformed into her scourge as she became a daily reader of Thomas à Kempis's *The Imitation of Christ*. Praiseworthy though that book is, those who were not preparing themselves for a monastery or convent were unlikely to see in it an immutable model for secular life. Ottoline did. Already susceptible to feelings of guilt about things over which she had no control, she allowed Thomas's teachings to fan the flames of her anxiety. 'Every thought, word, action and motive was subjected to [His] fierce burning light, none was kept back or hidden. My young being was scrutinised, scourged, and mercilessly pruned; all desire for food must be constrained, pleasant books put away, everything soft and pleasing renounced.'[9] Not satisfied with cutting her meals down to a few mouthfuls of toast or soup, she gave all her pretty dresses away and read nothing that was not religious. A modern psychoanalyst would probably suggest that she was taking drastic steps to ensure that she was noticed and loved.

Love was not forthcoming, but anxiety was beginning to be expressed by those closest to her. The family had been alarmed by Miss Craig's reports of Ottoline's appearance and they were not reassured by the news of her religious fervour. Society was thought to be the best remedy: Ottoline was taken under the efficient wing of the young Duchess of Portland and swept around the great houses of Mayfair and Piccadilly for a London season. When it became apparent that this was not having the desired effect, the duchess suggested that Lady Bolsover should take her daughter for a winter in Italy.

In February 1892, mother and daughter set off with two pet pugs and a nightingale to visit San Remo and Florence. En route, they paused in Paris where Lady Bolsover had heard that the French crown jewels were being sold. Remembering how enthralled Ottoline had been as a child by the royal trinkets they had discovered together at Welbeck, she bought her a magnificent pearl necklace which had once belonged to Marie Antoinette, together with some white muslin dresses. Thomas à Kempis had strong views about worldly ornaments; regretfully, Ottoline declined to wear them.

Neither of the travellers was well; by the time they reached Florence, Lady Bolsover had collapsed. Ottoline was in no condition to look after her. Her head ached, her body was burning and she could eat nothing. The doctor she summoned to attend her mother took one look at the daughter and called for a nurse. Urgent messages were relayed to London. Dimly, like a figure in a dream, Ottoline saw her brother Bill standing by the bed, telling her that she had nearly died of typhoid fever.

Nursing Lady Bolsover was clearly out of the question. Bill took over the arrangements for the time being, and it was he who decided that the home of their Aunt Louise,* high in the hills above Florence, would be the best place for Ottoline's convalescence. The sisters-in-law were not fond of each other, but as soon as Bill indicated that Ottoline would be alone, he was told that she must come and stay for as long as she wished.

To Ottoline, it was like stepping, however briefly, out of a nightmare into a fairy tale. The Villa Capponi was a beautiful little Renaissance palace looking towards Fiesole; Aunt Louise used it as her main summer residence in Italy – she owned another villa at Bordighera and an apartment in Rome – and shared it with her daughter Cecilia and the younger twins, Violet and Hyacinth. Her taste was much admired and the Villa Capponi was as impeccably furnished as her English home, Forbes House in Richmond. Ottoline, whose love of pretty things had not been entirely quenched by the teachings of Thomas à Kempis, was entranced by the villa and by the garden which her clever aunt had designed. (Years later, she used it as a model for her garden at Garsington.) Aunt Louise, a graceful woman with eyes as black as her silk dresses, was heart-warmingly kind and Ottoline struck up an instant friendship with Violet ('Vava'), a lively, pretty girl who shared her enthusiasm for poetry and Bible classes. A halcyon fortnight was only allowed to end when

---

* Aunt Louise, grandmother to the Hon. Elizabeth Bowes-Lyon, wife of King George VI and, since 1952, Queen Elizabeth the Queen Mother, had been twice widowed. Her first husband was Charles Bentinck; her second was Henry ('Chéri') Warren Scott. Cecilia, Violet and Hyacinth were the daughters of her first marriage.

Ottoline had promised to come to Florence again and to see them all in England. Her aunt's carriage took her back to Lady Bolsover's hotel in Florence.

The fairy story was over. Lady Bolsover's English doctor had used Bill as a courier to send her a highly recommended new medicine, but Lady Bolsover's illness was a complex one and the supposed cure had been a disaster. Always frail, she had become too weak to leave her bed or even to sit up without support. Bill had already left for England and Ottoline, still exhausted by her own illness, was confronted with the task of getting her mother back to London. A wheelchair was needed for every change of train. Railway carriages could only be managed with the use of a special ladder. Air cushions had to be inflated and fastened around the invalid's body to cushion her from the jolts. Henry and Bill came to meet the travellers at Victoria Station and conducted them to the house in Grosvenor Place, where Ottoline was left alone in charge of her mother.

Professional nurses were brought in when it became clear that the decline was irreversible, and, two months after their return from Italy, Lady Bolsover died. Ottoline had only left her once, when the duke insisted that she should attend the christening of his first son at Welbeck, an occasion which was celebrated on a handsome scale, with a hundred and fifty tenants coming to lunch in the Gothic Hall, dancing to the strings of Herr Gottlieb and his Vienna Orchestra, and tea and games for three thousand local children in the garden. Photographs of the house party show Ottoline looking at the camera with the desperate smile of someone whose nerves were stretched to breaking-point.

The end came only a few days after her return to London. She had known that it was inevitable. It did not lessen the pain. Twenty-five years later, she took up the tress of black-and-silver hair she had cut from the dead woman's head and wrote in her journal: 'I touch it again and again, with the same undying passionate love.'

The words express a commitment almost frightening in its intensity, even when we consider the exalted terms in which people of Ottoline's generation tended to speak of their parents. Neither Ottoline's husband nor her child nor her lovers could live up to the idealised figure that Lady Bolsover became in her memory. When she wrote her account of three years spent nursing a sick and demanding woman, she declared them to have been the happiest of her life. In her memoirs, however unfairly, she chose to show Welbeck as the source of all her unhappiness and her mother of all her joy.

It is difficult to share Ottoline's feelings, particularly in the context of her life at St Anne's Hill, when Lady Bolsover seems to have manoeuvred her into the role of unpaid nurse and companion, playing on her sense of guilt to keep her tied to the arm of her wheelchair. If we are to ask ourselves why, at the age of nineteen, Ottoline was lonely, shy, undereducated and devoid of self-confidence, the blame has to be laid at her mother's door. It had not suited her to have an independent daughter; although Ottoline did not know it, she had even gone to the lengths (on 17 May 1884) of cutting her out of her will to help ensure that she did not have one. (The lawyers, to their credit, had vigorously resisted this enigmatic decision.) The only period of freedom Ottoline had enjoyed had been at the Villa Capponi, where her mother had never intended that she should go. The motherly love in which she chose to believe could better have been described as selfish need. Still, Ottoline had been a ready candidate for the role of the willing slave; it was unfortunate that it led her to think that she had the right to expect the same degree of submissive devotion from her own, less tractable, child.

2

FROM DAUGHTER TO WIFE
1893–1902

'I was not critical of my family. I only felt a moral indignation and disapproval of their way of life . . . I was hampered by the terrible imprint of Thomas à Kempis who seemed burnt into me and made me believe that any pleasure – even reading – was wrong.'

OM to Francis Hackett, 21 April 1937

'I . . . clung to my solitary liberty. I believe in many women there is a strong intuitive feeling of pride in their solitary life so that when marriage really comes it is, to a certain extent, a humiliation.'

OM, *Early Memoirs*

The question 'What is to be done about Ottoline?' was answered by her mother's death and by the fact that she was now financially dependent on the duke; clearly, she must be taken back into the family circle in which, if treated with the firm affection used to train a nervous filly, she would soon come into line. Solitude seemed to have had a bad effect on her; at nineteen, it was time to start enjoying herself. She would become more cheerful and lively when she was comfortably settled at Welbeck with all of her responsibilities removed. All they asked was that she should fit in.

Grieving is a slow process; Ottoline was given no time to experience it. St Anne's Hill had not prepared her for a social life; sitting among the guests at Welbeck, she felt that she was taking part in a play for which everybody else had been helped to learn their lines. 'It is a perfect performance. To those who are beautiful and gay it is not difficult, the applause always complimentary and laudatory. Unfortunately, try as I might, I could never learn my proper part. I tried very hard; stage fright perhaps prevented me; but I could never take the cue...'[1] Shyness feeds on itself; Ottoline grew increasingly unhappy and unsure of herself. There was no intentional cruelty in the Bentincks, but there was a strongly-rooted dislike of personal conversation. It seemed best to them to behave as though nothing was wrong, and their silence confirmed her sense of alienation. 'I remember standing by my bedroom door as I was going out one day, and realising it so vividly that I said aloud to myself: "They do not like me. My presence among them is unwelcome to them."'[2]

Their dislike was a figment of her impressionable imagination, but there was certainly a degree of impatience and unease. Ottoline's religious fervour had not slackened, and she did not hide her disapproval of what seemed to her a selfish and purposeless way of life. The fault, on both sides, was a lack of communication and understanding; the result was a feeling of suppressed anger and estrangement. 'So there,' Ottoline wrote to an Irish friend in the 1930s, rounding off a description of her return to Welbeck, '– odd to think I was really *quite* alone. All that life gave me a permanent feeling that I couldn't really succeed – took away all confidence.'[3]

Once sensed, the imaginary lack of affection became as real as fact to Ottoline. If her family did not like her, the best thing seemed to be to inflict her presence on them as little as possible. She still went for daily afternoon rides with the duchess, but she took no further part in the social life of her brother and sister-in-law. Rebellion of any real kind was not possible. She had no idea yet what it was that she wanted from life. Vague dreams of doing good filled her mind, but it was hard to see how to accomplish them. It was all very well to wear shabby clothes and to travel third-class, but she did not need the duke to point out that she was helping nobody by making him look ungenerous.

A partial solution came from the duke's children's nurse, a stoutly religious woman who sympathised with her longing to help people. When Ottoline mentioned the Bible classes she had started at St Anne's Hill, the nurse suggested that she could do the same at Welbeck. A few friendly servants helped to spread the news and, on a cold January evening, a group of bashful young footmen sidled into Ottoline's sitting-room for a session of readings and hymn-singing. The duchess, listening outside the door, was ready to collapse with merriment, but the pupils evidently enjoyed themselves; by the end of a few months, Ottoline was speaking to gatherings of fifty or sixty. Her next venture of carving classes, run by a local craftsman, went equally well and helped Ottoline to regain a little confidence in her ability to help people. But affection and respect were no substitutes for the friendship she longed to achieve and social consciousness was too deep for there to be complete ease between the pupils and their timid young patron. They could not forget who she was. Her visits to their homes were remembered as awkward occasions of stilted conversation and embarrassing silences. Her dream of being accepted and welcomed without formality foundered on hearing the cold chink of teacups in tidy parlours. Here, too, she was an intruder.

Ottoline was not quite so alone as she remembered in later years. She had supporters in the family in the duchess's mother, Mrs Dallas-Yorke, and in the mother of Olivia ('Birdie'), her brother Henry's wife; perhaps because age made them more understanding, these two ladies were more tolerant of her reluctance to conform than her immediate family. When Ottoline was in London – Henry and Birdie had allowed her to keep some rooms at the top of Lady Bolsover's home in Grosvenor Place, now jointly owned by Henry, Bill and Charlie – she went on visits to Birdie's mother, Lady Bective, or to her Aunt Louise's home in Richmond. Here, while her aunt read or played the piano in a drawing-room filled with lilies and lined with sermons, Ottoline and her cousin Vava drafted the homilies which they were busily distributing to hospitals and temperance groups. (The only alcohol Ottoline ever touched was a glass of champagne several months before her death, when she was told that it would help her to regain her appetite.) But if one side of her nature found satisfaction in good works, the other, still unformed, longed for intellectual stimulation. It was a happy day for her when Arthur Strong became the librarian at Welbeck in 1896. Described by the religious historian Ernest Renan as the most remarkable man he had ever met,[4] Strong was quick to sympathise with Ottoline's longing for an education and kind enough to do everything he could to help. In London, he took her on long tours of the National Gallery; at Welbeck, he gave her informal tutorials on philosophy and literature with particular attention to Locke, Meredith and Browning, the poet all well-brought-up young ladies of that period were expected to enjoy. A stimulating mentor, Strong and his wife, Eugenie, a classical scholar, became Ottoline's devoted friends.

Having lost both of her parents, Ottoline began to look for substitutes. William Maclagan, the worldly old Archbishop of York, was the first of a series of older men who became surrogates for the father she had hardly known.

Ottoline was twenty-one when Maclagan made his first visit to Welbeck. Her unusual beauty was beginning to show itself. She was just over six foot – taller than most men – with turquoise eyes, wavy red-gold hair, a pale skin and a graceful, sliding walk. A large nose and the strong chin of the Bentincks prevented her from being a conventional beauty; her appearance conveyed something more rich and complex, as did her low voice with its inimitable inflections and hesitations. She was like nobody else and Maclagan, always ready to be charmed by young ladies of good family, was delighted to speak to her as 'your loving father' and to be invited to address the Bible classes for prostitutes which Ottoline had started holding at Grosvenor Place. Bishopthorpe, the Maclagans' Yorkshire house, offered a welcome alternative to Welbeck and two rooms were reserved for her whenever she wanted to visit. She went to Bishopthorpe at least eight times in 1896, but Maclagan's Easter letter to her that year was addressed to a place which Ottoline valued even more highly.

The Cornish Sisterhood of Truro, which she had discovered through Vava in 1895, was a thriving example of the active benevolence which Ottoline most admired. Comprising only seventeen sisters and three novices (all from fairly grand families), it was divided into a laundry house for penitents, a convalescent home for working men and a mission school for working girls. Supervising it was Mother Julian, a sophisticated woman who had taken her vows late in life and renounced none of her social connections. (The letters she wrote to Ottoline and Vava in 1895 and 1896 came from her family home in Cheshire as well as from addresses in Eaton and Grosvenor Squares.)

Ottoline was in danger of becoming a prig; Mother Julian wasted no time in telling her so and in advising her to exchange Thomas à Kempis for her own favourite author, H. G. Wells. Observing Ottoline's thinness and her untidy appearance, the elderly nun went on to warn her that self-discipline can easily be taken too far and that she was too young to spend all of her spare time poring over theology books. Tactfully but firmly, she guided her towards the notion that it was possible to love God without giving up pleasure. Obvious though that may sound to us, it came as a revelation to Ottoline. 'It is odd to remember,' she wrote later, 'that in that sisterhood was the place I found my youth and the encouragement to live with any gaiety.'[5]

It is clear that Mother Julian soon took over the role of Lady Bolsover in Ottoline's life; George MacDonald, author of some of the best-loved children's books of the time, became another substitute for her father. Vava Bentinck, once again, arranged the meeting in 1896; a few months later, Ottoline and she pooled their funds to buy an amber cigarette-holder for his birthday present. Their next plan, which was to adopt the MacDonalds' tubercular daughter and cure her with prayers, was politely declined, but Ottoline was comforted with the gift of a gold charm fashioned, so Mrs MacDonald assured her, in the shape of her husband's soul.

Maclagan was anxious about Ottoline's health; so, now, were the kindly MacDonalds. 'We – George and I – often wonder how you are getting on – bodily, I mean,' Louisa MacDonald wrote to her in 1897. 'Do let it – the mortal body – have its consideration from you.' They were right to worry. Ottoline had not taken Mother Julian's advice about looking after herself. She ate almost nothing, sat up until three in the morning with her books in an unheated room and set her alarm for five. Painfully undernourished, she admitted to suffering from agonising headaches. While no single cause can be identified for the ill-health against which Ottoline fought throughout her adult life, it had begun to show itself in a form very similar to her mother's – headaches, excessive fatigue, skin rashes and distorted vision – and seems to have been related to an unusually severe form of migraine, aggravated by any form of excitement or nervous tension. When Ottoline's friends spoke later of her courage, many of them were thinking of the trouble she had taken to hide her suffering from them.

Mother Julian, the MacDonalds and Maclagan did their best, but it was Ottoline's old governess who took the initiative and caused her to change the pattern of her life. When Ottoline visited her in the summer of 1896, Miss Craig not only suggested a Continental holiday but produced a suitable travelling companion, Miss Rootes, a long-toothed old lady whose expression resembled the patient glare of a sheep and whose attire for all weathers was a brown flannel suit with matching button boots. Having obtained the family's consent, Ottoline prudently expanded the party by inviting Hilda Douglas-Pennant, a distant relation she had met at the home of her Aunt Louise. Hilda, a clever but intense woman seven or eight years older than Ottoline, was already secretly fascinated by her and delighted by the opportunity to form a closer friendship.

The British female on tour was always an object of discreet amusement with her mushroom hat, veil and dustcloak, but Ottoline's party provoked outright hilarity. Miss Rootes wore her brown suit and button boots throughout the trip. Hilda spent half her time unpacking and repacking suitcases and the other half struggling to disentangle herself from her daily baggage of air cushions, sketching equipment and a collection of alarm clocks set to remind them of their schedule at hourly intervals. Ottoline, determined to devour every available scrap of culture, travelled in a voluminous scarlet cape lined with pockets in which to carry a library of suitable reference books. It was, she conceded, a battle of unfairly-weighted odds for anyone unlucky enough to bump into her.

Ottoline's little notebooks, her only record of events until she began to keep a journal in 1909, suggest that she became depressed in Cortina, where the spectacle of soaring granite mountains increased her sense of the triviality of human endeavour. The mood was transient; looking back in 1911, she remembered only the exhilarating sense of freedom. It was her first taste of independence and she revelled in it. 'Oh how wonderful it was,' she sighed in a nostalgic letter to Bertrand Russell that year. 'Hilda and I were very happy and I am afraid neglected

Miss Rootes shamefully ... we went to wonderful places, Ravenna, Viareggio, Bologna, Padua and then Florence and HDP and I went to Assisi and Perugia, Orvieto and other places and then to Rome where I stayed all winter with my aunt Louise – Mrs Scott – and Violet [Vava] who had an apartment there – and Hilda returned sadly home.'[6]

The Italian visit was, in short, a huge success. Hilda, ready with a poetical quotation for every scene, seemed an ideal companion and Ottoline looked at everything through her friend's eyes. If Hilda said that Miss Rootes was dull, so she was. If Hilda announced that Piero della Francesca and Andrea Mantegna represented the pinnacle of Italian art, so it was. Blinded by the revelation of Art (always written with a capital letter in her early notebooks) through her new mentor, Ottoline failed to notice that Hilda was infatuated with her. The infatuation was, on their first trip together, less apparent than later only because Hilda had no rival. Miss Rootes, stumbling in their wake with her sketchbook ready for suitable vistas, offered no threat.

Miss Rootes made one valuable contribution to Ottoline's life by suggesting that a bad education could be remedied, and independence maintained, if she went as an extramural student to university. Lack of qualifications was no hindrance. Philosophy, Ottoline decided, would suit her interests best. The duchess's mother added her support to the idea and the duke reluctantly gave his consent. In the bitter January of 1897, Ottoline travelled to St Andrews in Scotland where, since philosophy was not on the curriculum, she studied logic under Professor Ritchie.

Ottoline had no friends in St Andrews, but she was given no opportunity to be lonely. Squeezed together in the spartan rooms of 5 Murry Park were two pugs, a lady's maid, Hilda (who had insisted on accompanying her), and a tutor. The tutor and Hilda disliked each other on sight. Miss Hurlbatt made it clear that she had a low opinion of Hilda's intelligence. Hilda retaliated by declaring Miss Hurlbatt to be conceited and boring. As with Miss Rootes, Ottoline meekly bowed to her friend's superior judgement, but she was beginning to wish that Hilda would be less possessive and a little less condescending to those she judged to be her inferiors. It embarrassed her to see the way Hilda stared at the other students and how scornful she looked when Ottoline spoke to them. The lectures were stimulating ('I really did enjoy them and enjoyed the work,' Ottoline told Bertrand Russell many years later), but Hilda made it impossible for her to spend time with anyone else, the atmosphere at Murry Park was tense, and the bitter cold brought on one of her bouts of illness. By the end of two terms, she was ready to leave St Andrews.

There had been some consolations. She had proved to her own satisfaction that she could tackle a difficult subject; despite Hilda's efforts, she had made enough friends for several of her fellow students to visit her in London; she believed she had found a new paternal figure in Herbert Asquith. An old friend of Lady Bective's, he had been urged to call on Ottoline when he visited St Andrews, and had been at his most avuncular. Gratified by his approval of her wish to educate herself, and delighted by his promise to devise a reading course in Greek history for her, she happily agreed to meet him when she returned to London. Asquith had a part to play in Ottoline's life, both as an unwanted suitor and as an influential friend, but his time had not yet come.

In 1898, at the age of twenty-four, Ottoline fell passionately in love with a man 'who was not cut out on the ordinary cardboard pattern, who was subtle and free and daring and sympathetic'. It was a view she could never quite bring herself to abandon. 'He had great magnetic charm – irresistible to anyone as impressionable as I was,' she wrote in her sixties. 'It was wonderful to find anyone so unconventional whom one could laugh with. I *was* in love with him! And *how* I suffered!'[7]

She first met Axel Munthe at the Portlands' new London home in Grosvenor Square. The duchess, who had heard her friends speaking of him as a charming and brilliant man, was disappointed; Ottoline was as captivated by his sapphire eyes and his easy eloquence as by his accounts of the time when he had risked his life to work among the poor in cholera-stricken Naples. At forty, Munthe was old enough to satisfy her continuing need for a fatherly man. There were several meetings at Grosvenor Place and with Vava Bentinck at Richmond before Munthe invited Ottoline to come and spend the rest of the summer in Capri. Already committed to a quiet holiday with Hilda in Savoy, she gave him her address there.

They had barely settled into their hotel when a letter from Munthe arrived, urging her to come and stay at the little seventeenth-century residence of the bishops of Sorrento which adjoined his own home. Love made Ottoline unscrupulous. Hilda was needed as a chaperone if she was to seem respectable; with this in mind, she told her friend that they were going to Capri to visit a lonely old gentleman. No amount of objections by Hilda to the expense and inconvenience of travelling five-hundred-odd miles in the blazing heat of August could shake Ottoline's determination. They should and would go to Capri, at once.

If Hilda was sullen in Savoy and rigid with annoyance during the stifling train journey south, she was speechless when, on their arrival at the harbour in Naples, she saw Ottoline being tenderly greeted by a dapper little man with the face of a lecherous faun. This, she realised, was the sad old gentleman she had been asked to visit as an errand of mercy. She had been duped.

The Capri visit was a humiliating experience for Hilda. Neglected and excluded, she was forced to fall back on Ottoline's maid for company; Ellen Dormer, who had originally worked for Ottoline's mother, was ready to agree that her employer must be rescued from a dangerous libertine. Hopefully, Hilda led Ottoline into the garden and pointed to a statue of Fate. Was it not a terrible warning? Did she understand that she was ruining her name?

Ottoline was beyond the reach of Hilda's threats; years later, she was still using her memory of the first days in Capri as an example of the one time she had been utterly happy. The little palace of the bishops was almost as lovely as San Michele. The windows looked over one of the most beautiful bays in the world; the garden's cool arcades were constructed from the remains of an imperial villa; the hill above, leading up to the old chapel which Munthe had converted into a library, was a chirping paradise of butterflies and crickets, its air heavy with the scent of thyme. Munthe himself was the best of companions, romantic, solicitous and knowledgeable. Ottoline listened with rapt attention as he told her that 'what you give away you keep for ever' and that 'contentment and peace of mind thrive better in a small country cottage than in the stately palace'. It never occurred to her that such slick homily-making was inappropriate in a man who had the most expensive medical practice in Rome and whose house was crammed with valuable objects which were never given away. She had lost all critical faculties. She was, as she admitted later, completely besotted.

No hard evidence can be offered, but it seems clear that Ottoline slept with Munthe. Hilda's presence had blocked his progress during the first part of the visit; when they left Capri, Munthe announced that he would accompany them to Naples as their guide. They visited Sorrento and Pompeii as an uncomfortable threesome, but Munthe soon persuaded Ottoline to go for a walk without Hilda. He then declared his undying love and urged her to come back to San Michele alone with him for a few days. Ottoline agreed.

We slipped across the bay back to Capri in a fishing-boat; I lay covered over at the bottom and I can still hear Dr Munthe's voice encouraging the rowers ... Then after a day or two we turned homeward to England after spending a day and night in Naples, Hilda in the last stage of being shocked at Dr Munthe's freedom with me.[8]

There is no reason to question Ottoline's assertion that Munthe wanted to marry her, but he was a vain man with a high sense of his own worth. When Ottoline wrote from England to say that she was afraid that their religious beliefs were incompatible (Munthe followed no formal faith) and that she hoped he would be patient, he interpreted it as a slap in the face from a proud family. He underrated her fervour. Ottoline would never have allowed her family to stop her from doing what she wanted, but she could not marry a man who did not acknowledge her God. Perhaps it is as well that Munthe destroyed the flood of letters in which she poured out her love and her beliefs; they would have made harrowing reading. They did not harrow Munthe. He dismissed them as the ravings of a neurotic zealot. He visited her that autumn in England, but only to break the connection. An excursion arranged by Ottoline to show him her favourite haunts from the St Anne's Hill days was a dismal failure. Munthe made no effort to hide his boredom and his impatience to be gone. 'How much was my fault, how much his fickleness, I never knew,' Ottoline wrote later.

However, she was soon to find out. The Portlands, apprehensive of another lapse into ill-health, sent her to Florence in December to stay at the Villa Capponi, where Vava Bentinck, who had liked Munthe when she had met him in England and who sympathised with her cousin's misery, thought it was worth making one last attempt at a reconciliation. She and Ottoline had an excuse for visiting Munthe in Rome; Vava was willing to pretend that she wanted a course of treatment for the headaches from which she, like Ottoline, suffered. Half hoping, half fearing, Ottoline agreed that they should go together.

Munthe's Roman practice was in the house where Keats had once lived, on the fashionable Piazza d'Espagna. Here, lying among the heap of books in the waiting-room, Ottoline was dismayed to see her last present to him, a volume of poems. When, finally, she was called into the consulting-room, Munthe was brutal. He was angry with them for coming. He saw no point in further discussion. He had no intention of marrying a religious maniac. He suggested that she and her cousin should go back to Florence. Embracing her briefly, he led her to the door.

It was a sad end to Ottoline's hopes, but the pain had been far worse when she was alone in England, disapproved of by her family and unsure of Munthe's feelings. Now, faced with the truth, she was disconcerted by her sudden sense of relief, 'that odd sense of being born again, with power to win, unshackled to start afresh'. It took years for her to forget the humiliation of having been used and rejected;* in the short term, beautiful surroundings and new friends helped to lift her spirits. Florence in the spring was no place to be miserable and her aunt took good care to provide her with diversions.

---

* Nevertheless she kept the gold watch Munthe gave her by her bed for the rest of her life.

Knowing how much her niece longed to meet interesting people, Aunt Louisa put her in touch with a celebrated literary neighbour.

Vernon Lee, never known to her friends by her real name of Violet Paget, had lived in Florence for many years. Some people considered her to be the most brilliant conversationalist of her time; Henry James thought her 'as dangerous and uncanny as she is intelligent, which is saying a great deal'. The danger, if you happened to be young, bright and female, was that Vernon would encourage you to believe that you had an artistic eye and persuade you to become her unpaid assistant and housemate. '... Vernon was a tyrannical taskmaster,' Dame Ethel Smyth wrote in one of her entertaining memoirs, As Time Went On (1936), 'and the culte gradually discovered she was being lovingly and tightly bound by unbreakable cords to "OUR WORK". In the end of course there came a moment of violent disruption, and Vernon suffered deeply.' Her lesbian tendencies were repressed: the most a culte could expect was a kiss which one of them, unnamed, described as having been of the sacramental kind. 'You felt you had been to your first communion.'

Vernon was feeling lonely at the time when Ottoline entered her life. Kit Anstruther-Thompson, the most recent of the cultes, had grown tired of pronouncing on Greek statues and gone off to a less demanding relationship. Any new association was welcome and Vernon, while unnerved by the elegance of Mrs Scott and what she rudely called her 'Duchess-that-should-have-been manner', was immediately charmed by her niece.* Ottoline soon became a daily guest at her villa, Il Palmerino. The food was a disagreeable change from the elegant food at the Villa Capponi – Vernon's cook specialised in tongue stewed in chocolate and birds'-claw omelettes – but Ottoline never cared what she ate. She feasted instead on the afternoon symposiums, which included accounts of the recent and furious row Vernon had had with Bernard Berenson when he accused her of stealing his ideas (Ottoline prudently held her tongue about the fact that she had rather liked Berenson when he came to dinner with her aunt). When Vernon retired to write, she was sent off to the Uffizi gallery with another of the cultes, a stout and lively young art historian called Maud Cruttwell. Vernon was waspish about Maud's furry skin and her genteel 'Oxford' accent, but Ottoline, while startled by her fond-

---

* Vernon Lee seems to have been the only person ever to say an unkind word about Mrs Scott. It is true that she would have become the Duchess of Portland if her first husband had outlived the Fifth Duke, and possibly this contributed to the bad feeling between her and Lady Bolsover.

ness for wearing men's clothes and smoking cigars in public, thought her great fun. Between them, Vernon and Maud taught Ottoline a great deal, while persuading her that life without Axel Munthe could still be enjoyable.

Ottoline left behind her two extremely downcast ladies when she returned to England in April 1899. By September, she had received more than sixty adoring letters from Maud Cruttwell, who felt that her life had been transformed by their meeting. 'I want you to know that all the sympathy of your talking and – I must say – chiefly of your atmosphere – has braced me up and made me feel stronger and more resolute than I have ever felt in my life,' Maud told her, and added that she was even beginning to appreciate the beauty and value of 'the religion you love'.[9]

Vernon, too, was grieving at Ottoline's departure. In October, she wrote to propose that she should return and become resident *culte* at Il Palmerino.

I have often had a little passing dream of trying to give you the benefit (for you to amalgamate with your own personal views and traditions) of my additional twenty years of reading, thinking, and in practical life. I should like to talk to you about psychology, which is in great measure my study, and political economy, of which I know a little. I can teach you infinitely less than any person at Oxford, but I think we might *think* things out together, which is sometimes quite as fruitful.[10]

It is intriguing to speculate on the course Ottoline's life might have taken if she had accepted Vernon's invitation. It had much to recommend itself. She was becoming passionately fond of Italy. She longed to broaden her knowledge and the prospect of 'thinking things out together' had considerable appeal. But much though Ottoline liked and respected Vernon, she had no wish to be bound to her. She answered with a politely-worded refusal. A more direct overture two years later was again courteously rejected, but the friendship endured and, in 1902, Vernon Lee was one of the first friends to be told of Ottoline's engagement to Philip Morrell.

Ottoline had already embarked on a new course of self-improvement when Vernon wrote to her in the autumn of 1899. She had taken herself off to Oxford that May as an out-student at Somerville College, where (possibly under the influence of Asquith) she was studying Roman history and political economy. 'An Oxford don-na perhaps by this time,' the kindly MacDonalds twittered in a state of high excitement.

A month after Ottoline's arrival in Oxford, Philip Morrell was walking home from his day's work in the office of his father, a solicitor, when he saw a young woman on a bicycle riding slowly past him. The sight took his breath away. 'She was dressed entirely in white,' he wrote, 'and her pale face had a set and rather anxious expression as if concentrated on the art of riding a bicycle; but the most striking part of her appearance was the mass of deep copper-coloured hair . . . she was extremely beautiful.' He longed to know who she was. His curiosity was satisfied a few weeks afterwards when his mother told him that she had just had a visit from the sister of the Duke of Portland, a striking young woman with astonishing red-gold hair; she had wanted to see their collection of Italian paintings. Six months later, he met Ottoline again and managed to strike up a conversation. She invited him to come to her lodgings for tea, over which she admitted that she was having difficulty in keeping up with all the books she was meant to read, but Philip's offer of help was politely refused. Her room, he noticed, was old-fashioned, full of ferns and family photographs. In December, invited by his mother, Ottoline went to dinner at Black Hall, the Morrells' Oxford home, and outshone all the other women in a superb dress of black satin and rows of pearls. The male guests shared his dazzled admiration and, rather to Philip's annoyance, he was excluded from the circle who surrounded her. He did not persist. His life was still shattered by the recent suicide of his only brother and there seemed little point in a young solicitor's dreaming about the sister of a duke. For her part, Ottoline scarcely noticed him. He was friendly, sympathetic and handsome, but she was firmly wedded to the idea that her happiness depended on the company of older men. She still needed to fill the void left by her father's death, and Philip Morrell was not the man to replace him.

Herbert Asquith had briefly seemed to be a more satisfactory substitute. Asquith's marriage to Margot Tennant was not ideal; Margot's passion for socialising had left him lonely and with time on his hands after the Liberal Party's defeat in 1895. He had become acquainted with Ottoline at St Andrews; he was among her first visitors when she returned to England from Florence and he was in constant communication with her during her first term at Oxford. The outbreak of war in South Africa in October 1899 brought him an unexpected bonus. Henry Bentinck and his wife went out to organise a hospital for the wounded and the younger brothers soon followed them. Ottoline could not be allowed to stay alone at Grosvenor Place; instead she was sent to stay with Birdie's mother, Lady Bective, one of Asquith's most ardent admirers.

Ottoline had been thinking of Asquith as a friendly, informal tutor in the paternal mould. It had never entered her head to contemplate him as a lover. His letters to her have almost all been destroyed –

probably by Ottoline herself – but it seems that he judged his moment to have come when she was staying in Lady Bective's house. We do not know what happened, but it is clear that Ottoline was profoundly distressed by it. Abruptly cancelling her third term at Somerville, she fled to Mother Julian at Truro. By the beginning of April 1900, she was being treated for a nervous collapse at a nursing home in Maida Vale. In June, she went to convalesce at Lake Como, taking Hilda with her. In July, the family agreed that she should go to Giessen in Germany where she could be examined by Fritz Beigel, a specialist in nervous diseases.

Professor Beigel was no luckier than his many successors in identifying or curing Ottoline's illness, but he soon grew fond of his young patient and was more than ready to prescribe a cure of sun and travel which would keep her away from Mr Asquith. For the rest of 1900 and for all of the following year, Ottoline divided her time between Germany and Italy. The family approved; Asquith was piqued. At the end of her one brief visit to England in 1901, during which he persuaded her to see him several times, he gave her a present. *A History of the Peloponnesian Wars* was more of a bramble branch than a bouquet.

Ottoline was lucky in her travelling companions during her year abroad. In Sicily, she and Hilda were befriended by an eminent professor of Greek and his wife; in Rome, their archaeological guide was Eugenie Sellers, the formidably intelligent wife of Arthur Strong. Maud Cruttwell, delighted by an opportunity to escape from her taskmaster at Il Palmerino, took them on a tour of her favourite Tuscan towns, puffing a large cigar on the carriage box while Ottoline and Hilda shaded their faces under a canopy and discussed their futures. Hilda wanted them to take a house together in Bloomsbury, but Ottoline was not sure that she shared Hilda and Maud's enthusiasm for the single state. What, she asked cautiously, did Hilda think about marriage? Could that not be a way of developing oneself? Hilda produced an answer worthy of an Austen aunt. Well, she said, according to Ottoline's memoirs, '"I suppose the great thing in marriage is that it solves that question and naturally gives interest and occupation."'

It was not the response Ottoline wanted to hear. At twenty-eight, she was old enough to cherish her independence and to be sure that she would never renounce it, but she had begun to contemplate the possibility of marrying a man who would understand her need for freedom. When they returned to England in the autumn of 1901, she continued to give Hilda noncommittal answers. Her family made it easier for her by declaring that it was absurd to talk of living in shabby Bloomsbury when she still had a home with them. The Bentincks were away at Birdie's home in Westmorland when she returned; Ottoline had the house in Grosvenor Place to herself, a fact which Mr Asquith was quick to exploit until his place was usurped by a younger, unmarried man.

It was almost two years since Ottoline had first met Philip Morrell in Oxford; it is just possible that it was he who came to mind when she thought about the sensitive, undemanding kind of man who would not restrict her or force her into a conventional marriage. For the biographer, Philip remains a stumbling-block, a handsome, shadowy character whose words are seldom reported and whose personality remains veiled, but that very shadowiness also holds the clue to his attraction for Ottoline. Philip was too weak a character to dictate the form a marriage should take; in almost every respect, he was putty in her hands.

Philip had arrived in London in January 1901. His request to be taken on as a partner in the family firm of Oxford solicitors had been angrily rejected by his father who decided instead to despatch him to a minor branch of the firm in Bloomsbury, Philpott and Morrell. Living quietly in lodgings at 115 Piccadilly, Philip's only solace in a tedious life was the company of his two closest friends from Balliol, Logan Pearsall Smith and Percy Feilding, who encouraged him to join them in an antiques-dealing venture which they were running from a room in Pimlico under the name of Miss Toplady. But most of Toplady's business was done by Logan, acting as agent for his brother-in-law, Bernard Berenson; the company of his friends served only to remind Philip that, unlike him, they were free to do as they wished. By October 1901, he was admitting to them that he was desperately unhappy; a few weeks later, he met Arthur and Eugenie Strong and gladly accepted their invitation to a dinner-party when he heard that Lady Ottoline had already promised to come.

It seemed at first as though Philip was doomed again to be on the outside of Ottoline's circle of admirers that night; when she was not talking to Arthur Strong and Percy Feilding, she was monopolised by a rich and scholarly American, Harry Brewster, who shared her love of Italy. It was only when she rose to leave that Philip saw his chance. Grosvenor Place was on the way to his lodgings; Ottoline was persuaded to share a hansom with him. When she wished him goodnight, she suggested that he might care to visit her one afternoon.

Philip waited a week to pay his call. The sight of a man's hat on the hall table almost frightened him into leaving at once, but Ottoline appeared at the top of a flight of uncarpeted stairs (the house was being cleaned in the owners' absence) and called him to come up and meet Mr A———. Philip did not quite catch the name, nor did he recognise the burly, red-faced man who gave him a curt nod before leaving. Later, Ottoline casually apologised for his manner. Herbert Asquith! Philip was mortified not to have recognised him, and was staggered that she should treat a celebrated man with such easy disregard.

Philip did not know it, but the comparison with Asquith worked strongly in his favour on this occasion and on his subsequent visits. Philip showed none of Asquith's tendency to bully or molest Ottoline. Over a series of teas at Grosvenor Place, she persuaded him to tell her about himself. Sympathetic and concerned, she listened to his history of early illness, rheumatic fever, typhoid fever and, in 1891, a nervous breakdown at the end of three unhappy years at Balliol. In 1897, he had joined the family firm to please his father; the following year, he had been the shocked recipient of a package of bloody clothing after his handsome younger brother had shot himself. (Hugh Morrell had been ordered abroad in disgrace after seducing his commanding officer's wife; always highly-strung, he killed himself two days after leaving England.) Hugh had been his mother's favourite child, a fact of which Philip was left in no doubt when he broke the news to her and was told how much less his own death would have hurt her. The effect of this on a nervous and insecure young man is described in the unpublished memoirs Philip started to write after Ottoline's death; it is clear that he never fully recovered from it. He was, and remained, a little unbalanced. Pressed by Ottoline to tell her what he wanted to do with his life, he spoke of being an architect or, perhaps, doing something in politics. He was, she discovered, a secret Liberal in a Tory family, like herself.

It was clear that Philip had not yet found his true vocation, but everything he said suggested to Ottoline that his interests and ideas were similar to her own. Tall and unusually handsome with curling brown hair, a long, sensual mouth and soft blue eyes, he was made still more attractive to her by his unhappiness. Drawn though she had been to the company of older men who could instruct and advise her, she had lost none of her love of helping people. Philip was well-educated enough to play the tutor's role, but he was also the kind of man to whom she could imagine herself giving comfort and encouragement. It was as a brother rather than as a potential husband that she soon began to look on him; when he asked her to come and stay at Black Hall at the beginning of December, she gladly accepted. A little naïvely, she failed to see how such a visit would be interpreted by Philip's family.

The visit was a muted success. Ottoline had little in common with Philip's sisters, Margaret Warren and Frederica Morrell (later Peel), but she enjoyed the company of Harriette, his mother. It was from her that Philip had inherited his good taste, his love of beautiful furniture and his interest in artists and writers: Ottoline was intrigued to learn that Mrs Morrell knew Henry James and had been the model for one of his characters (the acquisitive Mrs Gereth in *The Spoils of Poynton*); she was too kind to smile when her hostess went on to hint at her own family's ducal connections. The link to an eighteenth-century Duke of Hamilton was tenuous, but Harriette was anxious to produce this explanation for Philip's air of good breeding, and Philip himself seemed happy enough with it.

Harriette's friendly manner did not mean that she was eager to relinquish her son. Hugh had been her favourite, but Philip was devoted and obedient. She was too used to her role as the adored woman in his life to wish for a female rival, least of all one whose ill-health and impractical approach to life suggested that she might become a ladylike burden on them all; it did not please her to think that Ottoline's aristocratic background would overshadow the tenured splendours of Black Hall.* She looked with a kinder eye on Philip's long-standing friendship with Logan Pearsall Smith, the member of a remarkable clan of Americans who had settled in England. Logan's friendship offered no threat to her and, obvious though his homosexuality was, she had never chosen to worry about his devotion to her good-looking son.

Logan was equally alarmed by the prospect of losing the man who had been his closest friend for almost ten years. His first literary work, *The Youth of Parnassus*, had been presented to Philip 'in memory of the hours and quarrels we enjoyed in polishing these phrases'. They had studied together, travelled together, relied on each other: if Philip married, Logan announced, he would never speak to him again. Less importantly, the Strongs made it clear to Philip that he was not good enough for their beloved Ottoline.

All of this discouragement was ignored by Philip. Usually hesitant and indecisive, he was determined to have Ottoline for his wife. On 19 December, hearing that she was going to Truro for a night, he decided to go with her and to propose on the way; unfortunately, he missed the train and had to fall back on the dramatic announcement that he would be leaving the country for France in a week. (His father had unexpectedly suggested that they should spend Christmas together at Pau.) Ottoline did not seem as upset as he had hoped; on the contrary, she congratulated him on the beginnings of a possible reconciliation. 'You must feel relieved that Pau is settled, don't you,' she wrote, 'and you have to make the plunge. I hope so much that

---

* The house in St Giles, Oxford, belonged to St John's College, although the Morrells had lived in it, as the university solicitors, since the eighteenth century.

it will fulfil all your best hopes ... Yours very truly, Ottoline C. Bentinck.'[11]

That letter was written on 21 December; despite its cool tone, Philip came to Grosvenor Place the following day and asked her to marry him. Ottoline refused to give an answer. The day after, she set off for Christmas at Welbeck. When she arrived at King's Cross Station, Philip was there with a bunch of lilies and a second proposal. 'Impossible,' Ottoline murmured as she climbed into the carriage. But her travelling companion, Mildred de Lotbinière (the married sister of Charlie Bentinck's wife), thought Philip looked far too charming to be dismissed. Her own sister's marriage was proving an uncommonly happy one; she used it to convince Ottoline that matrimony might, after all, be a very pleasant state. That, at least, was how Ottoline remembered it, but her letters show that she continued to feel uncertain. One, written on 24 December, raised the question of 'that old smouldering furnace' of the desire she had felt for Munthe and which she was perfectly aware was not showing any sign of flickering into life in this new relationship. She had not yet talked to Philip about Munthe:

About that my dearest I would rather no one else told you except myself. Hardly anyone knows and very few people care for the man or understand him and I should mind if you heard him abused ... indeed I do love you very deeply but I am not sure that is enough ...[12]

Five days later, she wrote again, promising him that she would make no final decision until he returned to England.

Ottoline came back from Welbeck at the beginning of January. Alone and worried, she decided to seek advice. Hilda had already shown herself to be strongly prejudiced against Philip; instead, Ottoline went to see Eugenie Strong. The interview was not a pleasant one; shocked by what she heard, Ottoline decided to confront Philip at once. 'I did so mind that conversation with Mrs Strong about you,' she wrote on the evening after their meeting:

She made you out so worldly and ambitious as if you would marry for money, 'to get on,' etc. Can you understand how it all shocked and hurt me, Philip? *It is not true is it?* By the bye, I don't know whether you know what I have. It is not much – £1500 a year. Oh how I loathe figures and anything to do with money – please don't say anything to me about it unless you need.[13]

It is hard to know whether Mrs Strong's suspicions had any sound basis; £1,500 a year was not a princely amount, but Philip was poor and it would have been reasonable to suppose that Ottoline's income came from a capital sum to which she would eventually become entitled. He knew that her mother had left her nothing more substantial than a handsome marquetry chest but it was inconceivable that Lady Bolsover would have made no financial arrangements for her child. Inconceivable but true, as later events showed. For the present, even £1,500 a year would make his own life easier. By 6 January, he had managed to persuade her that he had no interest in money or social position and Ottoline was sufficiently reassured to indicate that she might now accept him. 'I am naturally *very* timid of people,' she told him on 7 January, 'especially men, for I have known so few well and I think I can honestly say I have *never* felt the same confidence in any as I feel with you and it is *very* delicious to feel that I could say anything to you . . . You will be kind to me, still, won't you?'[14]

She struck a note of affection and trust rather than love and passion, but it was enough for Philip. On the following day, heavily scented with violet hair lotion, he climbed the stairs at Grosvenor Place to hear her answer. 'She gave her final consent yesterday afternoon,' he told his mother; two days later, Harriette Morrell received a letter from Ottoline, asking her to pray that she might make Philip happy. The next day, to Philip's mortification and his mother's astonishment, she announced that her final decision must depend on what Mother Julian said. Philip, furious, accused Hilda of having interfered, but Ottoline was adamant. It was between her and God, she told him, and she was not going to be bullied. As for his mother's feelings, he would have to deal with them himself. Even at this early stage, it was clear that Philip would never be allowed to dominate his wife.

It was the middle of January before Ottoline felt sure that she was doing the right thing in marrying Philip and agreed to set a date, 8 February, for their wedding. Apologising for the cruel conditions she had imposed, whatever those may have been, she was ready to lavish on him all the affection of her naturally loving nature. 'You are my *all*, my adored husband,' she wrote in one letter; in others she signed herself as 'your little wife' and told him how much she was longing for the time when she would be able to do all that she wanted for him.

The Bentincks had not yet met Philip, although the duke had made use of a friendly chaplain in Oxford to get a report on his family; John Singer Sargent, who was at work on a portrait of the duchess, was able to tell Henry James, who in turn told Harriette Morrell, that Ottoline's family thought Philip sounded to be a great improvement on Axel Munthe. A lunch for the Morrells was given at Grosvenor Square, an occasion which both Ottoline and Philip remembered chiefly for Charlie Bentinck's genial observation that he couldn't imagine anyone daring to undertake marriage to his sister. Birdie Bentinck, anxious to put Philip at ease, wrote to sympathise with him for having had to face the family all at once; still, she added, 'I don't think we are *really* formidable.' The duchess wrote to him, too, in a letter which accompanied her present of a charming miniature of Ottoline, telling him 'how sure I am now that our darling Ottoline will be as happy as the day is long with you. I think,' she added with what sounds suspiciously like malice, 'in so many ways, you are made for each other!'[15] The duke had no compliments to offer, but he gave his half-sister a present of a thousand pounds, while Henry produced a handsome pair of Georgian silver candlesticks.

The marriage took place in February 1902 in London, at St Peter's in Eaton Square, with members of the two families comprising the largest part of the congregation and with Ottoline wearing a full-sleeved dress with billowing silk panels that made Hilda Douglas-Pennant think of a ship in full sail as her friend glided past the pews to the altar. The duke, who gave Ottoline away, went to the station to see the couple off and to fill his sister's lap with all the new magazines before they departed for a night at the stodgily grand Lord Warden Hotel in Dover and another at Canterbury before beginning a honeymoon of two months in Italy.

PART TWO

Steps Towards Liberty

'I stepped out on February 8th, 1902, into the outer courts of my real life . . . I didn't leave a home or a mother.'

OM, *Early Memoirs*

3

MARRIAGE AND MOTHERHOOD
1902–7

> *'I have fallen in love with Lady Ottoline and can hardly think of anything else. I have rarely seen anyone so splendid. She is exactly like a Van Dyck, only Van Dyck never painted anything so lovely. Philip couldn't keep his eyes off her and no wonder.'*
>
> Louise Kinsella to Logan Pearsall Smith, 12 July 1902

Ottoline's honeymoon diary – a little white vellum-bound journal – is of interest precisely because it has no secrets to hide. It tells us that they went to the Villa Capponi before travelling on to Naples and to Rome, where Ottoline prayed that they might learn 'to edify one another' and made her contribution by showing Philip the catacombs and the Forum. On the way back to England, Philip made his by introducing Ottoline to the paintings of Puvis de Chavannes in Paris.

What one would like to know is whether they were enjoying a happy sexual relationship. It seems that they were not. Ottoline had already indicated to Philip that she did not feel the kind of desire for him that she had felt for Munthe; many years later, she wrote in her journal that the discovery that Philip did not find her physically attractive had been her first painful lesson in understanding him. There had, however, been some lovemaking on the honeymoon, or plans for it; on 6 March, Ottoline noted that they had been together to take advice from an English doctor in Florence; on a later date, she wrote that 'my Philip is wonderful and loving'. But the pattern for the future had been set. Sexual relations did exist between them, but they were not of a particularly satisfactory kind. It was not passion which bound them to each other, but loyalty, affection and need. The need was far stronger in Philip than in his wife; the more aware she became of his dependence on her, the more determined Ottoline grew to protect and defend him. Without her, she was convinced, he would never survive. 'Take him first,' she prayed in 1929 when she believed that she was dying. 'Let me be there to hold his hand as he sets forth, to say, "It is all right. I am coming with you."'[1] The sentimental style should not lead us to question her sincerity. She gave her love to other men who desired her more than her husband did, but nothing they could say would ever shake her free of the conviction that she and Philip belonged to each other. Describing the relationship of husband and wife in her memoirs, she compared it to that of a brother and sister and added: 'They are to each other comrades, and they do not part.'[2] That was her firm view of her marriage, and she never deviated from it.

The honeymoon was, nevertheless, a happy one. There were only two awkward moments. One was when Ellen Dormer, Ottoline's maid, lost her temper with Philip in Naples and was, at his request, sent back to England. The other was when they ran into the Berensons and heard that Logan, who was staying with them, had been amusing the guests at their expense. (Logan had a notoriously vicious tongue.) Mary Berenson, reporting to her mother that she had met the Morrells at Orvieto's railway station, gave a memorable description of Ottoline as 'a tall drooping figure in a fur coat and low neck hung all over with jewels and crowned by an immense poke bonnet, on which nodded and trembled an immense array of ribbons and funereal feathers and ends of lace'. Once settled into the railway carriage, she had removed the bonnet and replaced it with a lace shawl pinned to her hair with jewels before embarking on what Mary derisively called a 'culture' conversation with Berenson.* 'Altogether it was a "sight",' she concluded, before allowing that Ottoline had after all 'looked very sweet and nice'.[3]

Neither Ellen Dormer's outburst nor Logan's gossip marred Ottoline's contentment. Her own passion for Italy was complemented by Philip's enthusiasm. He showed no wish to quarrel with her religious beliefs. He treated her ideas seriously and enjoyed discussing them.

* Berenson had already met Ottoline in 1898 when he dined at the Villa Capponi and praised her charm, her beautiful voice and her 'perfect personal simplicity'. There may well have been a little jealousy in Mary's catty description. (Bernard Berenson to Isabella Stewart Gardner, 24 April 1898, *The Letters of Bernard Berenson and Isabella Stewart Gardner*, ed. Rollin Hadley [Northeastern University Press, Boston, 1987]).

He praised her embroidery skills – his own mother was a superb needlewoman – and did not object to her smoking cigarettes (a new vice) while he read aloud from Macaulay, Shakespeare or Gibbon. For the first time, she had an intelligent and sensitive companion whose criticisms were never cruel or mocking. Philip gave her the gift she needed most at that time, the confidence to be herself. To this extent, at least, he was justified in his later claims that Ottoline owed everything that she had become to him.

Back from Italy, Ottoline and Philip set about finding themselves a home. They settled first at 36 Grosvenor Road in Pimlico, a furnished house rented out to friends by Percy Feilding. In July 1902, Ottoline wrote to tell her little king, as she liked to call her husband, that she had found another house for sale just down the road, No. 39. Philip and his architect brother-in-law, Edward Warren, went to inspect it and the Morrells moved in at the end of the summer.

Time and the city planners have not dealt kindly with what was once a pretty stretch of riverside homes lying between Parliament Square and the Chelsea Embankment. Grosvenor Road today is an unappealing shambles of apartment blocks and building sites looking across the Thames at a concrete skyline. Only a few of the original houses remain and neither 36 nor 39 is among them.

Ottoline had little experience of running a house; never having cared about food, she left the housekeeping in the hands of a mediocre cook. (Menu-lists indicate a diet of risottos, boiled celery and rice pudding.) What she did have were strong ideas on decoration. Philip pruned and restrained, she liked to say to friends, but he exerted no influence over her idea of how a room should look.

Ottoline's design ideas were well in advance of the times. The typical English lady of 1902, dutifully following the principles laid out in such popular works as Mrs Jennings's *Our Homes and How to Beautify Them*, translated beauty as stately clutter. Originality was in short supply; had Ottoline met an Ogden Codman, she could certainly have done for the English what Edith Wharton did with Codman to revolutionise American homes through their book, *The Decoration of Houses*.

It is possible that Ottoline and Mrs Wharton took their ideas from the same source. Both women had become close friends of Vernon Lee in the 1890s – Mrs Wharton was at Il Palmerino in 1894, two years before she published her views on decoration – and they had both been influenced by Vernon's enthusiasm for the eighteenth-century Italian style and by her belief in the crucial importance of colour and proportion. It was Vernon Lee who encouraged both women to start buying old Italian furniture; it may have been her enthusiasm for the gardens of the Florentine villas which helped to inspire the formal Italianate designs carried out for Mrs Wharton at Lenox and by Ottoline at Garsington.*

But Ottoline's remarkable sense of colour was all her own. Evidence of it turns up everywhere: in her choice of sepia ink to enhance her beautifully curling writing on handmade paper the colour of old roses and the soft vermilion tissue used to line her envelopes; in the one remaining sealing-wax-red panel which allows us to guess at the effect of the Red Room at Garsington; in the chests full of rich materials purchased on her travels; in a sewing-box as pretty as a picture with all the orange, red, gold and lemon silk reels lying in carefully graded rows; even in the pinkish-grey material she chose for her maids' uniforms, setting them off with crisp white pinafores. 'You beat us all at colour,' one artist, Henry Lamb, told her. When Roger Fry sent her a Venetian-red lacquer box, he told her that only she would know how to set it off best. When Bertrand Russell goaded her into telling him why it was that she thought they were incompatible, she spoke not of emotional or intellectual chasms but of his blindness to the effect of the colours for which she cared so passionately. 'I cannot bear it,' she wrote. 'You see, I live so much by the eyes and that is really nothing to you.'[4]

Ottoline grew more confident about her instincts with each new home she took in hand, but even in those early days she revelled in trying out her own ideas. The Grosvenor Road hall was a vivid sunflower yellow and deep pink curtains of Chinese silk were hung at the drawing-room windows. When they were closed in the late afternoon, their colour tinted the pearl-grey walls to a shimmering rose.

If the flamboyant colours at Grosvenor Road suggest that the artistic side of Ottoline's nature was looking for an outlet, the puritan side which kept all luxuries away from the dining-table was still in control. Her diaries from 1902 to 1905 were filled with prayers, self-castigation and stern resolves to purify her spirit. Philip's enthusiasm for religion and good causes was proving weaker than she had believed; she turned instead to the company of her favourite cousin, Vava Bentinck. Ottoline was always welcome at Richmond and the open lawns of the landscaped garden at Forbes House offered a refreshing view to eyes starved of greenery: she was finding it hard to

---

* In practice, Edith Wharton's taste leaned towards a cold perfection which was the antithesis of Ottoline's heterogeneous creations and which caused Henry James to disparage 'an almost too impeccable taste'. It was in fiction, intriguingly, that she identified with Ottoline's more bohemian style. In *The Age of Innocence* (1920) Ellen Olenska transforms a drab room into something exotic by 'the skilful use of a few properties', a stretch of red damask, a Greek bronze, two startling roses and a few bright and curious objects. (Signet Classic edn, pp. 64–5) This is Ottoline's taste, but the imagination which visualises and approves it is Mrs Wharton's.

get used to living away from the countryside. Mother Julian was often to be found here; Vava, as affectionate as ever, was always eager to discuss projects for helping the poor and unenlightened. We can blame her rather than the worldly Mother Julian for the attacks of liberal conscience which afflicted Ottoline during this period. 'Why should not the State have evening schools, gymnasiums . . . dancing, botany, social science for both boys and girls?' she wrote in 1903. 'Why should all these good things be for the rich? He came to the poor to enlighten them.' Her husband would not have been pleased to discover how many of her entries had to do with her plans 'to strengthen and improve Philip . . .'

Priggish though she later thought she had been, Ottoline was working away with tremendous determination both at the improvement of her own mind and for those who came under the general heading of the unenlightened. Her engagement books for 1902 and 1903 show that she was initiating a scheme for urban women's libraries, organising talks at Grosvenor Road and trying to find work for unemployed girls and to ensure that they were in safe lodgings. In the mornings, a friendly Newnham don called Melian Stawell came to tutor her in Greek philosophy, poetry and French literature. Ottoline's lack of a formal education had already been amply compensated for, but she still drew up a new reading-list every month in a blue workbook. (The list was often startlingly eclectic: Plato, Stendhal and Montesquieu appear on one page, Lecky and Greville on another.) The concept of spare time was anathema to her; in the hours left over from her good works and studies, she went to art galleries and concerts at the Queen's Hall with Hilda and lectures on every subject from contemporary politics to Zen Buddhism with Logan Pearsall Smith. (Logan had rapidly changed his mind about Ottoline and now went about extolling Philip's wonderful, fascinating wife.)

Years later, Ottoline described these early years at Grosvenor Road as the happiest period of her married life. Bundles of letters testify to the heartfelt love she lavished on her husband. 'My Philip I do adore you so,' she told him in one written on 1 September 1902; 'all my life is yours . . . Indeed we are blended into one.'

Careful though she was not to say so in her letters, Ottoline was disappointed by Philip's apathy. She knew he loathed his solicitor's work; she felt that he was wasting his life. At thirty, he had achieved nothing, and he readily admitted that he lacked any real sense of purpose. In the past, he had talked of trying to become a politician; Ottoline quietly made up her mind to help him realise that ambition. All he needed, she thought, was encouragement and good advice. She could still remember the excitement of the time in 1886 when she was only just thirteen and her mother had taken her to stay with friends in Norfolk to see Henry's first election victory.* Politics were, in her view, a splendid field for a man as clever and high-minded as Philip. For suggestions about where to begin, she turned to the Pearsall Smiths, a family of Liberal supporters with an impressive network of political connections.

Logan and his sisters, Mary Berenson and Alys Russell, Bertrand Russell's first wife, were the children of two rich Philadelphia Quakers. The family had been obliged to leave England in the 1870s when the late Mr Pearsall Smith's preaching career was destroyed by a sex scandal, but they returned in the 1880s and settled at Friday's Hill, a rather ugly house near Haslemere in Surrey.

Ottoline had already won round Logan and had been passed by Mary, but her main supporter at Friday's Hill was Logan's widowed mother. Hannah Pearsall Smith liked Ottoline on two counts: she was religious and she was an aristocrat. Hannah, a best-selling religious author, had a great love of titles (she had once told an American friend that she could only contemplate living in England as a member of the aristocracy). Ottoline, a lady and a Liberal to boot, was always welcome at Friday's Hill and Hannah was delighted to be consulted about Philip's chances of being chosen as a Liberal. Her response was optimistic: a pleasant manner and a handsome face were, in her view, the most valuable assets a young would-be politician could have. Hearing that he was full of diffidence, she told Ottoline that she had just the friends to enthuse and advise him. She arranged a weekend when Sidney and Beatrice Webb could visit Friday's Hill at the same time as the Morrells.

Ottoline did not like the Webbs and her spirits were not raised by the discovery that they were near-neighbours in Grosvenor Road, but she was delighted to see the effect that they had on Philip. Sitting with Hannah over tea in the garden, the Webbs painted a glowing picture of the reformed England that would come into existence when Arthur Balfour was defeated and the Liberals restored to power with the help of intelligent, dedicated men like Mr Morrell. Philip was ready to be persuaded if they could only tell him how to finance this new career. His salary as a solicitor was meagre, and neither he nor Ottoline could look for help to their staunchly Conservative families. The Webbs had an answer ready. The Liberal League, formed that year under Lord Rosebery's presidency, had offered to subsidise candidates who were prepared to take on the fight for the most solidly-established Conservative seats.

Ottoline's next problem was to get Philip accepted by the League.

---

* Lord Henry Bentinck represented North-West Norfolk for the Conservatives from 1886 to 1892 and South Nottinghamshire from 1895 to 1906, and again from 1910 to 1929.

She had two powerful friends in the Party, Augustine Birrell and Herbert Asquith. Birrell, a charming and erudite man who had known Ottoline before her marriage, told her that the Webbs were right to suggest the Liberal League as Philip's best course. He could do nothing himself to help, but it was obvious to him that their best chance was to enlist the support of Asquith, Sir Henry Campbell-Bannerman's heir apparent as the Party's leader.

Ottoline hesitated. She knew that Asquith had seen Philip as his rival in the days when they were both visiting Grosvenor Place; he had been a forceful opponent of the marriage on the grounds that Philip was a weak character and thoroughly unworthy of such a wife. But Asquith had lost none of his old affection for Ottoline; for her sake, he agreed to see Philip and to put him in touch with the Chief Whip, Herbert Gladstone, while adding his own endorsement. (This in itself was a guarantee of success; Gladstone, who had been Asquith's under-secretary at the Home Office, was among his most loyal friends.) With the Chief Whip's recommendation, Philip was promised total political subsidy and adopted to stand in the Liberal interests, news which was only blighted by the fact that he was to be the candidate for South Oxfordshire.

It could not, from Philip's point of view, have been a worse choice. The area was dense with his relations, his parents' friends and clients of his father's firm; the seat for mid-Oxfordshire was already held by his Tory cousin, Herbert Morrell. It was bad enough for his family that he had joined the Liberals, whom they detested; that he should flaunt his treachery on their doorstep was intolerable.

The Morrells expressed their anger vehemently, but privately. Outwardly, things remained as they had been with long, tense visits to Black Hall during which Ottoline, who detested card games, read or embroidered while Philip played poker patience against his mother. The Bentincks could understand why Ottoline would want Philip to follow the same career as her brother Henry, but not why she should want to espouse the Liberals. They were not pleased, but since Philip's chances of winning in a solidly Conservative constituency were slight, they said little.

Fully aware that she had incurred the disapproval of her family, Ottoline remained jubilant. She had found a cause to fill the void in Philip's life; her only worry now was that he appeared to be so nervous in public. Struck by Bertrand Russell's eloquence when Logan took her to hear him lecturing on Free Trade Theory, she longed to hear her husband speaking with the same easy confidence. 'My darling Philip so disappointed that he was not better,' she wrote after one ill-starred speech, 'but he will improve and must learn.'

Years later, Ottoline regretted having pushed Philip into a career which put a huge strain on a shy and insecure character: 'He lacks the "drive" that comes from passion and concentration on one cause,' she wrote in 1912. '... If one could have seen more clearly and judged his capacities more accurately, I think it would have been better and more natural to him if he had devoted himself to literature and history and had not entered politics.'[5] Philip, who supervised the editing of his wife's memoirs, felt no need to delete this view of his pre-war career in politics. Reading, golf and evenings of bridge at his club – these were the undemanding pleasures of a man who did not respond well to the pressures of the arena into which his wife's ambitions had thrust him.

By 1912, Ottoline was already beginning to think that she had made a mistake. In 1903, her sense of what was good for Philip was directed by her own longing for him to be seen to do well. She was determined to do everything she could to ensure her husband's victory in the next election. It was vital, in those pre-broadcasting days, to make personal contact with as many of the electorate as possible, and this was what the Morrells worked at in every moment that Philip was free from the office. (His legal career did not end until after his victory in 1906, when Mr Morrell decided that a Liberal Member was a liability to the firm's name and ordered his son to resign.)

Free time meant weekends and evenings; Ottoline soon grew used to setting off at dusk for a three-hour drive into the country. They could never be certain what would be in store for them in the Oxfordshire villages, an enthusiastic audience of loyal Liberals or angry Tories armed with eggs and stones and ready on at least one occasion to turn the Morrells' cart over and land its occupants in the road. Commonest of all were the evenings when they were respectfully received by a group of silent farmworkers in a village hall. Resolutely speechless, they still felt at liberty to stare; Ottoline's striking looks and elaborate costumes were becoming a well-known attraction.

Canvassing also involved visits to the families who were helping to finance the Liberals. Mr Pears, the original beautifier of infant complexions, was sallow-skinned, reeked of cigar smoke and drove them out in a carriage upholstered in slippery sky-blue satin. Sir Frank Crisp, a rich solicitor, interested Ottoline more since he shared her reclusive relation's passion for underground buildings. The Fifth Duke's works had been large and sedate; Sir Frank's were of a playful kind. China hobgoblins and goggle-eyed monsters squatted by an underground lake on which the visitors were invited to row past sham mountains ornamented with porcelain chamois. Warned by the jovial Sir Frank of the imminent descent of a giant false spider on her hat as she and Philip rowed towards him, Ottoline's smile was a miracle of self-control.

More congenial to Ottoline and of greater consequence to her life were the visits to Newington, the Oxfordshire home of two rich New England ladies who never allowed their enthusiasm for the Liberals to interfere with their love of painting landscapes and of entertaining their friends.

Ethel Sands, who shared her manor house with Nan Hudson, offered a luxurious way of life to a select circle of literary, artistic and political friends, many of whom, like Henry James, Logan Pearsall Smith and Edith Wharton, were fellow expatriates; it was at Newington that Ottoline first began to dream of creating a similar existence for herself. 'The beauty of this place ravished me,' she wrote, remembering how she had first seen it in winter, rising from a grey mirror of floodwater, desolate and spellbound. In summer, Ethel's formal garden was full of roses and the well-proportioned rooms lay cool as an oasis behind long linen blinds, all pale silks with carefully-placed bowls of pastel-coloured flowers. It was not Ottoline's taste – hers was more rich and idiosyncratic – but she was charmed by the atmosphere of civilised tranquillity. Watching Ethel strolling in the garden with Edith Wharton and Henry James's brother, William, Ottoline decided that intellectual society was neither so remote nor so impossible to join as she had supposed. She was helped by Ethel's generosity with her introductions; William and Edith both pronounced themselves enchanted by her (a compliment which Ottoline did not feel able to return about Mrs Wharton, who struck her as a restless, worldly woman without depth). In bringing Ottoline together with her own most famous compatriot, Ethel was confident of giving equal pleasure to them both. Henry James adored meeting aristocrats; Ottoline had spoken of her longing to meet creative people.

For James, there must have been a curious sense of *déjà vu* when he first met Ottoline. Drifting through Ethel's pale rooms in one of the gracefully-draped Grecian-style dresses she favoured at that time and with her copper-coloured hair in a loose chignon that framed her long face, she spoke in a soft, eager voice of art, literature and the need to reform the social system. Was she not one of his own inventions, the beautiful Christina Light in her second incarnation as the politically-minded Princess Casamassima? This was his first reaction to the tall and exotically beautiful young woman who evidently shared Miss Light's determination to shape her own destiny. James was charmed and intrigued.

A strong mutual affection for Ethel, their hostess, helped to ease the way to an enduring friendship between the elderly James and the young woman he affectionately called his superfine princess. One of his last afternoons out in London was to have tea alone with Ottoline. She was invited to his country house in Rye and stayed with him at the Windsor home of James's friend, Howard Sturgis, while James in turn came to lend his protective presence to her London parties. Shocked by the insouciance with which she flung herself into the lively currents of bohemian society after the move from Grosvenor Road to Bedford Square, James saw it as his duty to warn her against such cavalier behaviour. Social position, in his eyes, was far too precious a possession to be squandered for the sake of procuring what anyone with money might buy, the company of artists and writers.

Ottoline was always amused by Henry James's frenzies of snobbery; in all other respects, he commanded her admiration and love. Entranced by the mixture of wit and melancholy which she shrewdly ascribed to his Irish ancestry, it was his humanity which made her read his books over and over again. 'It is not deeds, acts, that he values as important,' she wrote in an appraisal of his novels which astutely discerned the link with his psychologist-brother's work, 'but thoughts, personality, goodness, the "invisible man," and the conflicts of the spirits of good and evil . . . [His works are] lit by the penetrating lamp of love and understanding, and a sincere wholehearted compassion for tangled, shot-silk human nature.'[6]

Henry James spoke to Ottoline from another generation, but the painter and art critic Roger Fry was only seven years older than herself. Emotional, impulsive and articulate, he won Ottoline's heart at their first meeting at Newington in 1904. The unlikely product of an austere Quaker upbringing, Fry was an immensely attractive man; a wide grin, piercing eyes and a shock of unruly brown hair gave him the look of a scruffy overgrown schoolboy.

Fry had held his first one-man show and collaborated in the founding of *The Burlington Magazine* the year before he met Ottoline. Quietly humorous, he became passionate whenever the subject turned to art. Absorbed by his ideas on the relation between art and religion, Ottoline was intrigued to learn that he had only recently parted company with Bernard Berenson, his most influential mentor. They had already found that they had acquaintances in common in Logan Pearsall Smith and Ena Mathias, a new friend of Ottoline's who had known Fry at the Slade; talk of Berenson and Florence led them to discover that they had fallen under the spell of Italy at almost exactly the same moment, visiting all the same places in a state of cultural exaltation.

People always found it easy to confide in Ottoline – listening was one of her greatest gifts – and Fry was no exception. Helen Fry, a lovely Botticelli-faced painter whom he had married in 1897, had become mentally unstable. She had been in an asylum twice and, although the doctors pronounced her better, she had become almost speechless. (On a good day, she might speak a couple of sentences.) Fry had just accepted a new job which would take him to America, where he subsequently became curator of the Metropolitan Museum. Helen was to remain in England with their children. Since Ottoline seemed sympathetic and ready to help, Fry asked her to visit and write to his wife whenever she had time. Ottoline readily agreed. When Fry returned to England in 1907, he was eager to renew a friendship which was deepened by gratitude on his side and by sympathy on Ottoline's.

Newington was the seeding-ground for many friendships, but the most demanding of Ottoline's new attachments was far removed from Ethel Sands and her circle. Writing down the names of the people she thought had most influenced her life before she met Bertrand Russell, she chose only three: Mother Julian, George MacDonald, and John Cramb. In 1913, the year Cramb died, she told Lytton Strachey that he had been one of the most brilliant and extraordinary men she had ever met.

Cramb came into Ottoline's life late in 1903 when she had been married almost two years and was hungry for more mental stimulation than Philip was able to provide. Her visits to Newington offered a rare oasis in a desert of political functions. A talk was being given one evening in November about Madame Roland, the French revolutionary heroine, and Ottoline decided to go and hear it on her own at the Queen's Hall. During the interval, she was approached by a tall, fiery-eyed old man, a professor of modern history who, while his first passion was music (he thought nothing of going to a dozen concerts a week), was also an authority on philosophy, divinity, French literature and the medieval romance. Ottoline was fascinated by him; Cramb was enchanted out of his wits.

A lonely man with a crippled son and an invalid wife, Cramb was delighted to take on the role of Ottoline's new tutor. By the beginning of February 1904, he had become her regular companion at exhibitions and afternoon concerts. They met for lunches and teas in Piccadilly, near the Grafton Gallery, and went for long afternoon strolls in Richmond Park, during which Cramb developed the romantic notion that he was a gallant troubadour, Raymond de Ruyrémonde, sworn to the service of the exquisite Lady Alvora of Alvorédene. (The names were borrowed from the epic poem by Ariosto, whose portrait they admired when it was on loan to the National Gallery.) By the middle of May, his letters had become delirious outpourings of his love. He saw Ottoline in flowers, he felt her in poetry, he heard a waltz and instantly, 'je rêve, je rêve à Ushas, la déesse de l'aube – vois-tu, vois-tu, ma soeur, oui, toi, la soeur de mon âme . . .'[7] Cervantes would have been delighted by him; Ottoline began to grow alarmed and to look for an escape.

The friendship had come at a particularly sad moment in her life when she had lost a brother and one of her closest friends. Bill Bentinck, her favourite brother, had died on 4 November 1903 en route to India, from an infection caught in Africa during his service in the Boer War; Arthur Strong died of pernicious anaemia in February 1904. Ottoline went to sit with Eugenie Strong beside the body. It comforted her to think that, in John Cramb, she had found a man whose mind was, in its unworldly way, almost as remarkable as Strong's. But Arthur Strong had never been in love with her, while John Cramb was utterly besotted. Suggestions that he might take an interest in her friend Hilda were spurned; the news that she was to visit her mother-in-law at Black Hall for a few days produced petulant complaints and accusations: 'I am very tired of not seeing thee, very. But Oxford is medicinal. Is it? Hein?'

Cramb's ill-health was one reason why Ottoline was anxious not to end the friendship too abruptly. In between flirtatious promises in his letters to kiss 'tes ongles roses et pointus' (he was obsessed by her pretty hands), there were disturbing references to nervous collapses and to blindness, 'this eternal misery of my sight'. A less noble reason for wishing to continue seeing him was that Cramb, remembered by his pupils at Queen's College as an exceptional teacher, was giving her the education she had always wanted.

Ottoline's intelligence was instinctive rather than academic, but she had a passion for knowledge and a retentive memory which stood her in excellent stead when she encountered the quick and effortlessly allusive minds of Bloomsbury a few years later. Nobody seems to have wondered how it was that she came to be so well-versed in history, music and literature, yet they can hardly have supposed that she had gleaned so much from the governess at Welbeck and a little extramural study. Her morning lessons with Melian Stawell at Grosvenor Road had helped, but the real answer was that she acquired her knowledge during the year of her friendship with Cramb. Occupied though she was in helping Philip with his political campaign, she always managed to set aside at least two hours for reading every day.

Ottoline wanted to learn and Cramb was a superb educator. Urged to saturate herself in Balzac, she was introduced to the works of Diderot, Rousseau, Turgenev and Carlyle. (Cramb's taste was astonishingly diverse.) After making her compare Byron to Goethe, and persuading her to exchange Daudet for Zola, Cramb led her towards the mellifluous pleasures of French nineteenth-century poetry.

Baudelaire and Verlaine were his own favourites: Verlaine, above all, coloured the tone of much of his correspondence with Ottoline as he envisaged her, pale and still, a statue glimpsed behind the clear cold jets of fountains.

The image was poignantly appropriate. Ottoline was not made of stone, but she could not bring herself to see Cramb as a gallant troubadour. She did not want his love. Sorry though she felt for him, she saw nothing but tragedy ahead if she continued to play the part of Lady Alvora in the mind of this elderly and utterly unrealistic man. Cramb was already growing frantic at the thought of losing her by the end of the summer ('Why has thou no wish to return, hein?' 'Thou doest read my letters?'). Late in November, a year after their first encounter, Ottoline wrote to tell him that she had decided not to see him again. 'There is no friendship quite like this which has ended, none,' Cramb told her, but he did not protest. He did not forget the adoration he had felt for her, however: in 1908, when she sent him an affectionate letter, he told her that he was never without his photographs of 'Alvora Alvorissima' and that 'for every word I have written in this letter I have thought a thousand'. In 1910, Ottoline took her four-year-old daughter to visit Cramb at his dingy flat in west London and heard that her old admirer had been charmed by the little girl's 'grave, winged glances' back at him through the carriage window as they drove away.

The friendship had shaken Cramb's quiet, well-ordered life to the core, more so than he had allowed Ottoline to know. A telling image occurs in *Cuthbert Learmont*, one of the novels Cramb wrote under the pseudonym of J. A. Revermort, in which Mary Fotheringham, a tall and beautiful red-haired woman with a weakness for large hats and rich scents, is a thinly-disguised portrait of Ottoline. A moment comes when the hero (Cramb's fictitious self) is obliged to imagine Mary being made love to by her husband. The thought is so unbearable that he almost faints: it is described as being 'as though he lay pinioned on a floor of melting sulphur'. So, we may be sure, Cramb had tormented himself with the thought of Ottoline giving herself to Philip; only in fiction could he acknowledge the strength of his own desire for her. To Ottoline, Cramb had offered a chance to educate herself and to indulge the side of her nature which delighted in romantic fantasies. She made no reference to the friendship in her memoirs, although she persuaded Asquith to give Cramb's widow a pension. But she did not forget the effect he had had on her. 'He was a creature that was simply shaken with passion and fire,' she told Russell in 1915. 'His thought was unruly . . . but you would have loved his passion. I am very glad to have known him now.'[8]

It has been suggested by an earlier biographer that Ottoline's trip to Spain at the end of 1904 was a direct result of her relationship with Cramb: '... it happened with Munthe and it happened with Asquith; in fact whenever Ottoline had an emotional crisis, a trip abroad or a visit to a nursing home was sure to follow ... after she broke off from Cramb it is not surprising to find her and Philip leaving for a holiday in Spain ...'[9] The generalisation is too simple. Emotional traumas can be made to account for some of Ottoline's visits to sanatoriums and foreign spas, but not all; it is worth remembering that a general sense of being tired and run-down had been the English city-dweller's reason for escaping abroad since the 1860s. We would be embarking on a baffling journey if we tried to find a crisis behind each of Ottoline's many health-oriented journeys.

Her holidays with Philip, above all, do not belong in this misleading category. The visit to Spain did not take place until six weeks after she had ended her friendship with Cramb, but she had been planning it and studying Spanish three months earlier. This does not suggest an emotional collapse, nor were her feelings for Cramb so intense as to have provoked one. The date indicates that there were more mundane reasons for wishing to leave England. No one liked being in London in December and January in the era of peasouper fogs, when windows had to be kept permanently shut and nobody who could avoid it ventured out of their house. Ottoline had no desire to go to Welbeck for Christmas, and Black Hall was equally uninviting. Travel was cheap; they had never visited Spain; the prospect of warmth and sunlight was enticing. Here, rather than an emotional crisis over a man for whom she had only felt affection, is the obvious explanation for their journey to Spain.

It is more helpful to observe one small incident which took place during the holiday. The Morrells had only been married for three years and the trip to Spain could easily have been treated as a second honeymoon, but a young flamenco dancer who saw them together in Madrid instantly identified them as a brother and sister. Ottoline saw nothing odd in the mistake; she mentioned it in her memoirs only because it had amused her that the girl thought they were painters. In fact, the girl had intuitively grasped the nature of their relationship. It was not, and never had been, that of lovers. Trust and loyalty were important ingredients in their marriage; passion was not. When Philip shared a bed with his wife, he did so chiefly because he wanted a child and, above all, a son. Ottoline, while initially saddened by his evident lack of desire for her, had accustomed herself to it. When the platonic friendship with Cramb ended, she returned to Philip's side with gratitude for his tranquil, undemanding love.

MARRIAGE AND MOTHERHOOD

In August 1905, Ottoline discovered that she was pregnant and found a new house; the prospect of motherhood gave her considerably less pleasure than the thought of making a new home. 'Never did I feel that I was bringing a new and beautiful creation into the world,' she wrote. 'It seemed an invasion, a burden, an unknown existence breaking into ours and upsetting the wonderful intimacy and companionship of our life together.'[10] Philip, however, was delighted. The year 1906 promised to be a glorious one for him. The Tory leader, Arthur Balfour, resigned late in 1905 and January 1906 saw the Liberals back in power with Campbell-Bannerman at their head and victories in even the safest of the Tory constituencies. (This was a result of the electorate's furious response to Chamberlain's tariff proposals, which had been perceived as a threat to Free Trade.) In South Oxfordshire, Philip was voted in with a handsome majority (4,562 votes against Sir Robert Hermon Hodge's 4,050), a triumph which was marred by the icy response of his own family and Ottoline's. Mr Morrell's request that his son should dissociate his name from the family firm upset Philip less than a harsh letter from the duke, accusing him of turncoat politics and of having disgraced them all. Neither a private interview with the duchess nor a temporising letter to the duke from Henry Bentinck, who had lost his own Conservative seat, succeeded in lessening his wrath. Ottoline was informed that she was welcome to come and stay, but not if she brought her husband with her. The predictable result was that neither of the Morrells visited Welbeck until an invitation was issued to them both, in 1915.

House-moving plans provided a diversion from pregnancy and family rows. The new home which Ottoline had found was a handsome four-storey Georgian house in Bedford Square. She had always liked Bloomsbury, a pleasantly unassuming area of London, and she fell in love with the house on the spot. The prospect of paying £1,800 for the lease and another £300, by her own calculations, for the decoration, did not deter her. (The shock of Lady Bolsover's arrangements for her daughter was not disclosed until 1912 and Ottoline was still a fairly wealthy woman in 1905.) 'I think we should be very happy there,' she wrote to Philip in a letter which urged him to make a quick decision. He went to inspect the house that week, and gave his approval.

Bloomsbury had no wider connotations than as an area of London in 1906, the year in which the Morrells moved into 44 Bedford Square. Their neighbours in the handsome houses with their Adam-influenced interiors were professional middle-class families, a mixture of architects, surgeons, and elderly editors. The artists who later gave the area its vividness had not yet arrived – Augustus John, Henry Lamb and Duncan Grant were all living in Paris – and the Bloomsbury

Group lay in the future. (The young men who came to Thursday evening discussion groups at the home of Sir Leslie Stephen's children in nearby Gordon Square had not yet broken away from their own families.) What drew Ottoline to Bedford Square was not the prospect of a literary or intellectual environment, but the charm of owning a prettier and larger house than the one in Grosvenor Road, in a part of London she greatly preferred.

In Bedford Square, on the night of 18 May 1906, Ottoline gave birth to twins, a frail little girl weighing only three pounds and a healthy baby boy. Philip instantly named them after the twins in *Twelfth Night*; discouraged from being so pretentious by Ottoline, he chose Hugh, the name of his dead brother, for the little boy, while Ottoline named the girl Julian after her old friend in Truro. Unpleasant though she had felt the whole business of pregnancy and childbirth to be, she found herself being caught up in the mood of her husband's delight. She had never seen him so happy. 'Philip so dear and so proud of the little boy especially,' she noted and went on to say that this fair and beautiful child promised to become the centre of their lives. All their love was directed towards him; the doctors had made it clear that the little girl was unlikely to live.

The twins were only two days old when an ominous entry appeared in Ottoline's journal: 'We did not think the little boy very well in the morning.' He was worse on the following day; on 22 May, Ottoline wrote his name for the last time.

Little Hugh suddenly taken ill at 9 o'clock; sent for doctor; haemorrhage in the brain. Doctor came to operate; slowly sank, and died at 1.30. Agonising, cannot write of it.[11]

There were to be no more children. In February 1907, after nine months of ill-health which she had ascribed to nervous depression following the tragedy, Ottoline was found to be suffering from a dangerous pelvic infection. She was taken into Miss Nelson Smith's nursing home in Maida Vale and operated on at the end of the month. When she recovered, she was told to reconcile herself to the fact that any chance of another child had now gone.* Philip, who longed for a son, was almost unhinged by disappointment. Ottoline wrote bleakly in her journal of 'my barrenness of fruit' and buried her sorrow. Of

---

* Ottoline was as vague in her letters as well as in her journals and memoirs about gynaecological details. The operation may have been for fibroids or a tubal occlusion: her journals show that she continued to have unusually painful periods for another ten years. It is difficult to know whether it was deviousness or ignorance that caused her to be so evasive when Bertrand Russell told her, as he often did, that he wanted to have a child with her. Ottoline's early letters to him refer only to the social problems that they would encounter; they never suggest that she believed it to be physically impossible.

the vast circle of people who began to cluster around 44 Bedford Square in the summer of 1907, none were told what had happened. Julian, as a young schoolgirl, rather enjoyed parading the tragedy of 'my secret grief' for the twin brother she had never known; her parents preferred to mourn their loss in silence.

The principal victim of the little boy's death was his survivor. Philip's desire for a son was only partly assuaged by the existence of a daughter who, according to her own recollections, was encouraged by her father to look as boyish as possible by cropping her hair and dressing in masculine clothes. But in time Philip became deeply attached to his daughter; it was Ottoline who found it impossible to forgive her for having lived when Hugh, their darling, had died. In all her writings, both public and private, a clear picture emerges of a child being accommodated on the fringes of her mother's life. Julian flits through her mother's published memoirs like a ghost, significant only at the moment that she catches someone's eye. Nijinsky picks her up and whirls her round in his arms; Yeats tells her that she is very pretty; on such occasions, her mother is happy to praise her. But one of the principal reasons why Julian later became reluctant to allow her mother's private journals to be seen was because of the references to herself; here, Ottoline gave vent to all of her anger and disappointment that her daughter was, as she saw it, so hard, self-willed and undemonstrative of anything but a desire to have her own way. It is extraordinary but true that nowhere in Ottoline's writings is there a hint that she ever felt herself to have been at fault as a mother, and yet it is hard to think of anyone more eager to criticise herself than Ottoline was in every other respect. Not once, in 1913, when the seven-year-old Julian was left in a Swiss sanatorium for consumptive children for eight months, did Ottoline remark that such an experience was bound to have a traumatic effect. (She had, however, become genuinely loving and anxious the year before, when Julian was alarmingly ill.) She completely failed to understand why Julian should have been wilful and difficult on her return; the solution she found before sending her away to boarding school was to lodge her with a Morrell aunt.

We should not be too quick to condemn Ottoline. Julian was born in 1906, in an age when any family who could afford it left the care of their children to nursemaids and governesses. Ottoline's own unhappy memories of being compelled to participate in the grand parties at Welbeck could have influenced her decision to keep Julian away from Bedford Square. Neither she nor Philip wanted their frail daughter to have an urban childhood. Ottoline's own happiest memories were of her first years at East Court; it may have been the wish to create a similar kind of country upbringing for Julian that decided her in 1907 to rent Peppard Cottage, a low, pleasant house near Henley-on-Thames with a view across Peppard Common to tall beechwoods and, beyond them, undulating sweeps of downland. It is certainly possible that Ottoline had Julian's needs in mind. There was a garden for her to play in and the village was quiet and friendly; it was an added bonus that Miss Brenton ('Brenty'), Ottoline's lady's maid, came from the village and was ready to settle there as Julian's nurse. (The Brenton parents ran the Dog Inn at Peppard and were prepared to provide extra accommodation for Ottoline's visitors since the cottage only had one spare room.)

Peppard was very close to East Court, which may help to explain why Ottoline started to model herself on Lady Bolsover during the first two years of Julian's life in the country. Imitating her mother, she prepared suitable stories and poems for Julian as well as the 'Thought-Book' of improving maxims composed for her daughter's benefit. But Julian was as stubborn in her liking for pleasure as Ottoline had once been in her determination to renounce it. Sensing that religion was being used to fasten a yoke of duty around her neck, she shook it off. By the time she was five, she was able to show what she thought of a mother who cared only about improving the state of her soul. 'Whenever I make advances to her she turns and pushes me away,' Ottoline noted and went on to remark that Julian never rejected her father's embraces. From then on, she drew increasingly bitter comparisons between the devotion she had lavished on Lady Bolsover and the lack of feeling she observed in her own child.

One more thought should be introduced regarding Ottoline's role as a mother during Julian's early life. The knowledge, or even the half-knowledge, of adultery must affect a child's feelings towards its parents. Both Ottoline and Philip had affairs which took place on home territory in the period between 1910 and 1922. Julian was at Peppard in 1910 when Henry Lamb was living in the village and deep in an intensely complicated and passionate relationship with Ottoline. She was at Cliff End in Dorset with her mother in 1911, when Ottoline first slept with Russell. It is not possible to be certain when Philip started to have sexual liaisons with women who worked for them, but Julian must have been conscious of an atmosphere of whispering and secrets long before the situation reached its shocking climax at Garsington. That was in 1917. Julian was ten years old.

4

IMAGINATIVE IMAGES

'... I did rouse myself to go and see Ott. I was so much overcome by her beauty that I really felt as if I'd suddenly got into the sea, and heard the mermaids fluting on their rocks. How it was done I can't think; but she had red-gold hair in masses, cheeks as soft as cushions with a lovely deep crimson on the crest of them, and a body shaped more after my notion of a mermaid's than I've ever seen ... swelling, but smooth.'

Virginia Woolf to Vanessa Bell, 22 May 1917

Watching one of the artists at Garsington trying to paint Ottoline in the war years, Julian was heard to say that she thought the task impossible: nobody could make her mother look as wonderful as she did in real life.

Ottoline was, for many years, a woman of extraordinary beauty, though there are descriptions of the older woman, henna-haired, overpainted and dressed in clothes which make her look bizarre in the post-war decade. Cruel images are more tenacious than romantic ones, but it is important to be aware that there was nothing grotesque about Ottoline in her first years at Bedford Square. Quentin Bell, discussing her in a BBC radio programme on 9 May 1973, remembered having first met Ottoline when she was over sixty: 'She still kept something which must have been very much stronger, of course, when she was a young woman. Definitely one did feel that she was, or had been, enormously attractive.' Pressed by his interviewer, he said that even then, there had been 'something sexy' about her which fascinated him.

Portraits and photographs show that Bell was right; Ottoline in her mid-thirties had a sensual, charismatic quality which was made more intriguing by the fact that she seemed to be quite unaware of it. She may have been an imperfect mother to her little girl, but she offered an irresistible subject to artists in search of an unconventional model. Duncan Grant, Henry Lamb, Simon Bussy, Augustus John, James

Pryde, Dorothy Brett, Neville Lytton, Charles Conder; the list of artists who attempted to capture her on canvas is a long one. The attraction for them lay in the deliberate presentation of herself as a creature of fantasy which was so oddly contradicted by her lack of vanity. They were free to make what they would of her; Ottoline only objected once in her career as a portrait sitter, when she thought, a little unfairly, that Dorothy Brett had made her look like a prostitute.

We know that Ottoline had a passion for weird and wonderful clothes which may have been inspired by her eccentric ancestress, the Duchess of Newcastle. Hints of this enthusiasm were apparent on her honeymoon when Mary Berenson saw her swathed in lace and plastered with costume jewellery. The completed picture only emerged in 1905, the year before Julian was born; some of the credit for its success must go to the skilful needle of her dressmaker, Miss Brenton.

Brenty had worked for Ottoline since 1901; like all her female employees, she admired Her Ladyship (as she was always known to them) for her bold originality and loved her for her kindness and simplicity. A thrifty, practical woman, she was able to adapt the ideas which her employer took from paintings seen on her travels. Ottoline's part of the task was to provide postcard-reproductions or sketches and suitable materials; Brenty's was to decide whether the designs would work. 'I think the postcard very quaint and pretty but not the style for you' was her blunt answer to one notion. 'It is so difficult to keep out of the fashions as the narrow frocks do suit you so much,' she went on, 'but we must make our things quaint and unusual by the colouring or embroidering.'[1]

Quaint and unusual is as good a description as any for the extraordinary clothes which Brenty produced: with their huge puffed sleeves, embroidered bodices and sweeping satin skirts, they would have made the wearer look at home in a painting by Velázquez. The fact that they seldom cost more than three guineas to create is explained by the way they were produced. The materials were magnificent, but everything was in the general effect; seams were skimped, lining was not used, fastenings were minimal, hems and turnings were often only tacked into position. Made like theatrical props (some were copied from stage costumes, with Brenty being sent along to sketch in the audience) Ottoline's dresses were designed, not for comfort, but to stir the imagination of the viewer. They succeeded in doing so to a remarkable degree.

The first commissioned portrait of Ottoline was painted in 1905, not long after her trip with Philip to Spain, by James Pryde, an original, intensely imaginative artist whose theatrical compositions influenced the early stage productions of Edward Gordon Craig. Known to everyone as Jimmy, Pryde was much-loved in bohemian London for his good nature and his wit. 'Christ come to Chicago' was how he described Augustus John in a black billycock hat, while his summary of the artist's existence was 'a here-to-day and gone-to-borrow sort of life'.

Philip had already been urging Ottoline to get herself painted when Percy Feilding brought round 'a charming little picture of a lady sitting on a sofa', painted by Pryde. When it transpired that the artist and his wife were living in High Wycombe, not far from Oxford, Ottoline wrote to suggest that she and her mother-in-law might visit him from Black Hall; would the following Friday at two o'clock suit him?

Pryde was not at all sure that it did suit him. He hated the idea of being treated as a society painter, although Ottoline's striking looks and sweet manner, together with the promise of a seventy-pound fee, changed his mind. But he was no Sargent and his heart sank when he came for the first sitting at Grosvenor Road to find Ottoline draped on a sofa in an exquisitely intricate white lace dress chosen by Philip. Pryde's skill did not lie in representing minute detail; he had never in his life tried to paint lace. Losing his courage, he fled and only came back when he had found a friend, a photographer, who could do justice to the dress.

Cavendish Morton produced a superb series of photographs of Ottoline, some in the white dress and others, more strikingly, in pearls and black velvet, but Pryde felt guilty about having disappointed her. Later that summer, he visited Ottoline in Oxford and made some preliminary notes while they were wandering around the botanical gardens. A month later, he presented her with a portrait.

It is a curious picture, painted in deep shades of sepia and brown. Ottoline, draped in a heavy silk shawl and with one hand extended like a broken wing, stares enigmatically at the viewer from under the shade of a broad hat. On either side, she is flanked by two towering blocks of shadow, tall as prison gates and reaching to the full height of the canvas. The effect is both sinister and intriguing, as if the sitter had been trapped by her setting.

The lace dress was not forgotten, and Ottoline talked to Pryde about her love of fantastic clothes. If she wanted to own something really remarkable, he said, she should go and see Mrs Neville, Max Beerbohm's sister, who had made herself one of the most fascinating dresses he had ever seen. Ottoline took up the suggestion and discovered that Agnes Neville's famous dress had been sewn from silk panels painted by her friend Charles Conder. Agnes, seeing her eyes light up, suggested that they should visit him and see if he would repeat the experiment.

Ottoline looked forward to meeting Charles Conder. She had heard about him from Logan Pearsall Smith and also from Roger Fry, a great admirer at the time of Conder's atmospheric landscapes and of the silk fans on which he evoked the world of Watteau's *fêtes galantes*. It was a world which had been dramatically revived that year at a magnificent fancy-dress ball which the Conders gave at their home in Cheyne Walk. Ottoline, who met them a week or two after it took place, was forced to be content with Mrs Neville's descriptions of a room draped in the shades of Whistler's 'Nocturnes', of Arthur Symons stalking pretty boys in a gold Venetian mask and the young Baroness de Meyer playing Hamlet in black tights, while Conder exploited his own reputation for wildness and played his favourite villain, Balzac's de Rastignac.

Friends had warned Ottoline that Conder was debauched; meeting him, she thought them most unkind. Charmed by his blond good looks, his luminous eyes and his gentle, hesitant voice, she decided that he was one of the most unworldly and delightful men she had ever met. Smoking as he scribbled and shaded – he was never without a cigarette and a pencil, even at meals – Conder talked about his early years in Australia and his later ones in Paris, about Balzac and Wilde, and about the artists he knew and whom Ottoline was longing to meet. At least, she thought she was; she was unnerved by the exuberant drawings of nudes by Augustus John in Conder's room which the artist had bought when John was so poor that he had to lie in bed while his wife patched his only pair of trousers. Such poverty was awful to contemplate, but so were the drawings which she admired with averted eyes. In 1906, Ottoline was still prim enough to prefer Conder's gracefully-dressed females.

Conder was the only artist who painted Ottoline as she believed herself to be. Augustus John showed her as a sibyl and a gypsy in a ravishing series of watercolour sketches; Henry Lamb usually favoured the hagiographical approach with her eyes upturned in a soulful stare (although he also gave her a fanciful picture of herself as a naked dryad, swinging her legs from a branch in the Peppard woods).* Duncan Grant wanted to make a witch of her, turning her face into a white triangle rushing towards the jabbing point of her chin. Simon Bussy, Lytton Strachey's brother-in-law, tried for the same effect in a picture which suggests, despite its imaginative colour-

---

* This picture, given by Ottoline to Ena Mathias, is now in a private collection. One of the eleven children of a rich art-dealer, Ashley Wertheimer, Ena Mathias met Ottoline in 1904 and became a close friend. As the owner of the Claridge Gallery, she was often able to help find purchasers for the artists Ottoline wanted to help.

ing, that the sitter had a leading role in a Salvation Army band. Dorothy Brett used the visionary approach in a portrait which changed Ottoline's eyes to turquoises and made a fiery comet of her hair. But Conder simply transported her into his own world. When he took up the brush, he saw the woman he had been painting for years. It was surely a Conder picture that Ottoline had in mind when she described her feelings as she joined a noisy fancy-dress party in Gordon Square and wrote that 'perhaps, after all, I belonged to the time of hoops and loops and billowing skirts – a rare survival – one of those who were laughing from behind the trees'.[2] She had described Conder as a descendant of Watteau; when he looked at her, he saw one of the smiling, melancholy figures who stand apart from the *fête galante*. He recognised, as no other painter did, that Ottoline belonged to another age.

Conder had been ruining his health with alcohol for years. In the autumn of 1906, while he was undergoing treatment and Ottoline was helping his wife Stella to hang his pictures for a new exhibition, she met another artist, Neville Lytton. A delightful man whose love of painting was equalled by his enthusiasm for socialism, music and folk-dancing, Lytton wanted to paint her at once. Ottoline was unable to sit for him until after her gynaecological operation, but in the spring of 1907 she agreed to spend a couple of weeks at Crabbet, the stark and beautiful house built for Mrs Lytton's father, Wilfrid Scawen Blunt.

The painting, which showed Ottoline standing in a rich red dress against a dark background, was a success, and Ottoline was delighted to be serenaded by Lytton on his flute and by the young Hungarian violinists, Jelly and Adela d'Aranyi, who were staying in the house. She enjoyed, too, being taken to visit old Blunt in one of the woodland cottages to which he was still ready, at seventy, to carry off willing damsels; she wished she was an artist herself when she saw her young host sauntering through the bluebell woods in high boots and velvet breeches. She did not, however, feel the same enthusiasm for his wife Judith, who played real tennis, bred miniature dogs and Arab horses, and spoke to her guests, all with an air of absolute indifference. She talked to her tennis coach, but never to her three children, who were to be seen wistfully staring out of bushes in the garden as their beautiful mother, dressed in an Arabian robe, swept unsmilingly past. To Ottoline, who had strong views about how a hostess should behave, Judith seemed quite shockingly self-engrossed. It was not how she planned to treat her guests at Bedford Square.

5

BLOOMSBURY, LOVE AND ART
1907–10

'Conversation, talk, interchange of ideas – how good it was! . . . I gave myself in reckless energy to these people.'

OM, *Early Memoirs*

'Conventionality is deadness,' Ottoline wrote in her diary for 1907. 'Your life must break bounds set by the world. Be ye not conformed unto this world.' She was ready to break free. Devoted though Ottoline still was to her husband, the death of their baby boy had marked the beginning of a rift; her notebooks were full of wistful references to Philip's coldness and her sense that she had failed him. 'If I could only have a son,' she wrote. They seem never to have talked about it together; it was only when she had closed the door of her study at the end of the long Bedford Square drawing-room that she felt able to pour out her sense of failure. It was her fault, she thought, that Philip seemed always to be nervous and on edge; she blamed herself for being too stupid to be of use to him. 'I am not clever or capable enough to work alone,' she wrote, 'but I would love to help him more if he would let me. I wish this so much.' By 1907, she was feeling unhappy enough to think that she ought to end the marriage but, even in those early days, she did not dare to think of the effect that such a decision would have on Philip. Remote though he had become in the last year, she knew that he relied on her to stay with him, financially and emotionally: 'he cannot really go alone.'[*] Her best chance of finding happiness lay in looking for it elsewhere.

Ottoline's chief supporter in her project for a new life was Logan Pearsall Smith. Logan was in raptures about the new house with its

---

[*] Philip had no money of his own, now that he had ceased to work as a solicitor.

graceful staircase and views over the square from the drawing-room windows which Ottoline had boldly framed with lemon-yellow taffeta curtains in contrast to walls in her favourite luminous grey. He was charmed by the little pearl-grey retreat behind it which was her study, and by the curving doors set into the corners of oval rooms. Logan admired Ottoline's personality and looks as much as her taste; he hated to think of it being wasted on the Liberal fund-raisers and politicians who were her regular guests. She had begun to move in other circles – he had heard about her friendship with the Conders and of her liking for Lytton Strachey, G. E. Moore, Desmond MacCarthy and Charlie Sanger when she met them at London dinner-parties in 1905. Ethel Sands had told him of her successes with Henry James and Roger Fry at Newington; among the other friends that he knew of were the painter, Sargent, the Chestertons and Hilaire Belloc. Whatever Ottoline might say about being friendless, she was not lacking in acquaintances to invite to Bedford Square. She had often told Logan of her longing to do something useful for creative people; his sensible suggestion was that she could ask them to her home and introduce them to patrons.

Ottoline was ready to be persuaded. In the spring of 1907, she began issuing invitations to her famous 'Thursdays'. A few close friends were invited to dinner; slight acquaintances were told to come later and to dress as informally as they liked. Watching the writers and painters and musicians crowding into the drawing-room, planning who could be of most use to each of them, Ottoline felt that she had begun to discover her vocation at last. She could enhance the lives of people she admired. If they would only let her, she could help them. She had found what she wanted, the chance to live a life of active benevolence outside the conventions.

Ottoline's new friends were appreciative, amused and baffled. There was no doubt that her parties offered a dazzling contrast to the play-readings held at Clive and Vanessa Bell's nearby home in Gordon Square and the buns-and-cocoa evenings over which Vanessa's sister, Virginia Stephen, was shyly presiding in Fitzroy Square. Ottoline was not alone in her passion for the world of the French eighteenth-century court which was evoked in Conder's paintings. Emerging Bloomsbury modelled itself on just such a society of candour and love-intrigues, of games and masquerades. Ottoline's aristocratic background and her willingness to act as hostess gave her a leading role in the fantasy of re-creating that vanished world of intellectual frivolity, and there were times when the grey-and-yellow drawing-room was as sedately vivacious as one of the gatherings which she and her guests loved to read about. She seemed to be learning to play Julie de Lespinasse or Madame de Châtelet to perfection as she drifted from a group of politicians to ask young Jacob Epstein to discuss a possible commission with her art-loving brother Henry, or to coax Virginia Stephen into telling them about her recent encounter with Henry James at his home in Rye. But there she would be on the following Thursday with a Spanish shawl draped over bare shoulders and with that extraordinary red-gold hair – could it be natural? was anything about her natural? – pinned up in tortoiseshell combs, announcing that Gilbert Murray's 'Wind, wind of the deep sea' was the only line in English to express the passionate soul of the Greeks. So, what was she, a Madame de Châtelet roving through intellectual society in search of her Voltaire, or an echo of that charmingly bizarre ancestress she admired so much, the Duchess of Newcastle? The artists, sensibly, accepted her kindness without worrying about the contradictions in her behaviour and appearance; the literary world of Bloomsbury, while grateful for the aura of glamour she bestowed, could not rest until Ottoline had been analysed, discussed and judged.

Ottoline did not give her parties for the Bloomsbury Group, but for anyone creative whom she thought she could help. It was, nevertheless, among the Bloomsbury Group that she formed many of her closest friendships and found some of her most powerful enemies. They were lively recorders and it is on their evidence that biographers have tended to rely for their accounts of Ottoline. Before we discuss individual friendships, it is important to consider the point of view from which they judged the exotic outsider who had arrived in their midst.

The two main families of the Bloomsbury Group were the Stracheys and the Stephens. The strongest influence in the formation of the group in its earliest days were the Apostles, male members of the elite and secretive Cambridge discussion group to which Vanessa and Virginia Stephen had been introduced by their brother, Thoby, before his early death in 1906. Leading lights in the Cambridge society included many of the young men Ottoline had already met by 1907: E. M. Forster, Roger Fry, Desmond MacCarthy, Maynard Keynes, James Strachey and his brother Lytton, who later became one of Ottoline's best-loved friends.

The Stephen sisters were in their early twenties in 1905, when Thoby began bringing his Cambridge friends home. With them, they brought a candour which the girls were quick to imitate after Lytton, one memorable afternoon in 1907 or 1908, shattered their reserve by proposing that a stain on Vanessa's dress might have been caused by semen. It was meant as an act of grace; he offered them the chance to be at ease in a male circle. From that date on, Virginia wrote with mild exaggeration, 'the word bugger was never far from our lips. We discussed copulation with the same excitement and openness that we had discussed the nature of good . . .'[1]

The Bloomsberries' unease about Ottoline stemmed from their views about the nature of good. These derived from their reading of one chapter of G. E. Moore's *Principia Ethica* (1903), in which he emphasised 'the pleasures of human intercourse and the contemplation of beautiful objects'. Ottoline thought there was more to goodness than that, but Thoby Stephen and his fellow Apostles had chosen to ignore Moore's chapter on 'Ethics in Relation to Conduct', in which he stressed the need for the individual to obey general rules: the young Apostles believed that they had the right to stand outside any general rules, judging each case on its own merits. The conventional notions of good behaviour were rejected. 'We repudiated entirely customary morals, conventions and traditional wisdom,' Maynard Keynes wrote in his brief paper, 'My Early Beliefs'. 'We were . . . in the strict sense of the term, immoralists.'[2]

It was Moore's chapter on 'The Ideal' which was of particular interest to the Apostles. Here, he had written that 'personal affections and aesthetic enjoyments include *all* the greatest, and *by far* the greatest, goods we can imagine'. This was the declaration which they took for their credo. Moral obligations were rejected and *Principia Ethica* was hailed as having marked the birth of a new age of freedom. The book, interpreted in such a way as to put a seal of approval on a way of life he had never meant to condone, became the secular bible of Bloomsbury.

When the young Cambridge graduates began to meet regularly in the homes of Thoby Stephen's sisters, they continued to formulate and explore the new code of living they had discussed at university. Moore's technique of establishing the exact nature of the question was followed; the process would, they believed, invariably lead to the correct answer.[3] Since personal affections were held to be among the greatest imaginable goods, a large number of the discussions focused on emotional states. Love, while held to be of supreme importance, was only considered admirable if it was wedded to fundamental integrity. It was the concept of integrity which became the Bloomsbury substitute for morality. Integrity represented a state of absolute, unflinching honesty; without it, affection was held to be valueless.

High-minded frankness never stood more than a hair's-breadth away from the slander and spite into which it frequently degenerated. Maynard Keynes was anxious in later years to stress the purely intellectual level at which he and his fellow Apostles had conducted their Cambridge debates ('I can see us as water-spiders, gracefully skimming, as light and reasonable as air, the surface of the stream . . .').[4]

The conversations which David Garnett, a junior member of the Bloomsbury Group, described as displaying 'an almost gourmet-like love of the foibles of old and intimate friends' give us a clearer sense of the way that Ottoline was used as a topic for analysis and discussion. Snugly endorsed by Moore's words, Bloomsbury settled down to the game of character-assassination, and they played it with great skill. Eccentricities and weaknesses were seized on with delight and were, most strikingly in the hands of the Stephen sisters, Clive Bell and Lytton Strachey, embellished almost out of recognition. If Ottoline brought them the glamour of a Madame de Châtelet, she also offered them an irresistible subject who, in her wish to swim in larger lakes than their little, self-regarding fishpond, made herself a natural victim. For Bloomsbury, like the Apostles who regarded even those members who left Cambridge for London as traitors, was fiercely elitist. Ottoline's refusal to abide by their rules meant that she would always be treated, and judged, as an outsider.

With her bizarre clothes, her singular voice, her reverence for creative people and, above all, her religious faith, Ottoline was God's own gift to the quick and witty minds of Bloomsbury. The group, while entirely hostile to religion, had an odd prudishness about believers; when rumours that she was a woman of many love-affairs were followed by the news that she did not intend to discuss them in detail, they were shocked. She had shown a serious lack of integrity. She could be as discreet as she liked if she was chaste and religious; but if, as they believed, she was only a promiscuous woman who liked to pose as a saint, she had a duty to be frank. To fail in this duty was to risk being seen as a hypocrite and, as Leonard Woolf approvingly observed of his wife after her death: 'How can anybody of high critical standards fail to censure what seems trashy, trite, false or pretentious?' Woolf was living abroad when Ottoline first started to encounter his fellow Apostles and to entertain the Bloomsbury Group at Bedford Square; by the time he married Virginia Stephen in 1912, Ottoline was being condemned on all four counts.

Logan Pearsall Smith had rightly guessed that Ottoline's aristocratic background would be a valuable asset in her search for new friends. In Virginia Stephen's view, Ottoline's title added considerably to her charm. She was fascinated by the accounts of life at Welbeck which sounded to her like something out of a fairy story. 'There are merits in the aristocracy which don't appear to you – and manners, and freedom . . .' she reproached her when Ottoline expressed her dislike of the grand society Virginia found, from a distance, so enthralling. 'Is our world very small compared with yours?'[5] Ottoline was asked to lunch at Fitzroy Square and coaxed into talking about precisely the kind of people she wanted to escape from; Vanessa Bell, meanwhile, asked herself round to Bedford Square and gleefully reported that Ottoline had revealed all her secrets. She had never loved her husband. She had had nine love-affairs. She would have gone on to say a good deal more if it had not been for the presence of Philip.* Vanessa thought that Ottoline also had lesbian tendencies; she had admitted to preferring the company of women to men. Virginia, who was not impervious to beautiful, well-born bisexuals, felt that this added to her charm. 'Ottoline is slowly growing rather fond of me,' she reported to a friend. 'It is like sitting beneath an Arum lily; with a thick golden bar in the middle, dropping pollen, or whatever that is which seduces the male bee.'[6]

'This strange, lovely, furtive creature never has seemed to me to be made of common flesh and blood,' Ottoline wrote in turn of her new friend. There were other women with whom she felt more at ease, but it was Virginia who enchanted her, and who seemed so shiningly sincere when she said how she treasured their friendship and that she was longing for them to see more of each other. It took Ottoline several years to understand that these declarations would never prevent Virginia from helping to spread scandalous accounts of her behind her back, and to accept that Virginia's instability meant that she could not always be relied on in times of crisis. 'When I stretched out a hand to feel another woman,' Ottoline wrote in 1917, when she was badly in need of her friends, 'I found only a very lovely, clear intellect . . . life presents an insoluble problem to her. She flies above the earth but has no contact with heaven.'[7]

Friendship with Virginia was a challenge; it was a relief to Ottoline to know that not all of the Bloomsbury Group expected so much of her. Roger Fry, back from America in 1907, was full of gratitude for her willingness to lend him money and for her kindness to his wife, whom he was desperately contriving to keep out of an asylum. 'I feel more dumb than anyone about it,' he wrote to her. 'Nature seems so relentlessly cruel to those that she has made too finely.'[8]

Ottoline did not get to know Lytton Strachey well until both found themselves involved with the artist Henry Lamb in 1910, but the MacCarthys had become close friends of hers since their first encounter in 1905 or 1906, when politeness had obliged them all to feign delight at Dora Sanger's dinner offering of rotten fish in cold cheese

---

* One cannot help suspecting that Ottoline's reputation was being sacrificed to Vanessa's wish to show how much better she knew her than Virginia. It is inconceivable that she would have told Vanessa that she had never loved her husband when he was in the same room; if she had managed to have nine love-affairs, of which no hint exists in her private papers, it is incredible that Vanessa should instantly have been chosen as her one confidante.

sauce. Ottoline looked kindly on anybody with Irish blood like herself, and Desmond (whose forebears came from County Clare) was especially easy to love, a charming and kind-hearted dilettante whose romantic nature did not make him an easy husband to Molly, a small, lively, elegant woman famous for her lack of punctuality and her startling habit of darting without warning from one subject to the next. When Molly needed to be comforted, it was often Ottoline who came to the rescue. Even a brief dalliance with Philip in 1916 (revealed by Molly in 1932, and denied by Philip) was quickly forgiven: Ottoline had learned by then how hard it was for her own husband to resist a pretty face.

But it was with the painters who started to flock into Bloomsbury that Ottoline felt most comfortable. Walter Sickert came into her life when Ethel Sands began painting in his Fitzroy Street studio. A frequent guest at Ethel's dinner-parties, Sickert was a rumbustiously flirtatious man who charmed Ottoline less with his extravagant praises of her 'beautiful Florentine head' than with his readiness to tell jokes and sing music-hall duets. Duncan Grant, Lytton Strachey's cousin, quickly became one of the most exuberant attendants at her parties. A graceful, faun-like young man who was always ready to act in a charade, dance a reel or tell a story, Duncan was funny, observant and – this was unusual in Bloomsbury – utterly lacking in malice. He once horrified Ottoline by stating that selfishness was an admirable virtue; what he meant was that he always put his art before friends and lovers. Everyone who fell in love with Duncan – those who did included Lytton, Maynard Keynes and Vanessa Bell – was forced to accept the detachment which was the secret of his serenity.

Ottoline was never in love with Duncan Grant, but she was full of love for him. 'He is an adorable fellow,' she wrote in 1937, 'so simple and full of humour – a lovely character.'[9] She bought his pictures, told him he looked like his beloved Molière and swamped him with presents. Duncan, in turn, kept her supplied with specially dyed wools and silks for her embroidery, visited her regularly until the end of her life, passed on the nice remarks ('Virginia came here [Charleston] on Monday for a night and raved about you')[10] and defended her from mockery whenever an opportunity to do so arose.

And then there was Augustus John, his flamboyant character causing Bloomsbury gentlemen to draw up their skirts with maidenly shrieks as he stalked into their territory, handsome as a Celtic hero and rampantly heterosexual. 'Oh ... what a "warning"! as the Clergy say,' Lytton hissed to Duncan. 'When I think of him, I often feel that the only thing to do is to chuck up everything and make a dash for some such safe secluded office-stool as is pressed by dear Maynard's happy bottom. The dangers of freedom are appalling!'[11]

Augustus had come back to London late in 1907, following the death of his first wife. He had found himself a roosting-place at Whistler's old studio in Fitzroy Street and had, for the moment, decided to opt for the single life. Dorelia McNeill, the mother of two of his children, had given him little choice in this after making it clear that she preferred to stay on in Paris where she was being ardently pursued by Henry Lamb. Augustus's relationship with her was powerful enough to survive her interest in Lamb and his own cheerful readiness to go to bed with every attractive woman he met, but Dorelia was only occasionally in England at the time he got to know Ottoline.

Ottoline had first seen John's paintings early in 1906 when she was visiting Charles Conder's studio. She knew nothing about him then, but Conder praised his courage and zest for life. Augustus John, he said admiringly, was a man who would dare to do anything. He was a great artist – and he was also a great man.

Ottoline was intrigued by such hero-worship. A few weeks later, a chance encounter allowed her to form her own view.

One day that I was at Conder's studio, I found a tall, rather mysterious-looking man there. He seemed intensely silent and rather *méfiant*. His hair cut like a Renaissance picture, gold ear-rings and a black sweater high to his neck, he looked at everyone very intensely with eyes that absorbed what he gazed on. They were remarkably beautifully-shaped eyes, and were of that mysterious pale grey-green colour, expanding like a sea-anemone, and more liquid, more aesthetically and poetically perceptive, than any of the darker and more definite shades. His voice, when he did speak, was not very unlike Conder's, only rather deeper and more melodious, but like Conder's hesitating – and he also had the same trick of pushing his hair back with one of his hands – hands that were more beautiful than any man's hands I have ever seen. Conder murmured 'Augustus John.'[12]

Ottoline was dining with Ethel Sands at Lowndes Place in December 1907 when she had her next encounter with this mesmerising figure. Augustus had become a good deal more famous by this time (Ethel would not otherwise have invited him), but he hated getting dressed-up in evening clothes. When Ottoline came in, he was standing alone in the middle of the drawing-room, evidently wishing himself elsewhere. He recognised her with a look of relief and seemed pleased when they were put next to each other at the table. They talked about Conder, about painters and gypsies; before she left, John asked her to come to his studio the next day.

Ottoline went to 8 Fitzroy Street, but she prudently took Philip with her. The artist was in his most hospitable mood. There was an oil painting on his easel of a girl in a tight black dress standing on top of a mountain. Questioned by Ottoline, the artist said that he had called it 'Seraphita' and that it had been inspired by Balzac's uncharacteristically mystical novel. (Naturally, he did not say that the other inspiration had been the model, Alick Schepeler, his mistress of 1906.) Other guests arrived, but Ottoline could not tear herself away from the girl in black who 'made an impression of strange unearthly poetry and imagination'.[13]

Friends had already told Ottoline that John was wild and unreliable. She had sensed the darker, melancholy side of his nature; reading *Seraphita* at Peppard that winter, she noted that Balzac's theme was man's struggle between carnal desire and spiritual aspiration. This, she decided, was the clue to Augustus John's character. Earthy though he might be in his relationships, there was another side to his nature, a side which she resolved to work on and to help him, in her favourite new phrase, 'to develop'. John was travelling in France and Spain in March and April; in May, when he was back in London, Ottoline began to sit for him almost daily as his favourite model. By the end of the month, she had forgotten about trying to improve him and was pouring out all her own worries and secrets.

The big parties at 44 Bedford Square had presented Ottoline with a wide circle of acquaintances, but few friends she could confide in. From her own family she saw only Henry. Philip's sisters were not congenial and Harriette, while she had stopped referring to her daughter-in-law, infuriatingly, as 'our poor, dear, sweet Ottoline', was not affectionate. ('She will never be a mother,' Ottoline noted during this period.) Her new social life had distanced her from Mother Julian, Vava Bentinck and Hilda Douglas-Pennant; friends like Ena Mathias, and Griselda Baillie-Hamilton whom she had known at Truro, were busy with their own family lives. Philip, already immersed in his new political career, was also struggling to keep the peace in the Morrell family after his father died in 1908, leaving nothing to his children and everything to his widow; Julian was living at Peppard Cottage with her nurse. Ottoline was lonely and Augustus John, who was always ready to listen and sympathise, became the most important person in her life. Her days revolved around her visits to his studio. At the end of a particularly gruelling sitting on 30 May 1908, Ottoline told him that she had fallen in love with him.

John was in a difficult situation. He was attracted to her both as a woman and as a model; he had also become immensely fond of her. Relations between them were so affectionate that her admission came as no surprise, but knowing that he would never give up Dorelia, what could he do? Late that same night, he decided to send her a candid account of his feelings. 'While you were in my studio today I wished I could cry . . .' he wrote, 'with the delicatest and noblest of women loving me beyond my deserts. Do you know what a horror I have of hurting a hair of your head or bringing a shadow into your thoughts? . . . and you are trying to assure me you are just like others are!' He was not ready to blame himself for encouraging her. After all, 'one doesn't meet Ottolines every day', but neither did he relish a more intense relationship. 'We *can't* go on thus, darling that you are,' he concluded, 'you will only get unhappy and I shall hate myself. Don't let us spoil a beautiful thing . . . and let us be gay little heroes! Goodnight, angel. Elffin.'"[14]

Ottoline had been kindly warned, but she was in love. The affair went on, as much on paper as in life, with letters flying to and fro at a rate that was only matched, over years rather than months, by Ottoline's subsequent correspondence with Bertrand Russell.

In many ways, they were a well-matched couple. Both were voracious readers: their letters ranged from Plato's *Phaedrus* to Wordsworth and Dostoevsky. Augustus's exuberant manner hid a dreamy, idealistic strain in which he was ready to see Ottoline as 'a daughter of Heaven' and to tell her that 'I can only really approach you spiritually'. (4 June 1908) Like her, he had adopted a romantic style of dress which allowed him to identify more closely with the troubadours and gypsies to whom he was linked by temperament rather than by blood. (His father was a Welsh solicitor.) And, like her, he was an odd blend of parsimony and lavishness, skimping on his own needs to help his friends.

Ottoline did not find it easy to comply with Augustus's requests that she should, being an angel, act like one. 'Il faut être dur et simple – to give joy one must be happy oneself so – be happy!' he told her. (28 July 1908) She found it even harder to understand why she should not smother him with presents. Giving was so instinctive a way of showing her love that she could not comprehend why Augustus – and, after him, D. H. Lawrence – were too proud to enjoy playing the role of grateful beggars at a rich woman's gate. But some of her gifts did please him. 'You are the most generous woman in the world,' he told her when she offered him a splendid black hat to go with an earlier present of a cloak. It was sweet of her to send him flowers, and rugs, and a quilt big enough to cover the Great Bed of Ware, but he was embarrassed by the rings, the brooches (these included a beautiful opal) and a jewelled watch. Gently, he tried to wean her away from the idea that she could bind him to her with gifts. But, she said, she must do something for him. 'You *are* able to do so much for me in spirit,' he reassured her. 'And I, what can I do for you?' (4 June 1908)

He did do one thing which delighted Ottoline and which eased his embarrassment. Since she was determined to be generous, why should some of his poorer friends not reap the benefit? He told her about

---

* 'Elffin' was the nickname adopted by Augustus John during the most intense period of his relationship with Ottoline.

Henry Lamb, a young artist who he could assure her was 'no ordinary personage and has the divine mark on his brow'. (20 September 1908) He told her about Jacob Epstein, who was being forced to pay for the stone from which he had carved eighteen figures for the Medical Council in the Strand. The stone had cost Epstein almost all of his commission fee, and now the figures were said to cause offence to passing pedestrians and were threatened with being dismantled. Philip Morrell had been too busy with his father's will to help when Augustus wrote to beg him to find some 'recognised *moral* expert – such as a bishop for example', to defend the sculptures, but Ottoline's tender heart was touched. She went to see Epstein in his studio and, horrified by the evidence of his poverty, set out to do everything she could to remedy it. A garden statue was commissioned, friends were taken to see his work and urged to buy it; Epstein was invited to the Bedford Square parties and introduced to her brother Henry, an enthusiastic collector of modern works who wanted to give him some commissions.

Augustus had found a way to keep Ottoline profitably occupied, but he had given up warning her against becoming too involved with him. Not all of their correspondence has been preserved, but the relationship appears to have reached a climax in December 1908 when Augustus made it clear that there were other things in his life besides Ottoline's love. Hurt, she sent him a stormy letter; his response made it clear that he had seen the end of this particular road: 'I suppose my letter seemed perfectly fatuous! Well, it was *not written* in that spirit nor was there any irony in it. Its lightness was the merest transparent affectation not expected to take you in. I felt I was fated to cause you in the long run more pain than happiness – and that I could *not* acquiesce in. I dislike sailing under colours none of my hoisting.' (21 December 1908)

Augustus had a strong reason for wanting a less passionate relationship with Ottoline: Dorelia had arrived in London and, shortly before Christmas, a family home had been found in Chelsea for her, Augustus and the children. It was not an appropriate time for passionate meetings and love-letters and Augustus started refusing invitations to Bedford Square by explaining that he was anxious not to offend Philip. A week later, he carefully emphasised his new image as a respectable domestic figure, telling her on 26 December that Dorelia and he were 'bourgeois folk with carpets and front doors and dining-rooms'.

It did not come as a surprise. Ottoline had known for some time that Dorelia represented the steady centre in Augustus John's life. Five months earlier, after a lovers' tiff over whether Ottoline was going to keep a ring that he had given to her, she asked him to be frank about his feelings for them both. She received an honest answer. 'You are certainly wonderful, Ottoline,' he wrote, but 'no, I love no one more living than Dorelia and in loving her I am loyal to my wife and not [*sic*] else.' (undated)

Ottoline met Dorelia for the first time in March 1909, when John was painting her portrait at Church Street, his new Chelsea home. Then and later, she thought her beautiful and very un-English ('*very* like Leonardo's Mona Lisa'), but difficult to get to know ('very passive, almost oriental – *very* inarticulate').[15] Augustus wanted them to be friends and, while they never became close, they grew surprisingly fond of each other. Ottoline, having realised that Dorelia hated parties, contented herself with giving her presents, helping to choose schools for the children and inviting two of the boys to stay at Peppard for Easter. Dorelia in turn asked to accompany her on a trip to Paris to look at paintings and, some years later, to come and stay in the country on her own. She evidently enjoyed the visit: Ottoline wrote to Bertrand Russell to say that she was afraid Dorelia was never going to leave. In later years, Ottoline's diaries offer descriptions of the two ladies going clothes-shopping together (Dorelia loved pretty shoes) and of oyster-bar lunches in the City. Clearly, there was warmth between them, if not intimacy.

If Ottoline was still cherishing romantic dreams about Augustus in the summer of 1909, a visit to his caravan camp was all that was needed to disillusion her. 'Wanderers, you have the sunrise and the stars!' he had once written to her; in July, he offered her the chance to discover what he meant by paying a visit to the field near Grantchester where the Johns were living while he officially spent his time painting Jane Harrison, the redoubtable Newnham classics don, and unofficially made himself familiar with the Cambridge pubs. She would love it, he urged Ottoline. She would ride in a pony-trap and meet wild, charming people, real gypsies. Nothing could be more delightful than life in a field. Ottoline was not convinced. 'What do you mean by talking about boring!' John exploded and sent off a gypsy photograph to fire her imagination. (22 July 1909)

At the end of three months of moving in smart Liberal society and entertaining her widowed mother-in-law during a protracted visit to London (she came to be converted to Catholicism and stayed on to be amused with visits to smart shops and parties), Ottoline was feeling that she had had a surfeit of good behaviour. 'It was a relief to return to our ... own queer imaginative friends, our scallywags, as Virginia once called them.'[16] A visit to Augustus, a scallywag if ever there was one, could only be an improvement; she looked forward to talking to someone who would have been as saddened as herself by the death of Charles Conder earlier that year. At the end of July, ignoring Philip's disapproving looks, she set off in one of her best muslin dresses to catch the Cambridge train. Augustus, sporting a black eye and a grim expression, came to meet her, not in the promised pony-trap, but with a high gig and a horse over which he showed no gypsy mastery. The animal fell between the shafts before they had left the station and Augustus, having descended with great speed, obviously had no idea of how to get it back on its legs. Some grinning station employees came to the rescue, and they trotted slowly away through Cambridge towards the famous camp.

Here, Ottoline was forced to admit that Philip's forebodings had been prescient. It was a cold, damp day; the meadow was flat and drab; Augustus, recovering from a brawl the previous night, was dour. Ottoline was reduced to walking briskly up and down the meadow to keep herself warm while Dorelia and her sister Edie washed the clothes. Dinner was a crust of bread and some fruit. Late that evening, she made her excuses and took the train back to London. She arrived at Bedford Square feeling chilled, depressed and ready to agree with Philip that the vagabond life was more delightful in fiction than fact.

The visit to the camp ended any lingering dreams Ottoline may have had about Augustus and herself, but they remained on excellent terms. Augustus kept in frequent touch with her on his travels through a stream of lively notes and cards, but the altered nature of their relationship is clear from the fact that he was ready to tell her all about his visit to an Avignon brothel. Always aware of his shortage of money, Ottoline continued to support his work and to find buyers. (It was a source of hideous embarrassment to her when Birdie, her sister-in-law, accompanied Henry and herself to the studio and rounded on them both, in front of the artist, for buying such rubbish.)[17] There were many occasions when Augustus let her down. He would promise to visit and fail to turn up; he would undertake to paint Julian's picture and then forget all about it; Ottoline had long since accepted that he did not follow a conventional code of behaviour. He was not a person to whom the ordinary rules of time and place could be applied, she told Russell. She grew accustomed to the sudden call that would come for her when he felt lonely or depressed. Consulted about his health, she found him doctors, recommended nerve treatments and urged him to take better care of himself. Occasionally, she ran the gauntlet of his growing family's interested stares to pay a visit to his country homes. 'Lady Ottoline's inborn aristocratic arrogance . . . did not endear her to the lesser female members of the household,' wrote one of Augustus's stepchildren, who remembered spying on her in the garden 'while she waited for attention, seated in profile in the throne of the trap, the whip held like a spear . . .'[18]

'Do you know Cézanne's work?' Augustus had asked Ottoline in September 1908. Cézanne, who had died in 1906, was only just beginning to be appreciated by the English art world, but Ottoline did already know something of his genius from Roger Fry, who had been urging her to go and see his work when she next visited France. Writing in *The Burlington Magazine* earlier that year, Fry had set out his arguments in favour of Cézanne and against the English fear of new movements in art. ('What I do want to protest against is the facile assumption that an attitude to art which is strange, as all new attitudes are at first, is the result of wilful mystification and caprice on the artist's part . . .')[19]

Fry had often seen Augustus John and Epstein at Ottoline's Thursday parties and he had noticed how diligent she was in finding purchasers for young artists' work. 'She has been very good to me and has a real feeling for art,' he told his friend Dugald MacColl, the painter and critic who had recently been appointed Keeper of the Tate Gallery.[20] MacColl and Fry had collaborated in 1903 on the foundation of the National Art Collections Fund. In 1909, Fry persuaded MacColl and Charles Holmes, the new director of the National Portrait Gallery, to help him start a similar fund which would purchase the works of contemporary artists, exhibit them and, in due course, loan them to needy galleries. (One of the strongest incentives was a wish to encourage and promote Augustus John, whose portrait of Dorelia known as 'The Smiling Woman' greatly struck both MacColl and Fry when it was exhibited in February and March 1909.) Fry also approached Ottoline and, after introducing her to MacColl, suggested that she should join them.

Nothing could have interested Ottoline more. Her visits to Epstein's studio had opened her eyes to the real hardship of an artist's life, and her friendship with John had left her with a longing to do more to help his less successful friends. 'I feel strongly now that every penny one can save ought to be given to young artists,' she wrote after lunching with MacColl and Fry. 'At least, we who really feel the beauty and wonder of art ought to help them . . . young creators have such a terrible struggle.'[21] No. 44 Bedford Square was settled on as their headquarters and the scheme was hammered into shape in April 1909, with an agreement to enlarge their committee to ten. A year later, the original name of the Modern Art Association was changed to the Contemporary Art Society (CAS) with Ottoline's brother Henry acting as chairman from 1910 until his death and her art-loving young cousin, Lord Howard de Walden, as its first president. By the autumn of 1911 a scheme had been devised for two purchasers to be chosen to represent them, with complete freedom of choice, for periods of six months.

Ottoline was, from the start, a passionate supporter of the CAS. Bedford Square was handed over for its meetings even after a quarrel with Roger Fry had made it impossible for her to attend them. She gave parties to raise funds which, with a membership fee of a guinea a year, were badly needed; she allowed her drawing-room to be turned into a gallery on several occasions, and she acted as one of the purchasers in 1914. She did well for the CAS; her acquisitions included Gilbert Spencer's 'The Seven Ages of Man' and Mark Gertler's 'The Fruit Sorters'.

If on one level the CAS appealed to Ottoline's philanthropic spirit, it also offered her an opportunity to educate herself in a new field. Fry had told her that the most exciting modern paintings were in Paris; when Augustus John's friend Emily Chadbourne asked the Morrells to come and stay in her apartment at the Hôtel Crillon in the autumn of 1909, Ottoline jumped at the idea: few women were said to be better informed about modern French paintings than Mrs Chadbourne. Philip was busy; slightly to Ottoline's embarrassment, Dorelia announced that she would take his place.

She need not have worried. Nothing ever ruffled Mrs Chadbourne's composure. Did anyone's presence ever make a difference to this composed, remote woman, Ottoline wondered as she and Dorelia fidgeted in their hostess's luxurious, overheated rooms and dropped hints about the supper they had not had and which, on their first night, they failed to get? As an introduction to the art world of Paris, the stay at the Hôtel Crillon would have made up for ten nights of starvation. Mrs Chadbourne, one of the fabulously rich Chicago collectors at whom Berenson had discreetly jeered when he visited what he called 'the City of Dirt', took Ottoline everywhere and showed her everything. While Dorelia went shoe-shopping and visited her sister-in-law Gwen John, Ottoline was whisked from the Van Dongens and the Van Goghs at the Salon d'Automne to a magnificent private collection of Manets and Cézannes, to Matisse's studio, and on to the huge bare rooms where Gertrude Stein and her brother Leo had emblazoned the walls with their Matisses. The paintings were dazzling, but it had been a long day and the Steins were not easy hosts. 'It was one of those interminable evenings where we continually wandered round the room, and no one dared to talk, silenced perhaps by the clamour that seemed to shout from the walls. Mrs Chadbourne stood vaguely about with a bunch of flowers in her hand.'[22] They tracked down Picasso in Montmartre and went up to the top of Ambrose Vollard's house where, perhaps, Ottoline might have been reminded of her first day at Welbeck as the dealer silently dragged one treasure after another forward from the walls, ending with Cézanne's magnificent portrait of himself. Ottoline was ready to agree with Roger Fry by now that Cézanne was the master of them all: 'a vision that to most mortals would have been seen and forgotten in an hour was by him absorbed and held and re-expressed as by magic and made permanent'. Passionate lover of nature though she was, she thought that Cézanne's paintings of the rocks and villages of Provence used rhythm and pattern to make something 'so new, so illumined, that it surpasses the original'.[23]

Ottoline pursued her interest in Cézanne the following summer when she and Philip went to Provence. Augustus and Dorelia had urged her to come and stay at the house they had rented there at Martigues, but Ottoline, mindful of her husband's dislike of the gypsy life, decided to follow her summer cure at La Bourbole* with a visit to Marseilles to see the paintings of Philip's adored Puvis de Chavannes before settling him into the comfortable old Hôtel de Thermes at Aix. She did, however, promise not to go and see Cézanne's house until the Johns could make the day-long journey to Aix in their only form of transport, a donkey-cart.

Ottoline was charmed by the artist's old home, a miniature château on the edge of the town, and it amused her to see the two sober custodians shaking their heads at the sight of Dorelia, pregnant, barelegged and wearing sandals, sad evidence of poverty to their bourgeois eyes. The serenity of the house impressed her as much as the landscapes from which Cézanne had created his masterpieces, but she came away from Aix with a depressed feeling that Augustus had started to care more about drink than painting. His eyes were bloodshot and the only moment of the day's tour that she saw him looking cheerful was when he went off for a drink with a waiter from the hotel. Disapproving of his readiness to drown boredom in a bottle of brandy, she indulged in a bit of sermonising: 'No mistress, no lover is more exacting than the creative instinct. It must absorb and drive on, scattering out of the path extraneous pleasures, if it is to develop into greatness such as Michelangelo, Cézanne or Van Gogh.'[24] The greatness he would have achieved if she had been in charge of his life is the obvious subtext, but the old intimacy between them could not be renewed and she did not dare to reproach him in front of Dorelia.

Ottoline left Provence in the summer of 1910 burning with enthusiasm for the new French painters. Almost immediately, she was given the chance to help open English eyes to the splendours of Cézanne, Gauguin and Van Gogh. These, the three she most admired, were the artists who were most strongly represented at the famous exhibition which opened at the Grafton Galleries on 8 November 1910 under the title 'Manet and the Post-Impressionists'. (Eight Manets were shown to soften the shock of twenty Van Goghs, twenty-one Cézannes and thirty-seven Gauguins.)

The Post-Impressionist exhibition was the project of Roger Fry; his letters make it clear that Ottoline was closely involved in arranging

---

* More will be said on the subject of Ottoline's poor health in 1910 in the following chapter.

it from an early stage. She and Philip had moved on to Venice from Aix at the end of the summer; Fry wrote in September to urge her to come back to England via Paris so that they could review the Cézannes and Van Goghs he was planning to bring to England. 'My best time would be about Oct 5–15. Then we might go on to Brussels and see the exhibition.* Now do help to bring this about. It would make all the difference to me if we can arrange it.' Ottoline obligingly altered her arrangements and duly appeared in Paris dressed, much to the delight of Fry and Desmond MacCarthy, who had come with him, in one of her most unusual hats. Years later, Desmond was still fondly reminding her of the crimson tea cosy trimmed with miniature hedgehogs which had given them all such joy. Fry outlined the plan for the exhibition to her: Ottoline was eager to know what she could do to help. Writing to tell his old friend Goldsworthy Lowes Dickinson that Lady Ottoline was hoping to come and visit him in Cambridge, Fry added that he would like to accompany her. She was, he said, 'quite splendid . . . she'll face anything'. Impressed by her enthusiasm for the scheme, he asked Ottoline and her brother Henry to join the small executive committee whose objective now was to shake the Custard Islanders (his name for the unadventurous British art-lovers) into a livelier state of awareness.

Beliefs need to be tested and the Post-Impressionist exhibition was an excellent test of the sincerity of Ottoline's new-found enthusiasm and of her loyalty to Fry. Commercially, the exhibition was a huge success with an average of four hundred visitors a day during its three-month run. The public, however, were outraged. The gallery Complaints Book was filled; apologies were demanded from the Grafton's director; an elderly gentleman had to be helped out after collapsing with shock; ladies dissolved into shrieks and giggles; doctors gave lectures to explain why the paintings were the work of madmen. Wilfrid Blunt noted that the entire exhibition was only worth five pounds, and that would be for the pleasure of the bonfire the pictures would make. Eminent critics hurled abuse at Fry (even the loyal MacColl would not defend him) and it was not just the older artists who were quick to express their disgust. Eric Gill, who was only twenty-eight, thought his own sculptures vastly superior to the Matisses at the Grafton. Even Fry's old friends and fellow Apostles were unwilling to support him; Lytton's suggestion that the British art world ought to burn Fry as a heretic in the courtyard of Burlington House did not, at the time, seem one of his best jokes.

Outwardly calm and prepared to say that he did not give a damn for the opinion of his critics, Fry suffered intensely in private. 'I know

---

* This must have been the 17th 'Libre Esthétique' exhibition, which included important Post-Impressionist works.

that you will be grateful that it is being accomplished,' he had written to Ottoline in October; a week after the exhibition had opened, he wrote again to thank her for being with him on the traumatic first day and evening and for her steady support. 'I can't tell you how it helped me to have you at such a difficult time, to help and advise,' he told her. 'I don't think I could have done it without you . . .' (November 1910)

It was not in Ottoline's power to subdue the storm which was buffeting her friend, but she did what she could by making extra visits to Fry's invalid wife Helen and telling him to come to Peppard whenever he wanted. The loyalty and unswerving enthusiasm she had shown for their crusade brought her very close to Fry; he repaid it by trying to let her know how much her backing had mattered. 'The general life seems to have suddenly become more worthwhile,' he told her after seeing her on 23 November, 'and in all that you know how much you have counted – I don't mean only that but still quite tremendously in that. You've managed to give us all a quite new courage for effort.' To him, it seemed clear that her duty was to the world of art; it infuriated him to hear that she was committed to helping Philip with his campaign for a new constituency. (Having lost Oxfordshire to the Conservatives in January 1910, Philip had agreed to fight for the new Lancashire seat of Burnley in the second election of that year, in November.) 'There's such heaps of things that I want your help and advice on that I'm furious with politics,' Fry wrote in November; 'there are lots of immensely important things besides politics which will fail but for you, so don't kill yourself.' He went on to ask her to consider being on all his future Grafton Galleries committees and to urge her to think how much help she would be to him. It was an accolade which Ottoline treasured. Nevertheless, she wrote back to say that her duty was to see that Philip won the Burnley seat. Art, for the time being, would have to wait.*

---

* These letters contradict Virginia Woolf's statement in her biography of Roger Fry (1940) that 'a great lady' (Ottoline was the only woman involved) showed her loyalty to him at the time of the Post-Impressionist exhibition by asking for her name to be struck off the committee. She may have been misled by Fry himself since he was soon to become one of Ottoline's most venomous enemies.

6

A MAGNET FOR EGOTISTS
1909–11

'After eight or nine years one ought not to expect passion, and yet I can give it, and perhaps do miss it.'
OM, *Journal*, 23 January 1911

'I have always been a magnet for egotists,' Ottoline wrote in her last years; she was thinking in particular of the two men who first entered her life in the autumn of 1909, the year before the Post-Impressionist exhibition. Egotism was all that Henry Lamb and Bertrand Russell had in common; between them, they offered more scope than she had ever bargained for in her wish to give love to those who most needed it.

An intensely nervous and emotional temperament, together with a refusal to lead the quiet country life urged on her by every doctor she saw, were the chief reasons for Ottoline's lifelong ill-health; it is noticeable that her health was never worse than during the period of 1910–12 when she was trying to juggle her duties as mother and political wife with those of a leading London hostess, an influential patron in the modern art world, and the mistress of two exceptionally demanding men. She had grown understandably wistful about the lack of passion in her marriage; passion was now provided with a vengeance. But the price was a high one, with Lamb and, after him, Russell, drawing ruthlessly on her for the reassurance and solicitude they craved.

Was it worth it? What did they give her in return? What she wanted more than anything else, the knowledge that she was of real value to them and that, through her, they had achieved a better understanding of themselves. 'That gift of enlarging their natures and denying their appetites, enhancing their senses and evading their exigence,' her Irish friend Francis Hackett wrote to her in the 1930s after reading a prudently selected batch of their letters. 'O Ottoline, you are mysterious and by this intangible quality these most different men became exalted and resonant and in a way achieved. It is lucky for them that you were good.'[1]

The reader who knows that Ottoline's relationship with Bertrand Russell did not become serious until March 1911, at a time when she was doing her best to cure herself of her passion for Henry Lamb, will be puzzled by the fact that this chapter begins with Russell. There are two reasons for this. The first and more pedantic is that she had not yet met Lamb in September 1909, the month when Bertie first became aware of Ottoline as an immensely attractive personality with a power to change people's lives. The second is that this is an appropriate moment to remind ourselves of Ottoline's role as a politician's wife.

A general election was only four months away in September 1909, when Logan Pearsall Smith, a keen Liberal himself, decided to bring two like-minded friends together by introducing Philip to his brother-in-law. The conventional political career chosen by Philip had no attractions for Bertie Russell, but he was always prepared to use his superb mind and his famous name (his grandfather, Lord John Russell, was the great champion of political reform and, in particular, of the 1832 Reform Bill) to draw attention to the causes he espoused. His own mother had been an early suffragist and Alys, his wife, was a passionate supporter of women's rights. It was in order to raise interest in the women's cause that he had presented himself in 1907 as the last-minute Liberal candidate for Wimbledon. There was no chance of his winning a solidly Conservative seat and the local Liberal Party had been mortified to discover that they were only being used as a platform for his views on Women's National Suffrage. As an electoral campaign, it had been a fiasco; as propaganda, it was a great success, not least because of Bertie's beguiling manner. 'He is elegant, good-looking, courteous and enthusiastic,' one of the reporters noted. 'Slight in build, dark, and immaculate in dress, he wears a heavy moustache; above are a pair of eyes ready to twinkle into merriment.'

The Russells, speedily followed by Logan and his mother Hannah, had settled near Oxford. Hearing that Ottoline and Philip were staying with Mrs Morrell at Black Hall in September 1909, Logan persuaded his sister Alys to invite them over to her home at Bagley Wood. His memories of the Wimbledon campaign made him think that Bertie's energy and formidable eloquence could help to gain support for diffident, slow-spoken Philip. The last thing on this devoted brother's mind was the way that Bertie, trapped in a marriage to a woman he no longer desired, might respond to Philip's beautiful wife.

Ottoline's previous acquaintance with Russell was slight. Logan had taken her to hear him lecturing in 1904 and she had met him briefly when Philip was fighting for his Oxfordshire seat in 1905. But the visit to Bagley Wood was the first time she saw him in a relaxed setting, and what she saw impressed her. They were not the only visitors. Desmond MacCarthy was there; Vernon Lee, whom she had not seen for several years, dropped in to rebuke them all for not being more friendly towards Germany. Russell, Ottoline noticed, did not like to be lectured; he fidgeted and looked as if he was having difficulty in being polite.

Ottoline was mildly interested in Vernon's harangue, but it was Bertie who held her attention. 'Bertrand Russell is most fascinating,' she wrote that evening. 'I don't think I have ever met anyone more attractive ... His notice flattered me very much, and though I trembled at the feeling that in half an hour he would see how silly I was and despise me, his great wit and humour gave me courage to talk.'[2] Neither of them recorded what they talked about, but Bertie was sufficiently intrigued to coax her away for a long walk alone with him. 'I remember a day when you came to Bagley Wood and we had a talk on the way to the river,' he told her in March 1911; 'that was for me the beginning.' Perhaps they spoke of Philip; Russell later admitted that the first thing about Ottoline which had really impressed him was her passionate involvement in her husband's career. He was charmed, too, by her unusual beauty and presence, and by the soft voice with which she could effortlessly create an atmosphere of intimacy. Even in that short encounter, he felt that he was talking to a woman who held the secret of the happiness he craved. The feeling grew into an overpowering certainty in 1911, but it had already shown itself as a strong wish to know Ottoline better. When Ottoline went to visit old Mrs Pearsall Smith the next day, she met Alys, who passed on the message that Bertie would like to see her, and, of course, Philip, in London. Ottoline smiled politely, but gave a noncommittal answer. 'I really have not the courage for it,' she wrote, a phrase which suggests that she had guessed that Russell might want more than conversation.[3] She decided to change the subject when, sitting next to her at a dinner-party some weeks later, Bertie suddenly turned to her and said: 'There is always a tragedy in everyone's life, if one knows them well enough to find it out.'[4] It was as clear an invitation as he could give her to share the knowledge of his unhappy marriage. But the moment had gone. Ottoline had already become involved in the complex emotional life of Henry Lamb. The last thing she wanted was the additional burden of Russell's confidences.

Ottoline was not ready for the intimacy which Russell was tentatively feeling his way towards, but she was full of admiration for the energy with which he helped Philip to fight for his seat in the election of January 1910. In his autobiography, Russell remembered giving speeches in support of Philip at almost every village between Oxford and Caversham – a healthy number – and spending most of his days out canvassing. Philip and Ottoline bore the brunt of a rough campaign with two or three meetings a night and the danger of being stoned as well as heckled; Russell, meanwhile, was driven out of the house of one blustering Tory colonel, who threatened to set the dogs on him for mentioning that scoundrel, Morrell.[5] It was at one of the most violent meetings of the campaign that Ottoline first realised that he was not only brilliant, but fearless.

There seemed no chance of anyone being listened to, much less anyone so quiet and remote as Bertie Russell, but undaunted he stood up and began to speak. Catcalls, whistles and yells redoubled, but something in his passionate sincerity and intellectual force arrested them, and in a few moments, much to our surprise, he was being listened to with attention. Very seldom have I seen intellectual integrity triumph over democratic disorder.[6]

Although Philip was one of many casualties in an election where the Liberals suffered severe losses, Russell's valiant efforts did much to strengthen his friendship with the Morrells. Academic responsibilities compelled him to refuse Ottoline's invitation to come and help again in the campaign which led to Philip being returned to Parliament for Burnley, but he became a regular attender of the Bedford Square Thursday parties at which, for a time, he could forget his domestic unhappiness.

'I *was* in love with him,' Ottoline told Francis Hackett a few weeks before her death. Russell was the only man of whom she could say in her sixties that their rapport was still so perfect that they could answer each other's thoughts, but she was speaking of Henry Lamb, the man who Hackett had decided was a sulky troublemaker, 'capricious as a cocotte', after reading some of his letters. Ottoline preferred to remember him as having been like Stendhal's Julien Sorel, a moody boy with a genius for destructive love-affairs.

It was Dorelia who brought about the introduction, a fact which has led some to think that it was an artful bit of manipulation to distract Ottoline's attention from Augustus. But Dorelia had no cause for anxiety by the autumn of 1909 and it is more likely that she, like John, was thinking that Ottoline might be able to help their impecunious friend with money or commissions.

The two women had spent the afternoon of 2 October inspecting a suitable school for the John boys. On the way back, Dorelia said she wanted to leave a message for Lamb. His studio was in the house in Fitzroy Street where Ottoline had paid her first visit to John. Looking up at the windows from the taxi, she was relieved to find that she no longer felt any emotion. '"Thank God it is over," I murmured half aloud,' she wrote in a much later account of this memorable afternoon:

'Won't you come in for a moment? Dorelia sent me,' I heard a voice say. I awoke from the past and saw standing by the door of the taxi a figure that seemed to come from a vision of Blake, a pale, slim man, dressed in an old-fashioned mustard-coloured coat, a green and yellow silk scarf round his neck, an almost transparent face and pale golden hair starting back from his forehead in pale flames.[7]

'Little did one know what vicious hard envious vanity was lurking underneath,' she added to that ethereal portrait, and then cut it out again. Her love for Lamb was always stronger than her sense of his faults.

Augustus had told her that Lamb had an almost divine quality when he was urging her to help support him in 1908; his words had not prepared her for quite such devastating good-looks. Following him upstairs in dazed silence, she found herself in a poky room with Dorelia and a pretty model. She looked at the bed and the heaps of crumpled clothes and then again at Lamb, wondering whether to draw the obvious conclusion. His smile gave nothing away, but she noticed (or, probably, felt later that she should have noticed) that his lips had a cruel twist and his eyes were like ice. Recovering her poise, she asked all three of them to come back for tea at Bedford Square.

Lamb left for Cornwall a few days later, while Ottoline and Dorelia made their visit to Mrs Chadbourne in Paris. No letters exist for this period to help us chart the progress of the relationship, but they had clearly been in touch; by January 1910, Ottoline was describing Lamb as 'my new friend'. Sorting letters every day for the fund-raising Gladstone League for which Philip took on the job of secretary after the loss of his Oxford seat, Ottoline had time to think about Lamb. He had already given her some hints about a dark side to his character, but that was no discouragement. On the contrary, to a woman like Ottoline, the opportunity to exercise a benevolent influence over the Mr Hyde in Henry Lamb was almost irresistible.

Ottoline was not the only person to be fascinated by Lamb's presentation of himself as a fallen angel: Lytton Strachey had already marked him out in 1905 as unusually seductive and 'very, very bad'. Lamb was not really bad, only neurotic and very self-absorbed. Born in Manchester in 1883 of a respectable family who bored him, he eloped to London with a beautiful and promiscuous art student and enrolled himself at the Chelsea Art School, where he fell under the influence of Augustus John's charismatic personality. Flowing hair, gold earrings and velvet coats marked his rapid metamorphosis into John's most devoted follower, a process which reached its natural conclusion when he fell hopelessly in love with Dorelia while John, ever obliging, enjoyed a brief flirtation with Lamb's wife, Nina. By 1908, Nina had left and Lamb had formed a new attachment to Helen Maitland, a friend of Dorelia's. The fact that Helen was also being courted by Lamb's best friend, the Russian mosaicist Boris Anrep, did not discourage him at all; rivalry always stimulated his pleasure. Ottoline knew about both of these relationships ('all his heart is given to Dorelia,' she wrote in May 1910) when she fell in love with Lamb. The only piquant detail denied her was that the model for the Epstein statue she had recently purchased was Nina Lamb.

Ottoline's close friendship with Lamb was already being discussed in Bloomsbury circles in March 1910. Lytton Strachey, who still scarcely knew Ottoline, although he attended her parties, was not deterred from setting out to discover whether the handsome young artist might not prefer the company of a man. He saw Lamb, 'for the first time for ages', at a Bedford Square party on 1 March 1910. A week later, meeting Lamb there again, he plucked up the courage to flirt and was rewarded with an invitation to come to the studio and be drawn. Lamb's room, when Lytton visited it, was full of the rich coloured rugs and exotic flowers which he had noticed as being Ottoline's taste at Bedford Square, but the artist was not prepared to discuss his friendship with her. He allowed Lytton to stroke his cheek, which struck the suitor as a great mark of progress; the next time, however, Lamb flinched. On 25 March, Lytton was able to record a real triumph; he had persuaded Lamb to come to dinner at his home and the conversation, while James Strachey serenaded them on the pianola, had become most promisingly flirtatious. His hopes were promptly dashed again by the news that Lamb was off to spend the weekend with Ottoline at Peppard, alone.[8]

If Lytton had been on more familiar terms with Ottoline, he would have known that she, too, was suffering from Lamb's capricious nature. He could, when he was so inclined, be playful, funny and affectionate, but she was finding it impossible not to be wounded by his savage temper and exhausted by his fits of depression. 'H.L's friendship or rather the friendship given to him is a very great pleasure and joy to me,' she wrote in May 1910, but she did not underestimate the effort it was costing her to achieve it:

... It has been a hard struggle to get into touch with him for apparently he had heard me much derided ... and only by being very strong and generous, persistent and ignoring his bursts of fury could I get near him at all. He has however a very fine and beautiful nature threading through all his poor beaten vain sensitive self ... John and his set have done much to ruin and deface him and to make him disbelieve in good. If God will work in me may I be able to help him!

Ottoline was not yet ready to admit that she had fallen in love with a twenty-seven-year-old who conducted his life as though he was playing the junior lead in a Chekhov play. It was easier to believe that she was only concerned with rescuing him from the dangerous influence of John and Dorelia. Her object, she told herself, was to help Lamb to find the best in himself; with this in mind, she took him off on long walks across Richmond Park and Putney Common. At Peppard, confident that nature would calm him, she arranged afternoon drives across the downs and long walks into the beechwoods, armed with poetry books. It is impossible to be precise about when they became lovers, but it was certainly in the Peppard beechwoods that Lamb sketched her, naked, framed by leafy branches.

Philip had been a distant husband for almost three years. There is good reason to suppose that he had already started to be unfaithful himself, but discretion still has to be maintained about his early infidelities. Ottoline seems to have been unaware of them; certainly, she made no reference to them in her diaries or letters. She had already resolved that she would never leave him but, undesired by her husband, she was willing to give her love elsewhere. By the spring of 1910, she could think of nothing but Henry Lamb; when Philip unexpectedly chose *Antony and Cleopatra* for one of their evening reading sessions, she was able to listen contentedly to the story of a marriage which is sacrificed to a passionate and ill-fated love. She was so smitten that the main thought in her mind was that Lamb's letters were quite as magnificent as Shakespeare. 'No words of mine could describe this demi-angel as his letters do,' she wrote in her memoirs.[9]

It is hard to find much in these letters to justify Ottoline's enthusiasm and impossible to see anything but obsessive love in her belief that they were as fine as any that Russell wrote to her. 'Oh, my dear big lovely one,' Lamb saluted her in one; in another, he complained, with justification, of his lack of skill in 'this confounded unmanageable pen-art which comes and damps all expression'. Ottoline noticed none of the flaws. To her, the letters were evidence that she was indeed succeeding in her task of helping Lamb to become a better person.

'Oh Ottoline, you have done *all* for me, you have inspired every bit of worth I own,' began a letter written in the spring of 1910.[10] Consciously or not, Lamb held Ottoline firmly in thrall to him by his insistence that she, and only she, could rescue him from himself. This was the string he pulled to make her dance to his whim for the next two years. He had enmeshed her in a golden net, she wrote in one of the many passages concerning him which were excised from her memoirs after her death; it was only when she was trapped that she found she had been imprisoned by iron wire:

For no one had such power of tormenting a soul as Henry Lamb had. For half a day he would be angelic and enthrall one by his conversation, his humour and gaiety and his enjoyment of the moment, his wit and observation, his tenderness – then suddenly he would change and become a devil, full of spleen and cruelty, cutting one as with a knife, with his rude behaviour and cruel words. This might have been effective on the stage but in real life and directed to a sensitive individual [she was speaking here of his treatment of Lytton] it was really intolerable.

Ottoline was unable to be with Lamb as much as she would have liked in the spring of 1910. Early in April, Philip received a deputation from the Liberal Party in Burnley; they asked if he would be prepared to represent them in the campaign for the new constituency before the December election. Fighting for a seat was infinitely preferable to the desk-bound work he was doing for the Gladstone League: Philip agreed to make a preliminary visit to Burnley and Ottoline went with him.

Lying thirty miles north of Manchester, Burnley was a smoky Lancashire mill-town of the kind evoked in Dickens's *Hard Times* and Mrs Gaskell's *Mary Barton*. The town itself was chiefly composed of small black terraces, a few of which were lined with stunted black trees; Burnley children drew houses and trees in black crayon because they saw it as their proper colour. The big houses of the local gentry stood outside the town behind high walls; beyond and around lay the moors and crags and ravines towards which the townspeople felt a mixture of pride and terror. Edmund Spenser had written the gentle 'The Shepherd's Calender' here, but Burnley's people were more familiar with the tales of devils, witches, battles and grisly deaths handed down from the past.

Uncompromisingly ugly though the town was, Ottoline took to it at once, and, much to her pleased surprise, Burnley took to her. 'They are much more alive, vigorous and intelligent than the southerners,' she wrote during the two weeks she spent there with Philip; the local Liberal Party returned the compliment by telling Philip that his wife was just what the Burnley democrats wanted.[11]

The combination of a hectic round of political engagements and an intensely emotional relationship with Lamb took their toll; by the middle of May, Ottoline was in bed with migraine and psoriasis. But there was no time for rest: Philip wanted help with his speeches, she could not bear the thought of missing the June season of Mozart operas being conducted by Beecham, and Lamb, back in England after a fleeting visit to France with Helen Maitland, wanted all of her attention. Piqued by his refusal to give up seeing Helen or stop singing the praises of Dorelia, Ottoline suggested that he ought to think of finding a wife; Lamb's response was to invite her to come and spend a few days in Paris with him. Writing shortly after a visit to Peppard, he tenderly reminded her 'of that enchanted existence we enjoyed a few days ago' and which they could continue in Paris, if she chose. She chose not to risk it. Philip had at last begun to say that he wished she would spend more time with him and less with Lamb; Ottoline decided to spend the rest of the summer with him, visiting Aix and Venice. When she did eventually go to Paris, she was chaperoned by Roger Fry and Desmond MacCarthy.

Ottoline's first concern when she arrived back in England in September was that Philip should be in good spirits for what promised to be a tough autumn campaign, but Lamb's welfare was also very much on her mind. One of her most endearing characteristics was her determination to make life as agreeable as possible for those she loved. Comfort, in her view, was of crucial importance; nobody could be expected to create if they had to worry about where to live or how to afford to eat, as Lamb, like most artists, did. Her function, as she saw it, was to smooth away the creator's need to worry about such mundane problems. But the visits to exhibitions, concerts and operas which she arranged were transient solaces, and no amount of presents could reconcile Lamb to his cramped room in Fitzroy Street. He announced that he was thinking of giving up the studio and becoming a person of unfixed abode. He might, he said, move to France.

Ottoline was shocked into action, as Lamb may have hoped that she would be. He had already said how much he loved being at Peppard and that he always worked best when he was away from London. With Philip's reluctant agreement, she told him that he must come and make his home with them for as long as it suited him. A coach-house just down the road from the cottage could easily be converted into a splendid studio. Philip did not want him to share their home, but he could easily stay at The Dog and come to the cottage for his meals: a room in a country pub would be far cheaper than the rent on his London studio. Ottoline was also confident that she could persuade that benevolent art lover, Lord Henry, to give Lamb some lucrative commissions.

Lamb was ecstatic. 'You have put me on such a footing that I can look at all material and most moral difficulties straight in the face,' he told her: 'I can chirp, grow fat, live where I will and paint what I like.' (n.d. 1910) But Lamb was nothing if not volatile. 'Dinner with Roger [Fry] and P. and H.L. after Post Impressionist show,' Ottoline noted. 'Everyone was cross and upset and tired and it was not a great success. I went with H.L. afterwards and then there was a miserable journey down to Peppard. H. and P. like two dogs growling at one another.'* Lamb moved out of the cottage and into the studio the following day.

Visiting Goldie Lowes Dickinson in Cambridge the previous week, Ottoline had slipped off alone to have tea at Newnham with Jane Harrison.† Lytton Strachey was also there, exchanging notes on a Swedish massage cure which he and Miss Harrison had recently survived. 'Swedish massage as administered by a robust native is no picnic,' as Miss Harrison had found to her cost; she had been quick to take a tip from Lytton. '"Take my advice," he said; "as soon as they touch you begin to yell, and go on yelling till they stop."'[12]

Lytton was far more interested in hearing about Henry Lamb than in gossiping about massage techniques. Ottoline reported the latest development and, prompted by a spirit of mischievous boldness, suggested that he might like to come and stay at Peppard. She herself would have to join Philip in Burnley for the election at the end of November; her suggestion was that Lytton should come before then and, if it suited him, stay on to keep Lamb company. Lytton could hardly believe his good luck. 'He pondered it very seriously, drifted away, but after a few moments he came back to me and said, "Do you really mean me to come to Peppard?" and I said, "Of course I do."'[13] In love with Lamb though she was, she saw no danger in encouraging this friendship; the painter was far more likely to stay contentedly at home in her absence if she provided him with stimulating company. 'I cannot answer for his tempers but the thought of seeing you makes him very happy today,' she wrote to Lytton and added, in case he should change his mind, that the village taxi would be sent to meet his train and that the cottage spare room was ready.

Bravely though she had extended her invitation, her heart sank when she saw the visitor uncoiling his long legs from the taxi. To her journal, she was ready to admit that Lytton terrified her on the first days of his visit; it was a pleasant surprise to discover, as he began to relax, that there was a very different man hidden away behind the mask of forbidding shyness. 'It is hard to realise that this tall, solemn,

---

* An interesting example of the way the memoirs were revised by Philip. In the published version, we read that the journey was managed 'without any quarrel'.

† Jane Harrison, together with Gilbert Murray and Francis Cornford, was one of the Cambridge ritualists who argued for an origin in ritual of mythology, drama and religion. They were influenced by Sir James George Frazer's monumental work, *The Golden Bough* (published in twelve volumes between 1890 and 1915).

lanky cadaverous man, with his rather unpleasant greasy appearance, looking indeed far older than he is [Lytton was thirty, seven years younger than Ottoline] is a combination of frivolity and love of indecency, mixed up with rigid intellectual integrity,' she wrote after getting to know him better.[14] In 1910, she did not know him well enough to realise what a dangerous game she was playing in seeming to encourage his feelings for Henry Lamb. 'I wonder if it is possible for me ever to see the rightness of promiscuous love, transient flirtations,' she wrote after her first long conversation with him; she had not understood the strength of Lytton's need to win, not just the body, but the heart. To Ottoline, lying upstairs in her bedroom – her health had once again collapsed – it seemed only that her visitor was keeping Lamb entertained. 'I heard the duet of their voices underneath, laughing and joking, Lytton playing with him [Lamb] like a cat with a mouse, enjoying having his own sensations tickled by Lamb's beauty, while his contrariness adds spice to the contact.'[15]

Lytton had come to Peppard unarmed by any knowledge of what to expect; at the end of the first week, he was finding it difficult to make up his mind whether he was more in love with Lamb or with Ottoline. On the most superficial level, he was snobbish enough to enjoy referring to a duke's sister as his intimate friend. (One of his first references to Ottoline, in a letter to Duncan Grant, seems to have been made only to drag in the fact that her companions at an exhibition had been the Duchess of Portland and the Marquis de Soveral.) On a more agreeable level, he was overwhelmed by her generosity. A few months earlier, he had been ready to hate her for carrying Lamb 'off to the country with her under my very nose', as he lamented to Duncan Grant.[16] How could he hate her now, when she not only appeared to be ready to share Lamb with him, but gave him the run of her home? And such a home! It was, he reported to his younger brother, James, 'altogether exquisite':

Such comforts and cushions you never saw! Henry, too, more divine than ever, plump now (but not bald) and mellowed in the radiance of Ottoline ... She seems quite gone – quite! And on the whole I don't wonder. But his attitude is rather more cranky. No doubt it's a convenience, and a pleasure even – but then – Meanwhile Philip electioneers at Burnley.[17]

The grudging tone of that 'no doubt it's a convenience' tells us that Lytton was not altogether satisfied in paradise. He was undisturbed by Ottoline's evident passion for Lamb: whoever minded if their beloved inspired other people? It did not, however, please him that Lamb should be quite so attached to her. It was rather a relief when his hostess took herself off to the Thorn Hotel in Burnley, leaving Julian in the care of the maids and Lytton free to pursue his courtship over the first three weeks of November.

The letters from Peppard were Ottoline's only light relief in a month of hard campaigning. She rose at six, roused to her duties by the tumultuous clatter of clogs on the cobbled streets. She danced with Burnley councillors, kissed the mill-girls, offered her views on the worthless lives of rich landowning Tories and handed out publicity photographs. Lamb (his letters that month were almost all undated) failed to be captivated by her enthusiastic accounts of the warm-hearted people of Burnley. 'It all sounds very interesting,' he wrote, 'but I think I can content myself with no nearer approach than your accounts can give me.'

Lamb had good reason to be contented. Knowing his love of music (he was a fine pianist), Ottoline had arranged for a piano to be delivered. Julian, who adored Lamb, was being 'frantically amorous' and Lytton was proving such a delightful companion that Lamb begged Ottoline to write and urge him to stay a little longer, while lamenting that she was away so long. 'I burn to embrace you and cover your body with mine,' he told her on 20 November, but in the same letter, he said that he was thinking of asking Helen Maitland to come and stay at the Dog Inn.

Lytton, while reported by Lamb to be 'in great terror of exceeding the covenances' by staying too long, was also in a state of high satisfaction. Ottoline had told the cook to give him whatever he asked for to eat and showed no sign of minding when he wrote to tell her that Henry was 'lovely'; Lamb had invited him to come and sit every day for his portrait in the studio. All that was required to make his life perfect was that Lamb should respond to his physical advances. 'Extraordinary,' he reported to his brother James. 'I tremble to think of what an idyll it might be, if only – and even as it is – in fact I really have no notion *what* it is.'[18]

Lytton reluctantly left the cottage in early December. Tears were reportedly shed on both sides and Lamb was given the task of writing to convey his gratitude to Ottoline, both for 'the unparalleled joy of his visit' and 'for the new evidence of divine strength and love in you'. Lytton's own letter thanked her for the present of a vellum-bound book and for what he described as 'an interlude from the Arabian nights', since only conversation had saved Lamb from a fate he was evidently as anxious to avoid as the storyteller Scheherazade had been to keep her life. It was elegantly phrased, but Ottoline was too anxious to appreciate wit. Election night had come, and the results were unpredictable enough for Asquith to have come up to Burnley himself to urge support for Philip. Hearing distant cheers as she sat waiting for the results in the hotel coffee-room, Ottoline was sure that they had lost.

No cheering near the hotel, and sure enough the Boots brought word that 'Arbuthnot was in by nineteen' . . . My only thought was: 'Nineteen, nineteen. Why didn't we work harder?' But then he returned to say he was 'not sure' and in a few minutes Philip himself rushed in, excited and happy. The cheering was so great that I could not hear him and had to ask him to shout the result in my ear. He was in by a hundred and seventy-three. The crowd outside was like a sea, and the shouting and cheering indescribable . . .[19]

Lytton Strachey left England in December 1910, to spend four months building up his strength in a French sanatorium after 'une légère attaque de cholerine', to work on his first book, *Landmarks in French Literature*, and to puzzle over the complicated character of the man he called his 'très cher serpent'. Long letters arrived at Peppard every week from the Zander Institute in Nice, but Lamb's replies were dilatory and full of his personal concerns. 'He seems to be completely indifferent to everything that concerns me,' Lytton wrote despondently to his brother James. A year after his first visit to Peppard, writing to James again, Lytton had experienced nothing to alter his initial impression. 'He is the most delightful companion in the world,' he wrote, ' – and the most unpleasant.'

Ottoline, too, found it difficult to decide whether the pleasure of being with Lamb when he was in a sunny and affectionate mood was worth the misery he was capable of causing her. Always imperious, he expected devoted attention after her return from Burnley; it infuriated him to find that she had arranged to entertain a steady stream of visitors whose comforts took precedence over his own demands. All through December, the London train transported guests to Peppard: Desmond MacCarthy, Vanessa and Clive Bell, Virginia Stephen, Roger Fry; even Lamb's own arrangement to be visited by Helen Maitland was destroyed by the fact that she arrived with Boris Anrep. None of the guests were congenial to him. He did not conceal his annoyance and Ottoline was made to bear the brunt of it. He wanted to punish her for thoughtless behaviour.

It was the knowledge of his lack of mastery over her which galled Lamb most. He had worked hard to establish it. He had ensconced himself in her home, won Julian's friendship and gained Philip's unwilling tolerance; he had let it be known that the household maids and village girls were devastated by his charm and good looks. But he still had not subdued Ottoline. She went where she wished and when she wished. She invited her friends, not his, to stay, and while they lounged comfortably in the cottage drawing-room every evening, he was obliged to retire humbly to the inn. His cruellest shafts of scorn appeared to fall to the ground unnoticed. Philip, glowing with success from his Burnley triumph, was unassailably cheerful and Ottoline was far too proud to admit that Lamb's criticisms hurt her.

Lamb would have been angrier still if he had been allowed to look into Ottoline's journal. It might have amused him to know that Virginia had been offering the opinion that all artists were brutes – how much had Ottoline told her? – but not to learn that the two women had been analysing his defects. 'Guard against mésalliance,' Ottoline wrote after this interesting discussion. 'One can give to these inferior souls largely, generously, sympathetically, affection and tenderness, but not one's inner freedom. One can be their comrade but not their subject.'[20]

Strong though the signs are that Ottoline was trying to cure herself of her obsession with Lamb, she did not succeed. She wrote of him as a demi-angel, but there was something quite devilish about the way that he now began to exploit the fact that both she and Lytton were under his spell. There is no doubt that it was an effective ploy. Neither is there any doubt that he knew exactly what he was doing: on one occasion (in the summer of 1912), he sent Lytton a caricature which showed Lamb, the puppet-master and hangman, dangling his two victims from his strings. The caption read: 'When will he realise what he makes us SUFFER?' It is, on the other hand, fair to point out that Ottoline would never have enjoyed her close friendship with Lytton if it had not been for their mutual love of Henry Lamb, the chief subject of their correspondence from 1910 to 1913.

Artful though Lamb was at manipulating Ottoline's feelings, his strongest suit was the fact that he was always ready to let her know that, without her, he was lost. 'I do feel so miserable about my conduct to you these last few days,' he wrote, probably in December 1910:

I have been acting quite often directly against my wishes, compelled by something inexplicable. When we came out this evening, I really did want to talk to you and to ask your forgiveness for my cruelty, but something made me do and say the opposite. Please try to forget all I said. I am sorry for hurting you so much.

And above all I pray you not to despair of the ultimate effect of your influence on me; I see and feel and love so much its force on other people that I earnestly hope to receive it in full myself. I know, for instance, that I can only tolerate those who live about you, owing to that part of you which has filtered into them. I feel sure you could tame me and that with your help I could overcome myself. Do try patiently to help me and above all believe in my affection.

Lamb's appeal had a large measure of truth in it. He did love and admire Ottoline and he did believe that she could help him to achieve a kind of serenity. And every time he took up his scratchy pen and a scruffy sheet of graph paper to tell her that she alone had the power to transform his life, Ottoline capitulated. 'After all, I have come back to Peppard and have made friends with H.L.,' she wrote on 29–30 January 1911, at a time when she was sure that he had transferred his affection to Lytton. 'I believe there is something in our friendship, something that unites our souls . . . He certainly cares most for L. [Lytton]. He is fond of me in another way and a good way and the only way of doing him good is to keep myself in reserve . . . Let the physical side diminish and the Divine side increase – the other gives a gêne and discomfort.'

In February 1911, Henry Lamb started work on a commission for Lord Henry, 'The Lake', a vaguely symbolic picture which he described as 'the most complete of my productions'. His larger interest was in a full-length oil painting of Ottoline, standing, in a green richly-decorated dress and jacket which set off the pallor of her skin and the deep red of her hair. 'Your portrait is to be a sumptuous thing,' he told her. 'I will have nothing less: therefore don't grudge me for the hours you have stood and will spend standing.' Perhaps it embarrassed Ottoline to see her lover so obviously setting himself up against Augustus John who had also painted her free-standing in a deep green dress. Perhaps the long hours of standing motionless exhausted her; certainly, she showed little enthusiasm for the project. She came to the first sittings in a long cardigan which she kept on because it was too cold; she missed sittings because of other commitments; she pleaded illness, fatigue and boredom as excuses for remaining at the cottage. Lamb's own bad temper made modelling a particularly thankless task. She imported Boris Anrep's vivacious mistress, Junia (Anrep had now set up a *ménage à trois* in Paris with Junia and Helen Maitland), to render a weekend of sittings less disagreeable by reading to her while she posed, but a weekend was not enough to satisfy Lamb. It 'hardly means more than a couple of sittings under the best of circumstances', he grumbled, 'and how am I to paint face, hand, jacket and embroidery in that time?' Ottoline's patience was coming to an end. 'If he found a strand of hair in a different position to what it had been the day before he would make me feel that I had committed a most grievous offence against Art,' she wrote, 'and therefore I was grateful to Junia when she told him not to be so silly.'[21]

Henry Lamb's volatile behaviour was a contributing factor to Ottoline's increasing dissatisfaction with Peppard. The time had gone when she could look forward to the solitude of her long spells in the country; once a refuge, the cottage had now become a trap where she felt badgered and persecuted. If she went for a walk in the woods, she was accused of selfish indifference. If she went to the studio, she became the target for Lamb's complaints as the defects of the portrait were laid at her door. But there were other less emotional reasons for wanting to leave the village, fond though she was of it and gladly though she had presided over the fêtes and flower shows, the Christmas parties in the school hall. The cottage was simply not large enough for entertaining more than two friends at a time: it was, Ottoline wryly observed, very like trying to entertain in a beach hut, something nobody would dream of doing for pleasure.

Roger Fry, who had visited Peppard enough times to sympathise with the problem, appointed himself as the Morrells' chief housefinder. At the end of 1910, he had moved into Durbins, a house built to his own design. Its only flaw was that there were no congenial neighbours in the Guildford area. 'It's really a duty to look at houses here,' he urged Ottoline. 'I've already made inquiries and the agent understands exactly what is wanted and is looking out and will send me word.' (12 February 1911) Four days later, he wrote again to remind her that she had promised to visit Durbins in early March and to say that he had 'a great sheaf of houses' ready for her inspection. The dislike which Ottoline had bluntly expressed for two Eric Gill reliefs which Fry had just bought on behalf of the Contemporary Art Society did not lessen his eagerness to see her, or his pleasure in the purchase, although 'there's no one whose opinion I go against with more difficulty than yours and I always expect to think you are right . . . I'm so delighted you'll come on the 4th . . . If only it will be fine when you come and you'll stay on as long as possible.' (16 February 1911)

Perhaps Ottoline should have guessed that Roger Fry was falling in love with her, but her thoughts were fully occupied with Henry Lamb. The following month, with the speed of a comet, Bertrand Russell burst into her life, overshadowing everything else.

7

AN OVERWHELMING PASSION
March 1911

'It seems you or I must be ruined – perhaps both ... I love you with all my heart and soul, but I begin to fear you too.'
Bertrand Russell to OM, 28 March 1911

'Dearest, it is good that love has come to you – it would have been too terrible if your divine power of loving had never found an object. I feel utterly unworthy, but I do give you a love which is worthy of yours.'
Bertrand Russell to OM, 2 April 1911

On Saturday, 18 March 1911, Bertrand Russell wrote to Ottoline to confirm that he was looking forward to visiting Bedford Square the following day before setting off for Paris, where he was due to give a short course of lectures at the Sorbonne. It was a friendly note. Nobody who read it would have believed what was to follow from it, least of all Ottoline herself. Since Philip was away in Burnley, she invited two friends to dinner, Ethel Sands and Ralph Hawtrey. The guests left early and, for the first time, Ottoline found herself completely alone with Russell. She had sensed that he was unhappy; she had often noticed that he seemed to be controlling himself only by some ferocious discipline. When someone showed signs of wanting to confide in her, Ottoline's instinct was always to encourage them to speak and to offer all of the considerable sympathy and understanding of which she was capable. The result, on this occasion, was explosive.

After they had gone, we sat over the fire talking until late. It is difficult to clearly recall or to describe an evening that had so much influence on my life and on B's life. I certainly had not before this evening thought of him as anyone very intimate, but fate sometimes throws a ball of fire into one's life, stunning and overwhelming one.

I knew he was unhappy, and I knew he lived in a state of intense compression and strict inner discipline; one could see that, by the tense way he always sat – his hands clenched together – and by his erect attitude. I was unprepared for the outburst of passion that poured itself out upon me. I was overwhelmed, bewildered, and swept a certain distance. What had I done to remove the lid from this boiling cauldron? My imagination was swept away, but not my heart, although it was very much moved and upset. All Bertie's eloquence and passion was brought to bear on me, urging me to give up everything for him, and in spite of myself I was carried along in this spate of emotion. I could not convince him that to leave Philip and Julian was unthinkable.*

Russell's own account of the evening endorsed Ottoline's, while adding that only 'external circumstances' prevented him from making love to her that night. 'My feeling was overwhelmingly strong, and I did not care what might be involved. I wanted to leave Alys, and to have her leave Philip. What Philip might think or feel was a matter of indifference to me.'[1] In a letter which he wrote to Ottoline a fortnight later (31 March 1911), he confessed that his declaration had been as much of a thunderbolt to himself as to her:

I did not know I loved you till I heard myself telling you so – for one instant I thought 'Good God what have I said?' . . . and then I knew it was the truth. My heart spoke before my brain knew – and then love swept me on in a great flood and lifted me to the heights. It is strange to have been sure so quickly, but I knew at once that I could give you *everything* my nature is capable of.

To Bertie, the discovery of his love for Ottoline came as an intoxicating relief from his despair about his marriage to Alys Pearsall Smith. He felt like a prisoner whose door had been thrown open; all he had to do was to persuade Ottoline to walk to freedom beside him. Writing to her from the train to Paris two days later, he tried to convey his feelings. 'My heart is so full that I hardly know where to begin,' he told her.

The world is so changed in these last 48 hours that I am still bewildered. My thoughts won't come away from you – I don't hear what people say . . . I see your face always, tho' as a rule I can't imagine anybody's face. I love you very dearly now and I know that every time I see you I shall love you more . . . now I know what I have longed for. Only it is altogether extraordinary to me that you should love me – I feel myself so rugged and ruthless,

---

* Since this passage is frequently used for quotation, special attention should be drawn to the fact that it has been taken from the original typescript, revised for posthumous publication by Ottoline herself. It differs strikingly from the version edited by Robert Gathorne-Hardy and published by him in an appendix to the second volume of Ottoline's memoirs, *Ottoline at Garsington 1915–18* (Faber, London, 1974).

and so removed from the whole aesthetic side of life – a sort of logic machine warranted to destroy any ideal that is not very robust. My own ideals can endure my own criticism and thrive on it; yours, I believe, can also. But most people can't. People think me cynical, but that is superficial. The bottom feeling is one of affection for almost everybody. I often wish I could be more ruthless in feeling – it would simplify life.

I don't really know you yet. You must help me to. I want to know every bit, absolutely. (21 March 1911)

It was a remarkable letter, not only for the determination and eloquence with which it was written, but for the fact that Russell was already able to foresee what the main causes of division between them were going to be. His failure to respond to the aesthetic side of life, to the world of colour, imagination and sensation which she valued, was the deficiency which Ottoline would later find hardest to tolerate; he would use that 'logic machine' when he began relentlessly to batter the fortress of her religious beliefs. But in March 1911 it was the threat to her marriage, not her ideals, which frightened Ottoline. Nervously, she wrote back to tell him that while she did indeed return his love, she was not prepared to leave her husband. It was all so quick, she added. How could she suppose that he loved a woman whose mind was so inferior to his? In a second letter, she tried another tack. Secrecy was essential if they were to have a liaison. Philip must never be allowed to know of it. If Bertie could not bring himself to agree to this, then she would have to sacrifice the love she felt for him.*

Ottoline may have hoped that these conditions would have a cooling effect on Russell's ardour. They did not. His response was prompt and frank enough to show that he intended to obtain her. 'I have been told, and I believe, that your obstinacy is incredible,' he wrote from Paris on 23 March; 'so is mine.' In his letter of the previous day, he had told her that her love would be 'everything to me, and what I want even more – peace ... You could give me inward joy and expel the demons.' Now, he laid down the rules. This was to be an all-or-nothing love. It was absurd of her to worry that she was not clever enough for him. He was not prepared to consider a secret affair. She had asked him to think how it would reflect on her if she was known to be his mistress; she would, in his view, look worse if she was seen to have been intriguing behind her husband's back.

You do not 'survive' well in a position involving deceit ... You must, you

---

* Although she did not want Bertie to know of it, Ottoline had already told Philip of his love for her without admitting that she had also been profoundly affected. At the end of March, Philip was allowed to assume that Bertie's interest in her had subsided. It was not until the middle of April that Ottoline felt obliged to enlighten him about Bertie's feelings and, to a lesser degree, her own.

shall, be worthy of the love that is the best in you and me; you shall not kill the new-born infant ... My life is bound up with you, it is my last chance of real happiness, or of a life, that brings out my best. For you also – I *will* say it – such love is not to be despised. (23 March)

Ottoline was agonised. 'What was I to do?' she wrote in her journal retrospectively. She begged him to tell everything to Alys (which he did), then changed her mind. She could not contemplate leaving Philip who, for all their sexual incompatibility, depended on her for understanding and loyal companionship; she could not resist Bertie's declaration of his need for her. 'How could I allow him to return to the dreary life of self-repression that he had risen from? It seemed that I could not refuse to take upon me the burden of this very fine and valuable life.'[2] Editing her journals for the public eye, she did her best in sentences like these to convey that she had submitted to the will of Bertrand Russell in a spirit of duty; her letters make it clear that the act of duty was staying with the husband who depended on her to do so. Her feelings for Bertie were far more passionate than she was able to admit in her memoirs. 'Nothing can stop the force of my love coming to you and yours to me,' she wrote to him on the morning of 25 March when he was hurrying from his train to Bedford Square. '... My spirit *is* with you this moment and every moment. I understand you as I understand myself.' The meeting, however, was a stormy one. Not only did Ottoline reiterate her determination to preserve her marriage, but she admitted that she was still allowing Philip to come to her room to make love to her, when he so wished. This, for Bertie, was the final straw; if she was not even prepared to forbid Philip to enter her bed for his sake, he wanted no more to do with her. If they met again, it would be for the last time. Late that night, as she and Philip sat in their opposite chairs by the drawing-room fire, he reading a book, she writing her letters, Ottoline tried to explain to Bertie how unimportant she felt her sexual connection to her husband to be. There was no passion in it, only a matter of conjugal rights which she felt it would be wrong of her to deny, and from which neither of them extracted much pleasure. 'Philip does not *possess* me,' she wrote:

and what you object to is in *reality* no different from sitting in the same room with him as I am doing now, writing to you. I am as much my own free self as I always am, and I certainly feel farther from him then than I do often when he and I are talking together. I understand your imagination not accepting it, but I who know the facts know that your imagination is wrong ... (25 March)

Ottoline was doing her best to make him understand that sex was not a significant part of her marriage. Since, as she said, it had no more meaning for her than the act of talking to her husband, she could not understand Bertie's distress. She had failed to consider his own point of view. Bertie, who was in some ways more of a romantic than Ottoline, could not imagine anybody being able to endure sex without passion. He had only occasionally slept with his own wife out of pity since 1902, the year when he fell out of love with her; he found it impossible to suppose that Ottoline's feelings for Philip might be different. Since she loved him, she could not conceivably feel able to go to bed with Philip. From Van Bridge, the cottage near Fernhurst in Sussex which had been rented for Alys when he accepted the university room that went with a Cambridge lectureship in 1910, Bertie wrote again, asking Ottoline to go and take the advice of Evelyn Whitehead, one of his closest friends, and repeating his warning that he would end the relationship if she did not stop sleeping with her husband. He wrote, too, of his profound love, but Ottoline sensed now that she was being cudgelled into submission. 'You make me nearly obey you,' she answered on 26 March, 'but not quite.' She was not prepared to do as he wanted even though 'nothing keeps me here except my own will and conviction of what is right . . .' She would, if he wished it, go and visit Mrs Whitehead, if he in return would promise to see her again, 'if only for once more as you said . . . I long for you to take me completely once and let me pour myself into you.'

Two days later, obedient to her promise, Ottoline went to Carlyle Square, Chelsea, to talk to Evelyn Whitehead, the wife of Bertie's colleague and collaborator on *Principia Mathematica* (1910). A clever, imposing woman who liked to emphasise her Spanish blood by wearing heavy silk shawls and haircombs, Mrs Whitehead had become the most important woman in Bertie's life after his emotional break with Alys in 1902. A shrewd instinct about this intimacy prompted Ottoline to write to Bertie only that she had liked Evelyn very much and been impressed by 'her great affection and understanding of you'. To her journal, however, she confided that she had been uncomfortably conscious of 'suppressed mistrust and jealousy'.

The next day, the 29th, marked a climax in a week of intense activity. Ottoline had been brave enough to try to act as Bertie wished. She had told Philip, presumably for the first time, that she did not wish to share a bed with him. 'I asked him to sleep in his room. Oh Bertie, now this is said and one turns one's face away, it is torture. I can't express it . . . My only desire is to come to you, my beloved, and to give myself wholly to you if only for once.' She was waiting eagerly at Bedford Square for his reply when Evelyn Whitehead was shown in. 'Oh God how awful it was,' she wrote later, after her visitor had reminded her of her duties as a wife and mother before adding with, one suspects, considerable satisfaction, that Bertie, who was now staying at Carlyle Square, had decided that he could not bring himself to see her. In the unpublished version of her memoirs, Ottoline makes it clear that Mrs Whitehead had spared her nothing of Bertie's own account. She was told of Alys's misery and of how she had been standing at the window of the cottage, 'watching for the postman to bring a letter from me, and of Alys watching him snatch it from the postman's hand . . . she told me that very night Alys had come to him in tears.'³

Mrs Whitehead had doubtless been affected by the thought of Alys's misery and Bertie's guilt, but it was optimistic of her to suppose that she had the power to alter the course of events. By midday, a letter from Bertie had arrived at Bedford Square and when another followed, begging for a 'last' meeting the following morning, Ottoline wrote to agree. The meeting took place,* but the man to whom Ottoline chose to give herself on the evening of 30 March was not Bertie but her old friend, Roger Fry.

Fry had been urging Ottoline to join up with him, the Bells and Harry Norton, a Cambridge friend, on their springtime journey to Turkey, an invitation which Ottoline had good-humouredly refused. Vanessa Bell's ill-health had caused the projected trip to be revised; the current plan was for Fry and Norton to go on ahead, leaving at the beginning of April, and for the Bells to catch up with them at Constantinople. On 30 March, after an evening party which they had both attended, Fry came to Bedford Square and made some kind of declaration to Ottoline. (Her own account tells us only that 'he did give vent to great emotion just before he started for Constantinople'.) Later that night, Fry sent her a scrawled note in which he told her that he was 'still all amazed and wondering and can't begin to think – I only know how beautiful it was of you, how splendid . . . it's made me feel absolutely humble before you.' His next few letters from abroad suggest that he was thinking of running away with her and believed that it was what she, too, wanted. Ottoline's own diary entry for the evening of 30 March, which misleadingly appears in the Russell appendix of *Ottoline at Garsington*, clearly refers to Fry: 'Oh grant that it may be good . . . and do him good, not any harm.'

What was going on? Ottoline did say later that Fry was the only person she chose to confide in about her relationship with Bertie; she hoped, as one of Russell's friends, that he would be able to advise her. But Fry's letters make no reference to Bertie until his arrival in

---

* It is usually assumed that there was only one 'last' meeting, but the letters suggest two, one at Carlyle Square on the morning of 30 March, when Bertie was given an encouraging letter, and the second on 31 March (the morning after her puzzling surrender to Fry), during which Ottoline declared her total love.

Turkey, and it is difficult to imagine that the revelation of Bertie's love for her would have inspired him to write as he did on the eve of his departure. It is indeed impossible to put any construction on his first letter, or on the passionate ones which succeeded it, other than the obvious, which was that Ottoline had allowed him to make love to her and to believe that she loved him. Her letters to him have disappeared, but Fry's answers offer us a few clues about their contents. Certainly, she gave him the impression that she returned his feelings; was she, as Fry later suspected, simply using him as a decoy, hoping that gossip about her relationship with him would draw the hounds of Bloomsbury off the scent of her relationship with Bertie? 'I know you will decide right for us and together we shall have strength to do whatever you decide,' Fry wrote to her on 4 April. A week later, he was beginning to feel overwhelmed by her praises. 'Don't please think me too splendid,' he begged her; 'it frightens me for fear you should find you had liked a self-made image and . . . it's more comfortable to feel sure that one's just loved for being the queer mixture one is.' (13 April) If nothing else, these letters tell us that Ottoline was not yet ready to confide in him about Bertie.

On 29 March, Russell had sadly resigned himself to the fact that his next meeting with Ottoline was going to be the last. But, even before she came to meet him at Carlyle Square the following morning, Ottoline had made up her mind to end nothing, neither her marriage, nor the burgeoning relationship with Bertie, nor the old, unfinished love-affair with Henry Lamb. 'Dearest, my whole soul is flooded with joy,' Bertie wrote as soon as she had left the house; '– your radiance shines before me, and I feel still your arms about me and your kiss on my lips. You have become to me something holy . . . I will accept whatever of your time you feel you can rightly give, and I will not ask for more.' The next day, Ottoline sent him a little photograph of herself standing in St Mark's Square in Venice, small enough to keep in his pocketbook.

Bertie was overjoyed. Back at Van Bridge with Alys and Mary Berenson's two daughters, Karin and Ray Costelloe, he found it impossible to think of anything but Ottoline. He was glad now, he wrote, to know that the price of their love was not to be the sacrifice of the people who loved them; he was full of a sense of delight and wonder that he should be thought deserving of her love. The future was fraught with problems – would Alys be willing to keep her promise to say nothing to anybody for the time being? how would Philip react when he learned that they had not, as he had been allowed to suppose, parted for ever on 30 March? – but for the moment, they were in a state of rapturous mutual engrossment which made light of every difficulty. While Alys dried her tears, Bertie fretted about what present he should give to his beloved. Had she read Synge's *Deirdre of the Sorrows*, since 'nothing in literature seems to me to fit so well with what I have been feeling'? Matthew Arnold's poem 'Dover Beach' expressed his own painful yearning for a religious belief he could not rationally endorse, 'but it does not express yours'. What about Blake, or Shelley, 'the poet I have loved best ... he is constantly in my thoughts.' (5 April)

It meant a great deal to Ottoline to discover that Bertie shared her literary tastes – she knew the work of Shelley and Blake as well as he did and she had recently become an admirer of J. M. Synge's plays. It astonished her to find how much they had in common, even if Bertie spoke only of the importance of truth when she talked about her religious faith. 'Yes Dearest,' Bertie continued, 'we do seem strangely near in thought and feeling ... I have the sense that you will always understand me.' But what meant most of all to Ottoline was the knowledge that she had, in Bertie Russell, found the worthy object for a regenerating love that she had been seeking all her life. Through him, she could achieve miracles. He had told her so himself. 'I cannot really care without making what I care for a symbol of something universal,' he had written to her the previous day.

Life is like a mountain top in a mist, at most times cold and blank, with aimless hurry – then suddenly the world opens out, and gives visions of unbelievable beauty ... I do not mean unreal visions. I mean seeing the hidden things that may be made manifest. And I want to give the visions to others ... what I mean is somehow that you belong with religion to me, and that therefore I will make our love help me in trying to preserve ideals in me without what seems to me false belief – which is at bottom what I most want to do ... My whole being is one song to you of love and reverence.

The philosophy of mathematics had dominated Russell's mind until he met Ottoline. The year 1911 marked the end of what he described as his imprisonment in 'that cold and unresponsive love' and the beginning of his larger and, in the view of many people, more important career as a philosopher concerned with human matters. His love for Ottoline played a significant part in this transformation. Her influence over his character was, as he acknowledged in his autobiography, great; it was also 'almost wholly beneficial'.

PART THREE

Ottoline and Bertie

'I reach out to the stars, and through the ages, and everywhere the radiance of your love lights the world for me.'
Bertrand Russell to OM, July 1911

8

PORTRAIT OF A RELATIONSHIP
1911–16

'I have the very greatest fear that my life hereafter be ruined by my having lost the support of religion.'
Bertrand Russell, private journal of 'Greek Exercises', 27 May 1888

'I fear almost to say how much I love you for fear that should influence you towards me ... I only ask you to be courageous to hurt me if necessary, or rather not to think of hurting me, only to trust to my understanding and love.'
OM to Bertrand Russell, 27 May 1911

Ottoline and Bertie exchanged letters, sometimes at the rate of four each a day, until her death in 1938. They are an intimate record of a love-affair; they are also an invaluable source of information about Ottoline.

Passion was the grand theme of their letters in the first few months; the minor theme had more in common with a comic farce as they struggled to keep their affair secret in the middle of a gossip-loving society. Railway timetables were frantically consulted in order to allow Bertie to dart into a departing train as Philip climbed out of one arriving at the opposite platform. Meetings took place on park benches, at remote Underground exits, at drab London hotels where a bedroom could be hired for the afternoon, in village churchyards and in railway waiting-rooms. A more civilised pattern only emerged in the autumn of 1911, when Bertie found a small flat near Bedford Square. Philip Morrell always walked the dogs after dinner; as soon as he had left the house, Ottoline went to the flat; if the weather was bad or she was feeling unwell, an advance note would bring Bertie to her door as soon as he had seen Philip walk out of the square.

We may smile at the Feydeauesque picture conjured up by these complicated arrangements, but love cast a transforming glamour over the absurdity. A hurried lunch together of steamed chicken in the flat was sufficient to inspire pages of ecstatic recollection. Ottoline, always an eager pupil, thought that love had no greater pleasure to offer than sitting with Bertie in the beechwoods near Peppard and being allowed to ask him questions about philosophy and put forward her own ideas. For Bertie, too, these afternoons came to represent the happiest period of their relationship. Joyfully, their letters dwelt on the extraordinary rapport which existed between them.

If their minds were marvellously well-attuned to each other's interests and inclinations, their bodies were not. For all the freedom of her life and the strong desire to use her love in a constructive way, Ottoline did not have any real enthusiasm for sex. As recently as February 1911, when she was still tormented by her feelings for Henry Lamb, she had written longingly in her journal of her desire for a relationship in which sex or, as she called it, *volupté*, need play no part. 'Is it *la volupté* that tempts one out of one's Eden,' she had asked herself, 'or is there such a thing as mutual attraction without *volupté* that makes it possible for two creatures to help each other and yet keep their separate lives sane and uninebriated?' It was just this kind of relationship that she wanted to establish with Bertie. The fact that she did not find him physically attractive made the decision an easy one, particularly since Bertie, until 1914, suffered from a mild case of pyorrhoea. But Bertie, at the end of nine years of almost total celibacy, was not in the mood for a platonic affair. He liked sex and saw it as the natural corollary to any attachment he formed. It was not, then, on the physical level, an easy relationship, and it was not helped by the fact that Ottoline had a horror of sexual frankness. Even talking about love filled her with dread; she was always happier when her love-affairs could be shifted on to an ethereal level. Over and over again in her letters, we find her miserably apologising to Bertie for having been unable to talk in the way he wanted, for having seemed cold and withdrawn, and for having failed to make it clear how much she felt for him. Occasionally, she would manage to write in the intimate style that so embarrassed her; slight though the evidence is, it is sufficient to undermine the version offered in her memoirs of a total lack of desire on her part. 'I feel shy of speaking ever about *our physical union*,' she wrote to Bertie on 9 January 1912, 'but it is *most divine* and today it seemed more so than ever before.'

Such moments were rare and Bertie's patience was frequently stretched to its small limit. Not surprisingly, he drifted into relationships with other women during the long affair, while never intending to give up Ottoline. The pattern was always the same. He would tell her what was going on, or even what was about to go on. Ottoline responded with apparent delight that he should have found the possibility of happiness at last. Having given her approval, she retreated into her marriage, the needs of her child, her commitments – anything that would show Bertie that she intended to exclude him from her life. The message contained in her letters of kindly advice was clear: she would not stand in his way, but she was not prepared to share him with another woman. If he took a mistress, he would lose her. She would, naturally, always be his friend.

The result was predictable. Bertie would begin to think that a sexual relationship was not going to make up for the loss of Ottoline. There would be a passionate reunion – Ottoline's love for him was always most intense, and most sexual, when it had been threatened – and the newer relationship would shrink away. This pattern continued until 1916 when Bertie transferred his passion, but not his profound love, to a beautiful and promiscuous young actress – she was half Ottoline's age – Lady Constance Malleson.

Ottoline's relationship with Bertie would never have survived if sex had been its chief foundation. But the basis of her appeal to him was more complicated than that. 'You are to me the epitome of all the beauty of the world,' he told her in April 1911. 'You have a calm which I have never known before with such strength of feeling – it ... comes of large-hearted love and wisdom and knowing what is really important ... you achieve what I only aim at, and achieve by moments.' He was speaking of her religious faith.

It is impossible to appreciate the significance of Ottoline's beliefs to Bertie and, in particular, the way her religion influenced her behaviour, without understanding all that the loss of a credible God had meant to him. The death of religion offered a new social and intellectual freedom to the younger generation of the Stephen sisters, Maynard Keynes and Lytton. But Bertie, like Ottoline, had grown up in an earlier period of religious expansion; there was a world of meaning in the succinct distinction he drew between himself and Goldie Lowes Dickinson, his Cambridge contemporary, and the junior, exuberantly irreverent Apostles. 'We were still Victorian,' he wrote; 'they were Edwardian.'[1] Ottoline and Bertie were products of the Victorian age. The conventions and attitudes which they shared were stronger and more binding than their religious disputes.

Bertie had no memory of his parents; the woman who played Lady Bolsover's role in his life was his formidable grandmother, Lady John Russell, widow of the great reformer. While his older brother Frank went to public school, Bertie was educated by tutors at her house in Richmond Park. The atmosphere had been one of neglect and melancholy; religion was a way of life; self-denial was encouraged and practised with zeal. When he asked about his parents, both of whom had been non-believers, he was told to be thankful that they had died;

when he opened the Bible he received on his twelfth birthday, he found it inscribed with a reminder that God was always with him. 'Our God will still be yours,' Lady John reminded him again on the eve of his marriage to Alys, after urging him to cherish only holy thoughts.[2]

Bertie had been devoted to his grandmother. Her influence over him was quite as powerful as Lady Bolsover's had been over Ottoline. A quiet and contemplative child, he seemed destined to become as devout as she could have hoped, but an inquiring mind led him to start questioning the arguments for Christianity. By the age of eighteen, he had decided that he had no grounds for continuing to believe in God. This painful passage into scepticism was recorded in a journal which he disguised as Greek grammar exercises; he was twenty-one before he dared to admit to his grandmother that he could not accept a Being of whom he was shown no proof. Far from feeling liberated by this act of emancipation, he was filled with dismay. 'I have the very greatest fear that my life hereafter be ruined by my having lost the support of religion,' he wrote on 27 May 1888, when he was sixteen; three months later, after reading *The Mill on the Floss*, he wrote of his envy for Maggie Tulliver's ability to follow the teachings of Thomas à Kempis, if only because they seemed to promise a calmer and happier life.

The rational, intellectual side of Russell's nature made it impossible for him to accept a God whose existence could not be proved; the emotional side which was drawn to Ottoline searched for a compromise in mysticism. On its deepest and most enduring level, his love was less for the woman than for a vision sent to teach him how to bring the warring elements of his nature, the intellectual and the romantic, into harmony. 'I have seen a land of peace and have found some kind of union of reason and vision,' he told her on 12 August 1913, when he was composing *Mysticism and Logic*. But every time that emotion started to gain the upper hand, rational thought would reassert itself and Russell would see that his intellectual discipline had been threatened. The vision became a treacherous siren song and Russell remorseless in his determination to punish Ottoline for having led him astray by forcing her to admit that her muddled faith was a sham. Furious with her as much as with himself, he would try to bully her into admitting defeat; paradoxically, he continued to yearn for her to win, to show him how to escape through any loophole into her world, his grandmother's world, of enviable, serene belief. 'The longing for religion is at times unbearably strong,' he admitted to her on 27 December 1911; in the summer of 1913, when their relationship was at its nadir, he described a moment when he had found himself alone in a church and had started to pray. 'I can't justify it,' he told her, 'but it was a deep and sincere prayer.' (19 August)

Ottoline did not mind being attacked about her beliefs. 'The one thing I desire is for you to be ruthless with me and to be absolutely true to yourself,' she told him on 27 May 1911. 'Your whole life and work would be ruined if that was not so.' She never faltered in this brave attitude, but neither did she say that she would be swayed by his arguments. His mistake was to suppose that he could ever persuade her to rate intellect above feeling. 'What I don't understand is the purely intellectual part – how you can think it is true,' he wrote a few months later. To him, it was clear that what could not be proved was not truthful. Ottoline could love truth as he did, or she could believe in God; she could not do both.

Initially, he thought it unimportant that she was devout; in the space of a few months, her conversion to his own point of view became of crucial importance. His relationship with her seemed to him to embody the sublime love which could be substituted for dogmatic religion; if only he could persuade her to become agnostic, they could exemplify it. But then, if he succeeded, he would have killed the very quality towards which he was most strongly drawn, the dauntless courage of a woman who believed she was born for a purpose.

Russell's crusade was doomed to fail. The most striking aspects of Ottoline's letters to him are the intelligence and certainty with which she met his arguments. 'I might perhaps give up belief in a personal God,' she conceded after one of his most savage outbursts in December 1911:

but I could not ever, I believe, kill within me the stretching out to some spiritual 'Something' beyond myself. It is more real to me than any human being is. I suppose it is the same as what you call infinity, for all that fills me with delight in nature and all music and goodness and love is filled with it and expresses it.

I think there is a great possibility there may be at the back a personal Being very different from anything a finite mind can now conceive of – but this I know is quite non-certain and most things point to Him not existing, but I feel I could never say for certain that He does not exist . . . I cannot understand why you feel I must be dishonest and why you are so intolerant to my belief. It seems to me as if someone who did not care for music to be [sic] intolerant to anyone who cared passionately for it, and to whom it was a tremendous revelation of life. But I suppose it is different. (27 December 1911)

The religious dispute was sustained at this level of intensity for the entire length of their turbulent affair: Ottoline never compromised her beliefs. It was Bertie who, under her strong influence and in response to his desperate need to find an area in which they could reach agreement, gradually moved away from the cosmic loneliness he had bravely confronted in one of his early and most admired writings, 'A Free Man's Worship'. In 'The Essence of Religion', published in 1912, he argued, with Ottoline's approval, that the three most important elements of religion – worship, acquiescence and love – could exist 'without dogma, in a form which is capable of dominating life and of giving infinity to action and thought and feeling'.[3]

Russell did everything he could in later life to obliterate the most extreme examples of Ottoline's intellectual influence over him as she encouraged him to give voice to the mystical side of his nature. 'Prisons', the religious and emotionally-charged book which he planned and partly wrote in close collaboration with her, was abandoned and then either lost or destroyed. 'The Essence of Religion', into which some of the ideas to have been explored in 'Prisons' eventually found their way, was reprinted in a collection of writings with Russell's permission in 1961, but he told an interviewer two years later that it had soon come to seem too religious for his liking. *Mysticism and Logic*, which was clearly influenced by Ottoline, was allowed to appear without any disclaimers from the author, but instructions were given to prevent the publication in his lifetime of *The Perplexities of John Forstice*, an incomplete novel to which Ottoline contributed a section. He praised her in his autobiography for her influence on his character and, in particular, for the way her sense of humour had helped to cure him of priggishness and egocentricity, but he had no wish to recall how far from atheism his love had led him.

The intensely dramatic last days of March 1911 were followed by passionate declarations of love and the leisurely exchanging of life-stories. Ottoline had already made arrangements for an Easter seaside holiday in Dorset, but a meeting with Bertie was planned for 7 April, the day before she left. She suggested it; Bertie applied himself to the details with conspiratorial zest.

I think it is better to avoid places like Kensington Gardens, where we should meet all our friends. The only plan I can think of is to meet at some underground station exit and take a cab to some out of the way place like Putney Heath where we could walk if it was fine. This doesn't seem a very excellent plan, but I don't see anything better. If possible, I ought to get away by the 6.40 from Waterloo ... I would suggest Walham Green, which you can reach in about 15 minutes from Charing X underground ... (5? April)

The meeting was a happy one: it was lucky for them that the spring and summer of 1911 were unusually fine since there were to be a great many of these outdoor assignations. Ottoline, who had not yet said much about Lamb, took the opportunity to describe him as an unhappy young man in need of her friendship and support. Unsuspecting of the truth, Bertie was ready to be charitable and to agree that she should continue to exert her benevolent influence. He was too elated to grow easily anxious. Back at Van Bridge, while Ottoline set off for Dorset with Philip and their four-year-old daughter, Bertie could not even worry about the news that Alys had gone to London to talk to Evelyn Whitehead. 'I have a sense of great calm,' he wrote; 'whatever reasons there may be for foreseeing evil, I feel I can't be bothered to foresee it.' Alys's absence left him free to pour out his heart – and most of his history – to his beloved, for 'the moment I am alone I begin to live with you, Dearest', before blowing out the light and going to bed.

In her memoirs, Ottoline wrote of her delight at the thought of Bertie's arrival (he had arranged to join her in Dorset on the 18th); in fact, she had only been away for two days when she was wishing that he could come 'tomorrow evening or Tuesday for it would have been so lovely to have had you even for one night . . . I do long for you to come now but I won't think of it . . . we will wait patiently for the 18th – ten days off.' (9–10 April)

9

CONFIDENCES AND INTRIGUES
April 1911

'I feel just filled with utter thankfulness to you and worship. Darling darling Bertie.'
OM to Bertrand Russell, 28 May 1911

Miss him though she did, Ottoline was happy to be back at Studland, which she and Philip had discovered in February that year. Looking out towards Brownsea Island, it was a small and enchantingly pretty resort much frequented by writers and painters. A flower-bordered path wound along the top of the cliffs, the beaches were of soft yellow sand and Cliff End, the house they had taken for the month, was so isolated that Ottoline could behave as though she had the whole bay to herself, paddling along the shore with her hair in two long plaits to her waist and spending hours collecting shells on the beach with Julian. In the evenings, while Philip read, she wrote long letters to Bertie about her unhappy childhood, so similar to his own, and wondered, as he did, at 'the absolute accord and sympathy' between them. 'Oh *how* good it is and how wonderful.' (9–10 April)

Her letters were not entirely reassuring. She had managed to dissuade Lytton Strachey from inviting himself to stay at Cliff End (he was with Henry Lamb at the nearby village of Corfe), but it had been impossible to put off Logan Pearsall Smith, who had announced that he would be coming with his and Bertie's niece, Ray Costelloe. So far as Bertie knew, Logan was unaware of their relationship, but it was too much to hope that he could sleep under the same roof as Ottoline and Bertie without suspecting something. 'You must manage to get him away before I come,' Bertie wrote. 'Ray won't matter, she is unobservant . . .' (12 April)

Logan made his visit before the 18th and he went away in as complete a state of innocence as he had arrived, blessing Ottoline for her delightful hospitality. 'You have the gift of life,' he told her, 'and it is a temptation to your friends to become vampires, and take more from you than they ought.'[1] But it may have been this visit of Logan's which brought home to Ottoline the necessity of being honest with Philip. Until now, she had allowed him to imagine that Bertie's interest in her had subsided. She had told him of their decision to part, but not of the reconciliation which had swiftly followed. Philip was scheduled to leave Cliff End on the day Bertie arrived; the evening before he went, Ottoline admitted that she had promised to continue seeing Bertie and that he was coming to Studland for three days. She did not lead him to think that there would be any physical intimacy; nevertheless, his stoicism staggered her. '"Do you want to go?"' he asked her. '"You must if you want to." I felt hurt that he could even imagine such a thing. How could he suppose that I should wish to part from him with whom my life was entwined, to whom my love and confidence was given? The thought made me utterly miserable.'[2]

It is unlikely that Philip's character will ever be entirely clear to us. We know that he was not sexually attracted to Ottoline; we may wonder if he recognised that she needed the intellectual fire which he was unable to provide. We may even wonder if, since he was not a faithful husband, he really cared. Certainly, his words, if Ottoline remembered them accurately, were not of the kind that would normally be spoken by a jealous husband, and Philip could, when he wished, express himself with passion. All that can be said is that his response was astonishingly tolerant. Once apprised of the true situation, he promised his support and calmly continued with his plan to return to London, expressing only the hope that he would not collide with Bertie on the platform. He was spared that embarrassment: Russell's train drew in a few minutes after his own pulled out.

As prearranged with Ottoline, Bertie hired a cab from Swanage station and kept watch through the window for where she was waiting for him under a group of fir trees. The cab was ordered to go on with the baggage:

and we walked across heath and heather to the sea. He [Bertie] assumed at once that I was his possession, and started to investigate, to explore, to probe. I shrank back, for it was intolerable to me to have the hands of a psychological surgeon investigating the tangle of my thoughts, feelings and emotions which I had never yet allowed anyone to see. I felt like a sea-anemone that shrinks at the slightest touch. I forced myself, however, to be brave and to expose myself as much as I could bear . . .[3]

We should remember that Ottoline allowed her husband to read her memoirs and that she wrote them with this in mind. A better sense of the visit is gained from the fact that Bertie was scarcely on board the return train from Swanage before he was lamenting the torture of leaving her. 'I wanted to carry you off with me to some sunny Italian hillside,' he wrote yearningly, ' – to live in our love and think of nothing but beauty . . . Our three days were an absolute revelation of life and love.' (21 April) Glancing at his face in the compartment mirror, he could see the physical evidence of Ottoline's influence; she had persuaded him to shave off his moustache.* In a rare moment of self-preening – he was not a vain man – Bertie thought he saw a glimpse of Voltaire's features in the clean-shaven face with the lively eyes which Ottoline had told him were full of beauty and tenderness. She, for her part, had been touched by his affection for little Julian and delighted by the discovery that his love for the sea and the wild Dorset landscape was as great as her own. But most of all, she enjoyed being led into his mental world. She had read as much philosophy as she could before his arrival; her reward was to be engaged in rigorous discussion. She revelled in it, and the language which she chose to describe this suggests that the excitement of being with a man she knew to be her intellectual master was akin to a sensual pleasure.

It was exhausting but delightful for me to have my mind kept in strict order, driven on to the end of a subject, through tangled bushes and swamps, till it reached open ground. I often wriggled and rebelled, and wanted to hide under shady, sentimental willow trees, but this was never allowed. Bertie would take me metaphorically by the hand and pull me up and urge me on . . . tearing down old dusty growths in my mind, and opening dark windows that had been blocked up in the lower depths of my being.[4]

The fact that the physical attraction on his side was stronger than on hers hardly seemed to matter when they started talking. It was not Bertie Russell's body that she was in love with, but his spirit.

The beauty of his mind, the pure fire of his soul began to affect and attract me, and magnetise me with an attraction almost physical, carrying me up into ecstasies such as Donne expresses; his unattractive body seemed to disappear, while our souls were united in a single flame; the flame of his soul penetrated mine.[5]

Ottoline knew the importance of discretion. It was not just, as she claimed, a fear that Julian might catch his mumps which made her refuse to allow the ailing Lytton Strachey to come and convalesce at

---

* Ottoline had not seen the last of Bertie's moustache. It took permanent leave in December 1911.

Cliff End after Bertie's departure, but a terror that she herself might reveal more than she should. It was for the same reason that, despite Lytton's entreaties to her to come and visit him, she would only consent to change trains at Corfe on her way to London and walk up to the inn, from which he could talk to her, she said, 'out of the window, Romeo fashion'. She was full of good intentions, but the relationship with Bertie was less than six weeks old when it ceased to be a secret. She had spoken about it to Philip; by 22 April, Roger Fry knew enough to write to her from a Turkish village that 'it did seem such a chance for him [Bertie]. Now he'll never get quite away but I suppose she [Alys] still feels something. I don't think the merely conventional aspect would touch her.' Certainly, Fry had been told enough for there to be a striking change here from his passionate letters earlier in the month.

Back in London again in late April, with Bertie visiting her as often as he could escape from his duties at Cambridge, Ottoline lunched with Henry Lamb and informed him 'that I was transferring my love to Bertie. This,' she added with unconcealed satisfaction, 'acted like an electric shock and made him desire to keep me at all costs – too late, too late, for he had trampled on or [sic] destroyed our friendship.'

Lamb's first reaction was of outraged disbelief; how could she possibly prefer a dry little stick of a man like Bertie Russell to himself? How could he fight the demon of his ego alone? What about all the promises she had made to devote herself to his needs? Somehow – one would like to know how, but we are not told – Ottoline succeeded in calming him down and convincing him that she had love enough for both him and Bertie, if only he would be patient. Her arguments were persuasive; the letter that Lamb scribbled to her from Paris a few days later, on 3 May, was one of his most ecstatic. 'The waves of that frightful storm have hardly subsided in me yet and I can't see anything clearly,' he told her, 'how much you understood and changed or how much did I. I feel possessed with an immense adoring submitting love for you, my holy heavenly one! All the rest is vague and confused. I still hardly realise what happened. But oh my glorious lady, I do so profoundly want to fall at your feet and keep imploring pardon, instruction and love, still more love! . . . Do what you will, order me to do what you will – I only want to submit to you in everything.'

Lamb was staying with Boris and Junia Anrep in Paris; in the same letter, he urged Ottoline to come and join them. Surely she could leave her task of writing invitation cards – she was planning a large party for 18 May and the guests were always invited by handwritten notes – to snatch a few days of freedom?

Ottoline prevaricated. To Bertie, who was also 'longing for you, seeing you, hearing you, feeling you, thinking of your life, wishing for you wholly' (2 May), she sighed that Lamb was being very demanding and troublesome; to Lamb, she wrote that Philip would be upset if she went to Paris without him. 'What a dark mystery his power is these days,' Lamb jeered; 'the good Russians are very astonished that you are not considered old enough or sufficiently emancipated to go where or when you like!!! I am not.' He included a drawing of a male hand pointing commandingly at her and left her to decide whether he meant it for Philip's or his own. (7 May) Boris Anrep added a beguiling plea: 'Would it be impossible for you to neglect for a few days your home duties and by such a crime to buy our joy which is now mastered by the mournful spleen?'

To go or to stay? Unable to make up her mind, Ottoline slipped away from London to Cambridge to visit Bertie at Trinity College. 'It is obvious my bedmaker is quite unsuspicious,' he wrote after she had gone. 'She considers you tall, which is true if not penetrating... 'I don't think she sniffed your scent or thought me a gay dog.' (11 May 1911) His letter to Ottoline crossed with hers telling him that she was going to Paris for a few days to visit some Russian friends: once arrived, she was able to tell him that she had, by the merest coincidence, run into Henry Lamb. 'Next time you go to Paris, I hope that Lamb will not be there,' Bertie answered tartly, but he was too elated by G. E. Moore's presence at Cambridge to be deeply distressed. He had been reading *The Idiot* on Ottoline's recommendation and had been struck by the remarkable similarity between Myshkin and his colleague. 'His nature is transparent, crystal,' he told her, 'like a mountain spring – he always speaks the truth, because it does not occur to him to do otherwise, and he does it so simply that nobody ever minds... I wonder what you are talking about with your Russians.' (14 May)

The expedition was a great success. Ottoline went to all the new exhibitions and visited her favourite French dressmaker. On the last evening, despite her virtuous resolutions to lift her relationship with Lamb on to an asexual plane, she seems to have allowed him to make love to her before lecturing him on the benefits of chastity. She left Paris on 16 May; that night, Lamb wrote to remind her of 'that incredible little room where you, holy woman,* lay... and received me'. Six days later, he wrote again: 'I lay down in your bed, plunged my face in the pillow and breathed myself to sleep in your scents... Now goodbye – with an endless kiss, I embrace you. I think of you perpetually.' (22 May) As for her resolution to establish a platonic relationship with him, he was prepared to say that he admired her determination. He did not believe it would last. Paris had erased the anger he had felt at their meeting in London and he was not ready

---

* Probably a reference to the fact that Ottoline was staying at the small hotel known to her, Lytton and Lamb as 'The Holy Fathers' (Hôtel Saints-Pères).

to accept what he would later call 'the coincidence of my "chute" and B's ascendance'. Arrogantly and unwisely, he assumed that the affair with Russell amounted to no more than a passing infatuation; to his own satisfaction, at least, he had shown which of them was her master.

Back in London, Ottoline's first appointment was with Russell for a long afternoon in a Tottenham Court Road hotel. He went back to Cambridge, she to Bedford Square to prepare for one of her most formal Thursday parties. The guests for 18 May included Virginia Stephen and Roger Fry, both of whom had recently returned from the task of nursing Vanessa in the Turkish village where she had collapsed; the centre of attention and guest of honour was Winston Churchill whom neither of the Morrells knew well but who they felt would be a useful ally to acquire for Philip's career. Churchill looked very fine in his full-dress uniform – he was going on to a ball at Buckingham Palace – and he expressed a gratifying admiration for two of their Picasso etchings, but Ottoline was irritated to find that he wanted to talk of nothing but politics: 'He is very rhetorical,' she noted, 'and has a volcanic, complicated way of talking which is difficult to listen to, or to gather what he really thinks.'[6] She might have been amused to learn that this was precisely the complaint which Churchill had lodged against her friend Henry James.

There was no indication in Fry's behaviour that evening of anything but pleasure at seeing her. He made an arrangement to come and stay at Peppard in a fortnight's time (a plan which was cancelled after subsequent events). He did not mention Vanessa, although he had confided in one of his letters to Ottoline that he had become seriously worried about her sanity when she fell ill in Turkey. ('I know you won't say anything about all this,' he had added.) It was left to Virginia that evening to tell Ottoline that Fry had fallen in love with her sister while helping to nurse her back to health. Unaware of his night with Ottoline, Virginia had no qualms about expressing her approval; she had already told Ottoline earlier in the year that she thought Clive Bell was a bad influence on Vanessa. The following day, 19 May, Fry telephoned Ottoline to ask if he could come and see her. On 20 May, after a cheerful morning of antiques-hunting and a long lunch with Bertie, she returned to Bedford Square to find Fry waiting for her.

I expected to hear of the things he had seen and done. Perhaps we started at Constantinople, but very soon he travelled from there, for he suddenly turned on me with a fierce and accusing expression, commanding me to explain why I had spread abroad that he was in love with me. I was so utterly dumbfounded, for this thought had never entered my head ... He refused to tell me from whom he had heard this absurd story, indeed his behaviour seemed to me quite unbalanced and he paid no attention to what I said to him.

Whatever the cause, one of my most intimate and delightful friendships crumbled to dust that Saturday . . . I had never before realised what mischief a slander could do.[7]

That was the published version; no mention was made of the curious episode which had taken place at the end of March, or of the love-letters which Fry had written to Ottoline in early April. But she was not so guiltless as she claimed. Her subsequent correspondence with Lamb makes it clear that she had been discussing Fry with him and was afraid that he had passed her accounts on to Lytton. She had revealed something; what is not clear is whether the subject of her indiscretion had been Fry's passion for her or the confidences about Vanessa Bell's precarious mental state which he had begged her to keep to herself.

Ottoline did not immediately give up hope of regaining Fry's affection, as her memoirs suggest. To Bertie, who had already been told enough to believe that Fry was furious at being supplanted by himself, she wrote that she was doing all she could to make peace with him, 'for however rich one is in friends it seems wrong to lose a friend lightly'. (18 June) Her effort was doomed to failure, as she reported two days later. 'I telephoned to Roger whom I found was at the Bells and said that if he preferred it I was willing to wait, but should like a definite understanding some time. He said, "Oh, it would be much *nicer* to wait." What a word to use.' (20 June)

By the end of June, Ottoline was forced to accept that she had made a dangerous enemy, and one with a vicious tongue. She had begged Fry to be discreet about the affair with Bertie, warning him that Alys was likely to destroy her husband's academic career if silence was not maintained. Now, Bertie told her that Sidney Waterlow,* a man he hardly knew, had approached him and talked quite freely about the relationship with Ottoline. Since Waterlow was acquainted with both Vanessa Bell and Virginia, Bertie suspected them of having picked up some gossip and spread it. 'If the Stephens know it must be through Roger *before* I warned him to be careful,' Ottoline wrote.

By October, most of the damage had been done. Bloomsbury continued to attend Ottoline's parties, but her integrity was under a cloud. She was judged by all that Fry, Clive and Vanessa now said about her. She was seen to be indiscreet, promiscuous and untruthful; only Virginia, while always ready to participate in the latest round of gossip, was unwilling to condemn Ottoline as the villain of the piece. Feeling, perhaps, that he had done harm enough, Fry started to make friendly overtures; Ottoline was too hurt and angry to respond. 'I feel

---

* Sidney Waterlow was a Cambridge intellectual, a friend of Clive Bell's who had, in 1910, made an unsuccessful proposal to Virginia. (He was also a cousin of Katherine Mansfield's.)

more and more I don't want to make it up with Roger and the Bells,' she told Russell on 4 October. 'Somehow I feel that atmosphere to be really ignoble and Roger has so completely thrown himself into it – it has affected him.' The last straw had been the discovery that he was urging Ethel Sands to join the anti-Ottoline camp. Ethel had introduced them to each other; she was their mutual friend. To Ottoline, this final betrayal made Fry seem as contemptible as 'an untrustworthy dog, who softly pads up to one and licks one's hand, but who will nearly always turn and bite'.[8] She was still prepared to support him by going to his exhibitions and by buying hand-printed materials from the Omega Workshops,* but when the Contemporary Art Society held its meetings at Bedford Square, she took a book up to her bedroom and refused to come down until Fry had left the house. Meeting him in public, she found it impossible to hide her dislike – as did he. 'We had tea with Roger,' Virginia wrote after she and Ottoline had been to an exhibition at Heal's. 'I was very conscious of strain – Ott. languid, and taking refuge in her great ladyhood, which is always depressing. They seemed to have their quarrel before their eyes.'[9]

Trouble was blowing towards Ottoline and Bertie from a quarter which was, from Russell's point of view, still more dangerous. Logan, knowing nothing about the affair, had innocently informed Alys of the visit Bertie had made to Studland. Little realising the pain he was causing his sister, he had gone on to sing Ottoline's praises, and to say how helpful and sympathetic she had been about the loss of their mother. (Full of happy anticipation of a warm reception, Hannah Pearsall Smith had gone to meet her Maker on 1 May 1911.) Alys listened in speechless misery. She had persuaded herself that Bertie's love for Ottoline would not last, and that he would come back to her. This story of a visit to Studland was profoundly discouraging and it added to her unhappiness to think that she could not speak about it to her own brother. Bertie, accustomed to finding her in a state of sad resignation on his brief visits to Van Bridge, was alarmed by her manner. 'It is dreadful here – much worse than I anticipated,' he wrote to Ottoline on 21 May:

Alys is very wild and miserable . . . She began in great anger, threatening divorce. Gradually, however, she grew quieter. She is very anxious to tell

* She annoyed Vanessa Bell, however, by refusing to buy a set of Omega dining chairs in which she had been heard to express an interest. When Vanessa demanded a reason for her change of heart, she told her that Omega goods were too expensive. (Letter from Winifred Gill to Duncan Grant, 20 February 1967)

Logan – evidently his friendship for you galled her beyond endurance. Would you mind Logan being told? . . . perhaps he had better be . . . I cannot endure her misery.

Alys was too desperate to wait for Bertie's permission. Once informed, Logan was convinced that it was his duty to rescue his sister from an appalling situation. She could not be allowed to go on hoping that Bertie would return, but neither could she be allowed to continue participating in the conspiracy of silence. Two days after Alys's revelation, Logan went to see Ottoline at Bedford Square and told her that she had betrayed her friendship with his family. Still shaken by her encounter with Roger Fry, Ottoline was so meek that Logan felt slightly guilty after he had left her. 'I fear I was too hard and bitter,' he wrote to her on 24 May:

If I was, please forgive me and put it down to the feelings of a brother who has been the helpless witness for years of his sister's misery . . . I am inclined to think that I shall advise her to make a complete break . . . I hope that Alys will be able eventually to get entirely and perfectly free in some manner that will involve the least possible amount of suffering – there would be no thought, of course, of ever involving anyone we loved.[10]

To Ottoline, who saw no reason why the Pearsall Smiths should now look on her as someone they loved, it was clear that the break which Logan would be recommending to Alys would be a divorce, that she would be cited, and that Philip's political career would be ruined by the scandal, as would Bertie's at Cambridge. Philip, however, after being shown Logan's letter, thought that it offered room for negotiation. They had already arranged to go and spend the following weekend with Ethel Sands at Newington; it was Philip's idea that they should ask Logan over and discuss the situation with him in a friendly way. 'P. is quite cheerful and unmoved and thinks it will all subside,' Ottoline wrote to Bertie on 25 May:

They would only destroy a beautiful thing and have nothing left on their hands if they persisted . . . I don't feel *any* resentment to Logan. I only think him blinded by undisciplined emotions. I am sure he and Alys would be miserable afterwards if they ruined us all but they won't do it I am sure . . . Darling life, don't worry, I am quite at rest. I feel our life is very sacred and serious and their talk does not come within miles of it.

The charms of Newington, at its loveliest in early summer, with nothing more arduous to do than to play leisurely games of croquet with Ethel (who had promised her support) and Desmond MacCarthy, the only other guest, were enough to lull Ottoline into a state of false security. 'It is such a lovely night,' she wrote dreamily to Bertie on Saturday evening. 'The stars so bright and nightingales singing and owls calling and Desmond humming on, I lying in a chair thinking of you and sending my spirit to you . . .'

There are several versions of what happened after Logan's arrival at Newington on Sunday afternoon. Of the three, one being Ottoline's report to Bertie and another the edited account presented in the second volume of her memoirs, the most illuminating is given in her original draft. Wrongly dated as 26 May (it should be 28 May), it is the closest of the three to an eyewitness's account.

It was a horrible visit. Logan . . . came over on Sunday, and he and Ethel Sands discussed me and B for hours, and then both Ethel and Logan in turn pryed into every detail of my friendship with B, Ethel asking me intimate and indelicate questions which outraged me, but left me at the same time dumb and helpless. I was in fact arraigned by them. They told me I was killing Alys. It was all perfectly horrible. Logan threatened divorce proceedings. I had to sit still while their dreadful voices discussed and probed. Philip and Desmond were playing croquet on the lawn. At last Philip came and joined us. This was an immense help to me, for he understood the real position and would defend me from the pryings and bullyings of these two American puritans. I was astonished that Logan and Ethel Sands, who in conversation is so free, cynical and libertine, should when faced with an occasion in real life that needed understanding and tolerance fail so completely. I had always thought that Ethel would have stood by me . . . but I was much mistaken. Logan ended by taking me aside, and pouring into my ear a torrent of abuse of B. and warning me against the consequences of the immorality of my conduct. He said that if we remained friendly with B. he could never enter our house again, also that my old friends would cut me.[11]

Logan had come to Newington armed with conditions. The most important of these was, if he could only have known it, far from unwelcome to Ottoline. She was not, as has been explained, sexually attracted to Bertie. It was no great hardship to her to obey Logan's command that she should never spend a night with him; she was only angry at the idea that she should be expected to take orders from the Pearsall Smiths.

Even though Logan had made it clear that he wished to terminate his friendship with the Morrells, Ottoline did not fully understand what an implacable enemy they had made. It mattered nothing to Logan that Bertie's marriage had broken down long before he met Ottoline; to him, it was a disgusting example of two English aristocrats thinking that they could do just as they pleased and supposing that they were going to be allowed to get away with it. From 1911 until the end of his life, Logan did everything he could to make sure that they and, in particular, Ottoline did not go unpunished. He began by telling Evelyn Whitehead that Philip only condoned the situation because he was penniless and could not afford to lose his wife's goodwill. He went on to spread venomous accounts of Ottoline to anyone prepared to listen. 'Again and again I have found proof of his malign influence,' she wrote in her memoirs:[12] Robert Gathorne-

Hardy, who acted as Logan's secretary for many years, described his hatred as 'a monstrous, undiminishing monomaniac obsession, which was very close to madness'. As a close friend of Ottoline's, whose memoirs he later edited, Gathorne-Hardy finally had to ask Logan never to talk to him about her in order to protect himself from the flood of vicious inventions.

'I feel awfully sad tonight,' Ottoline wrote in her long account to Bertie of Logan's visit and the conditions he had imposed. Bertie, while irritated that Logan should compel him to trail to and from a hotel in Henley on 30 May instead of spending the night with Ottoline at Peppard as he had planned, was ready to take a more cheerful view. One of his own greatest worries had been that Ottoline would be named in a divorce suit and that he would be put in a position where resignation from Trinity was the inevitable outcome. But when Alys and Logan visited him together the day after the Newington encounter, they took what seemed to him to be a fairly reasonable line. Alys was ready to agree to an informal parting on grounds of incompatibility; nothing would be said about Ottoline so long as she never slept under the same roof as Bertie. In his view, they were safer than ever before. 'Dearest, dearest, don't be depressed,' he comforted Ottoline; 'the Smiths have shot their bolt . . . forget the horrid things and think only of our love, which they cannot sully.' (29 May) A day together reading Spinoza in the Peppard woods was all that was required to draw the lovers back into their world of private joy, away from the squabbling and bitterness which had threatened to destroy it. 'I can never *tell* you what you are to me,' Bertie wrote as he travelled back to Cambridge, 'it is something beyond words altogether':

All this time I had a solemn almost religious feeling – there is something about our love that seems so much greater than I am that I hardly understand how I can feel it . . . Goodbye my heart – my love for you is as deep and boundless as the sea. I cannot tell you how great it is, but I know you know. Yours in utter devotion,

B

10

THE IPSDEN CRISIS
1911–12

'Living without any religious beliefs is not easy. Darling, my love to you is rather terrible really – it is so absorbing and so necessary to my life.'
Bertrand Russell to OM, 17 July 1911

Ottoline's relationship with Bertie had become the most important thing in her life by the summer of 1911, but it did not mean that she was prepared to relinquish all other friendships. One which was at last flowering into intimacy was with Lytton Strachey.

Lytton had not forgotten the pleasure of his first visit to Peppard during the Burnley election; denied the chance to stay at Cliff End, he succeeded – with difficulty – in pinning Ottoline down to a date when he could visit her, for the weekend of 5 June. Perfect weather, a second visit later in the month and the absence of Lamb, who was in France, helped to thaw the careful formality which had marked their correspondence (or, at least, Ottoline's side of it) until then. Ottoline said nothing about Bertie until three months later, when she urged Lytton to be discreet 'for the present' (2 August); in June, they were more interested in discovering each other's impressions of Lamb. Ottoline thanked Lytton 'for your friendship to me as well as to H.L.', adding that she, too, thought him 'very wonderful and beautiful'. (6 July 1911) She was referring, presumably, to his looks rather than his behaviour, since she casually inquired on 21 July whether Lytton had heard the latest gossip: 'Did you hear he raped Dorelia's sister?' Lytton, meanwhile, begged Ottoline to bring back reports of his new hero, Nijinsky, when she went to Paris in July; he was infuriated when, after telling him that she had thought the dancer 'rather spotty' when she first saw him in Venice, she admitted that, although she had seen him in *Spectre de la Rose*, she had been too enthralled to find herself sitting next to Diaghilev to look at the stage.

By way of compensation, she promised to get Lytton invited to Newington when she returned to England: he had expressed a great wish to find country houses where he could be in congenial company and allowed to work on his book. 'Mr Strachey' and 'Lady Ottoline' were no more; by the end of June, they had transformed themselves into eighteenth-century characters. Lytton was 'My dear Monsieur Le Comte', while Ottoline had become his 'plus chère des Marquises'.

The fact that Philip had taken his side against Logan in the discussions at Newington did not make Bertie Russell any more eager to meet him; accommodating though Philip had been, he was still Ottoline's husband. For two months, Ottoline had contrived to keep the two men apart, but it could not last. Bertie was visiting Ottoline alone at Peppard on 7 June, when Philip unexpectedly returned from London. He stayed for only a couple of hours, but it was long enough to make Bertie feel deeply embarrassed. 'I thought Philip felt my presence almost unendurable,' he told Ottoline on 9 June, 'and, thinking so, I admired his behaviour very much indeed. I felt a sense of shame in his presence – not reasonably but instinctively. I am glad the first meeting is over – it will be easier another time.' He was tempted to be less gracious when he followed the Morrells on a visit to some mutual friends, the Phillimores, and heard from his hostess that Ottoline and Philip were a devoted couple, always embracing and calling each other by affectionate endearments. Bertie was not pleased, but he was already alert to the danger of ever seeming to criticise Philip. Ottoline did not allow it; on the contrary, Bertie had discovered that she was touchingly grateful if he could manage to say something kind about her husband. He did his best. 'It was nice having a few comfortable words with P.,' he told Ottoline after a second short encounter with Philip, at Bedford Square. 'I felt quite at ease, and so did he apparently. It is a very good thing – really you have managed us both so amazingly well . . . No praise of P. wd. rouse jealousy in me.' (16 June)

There was some wishful thinking in that declaration, but Ottoline was also susceptible to an occasional fit of jealousy. She was almost thirty-eight and she could not help feeling uneasy when she thought of all the pretty and clever girls Bertie must meet at Cambridge. 'No, I have not talked to any charming muslined young ladies,' he reassured her. 'Miss Harrison is the only lady I have talked to at all . . .* My dearest heart, your jealous shade would not find much

---

* Jane Harrison certainly did not fit into the category of 'charming muslined young ladies': Ottoline would have felt no alarm.

material – it would find your image burning whenever it appeared.' (12 June) As evidence of good faith, he told her that he was going to give her a ruby engagement ring for her birthday present. More presents followed: Ottoline offered him a heart-shaped locket holding a piece of her hair, while he gave her another (minus the hair) which had belonged to his mother.

Bertie's meeting with Jane Harrison had been a trial run for the part he was required to play in order to protect his wife and Philip Morrell from gossip. Everyone knew by now that he and Alys were living apart, and in Cambridge, where there was as yet very little knowledge of the affair with Ottoline, there was limitless scope for guessing what could have led an attractive man suddenly to break away from his wife. Miss Harrison had decided that the wife of a Cambridge don must be behind the rift; her purpose in summoning Bertie to call on her at Newnham was to question him directly and to get a straight answer. She failed. 'They will have a job finding that Cambridge lady I am supposed to be devoted to,' he reported to Ottoline with glee. 'Miss Harrison was very friendly and obviously quite reassured ... It was helpful talking to her, because I had to give a false impression favourable to myself.' (12 June)

Evading Miss Harrison's questions was almost a game, but Bertie felt less comfortable about accepting the kindly commiserations of his own relations on his marital misfortune. 'I hate this injured martyr business,' he admitted to Ottoline on 14 June, 'but it can't be helped. It is funny that the welfare of Philip and Julian should depend upon my assuming virtues I don't possess – but since it is so, may God give me strength to play the hypocrite ... pretending to be heart-broken when one is filled with happiness is rather a dirty business. However as it has to be done I get my fun out of it.'

Selflessness was not Bertie's strongest point, but he was quick to blame himself when he visited Ottoline two days later at Bedford Square – it was her birthday – and found her lying on a sofa, chalk-white and biting her lips with pain. It was his fault, he told himself; he should have given more thought to the strain she had been under. His sympathy turned to irritation when Ottoline made it clear that no illness was going to stop her from holding the huge fund-raising party that she had promised to the Contemporary Art Society. He did not, in principle, disapprove of her wish to help struggling artists, but it enraged him to see her exerting herself for people like Fry who seemed to make such a poor return for her friendship.

There were two things which Bertie had failed to grasp about Ottoline: her determination to override her ill-health, and her capacity for enjoyment. He had seen the serious, almost puritanical side of her nature, but he had not realised that there was an equally strong streak of the bohemian in her character and that, if she wanted to express it, nothing would prevent her. Bertie had scarcely sent off a tender letter to 'my dearest bed-ridden old woman', urging her to rest and wishing he could nurse her ('I am a very good sick nurse – quiet and unfussy') before Ottoline was caught up in a flurry of social engagements. 'What a mad place London is now,' she sighed after entertaining a troupe of Spanish flamenco dancers; he was not sure whether to believe her or not when she wrote three days later to tell him that she was at the mercy of her friends and envied him the peace of his Trinity rooms at Nevile's Court.

There were other and more sedate engagements. The night before the CAS party, Ottoline went with Ethel Sands to hear Philip make his first speech in the House of Commons ('excellent, and his voice beautiful'); on 22 June she went to see George V being crowned. Ottoline, who had an ill-formed but sincere contempt for everything to do with the monarchy, would have stayed away if Philip's position as an MP had not required that his wife should be present. Perched in one of the highest seats in the Abbey, she had to squint to see the trail of figures moving slowly towards the Coronation Chair. Her eyes were hurting and her thoughts were troubled by an uncomfortable interview which had taken place on the previous day. The duke had made a brief visit to Bedford Square and had, without saying anything specific, let her know that he did not think her style of life did credit to her family. He suspected her of having aroused her brother Henry's increasingly Liberal sympathies and encouraged his dabbling in modern art, pictures of the sort which struck the conservatively-minded duke as being in very poor taste. Ottoline was calmly defiant during the interview, but she could not help feeling that she had been left looking more foolish than dignified when the duke made his departure: 'Those people have the way of making one feel small for the moment,' she admitted to Bertie. Back from the Abbey, she hurried to her desk to give vent to the rebellious feelings that had built up during the coronation service. 'I am *utterly* exhausted by that puppet show. It was hateful and I am more Republican than ever . . . all through that dreadful ceremony I was talking to you . . .'

Russell, while ready to joke that any eye malady which prevented her from seeing George V crowned was 'a judgement of heaven', was much more worried about his latest talk with Evelyn Whitehead. No reader of his letters can help suspecting that this lady was quietly enjoying her position of power as the prime gatherer of all gossip relating to the love-affair. Having summoned Bertie to Carlyle Square on 21 June with intimations that there was fresh cause for alarm, she had primed him with all the latest information. Fry, with whom she had had a lengthy interview, was said to be 'thoroughly friendly both to you and me', Bertie reported, 'but hurt through his caring for you'. His continuing goodwill, suggested Mrs Whitehead, depended on his being kindly treated by Ottoline. Logan and Alys were said to be furious that Ottoline should have written a friendly note to their niece, Karin Costelloe, whom she knew and liked – 'apparently from you they resent the slightest thing towards Karin'. More disturbingly, Jane Harrison, who Russell had confidently supposed to be cured of her suspicions, was still convinced that a Cambridge don's wife was involved and had started to name likely candidates. 'Mrs W. thinks the [Pearsall] Smiths may still let out the truth, on the ground that they must protect innocent women wrongly suspected,' Bertie reported. 'Apparently Mrs Cornford has been mentioned.' (21 June 1911)

If Evelyn Whitehead hoped (and, given her own possessive affection for Russell and her lukewarm enthusiasm for Ottoline, it is reasonable to suppose that she did hope) to frighten Russell out of continuing his affair, she did not know her man: difficulties only increased his sense of the inestimable value of Ottoline's love and strengthened his determination to preserve it. 'I feel as if I had always known you and always loved you,' he told her in the same letter of 21 June, 'and I cannot imagine any other life. Everything in me belongs to you – all my hopes and ideals and all my strength and weakness – everything I have to give is yours ... Goodbye my Life. I love you more and more completely and utterly. I *will* do great things for you – greater I hope than I have done without you.'

'For you' in Bertie's mind also meant 'with you'. 'It is the force of your belief in the spiritual things that is such a strength to me – and it is by that you help everyone you have to do with,' he told her in a letter of 6 August. It was that force which he now wanted her to direct only at him.

He had begun in May by sending her some of his essays, one on William James's study of pragmatism, another on Spinoza; now he started to tell her more about his work and about the people who had influenced or interested him. She heard about Philip Jourdain, a clever young mathematician whom Bertie often visited at the Dorset village home to which illness confined him. She read some early letters from which Bertie wanted her to understand how valuable Evelyn Whitehead's support had always been to him. She was invited to comment on his early 'The Free Man's Worship' and asked whether she would like to have an early look at some chapters of the cheerfully nicknamed 'Shilling Shocker',* later published as *The Problems of Philosophy*.

---

* It is not clear when the book acquired its nickname, but Ottoline's letters show that she also referred to Lytton's manuscript for *Landmarks in French Literature* as 'the

Ottoline's responses were enthusiastic, but cautiously general. She did not have an academic mind. She relied on her instinct when she was looking at paintings or reading novels and poetry, but instinct could not get her much further in philosophy than telling her that Spinoza's idea of an intellectual love of God was an appealing and congenial one.* Hearing that the Shilling Shocker would not be dealing with the areas which most interested her, religion and morality, she could only summon up a half-hearted interest in reading it, especially since the continuing problems with her eyes made any form of reading painful. Bertie comforted himself with the agreeable prospect of teaching her more about philosophy (as she eagerly asked him to do) at a later date in the summer, and with the thought that his writing was going along at a splendid rate. 'I have got into the right vein, and can write easily,' he told her, 'only as I have to keep off religion and morals I can't write anything that wd. interest you very much and this worries me.' (26? June 1911) Religion would have to wait; in the meantime, he amused himself by converting lessons in geometric proofs into tender declarations.

Axiom I. The attraction between one and another person is directly proportional to the merit of the other person and inversely proportional to the square of the distance between us. Axiom II. O. is one object of infinite merit. Axiom III. The distance between O. and M is zero. The pupil is expected to construct both the proposition and its proof from the above data, remembering that the letter 'O' stands for the 'object'. I have endeavoured to produce belief in the proposition by the intuitive method, which points out the number of facts not explicable by any other hypotheses, but in the end the geometrico-deductive method is the best. It is hoped that this method will produce the desired results in the reader. (19 July 1911)

Such a prettily encoded love-letter would not have aroused more than bewilderment in the mind of a third party. It was unfortunate that the letter which was waiting for Ottoline when she arrived for a weekend at Black Hall towards the end of June was written in a more nakedly passionate vein. 'Fancy my dismay,' Ottoline wrote after her mother-in-law had sharply inquired who her Cambridge correspondent was:

Luckily I was fairly wary, for I said, 'Oh, I expect Lytton Strachey.' She then went on to say that she had opened a letter from Cambridge. I asked

Shilling Shocker' in her letters to Strachey that year.
  * Bertie had chosen the seventeenth-century Dutch philosopher as the man whose writings they could study together with the least risk of falling into disagreement. Writing to Alys on 28 January 1894, he had noted that he was currently captivated by Spinoza's 'rich voluptuous asceticism based on a vast undefined mysticism'. Writing to Ottoline on 8 March 1912, he told her that 'Spinoza has it all – intellect and love. It *can* be done.' (See Kenneth Blackwell, *The Spinozistic Ethics of Bertrand Russell*, Allen & Unwin, London, 1985.)

her how she knew it was for me, and she said, 'By the way it began.' I have just looked it up and you began 'My darling' and you wrote on Trinity paper, but did not post it in Cambridge but in London. So she took in a good deal! Think what a scandal now she will weave round Lytton S. and me . . . (26 June)

Bertie, free from the awkwardness of dealing with the formidable Mrs Morrell in person, was hugely entertained by the notion of Lytton as a suspected lover. 'I think you ought on the spot to have told her how severely you had written to Lytton telling him to recollect himself,' he wrote back on 28 June. 'Shall I write to him telling him to appear dying of love – doing his best to conceal his grief, but alas unable to do so?' As a happy afterthought, he signed the letter, 'Your loving Lytton'.

Bertie's expectations of having Ottoline all to himself when he made a brief visit to Peppard at the end of the month were crushed. Henry Lamb still had his studio in the village and his arrival there from France coincided precisely and unfortunately with Bertie's visit to the cottage. Lamb had no intention of being excluded. Remembering the ease with which he had been able to persuade Ottoline to join him in Paris only a month earlier, the intimate evenings, the leisurely walks in the gardens of Versailles, he still could not believe that Russell had taken his place. Determined to establish superiority, he attached himself to Ottoline's side and ignored all of Bertie's snubs and hints that he might be better employed in getting on with some painting. More maddening to Lamb than anything else was his rival's refusal to take him seriously; irritated though Bertie was by Lamb's intrusiveness, he could not see him in any light but that of a neurotic young man who was trading on Ottoline's kindness.

Seeing the two men together only confirmed Ottoline's sense that she had taken the right course. Bertie, not Lamb, was the man to give her the sense of purpose she craved more than any physical passion. 'Darling darling, it is I who long to *thank you* for all you give me with and in your love,' she told him when he had, most unwillingly, departed. '. . . I know it feels as if I had *arrived* at what for years and years I had been seeking for. All the feeling of uselessness and a deep sense of self-conscious failure has gone . . . you give me and encourage in me the sense of greatness in life and of right proportion and value.' She went on to say that she had spoken most severely with Lamb and had made it clear that she would not tolerate his intruding on her time with Bertie. 'I am *very* sorry for him,' she added, 'but it will not I think be bad for him.' (1–2 July)

Lamb had been demoted to second place, but there were ways in which Ottoline still found him the more congenial companion. During the two weeks that he remained in England, they went to exhibitions together, saw the Russian Ballet in its first London season, and argued about novels. 'He talks and talks and it helps him, I think,' she wrote three days later. 'He is very interesting – he makes his own aims, desires, feelings so abstract that they *are* interesting, quite like Spinoza!! . . . He says he needs my friendship very much.' Touched by this new spirit of meekness, she begged Bertie to be friendly to Lamb when he visited Peppard again on 7 July and to believe that 'his good ideal side has expanded in a wonderful way . . . I wanted to tell you before you come how different he is and how hard he is trying to be unselfish so that you may feel kindly to him tomorrow.' (6 July)

Bertie was not impressed by the stories of Lamb's conversion, but he held his tongue. Even the news that Ottoline was to cut short her day at Peppard with him in order to go to the ballet with Lamb in London that evening did not trouble him. Ottoline had been careful to say that they always went out in a threesome with Philip, which was true, and that it was Philip who 'is always so amused by him and spoils him more than I do really', which was not. (1–2 July) How could Bertie be jealous of a man who was presented to him as a capricious child? The very fact that he felt able to write to Ottoline that month and tell her how distraught he would be if she ever fell in love with another man suggests that he had ruled out any likelihood of her being in love with Henry Lamb.

A more serious cause for impatience and unhappiness was stimulated in Bertie's mind by the presence at Peppard of Ottoline's five-year-old daughter. Neglected by her mother and cosseted by Brenty and the maids, Julian was a pretty, affectionate child who was as willing to make friends with Bertie as she had been with Henry Lamb. Unprompted by Ottoline, Bertie found that he was becoming as attached to her as if she had been his own child. He took care to find presents to please her – a book of Edward Lear's nonsense rhymes was one which did – and to encourage her to come and chatter to him in the afternoons when her mother lay resting upstairs in a darkened room, but no amount of wishful thinking could make Julian his, and he longed for a child. Every time Ottoline told him that her erratic 'Lady' had failed to arrive on the appointed date, he found himself hoping that she might be pregnant. He knew that she had had an operation which made this unlikely, but she had never told him that it was impossible. When he first raised the subject, Ottoline did her best to put him off. She would, she said, be 'very very happy' to bear him a child, but he must consider the likely effect on poor Alys and also the fact that she was not over-fond of children. 'You know, don't you, that I have hardly any maternal instinct and I always have the fear that I should not be a good mother.' (1–2 July)

Her excuses were not good enough. In his next letter, Bertie wrote that he could not keep the thought of a child out of his mind when he was making love to her; he could not believe that she did not secretly feel the same longing. It seemed that she did. 'Yes my darling, it was in my thoughts too all the time you were here,' she assured him, 'and I was too shy to say anything.

Darling I *do long* for it too but I would rather it did not come *yet*.
I think the strain would be very great. I know you understand but ... I don't know if it ever would be possible for me on account of the operation ... I want you to *know* that I shall absolutely understand if in the future the longing for a child is too great and you make other ties. (5 July)

This was not at all the response Bertie had anticipated and he was horrified when it was followed by another letter in the same vein, in which Ottoline appeared to be saying (doubtless with her thoughts on Henry Lamb) that their relationship need not exclude 'affection and *love*' for other people. Having already noted that she intended to be understanding about his need to make 'other ties', he hastened to warn her against too great a degree of tolerance. 'Believe me, I *know* I am right in saying it is better I should avoid intimacy with other women,' he answered. 'You will make a grave mistake if you go against this knowledge ... It is quite immeasurably more important to my welfare that I should maintain my exclusive love for you than that I shd. have a child by someone else.' As for the idea of his sharing her love with another man, he would not alter his opinion of her, but 'I should not continue to give love. Altogether, you would have a first-class tragedy on your hands.' (16 July)

Bertie was staying with the Phillimores when he wrote this letter and his hostess's tactless accounts of Ottoline's devotion to Philip had not raised his spirits, but he himself was quick to recognise that his depressed state had been chiefly brought on by work. His unsatisfied longing for children now diffused itself into a mood of uncontrollable despair with which Ottoline was to become wearily familiar over the next four years. It all poured out. He had ruined Alys's life. He felt old and helpless (he was thirty-nine) – 'the feeling of the doomed Titan wearily upholding a world which is ready to slip from his shoulders into chaos' – and nothing in the world seemed to be worth living for, except his Ottoline. 'Oh my beloved, my soul turns to you out of this strange and incomprehensible pain ...' he wrote to her on 17 July; 'the moment anything troubles me about you, it opens the floodgates to all the sorrows of mankind. Living without any religious beliefs is not easy. Darling, my love to you is rather terrible really – it is so absorbing and so necessary to my life. And I dread your feeling oppressed by it, and feeling that it is a prison. It shan't be a prison to you my Dearest if I can help it.'

There were to be many occasions when Ottoline would feel trapped in the gloom of Bertie's black phases, but she had experienced few of them in the summer of 1911 and she was too full of love herself to be cast down, and too conscious that her own aversion to motherhood had contributed to his sadness. Sensibly, she urged him to look forward to the happy times they would have together when he carried out his plan to take rooms at Ipsden, a village near Peppard, from 23 July. (Philip, ever-obliging, had only remarked that Ipsden was a bit on the distant side for the daily bicycle rides Bertie planned to make to Peppard.) The weather was magnificent and the countryside was looking glorious, she wrote: how could they possibly be anything but happy?

The ingredients for a crisis were there and it came soon after Bertie's arrival at Ipsden. Russell later described it as a religious dispute, but there was more to it than that. This was their first real quarrel, generated by Bertie's frustration and Ottoline's decision to tell him what she wanted from the relationship; both of them looked back on it as the time when they discovered the true depth of their love for each other. Ottoline's own needs were recognised by Bertie and they resolved to embark on a new project, a book which would belong to both of them. He would be the author; Ottoline would be the guide. The book was intended to strike a balance between her belief and his scepticism; they saw it, and lovingly described it to each other, as their child.

The letters from both sides written after the Ipsden crisis show that their love had indeed been strengthened, a new level of intimacy and understanding achieved. It was now, Ottoline wrote in a state of bewildered joy, 'as if there was not one thought or shade of thought in me that you would not understand and share. Our child is a great joy. I believe it has come out of our *complete* union just as much as an ordinary child would have ... My darling darling Bertie. My thoughts are with you every moment. I adore you.' (28–29 July)

Bertie's letters of this period chime in as sweetly with hers as though they had been written in the same room. 'Often I can hardly know whether it is your thoughts or mine that I am expressing, they seem so much the same,' he told her on 6 August. For him, too, the crisis had brought new certainty and a sense that the 'inward tie' between them would never be broken. 'You liberate my best,' he wrote to her on 28 July:

and make me know a wisdom to which my whole being responds; I feel that at last I see the world as it is natural to my best to see it. I have been slow to achieve inward harmony, and but for you I might never have achieved it. But now I possess it ... And out of this inner harmony I feel the power to give a great gift to the world – our child.

This child, the infant who was discreetly buried by the older and – in his intellectual and religious attitudes – harsher Russell, was 'Prisons'. The seed was planted in the letter of mid-July where he had expressed the fear that his love might become a form of imprisonment to Ottoline; the imaginary bars were now dissolved by an exultant sense of liberated potential. Nothing seemed impossible. 'I reach out to the stars, and through the ages, and everywhere the radiance of your love lights the world for me,' he proclaimed in an undated letter at the end of July.

'Prisons' was designed to demonstrate the value of a non-doctrinal religious attitude to the world, a theme to which Russell returned with a greater measure of success in 'Mysticism and Logic'. In early August 1911, he was intoxicated both by the idea and by the chance it offered him to work with Ottoline without compromising his position as a non-believer. By concentrating on the value of a religious attitude, the difficulty of Ottoline's convictions could be avoided. He had never disputed the attitude, only the grounds for a belief. 'The result will be extraordinarily Platonic,' he told her as he started to plan the book: Ottoline was thinking along similar lines. 'I feel something straightforward,' she wrote to him by the same post; later in the week, she told him how glad she was that he would use some of the ideas for the book in the last chapter of *The Problems of Philosophy*. 'How anxious I shall be to know how that final chapter fares – I feel awfully anxious over that child.' (11 August) 'Prisons', she was convinced, would have a transforming effect on many people; she foresaw it as the inspiration which would, in one of her most splendidly vague phrases, 'lift them out into life and freedom and love and union with others and service'. (12 August) Bertie, doubtless, knew just what she meant.

He was working fast. By 18 August, he had finished writing *The Problems of Philosophy* and drawn up a plan for 'Prisons', to which he now wanted to give the new title, 'The Religion of Contemplation'. He went to work at once; by 29 September he had a typescript ready to show her, of which a copy also went to Alfred and Evelyn Whitehead. (Neither has survived.) Ottoline, while worried by the fact that he had given scant consideration to some of the less intellectual elements, approved. The Whiteheads did not like it, and said so as kindly as possible. Evelyn's main objection was that the emotional and intellectual parts were insufficiently integrated. She could not pretend an enthusiasm she did not feel. 'I knew in my instincts she would not like it,' Bertie reported to Ottoline on 18 October. 'She says the beauty of the Free Man's Worship is lacking.'

A partly revised manuscript was in Ottoline's hands by March 1912. It was Bertie's wish that she should read it and comment as frankly as she liked, with particular attention to the religious aspect. It was, as he had already told her, closely based on his observation of her; in it, she would find a clear reflection of the feelings he had so eloquently expressed in his letters. Its intention was to show that it was possible to achieve a state of union with the universe whatever one's convictions about the nature of the universe might be. It was possible, in other words, to find a religious attitude which was independent of all beliefs.[1] In his notion of the highest state, the contemplative vision, Russell described the transfiguring sense he had experienced in his love for Ottoline. This was presented in grandiloquent terms as the final state of freedom from the prison of self.

And above all is the contemplative vision; partly sad, partly filled with a solemn joy, wholly beautiful, wholly great: the vision of all the ages of the earth, the depths of space, and the hierarchy of the eternal truths, met and mirrored in one mind whose being ends almost as soon as its knowledge has come to exist.[2]

Understandably, Ottoline was impressed by the splendour of the vision. After reading the chapter on religion, she wrote to tell Bertie that it was 'very very beautiful – more so than I had remembered' (5 March 1912), but she was not wholly uncritical. What did he mean by impartial worship? Could he give more thought to the idea of diversity in individuals, and to the idea that each person could only hope to become a complete whole by trying to 'learn what is best for him ... *Individuality is so precious*,' she added, in case he had missed her point. No longer intimidated by his brilliance, she had no qualms about criticising his prose. 'I don't like "useful". It jars,' she noted on one page, and on another, 'The sentence of the top paragraph "What promotes" etc., does not end very well, does it?' 'Reverence', she thought, was a better word to use than 'worship'. (6 March 1912)

She could have saved herself the trouble. Russell, already immersed in his next project, no longer had his heart in 'Prisons'. The Whiteheads' cool response had troubled him and his new friendship with his intellectually ruthless pupil, Wittgenstein, was causing him to reappraise the emotional content of the manuscript. He had already incorporated some of its ideas into *The Problems of Philosophy*; now he decided to scrap 'Prisons' and salvage the best of it for a shorter paper. In February, he had told Ottoline that he was thinking of publishing the religious chapter separately and that she should read it with this in mind. On 11 October 1912, it was printed in *The Hibbert Journal* in a revised form as 'The Essence of Religion'. Ottoline admired it greatly, but Russell was still uneasy. When Wittgenstein upbraided him for its lack of precision and for the use of vague and general language, he found himself unable to disagree.

THE IPSDEN CRISIS

The new mental rapport achieved after the Ipsden crisis of July 1911 had the added benefit – from Ottoline's point of view – of putting Bertie into a less demanding frame of mind about sex. Until then, his attitude had been that of a starving schoolboy offered a tightly-wrapped box of chocolates; now, his physical needs were shifted on to a more exalted level by the plans for their 'child'. Their embraces were made more tender by 'a sacred and mystical joy . . . the physical is swallowed up in the other'. Ottoline's body was no longer mere womanly flesh to be caressed and penetrated; desire and act were fused in one extraordinary and almost metaphysical experience. 'I feel you as the gateway into a transfigured world through which all the glory shines before me,' he told her. 'You wouldn't believe how hard it is for me not to be mythological about you.' (August 1911)

Being an object of mythological worship was easier than being the object of intense sexual desire. Ottoline had been secretly entertaining the idea of going on a long summer holiday with Philip, but now, happy with Bertie's new and more manageable attitude, she changed her mind. Her letters grew correspondingly light-hearted. Bertie was addressed as 'my darling Frivolous Philosopher' and twitted merrily about the Cambridge ladies. Had he heard from 'the adorable Miss Lindsay'? And how had he enjoyed having dinner with 'the dangerous one', the Mrs Cornford Miss Harrison still suspected of being his secret mistress?* And, dear heavens, he surely wasn't going to fall under the influence of her least favourite of the Romans? 'Oh no, don't taint yourself with that dreary Marcus Aurelius!' (6 August 1911)

A few months before, Ottoline would never have dared to offer such a dismissive remark. Her new-found confidence was partly due to the fact that Bertie had started reading chapters of *The Problems of Philosophy* aloud to her and encouraging her to tell him whenever she found it heavy or difficult to understand. The uncommon clarity of its style owes a good deal to Ottoline's insistence that she must be able to follow every point he made, and to the questions which she insisted must be given lucid answers.

While Russell was sighing over Mrs Cornford's stewed fruit, Ottoline had been visiting her brother Henry, the chosen favourite of her family. Fond though Henry was of his strong-minded wife, Birdie, he had a dreamy, contemplative streak and he shared his sister's passion for solitude. With this in mind, he had bought a tiny isolated house

---

* He hadn't. Mrs Cornford was a granddaughter of Charles Darwin; her mother was a close friend of Jane Harrison. Like all the Darwins, she kept a frugal table and Russell, who put quantity before quality, reported to Ottoline on 6 August that he went home hungry and bad-tempered after dining on soup and a few slices of cold meat and stewed fruit.

at Churn on the Berkshire downs which served as a retreat when he wanted to sketch and read and walk. Staying alone with him for a few days, Ottoline found it hard to believe that this was the brother who had once cared for nothing but hunting and shooting and who she had found so intimidating when she was a young girl. The new and more mellow Henry was a liberal-minded Conservative who sympathised with her political views and liked nothing better than to talk about paintings. Much later, Ottoline would undergo a similar change of heart about the duke; for the present, she was thankful to find herself so much in sympathy with at least one of her family. They talked together about Henry's only sadness, his lack of children, a subject which had also been occupying Ottoline since her conversations with Bertie early in July. But 'he finds a great deal of happiness in doing social reform work', she told Bertie. '. . . He has a great love of humanity and great tenderness and sympathy and really cares to help do good.' (4–5 August)

To Bertie, who liked Henry very much when he met him that month, this was a cue to make a few suggestions to Ottoline about curbing her own passion for helping people. It was, he thought, bad for her health. 'I don't think you ought to do *much* in the way of active philanthropy,' he told her on 6 August, 'partly because your strength is too small, partly because your impulse is to the spiritual things . . .'

Russell was brilliant, but he was not perceptive. It seemed to him that Ottoline ought to be satisfied by the opportunity to work with and through him; 'Prisons', he reasoned, would be her gift to humanity as much as his. There was no need for her to worry about making her own contribution. But the idea of active benevolence was too deeply engrained in Ottoline to be easily relinquished. She had no respect for her own mind, dismissing it as 'a calm slow brain, without charm of brilliancy', but she wanted to apply it to human situations, not to abstract hypotheses. 'Life, life is what we are here for and to live it well,' she wrote in her journal, 'not to go into a room and think about it all.'[3]

Russell was right to be anxious about Ottoline's health. Her local physician in Henley, Dr Wainwright, could only suggest a quiet life in the country with plenty of sleep, but the sale of Peppard in August made that impossible and the pain of daily violent headaches and constant exhaustion, combined with shooting pains behind her eyes which prevented her from reading, drove Ottoline to consult a series of London doctors. Neuritis, an umbrella term for any nervous illness which could not be convincingly identified, was proclaimed to be the trouble; she was urged to spend the autumn in a foreign spa. Marienbad was chosen and Ottoline asked Philip if he would mind Bertie joining her there for the first two weeks. Philip, who had arranged to follow later, gave his consent. Ottoline left on 29 August and Bertie, travelling second-class in an attempt to escape meeting any of his friends, set off after her within two or three days.

Ottoline and Bertie's first holiday abroad was not a success. The Prussian manager of Ottoline's hotel made it clear that he disapproved of their connection and tried to ban Bertie from visiting the establishment. Ottoline's attempt to remedy the situation by getting a friendly fellow guest to intervene was disastrous. The guest, then the Solicitor-General, was Mr Rufus Isaacs: the hotel manager detested Jews. His first act on the arrival of Philip was to inform him that the gentleman who had just left for England had been going into his wife's room every day and to point for his evidence to the cigarette burns on the bedroom sofa. Philip smiled, paid for the damage, and said that he was glad that his wife had not lacked company. Only Bertie was unable to admire Philip's gallantry. Certainly, he had been 'wonderfully generous' about their affair, but he did not want to feel indebted to a man he secretly despised. 'P. does not want of you what men usually want,' he wrote to Ottoline in a superior tone on 12 October. '... I firmly believe it is a relief to him to think that you get from elsewhere what he can't give you.'

The manager's disagreeableness had cast a pall over Marienbad. Shortly after his own arrival, Philip decided that a tour of some more congenial cities would distract Ottoline from the distressing news that her old friend and mentor, Mother Julian, had died. By the end of September, they had visited Prague, Milan, Pavia and Lausanne, where Ottoline found a new and encouragingly optimistic physician, Dr Combe, who had been recommended by Ethel Sands. 'I cannot tell you what a relief it is to me to feel I have this to fall back on if I am not better in the next few months,' she wrote to Bertie on 14 October. But Dr Combe's warnings against over-exertion were promptly overruled: in Paris, there was a new exhibition of Cubist paintings to be seen, the Anreps to be visited and Nijinsky to be watched; back in London, she plunged into a swirl of activity. Lytton Strachey was pining for tales of her travels; a visit from the elderly Henry James involved meeting him at the railway station and chaperoning him across London. Duncan Grant's new murals had to be inspected at the Polytechnic; the CAS wanted to borrow Bedford Square for a committee meeting. Only when all of this had been dealt with could she turn to the pleasurable task of helping Bertie to organise life in his new London flat.

Bertie had not been having a good time in Ottoline's absence. The news that Evelyn Whitehead, a psychosomatic victim of pseudo-angina, was at death's door (she made a speedy recovery), had been followed by the news that Roger Fry was making trouble again. Having done his best to redirect Ethel Sands's sympathy towards Alys as the victim of Bertie and Ottoline's heartless cruelty, Fry had hurried off to tell the same story to one of Bertie's closest friends, Goldie Lowes Dickinson, garnishing the truth with a sauce of malicious invention. The fracas had not prevented Bertie from working – nothing ever did – but it had stiffened his resolve to find a London flat where he and Ottoline could meet without the constant fear of being spied upon by one of their mutual acquaintances. He had finally settled on a dingy *pied-à-terre* in the appropriately named Russell Chambers, in Bury Place.* Its location, two minutes' walk from Bedford Square, was its only charm.

Alys allowed her husband to take what he wanted from Van Bridge; Bertie took only his books and a few things inherited from his grandparents – a desk, a table, some linen and silver. The rest had to be supplied from scratch. Creating a home from nothing was just the kind of challenge Ottoline enjoyed: 'I love planning all the things for you and feel so proud to do it for *love and joy*,' she wrote to Bertie on 3 November after a lengthy joint shopping expedition. A week later, ignoring Henry Lamb's angry complaints that she never had more than half a day to spend visiting his new Hampstead studio, she rushed back from Black Hall to snatch two hours with Bertie in the semi-furnished flat. 'Wasn't it wonderful today? ... My Bertie I *do* love and cling to you,' she scribbled that afternoon (10 November) before hurrying off to ransack the antique shops of Chelsea for gifts to lavish on him, while her cook was delegated to purchase all the 'unknown necessities' in the broom and saucepan category. 'The chest of drawers for £3.10s. sounds just the thing,' Bertie wrote, but her generosity appalled his frugal mind. 'Darling, it is not I that will be ruined but you, if you give me such a mass of things: rug, basket chair, pretty old chairs – what will become of you?' Secure again in the sense of her total love, he could afford to add a few kind words about 'poor Lamb' and his bad temper. 'What selfish creatures men are who have never had to accommodate themselves to other people.' (14 November)

Accommodating other people's needs was again taking a toll of Ottoline's health. Nevertheless, after setting up Bertie's flat and smoothing Lamb's ruffled pride with a promise to see him alone on her return to London, she found time to comfort a distraught Hilda Douglas-Pennant for being jilted at an age when marriage had seemed past hoping for, before setting off with Philip to visit his constituency in the North. 'I kept thinking of you all the time and wondering what

---

* Often wrongly referred to as Bury Street. 34 Russell Chambers is substantially the same today as it was in 1911.

you would think of it all,' she told Bertie after her return from the Burnley tradesmen's dance where she had joined in an ebullient charade after drawing famous names from a hat. Blessed with a strong sense of humour, she played Hamlet's mother with glee and was highly amused to see another 'Lady Ottoline' capering round the room in the arms of Burnley's football hero among a covey of pretend dukes and duchesses. It was a treat, she said, to be among people who enjoyed themselves so much; she and they had laughed until they cried.

Lamb, not satisfied with the fact that he had Lytton Strachey's devoted attention, was still pestering Ottoline with demands on her time, lacing his entreaties – 'O do not stint me! I am insatiable for more life with you and in you' – with complaints: 'Must I wait for the age and fame of a Henry James before I am to be allowed the general concession of private attention?' Time and experience had immunised her to his darts of petulance; she had a larger crisis on her hands. Shortly after her November visit to Burnley, Bertie prepared to attack her religious beliefs. During her absence in Europe, he had been pondering the incompatibility of her emotional conviction with his rational attitude. It was not her belief in God which worried him so much as her belief that to feel something was a good enough reason for holding it to be true, he told her on 20 November. 'My view is that passionate feeling is often a sufficient ground for judging things good or bad, but not for judging that they exist.'

The gauntlet had been thrown down, but Ottoline was in no hurry to pick it up. She tried to distract him with tender notes (just 'A kiss and my love' sent to 'My beloved Bertie'), and playful references to the final departure of his moustache. 'Do tell me what your friends the Whiteheads say about your new face,' she urged him. The reply was disconcerting: Evelyn Whitehead had commented that he looked just like Philip Morrell, a remark which annoyed Russell nearly as much as her observation that the revised 'Prisons' had 'the dullness that comes to middle-aged men when they marry'.

The quarrel was postponed by these tactics of evasion, but not for long. Russell went to the Whiteheads for Christmas while Ottoline, always unlucky on the ritual Black Hall visits, enraged her mother-in-law by collapsing into bed with a headache. 'I feel she hates me when I am not well,' Ottoline mournfully noted in the first of several letters bewailing her inability ever to please the old lady. Bertie was only moderately sympathetic; he was too impatient to have her answer to his religious queries.

They met on 27 December, reaching the Bury Place flat in time for a late lunch. Ottoline was still weighed down with the gloom which always descended on her at Black Hall and which had been deepened this year by her mother-in-law's pointed questions about her private life. Bertie, fresh from a traditional Christmas with the Whiteheads complete with charades and songs around the piano, was too impatient to be affectionate. After a perfunctory greeting, he went straight to the point. Was she ready to admit that belief based on feeling was an act of intellectual dishonesty? Would she agree that faith without proof was unworthy of his respect? The only response he got to his inquisition was that she felt ready to kill herself.

Sitting in the train on the way back to Oxford, Ottoline began writing a defiant letter. Did Bertie realise how humiliating it was for her to be treated as an erring fanatic? Didn't he understand the impossibility of explaining what her religious feelings meant to her? 'I don't know that I should ever be able to make you see what I felt any more than I could now see your adored mathematics,' she wrote bitterly – and then crossed it out. By the time she had reached Oxford she could think of nothing but the pain of losing him. Hurrying into the post office, she scribbled a quick 'Bless you' on a telegram form; she reached Black Hall to find an agonised letter from Bertie, begging for her forgiveness.

Letters flew to and fro at an even dizzier rate than usual over the next few days, but it was Bertie who was driven to seek a compromise. On 2 January 1912, in a letter which was an astonishing exercise in back-pedalling, he told her that his own need for religion was as great as hers and that it was just because she was religious that he loved her so much. As a proof of his good faith, he arranged to introduce her to his most devoutly Christian friend, Lucy Silcox, the headmistress of a girls' school which he thought might one day suit little Julian.

Miss Silcox, who raved about Ottoline's beautiful face and soul when they met on 9 January, was seeing her at her best. With the quarrel behind her and the battle apparently won, she was at her most relaxed, full of sweetness, full of love. She could not be expected to know that the battle had scarcely begun, or that one of the main protagonists would be a young man she looked upon as her spiritual ally. His name was Ludwig Wittgenstein.

11

TRIANGULAR RELATIONSHIPS
1912–13

'Passionate curiosity to see, to know and to understand more and more of life, is what leads me on.'

OM, *Early Memoirs*

In the letters, it was always God's fault. If only Ottoline could stop putting her faith in the unprovable; if only Bertie would not go on insisting that she should accept nothing unless it could be proved, they would have no cause for their quarrels. That was what they told each other. But there were other, less easily admissible factors at work.

One of these has already been indicated. Ottoline was far more excited by Bertie's mind than his body, and the times when she was happiest with him were when he talked about philosophy to her in the Peppard woods, or when they strolled along the sands at Dorset, discussing poetry, childhood memories, dreams and plans. Now that he had acquired a London home, these moments shrank away. Bertie did not come racing up to London in order to talk, but to make love to his adored mistress. In his letters, he called her 'the mother of sorrows' and told her that his love was something abstract, akin to worship. That was true, but he also had a strong physical desire for her and by 1912 he was becoming aware that it was not fully reciprocated. She always had a convincing excuse ready, but she was not a good actress and she could not pretend what she did not feel. In a letter written on 30 January 1912, Bertie told her that one of his greatest difficulties was with the feeling that she took nothing from him, while giving everything. He was being perfectly sincere, but it struck her as a painful irony. 'The dreadful thing is that just to him

I cannot *give*,' she wrote in her diary. 'It is almost entirely, I believe, his appearance – and I cannot control it. But I must control it.'

The second problem underlying the passionate disagreement which flawed their relationship from December 1911 until the beginning of 1914 is more easily identified with hindsight. Ottoline heard more than any other of Russell's correspondents about his friendship with Ludwig Wittgenstein, but she never understood how much he was responsible for the increasing violence with which Bertie repudiated her concept of his vocation.

Wittgenstein was twenty-three when he first erupted into Russell's life in the autumn of 1911. A small, luminous-eyed Austrian carelessly dressed in patched flannel trousers and an open-necked shirt, he came directly to the purpose of his visit. He had read Russell's *The Principles of Mathematics* while in his first year in England as a research student at Manchester (where, coincidentally, one of his tutors was Henry Lamb's father): his interest in the problems it raised and, in particular, in Russell's challenge to what is known as the theory of classes, side-tracked him from his first ambition to design an aeroplane. In April 1909, Wittgenstein had sent his own solution to the theory to one of Russell's mathematical colleagues, Philip Jourdain; in the summer of 1911, he visited the logician Gottlob Frege, a man who he knew was greatly respected by Russell. It was at Frege's suggestion that he approached Russell to ask if he could study with him in an unofficial capacity.

Russell had very few pupils who wished to study mathematical logic, and Wittgenstein's manner impressed him; he agreed to take him on, a decision which he immediately regretted. 'My German friend threatens to be an infliction,' he told Ottoline when Wittgenstein descended on him again the following night; a fortnight later, one of his seminars was reduced to chaos by Wittgenstein's refusal to agree that they could exclude the possibility of a rhinoceros's presence in the room.* 'He is armour-plated against all assaults of reasoning,' Bertie told Ottoline crossly; 'it is really rather a waste of time talking with him.' (16 November 1911)

His exasperation was short-lived. By the end of the month, Ottoline heard that Wittgenstein was, after all, 'literary, musical, pleasant-mannered (being an Austrian) and I think *really* intelligent'. The young man had started to show himself in a more human light; his

---

* It is not clear what the philosophical basis of this strange disagreement was, but it is most likely to have been connected with the view held by Wittgenstein at that time: that the world consisted not of things but of facts. He was probably wrestling with the difficulty of working out what sort of a fact the absence of a rhinoceros could be. (See Brian McGuinness, *Young Ludwig*, Duckworth, London, 1988, p. 89.)

father was anxious that he should continue with engineering; for himself, Wittgenstein was full of doubts about whether he had the makings of a philosopher. Russell tried to reassure him. After reading the essay which was handed in at the beginning of the winter term, he began to think that he had a genius on his hands. 'I shall certainly encourage him,' he told Ottoline on 23 January 1912. 'Perhaps he will do great things.'

It was presumably on Russell's recommendation that Wittgenstein was accepted as a member of Trinity College the following week, but acceptance did not make him more docile and there were moments when Russell asked himself whether, despite his genius, he was worth all the trouble; on the whole, however, he was enthralled and stimulated as the nightly discussions expanded into lunches, teas, visits to concerts and long strolls through the water meadows and woods outside Cambridge. 'I like Wittgenstein more and more,' he told Ottoline on 16 March. 'He has the pure intellectual passion in the highest degree; it makes me love him. His disposition is that of an artist, intuitive and moody. He says every morning he begins his work with hope, and every evening he ends in despair – he has just the sort of rage when he can't understand things that I have.' It was gratifying to know that G. E. Moore, for whose judgement Russell continued to have immense respect, shared his excitement. 'Moore says he always feels W. *must* be right when they disagree . . .' Ottoline learned on 5 March 1912. 'I am glad to be confirmed in my high opinion of W.' Bertie went on: '– the young men don't think much of him or if they do it is only because Moore and I praise him.' When Wittgenstein's sister visited him in Cambridge that summer, she was thrilled to be taken to tea with Russell and to hear that he expected the next important step in philosophy to be taken by Ludwig.[1]

For Ottoline, Bertie's interest in Wittgenstein brought a welcome diversion from being lectured on her religious beliefs. She liked everything she heard about this odd and brilliant young man who came to his discussions armed with bouquets of roses and lilies-of-the-valley and then stayed to argue through the night. Nothing, in her view, was more important in life than to respond to it with passion and energy; for that alone, she was ready to think that Wittgenstein was splendid. 'What a dear Wittgenstein is – I *love* him!' she wrote enthusiastically on 8 March. 'I am awfully glad Moore thinks so highly of him too.' Bertie must not be too impatient with him, she counselled a day later, 'for such people are so rare and they seem like meteors across the earth – England does not produce such reckless ones as he seems to be . . .' Everything Bertie told her suggested that he had found a friend after her own heart. Wittgenstein shared her passion for Thomas à Kempis, her admiration for the religious writings of William James, her love of childish jokes and her disregard for conventions. He liked Blake, one of her favourite poets; he adored Beethoven, Brahms and Mozart, her favourite composers; he was as fond as she of music halls. Like her – although we cannot be sure that she knew this – he had rejected the security of a rich family background. Reading Russell's letters, Ottoline felt that their talks must be very similar to her own arguments with Bertie. 'The things I say to him are just the things you would say to me if you were not afraid of the avalanche they would produce,' he told her, 'and his avalanche is just what mine would be.' (March 1913)

It did not surprise Ottoline when Bertie admitted in August 1912 that his feelings for Wittgenstein were those he would entertain towards a son. A year later, it became apparent that paternal affection was entwined with a more complicated emotion; as he fell more and more deeply under the spell of Wittgenstein's nature, Bertie began to see their relationship as a mirror to his own love for Ottoline. He 'affects me just as I affect you', he told her on 1 June 1913; 'I get to know every turn and twist of the ways in which I irritate and depress you from watching how he irritates and depresses me; and at the same time I love and admire him. Also I affect him just as you affect me when you are cold. The parallelism is curiously close altogether.' Russell was already aware of Wittgenstein's homosexual nature – it was one of the reasons that he was nervous of exposing him to the promiscuous attentions of the Apostles; it now began to look to Ottoline as if Bertie himself was falling in love. His next letter struck her as sounding very like one of Lytton Strachey's outbursts when Lamb had treated him unkindly. Wittgenstein had gone off in a temper after accusing Russell of insincerity and being told to practise self-control. Russell had waited for him to come to a concert and had grown terrified that he might have committed suicide when he failed to appear. He had left the concert, hunted everywhere, finally found him and 'told him I was sorry I had been cross . . . His faults are exactly mine . . . always analysing, pulling up by the roots, trying to get the exact truth of what one feels towards him. I see it is very tiring and deadening to one's affections.' (5 June 1913) At one point during this week, Bertie said something which led Ottoline to commiserate with him on the painful intensity of his feelings. 'Yes, it is dreadful to feel as you do about Wittgenstein,' she wrote on 11 June, 'but it is not a thing you can control is it? But I know how much you must mind it. If only you had Lytton's composition, how satisfactory.'

Increasingly aware of his depressive nature – Wittgenstein admitted to having contemplated suicide almost every day of his life – Bertie's own recommended antidote was riding, which Wittgenstein dutifully took up, but concern soon made Bertie turn to Ottoline for advice. Her first suggestion was a visit to Dr Roger Vittoz, the nerve specialist who was giving her lessons in thought-control in the summer of 1913;

since Dr Vittoz was in Switzerland and Wittgenstein was in Cambridge, she had another, more practical suggestion to make: Bertie was startled to receive a large packet of cocoa tablets from Lausanne with the news that hot chocolate was the best thing possible for Wittgenstein's nerves. Their effect was not reported.

Hearing always of Wittgenstein's troubles, it did not occur to Ottoline to connect Bertie's own despairs and sudden changes of direction with his pupil's influence. In the autumn of 1911, Bertie had been intensely excited by the idea of writing 'Prisons'; at the beginning of 1912, he had been seeking her advice on the chapter she most admired, but when it appeared in print later that year as 'The Essence of Religion', he was quick to dismiss her praises: Wittgenstein had accused him of being 'a traitor to the gospel of exactness'. In the spring he was elated by the progress of a new collaborative work, a novel which was to be a spiritual autobiography and to which Ottoline was to contribute an episode; by the end of the summer, he was finding excuses to abandon the book. In the summer of 1913, when Bertie relinquished one of his most ambitious projects, a book on the theory of knowledge, he did so only because Wittgenstein had proved that the first six chapters were based on an untenable theory. (Bertie had believed that the theory of types on which *Principia Mathematica* was founded could be based on the theory of judgement employed in the new book: Wittgenstein showed that the two theories were incompatible with each other.) It was, for Bertie, as agonising an experience as it would have been for Ottoline to have the grounds of her religious faith destroyed; his confidence was shattered. He tried to explain how he felt, but it was impossible for Ottoline to grasp that his despair that summer had less to do with her than with Wittgenstein's abrupt destruction of a book based on years of work.*

Ottoline's relationship with Bertie in the pre-war years suffered, in short, from the fact that he was being pulled in two directions. If he wrote in the way Ottoline wished, Wittgenstein accused him of dishonesty and sloppy thinking; if he turned back to pure philosophy, he exposed himself not only to Ottoline's displeasure but to the merciless clarity of his pupil's judgement. In Wittgenstein's view, the only

---

* Describing the events of 1913 to Ottoline three years later, Bertie told her that Wittgenstein's criticism, 'tho' I don't think you realized it at the time, was an event of first-rate importance in my life, and affected everything I have done since. I saw he was right, and I saw that I could not hope ever again to do fundamental work in philosophy. My impulse was shattered ... I became filled with utter despair, and tried to turn to you for consolation. But you were occupied with Vittoz and could not give me time.'[2]

field over which Russell had total mastery was mathematical logic; in Ottoline's view, he had a clear duty to use his intelligence for the good of humanity, to 'give out a philosophy that would help people to make all their life religious'. (15 March 1912) If Wittgenstein had had his way, Russell would never have written a word about religion and morals; if Ottoline had been allowed to have hers, he would have written about nothing else.

Ottoline had cause to be in low spirits at the beginning of 1912. Julian, not yet six, was thought by everybody to be too pale and listless to be well, while her own headaches and eye-pains had returned with blinding force. In February, she could bear it no longer and went to Switzerland for two months of further treatment, staying in a small hotel in Lausanne while Dr Combe and his colleagues tried out some of the bizarre cures for nerves which were then in fashion. The most disagreeable, based on the notion that the nervous system was affected by the mucous lining of the nose, was rhinosurgery. When bits of bone had been snipped out of Ottoline's nose with no improvement to her health, the doctors resorted to the use of electric wires which were pushed up the nostrils to cauterise the flesh, causing the patient agonising pain and bringing no relief.

Diversions were few. After decorating her drab room with silk shawls and reading her way through Bertie's gift of an abridged Spinoza (not, she admitted to Lytton, the easiest of reading for an invalid), she was reduced to embroidering a picture of 'Deirdre of the Sorrows' which Lamb had designed for her and talking to her new maid, Cookie.

Ottoline's main entertainment in Lausanne derived from her correspondence with Lytton Strachey. His first book, *Landmarks in French Literature*, had just been published. Writing to praise it in February, Ottoline rebuked him for imagining that she could ever think him dull. Had he not given her one of the most enjoyable afternoons of her life just before Christmas, when she let him hold a tea-party at Bedford Square and came to it herself as one of the guests? 'Please do not think you would ever bore me. It is all the other way about,' she assured him, before going on to picture the newly-published author's dazzling life in London as he pranced out, so she supposed, in a purple coat with a green velvet collar. He was not to take any notice of her when she worried that Henry Lamb and sociability would interrupt his working hours. She had not meant to offend him: '*Please* forgive my stupid heavy footedness ... I am an owl!' (28 February 1912) Writing again two days later, she wondered if she could tempt him to visit Lausanne with descriptions of a 'young Apollo' who played the piano in the hotel and sprang up the stairs like a dancer. She was sorry that her writing was so erratic: he must put it down to the changes in her moods. Had he heard that Henry Lamb and Ka Cox (a friend of Rupert Brooke's who had also fallen in love with Lamb) had been holding long conversations about 'contemporary relationships'? she asked him on 13 March. 'I wish I could have listened at the keyhole – did you?' Musing on the art of friendship in the same letter, she told Lytton that she was reading about Voltaire and wondering if it was possible to establish that kind of society again: 'all our relationships seem so loose, so ragged and inadequate . . . Is it London and all its chaos and hugeness that tyrannises over us and divides us?' By 22 March, she was getting ready to pack her things when the post arrived, bringing with it 'your dazzlingly delightful enchanting letter – oh, if you only knew the happiness your letters bring!'

Letters from Henry Lamb brought her less joy. His new practice of going on daily rides with, among others, Philip Morrell, had led him to the view that Philip was a charming character who deserved better treatment from his wife. 'I do like him so very much,' he wrote to her, 'but what a pity that he should be so friendless.' He went on to accuse her of monopolising anybody interesting they happened to meet, while poor Philip was abandoned. 'What a sad sacrifice!' (20 March 1912)

It was hardly for Lamb to say it, but his words touched Ottoline on a raw nerve. She had not taken Philip's friends away from him, but she had imposed her own without any particular consideration for his feelings. It could not, she thought, be agreeable for Philip to feel that she was always silently comparing him with Russell. With this in mind, she started to fill her Lausanne diary with admiring references to her husband in the hope that he would read it and feel happier. 'I have beautiful letters from Philip every day . . .' she wrote, tactfully omitting any reference to Bertie's more lyrical epistles. 'There is no one I have ever met that approaches my darling Philip . . . He has such a remarkably *fine* good mind, combined with the best character in a man that I have ever known.'[3] Writing to thank Bertie for taking the time to read one of his letters, she said: 'I am glad you like P's letter, though it's so dull.' (18 March) On another occasion, she apologised for having bothered him with her concern about her husband's unpopularity. 'It *was* difficult for you, but it was a relief to talk it over . . . It makes me awfully sad that he is not more appreciated or understood.' (12 February 1912)

Russell was not inclined to be sympathetic. Philip had a loyal wife; she had a devoted husband and an adoring lover. Surely the one to be pitied was himself, reduced to making do with such scraps of time as she could spare. 'Seeing that you, who have the whole of two men, would suffer greatly if you only had one and a half,' he told her in

April, 'you can perhaps imagine that it is hard to be content with a half, which is three times less than what would *not* content you.' Thwarted of his hopes of meeting her in Paris on her return from Lausanne (quite impossible, Ottoline said firmly; what did he imagine they could do with her maid in the next room?) he decided to walk off his ill-humour in Dorset.

The weather was not kind that spring, but it matched Russell's mood. Glowering down on the lonely crags of Portland Bill, he decided that this was the face of nature he could best appreciate, 'tumultuous, cruel, unchanging and inhuman'. The further he tramped, the more savage he felt. 'I doubt if ever you know how nearly I am a raving madman,' he announced from an inn at Christchurch. 'Of all the characters I ever read about in fiction, none was so intimate to me as Rogojine.* It is only intellect that keeps me sane.' (24 March) Opening the pile of letters awaiting her arrival in Paris, Ottoline was dismayed to find herself accused of prolonging her absence for her own pleasure. 'What *do* you mean by "trailing my coat"[?]' she asked despairingly. 'Please don't be X with me . . . *of course* I am longing to get back. I think it was the toothache that made you write so.' (24 March 1912)

By the end of May, they had kissed and made up for perhaps the twentieth time in their volatile relationship. Ottoline set off with Philip for a visit to her brother Henry and his wife at Underley Hall, their home in the Lake District. While she seethed on Henry's behalf (the house belonged to his wife and she was always ready to show who ran it), Russell packed his bags in expectation of joining Ottoline for a month in Lausanne when she returned there to continue her treatment. Philip was promptly informed and said to be 'very glad, as he thinks you will look after me'. The mere mention of Philip's name triggered a new explosion:

Ottoline: You mistake me – I do know what you feel and what you suffer. Oh Bertie, don't despair. Take at least what I give you . . . I feel you would rather not come to Lausanne. (31 May 1912)

Russell: I know you are meaning to speak the truth, so I think you don't know what words mean. I will try to take what you give me; at Lausanne the outward circumstances may make it easy to put up with its being so little . . . loving you is like loving a red-hot poker, which is a worse bedfellow than Lytton's umbrella; every caress brings an agony. (1 June 1912)

This was not a promising start and Ottoline had uneasy memories of their spell abroad together the previous year. This time, however, everything was perfect. Russell ensconced himself in the hotel on the

---

* Rogozin appears in Dostoevsky's *The Idiot* which Ottoline had urged Russell to read the previous year.

other side of Lausanne where Edward Gibbon had once lived, and spent his mornings writing in the garden. The afternoons were spent with Ottoline, talking, reading, going on leisurely expeditions. For her birthday treat, he took her to Geneva and bought her a little blue enamel watch which she wore until her death. From Geneva, they went on to look at Voltaire's home at Ferney and to stroll under the poplars in the park. Did she remember it all as well as he? Russell asked the following summer. 'The extraordinary beauty of the evening as we came back into Ferney after being in the fields – one of those moments of inward and outward peace, when time stands still for an instant . . . How happy we were.' (23 May 1913)

Ottoline had every reason to be happy. Her health was always affected by her emotions and she was astonished to find how well she responded now to the treatment which had proved so ineffectual three months earlier. Her fear of being disliked – a fear which she freely admitted amounted almost to an obsession – seemed absurd in the face of a flood of affectionate letters from the friends who were missing her. Lytton, riveted to hear that she had at last met Nijinsky while visiting Mrs Chadbourne in Paris, was making playful threats to come and be her maid in Lausanne if he couldn't coax her to return. 'Why can't I appear tomorrow in the yellow drawing-room, and take you off for a flaunt down Bond Street? Well, you *will* come back? You won't vanish altogether with an Apollo from Transylvania who'll whisk you off to his castle in a chariot and six? Shall I see you before the end of the month?' (7 June 1912) Virginia wrote to announce her engagement to one of Philip's riding companions, Leonard Woolf. 'Do you like him?' she asked. 'I hope so, because I want to be a friend of yours all my life.' (June 1912) Even Lamb was dulcet: would it please her to hear that he had a new painting ready as a present?

The chief source of her contentment lay in Russell's new tractability. She could say nothing wrong. Away from Cambridge and Wittgenstein and encouraged by Ottoline to saturate himself in the beauty of nature, he began to think that he did have something to offer the world as a religious philosopher. With Ottoline as a willing collaborator, the spiritual autobiography which he had contemplated during his walks in Dorset now began to take shape as a short novel.

The Perplexities of John Forstice is the story of a widowed scientist who sets out to find rational justification for believing that science and religion (religion in the broadest sense of reverence preferred by Ottoline) were not mutually exclusive. In it, Bertie fictionalised the difficulty of reconciling his intellectual and emotional aspirations while Wittgenstein and Ottoline pulled him in opposite directions. As a work of literature, the merit of *Forstice* is fairly slight, although the speakers representing different philosophies of life are skilfully presented; its interest for us lies in the contribution which Ottoline made with her description of Catherine Belasys, the Mother Superior of a convent.

Basing her portrayal of Sister Catherine on what she knew of Mother Julian's unhappy life before she became a nun, Ottoline described her as a woman whose worldliness had been 'purged in the fire of suffering, leaving it passionate still . . . passionate to *give*, not to receive . . . Was there regret for all she had missed? Sorrow and anguish for the pain she had caused, yes, perhaps – but above it all . . . there was a faith, obstinate and unfailing.' (28 June 1912)

To Bertie, it seemed that Ottoline had, with great insight, conveyed his own sense of herself in her evocation of Mother Julian. His alterations to her part of the story were few. The first person was changed into the third; a speech on the transfiguring power of love was inserted where Ottoline had left a gap with the simple instruction: 'Talk.' Drawing on one of his letters to Ottoline, he gave Sister Catherine 'a voice which held an agony of compassion for all the sorrows of mankind'. In an earlier description of her, he drew on another of his letters to present Sister Catherine as possessed of a beauty that 'spoke to the soul, not to the senses. All the sorrow and joy of the world lived in it . . . she seemed always to me the immortal mother of sorrows.'[4]

The descriptions of Sister Catherine are strikingly lyrical, but the most remarkable thing about *Forstice* is that a man renowned for the clarity of his thought and the beauty of his prose could have become trapped by his own confusion into writing in such a leaden style. At the time, however, Bertie was delighted; in *Forstice*, he thought he had demonstrated that it was possible to satisfy both of his mentors – and both sides of his nature. 'The discovery that love of truth springs from reverence has made a bridge for me between intellect and vision,' he told Ottoline on 26 August.

Bertie took the view that the best part of the novel was Ottoline's contribution; friends who were shown the work without being told of her collaboration agreed with him. But praise for the whole was disappointingly faint and he was hard at work on a new project by the autumn of 1912. *Forstice* was not dropped altogether – Joseph Conrad was shown it and praised the opening and conclusion in the summer of 1914 – but no further work was done on it. Later, appalled to think that he could ever have admired *Forstice*, Russell forbade it to be published until after his death and laid the blame firmly on Ottoline for the fact that it had been 'very sentimental, much too mild, and much too favourable to religion'.[5]

Ottoline had always recognised her own limitations as a writer, and she longed to transcend them. If Bertie had set out to think what would be most likely to make her happy, he could not have hit on a better idea than to ask her to collaborate with him on a quasi-religious project. (She had only been enrolled as an adviser on 'Prisons'.) Having never attempted anything more ambitious than some modest pieces of prose on moods and nature, she was as delighted to find how easily she could describe Mother Julian and her setting as by Bertie's surprising gentleness. The letters she posted across Lausanne to his hotel reflected a new mood of hope and confidence about their relationship:

It all comes back to this, that every moment is so full of a *great infinite* happiness. It has meant very much to me that I could help you . . . it has made me feel I can give you something else besides great pain.

I am *really really* happy now, darling . . . I feel so full of hope now for the future . . . if only we can keep the peace and depth of it in the days to come. (29 June 1912)

The journals told a very different story. No mention was made of the novel. The account went straight from a day at Ferney (where she wrote of Bertie's happiness and omitted to refer to her own) to a bland allusion to a pleasant day at Versailles before her return to London. Every reference to Bertie was preceded or followed by a eulogy of Philip's superior virtues and a forcefully-expressed preference for Philip's company. Read against the background of her adoring letters to Bertie, it is impossible not to conclude that the journals were being composed at this time for her husband's eyes. They offered a carefully edited version of the truth which was intended to boost his morale.

Further evidence of Ottoline's protective attitude to Philip is to be found in an incident which took place in mid-July, after her return to England, and which marked – at last – the end of her friendship with Henry Lamb. On 1 June, Ottoline had been joking to Lytton about how they would 'throw the beautiful Henry to Diaghilev to keep him quiet' when Nijinsky arrived in London, leaving Lytton free to court the Russian dancer. Lamb's behaviour the following month put an end to that frivolous scheme; there was no longer any question of his visiting Bedford Square.

I believe it came through his happening to hear Philip, who he liked, speaking of him as 'Little Lamb' to me, for he made a violent attack on him, saying very rude and violent things about Philip. At this I lost my temper – a very rare thing with me – and told him that he could not come to the house if he abused Philip, and I took him by the shoulders and shook him. Next day I received a note from him so bitter and odious that the wording is engraved on my memory.[6]

The shaking and the allusion to his height (he was considerably shorter than Ottoline) had been too much for Lamb, whose furious letter ended with the announcement that he had at last learned to pity her as a neurotic hypochondriac who could always be cured by a few parties. 'I think he is partly insane from egotism and vanity,' Ottoline confided to Bertie on 19 July, a view which was confirmed when Lamb telephoned the following week in a state of despair because he had not been asked to her Thursday party. He remained uninvited. The old intimacy had gone, but Ottoline, who wrote to Lytton on 16 July that she would never stop loving Lamb, 'whatever happens', found it hard to accept that the time for reconciliations had passed. She deserved it all, she wrote sadly to Lytton on 17 July, the day of the quarrel; Lamb had called her 'the scarlet woman', and he was right. Generous to the end, she sent her good wishes for the summer holiday which Lytton was planning to take with Lamb in Scotland.

Lamb's desire not to miss a Thursday party was understandable; with Nijinsky in London, Ottoline's gatherings had never seemed more alluring. To Bertie, who had been in touch with Dr Combe and had heard his views on the necessity for Ottoline leading a quiet life (see Appendix II), she teasingly defended herself by saying that she really couldn't miss the chance to show off a few celebrities and her pretty yellow rugs at the same time. But the real pleasure and excitement was, as it had always been, in bringing together people who would help each other forward or enrich each other's lives; it was this that she described as her instinctive, unreasoning passion.

Of all the artistic manifestations of the pre-war years, none caused so much excitement in London as the Russian Ballet. It was the Portlands' old friend Lady Ripon, a woman as famous for her affairs as for her love of dance, who made sure that Diaghilev and his troupe were properly welcomed by the philistine English in 1911. Having expected a circus act enlivened by bounding Cossacks, balletomanes were captivated by the exotic costumes and sets of Leon Bakst and by the daring choreography. Nothing so sensational had been seen for years; when the Russian Ballet returned in 1912, the names of the leading dancers, Karsavina and Nijinsky, were on everyone's lips. 'They, if anything, can redeem civilisation,' Rupert Brooke told a friend; the dance critic of *The Times* urged readers to welcome 'a whole range of ideas such as have never been seen before'.

Ottoline had never liked ballet; the old-fashioned ones that she had endured struck her as sentimental and artificial. Lytton's enthusiasm for the Russians had, she suspected, more to do with the muscular beauty of the male performers than their art. She had liked Nijinsky

TRIANGULAR RELATIONSHIPS

when she met him in Paris in June 1912, but it was, she wrote in her memoirs, only when she saw him in *Carnaval* that she joined the worshippers:* 'I was completely converted . . . he seemed no longer to be Nijinsky, but became the *idea* which he was representing.'⁷

Nijinsky made his first visit to Bedford Square on 12 July, when he and Leon Bakst came to tea after watching a game of tennis in the square's gardens where Ottoline had been lying on the grass, writing letters.† They returned the following week with Diaghilev, anxious to know whether his protégé was moving in the right circles. 'Duncan G[rant] of course became at once their pet – I saw Nijinsky looking him all over!' Ottoline reported to Lytton on 20 July. '[Frederick] Etchells, too, in spite of spectacles, I think was found attractive . . . I only asked very few – Duncan, Adrian [Stephen], Etchells, Epstein and Mrs Hilda Trevelyan who talks good French.' Bedford Square was approved by Diaghilev and, on 27 July, Ottoline gave her largest party of the summer with the dancer as her guest of honour. 'Come up in good time, won't you?' Ottoline wrote to Lytton, who was a little cross at not having been asked to the first party. 'Let *me* powder your nose! Who else would you like to ask or like me to ask to set you off?' (24 July)

Grateful though the guests were to be allowed to feast their eyes on the exotic visitor, Nijinsky's shyness and lack of English presented an almost insurmountable barrier; the fact that he was quick to express a preference for spending his afternoons at Bedford Square alone with Ottoline, who spoke excellent French, did not do much for her popularity. Lytton, taking his cue from her accounts of 'my adored Waslaw', spread the news that poor dear Ottoline was 'gaping and gurgling like a hooked fish' on the dancer's line.⁸ He did her an injustice. Ottoline, who later, together with Philip, helped to start the Nijinsky Foundation to raise money for him and his family (the committee held its meetings at the Morrells' home in its first two years, 1937–9) became one of the Russian's kindest friends. Her account of him in the memoirs is one of the most understanding that we have. 'He always seemed lost in the world outside,' she wrote:

and as if he looked on as a visitor from another world, although his powers of observation were intensely rapid . . . It was not easy to talk to him as he didn't speak English and his French was very vague, but we managed to understand each other, and he was glad, I think, of real understanding and appreciation of his serious work . . . There were at this time fantastic fables about him; that he was very debauched, that he had girdles of emeralds and

---

* But Ottoline's letters to Lytton suggest that it was *L'Après-midi d'un Faune*, which she saw in Paris in 1912, which converted her.

† This scene, recorded in Ottoline's memoirs, evidently inspired the poem by William Plomer reproduced in Appendix I.

diamonds given to him by an Indian prince; but, on the contrary, I found that he disliked any possessions or anything that hampered him or diverted him from his art ... He gave me a photograph of himself as he was in ordinary life and another to put by its side, as he was in *Petrushka* ... 'the mythical outcast in whom is concentrated the pathos and suffering of life, one who beats his hands against the walls, but always is cheated and despised and left outside alone.' ... Many years later, I found in Charlie Chaplin something of the same intense poignancy as there was in Nijinsky.[9]

Visiting the dancer in Paris in the 1920s, after he had been diagnosed as a paranoid schizophrenic, Ottoline was reminded of his vivid description of the Petrushka outcast as he sat in silence but with intelligence still seeming to flicker in the haunted eyes. She had the impression that he knew what was happening but was unable to break through the wall of silence he had imposed on himself.[10] It was better to remember him as he had been in the summer of 1912, staring enraptured at the tennis players or dancing around the drawing-room with little Julian in his arms.

While Nijinsky transformed her attitude to ballet, Bakst provided her with new inspiration for theatrical clothes. Several photographs of Ottoline after 1912 show her wearing an intriguing costume of tight silk trousers and a straight knee-length tunic. On a visit which she made to Vanessa Bell and Duncan Grant in 1916, she was described as having appeared at breakfast in a dress which 'might have been designed by Bakst for a Russian ballet on a Circassian folk-tale theme. Russian boots of red morocco were revealed under a full, light-blue silk tunic, over which she wore a white kaftan with embroidered cartridge pouches on the chest, on to which fell the ropes of Portland pearls.'[11]

Bloomsbury was not immune to the law by which the party-givers of Kensington, Mayfair and Chelsea put the furniture under dustsheets from the end of July until the summer heat began to wane. The beginning of August 1912 saw Lytton setting off in a mood of happy expectation for his holiday with Lamb while Ottoline steeled herself for two weeks at Black Hall ('very distasteful to me – but economical!' she told Lytton) followed by a visit to Broughton Grange, an Oxfordshire manor house which had belonged to Philip's family for two hundred years. Harriette Morrell had often suggested that it might provide a viable alternative to the cramped space of Peppard; Broughton had the additional advantage of being only a few miles from her own Oxford home.

Even the dullness of the last lunch in London, to which she had been summoned to translate Mrs Chadbourne's unremarkable observations on ballet to Leon Bakst, took on a rosy colour when Ottoline looked back on it through the veil of gloom which enveloped her stay at Black Hall. Dorothy Warren, Philip's niece, revealed that none of the Morrell family liked her and that 'Granny' thought she was a dreadful mother. Granny's feelings had already been expressed about Ottoline's ill-health and her reluctance to play poker patience every evening; her affection for her daughter-in-law was not increased by the fact that she had recently learned from Philip of Ottoline's involvement with Bertie. Full of resentment, Harriette Morrell did not try to hide her indignation; in one letter to Philip written in November 1912, she bluntly told him that he had made a very bad choice of wife. The lack of warmth was mutual: Ottoline confided to Bertie that she thought Philip's mother extraordinarily selfish for refusing to let Philip have so much as a footstool from her magnificent collection of furniture. Ottoline's letters to Bertie were full of complaints about the society in which she found herself, but the worst news came towards the end of the visit. When they moved on to Broughton, Harriette intended to go with them. 'She proposed herself and said, "I shall stay a week,"' Ottoline groaned to Bertie. '. . . I must grin and bear it . . . I think I shall try and collect *every* other friend possible and get them to come at the same time . . . so that they can all talk to her by relays.' (7–8 August)

They arrived at Broughton on 16 August and Ottoline busied herself with cleaning up the dusty rooms and deciding which were the most easily habitable – it had been badly neglected by the Morrells' tenants – while Philip romped with Julian under the tall trees in the garden. He, evidently, adored the house where much of his childhood had been spent; at first, Ottoline did not find it impossible to imagine living there. 'I think the country looks very charming, very secluded and old-fashioned,' she reported to Bertie on 16 August; 'perhaps I will grow fat and sleek and selfish if I live here much . . . I find I am longing to take you country walks, so do come, won't you. The trees and air and stillness are so delightful and will be a happiness to you too, I know, darling.'

Bertie needed no second bidding, especially when he heard that Philip would be out playing golf every day. Dissuaded by Ottoline from purchasing a motorbike for his visits, he meekly agreed that a hackney cab would serve the purpose quite as well. The weather was not propitious for romantic assignations – it rained relentlessly every day that he came to Broughton – but the lovers were still too full of happy memories of their month in Lausanne to care. Walking along the dripping lanes or huddling in the doorway of Broughton church, they made plans for Bertie to start looking for lodgings nearby, and talked about the miracle of their love. 'Isn't it wonderful, our union,' Ottoline wrote rapturously on 29 August. 'We seem to *grow* more and more into each other. No words can express all that your kiss makes me feel . . . It is just *heaven*.' Her only regret was that her letters were always 'so idiotic compared with your wonderful ones'; Bertie was quick to reassure her. Had she not written the best part of *Forstice*? Didn't she know how he adored her letters? 'I slipped away from all the mathematicians one moment,' he wrote when he was presiding over a session of their fifth International Congress in Cambridge on 22 August, 'and found your letter – oh such a joy it was – I kissed it madly many many times my Dearest Love.'

Bertie's temporary surrender to her vocational desires for him – he was even toying with the idea of writing a little history of the saints – could not dispel the increasing despair Ottoline felt as she stared out of the windows and tried to envisage a future at Broughton. Philip was locked in his memories of the house; try as she would, she could not share his enthusiasm. The views were quiet to the point of dullness; the long dark drive made it feel like a hermitage; the rooms, while pleasant, were unremarkable. It was a house without romance. Ever since Ottoline had fallen in love with Bolsover's fairy-tale keep on a hill, she had dreamed of finding a home in which to recapture something of its grace. This could never be done at Broughton. 'I tried bravely to hypnotise myself into liking it and pretending that we should be very happy there,' she wrote in her journal, 'but it was all useless, and I knew it was a hollow sham on my part.'[12]

An unexpected diversion presented itself in the form of a heartbroken visitor. Lytton's summer holiday with Lamb had been extended by a visit to Ireland, where glorious views were no solace for the awfulness of Lamb in one of his blackest moods. It rained every day and every night and, as they had decided to share a bedroom in a small and isolated hotel, there was no escaping each other's company. Cowering under a rug on the pretext of a chill which at least allowed him to stay in bed, Lytton plotted an early escape. 'I thank the Lord daily and hourly that I am *not* (no, I really am not) in love with him,' he wrote to a sceptical Ottoline on 14 August. '. . . Don't be surprised if I suddenly arrive at Broughton pale and trembling.' Oxfordshire was a long haul from the north-west coast of Ireland and Lytton had never been known for his consistency where Lamb was concerned, but a dramatic telegram reached Broughton four days later: 'Shall arrive tomorrow wire train later in need of your coraggio as well as my own.'* The following afternoon, a lank, red-bearded figure was let in by the maid and announced as Mr Strachey. Julian stared with interest at their peculiar visitor, so comically like one of her beloved

---

* *Coraggio*, meaning courage. Those were the days when it was thought elegant to break into Italian phrases; E. F. Benson's Lucia was the fashion's best-known exponent in fiction.

Mr Lear's drawings that she almost burst out laughing. (Lytton had grown his flowing ginger-brown beard since she had met him at Peppard in 1910.) Harriette Morrell winced and turned away as he fell into Ottoline's arms with a twittering cry; Philip murmured a word of welcome and fled.

Neither of the Morrells wanted Lytton to stay: Ottoline ignored them. A private sitting-room was prepared for him to work in and he was told to treat Broughton as his home for as long as he wished. Asked when their guest was thinking of leaving, she would not commit herself to an answer. 'Lytton has begged to stay until Friday,' she told Bertie on 3 September. 'P. is rather annoyed at his staying on but it was difficult to say no . . . Dear P. is very nervy and masterful sometimes and it tires me very much.'

Ottoline was already aware of Lytton's brilliance, but it was not until his visit to Broughton that she met the aspects of his character that she came to love best: the low-voiced, serious Lytton who came to the fore when he was reading aloud, and the giggling madcap who delighted in absurd jokes, gossip and games as much as she did herself.

At night Lytton would become gay and we would laugh and giggle and be foolish; sometimes he would put on a pair of my smart high-heeled shoes, which made him look like an Aubrey Beardsley drawing, very wicked. I love to see him in my memory tottering and pirouetting round the room with feet looking so absurdly small, peeping in and out of his trousers, both of us so excited and happy, getting more and more fantastic and gay.[13]

Lamb, the subject of many of their talks, made his own contribution by sending Lytton the drawing already mentioned of himself dangling his two helpless lovers from his puppeteer's strings. Ottoline was more amused than annoyed; her main concern was to reassure poor Lytton, shifting daily between hope and despair. Every day letters went off to Ireland, begging for another chance, pleading forgiveness for a poor child: 'Won't my papa come and open the door, and take me up into his arms again?'[14]

Papa would not come, but Lytton was feeling sufficiently recovered to write to his former love, Duncan Grant, suggesting that he might like to come and help relieve the tedium of life at Broughton. Rather staggered, Grant added a polite query to his refusal – was Lytton now the master of the Morrells' home and thus in a position to draw up their guest-lists?

He was not and even Ottoline was beginning to wonder if he would ever go. That question was answered only by their own eventual departure to Lord Henry's Berkshire cottage and by an unexpected offer from Alys Russell to lend Van Bridge to Lytton for a fortnight. Slightly guilty about the relief with which he had been shown the door, Philip sent a kind note after him, apologising for having been such an absent host. They were still hopelessly undecided about Broughton, he added, '... whether house or garden have any "capabilities" out of which something might be made; and if so, whether it would ever be good enough to outweigh the sordid dulness [sic] of the country around; whether Ottoline, with her romantic soul, could ever be happy there, whether any friends one liked would ever come and see us there a second time...'[15] Evidently, it was not only Ottoline who was uncertain.

They were not parted from Lytton for long. He had decided that two things were required to raise his spirits. The first was a bold change of appearance, the second a strenuous cross-country tramp which would bring him within striking distance of the Morrells at Churn. Warning was given of his imminent descent.

Very exceeding secret. I shall be ... in earrings! Yes! HUSH! ... Oh, *I* like them very much – so far – But of course civilised society – imagine its comments! I shall arrange my locks so that Pipsey* shall not see them – and you are *not* to tell him or anyone else,
Your eighteen year old Lytton
(25 September 1912)

He arrived three days later with a knapsack on his back and wearing yellow corduroy shorts. A proud toss of his burnished locks revealed the promised rings. Ottoline was entranced. 'What squeals of laughter and giggles and fun we had about it all,' she wrote. '... I was sad when he left, he was so well and full of fun and life and youth, adorable; and he and I and Philip had such delightful talks together.'[16] Lytton's malice was always enjoyable when someone else was the target; it amused Ottoline to hear Fry dismissed as 'a most shifty and wormy character', of Clive Bell 'strutting around in dreadful style' as the great art expert (he was helping Fry to set up the second Post-Impressionist show) and of Lamb as an unscrupulous brute: 'a more callous fiend never walked the earth'.

So witty, so charming – and so volatile. Could this really be the same man who had sobbed on her shoulder at Broughton? Could she really believe his vows of undying friendship? 'My nerves have got so shaken up lately by Roger and Henry,' Ottoline wrote to him on 25 October; 'I live in dread of you also shaking me and casting me off. Oh please don't. I should mind it too much.' Lytton was quick to promise that her humble servant would always be there 'to assist you to the best of his ability – and you will do the like by him, I hope. Our great-grand-children will see us gallivanting down Bond Street as nonagenarians, and gnash their teeth with envy.' (October 1912)

---

* Pipsey was the nickname given to Philip by their Bloomsbury friends.

TRIANGULAR RELATIONSHIPS

The only blight on Lytton's stay at Churn had been the fact that it collided with a visit from Bertie. Ottoline knew where her priorities lay and Lytton, who was by now reasonably well-informed about the relationship, had to settle for taking second place to 'that wretch Bertie'.

Wretched would have been the more appropriate word. '*Don't doubt that I love you always*,' Ottoline wrote, but such reassuring words were useless when Bertie fell into one of his depressions. What comfort was it to him to hear of her love when he always had to wait for her to spare the time from Philip? Was she never going to realise how much more valuable was the time she spent with him? While they were sitting on the downs, he broke down and cried.

In a long section which was excluded from her memoirs, Ottoline tried to analyse the problem. She did love Bertie, and she reproached herself bitterly for making him so unhappy and yet she could not help wishing that he would be a little less earnest. He seemed utterly unable to understand the other side to her character, the 'wild bohemian artistic side which never gets a look in except in my extravagance about colour and dress and pictures'. It was ironic that Philip, to whom she had committed herself, should be so detached ('any deep stirrings of passion rather bore him') while Bertie gave her a passion from which she was always drawing back. 'There must be some coldness of heart in me that I cannot fathom,' she concluded.[17]

Perhaps – it is never easy to be sure – she was dwelling on her lack of passion for Philip's benefit; how else are we to explain the fact that, only a month later, she was back in Lausanne with Bertie and telling him (on 23 October, when he returned to England), that she had never been so deeply in love with him?

While Bertie, back in Cambridge, worried over the dangers of introducing Wittgenstein to the Apostles who wanted Russell's brilliant and attractive young protégé to join them, Ottoline tried to deal with a last firecracker from Henry Lamb. Earlier in the summer, he had sent her a peace-offering of a picture of himself, naked, as a present.* Now, to his chagrin, he discovered that she had allowed Clive Bell to borrow it for an exhibition. 'Bell's bad faith is bad enough,' Lamb wrote, 'but what am I to think of your lack of understanding and imagination?' (7 November 1912) The explanation (Bell had taken the wrong picture from Bedford Square in her absence) was coldly received. Having heard that she was being treated (for her liver) with

---

* As late as 1956, Lamb was still trying to prevent this picture, 'The Walker', from being loaned by Ottoline's daughter for an exhibition at the Leicester Galleries.

radium injections diluted with milk, Lamb spitefully added that the best cure for her ailments was a dose of London society.

Predictable though Lamb's outburst was, Ottoline was depressed to think that she had earned herself another enemy with a spiteful tongue. Her fears that she was becoming the target of malicious gossip were not groundless – Molly MacCarthy wrote to Clive Bell that month (November), specifically to request him to stop spreading unkind stories about Ottoline. But there was nothing to be gained from worrying about it. 'I find that I rely more and more on you,' Ottoline told Bertie on 20 November, 'and am inclined to let "friends" drift away... The thought of you and your love is such a quiet conscious happiness to me...' Bertie, while moved, was temporarily too anxious about Wittgenstein's brief involvement with the Apostles to think about love. More prudish than Ottoline about homosexuals, he could not understand why she did not share his concern at the thought of his protégé falling under the influence of Keynes and Strachey. To his annoyance and surprise, Ottoline counselled leniency. Wittgenstein was young; what harm could there be in his making a few friends nearer his own age? Even after Wittgenstein had left the Apostles, she gently reproached Bertie for having been too harsh about poor Lytton. 'I have tried to buck him up...' she wrote to him on 28 November. 'He really has such a fine and noble spirit.' She was not to know how confident Lytton had been of scoring a victory with Wittgenstein. Following his visit to Churn, he had written to a friend that Bertie was looking haggard and 'about 96' since Wittgenstein had shown his preference for the Apostles. 'Bertie is really a tragic figure,' he added smugly, 'and I am very sorry for him; but he is most deluded too.'[18]

Ottoline's main preoccupation in the winter of 1913 was Julian's health, and it was for her sake that the Morrells decided to spend a quiet winter in the country. Broughton had been ruled out but Breach House, belonging to Philip's sister, Margaret, provided a good base in Berkshire from which to look for a more permanent country home.

Tuberculosis now began to be discussed for the first time as a serious possibility: Ottoline, never having shown much concern for her daughter before, became passionately maternal and the spiritual yearnings of her earlier letters to Bertie were replaced by copious references to her daughter. Julian was learning the piano, had danced nonstop at a little party arranged for her, had been so brave when she fell off her pony, had started to come into her mother's room in the evenings to watch her getting dressed for dinner. Augustus John had promised to come and paint her, for 'she looks so extraordinarily beautiful just now'. (Augustus forgot his promise and Dorelia came instead.) The new nanny, Mildred ('Billy') Townshend, was a difficult woman, but worth the irritation because Julian so loved her. The reformed mama even began adding to the 'Thought-Book' of sayings and prayers for Julian to study.

Life at Breach House was shaped by this new devotion to the child. Bertie, who had often rebuked Ottoline in the past for not being an affectionate mother, could hardly accuse her now of spending too much time with Julian; instead, on his second visit, he lashed out with one of the cutting remarks of which he was always capable when he lost his temper. It was a pity, he said, that she spent so much time reading books; he could assure her that it was a complete waste of her time. In her journal, Ottoline noted that it was one of the most hurtful things he had ever said, not least because of the contempt in his voice, but she made a quick recovery. By 4 March 1913, she was able to look forward to his arrival at the local inn and to say that he 'had found a way to win' her, and to make her feel so happy that any thought of breaking with him had left her mind.[19]

Concern for Julian gave Ottoline an opportunity to be unsociable; the few visitors who asked themselves to Breach House were disconcerted to find their hostess sitting placidly by the drawing-room fire with her box of silks and her books, describing the pleasures of a sequestered life with an enthusiasm which boded ill for the future of Bedford Square parties. Mrs Morrell came to inspect her favourite grandchild and to reproach Ottoline for having encouraged Dorothy Warren to think she could make a career as an actress; apart from Bertie's discreet appearances, Dorelia, Molly MacCarthy, Duncan Grant and Lytton were the only visitors. 'Do you remember a delicious walk we had in the winter and how we laughed?' Molly wrote to her later. Molly had evidently been on good form, but Lytton was deep in depression about his work and his social failure. 'I sat on my bed and he stood beside me, looking so dejected and despondent,' Ottoline wrote on 24 January; 'he seems to feel baulked in his life, doubtful about his writing; he says that he is no good at conversation so that he could never be a social success, that his small voice would prevent his going into politics, which he would rather like to do, but how could he ever make speeches with his thin tiny voice?' As he poured out this mournful tale, she longed to be able to show her sympathy by giving him a friendly hug. There had been an earlier occasion when Lytton had noticed her flinching when he kissed her cheek; now, once more, she shrank from contact and wondered how she was ever going to reconcile this physical fastidiousness with her longing to encourage and help her friends.

One of the reasons why the Morrells had been glad of the loan of Margaret Warren's home for the winter was that they were no longer comfortably able to rely on the prospects of Ottoline's inheritance. In May 1884, when Ottoline was ten years old, her brother the duke had taken out a life insurance policy on himself of £100,000, to be released to Lady Bolsover's children when it expired in 1912. The family letters, copies of which were now sent to the Morrells, show that on 16 May 1884 Lady Bolsover had made it clear that she wished this sum to be shared between her sons; none of it was to go to her daughter. The lawyers had pleaded with her to change her mind, but she was adamant. Instead of the handsome legacy which had been anticipated, Ottoline received £6,000, her share of the proceeds from the sale that year of her mother's old London home in Grosvenor Place. Ottoline, while still far better off than most of her Bloomsbury friends, was no longer able to be carefree about money.* It was with the knowledge of this setback that she and Philip began looking for a country house of their own while they stayed at Breach House.

Ottoline had caught her first glimpse of Garsington one moonlit evening in 1903 when Philip's sister Frederica, who owned some land there, was driving her back from a political meeting. Only five miles from Oxford just off the London road, it was an unusually pretty village, winding over the side of a hill up to the point where a Norman church overlooked a panorama of fields and wooded hills. There was already a strong family connection; the Morrells had been landowners in Garsington since the end of the eighteenth century. Philip, who shared his wife's enthusiasm when they made a second visit to the village in 1912, thought they might build a small new house; Ottoline instantly set her heart on the manor, a beautiful Tudor building framed on its forecourt by towering yew hedges. Once known as Chaucers, it stood on land which had belonged to the poet's son. The present owners had leased it out to a farmer, Joseph Gale who, happily for Ottoline's plans, died in January 1913. His daughter intended to remain at the semi-ruined manor house until the expiry of the lease in 1915, but the Garsington estate was put on the market. Lord Henry was ready to lend his sister £2,000 and on 15 March 1913, the Morrells paid £8,450 to become the owners of a dilapidated manor house, two farm homesteads, half a dozen cottages and 360 acres of farmland. The sale of a picture which Philip had bought and on which, with some difficulty, he now recovered the proceeds (his mother sold it as her own) allowed him to buy out Frederica's share of the Garsington

---

* Ottoline continued to receive an allowance of £200 a year from her half-brother, while the childless Henry, shocked by the revelation of their mother's strange behaviour, promised that he would take care of Ottoline's daughter in his will.

estate. By selling off half the land, Ottoline and Philip calculated that they could just afford to restore the house and start running the farm. Nothing could be done, however, until Miss Gale's lease ended in 1915. In the meantime, Ottoline's London friends could look forward to two more summers of glorious parties in Bedford Square. Of Ottoline's financial setback, they knew nothing at all.

Five months at Breach House followed by a week of fund-raising in Burnley gave Ottoline a hunger to be in London again; back at Bedford Square in April 1913, she grew intensely social. The high spots of a busy month were the making of a new friendship, with Gilbert Cannan, and the renewing of an old one, with Vanessa Bell. 'I went to tea with Ott.,' Vanessa reported to Roger Fry on 8 April. 'We had a most touching scene! She kissed me warmly and said how nice it was to be friends again. That the whole thing had been so dreadful, but we agreed that there was no need to go into that again! Then she kissed me passionately on the lips! And so we made friends and sat and had a long talk about things . . . I think she is really very nice though muddleheaded. One mustn't expect her to be clear about anything.'* Fry was galled; Ottoline had shown no sign of wishing to welcome him back into her house.

The friendship with Vanessa was restored, but it never became intimate. Ottoline did her best to believe that it was naïvety rather than mischievousness which inspired Vanessa to turn to Asquith at a Bedford Square dinner-party and ask if he took any interest in politics. A 1916 visit to Vanessa and Duncan Grant's home in Suffolk left her shuddering at the dampness and squalor of Wissett Lodge and amazed by Vanessa's pleasure in such merry japes as allowing her guest's cigarettes to be lit with firecrackers, but she tried to be tolerant: 'untidiness in sunshine does not matter . . . I enjoyed my visit all the same, for they were all free and gay.'[20] Such good-humour was quite beyond her hostess. 'We're recovering from Ott. whose visit nearly destroyed us,' Vanessa announced; '. . . I've decided that woman isn't for me. I can't stand it and hope I shall never spend more than a few hours at a time in her presence again – or at the most one weekend a year. This is final.'[21]

Thanks to the tactful interventions of Duncan Grant and Virginia,

---

* There is some confusion about the date of the reconciliation. Sandra Jobson Darroch (*Ottoline*, Chatto & Windus, 1976, p. 32) dates Vanessa Bell's letter to Fry as 8 March 1913. However, on 7 April 1914 Ottoline wrote to Bertie saying that Vanessa had just asked if they could be friends again, and that she had thought it 'much better to make it up. Divisions are very stupid in this life.'

Ottoline was never aware of Vanessa's contempt for her. She did not know how angry Vanessa grew when Lytton said that he thought Ottoline was creative, or how maliciously she was described in Vanessa's letters to her sister, or how Vanessa's children were encouraged to perform parodies of her before audiences which consisted principally of Ottoline's friends. Blissfully unconscious of all this, Ottoline continued to admire her dedication. 'Vanessa is beautiful as a Watts painting or a William Morris drawing,' she wrote. 'Her character seems to me like a broad river, not worried or sensitive to passers-by. She carries along the few barques that float with her . . . but the sea towards which she flows is her painting, above all the thing that is of importance to her.'[22]

Gilbert Cannan made his first visit to Bedford Square ten days after the *rapprochement* with Vanessa. His hostess was instantly charmed by a young man who seemed so clearly destined for a brilliant future. Her literary judgement was usually astute; the best that can be said in this case is that it was shared by Henry James, who thought Cannan one of the most remarkable writers of the younger generation. But James was always susceptible to handsome young men with good manners.

Racking her brains in later life to remember why she had been so eager to help Cannan, Ottoline decided that it must have been because he was being given a hard time for eloping with the middle-aged wife of J. M. Barrie, his mentor. An ex-actress, Mary Cannan was a lively, striking woman, strong-featured, strong-minded, and devoted to her young husband. Ottoline could not bear her. Cannan, she reported to Bertie on 18 April, was a charming young man, looking rather like a gentle Galahad as he shook his mop of fair hair and gazed into space, but Mary '– dreadful. I cannot think what can have made him go off with her except pity.' Instead of having interesting things to say about the theatre, she had talked about nothing but upholstery. When they came to dinner the following week, Ottoline did her best to banish Mary by telling her how tired she looked and urging her to go home and get a good night's rest. Mary offered a martyred smile, and stayed until midnight. 'Cannan is most attractive but I didn't talk to him,' Ottoline crossly reported; 'I feel it hopeless to try to make friends with him while his wife is there.' The following week brought a happy inspiration. The Cannans only had a country house; she had a London bedroom with a single bed. It was put at Cannan's disposal, and gratefully accepted. It goes without saying that the Bloomsbury gossips had a field day speculating on the nature of the friendship.

Julian's health remained too worrying for Ottoline to allow herself more than a month in London. She still had great faith in Dr Combe; at the beginning of May, she and Philip took Julian to Lausanne to see him, accompanied by a dour-faced Nanny Billy, who had never left England before. It was gratifying to Ottoline to find that the doctor's proposals corresponded with her own ideas; the little girl's strongest chance of recovery from what he now diagnosed as a liver ailment lay in peaceful surroundings, a careful diet and plenty of sun and exercise. The best of the Swiss child-clinics was at Leysin above Lake Geneva, where she could be taken in for a minimum of six months from October. (Rather young to be going to the University of Leyden, was she not? queried Lytton, struggling to decipher Ottoline's curlicues and dashes.) Nanny Billy agreed to be a martyr to duty and go with Julian to Leysin in exchange for a two-month summer holiday, during which Julian would be cared for in England by a clever but most unnannylike young Swiss girl, Marion Colomb, to whom Ottoline had taken a great fancy.

Hearing that Mlle Colomb was longing to meet a famous philosopher, Bertie remained sceptical about the whole enterprise; nannies should not be chosen for their brains and he had heard too many complaints in the past about how Julian interfered with her mother's plans to treat Ottoline's new-found concern for her with much seriousness. The notion of sending the little girl off to Switzerland struck him as cruel and absurd. 'You said it was a "fad of the rich" which was *horrid* of you!!!' Ottoline reproached him. She was eager to correct him: an old man she had met at the hospital had told her that Combe's writings and discoveries were 'quite marvellous ... especially wonderful about children'. (12 June 1913)

Reading Ottoline's memoirs and letters of the summer of 1913, the sense of a double life becomes overwhelmingly strong. On the surface, to be returned to in the following chapter, she was spending June and July in London in a whirl of social activity. Privately, she was riding out one of the worst storms of her life as Russell raged and beseeched and threatened in turn. She did not collapse; on the contrary, she made it abundantly clear that it was Russell, not she, who was dependent on the survival of their relationship. The man responsible for this new and most impressive resilience was Roger Vittoz.

Vittoz began treating Ottoline in May, after Philip had left his wife and daughter at Lausanne. No doctor could give Ottoline the good health she craved; what Vittoz offered instead was a way to control the emotions which played havoc with her physical well-being. His book, *Treatment of Neurasthenia by Teaching of Brain Control* (1911), suggested that nervous ailments could be controlled by simple mental exercises in which the patient learned to visualise a scene, a series of numbers or letters, and then to focus on eliminating a small part of it. As the patient grew more adept, a similar exercise was employed to control an instinctive response to powerful feelings. Joseph Conrad and William James both spoke highly of the influence which Vittoz had on their lives; in her memoirs, Ottoline wrote that Vittoz's treatment had a lasting effect in helping her to deal with traumatic experiences.

The letters which Ottoline wrote to Bertie from Lausanne in the last weeks of May suggest that she was practising her eliminating exercises with success, for she responded only to the cheerful parts of his letters. Seeking sympathy for his disputes with Wittgenstein and his worries about the 500-page opus on knowledge which he had started to write, Bertie was disconcerted to be met with accounts of boat trips, mountain walks and even of a young German confectionery-seller who had fallen in love with Ottoline when she took Julian to a circus matinée. Bertie only heard that Franz Kramer was besotted and had to be discouraged; Ottoline's private papers suggest that she had to use all of her new self-control not to have an affair when Kramer followed her back to England in June. A charming and handsome young man who came for a day 'of child-like divine love' (13 June) and also enjoyed several family meals at Bedford Square, he reminded Ottoline of the missing element in her relationship with Bertie, but she was more amused than infatuated, entertaining Lytton with accounts of 'the chocolate boy' and his pursuit of her to London.

Hints of this holiday flirtation did not trouble Bertie so much as a growing sense of her indifference. He did not think of blaming Vittoz; he only knew that he needed more than Ottoline seemed ready to give him. He wanted children. He wanted her to understand the agony it caused him when Wittgenstein demolished the ground on which he had planned to establish his new book, *The Theory of Knowledge*. He wanted, above all, to feel that she desired him as much as he did her. All through June, he saw nothing but a busy hostess for whom he was little more than part of a well-organised schedule. At the end of the month, there was a confrontation which caused him to declare that 'a scene of such degradation as yesterday's makes it impossible to stand spiritually upright in a person's presence again', and to add that he could no longer continue pretending to be happy in order to please her. They did love each other, he knew that, and she had been 'divinely patient and gentle', but neither of them gave the love which the other wanted. He was going to spend July with the Whitehead boys in Cornwall. Perhaps it was a good time to make the break. It was no good her expecting him to control his desire for her: 'instinct is too strong for me. However I behave, nothing but insanity lies ahead of me if we go on ... Nothing lives in me today but the fear of madness.' (28 June 1913)

Ottoline had heard it all before and she knew that Bertie was capable of changing his mind within a week. (It was, in fact, less than a day before he sent a telegram begging her to come to Cambridge.) It was silly of him to talk about insanity; 'that is *absurd*,' she wrote to him firmly after his letter reached her that night. 'It is simply nerves like I have had myself often . . . Naturally I should like to see you on Monday, but not if it is bad for you. You must decide . . . This all sounds so cold and hard but I am writing under difficulties and cannot express myself. I love you, love you my darling and only feel *intense* love and sympathy . . . My *darling Bertie*.'

This was the tone Ottoline adopted throughout Bertie's stay in Cornwall. Vittoz would have been proud of her. She was kind, dignified – and inflexible. When he modified his threat of separation to weekly meetings, she applauded his good sense. When he accused her of being unfeeling, she cheerfully agreed: 'Yes, I dare say it is true about my want of surrender – I have had in a way to build myself up on the other side to protect my health!' (25 July) Stung by such a buoyant display of independence, Bertie responded in kind. Returning from Cornwall, he announced that he was going to spend August walking with Charlie Sanger in the Alps before joining a group of friends, and that he would not be in touch. He preferred not to think about a woman who had no wish to be with him and who 'would rather ruin my life and work than be very much with me'. (10 August)

Not even the Vittoz exercises could prevent Ottoline from being distressed by such an unfair accusation. She was tired of being bullied, and she told him so, making it clear in a sixteen-page letter from Black Hall, where she was spending August, that she was no longer prepared to tolerate it. She wrote of ending the relationship – and added that it could only continue if it became platonic.

All Bertie's resolutions of detachment faded when her letter reached him in Italy; on 18 August, he wrote to admit that despite all he had said, 'I cannot face losing you . . . You hold the deepest depth of me, which no one else has ever touched, and from which no one else will ever dislodge you.' He was speaking the truth. None of his other love-affairs aroused the same spiritual intensity and naked emotion; no other woman fired his imagination so powerfully or enabled him to express his feelings with such ease. But he craved physical intimacy. Eight days later, he wrote to say that he had met a pretty German woman, a Frau von Hattingberg. He did not yet feel ready to have a physical relationship with another woman, but he wanted to warn Ottoline that this was becoming a real possibility.

12

INDIAN SUMMER
1913–14

'It is worth all the sufferings of hell to love as this.'
OM to Bertrand Russell, 20 January 1915

'Sometimes I feel that I have a terrible strength inside me.'
OM, *Early Memoirs*

'I do not regret my undertaking the Bertie affair,' Ottoline had written in June 1913 as she reluctantly abandoned her Swiss course of treatment with Dr Vittoz to travel home. 'It was the courageous thing to do . . . this really is the great thing in life, to risk censure and failure, and to step out with courage.' Vittoz had taught her how to control the emotional storms which Bertie was brewing up for her, but to learn self-control was not the same as to know peace. Her first reaction to the news that Bertie was going to Cornwall with the younger Whiteheads was of relief. 'I find an awful gap, and feel as if my occupation had gone,' she admitted on 6 July, but '. . . now I must pull myself together and work and read hard, and get my mind alert and detached.'[1]

Bertie's absence left Ottoline free to enjoy the end of the London summer, to study Italian (in order to read Dante), to be painted by Lytton's brother-in-law, Simon Bussy, and by Duncan Grant, and to go to one of Lady Ripon's smart lunches for the Russian dancers. (This was the occasion on which Diaghilev was horrified to hear Nijinsky drawing comparisons between Ottoline and a giraffe, before asking when he could next come to Bedford Square.)

It was not the prospect of meeting Nijinsky that brought Asquith's daughter Violet to Bedford Square so often that summer as much as the opportunity to talk to three great conversationalists, Henry James, Desmond MacCarthy and Wyndham Lewis. Fourteen years younger than Ottoline, Violet was the most brilliantly eloquent of the Prime Minister's children; having made up her mind to become Ottoline's friend, she invited her twice to stay at The Wharf, the family's country home in Oxfordshire. Flattered at first, Ottoline was quick to look for something more than scintillation in Violet's talk. She did not find it. Even when Violet spoke of an event as tragic as the recent death in an accident of her fiancé, the son of Lord Aberdeen, she seemed to be anxious to create an effect. 'I don't think we shall ever become intimate...' Ottoline wrote; 'we have such very different values in life. She really admires worldly success, and I never feel that matters.' She went on to compare the Asquiths' verbal accomplishment with the loquacity of her old friend, Henry James. There was no doubt that James took quite as much delight in hearing himself talk, but there was a solid fund of wisdom and experience behind his playful verboseness, while the Asquiths talked only to dazzle.[2]

Ottoline was moving in several different social worlds, as she loved to do. Henry James did not approve. An anxious guardian of convention who would have preferred to think of Ottoline visiting Welbeck rather than going to The Wharf or having ballet dancers to tea, he was appalled to hear that she was planning to visit his Polish country neighbour, Joseph Conrad. Up and down the grey drawing-room of Bedford Square he paced, his plump white hands gesturing his dismay. '"But dear lady... But dear lady..." he remonstrated, "he has lived his life at sea,"' although Conrad had spent more than ten years living tranquilly ashore; '"Dear lady, he has never met 'civilised' women. Yes, he is interesting, but he would not understand you."'[3] It was just the sort of remark to make Ottoline even more determined to meet him. No match for a strong-willed English lady, James agreed to write a letter and, having been given a date, Ottoline set off for Ashford, dressed, at Desmond MacCarthy's suggestion, in an elegantly eccentric dress. 'That was not difficult for me to supply,' she gaily observed, 'for my trouble was always to appear conventional and discreet.'[4]

The meeting was a huge success. Contrary to James's description of a rough-spoken sailor, Conrad struck her as having the air of a Polish nobleman. His manners were exquisite; his wife was kind and friendly, and she was cordially urged to come again soon. 'I stayed until 5, awfully nervous that I was there too long,' Ottoline reported to Bertie on 11 August:

but for myself I loved every moment. I told him that it was you who had given me his books and I described you a little and he said, 'Oh, I like mathematicians'... I know you would *love* him. I do... He was so easy to talk to. He said his writing was a terrible effort to him, but that is obvious. He also said that his health never recovered from the Congo. It was such a terrible moral shock to him. I longed to know more... Do go and see him when you come back. I felt underneath sadness that he was not more appreciated, and a fear that he wrote on too much the same as before.

There were further visits over a period of many years, but it was this first one which gave Ottoline the lasting impression of a man both frank and withdrawn, 'a tangled, tortured and very complex soul'.[5] Describing him in her memoirs eight years after Conrad's death, she found that 'even now, as I write this, I feel almost the same excitement, the same thrill of having been in the presence of one of the most remarkable men I have ever known'.[6] Reserved though Conrad was, he was quick to respond to the obvious sincerity of her interest and he liked her for the courtesy she showed to his wife, rudely ignored by most visitors. Ottoline's own account of her talks with him makes it clear that he felt utterly comfortable in her company and that there was no formality in their conversations about life and books.

It was only the English who were unable to take Ottoline seriously because she enjoyed looking theatrical; to Conrad, as to all her other European friends, it would have seemed absurd to judge her mind by her appearance. But something about her clearly attracted him enough to make him want to show off; the stories he most enjoyed telling her were of his wild days in Marseilles. He told her, too, of how he had first fallen in love with the sea when he went to Venice as a young boy, and of his struggles to learn English from the newspapers when he was living in a seaside inn. On another, later, visit, he confessed that he would always rather be among soldiers and sailors than intellectuals; she liked him for that. 'It was the simple adventurous Englishmen that he liked,' she discovered, 'but as a rule Conrad's talk was gay and witty. He liked to surprise you by some slight, swift sentence. I remember how, when we happened to talk of poetry and I was urging him to read T. S. Eliot's poetry, he professed that he never read it – "Oh, I'm not caught by poetry," he said, "not I."'[7] Was he joking, or not? With Conrad, half the charm was that she could never be sure.

Russell was fascinated by Ottoline's account, so much so that he went to see Conrad himself shortly after his return from Italy, but he was not ready to let go of the main subject on his mind. His resolve to put love out of his thoughts had crumbled as soon as Ottoline's letter of 16 August reached Verona; for the rest of the month, her stay at Black Hall was turned into an exhausting period of having to defend herself for not allowing him to have the complete monopoly of her time. Buoyed up by her Vittoz exercises and by livelier society than Oxford was usually able to provide in the high summer (Vernon Lee, Eugenie Strong and Ethel Sands were all there), Ottoline felt confident enough to stand up for herself with vigour and to tell him he had no right to accuse her of behaving like Augustus John who, in her view, 'kept his two women like slaves'. Who did he think was the slave in their case? 'I know I feel with you and P[hilip] that it is I who try to serve you both . . . I don't eat you up for my own use and pleasure . . . you say I want two people's whole devotion. I really don't get much devotion from P.' (21 August)

While Ottoline wrote about devotion, Bertie continued to brood about sex. What he really wanted from her was some sign of desire and it was not forthcoming: now, on the rare subsequent occasions when he succeeded in persuading her into bed, he was instantly made aware that this had been an exception to the rule. 'Yes my darling, I did love our day together the other day and I don't regret anything,' she told him on 22 October, 'but somehow I have an *instinctive* feeling that it is better not to let it happen in the future . . . our relation and intimacy has been so much better since it has stopped. But don't think I am unhappy because of the other day. I feel that [it] is worthwhile to make any sacrifices to keep it good.' Faced with such resolute coolness, it is not surprising that Russell grew increasingly restless. He reminded her that her behaviour might drive him 'to seek affection elsewhere, tho' I shd. always have the sense to keep out of anything serious' and hinted that their Christmas plan to meet up in Rome might be affected by the fact that Frau von Hattingberg was also going to be there. (26 November) If Ottoline was distressed, she kept it to herself.

It was probably as well for their relationship that Russell and Ottoline had little opportunity to meet during the autumn of 1913. He was working on the course of lectures he planned to deliver at Harvard the following spring while Ottoline was keeping her promise to spend some time among Philip's constituents. At the end of September, she went up to Burnley with Julian and the young Swiss girl, Marion Colomb, who was standing in for Nanny Billy. Ottoline took time off to explore the town, an inferno of sooty darkness dominated by the factory hooters and the clang of machinery. 'I *cannot reconcile myself* to thinking it is good for thousands and thousands of human intelligent creatures to live as these people live,' she wrote to Bertie and went on to tell him about the appallingly high rate of infant mortality and the lack of any form of welfare or rudimentary education for the mill-girls. (24 September) But these were just the kinds of things she could get something done about, Bertie told her when she expressed concern at the fact that they had no library, nobody to care about them. She took his words to heart. It was at her prompting that Philip, for Burnley, and Lord Henry, for South Nottinghamshire, started to press for an increase of women inspectors in factories and for a law to enforce the paying of compensation to the victims of factory accidents or, in the case of death, to their families.

Ottoline had been particularly distressed by the discovery of the number of young children whose deaths were taken as a matter of course in Burnley; it was impossible not to think of her own small daughter and of how cautious the Swiss doctors had been in their promises of a complete recovery. Julian was to start her course of treatment at Leysin in October; at Philip's suggestion, Marion Colomb stayed on in England. In later life, Ottoline was devoted to Marion, but at the time her intelligence and beauty could not make up for the fact that she was both lazy and unresponsive. Philip suggested that she ought to be introduced to the sights of London and to interesting people: Ottoline did her best. A tour of Lincoln's Inn, of the Catholic cathedral in Westminster and of Hampton Court were received with the same vague and incurious stare as a visit to Boris Anrep's new exhibition and a dinner with the hospitable MacCarthys. She refused to respond to the interest of the ex-Apostle Harry Norton, thought by Ottoline to be a perfect husband for her; she seemed, on the other hand, to be attracting a good deal more attention from Philip than was proper. But nothing stirred her. 'She is so frightfully passive,' Ottoline crossly noted. 'I long to shake her.' Lytton, too, was in a mood which was getting on her nerves. Capering around in her high-heeled shoes at Broughton or flaunting his new earrings at Churn, he was an enchanting companion; now, he was willing to do nothing but wrap himself in rugs and grumble about his health. Nothing could be done with him. Everything she suggested was 'so "difficult" to do', she complained to Bertie on 16 October. 'To go to the Tate Gallery is beyond his powers.' Hunched on his sofa with his long beard straggling down his blanket, he looked so old and depressing that she could not imagine what she had ever seen in him to charm her.

Lytton roused himself the following month when the Morrells set off for Italy, leaving him to wail at the dullness of London without his favourite hostess. What could it be that had taken her away from her social duties? he demanded with the gossipy asperity that never failed to amuse her. Was she having an affair? 'An escapade with John? Or an amorous adventure with an ice-cream boy?' (21 November 1913) Nothing so exciting, Ottoline demurely responded. She had merely decided to spend Christmas with her husband in Rome before they went to see their sick daughter. Lytton was not to be trusted with more information than that.

Bertie arrived in Rome, as they had planned, on 15 December and for the first four days, all went well. Ottoline found excuses to leave Philip while she and Bertie went on tours of the city and even on a day-long excursion into the country. But when Bertie appeared for their tryst at the Sistine Chapel to find that Philip was standing at her side, all his old insecurity returned. He had already issued his warnings about the German lady, who was due to arrive in Rome at any moment; now, he warned Ottoline that she must prepare to be betrayed just as, in his view, she had betrayed him. (Frau von Hattingberg's willing participation was taken for granted.)

There had been vague threats of infidelity before, but this sounded serious. Ottoline was torn between her wish to see Bertie happy and her desolation at the thought of losing him. She was going to Florence from Rome for a few days with Vernon Lee and then on to spend Christmas with Julian at Leysin; before leaving Rome, she arranged with Bertie to meet him in Switzerland, in a little village called Aigle, not far from the child-clinic. But first, sitting in the train bound for Florence on 21 December, she wrote to try to show him how much she cared:

I hope you won't find her *too* nice, but that is selfish of me . . . don't be too impatient or too much in a hurry to plunge into things. My darling darling love – I wish I could satisfy you more. It makes me so unhappy that I don't. I *long* to – and with all my soul . . . My darling darling, I *do* love you.

It may have been that Liese von Hattingberg was not so easily persuaded as Russell had expected; it may have been that she could not hold a candle to Ottoline. In Russell's later recollections, there was a liaison of some kind; at the time, he admitted that it had not been much of a success. 'I like her,' he told Ottoline at the end of December, 'but she does not touch my imagination, because I feel I can see all round her. I am not in love with her, and shall not be, nor she with me.' The discovery did nothing to raise his spirits. He arrived at Aigle in such a miserable mood that Ottoline decided that they must part, not for her good, but for his: 'about my own feelings I feel they must not come in,' she added to this declaration, posted after he left for England. 'I cannot well put into words all I feel – all the utter sadness and pain of separation to me.' (5 January 1914) She only ever had to use threats for Bertie to realise that he could not live without her. 'It would be spiritual suicide to give you up for the sake of peace,' he told her in his answer. 'It would not matter to give up physical things, and it would not matter to have other relations if they were compatible with our spiritual union – but that must not be broken. Whatever the pain, love is a sacred thing . . .'

The pain, in Bertie's tormented mind, was all his own; having chosen from the first to see Ottoline as a woman of unusual resilience, he seldom felt any qualms about the pain his behaviour might be causing her. The rest of her life concerned him only when it threatened to intrude on their relationship. One would expect the letter of a lover to the mother of a sick child to contain at least a passing reference to Julian and to Ottoline's anxiety about her. There was none. As to his readiness to give up 'physical things', Ottoline had only been back in England for a few days when he insisted that she should go to a doctor and have her child-bearing potential reassessed.

Ottoline was examined by a gynaecologist on 12 February 1914. She hated having it done; she had never wanted to confront the truth about her operation in 1907. He gave his verdict: 'there was absolutely *no* possibility, or practically none, of having a child.' Bertie's response was more than usually selfish; it was, he told her on 13 February, dreadful for him to know that he must relinquish all hope. Her news had left him feeling that everything was 'so useless'.

To be forced to undergo such a traumatic experience and then to receive such a heartless letter should have strengthened Ottoline's determination to put an end to the relationship: in fact, it had the opposite effect. On 24 February, she wrote him a long and loving letter, telling him that they could not be 'more fundamentally intimate with anyone on earth than we are with each other . . . the tie is too strong ever to be broken . . . you really have made a huge change inside me and are really important to me – I don't mean only in a personal way, but in building up something fine and good and religious inside me.' It sounds as though she was particularly anxious to affirm her love for him because a long separation loomed ahead. At the beginning of March she returned to Leysin while Bertie set sail for his three months of lecturing in America. The prospect of absence made both hearts grow fonder than they had been for some months. 'It is awful to have to leave you now,' Russell lamented. When he returned to England in June, he proposed to become an absentee lecturer from Cambridge and spend all of his time in the flat near Bedford Square.

Julian had thrived at the clinic in her mother's absence; photographs of her at Leysin show a strong little girl with cropped hair and a confident smile. She had made friends with a child in the next-door room. She knew all the doctors and nurses by name. Used to getting her own way with the devoted Nanny Billy, she screamed or sulked when Ottoline failed to comply with her demands for expeditions and shopping trips. Ottoline's sympathy was short-lived. It was bitterly cold and her circulation was bad; she was missing Bertie; there was nothing to do except read and write letters and, with Nanny Billy off on a well-earned holiday, there was no escape from Julian's tantrums. Well-meaning friends were anxious for news of the little girl's welfare: 'They all write condolences,' she told Bertie, 'and I have to write reassuring postcards.' (10–11 March)

The doctors would not hear of Julian leaving the clinic until mid-April, however healthy and brown-limbed she might appear; to Ottoline's dismay, they made it clear that they thought it her duty to stay at Leysin until then. A doting mother would have sensed how much love and support would be needed by a six-year-old child who had been exiled to a foreign hospital for almost half a year. Ottoline saw only that keeping company with a cross little girl was 'very tiring work if one isn't accustomed to it'. One wasn't: nannies were meant to look after this side of life. After staying for less than three weeks, coolly noting that Julian was distressed by her departure, she handed her over to Nanny Billy and returned to London.

Excuses can be found – she may even have subconsciously wanted to prove that she was a bad mother after the gynaecologist's diagnosis – but it was not kind behaviour and it contributed to Julian's enduring conviction that her mother disliked her, a conviction which was strengthened when she discovered that she was to spend most of her first year back in England under her Aunt Frederica's roof as a guinea-a-week boarder.

Three weeks at the clinic had given Ottoline a taste for gaiety; she was in her most ebullient mood as London plunged into its last riotous months before the war. Bertie was not on hand to chide her for deserting him, and life had seldom seemed more full of enticements. 'Everything seemed easy and light,' she wrote, 'as if the atmosphere had something electric and gay in it, imbuing everything with a lovely gay, easy quality, absorbing from it the worry and care and fret, and gilding it with possibilities of growth.'[8] Nijinsky, now married, had returned from touring South America with Diaghilev to set up his own ballet company; this rapidly proved too serious in its intentions for the commercially-minded management of London's Palace Theatre, which took the first opportunity to terminate his contract. Lady Ripon, furious with Nijinsky for having married a woman she described as an avaricious, anaemic Hungarian, had no sympathy; Ottoline's kinder heart was touched by the plight of the little dancer and his pregnant wife. In 1913, everybody had wanted to know him; now, nobody did. 'The world is a ruthless place to the artist who is not vulgar and pushing,' she wrote to Bertie at Harvard on 29–31 March; '... He is such a *pure* artist that I hope he won't go under. I am thankful he has such a delightful wife.' She went to visit them with her arms full of flowers and took care to invite them to the weekly parties where old friends and new chattered and danced to the music of Philip's new toy, a second-hand pianola, which freed him from the obligation of talking to the guests while he played for them.

Ottoline's quarrel with Roger Fry had not prevented her from continuing to be a staunch supporter and adviser to the Contemporary Art Society; in the summer of 1914, to her delight, she was appointed as their official buyer for six months.* One of the first purchases she made was of a farmyard scene by a young artist called Gilbert Spencer. A few weeks later, she decided to take Philip down for the day to the small house at Cookham in Berkshire where two tiny, red-cheeked men introduced themselves as Stanley and Gilbert. After lunch and an inspection of the studio, a converted bedroom where Ottoline picked out a selection of drawings for her own collection, the Morrells were escorted on a walk along the river-bank by the brothers and their old father, all rattling away with such vivacity about music and art that the last train to London departed unobserved. The Spencers were ready to faint with shock when Philip solved the problem by blithely hailing a passing taxi: nobody in Cookham had ever contemplated such an extravagance.

The brothers were quick to discover the warmth and goodwill hidden behind Ottoline's strange clothes and her shyly languid manner. She, too, was charmed by this family of brilliant midgets whose passionate discussions of music and paintings contrasted so remarkably with their simple way of life and their practical knowledge of the countryside. *Don Giovanni* was playing at Covent Garden the week after her visit to Cookham and Lady Ripon had offered her the Grand Box for the evening; remembering the Spencers' love of Mozart, she persuaded them to put aside their hatred of London and come to the opera. Clothes presented a difficulty, but two of her smallest male friends agreed to lend their suits. The suits were not quite tiny enough, but a careful arrangement of Ottoline's most voluminous silk cloak allowed Stanley and Gilbert to escape inspection as they scuttled up the stairs and into the dark. 'Once we were in the grand box we were safe, and I breathed happily. Their two ruddy faces and unkempt heads of hair just arose over the front, and their old father with his long white beard, and the mother, neat and trim in black with a white silk crochet collar, made I expect a comic picture – but nothing mattered. The music was divine, the performance the best I have ever seen or heard, and we were all perfectly happy.' Later, she was amused to hear that Lady Ripon had been bombarded with inquiries about the strange-looking party in her box.[9]

Hearing of Ottoline's eagerness to find the work of new artists for the CAS, Gilbert Cannan asked if he could show her the paintings of a brilliant young Jewish artist who was desperately in need of encouragement. Mark Gertler had learned his technique from pavement artists in the East End of London. William Rothenstein had

---

* 1915 is often given as the year in which Ottoline acted as a CAS purchaser, but her records leave no room for doubt that the earlier date is the correct one.

helped him to get into the Slade and he had recently been taken up (perhaps because of his Botticelli face) by the ever-generous Edward Marsh, patron saint of all struggling young artists and poets at that time, but he was still virtually unknown and very poor. Standing in his attic studio in Spitalfields, Gertler was shaking with excitement when he heard the visitors being shown up the stairs. Gilbert Cannan had not prepared him well; he was struck speechless by the vision of Ottoline towering over him in a purple-feathered hat and softly asking him to bring his painting of a fruit stall to her home to be seen by a few critics and painters. Gertler, naturally, was ready to do so and Ottoline went home to write about a boy 'who, with his small delicate frame and shock of dark curly hair looked almost like a girl, but who was in reality passionate and ambitious and exceedingly observant and sensitive'.[10] When he came to tea the following week, she listened with particular interest to his confession that he felt lost both among his own people and in the smarter social circle into which Eddie Marsh had been trying to draw him. His admission echoed her own sense of having a passport to several worlds and belonging to none.

The end of April found Ottoline in a very different milieu, but one to which she was becoming increasingly attached. Her happiest moments on her last trip to Burnley had been when the mill-girls started to give her impulsive hugs and kisses when she visited the weaving-sheds, and her Saturday afternoons at the football ground. Now, the news came that Burnley's football club had made it into the Cup Final and the fans came south in a stream of charabancs to cheer their boys on. Ottoline was thrilled. She showed them round the House of Commons with Philip before going off to the Crystal Palace to see them win the match ('more than I ever expected!'); at the celebration dinner which followed at the Connaught Rooms, she drank out of the victory cup, made them all sign her menu-card, and was immensely flattered when the team begged her to go north with them to join the triumphant parade into the city. To bring them luck, they said. 'They look on me as their mascot!' she told Russell with glee on 27–28 April. 'So there! I am really going up in the world, aren't I? ... It is an odd situation that sort of life invading the London life – I really think Burnley is nicer.'

The comparison in Ottoline's mind was with the Asquith set she had come to know the previous summer. It was they who were also in her thoughts on 1 June when she wrote in her diary that she was only interested in genuine friendships and that she was determined to see that Bedford Square remained free from 'foolish gossip and spite ... This all sounds very priggish,' she added: 'perhaps I am catching it from Bertie.'[11]

Philip's career did not allow for too much scorn; on the contrary, her eagerness to promote it made her a regular attendant at the

Asquith court. In April, she had been one of the honoured few to be invited to Violet's twenty-sixth birthday party at Downing Street; in May and July, she gave parties in the Prime Minister's honour and stayed at The Wharf again, wearing, on one occasion, a feathered turban and green silk trousers to show off her uncommonly long legs. Outshining Margot was never a good idea, but Asquith was enchanted and Violet professed to think her one of the most wonderful women she had ever met. 'Dearest, you don't know how different life is with you in it,' she gushed in May and, a few weeks later: 'I long to be with you above all people.' Violet took a strong interest in politics and during this period she was Ottoline's best informant about the Ulster crisis, which threatened to put her father out of power.* (Talking to Ottoline at The Wharf on 28 June, Asquith confessed that he had welcomed the assassination of the Archduke Ferdinand and his wife at Sarajevo that week as a diversion from the Irish problem!)

Of the two parties which Ottoline gave for Asquith that summer, the one in May was the smartest and largest, an occasion from which the frolicsome young were firmly excluded in favour of the great, the good and the interesting. Lytton, lying modestly in the third category, struggled to sound grandly detached in his diary. He could not, however, resist boasting to his brother James about the way Ottoline had singled him out and led him to Asquith's side. The company had been 'most distinguished and the whole affair decidedly brilliant', he told James after throwing in an account of the tête-à-tête he had later had with Lady Howard de Walden, the music-loving young wife of Ottoline's cousin. Even Ottoline was allowed to have been 'remarkably at her ease' in a dress of gold brocade. Lytton was impressed.[12]

The second occasion was a small dinner party given in July, ostensibly because Asquith had professed a desire to meet Russell on his return from America. The Prime Minister's letters to Venetia Stanley suggest that Ottoline may also have been providing a little cover for their discreet relationship: 'Do come to Ottoline's,' he urged Venetia. 'Couldn't you even manage dinner there? Do try.'[13]

Why, with such close connections with Asquith and with an unblemished record of loyal support, did Philip Morrell fail to gain a more influential position than that of Member for a small and relatively insignificant constituency? Anti-armament views were no disqualification from power before the war and the irritation which both he and Ottoline felt at what they saw as Asquith's inept handling of the Irish situation was never publicly expressed. One possible expla-

---

* This was the Home Rule crisis: the Liberal Party had committed itself to supporting Home Rule from Dublin, while the Conservatives supported the Ulster Protestants in their fierce opposition to the scheme.

nation suggests itself in a letter from Ottoline to Bertie of 18 June.

> I have had rather a fright about Philip. He arrived here last night at 9 o'c saying he had had a 'horrible and awful experience'. It turned out that one of these odd excited times had come on him while he was speaking in the House and he had said all sorts of things he had not meant to say. It was on Persia. (It does not read too badly in Hansard . . .)* but altogether it upset him too dreadfully and for hours he was very ill. I walked him up and down and I am thankful to say he did not turn against me. He really was not nearly so bad as before. I sent for a doctor. He thinks it is purely nervous trouble.†

It was evidently not the first time Ottoline had been made aware that Philip suffered periods of mental instability, but it may have been this unfortunate episode which put an end to any chance of his being elevated from the back benches to Asquith's Cabinet.

The pleasure of discovering an apt and congenial pupil at Harvard in T. S. Eliot had not been much compensation for the lack of attractive female company during Russell's three-month stay in America. As far as Ottoline knew from his letters, he had been counting the hours until he saw her again. Her suspicions were not aroused when her lover casually announced that he would be visiting a Chicago family called Dudley just before his return to England, although she might have picked up a hint of possible trouble from his reference to having known one of the Dudley girls some years earlier. On 1 June, the day before he set sail, Bertie wrote again, to assure her that 'I am longing to be with you again, my Dearest' before dropping his bombshell. After finding in the space of a few hours that 'I care for her a great deal', he had spent a night with Helen Dudley. She would be coming to England at the end of the summer. 'I do not want you to think that this will make the very *smallest* difference in my feeling towards you,' he hastened to add, 'beyond removing the irritation of unsatisfied instinct. I suppose it must give you some pain, but I hope not very much if I can make you believe it is all right and that she is not the usual type of American . . . The impulse that came over me was like the impulse to rescue a drowning person. And now, Darling, goodbye until we meet and do not let this prevent the happiness of

---

* Hansard's parliamentary reports were designed to present the speeches in an intelligible form, not to provide a verbatim account.

† It was fashionable in pre-war years to ascribe mental illness to a nervous condition; this is clearly what Ottoline had been given to understand, and why she was reassured.

meeting if you can help it. My deepest most intense devotion is with you always.'

Ottoline did not reproach him. Noting that Bertie blithely supposed that he would now be able to keep both relationships running in tandem, she told him in unemotional terms that this would not be possible. Nobody could be more pleased than she to hear of any relationship which might bring him 'more real *happiness* than you have ever yet known', but he must expect no more from her than that approval. As to their own reunion – 'When you and she have settled your life and are unified and solidified I think we could meet . . . I should like to be friends with her as far as possible. If you very greatly desire to see me I will do so, but I think for *both* our sakes it is *better not*.' (12 June 1914)

It was the response Russell should have expected from a proud woman, but it was not the one he wanted. It had never been his wish to lose Ottoline; on 23 June, he wrote again to seek her approval of his keeping another woman as his mistress, while retaining a spiritual friendship with her. 'If you could believe it, I could really have a much better relationship with you (if your nature permits it),' he told her, 'if I were not dependent wholly on you for what it is so hard for you to give . . . Physical instinct, at least in me, is not satisfied by the physical act alone, but cries out for constant companionship, especially in the night.'

If she could believe it; if her nature permitted it. It should come as no surprise that Ottoline was unwilling to give him an answer. The reference to the nights which they had promised Logan Pearsall Smith they would never share was a cruel cut, but she may have been shrewd enough to guess from the way Bertie was talking about Helen Dudley that she was never going to become serious competition. Two weeks later, Bertie was expressing the hope that Helen would find somebody else to love when she arrived in England. By mid-July, he was talking of going to Europe for August; Ottoline gracefully forbore to comment on the convenience of a holiday which would remove him from England just as Helen and her father arrived.

In his autobiography, Russell claimed that it was the shock of war which killed his passion for Helen; his letters make it clear that his passion had already dwindled to the height of a match-flame. The chief reason for this was Ottoline's response. On 11 June, before hearing of his involvement with Helen, she wrote to tell him that she wished their relationship to become entirely platonic; when Bertie arrived in London four days later, she arranged to come to his flat. Neither of them was quite sure what to expect; neither could have anticipated the ecstasy they evidently enjoyed. Jealousy of Helen may have played a part in heightening Ottoline's feelings; so, less romantically, may the fact that Bertie's pyorrhoea had been treated while he was in America. All that is certain is that their sexual relations now entered a new phase of blazing intensity which obliterated the image of Helen Dudley.

The threat of war had been hanging in the air for weeks; when Ottoline visited The Wharf on 25 July, she was surprised to find that only Edwin Montagu, the Financial Secretary to the Treasury, appeared to think that Britain would be playing more than an observer's role. The German threat to Belgium was mentioned, but Ottoline noted that Asquith and his colleagues were eager to absolve themselves of any duty to lend assistance. Three days later, Austria and Serbia were at war, Russia was mobilising her troops and France was expected to follow suit, but when Ottoline went to tea with Violet Asquith, she heard that the Foreign Secretary, Sir Edward Grey, had still given no hint about Britain's likely involvement.

War was in everybody's thoughts and Ottoline was shocked to find that although most of her friends were in favour, none of them had any clear understanding of what the conflict would be about, other than the humiliation of Germany. 'Things look blacker and blacker,' she wrote on 31 July to Bertie, who shared her anxiety. 'We had a few people in last night, Hawtrey and Eddie Marsh and Humphrey Paul and Lytton – all of them desperately jingo, longing to rush into the war at once. It seems absolute madness to me. They attacked Philip violently because he was in favour of keeping out of it . . . It seems quite extraordinary that a thing that affects every human being in this country should be decided by quite vague ententes and without any consultation with democracy . . . there is a passionate desire to annihilate Germany.'

Two days later, France and Russia were formally at war with Germany. Looking down from the Bedford Square windows at the bands of young men singing the Marseillaise and waving flags as they marched past, Ottoline felt sick with horror. To be so young and so thirsty for bloodshed without any knowledge of what it was that they were undertaking . . . The following day, she told Philip that he would have to address the House of Commons on the need to remain neutral.

It must have taken Philip enormous courage to make such a speech when his colleagues were burning for involvement. He had already heard the House roar approval for Sir Edward Grey's declaration that Britain would enter the war if Germany dared to invade France or Belgium. Ottoline was watching from the Ladies' Gallery as he made his protest. 'I can never forget seeing him standing there alone with nearly all the House against him, shouting at him to "Sit down",' she wrote.[14] Ignoring them, Philip spoke on, to warn them that they were being asked to go to war not because of an invasion but because the presence of some German troops in a corner of Belgium was providing an excuse to attack a country whose ambitions were feared by the British. Honour, he went on, had nothing to do with it. If Britain entered the war, it would be wise for them to consider the support they would be giving to Russian despotism. He was greeted with howls of scorn. Nevertheless, his speech provided a rallying post for the small number of MPs, including Ramsay MacDonald (Labour) and Arthur Ponsonby (Liberal), who were opposed to hasty intervention. In Burnley, the Liberal Committee met and wrote to tell Philip that they had given him a vote of confidence, before spoiling the effect by revealing that the vote had been a secret which they asked him to keep. The truth of it was that his brave speech had destroyed any remaining hopes of a larger political career.

Russell had gone to the House from his flat in the hope of hearing the speech. Having failed to gain entrance to the Public Gallery, he had to wait until the next morning for Ottoline's account while they wandered listlessly around the streets of Bloomsbury. The news they had dreaded hearing came at midnight. Britain was at war.

It cannot be easy to hold fast to your beliefs when the tide of patriotic fervour is rushing against you. To do so requires integrity, commitment and courage. These were the qualities which were singled out in the hundreds of tributes which arrived at Gower Street after Ottoline's death. She could suffer agonies of indecision over a guest-list or a piece of material; in a crisis, she never doubted where she stood. 'Sometimes I feel that I have a terrible strength inside me', she once wrote almost guiltily, but she had no cause to be ashamed of it. Russell had always admired her courage; in the early stages of the war, she became his rock, the only person he could rely on to remain true to her beliefs. She was 'a very great help and strength to me,' he wrote in his autobiography. 'But for her, I should have been at first completely solitary, but she never wavered either in her hatred of war, or in her refusal to accept the myths and falsehoods with which the world was inundated.'[15] His tribute is confirmed by one of Ottoline's earlier war letters, in which she asked him to prepare a short manifesto for the dissident Liberal MPs – 'not for the purpose of embarrassing the Government now, but so that at a future time we may bring pressure upon them in favour of peace.' Fearing that even Bertie was beginning to waver, she urged him to stick to his convictions. 'Yes, it is *hard* when everyone argues against one . . .' she told him, 'but I do *really* feel firmer than ever . . . I feel I would like to do all in my strength in the years to come for the cause of universal peace.' (7 August 1914)

Ottoline had already made a start by letting it be known that there would be no compromises. 'I find it very difficult to see my old friends who are in favour of war,' she wrote in her diary. 'It is almost impossible to talk to them without quarrelling, and I feel a disgust for them, that they can be carried away by such a terrible false emotion, and not divine the inner horror of it all.'[16] While Russell reeled under the shock of finding that even his old friends the Whiteheads thought that the right course had been followed, and that Wittgenstein, who had enlisted in the Austrian army against Russia on 7 August, must now be considered as one of the enemy, Ottoline resolutely cut herself off from anyone who did not share her views. Lytton, whose attitude at this time seemed to her 'quite inhuman and cruel', found himself temporarily excluded from her home; Violet Asquith was told that she must start looking for other friends. While there was no direct confrontation with Harriette Morrell, Ottoline made it clear that she could not condone her anti-German fervour. The only family towards whom she was unable to feel any hostility for supporting the war was her own; her brother Charles's endeavour to be sent to the Front was the understandable response of a professional soldier; she was full of sympathy for the Portlands when their older son, Lord Titchfield, went out to Belgium in the Life Guards. (The younger son, Morven, was still a schoolboy.)

The arrival in London on 8 August of Helen Dudley and her father briefly diverted both Russell and Ottoline from larger matters. Bertie was in a state of panic; his first reaction was to rush to Ottoline and beg her to rescue him in whatever way she thought best. To be given power in such a situation was not disagreeable; Ottoline agreed to do what she could. First, she told him, he must explain his feelings, or rather, his lack of them, to Helen; in doing so, he must be sure not to refer to her by name. If no connection was made, it would be the easiest thing in the world for him to suggest that Helen might like to meet an old friend who could help and advise her.

All went according to plan. Russell, while not quite up to telling Helen that he did not love her, managed to convey his need for a period of reflection, after which he beat a hurried retreat from London for a few days. On 13 August, Ottoline kept her part of the bargain and invited Helen to come to tea. Miss Dudley was not quite what she had expected: 'an odd girl of about twenty-seven, rather creeping and sinuous in her movements, she had a large head, a fringe cut across her forehead, a very long chin, rather underhung, with thick lips.'[17] Privately, she found it hard to imagine what Bertie could have seen in her, but she told him in a letter written that evening that

Helen 'had a fine side in her' and that she would certainly invite her again if he thought it would help.

Helen was most gratified by Ottoline's concern for her welfare. After her father's return to Chicago, she arrived at Bedford Square with a large number of trunks and asked if she could be allowed to stay. 'What could I do but acquiesce?' Ottoline wrote.

The boxes were filled with masses of very over-decorated cheap and vulgar underclothing and dresses. Her room in fact was rather like a secondhand dress shop. I was extremely sorry for her, coming over with such hopes and preparations for a honeymoon. She seemed almost like a beaten caged animal, for she would endlessly pace up and down her room like a panther, pouring out all her disappointment and handing me B's letters to read.[18]

The letters were a shock. Ottoline had not expected to be shown near replicas of the ones Bertie had written to her. 'The disillusionment is devilish hard to go through,' she admitted to herself, but pride forbade that she should let Bertie know how much he had hurt her. She remained brisk and practical: 'After all I suppose the vocabulary of love is limited!!' she wrote with a brave stab at insouciance before trying to reassure him about Miss Dudley. '. . . I think she will get over it. She is full of vitality and may fall in love again perhaps before very long.' (22 August 1914)

This was too optimistic. Helen was a tenacious young woman and she was not yet ready to believe that the battle was lost. When Russell refused to answer her letters, she took to going to Bury Place and hammering on the door of his flat. She always knew when he was there, she told Ottoline with painful honesty; she could hear him breathing on the other side of the door. What she did not know was that it was often two people who were listening in silence as she begged for entrance. 'It was wonderfully happy today,' Bertie told Ottoline after their meeting on 25 August, 'tho' it was painful when Helen rang at the door – it seemed so intolerably brutal.'

The presence of Helen and the fact that the lovers were conspiring to discourage her added a new edge of excitement to their affair. Ottoline's letters were more overt and directly passionate than they had ever been before. 'Yes, indeed,' she wrote on 26 August, the day after Helen's fruitless assault on the flat, 'nothing has ever been so wonderful as these moments. We are absolutely one, all the hindrances and barriers gone and just the absolute union between us. All my being, spiritual and [emotional? *illeg.*] and physical flowed with you . . . I felt it so yesterday but it grows and grows . . . I wish I could come round to you myself tonight, but it is impossible. My darling darling love . . .' Two days later, after assuring Bertie that he was doing the right thing in refusing to see Helen – 'far better to be firm' – she returned to the new joys of their physical intimacy, telling him 'how wonderful every time is to me, my darling . . . I love to feel that you take possession of me more and more.' (28 August)

Helen was no longer a threat, but she was getting on her hostess's nerves. She had high hopes of making a name for herself as a poet and there were many occasions when Ottoline returned home to find that her guest had taken over the drawing-room to entertain a visitor, a sheaf of poems on her lap while wreaths of cigarette-smoke coiled around her head. The fact that the visitor was invariably male suggested that Helen was less devastated about Bertie than she liked to claim, but every night there was a tap on the bedroom door and in she came for another embarrassing conversation about her love for him. It was a situation which discomforted Ottoline, but she could not help thinking that Lytton would be amused by it. Rashly, she dropped a hint of what was going on and was paid back a week later when, to her horror, Henry Lamb telephoned to ask for more details. There was nothing for it but to swallow her pride and write a grovelling letter to Lytton, begging him not to tell anybody else and assuring him that there was, despite what she had said, 'nothing in it as regards B.R.' who would be in '*great trouble*' if Alys Russell heard of this new involvement. (30 September)

By mid-September, Ottoline had decided that Helen must live elsewhere. After being sent to stay with the Cannans as a paying-guest at their country home, she was encouraged to take rooms of her own in Chelsea, well out of reach of Russell Chambers. Bertie was no longer interested in helping her, but Ottoline went to the trouble of finding her a job and continued to invite Helen to Bedford Square at least once a week.

It is hard to be sure how much Helen ever knew about Ottoline's relationship with Bertie; it may have been that she remained completely unaware of it. When she returned to London from a fortnight's visit to America at the beginning of 1915, Ottoline was her first port of call. 'Fancy Helen being back! What a bore!' was Bertie's cool response; he was irritated to find that Helen had been invited to Garsington a few months later when he too was visiting Ottoline's new home. Absence had not lessened Helen's passion and other guests claimed to have heard her knocking at Russell's door, begging to be let in.

Helen Dudley's subsequent history was a tragic one. In 1924, she was diagnosed as having multiple sclerosis. When Bertie visited the Dudley family in 1927, they told him that Helen had suffered a total mental collapse. She never recovered. Until insanity set in, she had remained unswervingly affectionate in her memories of Russell. 'Her sweetness of temper was remarkable,' Ottoline wrote in her memoirs, 'and I don't believe she ever felt a grudge against Bertie. She accepted what came.'[19]

Helen Dudley had scarcely been despatched from Bedford Square before another triangular relationship began to take shape: the curious twist to this one was that it was engineered by Ottoline.

Vernon Lee arrived in London from Italy in October 1914. Accompanying her in the familiar role of the *culte* was a girl whose slightly Spanish beauty gave her the look of a much younger Evelyn Whitehead. Her name was Irene Cooper-Willis. Ottoline, meeting her at lunch with her old friend, was struck by her intelligence and composure and shocked by the way she allowed Vernon to bully her. After taking Irene to a Bernard Shaw lecture, she arbitrarily decided that Bertie was the man to emancipate her; at the end of three weeks of fruitlessly urging him to take this interesting young woman out for a meal, she succeeded in bringing them together at a Bedford Square party where, according to one observer, Russell showed every sign of being enthralled by Irene; she, rather less so. Initially, her coolness intrigued him. By the end of December, Bertie had decided that she would suit his physical needs very well; in the meantime, he began to employ her as a part-time research assistant. Already impatient to quit his post at Cambridge and embark on a course of political lectures, he was soon looking on Irene as a potential part-time consort in his new life. He had not yet discussed the matter with her, but Ottoline was confident that she would be in favour of the idea and that she would, in time, provide him with the children he so desired. Vernon, while unaware of the future that was being plotted for her companion, grew nervous enough to announce that it was time for them to return to Florence. 'I think you ought to urge her [Irene] to stay,' Ottoline told Russell.

By the beginning of January 1915 Bertie was growing alarmed at the way Ottoline was urging him on. It was true that he had initially sought her approval of his affair with Helen Dudley, but he had never intended that she should be quite so active on his behalf. Ottoline, too, having heard that Irene was beginning to respond to Bertie's advances, grew anxious. What if she should turn out to be something more than an obliging vessel and child-bearer? Could she really trust herself to rise above jealousy? When Bertie wrote to accuse her of trying to get rid him by palming him off on another woman, Ottoline met the charge with passionate indignation. All she wanted, she told him on 9 January, was his happiness: surely he could understand that her only motive was one of generous concern. 'I know she could not fully satisfy you, but I saw, and *you said* she made you happy and kept you from feeling lonely ... and naturally I wanted [you] to feel that

I *understood* and that really I don't think it would interfere in what is so infinite between us.'

Perhaps it took only the thought of losing him altogether to trigger her emotions; certainly, Irene seems to have been responsible for a new surge of desire between Ottoline and Bertie. On 15 January, Ottoline told him that she wanted to break the embargo and spend a night with him. On the 17th, Bertie wrote a note on her letter: 'This Tuesday evening was the gate of heaven.' Ottoline, too, was in a state of ecstasy. 'Last night I could only go on my knees in deep awe and thankfulness that such wonders had been given to one,' she told him on 20 January. 'It was simply unearthly, wasn't it? Every *moment* of it up to the last ... It is worth all the sufferings of hell to love as this.'

The plans for Irene had not been abandoned, but Ottoline now saw them in the light of a test of her love. 'These days of happiness make it in some ways more difficult,' she confessed, 'but I *will* be good. I *will* be good. I *will* be good.' True to her word, when Irene came to Bedford Square to ask what she ought to do, Ottoline talked only of Russell's loneliness and said that she must do whatever she felt was best for them both. It was Bertie himself whose romantic soul was crushed by the icy calmness of his prospective mistress. The relationship had not progressed beyond discussions and a few embraces. His inclination to carry it further ended on 18 January when he received a friendly but rather governessy letter from Irene, saying that she would be quite ready to have an affair with him if it did not interfere with any other relationship. '"I should be very unhappy if your caring for me in any way diminished your friendship for Lady Ottoline, to whom, besides, and to Vernon, I owe you and most else,"' she went on in a letter which Russell promptly related to Ottoline. He continued to employ her, but he was no longer interested in making love to a woman who showed herself to be so lacking in passion. 'I have a real and great affection for her,' he told Ottoline a few days later, 'but I do like people to be willing to shoot Niagara.'

The situation had resolved itself painlessly by the end of February. Russell and Ottoline continued to celebrate the new-found glory of their love while Irene quietly, and perhaps thankfully, withdrew. 'Irene does not come to the Thursdays now,' Ottoline noted on 19 February 1915. 'I expect what you said is true. She finds us too complicated!'

13

NEW FRIENDS, NEW FOES
1914–15

'I put on my great full yellow silk embroidered dress on our last Thursday evening, and made my curtsey to the company, and said to myself and Philip, "This play is ended," and with a sad heart put out the lights . . .'

OM, *Early Memoirs*

When the war-fever of August subsided, there still remained the question of patriotic duty. Lord Henry Bentinck, who detested violence, reluctantly followed his younger brother to the Dardanelles.* Duncan Grant entered the National Reserve. Clive Bell talked of getting himself attached to the Army Service Corps, a non-active unit. Henry Lamb went to work in a French hospital being run by Lady Guernsey before he was sent to Salonika with the Northumbrian Field Ambulance Corps. Stanley Spencer joined him there, as a private, in 1917. Lytton salved his conscience by knitting scarves for the soldiers, while taking German lessons in case the other side should win. But the early jingoism had gone. Among the Bloomsbury women, only Molly MacCarthy was unexpectedly warlike.

By October, Ottoline had decided that it was hopeless to continue opposing what had already come to pass. 'I think one must simply face things as they are and not discard possible action for an impossible

---

* Lord Charles Bentinck, although wounded, served throughout the Gallipoli campaign in the 9th Lancers. Lord Henry was invalided out of the Derbyshire Yeomanry in the summer of 1915. One of his odder memories was of the nightly visit paid to him by his former manservant who came through the trenches to ask if he could be of assistance. 'He would ask this as if he had just laid out Henry's clothes.' (*Ottoline at Garsington*, p. 46)

ideal,' she told Bertie on 30 October 1914. She was already involved in the Union for Democratic Control (UDC) which had been holding meetings in the Bedford Square drawing-room since August, but their talk of starting a new pacifist party seemed as futile to her as it did to Bertie, who bitterly compared their efforts to those of a party of fleas trying to build a pyramid. She thought of organising another group with Russell, Lowes Dickinson and the Sangers as founder members, but this did not progress beyond informal discussions.

The idea of turning Garsington into a refuge for pacifists had not yet taken shape (Farmer Gale's daughter was still, technically, in residence there); in the meantime, Ottoline searched for a way to be of practical use until the society called 'Friends of Foreigners' put her in touch with half a dozen families whose lives had been destroyed by the war. Her job was to comfort and help the frightened women whose only crime had been to marry Germans and whose husbands were now being interned. All were viewed with suspicion by their neighbours; many were threatened with eviction and barred from even the most menial work. Their helplessness aroused Ottoline's sympathy and indignation and she worked hard to secure money for them as well as taking practical gifts of clothing and food to their homes in the East End of London. In December, encouraged by Ottoline, Russell started accompanying her on her visits before making others on his own initiative. Depressed by the fact that he was obliged to go on teaching at Cambridge when many of the younger dons had left and his own class had shrunk to a handful of foreigners, he was grateful to Ottoline for having found this role for him. As a token of esteem, he gave her a treasured personal possession, a single and valuable pearl of his mother's to add to her own necklace.* Knowing that she was often worried about money, he made her promise to sell it if she was ever in need.

Another obvious way to give immediate help as a pacifist in the war was to offer housing to refugees. The first to arrive at Bedford Square was a strapping young Belgian who was asked to leave after he had spent a week regaling his hosts with highly-coloured tales of German atrocities. The second, Valentine Tessier, was a French actress who was trying to earn her living as a language teacher in London. Indolent and flirtatious, Valentine soon found a rich lover who was ready to house her elsewhere. Ottoline, who had not enjoyed

---

* Ottoline's pearl necklace is so often mentioned in the memoirs of her friends that it is worth correcting a misapprehension on their part. The pearls, supposed by all of them to be 'the Portland pearls', were, apart from Russell's addition, those which Lady Bolsover bought for her daughter in Paris in 1892 and which were believed to have belonged to Marie Antoinette. Ottoline wore them on all occasions until 1918, when they were sold to help rescue Garsington farm from bankruptcy; after that date, she wore a cheaper substitute.

her habit of reciting sentimental French poems to their dinner guests, felt that she had had a lucky escape.

The third and most acceptable visitor was Maria Nys, a sixteen-year-old whose round white face was framed in cascades of dark ringlets and whose lower limbs were swaddled in the thick leggings and ginger-yellow button boots her mother thought necessary to fend off the dangerous English climate. Maria was the oldest child of a Belgian industrialist who had persuaded his wife and four daughters to seek refuge abroad. It was Madame Nys's brother, George Baltus, painter and professor of art at Glasgow, who had put her in touch with Ottoline; having already succeeded in housing herself in a Kentish rectory, Madame Nys sent Maria to Bedford Square in her place.

In her biography of Aldous Huxley, Sybille Bedford describes Maria (who later became Huxley's wife) as having been completely 'bowled over by Lady Ottoline. She was fascinated, she was dazzled – she adored.' Licensed to call Ottoline 'Auntie', she sometimes addressed her as 'Maman'. She devoted herself to her with a passion bemusing to the friends who thought of Ottoline as the most unmotherly of women. An early letter, written from Durbins where she had been sent for a fortnight as a companion to Roger Fry's children, shows that Maria had already singled Ottoline out as her adored mentor. Did Ottoline think she ought to take Mr Fry's advice and read *Anna Karenina*? she asked. Did she know how long the eight days seemed since they last saw each other? She had never had so much freedom and she liked Mr Fry and 'Vann' (Vanessa Bell) and everybody very much, but 'je ne suis attachée à personne comme à vous . . . je les aime en riant. Je suis vraiment trop enfant, c'est pourquoi [je? *illeg.*] *chère Maman* en vous remerciant encore pour *tout* ce que vous faites pour moi . . . votre petite fille aimante.' (9 December 1915)

Ottoline came to mistrust Maria's gushing spontaneity. Her memoir observations (written after she had decided that Maria had encouraged Huxley to parody Garsington in *Crome Yellow*) show little warmth. 'She was intelligent and sympathetic,' she wrote, 'but she was entirely devoid of wisdom or poetry or any religious insight . . . She was so completely foreign that she had no understanding of English ways or traditions, and in this she has never changed.'[1] But this was the judgement of later years. There must have been considerable kindness in her earlier behaviour to prompt this tribute, sent from Maria to Edward Sackville-West a month after Ottoline's death: 'I daresay you don't know just how much she was to my life. In spite of the agonies of those young loves, it was my greatest . . .'[2]

The war which wiped out a generation of British youth was also effective in destroying the last traces of a social world in which etiquette had governed behaviour. Until 1915, Ottoline's knowledge of young people had not extended beyond Bloomsbury and a nodding acquaintance with the Neo-Pagans' dream of turning the world into a sexy earthly paradise, the 'Heaven of Laughter and Bodies and Flowers and Love and People' which Rupert Brooke had blissfully extolled in a letter to his friend Jacques Raverat. War brought in a different mood, of ribald darkness, in which the yoking together of bodies and flowers suggested corpses and the bleeding symbol of the Flanders poppies. Brooke, like Ottoline herself, had been taught to believe that love was stronger than hate, that beauty was more powerful than the desire to kill. 'Now that ideal was broken like a china vase dashed to the ground', as one young observer wrote. 'The contrast between That and This was devastating... The war-time humor of the soul roared with mirth at the sight of all that dignity and elegance despoiled.'[3]

This was the spirit which infected the Thursday parties which Ottoline started to give again in December 1914. The guest-list, ruthlessly pruned of warmongers, was a wonderfully eclectic mixture of old society friends, politicians, the Bloomsberries, artists and students; the mood was barbarously young, and grew more so as the night wore on. David Garnett, a new attendant at the parties, described a typical evening as starting with a dinner for, among others, D. H. Lawrence and E. M. Forster before a brief concert in the drawing-room, often given by the d'Aranyi sisters, to whom Ottoline showed her gratitude by lending them the house for their public concerts. Between nine and ten, Philip, smooth and smiling in a braided smoking jacket of brown velvet, took his seat at the pianola while Ottoline and her new maids, Millie and Edith Ellis, carried in her trunk of fantastic costumes;* the younger guests of the evening would drift in from the square, and the dancing would begin. Not formal dancing, but any kind of improvised movement that fitted each dancer's mood as Philip changed the pianola rolls from a Hungarian Dance to Mozart or even to 'Get Out and Get Under', Ottoline's favourite of the old music-hall tunes. 'It was odd to see how each one expressed their personality as they danced,' Ottoline wrote in her own account of those evenings.

Duncan Grant was almost fierce, but full of humour and grace, as he bounded about like a Russian ballet dancer, or wound in and out in some intricate dance with Vanessa Bell or Bunny Garnett, who looked really fierce and

---

* Millie and Edith Ellis were the daughters of Lady Bolsover's old coachman. They wrote asking Ottoline for employment after their parents' deaths, and became the mainstay of her household. Edith was the cook at Garsington; Millie, technically a parlourmaid, was both housekeeper and Ottoline's chief confidante.

barbaric in bright oranges and reds, a gay-coloured silk handkerchief on his head. Duncan's special dance was one of Brahms's Hungarian Dances ... When there was a general mêlée, Bertie Russell would be dragged in by one of the Aranyis. It was very comic to see him – a stiff little figure, jumping up and down like a child, with an expression of surprised delight ... and then Lytton Strachey exquisitely stepped out with his brother James and his sister Marjorie, in a delicate and courtly minuet of his own invention, his thin long legs and his arms gracefully keeping time to Mozart ... I remember dancing a Spanish dance with Augustus John.[4]

The younger visitors brought an exciting feeling of liberty to the parties. They also introduced a new set of rules of behaviour. Cigarettes were ground out under the tapping heels. Bottles were smuggled into the house in overcoat pockets and unceremoniously dumped beside Ottoline's Chinese bowls of pot-pourri. One young lady, attempting a spirited pirouette, struck David Garnett in the face and gave him a black eye. Another guest, embarking on a high-stepping dance with his hostess, tripped on her skirt and brought her crashing to the ground in his arms. Vanessa Bell, waiting at the door to be escorted home by the new love of her life, Duncan Grant, left the house alone after seeing him being passionately embraced by the beautiful raven-haired Jelly d'Aranyi, a girl of half her age.

Vanessa and her contemporaries, all of them now in their mid-to-late thirties, had known Ottoline at the height of her beauty. The young intruders looked at her with fresh eyes. They saw the splendour. They were impressed by the surroundings and by her friendship with so many eminent people. They admired her vigorous opposition to the war. But she was not one of them. What Ottoline intended only as a sympathetic interest in their welfare was interpreted as a desire to manipulate them. Behind the friendly manner, they began to sense an iron will which would break them if they did not bend to it by behaving as she, not they, wished. Apprehensiveness tainted the sense that they had been let into an enchanted world.

One of the first of the new guests to succumb to Ottoline's charms became one of her most unkind critics. David Garnett was an amiably gauche young man who had not yet discovered his talent for writing. He met her on his first visit to the Bells at Gordon Square in January 1915. Ottoline was among the guests who stayed on to watch an extract from Racine's *Bérénice*, staged with Duncan Grant's giant cardboard puppets and recited in mellifluous French by various Stracheys. Ottoline was curious to meet the son of Constance, the woman who had translated Chekhov, Turgenev and Dostoevsky; before Garnett left, he heard her purring out the magic words in 'a cajoling drawl: "Do come to a party I am giving after dinner, next Thursday, Mr Garnett. Why do they call you Bunny?" Her words and instant invitation turned my head.'[5]

Garnett never became a close friend of Ottoline's and many of the things he later said about her in his autobiographical books were a mixture of hearsay and invention. It is he who has left us with the picture of Ottoline pushing herself uninvited into Lydia Lopokova's dressing-room while Garnett trailed bashfully in her wake, of Ottoline looking like a circus clown on her visit to Vanessa and Duncan at Wissett Lodge, of Ottoline poisoning her guests with a dinner of diseased peacock, of Lytton Strachey begging him not to pass a bit of gossip on to Ottoline, because she 'would immensely enjoy maliciously spreading a story at his expense'.[6] The truth? Garnett had sensibly attached himself to Ottoline's ballet-party because he knew she always went to see her friend Lydia after the performance; the circus clown had been rather beautifully dressed in a silk tunic and trousers; the peacock was a turkey which had, indeed, gone off; the only stories Ottoline ever told about Lytton were designed to enhance him in the eyes of her friends. Garnett's close friendship with both Lytton and Vanessa provides the most plausible explanation for his later delight in guying Ottoline. Like Dora Carrington, he started vilifying her only after he saw how readily his older friends did so; to defend Ottoline was to risk being mocked with her. And so, prudently, perhaps, the young changed their tune. The following account by Garnett bears the hallmark of the Lytton–Vanessa view of Ottoline:

> Spiritually her best quality was generosity: her worst, meanness and the love of power. The good and evil in her waged frequent warfare. Balanced between them was her strong schoolboy's sense of humour, which was, however, almost always malicious and never, as far as I can remember, at her own expense. If her love of power, or longing for love (often the same thing in her) were not aroused, her generosity would have it all its own way. Those whom she merely liked were indebted to her for a hundred acts of kindness, sympathy and help. When, however, her passions became more deeply involved, it was another matter. Love can be tigerish and those whom Ottoline loved were lucky if, sooner or later, a tiger's claws did not rend them in pieces.[7]

After these bold assertions, it was necessary to produce examples of his subject's tigerish ferocity, and here David Garnett found himself in difficulties. The only evidence he was able to produce did not add up to much. After breaking a dinner engagement at Ottoline's house at the last moment, he claimed to have apprehended that he might be 'torn limb from limb' in properly tigerish fashion when he received a telegram to say that she had not quite understood the message which Philip had passed on to her.[8] As tigers go, this might set a record in docile performances.

Many of the young women who came to Ottoline's parties that year were the boyishly-dressed girls who had gone to study art at the Slade at the same time as Stanley Spencer and Mark Gertler and who gained their name of 'cropheads' from their uniformly short haircuts. Two of them quickly grew closer to her than the rest.

Ottoline had already met Dora Carrington in May 1914, when Mark Gertler asked if he could bring her with him to see *The Magic Flute*; she soon learned that this sturdy fair-haired girl with china-blue eyes and a skin like apple-blossom was the object of his adoration. He was not the only man to fall under her spell: Ralph Partridge married her, Gerald Brenan had a passionate affair with her and Lytton Strachey was willing to spend the last fourteen years of his life with her. The torture for Gertler was in the fact that, while Carrington was deeply attached to him as a friend, one sexual encounter had been enough to convince her that they should never repeat it. 'I do love you,' she told him in a cruelly honest letter, 'but not in the way you want. Once, you made love to me in your studio, you remember, many years ago now. One thing I can never forget, it made me inside feel ashamed, unclean. Can I help it? I wish to God I could. Do not think I rejoice in being sexless, and am happy over this. It gives me pain also.'[9]

Gertler was devoted to the new patroness who praised his pictures, opened her home to his friends, sympathised with his sense of alienation and delighted in his gift for mimicry and story-telling. Carrington began by seeing Ottoline through his eyes and sharing his sense of shock at the discovery of how viciously she was mocked behind her back. 'I have just come back from spending three days on the Lewes downs with the Clive Bells, Duncan [Grant], Mrs Hutchinson and Lytton Strachey...' she told him in December 1915. 'What traitors all these people are! They ridicule Ottoline!... I think it's beastly of them to enjoy Ottoline's kindnesses and then laugh at her.'[10] But that was before she fell in love with Lytton and allowed her judgements to be guided by his.

Closer to Ottoline in age and background was Dorothy Brett, Carrington and Gertler's inseparable comrade and go-between. She was the thirty-two-year-old daughter of Lord Esher, friend and adviser both to Queen Victoria and Edward VII. Like Ottoline, Brett had broken away from her family to immerse herself in an exuberant and, as it seemed to her, less class-conscious world when she enrolled at the Slade in 1910. Brett's first encounter with Ottoline came about when Gertler took her and two other friends as his masked mystery guests to one of the Bedford Square parties in January 1915. Brett ran away again almost as soon as she had been coaxed into Ottoline's drawing-room, but Gertler was confident that she had made a good impression. 'I've never seen Brett look so well as she did that night...' he reported to Carrington; 'we couldn't altogether have been a failure.' He was right. Ottoline had been intrigued by her first glimpse of the young woman Gertler called 'the virgin aunt', who looked so startlingly young with her little rabbit's mouth, her round pink cheeks and tiny *retroussée* nose.[11] A week later, she received a letter from Brett, promising to be a reformed character on her next visit (it was indigestion, not shyness, which had caused her abrupt departure), and to behave 'like a perfect lady – I have misgivings about my clothes, but will put on the best I have'. (7 February) With her letter, she sent two drawings of herself, one as a scruffy teenager, the other, just in case Ottoline had failed to discern her background, as she might have dressed for a dinner-party at Welbeck. The letter and drawings were passed on to Duncan Grant. A scribbled note from Ottoline on the envelope read: 'Duncan dear, do come and meet this person.'

By March, Brett had become a regular attender of the Thursdays from which her friend Gertler had temporarily been banished for disorderly behaviour. (He had, by his own impenitent account, smashed one guest's spectacles, pulped Marjorie Strachey's foot on the dance-floor and left Maria Nys with an arm that was purple with bruises.) Brett, as a more sober guest, was rewarded by being invited to tea to meet one of her heroes, Augustus John. The occasion did not go well. John was uncommunicative – perhaps his thoughts were with the painting of Ottoline on which he had just started work again – and Brett was crippled by shyness. 'I felt just like a suet pudding – all stodge and no currants . . .' she wrote to her hostess, 'and John!!!! at the mere sight of him I was in forty thousand flusters = and thus do I apologise for my dullness = and I sit alone in my little studio and weep over my dullness.'

Deafness put a strain on Brett's social life, but she was neither so dull nor so stupid as she liked to pretend. Portraying her as Jenny Mullion in *Crome Yellow*, Aldous Huxley gave her the role of the shrewd observer whose secret diary is a lacerating testimony to her sharp judgement, but whose deafness always keeps her at a distance. In Brett's own memoirs, she hints that her deafness was, in part, a psychological condition and that it grew worse at the time when she made her entry into the Bedford Square group of 'engagingly frightening intellectuals who made up the world of painting and literature'. Brett was torn between her longing to be involved with them and her own insecurity: 'Much of the time I felt utterly terrified of the life around me and the life that at the same time I was loving to lead.'[12] But there was nothing frighteningly intellectual about Ottoline, well-read though she was. Her gift for sympathy encouraged Brett to start confiding in her and Ottoline, in turn, was pleased to have found a woman-friend with whom she felt completely at ease. 'Her deafness gives her an instinctive power of knowing one's thoughts,' she wrote. 'I love her and feel that she is one of the very few people I have met lately that I could be intimate with, and who could take a part in my life. I usually feel as if I were an eternal elder sister but with her I feel more on a level and that is a relief ... we have great fun together.'[13]

From Ottoline's point of view, the relationship in its early stages was as simple as that, but not from Brett's. Sean Hignett, Brett's biographer, makes a convincing argument for her fear of male relationships stemming from an unpleasant adolescent experience with Lord Harcourt, a friend of her father's who was always known as 'Loulou'. Significant, too, may have been the well-known fact of her father's homosexuality and the presence in the household of a series of young men whose role was not well-disguised. Men frightened Brett, but she was drawn to the kind of women who attracted them. At fifteen, she fell in love with a pretty actress called Letty Lind and stowed away a rope-ladder and a complete suit of boy's clothes in preparation for a fantasy elopement. As a girl of twenty-three, she became obsessed by Margaret Brooke, the exotic Ranee of Sarawak whose son married Brett's younger sister, Sylvia. (The Ranee, a woman of formidable character, had initially ordered him to propose to the older daughter, an instruction he chose to ignore.) Brett's relationship with Ottoline quickly developed into a girlish crush on a woman who was both powerful and intensely feminine. Lesbianism played no part in Ottoline's life, but she was effusively affectionate to the women she liked (Gertler wrote to a friend of an evening at the theatre when he had been embarrassed by the way Ottoline had hugged and kissed Brett) and she did nothing to discourage her admirer. By mid-1916, when Brett had become an almost permanent resident at Garsington, she was writing several letters a week in her absences and signing them 'your very very devoted Brettie' while announcing that she was the sheathed sword to Ottoline's 'passionate burning flame'.

But as with Carrington, so it was with Brett. Away from Ottoline's company, ever more confident in her own friendships, she soon found it irresistible to join in the glorious game of character-blackening. 'A bright fire burns in the tiny sitting-room,' she wrote in *Lawrence and Brett: A Friendship*, a memoir published as an open letter to the dead Lawrence. 'Gertler, you and I sit in a row in front of the fire discussing O. our mutual friend and enemy. I, terribly shy, in agonies of nervousness; you gentle, gently coaxing me out of my shyness. You sit very upright with your hands tucked under your thighs. We sit drinking tea, tearing poor O. to pieces. We pull her feathers out in handfuls until I stop, aghast, and try to be merciful, saying, "we shall leave her just one draggled feather in her tail, the poor plucked hen!" ... that is all I remember.' For Ottoline, reading the book with horrified disbelief in 1933, it was more than enough.

It was in December 1914 that Ottoline discovered a newly-published volume of short stories called *The Prussian Officer* by D. H. Lawrence, whose first novel had already attracted her interest. The stories, with the exception of the title one, were set in rural Nottinghamshire and reading them gave her a pleasurable shock of recognition. Lawrence had grown up in a grimy hill-town in the Midlands, but many of his days had been spent bicycling and walking through the country lanes and tranquil hamlets stretching to the north; the names of Bolsover and Welbeck were as familiar a part of his memory as the mining villages through which Ottoline had ridden as a girl. Stories such as 'Daughters of the Vicar', 'Shades of Spring' and 'A Sick Collier' took her back to the time when she had dreamed of making friends with the families of the colliers and estate employees. Here were their lives, affectionately evoked by someone who knew them well and who evidently shared her love of nature. Ottoline was enthralled. After urging Desmond MacCarthy to read the stories and to let her know his reaction – it was in the affirmative – she lent her own copy of the book to Bertie. But to enjoy the stories was not enough; she wanted to meet the author. By the beginning of January, she had persuaded somebody (probably Lawrence's country neighbour, Gilbert Cannan) to bring him and his wife to dinner at Bedford Square; by the end of the month, she had been asked to come with Maria Nys to their new home, a cottage in Sussex.

Lawrence in London was something of a liability: an introduction to Duncan Grant had already resulted in a tirade against the *Bérénice* puppets and other 'silly experiments' which she was expected to pass on as constructive criticism. But back at the cottage in Greatham, Lawrence relaxed and became the most congenial of hosts, cooking most of the meals himself and taking Ottoline off on long walks across the downs. He had made her feel extraordinarily happy and at ease, she wrote later, talking to her not in the flat voice he had acquired in London but in Nottinghamshire dialect, about the scenes he had described so vividly in his work. 'It was impossible not to feel expanded and stimulated by the companionship of anyone so alive, so intensely interested in everyone and everything as he was.'[14]

It would be easy to see this new friendship as another case of Ottoline's finding a new talent in need of being encouraged. That is not how it was. Lawrence had become a minor celebrity since his debut in Madox Ford's *English Review* in 1909. In 1913, he had started what was to become a famous friendship with John Middleton Murry and Katherine Mansfield, to whose literary magazine, *Rhythm*, he was a regular contributor; since writing for Edward Marsh's *Georgian Poetry* series, he had acquired two more useful supporters in the Prime Minister's son, 'Beb', and his wife, Lady Cynthia Asquith. He was not in need of a patron, but Ottoline's image as an aristocratic patroness added to her romantic appeal. It fascinated him to think that he who had sat as a boy listening to the old Welbeck servants talking about Ottoline's family should now be hearing her version of life at the great house. 'It *is* rather splendid that you are a great lady,' he told her when she tried to apologise for her connections. '. . . I really do honour your birth. Let us do justice to its nobility; it is not mere accident. I would give a great deal to have been born an aristocrat.'[15] But it was not snobbery which prompted this declaration so much as a passionate love of the English tradition in which class still played a part, a love which would later make him see the manor house of Garsington as a symbol of all that the war was eroding, 'of old things passing away . . . this house of the Ottolines – it is England . . .'[16]

Lawrence was never in love with Ottoline, but the feelings which she inspired in him had something in common with Russell's. Bertie had mythologised her, calling her the mother of all the sorrow and love in the world and, in his early letters, urging her to throw off the shackles of mundane life for the nobler role of his muse. Lawrence, too, wanted to put her on a pedestal. 'Primarily, you belong to a special type, a special race of women: like Cassandra in Greece, and some of the great women saints,' he told her on 1 March 1915. In a letter to Cynthia Asquith about Ottoline, he showed a perceptiveness which suggests that he understood her predicament better than Russell. Urging Lady Cynthia, on 16 November 1915, to go and stay with Ottoline (she had not, in fact, been invited), he told her that Ottoline's achievement in breaking away from her background had not helped her to find a substitute for it. 'Her life is in a way lost,' he wrote after correcting himself for having described Ottoline as 'unreal'. '. . . If you [want to] know her, be patient and go to the real things, not to the unreal things in her: for they are legion. But she is a big woman – something like Queen Elizabeth at the end.'

Frieda Lawrence bore no resemblance to Queen Elizabeth, but her character was every bit as strong as Ottoline's. A daughter of Baron von Richthofen, she was easily riled by her husband's respect for Ottoline's family and she made no bones about her dislike for what she disdainfully called their soul-mush relationship. Lawrence and Ottoline could rattle along in a pleasantly vague way about God's expression of himself in nature for hours on end. Frieda, who liked things to be clear-cut, took no part in these discussions, but she did not want to be excluded from any aspect of Lawrence's life. Ottoline's friendship was never a discreet gift and it would have irked any wife, let alone one of Frieda's possessive character, to see her husband being lavished with presents more suited to a lover than a friend. 'L. loves his opal,' she told Ottoline in February 1915, but did Frieda love her for sending him jewels? It was not easy for her to appreciate the virtues which her husband tactlessly extolled or to feel the same joy at the discovery that Ottoline and his sister shared a birthday, particularly when she found out that Ottoline thought their marriage disastrous and that she, Frieda, would be the ruin of Lawrence. 'I told her what I thought of her,' Frieda reported to Cynthia Asquith on 20 May 1916, after her suspicions had been confirmed. 'All her spirituality is false, her democracy is an autocrat turned sour, inside those wonderful shawls there is cheapness and vulgarity.'

Frieda's furious dismissal of Ottoline is no more reprehensible than Ottoline's immoderate dislike of Lawrence's wife. It should have been easy to pity a woman who took refuge in such absurd announcements as '"Do not forget, Lorenzo, I am a baroness,"' or 'in a loud, challenging voice, "I am just as remarkable and important as Lorenzo."'[17] But Ottoline and, by her own account, Philip made the grave mistake of deducing from Frieda's bullying manner and Lawrence's fretful submissiveness that it was safe to tell their friends how much happier Lawrence would be if he left his wife. 'Poor Lawrence, what a distraught creature he is underneath,' Ottoline wrote in the summer of 1915; 'the constant friction and fighting with Frieda will wear his nerves out in time. I fear he will have to kill all his gentle tender side, so as to have peace with her . . . But he will never part from her, he is too moral, and is bound to her by some need of his nature.'[18]

Some need of his nature! Should we wonder that Frieda was angry at being dismissed so contemptuously? Certainly, their marriage was not like any other Ottoline had yet seen. In her own family, disagreements were always suppressed in public. Neither Dorelia John nor Junia Anrep went in for shouting matches. Alys Russell had made no public display of her anger or her grief. Infidelities never prevented Clive and Vanessa Bell from maintaining friendly public faces. Virginia and Leonard Woolf seemed eminently capable of arguing without losing their tempers. Not so the Lawrences. Frieda's later memory of a marriage in which all the quarrels had been conducted in private was the product of wishful thinking: as a couple, they were noisy, dramatic and exhausting, ready to stir up a typhoon in any teacup that came their way. A good deal of the arguing had to do with Frieda's insecurity and her fear of being excluded. If she took offence

– and she frequently did – it was up to Lawrence to secure the apology or change of situation. When Russell failed to answer a letter from Frieda it was Lawrence who had to reproach him. When E. M. Forster cheerfully refused to 'have dealings with a firm' after Frieda started adding postscripts to her husband's letters, Lawrence was obliged to warn him that there are 'some things you should not write in your letters'. Even when Lawrence proposed himself to lunch on his own at Bedford Square, he was forced to add that Frieda, too, 'will come without me, to see you'. There was probably a large measure of truth in Ottoline's later suspicion that Frieda was responsible for their break with her in 1916 when they went to live in Cornwall, and that Lawrence had allowed his wife's view of her to influence him.

Ottoline's memoirs make it clear that she did not understand their marriage. She did not make much effort to do so. Frieda was six years older than Lawrence, thirty-five to his twenty-nine when they first met Ottoline. His adored mother had died in 1910; Frieda's role was the dual one of mother and mistress. She was a handsome woman and a passionate one; her life was lived on the tempestuous emotional level of one of Lawrence's superhuman fictional creations. She was not faithful; she was ferociously loyal. (If David Garnett had not used his tigress image for Ottoline, he might have employed it a good deal more convincingly for Frieda, who even looked the part with her reddish-blond hair, wide-set flaring eyes and large, well-exercised limbs.) She left a comfortable if undemanding life in Nottingham with her first husband, Professor Weekley, to live in a hand-to-mouth fashion on Lawrence's meagre earnings; she relinquished her children; she survived in the difficult position of being the German wife of a man who told Ottoline that he would gladly kill two million Germans (but who also described himself as a proverbial exaggerator); she gave him, unstintingly, the kind of love he needed to fuel his imagination.

Ottoline knew all of this and she chose not to take it into account. Why was she so hostile? Perhaps for the following reasons. She met the Lawrences in January 1915 when her relationship with Bertie was in its last and most powerful physical phase, when she was writing of their lovemaking that 'all passion that has been burnt white seemed in it and all the experience of our lives ... I was you – *one* with you, my love.' (16 January 1915) The passionate, noisy Lawrences brought home to her the well-mannered bloodlessness of her own marriage in a way that cannot have been registered without feeling. The life of the ex-Mrs Weekley forced her to make a more painful comparison. Frieda had given up a decent husband and the children she adored because she fell in love with a man who was not prepared to settle for an extra-marital liaison. Russell had fought and pleaded with Ottoline to do the same for him, and she had refused. Now, more in love with Bertie than ever before, still living on stolen half-hours and a daily exchange of letters, she must have been tortured by the constant comparison with the freedom achieved by Frieda's brave leap away from convention and security. Of course she never said so in her memoirs – how could she, with Philip supervising them? – but such feelings would help to explain her unreasonable hostility to Lawrence's wife and her eagerness to condemn the marriage.

Ottoline's and Frieda's dislike of each other was not declared until 1916; Lawrence was eager for them to be friends and, initially, they did their best to live up to his expectations. On Ottoline's first visit to Greatham, Lawrence told her how unhappy Frieda was to have been severed from her children. Weekley, a deceptively jocular man, had flatly refused her pleas to see them since May 1912; in the summer of 1913, the High Court awarded him sole custody and deprived Frieda of all rights of access. Ottoline was horrified by the story. If there was anything she could do . . . a few days later, Lawrence wrote to propose a scheme by which she might help. Weekley had written a book which would give her an excuse to ask him to visit her; she could then suggest Bedford Square as a place where mother and children could meet, if only for an hour. Ottoline promised to do all she could, earning herself a brief burst of affection from Frieda: 'I am so grateful to you that I could sing . . .' she wrote on 17 February 1915. 'Your help means such hope to me.' But their expectations that Weekley would be seduced by Ottoline's fine name were disappointed: the scheme came to nothing.

Lawrence had other plans for her. During the Christmas of 1914, Lawrence and Frieda had given a party for Katherine Mansfield and Middleton Murry, the Cannans, Gertler and their Russian-Jewish friend, Samuel Koteliansky (always known as Kot). They had feasted and danced, and Kot sang his favourite Hebrew song, 'Ranani Sadekim Badenoi'. It was Kot's song which gave Lawrence the name for the society of friends with whom he wanted to 'sail away from the world at war and found a little colony' called Rananim in, of all unlikely places, Florida. Their emblem was to be a black phoenix.

Ottoline heard all about Rananim on her visit to Greatham. Perhaps she mentioned the imminent move to Garsington; perhaps she gently pointed out the impracticality of establishing a commune in a distant country none of them knew. Certainly, by the time she left, Lawrence had decided that Oxfordshire was a more convenient location than Florida and that Ottoline would be just the person to help establish his utopia. 'I want you to form the nucleus of a new community which shall start a new life amongst us,' he told her in a letter written almost before she was out of the door, '– a life in which the only riches is integrity of character . . . We can all come croppers, but what does it matter? We can laugh at each other, and dislike each other, but the good remains . . . I hold this the most sacred duty – the gathering together of a number of people who shall so agree to live by the *best* they know, that they shall be *free* to live by the best they know . . . We will have no more *churches*. We will bring church and house and shop together.' (1 February 1915)

Lawrence's mind was full of confusion during those winter months – he even went so far as to enlist the help of a psychiatrist – and the notion of Rananim was too muddled to find much of a following among his friends. (When it was finally established, in 1924, in the Sangre de Cristo mountains north of Taos in New Mexico, it consisted only of the Lawrences and Brett.) But Lawrence clung to the idea that Garsington could become a refuge for 'a little society or body around a *religious belief which leads to action*', a tranquil country court of which Ottoline would be the queen. 'You must be president,' he told her. 'You must preside over our meetings . . . Garsington must be the retreat where we come together and knit ourselves together.' It would be, he thought, 'like the Boccaccio place where they told all the *Decamerone*'.[19] It was an apt analogy for his dream of escaping the horrors of war; Boccaccio's little court of storytellers had fled from the plague.

Ottoline had a more sensible suggestion to make. The cottage at Greatham had been loaned by a friend, Viola Meynell. When the Lawrences had to leave it, why should they not borrow one of the Garsington village houses? They could have a three-roomed gardener's cottage, if they liked.* They did like, but not, Lawrence said hurriedly, to own. Ownership (which had never been suggested) would go against his principles, but if Ottoline could see her way to installing a proper bathroom, a big workroom, decent heating, and adequate furnishings – then he would insist on paying six per cent of the costs. Restoring Garsington had swallowed up a large amount of Ottoline's money, and these were not cheap proposals. Abandoning her offer of the cottage, she made another suggestion, one which she thought would appeal to Lawrence's passion for all things medieval. There was a habitable monastic building adjoining the manor house – perhaps that would suit their purposes better? This time it was Frieda who 'required so much done that it would have cost far more than we could afford'. Appalled by her demands, Philip was finally driven to tell Lawrence that he would have to foot the bill himself. 'Enough, enough,' Lawrence raged; 'while this thievery and abomination lasts, I would not have a moment of hired work done for me. Let us have it all left until there is some decency on the face of the earth again.'[20] With that, the dream of Rananim at Garsington fizzled out;

---

* This was later occupied by Clive Bell when he came to work on the Garsington farm between 1916 and 1918.

when the Lawrences made their first visit in June, they stayed in the manor house as guests.

Lawrence did not allow financial setbacks to crush his enthusiasm; his next scheme was for a course of lectures on ethics and immortality which he planned for the autumn of 1915 and which were intended to provide the foundation for a new society. His co-speaker and fellow founder member of the new society was to be Russell.

Bertie had been the first to hear of Ottoline's new friendship; when she took him to Greatham in early February, she was delighted to find that his enthusiasm for Lawrence almost exceeded her own. '"He is amazing; he sees through and through one,"' Russell exclaimed as they drove away; when Ottoline answered, '"Yes. But do you think he really sees correctly?"' his answer was unhesitating. '"Absolutely ... he sees everything and is always right."'[21]

Lawrence appealed to the side of Russell's nature which was drawn to Ottoline, the side which moved instinctively as a moth to light towards people whose judgements and aspirations were rooted in a strong religious belief. Still in a state of uncertainty about his own course of action, whether to leave Cambridge, whether to commit himself to political writing, Russell was immensely attracted by Lawrence's energy and passion, by the quality which Ottoline described as 'a fire within him, a fire which flames into excitement and conviction when a subject or a controversy strikes a light'.[22]

Years later, Russell looked back on his Lawrence period as a time when Ottoline had somehow persuaded two men of dramatically opposite views that they should admire each other; it had not taken either of them long, in his memory, to identify in the other 'a positive force for evil'. His summary is glib, but the conclusion cannot be disputed. Ottoline, having persuaded herself that the portrait painted of her in *Women in Love* was Frieda's work, remained full of affection for Lawrence; Russell's eventual rejection of him was violent and absolute. He did not want to remember that Lawrence, like Ottoline, had spoken to that part of him which longed to share their religious passion.

At the beginning, Lawrence could do no wrong. When he visited Cambridge in March and expressed his loathing for the homosexual community he found there, Russell eagerly supported him. 'Lawrence has the same feeling against sodomy as I have,' he told Ottoline; 'you had nearly made me believe there is no great harm in it, but I have reverted; and all the examples I know confirm me in thinking it sterilizing ... Lawrence is wonderfully lovable,' he went on. 'The mainspring of his life is love – the universal mystical love – which inspires even his most vehement and passionate hate.'

There were, nevertheless, elements of Lawrence's character which Russell did not like. He missed the wit which had tempered even his harshest arguments with Wittgenstein, he was maddened by his contempt for any form of rational discussion, and he recoiled from Lawrence's insistence that he should acknowledge 'the powerful malignant will in him . . . the passionate evil that is in us'. And there were his friends. While Ottoline had been flattered and excited by her introduction to Murry, Katherine Mansfield and Kot, Bertie was disgusted, pronouncing all three of them to be 'idle and cynical. I thought Murry *beastly* and the whole atmosphere of the three dead and putrefying.' The encounter was followed by a discussion in which Lawrence asserted that London was a 'fact' and not a 'truth' and that he had only to say so to get it pulled down. Russell drily suggested that they should adjourn to Trafalgar Square and put his theory to the test. 'His attitude is a little mad and not quite honest, or at least muddled,' he told Ottoline; 'he regards all my attempts to make him acknowledge facts as mere timidity, lack of courage to think boldly . . . The trouble with him is a tendency to mad exaggeration.'

By July, Russell had modified his criticisms. He went to stay with the Lawrences for two days and was struck by the sincerity with which Lawrence declared Ottoline to be a woman of visionary powers. 'He is quite right,' Bertie told her. 'He feels all your quality as no one else seems to. It makes me love him.' Lawrence had shown him a draft of his philosophical writings, blithely entitled 'Morgen Rot' (Red Dawn), and he had liked them, '*very much*'. They had started making plans for the autumn lecture course. 'We have almost sworn *blutbrüderschaft*,' Lawrence told Ottoline a few days later. 'We will set out together, he and I . . .'

'Could anything have made these two fine passionate men work together for the country and the causes they both so desired?' Ottoline wondered in her memoirs twenty years later. 'I doubt it – they were both too self-centred and too intolerant of criticism . . . And though both of them were fond of dominating, and both were convinced that they were infallibly right, Bertie was not in the habit of submitting himself intellectually to anyone.'[23]

The time of the lecture course approached. Russell was irritated by Lawrence's arbitrary revisions to his work and maddened by his impracticality: how could he think that it would solve 'the whole economic question' to nationalise industry, communications and land all 'in one fell blow'? But it was Lawrence, smarting from the sense that he was being treated as a working-class clown who could be relied on to perform for the gratification of the aristocrats, who struck the death blow. Russell sent him an essay which stressed the dangers of a long war without making any reference to the social factors which had helped to bring it about. He expected a few objections; nothing had prepared him for the diatribe that followed. 'You are too full of devilish repressions to be anything but lustful and cruel,' Lawrence wrote. 'The enemy of all mankind you are, full of the lust of enmity. It is *not* the hatred of falsehood which inspires you. It is the hatred of people, of flesh and blood. It is a perverted, mental blood-lust.' For good measure, he added the information that a woman who had attended one of Russell's peace meetings had asked him how any man with such an evil face could mean what he said on the platform. When Russell had absorbed the shock, he decided to end the friendship. Lawrence's apology was ignored; Russell refused to accept the idea that only a difference in attitude stood between them. The difference, according to his later and harsher view of Lawrence, was that the mystical philosophy of blood-consciousness 'led straight to Auschwitz'. Like Ottoline, he became convinced that the real villain, the creator of the ideas for which Lawrence was only the mouthpiece, was his wife.

Ottoline was able to sympathise with Russell's anger in 1915; she knew what it was like to be on the receiving end of one of Lawrence's epistolary lashings. On 16 April, a few weeks before the move to Garsington, she had spoken to Maria Nys about the possibility of sending her away, perhaps to further her studies. When she came back from an expedition with Russell late that evening, Maria collapsed. She had tried to kill herself with a massive dose of sleeping pills. (The fact that she waited until Ottoline came home before swallowing them suggests that she did not plan to die, only to show her despair.) A doctor was fetched and Ottoline took her to a nursing home for the night. Lawrence was fond of Maria; there was no doubt in his mind where the blame lay. 'I'm not sure whether you aren't really more wicked than I had first thought you,' he told Ottoline on 23 April; '... she lived under the dominance of your will: and then you want to put her away from you ... *why* will you use power instead of love, good public control instead of affection? I suppose it is breeding.'

Ottoline was more forgiving than Russell. When she went to the Derbyshire spa-town of Buxton on 19 April to try to cure the rheumatism that had been plaguing her, she spent her evenings reading the second half of *The Rainbow*, on which Lawrence wanted her opinion. To him, she was cautiously enthusiastic, but she expressed strong reservations to Bertie. 'It is too *intensely* sexual,' she told him on 27 April, 'and I don't like it ... But one feels he *is* great and has probably a grt. future if he could see the world more.' The writing struck her as being slapdash; she was shocked to find the word 'fecund' repeated twelve times on one page. Had Bertie been guilty of such carelessness, she would have said so at once; she did not feel capable of such frankness with Lawrence.*

* The Russell–Lawrence letters quoted here are taken from *Ottoline at Garsington*, op. cit., pp. 55–74.

Bertie had been dreading the move to Garsington; correctly, he foresaw it as a move which would gently, insidiously, loosen the intimacy between them. Ottoline was telling him that 'our love is a rock on which I rest and lean', but she also admitted that she was nervous at the thought of having him to stay there except in Philip's absences. Her visit to Buxton seemed a last chance to spend a few days together; he was determined to make them memorable.

Taking Ottoline on a surprise outing to Bolsover was a present which gave her more pleasure than any other she had from Bertie. Nothing was said, but it was a way of acknowledging the kind of life which had produced them and to which they still, on a perfect spring day, were ready to pretend that they belonged. Wandering through the panelled rooms of the castle's keep, Ottoline saw the colours for her Garsington rooms; strolling into the walled garden and along the old paved forecourt, they fell into a game of make-believe in which Russell was Bolsover's owner, the Duke of Newcastle, planning a masque for a visit by Charles I, and Ottoline his adored second wife, Margaret Lucas, 'the dear, generous, kind, eccentric lady' Ottoline loved above all her ancestors.[24] The following day (26 April) Bertie left, and Philip arrived to show her the caverns of the Peak District. The plunge into Stygian darkness after Bolsover's airy grace was a bad exchange. Back at Buxton, Ottoline wrote to tell Bertie that it had been a dreadful experience, 'grim and horrible – and terrible'. (27 April) Always superstitious, she would look back on it two years later as an omen of what was to come.

PART FOUR

Garsington

'*Garsington was a theatre, where week after week a travelling company would arrive and play their parts . . . How much they felt and saw of the beauty of the setting I never knew. Not very much perhaps . . .*'

OM, *Ottoline at Garsington*

14

A PORTRAIT OF GARSINGTON 1915–28

'Garsington, which was upon an hill and could not be hid, became a target for many arrows, all the sharper because there was envy as well as dislike behind them.'

L. A. G. Strong, Green Memory

'So to the steps up the porch, through the doorway, and into the interior, fragrant with all the memories of old age, and of by-gone, remembered lustiness.'

D. H. Lawrence to OM, 1 December 1915

No English country house of the war years is more famous than Garsington, and when the Morrells arrived there in 1915, they ushered in a decade of colourful patronage. L. A. G. Strong, one of the many Oxford undergraduates who looked upon it as a second home, offered this description:

The first view of the house was always a shock of delight . . . In the summer, one came up the hill to a garden graceful and formal as its swimming pool, to take tea upon a lawn under a tree in whose branches peacocks were standing, looking across at a house that had been warmed and mellowed by hundreds of summers, enjoying an ease that did not seem to belong to time or space.[1]

Ottoline made her first visit to her new home in October 1914. Farmer Gale and his heirs had done nothing to ruin it, but neither had they done anything to preserve it. One huge and glorious ilex tree stood in a shapeless acreage of grass at the lower end of which an old oblong fishpond lay choked with weeds; rough holes had been cut in the hedge separating the garden from the orchard so that Gale could keep an eye out for boys who went 'scrumping' for his apples. In the house, Ottoline found that the floorboards had rotted away, the windows had lost their glass, the doors had fallen off their hinges. It was a discouraging sight, but she had set her heart on Garsington and its neglected state did not deter her. By the end of the month, the garden was being dug up and landscaped; by mid-December, the floors had been ripped out and the windows were being given new frames.

The speed with which the magnificent garden of Garsington was created was remarkable. By 1 June 1915, when the Morrells had only been living in the house for a fortnight, Ottoline sat down to record their progress. 'Philip has cleared the fishpond and restored its old oblong shape, putting back the stone coping, and then we hope in time to terrace the slope down from the house. It is already much more beautiful, we have made one terrace and a walk round the pond, and in the autumn we are arranging to plant yew hedges that will grow like a tall, dark wall round the water. It is more Italian than any other place in England that I have ever known – partly I suppose through being high on a hill and having a few dark cypresses already in the garden.'[2]

It may have been this Italianate quality which first drew Ottoline to Garsington; it was certainly Italy which was present in her thoughts as she started to shape and plant her garden. The memory of it had always been there; she only had to see clipped box hedges to be back at the Villa Capponi with her Aunt Louise. 'I find that the places I want to have sink down into my memory and have built themselves into my being like stones impregnated with beauty and romance,' she once wrote. 'I drank then of the elixir of Italy – I drank so deeply of it that it has never left me.'[3]

Ottoline had seen a great many Italian gardens before she came to Garsington. Like Edith Wharton, she had been particularly struck by the subtle integration in the Tuscan villas of house, garden and landscape; the artful placing of terraces to give variety of effect; the use of walls of box and yew to create areas of dense shadow at the end of which a landscape view was gracefully framed; the shock of a Persian carpet of colour in a walled flower garden; the soothing harmony of dark lakes and marble statues. All of these features are typical of the villas surrounding Florence; all reappear in the garden at Garsington. Most striking is its similarity to Mrs Scott's garden at the Villa Capponi, 'a delightful interior with one corridor leading to a long green lawn and lemon garden and another towards the vast terrace from which you descend to a walled garden and others beneath it, ending in a swimming pool hedged in by cypresses'.[4]

The chief charm of Ottoline's garden was its lack of ostentation and the use of space to create a startling variety of effect. From the east side of the house, a stone terrace completed in 1926 led down to the main lawn. Beyond it, two pineapple-capped pillars showed the way into a large enclosed flower-garden of twenty-four square box-edged beds separated by narrow grass paths and flanked by slender pointed yews like witches' caps. The beds were filled with brilliant colour, with phlox and montbretia, zinnias, marigolds, sunflowers, red-hot pokers and snapdragons, all the blazing reds and yellows of late summer. At the far end of the flower-garden, under a wall smothered with climbing roses, a herbaceous border was filled with day lilies, oriental poppies, foxgloves and roses. Below this, the hillside was flattened out for a tennis lawn surrounded by beds in which the dominant colours were the soft mauve of lavender and the yellow of roses and forsythia: at the eastern end, a handsome old stone dovecote with a tiled roof was left in situ. From here, a shady avenue led the way down to the garden's most Italian feature: a centrepiece was placed in the rectangular fishpond in the form of a stone platform from which a recumbent statue and attendant cherub looked down into the water. Long walls of clipped yew were set back from the water; on each side, niches were shaped to frame Italian marble statues, bought in England between 1915 and 1920. ('It is said that if the Morrells had to choose between adding a bathroom to their house or a statue to their garden, they would choose the statue,' Lord David Cecil noted with amused approval.) At one end of the pool stood the boathouse which had started life as a wooden pavilion in the garden of Peppard. Below it, a second yew hedge created a shady pathway; here, Ottoline adapted the idea of Mr Gale's orchard peep-holes to make *clairvoyers* looking out across the valley to the distant fields.

The last area of the garden to be laid out was to the west of the pond, beyond a faintly classical wooden summerhouse designed and built by D. H. Lawrence. Here, a carpet of wildflowers and drooping willows surrounded two natural pools fed by the many springs in the hill. East of this area, and directly below the drawing-room windows, lay the broad swathe of lawn on which guests drowsed and talked on summer afternoons. To the side of this Ottoline planted an avenue of lime trees leading up to the house.

Not everybody appreciated her work, but while many visitors sharpened their pens on the more eccentric aspects of life in the garden of Garsington – the peacocks screaming from the branches of the ilex tree; Ottoline in high-heeled scarlet shoes and billowing dress, her hat swathed in a veil of tulle – few were immune to its enchantment. Lawrence's return for the endless small acts of friendship which Ottoline performed for him were (apart from building the summerhouse) the extraordinarily beautiful descriptions of 'the old manor lifting its fair pure stone amid trees and foliage' with which he filled his letters to her in 1915. Sitting in the house at the end of that year, he looked through the windows at 'the wet lawn drizzled with brown, sodden leaves . . . the blue, hazy heap of the distance, under the accomplished morning', and told her that it was 'the vision of all that I am, all that I have become, and ceased to be. It is me, generations and generations me . . . every lucid pang of my coming into being.' (1 December 1915) It was to Lawrence that Ottoline turned when she wanted words for the pleasure of walking into the garden at dusk, or of watching the carters tossing sheaves on the wagons as lightly as bundles of feathers at the end of the day.

Dorothy Brett's contribution was to do a painting of all the Garsington visitors sitting out on the lawn under a canopy of parasols and blue umbrellas; Carrington, while she was quick to learn to jeer at the absurdity of life in 'Shandygaff Hall', never lost her sense of the garden's mysterious charm.

Aldous Huxley, staying at the manor in the summer of 1916, found it more agreeable to spend his nights lying on the leads between the gables and the central chimneystack of the roof than sleeping in a small hot room at the top of the house. Here, he and 'an artistic young woman', who was most probably Carrington, lay 'singing folk-songs and rag-time to the stars . . . while early in the morning we would be wakened by a gorgeous great peacock howling like a damned soul or woman wailing for her demon lover, while he stalked about the tiles showing off his plumage to the sunrise'.[5] In *Crome Yellow*, he drew heavily on his memories of the garden, describing the contrast between the dark avenues and the bright flower-garden as having been 'like passing from a cloister into an Oriental palace'. In another passage, he wrote of its being 'as beautiful by moonlight as in the sun. The silver of water, the dark shapes of yew and ilex trees remained at all hours and seasons, the dominant features of the scene . . . the [flower] garden was like a great tank of warmth and perfume and colour.'[6] It is a picture to which we can add the Russian image of Aldous the woodsman – he steered clear of the farm-work on which the other Garsington pacifists were engaged – striding out into the garden in dark-brown corduroy jacket, fawn breeches and yellow stockings to lop branches off the ilex tree for the household fuel.

Aldous's sister-in-law, Juliette, spent two years at Garsington as Mlle Baillot, Julian's young governess and companion. Since it was still considered vital for Julian's health that she should remain out of doors as much as possible, they became familiar with every nook and corner of the garden in all seasons. In her memoirs, Juliette described it as having been 'immediately enchanting, with a brooding austerity I came to love more and more'.[7] To her, we owe the images of stocky little Carrington posing as a nude statue by the pool – Juliette failed to add that she, Ottoline, Maria Nys and Brett were also posing unclad for the camera that afternoon – and of Ottoline taking her afternoon swim in a pink maillot covered by a rainbow-coloured tunic. (Vanessa Bell, hearing of the tunic, embellished her own second-hand account of Ottoline bathing in the pool with high heels, girlishly shrieking of being quite naked under the dark water if Duncan Grant cared to dive and take a peep.)

Ottoline's own happiest memories included the balmy summer evenings when she carried a Chinese lantern out into the garden, swinging it above the flowers to make them glow, and of the afternoons when she and Katherine Mansfield laid piles of cut lavender to dry and gathered sweet-smelling herbs for Ottoline's jars of pot-pourri. Sometimes, Ottoline sat quietly by on one of the garden seats, watching as Katherine 'walked up and down under the house where the night-scented stock had opened its pale nocturnal flowers, fanning herself with a little black transparent fan, holding it up before her creamy face . . . I believe,' she added, 'these lovely days and nights in the garden at Garsington almost came up to scenes that she would admit as worthy to be part of her life. At the time I felt that she was the one person there who felt their poetry and beauty as I did.'[8]

Ottoline was not wrong. The love which she herself inspired for a time in Katherine Mansfield also embraced her setting. With typical impulsiveness, she had armfuls of jasmine and roses delivered to Katherine in London, and the scent prompted the images which filled the grateful letters which went to Ottoline in 1916 and 1917, when she wrote that ' "I positively lead another life with you there bending over the flowers, sitting under the trees . . ." '[9]

Lytton Strachey's response was more complicated. Ottoline's descriptions of the garden she was making filled him with happy anticipation. 'I imagine wonders,' he told her on 8 June 1915, 'ponds, statues, yew hedges, gold paint . . . you needn't be afraid of my Critical Eye – for the simple reason that it won't be able to find anything to criticise!' While Lawrence briefly dreamed of the garden as an exquisite imitation of a Renaissance court, the descriptions of avenues, clipped hedges, elaborate parterres and shady enclosures suggested to Lytton that Ottoline had created a setting of the kind to which he felt best suited. In his essays on eighteenth-century French civilisation, he had conjured up the pleasures of country life in the châteaux of intelligent, social women, a sophisticated world of concerts and masked balls, plays and endless conversation. It was a world more real to him than his own. Dreaming of the house he had not yet seen, he saw himself stepping through a mirror into the past to join an ideal society over which Ottoline, charming, eccentric, sympathetic and generous, would effortlessly preside, the perfect chatelaine. Unfortunately, the visions of the guest and his hostess were in conflict. Ottoline had not come to Garsington with the idea of making a court. Her own simple wish was that Garsington should become a wartime refuge in which every guest would be happy after their own fashion; all she cared for was that they should work at whatever they did best and enjoy themselves in any way that pleased them. Concerts and intellectual debates had no more of a role in her idea of how her home should be enjoyed than ragtime dancing and swimming and messing about in boats.

Nothing Ottoline created pleased her so much as her garden; her pleasure in it was a secret joy to be hugged to herself in times of loneliness and disappointment – and there were many such moments in the years at Garsington. 'It was indeed a ravishing decor,' she wrote after the house was sold, 'recalling to one a Watteau or a Fragonard, a Mozart opera, an Italian villa, a Shakespeare play or any of the lovely worlds that poetic art has created'. She continued:

And now that it has been left behind I am too sensitive to ask any of those who came, 'Do you remember sitting in the loggia, or standing on the stone terrace and looking down on the garden and the great spreading ilex tree? The peacocks flying there to roost, their long tails hanging behind, and the grey statues against the dark yew hedges and the pond where white bodies plunged, swam, and feathery poplars and elms beyond. Did you feel as I often did, this is too beautiful, it cannot last? . . .

How often have I pulled the curtain aside and leant out gazing, gazing at the moonlight cutting across the gates, blue-white, green-white, opalescent. And then – drawn by the magnetism of this beauty I would creep down and open the old front door and wander out, like a ghost into the silent world and watch the white flowers bathed in a still more luminous white light, and then on to the terrace, where the house seemed as if it were a piece of sculpture abstracted or taken out of time. I see it always in my memory.[10]

'Very remarkable, very impressive, patched, gilded and preposterous' was Lytton's first impression of the restored manor house. 'The Bedford Square interior does not suit an Elizabethan manor house in the wilds of Oxfordshire,' he added for good measure.[11] Desmond MacCarthy, visiting Garsington in winter, saw it as a charming toy, a 'wonderful lacquered box, scarlet and gold, containing life-size dolls in amazing dresses'. Ottoline used the similar idea of a jewellery box in describing it as 'a square casket, enamelled inside with reds and greens and greys and golds'. In Siegfried Sassoon's recollection, 'There was a sort of sumptuous homeliness about it all, for everything in the manor house was arranged with instinctive tact and in harmony with its moderate proportions. Its interior structure was charmingly ancient and irregular and its character had been lovingly preserved.'[12] At the opposite extreme, writhing at the memory of Ottoline as his benefactress, Clive Bell described it as 'that fluttering parrot-house of greens, reds and yellows'.

Garsington was, in most respects, agreeably conventional; it had never been part of Ottoline's scheme to print her image on every part of it. The attic floor occupied by the maids, Julian, and the younger guests boasted nothing more startling than a route to the roof. The main bedrooms on the first floor were airy and comfortable. Ottoline's little study looking down on the garden was a private haven decorated in green and gold, book-lined and piled with cushions.

The real transformation was in the ground-floor rooms; the inspiration behind them was Ottoline's recent visit to Bolsover with Russell. While Philip pondered the practical aspects of window-frames, doorjambs, shelving and stone-laying, Ottoline donned a holland overall and went off with her assistant, an enthusiastic chain smoker called Percy Wilkins, to pursue the perfect colours for each room. Percy's job was to bicycle to the Oxford paint-sellers, fetching the sample tubes from which they dabbed and mixed in search of the translucent sea-green and the rich Venetian red for the two sitting-rooms. The hall was painted a pearly grey to which Ottoline added streaks of pink to create the effect of a winter sunset. The final touch was one in which visitors were encouraged to take part, the painting of a thin gold line around each of the small wooden panels in the Red Room which were now resplendent with colour. Julian's young governess arrived to find herself looking up at a plumply beautiful schoolgirl (Maria Nys) balanced on a ladder, paintbrush in hand; Russell was persuaded to make a stab at gilding the ceiling beams and Lawrence spent most of his first visit working on the wall panels with an egg cup of gold paint. Frieda, none too pleased to see her husband slaving away so merrily on Ottoline's behalf, sat on a table swinging her legs and telling them they were wasting their time. 'Of course to her, who hadn't a home, and who carries her belongings round the world in a few trunks, it seems absurd to spend time and trouble on making a house really nice,' Ottoline noted.[13] Frieda had an unerring instinct for annoying her.

Ottoline and her maid, Evelyn (Eva) Merrifield, had been sewing curtains all through the winter of 1914. When the paint was dry, it was only a question of deciding which colour of material to add to each room before they tackled the arranging of the furniture. 'This', in Ottoline's memory, 'was a dreadful task, for each piece of old furniture has such a definite character and mind of its own that if it doesn't like a room it is hopeless to induce it to look well or happy. It asserts itself and has to be moved elsewhere.'[14]

Neither the praisers nor the detractors of Garsington have been forthcoming in their accounts of how the house was furnished; the most we find is a vague allusion to its having been full of 'bric-à-brac', although mention is made of some good contemporary pictures; the fact that the 'bric-à-brac' included a superb collection of Italian eighteenth-century furniture seems to have passed unobserved. Fortunately for us, there are still illustrated copies of the inventory of the 1928 sale when most of the house's contents were auctioned. Reading through it, we can catch a ghostly impression of Garsington in its prime.*

Standing in the lobby between the two sitting-rooms is the pianola, complete with some fifty rolls of music-hall songs, waltzes and a rousing selection of classical pieces suitable for exuberant dancing. Beside it in a corner is the little 'Planex' flash-camera with which Ottoline snapped her visitors on the best-quality German film, field glasses for walking expeditions and the lantern which was carried out into the flower-garden on summer nights. The floor of the entrance hall is bright with Persian carpets and against the wall is the wind-up gramophone which gradually took the place of the pianola. In the dining-room beyond, a black and gold Coromandel screen hides the kitchen entrance; guests faced each other across a long refectory table, sitting on plumply upholstered Italian chairs. Small red shades protect the candles from draughts and increase the sense of comfort on winter evenings. A Welsh oak dresser stands against one wall; the room is reflected from another wall by two pretty Venetian pier glasses.

The hall leads forward into the Green Room and, beside it, the Red Room, where the walls are the colour of vermilion sealing wax. The colour and the bold mixture of periods in the furniture make the room feel warm and friendly. A corner cabinet is full of the blue-and-white Nanking china which Philip had collected since his Balliol days. A sewing box holds Ottoline's silks and cotton reels, arranged in graded rows; some of the chair covers in this room were worked by her from Duncan Grant's designs. Rolled up behind a sofa ready for the

---

* Much of the furniture was eventually transported to Gower Street, the Morrells' last home.

evening's work is the magnificent flowered bedspread which Ottoline began embroidering in 1916, a brilliant jungle of silk leaves and blossoms which took ten years to complete. Samarkand rugs spatter the floor with yellow and crimson. There are a mass of occasional tables for ornaments, lacquered cigarette boxes, paperknives for cutting the pages of new books. A big Chinese jar in the corner is filled with an almost overpoweringly rich pot-pourri; card tables and backgammon boards are a reminder of Philip's passion for games. Two Chippendale-design easy chairs with high backs flank the fireplace; Ottoline liked to sit in one of them when she was alone in the evening, sewing or reading by the light of the oil lamps.

The broad wooden staircase from the hall leads up to a gallery along which Ottoline hung many of her favourite pictures: Conders, Johns, Grants, Henry Lambs, Spencers. There are none of the landscapes, hunting prints or family portraits that might seem at home. The floor is gaudy with oriental rugs again; jars of pot-pourri stand between Italian chests.

Ottoline's own bedroom overlooking the garden is simply furnished; none of the bedrooms is ornate. The marble washstand in the corner of one of the guest rooms is set with green Copeland china; the hot-water can at the side has a cover crocheted in coloured squares. The bed, a wooden four-poster, sports a satin quilt and a tapestry bedspread. There are a couple of armchairs by the fireplace, a writing-table and a small wooden stand of books chosen by Ottoline to suit the taste of the visitor. In her own room, a screen allows a favourite guest to sit and chat by the fire while Ottoline undresses, climbs into her small white bed and props herself up against a pillow, ready to start writing her journal or letters.

Garsington was full of beautiful things, but it was not luxurious. The oriental rugs lay on cheap green haircord. The curtains, while of rich colours, were of the most inexpensive materials. The floors of the two bathrooms were covered in linoleum: water was pumped up once a week from the spring which served the village.* When Ottoline made one of her rare visits to Welbeck and heard the ladies discussing the length of time needed for a bath, she was tempted to announce that she only had a proper bath twice a year, making do with the garden pool or a bowl of hot water in her room. Food at Garsington was plentiful, and plain. But it was a house which always felt like a home, and it became a haven to Ottoline's friends. 'You can't think how

* The second bathroom at the top of the house was installed for the use of the maids.

grateful I am to your Manor House for its sheltering arms,' Lytton wrote after a Christmas visit. 'What a lucky person I am to have such a refuge to fly to. It was a delightful oasis of a time ... How kind you are to us all, you and Philip, almost too kind I sometimes think!' (28 December 1916)

Looking through the letters and memoirs of the mass of visitors, it seems that they were always too busy with gossip and scandal to spare much time for their surroundings. 'Oh I tell you I had to have a mental bath when I got home, as well as a bodily,' Dorothy Brett's sister the Ranee wrote to their father, failing to add that her own moral contribution had been to use the house as a trysting-place for her young airman-lover, although he had not been invited. Virginia Woolf, visiting in 1917, the year when Bloomsbury had picked up the scent of Philip Morrell's liaisons, was impressed by Ottoline's gallant maintaining of appearances. Her account was more generous than most. In it, she painted a picture of the Red Room at night: Aldous toying with the green marble discs at the draughts table; Brett in trousers, puffing her churchwarden pipe; Ottoline resplendent in velvet and pearls and flanked by two of the pug dogs; Lytton sprawled back in a vast chair. It had been a cold Sunday and her chief impression, apart from the overheated air and the rich scent of pomanders, was of people moving slowly in droves from room to room, 'from drawing-room to dining-room, from dining-room to Ottoline's room' in sedate rotation. Virginia's cousin Fredegond Shove, whose husband, Gerald, was a former Apostle who had joined the Garsington pacifists, had come in from their estate cottage in the morning; in the evening, Ottoline and Virginia sat alone by the fire. There had been talk, but no revelations, about the difficulties with Philip; Ottoline was always a little more discreet than Virginia would have liked. 'The horror of the Garsington situation is great of course,' she concluded, 'but to the outsider the obvious view is that O. and P. and Garsington house provide a good deal, which isn't accepted very graciously ... Ott. deserves some credit for keeping her ship in full sail, as she certainly does. We were made immensely comfortable; a good deal of food; the talk had frequent bare patches, but then this particular carpet had been used fairly often.'[15]

Virginia's letters of thanks to Ottoline were always full of praises – the beds were voluptuously comfortable, the guests 'wonderfully interesting' – but the hospitality was too orderly for her own taste. It felt to her as if a little section of London society had been transported to the country and denied the pleasures of country life. It offered no fillip to her imagination; she was only teasing when she told Ottoline that *Mrs Dalloway* was going to be her Garsington novel. Her husband Leonard was put in mind of another book after his first visit; he felt that he had learned what it would be like to spend a week at Peacock's

Crotchet Castle, he said, where the guests never descended from the heights of theoretical discussion. It is unlikely that he intended to convey a compliment by the analogy.

The most evocative descriptions of life at Garsington appear in Juliette Huxley's memoirs, *Leaves of a Tulip Tree*. Only nineteen when she applied for the job of Julian's governess, Juliette's interview took place in the waiting-room at Oxford railway station; to her relief, since she had no teaching experience, Ottoline seemed far more interested in hearing about the ambulances she had seen coming to meet the boat at Dover on her arrival in England. She was told that the job would not involve much formal teaching; she was only required to keep Julian amused and stimulated, and to improve her French.

From 1915 to 1917, Garsington was Juliette's home and Ottoline the romantic and glamorous heroine she worshipped with unswerving adoration; to describe her she borrowed Stephen Tennant's later account of 'a Renaissance princess, lock, stock and barrel'. Ottoline was famously kind to anyone who worked for her (Jane Powell, her old nurse, was regularly invited to Garsington and treated as an honoured guest): Juliette was never made to feel that she was an employee. In the evenings, after Julian had gone to bed, she put on the Fortuny dress which Ottoline gave her when she admired it, and joined the guests for dinner. Nobody questioned how she and her charge spent their time or reproached them for leaving the stuffy little schoolroom at the top of the house to go bicycling or to swim in the pool. Watching Juliette dive into the dark water with her long hair unpinned from its usual flaxen braid, Ottoline was reminded of a water nymph or one of Crivelli's silver-skinned saints.

Juliette's evocation of Garsington was written many years later, but it is wonderfully vivid. She writes of Ottoline's nonchalant skill as she guided a phaeton through the crowded streets of Oxford, 'sitting high, in her wide hat, holding the horse at a proud pace', and of the evenings when she took her turn to read aloud as they sat by the fire in the Red Room, of her bending over Philip to change the pianola rolls while the guests danced, of the excitement of dressing-up when the big chest of elaborate costumes was pulled into the hall. In a lengthy set piece, she describes an evening when a huge party of guests had assembled at the house. Dinner was at the long dark oak table, with the candles gleaming behind their red paper hoods. The conversation was quick and brilliant, punctuated by Clive Bell's shrill laughter and Bertie Russell's high cackle as Mark Gertler did one of his flawless imitations – he was good enough to compete, on a much later occasion, with Charlie Chaplin – while Maria Nys and Juliette watched and adored. When the guests were having their coffee in the Red Room, Philip went to the pianola and began to play one of the

Hungarian Dances. 'Soon the party drifted out to the lawn: there was a full moon, stars in a great still sky and the dark ilex tree brooding like an ancient god. The music floated, powerful and alluring, through the open windows, its rhythm pulsating; one after the other, the guests obeyed the compulsion . . . shawls became wings, smoking jackets and ties abandoned to a strange frenzy of leaps and dances by the light of the moon.'[16]

There was no doubt in Juliette Huxley's mind about who was the presiding genius of the house. It was, in her words, 'a habitable work of art' and it was Ottoline who had created it and given it something of her own character. 'She gave the breath of life to her decor and within these walls which reflected her personality she moved with her own particular dignity . . . words cannot convey the radiant essence of her influence.'[17]

It was not without reason that Carrington cheerfully referred to 'The Manor Arms' and 'Garsington Pub', although neither of her hosts drank alcohol. 'How did we ever house such a company and feed them in those lean war days?' Ottoline wondered later. Every Friday, they poured down from London, some by train, others on motorbikes, bursting into the hall and calling for towels before they raced down to the pond or spread themselves over the lawn to whisper the latest bit of gossip about their hostess. To turn the pages of Ottoline's tiny Visitors' Books, hardly larger than pocket diaries, is to have the impression that the world and his wife came to the manor house, and the books are not a comprehensive record. Never doubting that their hostess was a woman of prodigious wealth, hungry visitors from undernourished wartime London expected lavish hospitality from the moment they arrived at Wheatley station to find Yeates, the coachman, waiting with the Garsington phaeton. Lytton, having once been asked if he could manage to bring butter with him because supplies were so short, turned on Ottoline in a rage because his breakfast was not big enough. He was, however, appeased when Ottoline had six eggs, fish, ham, scones and everything else that could be found at short notice sent up to his room as a second sitting. (Lytton, to be fair to him, was used to special treatment: 'You shall be coddled and comforted and loved and petted up to the highest powers,' Ottoline had promised him on 19 November 1916, shortly before this visit.)

Ottoline's fondest memories of Garsington were not associated with being a hard-working hostess. She described some of them in her memoirs: driving into Oxford on a bright winter night with the moon on her face and a rug tucked over her knees; taking picnic baskets for a long afternoon expedition; riding on the merry-go-round at Abingdon Fair or, late on a warm summer evening, riding her bicycle through the winding lanes where the air was heavy with the scent of hawthorn blossom. In the villages around Garsington, they called her 'the Gypsy Queen'.

A shortage of bedrooms in the manor house meant that the Morrells seldom had more than four guests under their roof at one time. Aldous Huxley had his own attic room in the manor after August 1916, but Dorothy Brett and Mark Gertler were separately installed in the old monastic building (it had once been used as a cowshed) attached to the house. Fortunately for Ottoline's hospitable intentions, the estate included several cottages and, opposite the manor, the Bailiff's House, into which large parties could overflow. It was here that Philip was quick to arrange a set of rooms for Russell, a generous action which helped to solve the problem of entertaining a man who was now fairly widely known to be his wife's lover.

The Bailiff's House, thoughtfully equipped with a resident housekeeper, became the chief nesting-place of the conscientious objectors (COs) who came to live at Garsington in the summer of 1916. Philip, a tireless advocate of their cause, was able to offer them work which would save them from further harassment. (Farm-work was deemed by the Government to be of national importance.) Fredegond and Gerald Shove were the first to arrive; Clive Bell followed a few weeks later. A Mr and Mrs Galloway were installed in another cottage which was hurriedly done up for them; Chappelow, a poet and aspiring opera-singer, was given Russell's rooms for a time, at the latter's request. Last to come was a zealous baker who rose at cockcrow each morning to knead dough for the village before putting in a full day on the farm.

The baker was the exception to the rule. Farmworkers have seldom sounded so lazy and incompetent as the conscientious objectors of Garsington proved to be. Chappelow retired to his room with a cold after being asked to try chopping small logs or flattening molehills. Clive Bell was prepared to do a little light hoeing with the village women, but Gerald Shove, who Lytton had once proposed to Philip for a private secretary, was a woefully inefficient keeper of poultry. Having successfully killed off half the hens, he tried to form a union for less work and higher wages. The villagers refused to join it and the scheme collapsed.

From the COs' point of view, it was an unsatisfactory way of life. They were not cut out to be paid labourers. None of them shared

Philip's love of pig-farming* and most of them, regardless of their inexperience, felt that they were being exploited as cheap labour under the guise of idealism. Ottoline's rapturous enthusiasm for helping in the harvest field charmed the villagers; to the COs, it was as inappropriate as Marie Antoinette's fancy for tricking herself out as a shepherdess. Her pleasure made a mockery of their obligation. Their discomfort was the product of an ambiguous social role. If Clive Bell had been asked whether he ought to be discussing Molière on the Garsington lawn with Lytton or taking instructions from a hedge-cutter, his answer would not be difficult to predict. In a country which was still rife with class-awareness, these middle-class intellectuals were not at ease among the straightforward people of Garsington village. A Tolstoyan community would have suited them better than a feudal estate where the new squire and his wife were treated with affectionate deference. The COs left little impression behind, although Clive Bell had rather fancied himself as a killer of hearts among the farm-wives. Asked for their views by the author, the older inhabitants of Garsington would only say that the pacifists had not treated the Morrells as well as they should have done.

A portrait of Ottoline at Garsington which omits any mention of her relationship with the village is only a pencil sketch; what emerges from the villagers' accounts is the impression that she was duplicating the kindly and active role played by her mother at East Court and, on a rather larger scale, at Welbeck. The Morrells were never perceived as intruders; Philip's family had, after all, owned land in the village for more than a century. Schoolboys bowled their iron hoops up and down the streets; the old village stocks were still on the green. It was a richly traditional community of the kind which welcomed benevolent patronage and which believed that the aristocracy had as good a right to be eccentric as any of themselves. Bloomsbury ridiculed Ottoline for her lack of conventionality; Garsington loved her for it.

On the day that she arrived at Garsington, the bell-ringers pulled on their ropes from morning to sunset. They had missed having a squire at the manor and Philip and Ottoline were ready to do what was expected of them. One of their first actions was to build a village hall in memory of Philip's father, to be used for dancing, Christmas

---

* Pig-farming played a central part in the village's life; almost every cottage in Garsington had its own sty. There was tremendous excitement when the Duke of York (later George VI) came to open a local bacon factory and lunched at the manor. The Duchess, later Queen Elizabeth the Queen Mother, was Ottoline's first cousin.

parties and as a meeting-point for the village boys. A caretaker was installed to keep order and Ottoline contributed a grand piano. The garden pool was handed over for weekly swimming lessons for the village school and a library was set up by Ottoline at the manor, from which the children could withdraw a book a week. In the school, she not only set the essay competitions but, after hearing that none of the children had toothbrushes, gave them lessons in dental hygiene, together with prizes for diligent cleaning. (Odd though this sounds to modern ears, those were the times when it was thought generous to offer a young man a full extraction and a set of false teeth for his twenty-first birthday present.) Mrs Ada Eden, one of the pupils still living in the village, remembered that the promise of prizes had been almost as exciting as the visits Ottoline made to the schoolroom, exuding 'a most gorgeous heavy scent' and wearing 'bright red shoes with very high heels'.

Talking to the author, Mrs Eden recalled how she sometimes used to see Ottoline 'flying up the road in her carriage and pair' to collect guests from Wheatley station, taking the steepest corner on one wheel, 'a whip in one hand and the reins in the other', and of the day when she came to the cottage and knelt by the fire, toasting bread and spreading it with farm butter for Mrs Eden's sick father, who had been refusing to eat solid food for six weeks. 'After that she was always sending chicken broth, brandy and calf's-foot jelly to help him get well – oh, she *was* a love!' Mrs Eden interrupted herself.

Relations between the church and the manor were polite but restrained. Every Sunday, Philip and Ottoline walked up the hill to the church where Philip read the lessons; every Sunday, Mr Horne the vicar directed his sternest sermons at the Morrell pew.[18] A truce was called each summer for the Sunday-school outing when the vicar led the procession in a wheezing black car while the children rode behind in a brightly-painted wagon loaned by the Home Farm and drawn by two shire horses.

Christmas was the time for which the Morrells were best remembered. A gigantic tree lit with hundreds of wax candles was set up in the big barn at Home Farm; stacked underneath it were the presents, each bearing the name of the child in Ottoline's decorative hand. After the tea of jellies and cakes, there were games and dancing; on the following day, Ottoline went to each of the cottages with presents for the family: sweets for the children, a striped shirt for the husband and a red flannel petticoat (still standard country underwear in those days) for the wife.

The Witcomb family had preferential treatment. Mollie Witcomb was born in Garsington in 1921. Her mother had been a parlourmaid both at Peppard and at Bedford Square until she left to get married in 1914. The oldest child, Philip, was Philip Morrell's godson and in

1917 he offered Mrs Witcomb and her four children a cottage opposite the manor house. The older children remembered how Philip used to come across in the evenings to see them before they went to bed; the younger ones recalled being taken over to see Ottoline every Christmas, lying in the boudoir 'in a lovely floaty negligée' and waiting to give them their presents. For their mother, it was always stockings or long kid gloves; for the children, there were books with affectionate inscriptions. Miss Witcomb retains vivid memories of Ottoline's appearance, not least of the time she came running down the steps from Dorothy Brett's studio 'wearing a costume such as one might see in a harem with Turkish trousers and her hair was bright green – I thought she looked marvellous!'

Many of the village stories about Ottoline are fragments of anecdotes, but all of them suggest that Ottoline was a much-loved figure and that the village relished the eccentricities for which her guests were so quick to criticise her. They liked it when she climbed on a steamroller and drove along the village street, tooting its horn; they were thrilled when two young pilots came to lunch with her and landed their plane in Church Close. 'You may wonder how so exotic a creature was received in a small village,' Miss Witcomb wrote. 'Remarkably, in spite of their pacifism, I never heard any of the village people say a word against the Morrells. Lady Ottoline brought such colour into our lives and we missed them greatly when they left.'[19]

15

THE FIRST YEAR AT GARSINGTON 1915–16

'Stagnation is what I fear; adventure and failure are far, far better.'
OM, *Journal*, February 1913

One unexpected happening soon after the move to Garsington was a cautious reconciliation between Ottoline and her family. There had been little to bring them together over the past decade, but the news that gentle, idealistic Lord Henry had been sent to Gallipoli was of grave concern to them all. The Portlands knew how fond Ottoline was of him and it was with the kindest of intentions that they asked her to visit them during her cure at Buxton in the spring of 1915; Welbeck was only an hour's drive away.

'I dread it more than I can say,' Ottoline admitted to Bertie, who knew what an unhappy misfit she had always felt there in the past, but the visit went well enough for her to go again the following week. It was a relief as well as a surprise to find that her fellow guest, the Comtesse de Baillet Latour, who lived at Welbeck from 1914 until 1920, was just as vehemently opposed to the war as herself, and that they were not rebuked for speaking their minds. Always susceptible to the company of pretty women – Elisalex de Baillet Latour was considered one of the most beautiful women of her day – and delighted to see Ottoline enjoying herself, the duke, too, decided to be in favour of peace, if only around the dining-room table.

If Ottoline still rebelled against the rigid formality of life at Welbeck, she confined her disapproval to her letters to Bertie; the Portlands, in turn, forbore to comment when she swished down to dinner tightly sheathed in scarlet taffeta. (An overlay of lace remained the evening convention in those days.) As a Liberal hostess to Bloomsbury and – so they had heard with deep embarrassment – the mistress of, at the least, Augustus John and Bertrand Russell, they had not felt inclined to keep in close touch with Ottoline. Yet the imminent move to Garsington suggested that she was finally opting for a respectable way of life. Safer subjects could now be discussed and disagreements buried in talk of gardens, neighbours and the charms of their pug-packs.

Friendship thrived at this undemanding level and Ottoline was touched by the duke's eagerness to see her new home. He made his first visit the day after her own return in mid-May, and pronounced it to be entirely to his own taste. 'He was really charming and admired everything,' she reported to Bertie, but she was anxious that his next visit should not coincide with that of her birthday guests. Posterity has been robbed of the pleasure of hearing how the conversation might have gone between Bertie, Lawrence and the duke.

The birthday weekend did not augur well for Ottoline's hopes of turning Garsington into an oasis of serenity. It took only one stroll around the garden by Lawrence and Ottoline on their own to bring Frieda's quick temper to boiling-point. On the second night, there was no escaping from the sound of thumps and shouts in the Lawrences' bedroom: Frieda made a grand exit the following morning. 'I shall always see that unhappy, distraught, pathetic figure standing in the hall hesitating whether he should remain here or whether he should follow her to London,' Ottoline wrote. 'Philip strongly urged him to assert himself and leave her. Of course he didn't . . .'[1] She grew more indignant still when, a few months later, she read some of Lawrence's poems to his mother across which the tempestuous Frieda had scrawled a curse: 'Damn you that you should write this about another woman.'

The Lawrences were followed by a steady flow of visitors, among them Duncan Grant, Mark Gertler and Maynard Keynes who spent four weeks at the manor house while he was recovering from appendicitis. Broad-minded though she was, Ottoline had not often met anyone so rapaciously homosexual – 'that satyr Keynes,' she called him in her journal, but he proved to be a captivating guest. Sitting beside his deck-chair on the lawn, she wondered how to define the subtle quality of his charm, 'a detached, meditating and yet half-caressing interest in those he is speaking to, head on one side, a kindly tolerant smile and very charming eyes wandering, searching and speculating, then probably a frank, intimate and perhaps laughing home-thrust, which may or may not illuminate one's own self-knowledge'.[2] Keynes enjoyed his convalescence; he made many return visits.

Lytton Strachey had been urging Ottoline to invite him to Garsington since her arrival in May. His curiosity was satisfied in July when Ottoline felt that the house was ready to pass the test of being scrutinised by her most critical friend. Lytton's first visit was made with Duncan Grant and Vanessa Bell; two weeks later, he returned with Clive Bell and his mistress, Mary St John Hutchinson, together with a sprinkling of the cropheads.

Photographs of Lytton on his visits suggest that he enjoyed them. In most, he is comfortably seated in a deck-chair under a tree, sometimes with a quilt over his knees, often with a parasol over his head, reading a book or deep in conversation. He looks cheerful. His thank-you letters to Ottoline range from the ecstatic, in which only 'the tongues of angels' could convey his joy, to the jocular, in which she was invited to imagine him so transformed in health by his stay that he was bounding over Hampstead Heath 'like a gazelle, or a Special Constable'. Lytton's letters to his friends tell a different story, of detestable fellow guests, brainless hosts, squirming pug dogs, hateful games and – the final straw – ragtime dancing. But he made no effort to leave and Virginia was one of the few to ask the obvious question: if he was so anxious to save her the agony of visiting Garsington (she was sufficiently put off by his accounts not to go there until 1917), why was he always going to stay, not just for weekends, but for weeks on end?

Virginia's question was a fair one and Lytton's response, that he needed country air, was not convincing. The truth was that, while unwilling to relinquish his dream of the country salon which Ottoline might have presided over, he still found Garsington more congenial than he was ready to admit. He had no country home of his own until 1918; what Ottoline offered was a civilised and – in the austerity of wartime – luxurious way of life in which he was free to participate whenever he felt inclined. A pleasant bedroom on the first floor was reserved for his use, except for the rare occasions when there was a much older guest who could not be farmed out to one of the cottages or the Bailiff's House. Ottoline was generous, and Lytton was, after his own strange fashion, grateful. Writing to his mother in 1915, he felt no constraints about telling her that he was having a splendid Christmas in a comfortable house full of agreeable people; going on to describe a party which Ottoline had given for the children of the village, he was full of admiration for her energy and kindness. But when it came to praising Ottoline's hospitality to his friends, self-consciousness overwhelmed him. How they would laugh at him! How much better that they should laugh at Ottoline.

The note of scorn was quickly sounded. Writing to David Garnett from Garsington during his second visit on 25 July 1915, Lytton told him that it was 'not particularly enchanting' and that he was dreading having to leave his room to make his way through a sea of pugs to have tea with the other guests on the lawn. Despite his dissatisfied tone, Lytton liked the house enough to spend most of the summer there, writing in his bedroom, resting on the lawn or taking short strolls through the village (where his straggling beard earned him the nicknames of 'Christ' and, more perceptively, 'Judas'). Ottoline, blissfully unaware of the jeering reports with which Lytton was regaling her friends, was delighted to see how well he had settled in. In her journal, she wrote that he was full of good humour because his work was going well, and that he was 'an adorable companion'. On one rainy day, he had read her Dryden's *All for Love*: 'We sat together a whole afternoon racked with emotion and enjoyment of it . . . He is a wonderfully sympathetic friend.'[3]

There was nobody more congenial than Lytton when she wanted to talk about books or to have the past illuminated with mannered wit, but it was to Lawrence that she turned for a sympathetic understanding of the countryside she loved. 'I find the purely intellectual people who have grown away from nature so dead,' she wrote after one of Lytton's longer visits; at such times, she longed to be with Lawrence, who could walk with her for hours and talk about nothing but what they saw.

As Ottoline became increasingly immersed in country life, it was inevitable that she should have started to draw comparisons between Lawrence's intuitive sympathy and Bertie's cooler, sharper mind. In June, they were still finding time to spend ecstatic nights together in London, with Ottoline writing that she longed for the next occasion; by mid-July, Bertie's fears that Garsington would divide them were being fulfilled.

The irony of the Garsington situation was, in Bertie's view, cruelly apparent. Through all the London years of their affair, they had been forced to seize on every moment of Philip's absence for their meetings. Since the move to the country, Philip had mysteriously begun spending weeks at a time in London. (The ground floor and drawing-room of Bedford Square had been kept for the Morrells' own use, while the rest of the house was rented out.) Time had never been more generously available to Ottoline and Bertie than when their relationship started to decline.

'Why then are you both so downcast, both you and Russell?' Lawrence asked on 19 July. Analysing the relationships of his friends was not his strength; the conclusion he drew from their glumness was that they were losing faith in his plans for a new kind of England. His eyes fixed on the future, he remained blind to the true cause of their despondency.

The more Ottoline saw of Bertie in a country setting, the more depressed she grew by his refusal to respond to it. She did not do well at hiding her feelings. 'Bertie and I had a walk in the rain yesterday,' she wrote. 'He gets dreadfully on my nerves, he is so stiff, so self-absorbed, so harsh and unbending in mind or body, that I can hardly look at him, but have to control myself and look away. And of course he feels this, and it makes him harsher . . . What can I do? I feel I *must* be alone and go my own way to develop my life, my own internal life.'[4] But when Bertie wrote to her on 27 July to urge her to admit that she disliked him and thought him a bore, she was overcome with remorse. 'It is *not true* . . .' she wrote back two days later. 'You *know* I love you.' Bertie could not be comforted. Garsington *had* altered the nature of their relationship. Things could never again be as they were, and he knew it. Ottoline had been lonely and unfulfilled, in his perception, when they had first met. It had been up to him to reassure her and to teach her not to be afraid of him. Now the roles were reversed and it was not a pleasant sensation. Writing to her on 9 September, he described himself as paralysed with terror in her presence, 'stiff and awkward from the sense of your criticism . . . it makes it impossible for me to be natural before you, though sometimes it makes me exaggerate the things you hate.' It was, he suggested, very much her fault that he was always in low spirits when he visited Garsington, since it was due to his being 'constrained and frightened' whenever she was with him.

Readers will be familiar enough with the pattern of the relationship to predict the consequences of their estrangement. Ottoline, reluctant to take responsibility for his unhappiness, ascribed it to nerves and suggested mental exercises; Bertie instead resorted to a little philandering, having dressed it in the more becoming costume of philanthropy.

He had met T. S. Eliot as his pupil at Harvard in the spring of 1914 when the younger man was a postgraduate working in the philosophy department. Since then, Eliot, nicely described by Wyndham Lewis as looking like 'a very attractive young Prufrock', had been completing his studies at Merton College, Oxford. Supported by Ezra Pound in London and Harriet Monroe, the editor of *Poetry* magazine in Chicago, he had begun to establish his reputation as a remarkable poet while Russell, having renewed the friendship, looked on with avuncular interest.

Two weeks after his marriage in June 1915, Eliot invited Bertie to lunch to meet his wife, Vivien. Stylish and quick-witted, she struck him as a most unlikely wife for the laconic New Englander; when she instantly drew him into a discussion about the marriage, he was intrigued. 'She is light, a little vulgar, adventurous, full of life,' he reported to Ottoline in July; '– an artist I think he said, but I should have thought her an actress . . . I think she will soon be tired of him.'

Vivien's highly-strung nature and flirtatious manner did not detract from her charm in Bertie's eyes. (He was strongly tempted to succumb to Katherine Mansfield's display of similar characteristics the following year; Katherine, like Vivien, was a stylish dresser with a quick mind and a sexual quality that was as strong as a scent.) He was devoted to Eliot, describing him to Ottoline, as he had Wittgenstein, as being almost like a son to him, but his interest in the marriage was ambivalent. It was kind of him to offer in September to share his tiny flat with them; it was generous to give Eliot £3,000 in engineering debentures; it was not in quite the same altruistic spirit that he encouraged Vivien to treat him as her confidant.

In September 1915, the Eliots travelled down to Eastbourne. Shortly after their arrival, Vivien sent Bertie a letter which he described to Ottoline as being close to suicidal; two months later, he told her that Mrs Eliot was 'a person who lives on a knife-edge, and will end as a criminal or a saint – I don't know which yet'. At the end of the year, hearing that Vivien was in a state of nervous collapse, he insisted on taking her to Torquay for a week to restore her health. What happened during that week is still hidden from view in the Eliot Archives. Whatever it was, it had a beneficial effect. Eliot, who was employed as a master in north London at Highgate Junior School, was overwhelmed with gratitude when Bertie paid for him to travel down and spend the following week with his wife. 'I often wonder how things would have turned out but for you,' he wrote in a letter Russell proudly included in his autobiography; '– I believe we shall owe her life to you, even.'

Ottoline knew Bertie well enough to doubt that his concern for Mrs Eliot and his wish to be with her was prompted entirely by her nervous condition. She was not, or so she frequently assured him, in the least hurt by his interest in Vivien, but neither was she prepared to have her to stay at Garsington. The meeting with Vivien, when it finally took place in March 1916, was a carefully arranged London dinner at which both Philip and Eliot were present. It was not a success. Eliot was withdrawn; Vivien struck Ottoline as being utterly unworthy of Bertie's interest. She was 'of the "spoilt kitten" type, very second-rate and ultra feminine, playful and naïve, anxious to show she "possessed" Bertie. When we walked away from the restaurant she headed him off and kept him to herself, walking arm-in-arm. I felt rather froissée at her bad manners.'[5]

Ottoline was no nurser of grudges. In later life, she became a staunch ally of Vivien Eliot's, but there was no room for friendship in the autumn of 1915. Ottoline's main concern then was to keep Bertie's mind in a cheerful state and to protect him from scandal at a time when the warmongers would have been happy to tarnish the name of their most eloquent opponent. All of her considerable influence was directed to this end. She would not allow him to blame himself (as a shocked Irene Cooper-Willis would have had him do) for the discovery that Helen Dudley was having a nervous breakdown

('She hasn't been well for years and I don't think the trouble with you was the whole cause of it . . . I hope you will put it behind you . . .'). She urged him to go on showing her his lectures which, she assured him, were '*very* good – quite wonderful' and to depend on her as he used to do, for 'oh my darling one, we do need each other and if only you will trust me, indeed I won't fail you'. (18 November 1915) In fact, nothing worried her more than Bertie's relationship with Mrs Eliot and the possible consequences of it. In September 1915, she sat down at her desk to write him one of her most sober letters.

My darling,
I was awfully glad to hear from you this morning, but I am rather worried about the Eliots. I am so afraid of what might happen if she became in love with you which is evidently quite likely . . . I feel you are running a very great risk and I beg and entreat you to be awfully careful – for if you want to do any lecturing or public work any scandal of this kind would entirely damage it and I don't suppose she is worth it.

Anyhow I don't think it would *help her* and help towards making the joint Eliot life happier to let her fall in love with you. I expect in a way it may have made her already more critical of Eliot. Don't think I want to interfere or to stop you but I feel *very* strongly that in getting her confidence you are rather separating her from Eliot – and besides that running an awful risk for your reputation . . . Please don't think I am cross, for I am not one bit, only I know you are led on by yr. sympathy and by yr. longing to set people straight and the big things you *can* do are more important.[6]

In the autumn of 1915, the autumn when the order was given to retreat from Gallipoli and when Asquith was struggling to retain his authority over a restless Cabinet and a weary, nervous country, Maria Nys (her hair now cropped by Philip) got scant sympathy from 'Auntie' for her homesick letters in her first term at Newnham College, Cambridge. Ottoline's thoughts, when she was not fretting over Russell's reputation, were all taken up by the needs of her friends.

Among a series of vicious attacks launched on the Asquiths during this autumn, the most unpleasant came from Oscar Wilde's ageing darling, Lord Alfred Douglas. In October, Douglas was prosecuted for publishing an outrageously libellous portrait of Wilde's literary executor, Robbie Ross. Ross, who had been a friend of Ottoline's since the early days of the Contemporary Art Society committee, was revealed during the trial to be a frequent visitor to Downing Street. Douglas, dissatisfied with the trial's verdict, saw an unmissable opportunity to renew the attack and make more dangerous trouble; he insisted, loudly, publicly and frequently, that the Prime Minister should step forward and denounce his friend as a depraved homosexual. Nobody who knew the history of Douglas's long campaign to ruin Ross would have dreamed of doing any such thing. Ottoline was among the supporters – they included Shaw and Wells – who rallied to Asquith's call and, far from denouncing Ross, testified to the unimpeachable quality of his character.*

Ottoline's second concern was with Lawrence. *The Rainbow*, heavily revised since she had first read it in the spring, was published on 30 September 1915. Both Lawrence and his publisher, Algernon Methuen, had been apprehensive about the response and their misgivings were well-founded. The reviewers were almost unanimous in their condemnation: one, James Douglas, declared it to have 'no right to exist in the wind of war. It is a greater menace to our public health than any of the epileptic diseases which we pay our medical officers to fight . . .' Lesbian scenes and Ursula Brangwen's mockery of a soldier's uniform were not congenial to the wartime climate; on 3 November, the Director of Public Prosecutions started proceedings to have all remaining copies of the book destroyed. The magistrate, a man whose own son had recently been killed at the Front, was not inclined to be sympathetic and it did not help Lawrence's case that the book was dedicated to his German sister-in-law. Methuen was fined ten guineas and ordered to withdraw the novel.

On 8 November, five days before the final hearing, Lawrence was staying at Garsington. Expecting rage and bombast, Ottoline was astonished by his resignation. He did not want to talk about the book: instead, every day, he went for long walks across the fields or helped her to set iris bulbs around one of the garden pools. The passports which would take them to Rananim in Florida had come through. While part of him longed to be gone, another part ached with sadness at what he would be leaving behind. 'My God, it breaks my soul –' he wrote to Cynthia Asquith from Garsington; 'this England, these shafted windows, the elm-trees, the blue distance . . .' (9 November 1915)

Ottoline had not thought that the new novel was his best work, but because she passionately believed in freedom of expression, she urged Philip to present their friend's case in the House of Commons. At the same time, she quietly set about raising money for Lawrence's journey to Florida, contributing £30 herself. 'It seems an awful pity that we should lose him as he is a real genius – isn't he?' she wrote to Edward Marsh in one of her appeals for funds, 'but I don't think he would live through the winter if he remained.' (12 November 1915) Knowing that Bertie had not forgiven Lawrence for accusing him in September

---

* This unexpected response drove Alfred Douglas to new peaks of irrational rage. Among the stream of abysmal poetry in which he heaped public abuse on Asquith's head that autumn, the most vitriolic effort accused the Prime Minister's wife of being a lesbian and her husband of filling Ross's pockets with money while other 'honest Englishmen' went to their deaths. The connection between these bizarre accusations was not, however, made clear.

of being inspired by 'a perverted, mental blood-lust', she tried to appeal to his better feelings by invoking his pity. 'He is,' she told him, '*awfully* sad.'

Philip did his best. He raised the subject twice in the House, on 18 November and again on 1 December, but without success. A note on the Home Secretary's brief ('As to a Mrs Weekley living at address of D. H. Lawrence, see 352857') suggests that the German connection rather than the offending book was the chief cause of the trouble. According to Aldous Huxley, writing to his brother Julian in December 1915, all Methuen's copies of *The Rainbow* were burned by the Public Hangman outside the Royal Exchange.

On 15 November, in a mood of black despair, Lawrence had written to tell Ottoline that he was sending her a bundle of manuscripts to look after for him. Among them was *The Rainbow*, which she was to keep, destroy or sell: he never wanted to see it again. More precious to Ottoline than the ill-fated manuscript was the paragraph which ended Lawrence's letter: 'I rather like Clive Bell – not deeply. He says it is tragic that you can never have any *real* connection with anybody. I did not say that there was a *real* connection between you and me. Let them not know – swine. But there *is* a bond between us, in spirit, deep to the bottom.' (15 November 1915)

And why, one wonders, did he not want 'them' to know about it? It would appear to have been the usual story. Affectionate in her presence and in his letters, Lawrence was not above jeering at Ottoline behind her back. On 7 December, he told her that Gertler and Brett were coming to tea with him in London. This was the tea of which Brett wrote, many years later, that they had sat around the fire, 'tearing poor O. to pieces' and after which Lawrence, alarmed by the thought that Ottoline might get to hear about it, wrote to avert the danger by laying the blame on his visitor. 'Don't trust Brett very much,' he told Ottoline on 12 December; 'I think she doesn't quite tell the truth about herself to you.' Neither, it seems, did he.

All through December, Ottoline continued to go out of her way to find ways of helping Lawrence – and to tell anyone who cared to listen how saintly she thought he was for putting up with such a termagant of a wife. 'If only we could put her in a sack and drown her,' she wrote to Bertie, and he agreed.

On 6 December, she was visited for the first time by Aldous Huxley, a Balliol student who old Mrs Morrell had told her was longing to see Garsington. Harriette Morrell had been far from pleased to learn that her granddaughter, Dorothy Warren, now planned to join Lawrence's Florida community; it was with a wish to placate her that Ottoline hurriedly wrote to invite Aldous to lunch. Shyness created the impression that he was aloof and a little critical of them all, but what else should one expect of a member of such a brilliant family? Ottoline thought as she sketched in his background for the benefit of Juliette Baillot. (Maria was not yet back from Cambridge.) Aldous made his second visit the following week and revised his first impression of Ottoline as an overwhelmingly affected woman, 'arty beyond the dreams of avarice'. The affectation was, he perceived, a nervous veneer; nobody could have been kinder to him than Ottoline when she took him off to sit on the green sofa in her study and encouraged him to talk about himself.

There was much to tell. Aldous was only thirteen when his adored mother died in 1908; three years later, an infection temporarily blinded him; it left him with only the partial vision of one eye. In 1914, shortly after his arrival at Balliol, his brilliant, charming brother Trevenen had hung himself. It was causing him bitter humiliation that, at a time when most of his university friends had gone to fight, he was too blind to be eligible. He did not have his brother Julian's clear sense of direction. He had published some poetry; he had even, at the age of seventeen, written (in braille) an eighty-thousand-word novel, but he was not sure that he wanted to commit himself to a literary career. He did, he added, rather like playing jazz piano. Lawrence, Ottoline thought, would enjoy the company of this unusual young man, one of the few she had met who towered above her in height; if Aldous had thoughts of becoming a novelist, what better introduction could she give him? The next time she saw Lawrence, she suggested that he might like to ask Aldous to tea in London.

The meeting was a success. 'I like Huxley *very* much,' Lawrence reported on 22 December. 'He will come to Florida.' Aldous, too, was impressed, although he was sceptical about Rananim. The philosophy of blood did not attract him, but still – 'one can't help being very much impressed by him. There is something almost alarming about his sincerity and seriousness – something that makes one feel oneself to be the most shameful dilettante, persifleur, waster and all the rest.'[7]

Lawrence had friends of his own who he was impatient to have to stay at Garsington, and who he took there, rather to Ottoline's annoyance, at the beginning of December. Devoted to him though she was, the visit was an imposition and his friends were not the guests she would have chosen to entertain. Hussein Suhrawardy merely puzzled her when he compared her to a Persian princess, grand and cruel, but she was actively repelled by the other two. '[Philip] Heseltine is tall and blonde, soft and so degenerate that he seems somehow corrupt,' she wrote. 'Kouzoumdjian . . . has a certain vulgar sexual force, but he is very coarse-grained and conceited . . .

He and Heseltine seem to pollute the atmosphere, and stifle me, and I have to escape from their presence."[8]

It was not a comfortable visit. They took out the dressing-up box and played games, but Frieda got on Ottoline's nerves and Lawrence was torn between the pleasure of dressing to compete with the Garsington peacocks and the guilt of allowing himself to indulge in such escapist antics. It mortified him to see what a bad impression his friends were making on Ottoline. When, with scant enthusiasm, she agreed to allow them to come again the following week, he wrote begging her to be patient and to look for their merits, not just for their defects.

Ottoline's last good deed that month was to submit to Lawrence's request that she should ask his friend Middleton Murry to stay. Katherine Mansfield was away in France, grieving over the recent death of her brother; it upset Lawrence to think of Murry spending Christmas alone in London. An invitation was dutifully issued and as dutifully accepted. 'Bertie Russell, me and Clive Bell,' Murry wrote in a gloomy letter to Katherine on 23 December, the eve of his departure for Garsington. 'Feasts of intellect, I don't think.'

Christmas was far from being the sober affair Murry had anticipated. Ottoline's birthday house-warming had not been the success she had hoped for; this was her chance to make up for it. Two cottages and the Bailiff's House were pressed into use for the biggest house party yet. Murry, writing to Katherine from an attic room in one of the cottages, loyally refused to say more than that 'he was not having a bad time'; in fact, he was having the time of his life. Lytton was there, and Keynes and even, briefly, the philosopher George Santayana. The Bells, respectably reunited for such a traditional occasion as this, were visiting with their sons Julian and Quentin; Lytton brought along a brother and sister. Lord Henry, still very pale and withdrawn after his experiences at Gallipoli, came for two days. And, for once, there were no squabbles. Russell and Lawrence, in a sudden rush of Christmas goodwill, combined to send Ottoline a gift which outdid even her own wild generosity. Their quarrels were not her fault: this was their graceful apology for disappointing her. 'It is a beautiful present and I am ever so delighted to have it,' Ottoline wrote gratefully to Russell, 'but I felt very unhappy too for I fear it was awfully expensive, and I felt so worried and unhappy at you and L. paying so much when I

---

* Philip Heseltine (1894–1930), who later became involved in satanism, significantly took the name of Peter Warlock for his short career as a composer of songs and airs, the best known being a Yeats cycle, 'The Curlew'. Dikran Kuyumjian (1895–1956) is better known as Michael Arlen, the pseudonym under which he wrote several novels, including, in 1924, the popular *The Green Hat*.

know you were both so poor ... I thank you *ever* so much.' (January 1916)*

It was a splendid Christmas. The first village Christmas party was held in one of the farm barns and on the same day all the servants and several of the village families were invited to a dance in the manor house. In the daylight hours, the guests went out for long walks across the wintry fields, talking, talking – Murry had never imagined that people could devote so much time to talk as they did at Garsington. In the evenings, there were charades and one-act plays of which one bore the mock-heroic title, 'The Life and Death of Lytton'.

To Murry, by far the youngest of the guests, they seemed like creatures from another world, 'fantastic and fin de siècle...' he reported to Katherine. 'I am very much like a babe in the wood.' Most fantastic of all was Ottoline, and Murry was overwhelmed by her warmth and kindness. When he left Garsington on 28 December, armed with £5 to help him on his journey back to Katherine in France, his last glimpse was of Ottoline running like a deer across the forecourt to wave him goodbye. It was a gesture, he told her, which had warmed his soul: 'the memory of it warms me now.' (January 1916) Katherine added a postscript of her own: 'I have been wanting to write to you ever since the day Murry came and said "There's a perfectly wonderful woman in England" and told me about you ... I long to meet you. Will you write to us again?'†

Ottoline knew that Katherine and Murry were planning to return to England in April to take a cottage in Cornwall next to the Lawrences, near St Ives. (Frieda's status as an enemy alien had caused the authorities to refuse them permission to leave the country for Florida, or anywhere else.) Murry must also have indicated to his hostess that Katherine shared her dislike of Frieda, for Ottoline's next letter was addressed to her and solicited sympathy about Frieda's latest outburst.

The fault was one of indiscretion on Ottoline's side, brashness on Frieda's. Most unwisely, Ottoline had confessed her dislike of Frieda to Philip Heseltine on his second visit to Garsington; staying with

---

* The present was a large folder of reproductions of the paintings in the sacred caves of Ajanta in India.

† Both Lawrence and Beatrice Glenavy, a friend of Katherine Mansfield's, mention an earlier occasion on which they had taken Katherine late one evening to Bedford Square. In Lady Glenavy's memoir, *Today We Will Only Gossip* (Constable, London, 1964), she wrote that Katherine and she had been wandering around the drawing-room looking at the pictures and furniture when Katherine 'said softly to me, "Do you feel that we are two prostitutes and that this is the first time we have ever been in a decent house?" I knew she was acting a part and wanted me to join in the game.' (p. 80) Ottoline's journals confirm that this semi-encounter took place in the spring of 1915.

the Lawrences in Cornwall, Heseltine reported what she had said. Lawrence shrugged it off, but Frieda wrote a furious letter indicating that she was not prepared to put up with Ottoline's interference in their marriage. It was a small and silly incident, but it marked the beginning of the estrangement which led to the portrait of Ottoline as Hermione Roddice in *Women in Love* before the end of the year.

In August 1914, a man had to be five feet eight inches to qualify as a soldier because the response of volunteers had been so overwhelming. By the end of 1915, the horrors of the Marne, Ypres and Gallipoli had sunk in. No amount of stirring propaganda could disguise the unglamorous facts of disease, mutilation and death. The acceptable height was dropped by five inches, but volunteers continued to hang back at a time when the leaders were desperately anxious to swell the ranks. The image of a tank whose engine only turned over when it was fed with a steady stream of bodies is not an exaggeration of the common view of the situation two years into the war. The body supply could not be allowed to dry up.

A national register had been compiled in 1915. It showed that well over two million single men of military age could still be recruited. The Derby scheme for Pals' Battalions in which 'those who joined together should serve together' attracted nearly a quarter of this number. It was not enough. On 23 January 1916, the Military Service Act which was to enforce recruitment by conscription passed its third reading. Philip Morrell was among the thirty Liberals who fought to see that it contained adequate provision for pacifists. When the new law was implemented in March, it granted exemption for anyone who could satisfy a tribunal that they were medically ineligible, were doing work of national importance or were unable to bear arms on the grounds of conscience. In practice, however, the bill proved to be far harsher than these clauses suggested.

The Military Service Act produced a new kind of pacifist or, rather, it forced pacifists to redefine their beliefs. They did not regard the war itself as an evil. They believed that it was wrong to establish militarism in Britain for a war which aimed to put an end to militarism. The end was acceptable; the means was not. It was a view which was strengthened by the pitiless insensitivity of the tribunals and by the brutal treatment of men and women who were prepared to go to prison and even to die for their beliefs.

The hero of all those who opposed conscription in 1916 was Bertrand Russell, now wholeheartedly committed to fighting the battles of the No-Conscription Fellowship (NCF) from the lecture platform. Only the absent Lawrence was disdainful. ('I don't believe your lectures *are* good. They are nearly over, aren't they.') To the pacifists and to soldiers like the young actor Miles Malleson whose brief experience of war had left them baffled and uncertain as to the rightness of supporting it, Russell's lectures were wonderfully lucid. Malleson, standing at the back of the hall, listened for the first time to 'a passionate and reasoned argument that the slaughter of my generation should be brought to an end as soon as possible'. Lytton Strachey, nervously awaiting his own tribunal, dropped his cynic's mask to say of Russell: 'I don't believe there's anyone quite so formidable to be found just now upon this earth.'

Philip Morrell, in his quieter way, was equally courageous. Much to the disgust of his Burnley constituents, he frequently voiced his disapproval of the conscription bill in the House and did everything in his power to help his friends to outwit the tribunals. As a landowning farmer, he could testify that they would be doing work of national importance by tilling the Garsington fields; as a politician, his name added weight to their pleas for exemption.

Ottoline had never been more proud of the two men she loved best, both illuminated now by a sense of purpose. While Russell enthralled the lecture-rooms and expressed the views his audiences felt but could not clearly articulate, Philip threw his energies into defending the COs, using his legal training to help them to prepare their cases. The much-mocked 'Pipsey' of the Bloomsberries' letters was suddenly a man of influence. Vanessa Bell, fretting over the outcome of Garnett's and Grant's appeals, turned to Philip for help. Keynes's well-intended announcement that Mr Garnett's was a special case because his mother had visited Tolstoy misfired; Philip's staider observations proved more effective at the Ipswich appeal on 19 May. Permission was given for the two men to embark on a fruit-farming scheme at Wissett Lodge in Suffolk, where they were joined in due course by Vanessa and protected by a sheepdog named, appropriately enough, after Duncan Grant's chief patron, Lord Henry Bentinck.

Carrington, a guest at Vanessa Bell's house party at Asheham in Sussex late in 1915, tiptoed into Lytton Strachey's room with the idea of snipping off his magnificent beard. He opened his eyes as she bent over the bed; she fell instantly in love with him. That is how the story is always told, although Carrington wrote after his death to thank Ottoline 'for those days at Garsington when I grew to love him'. Certainly, the incident took place and Gertler was dismayed to learn that Lytton, who had been unsuccessfully pursuing him in 1915, had now stirred Carrington's heart. 'A man so contemptible as that ought not ever to make one miserable or happy. And so I shall try to forget it,' she told Gertler in December, but by the spring of 1916 it was clear that she was unable to put Lytton out of her mind. Her visits to Garsington that year were frequent and it was during the summer that Lytton decided to risk spending a week or so alone with her at Wells. The relationship would, of course, be platonic. It could not be otherwise for, as he told his brother James on 31 May in a language that still had all the thrill of novelty, 'cunts don't particularly appeal to me . . . they make me uneasy'.

Carrington was far from Lytton's thoughts in the early part of 1916. It was a measure of the Government's desperation that they reckoned it worth their time and money to force such an unsoldierly man into uniform. Lytton had, after an early phase of enthusiasm for the war, stopped knitting scarves for the soldiers and joined the pacifists. He attended Russell's lectures and took advice from 'Pipsey' Morrell on how best to prepare himself for the inevitable call-up. It came in February and Lytton was nervous enough to treat it seriously. 'I wish I could appear for you, but I feel a man would be better,' Ottoline told him in an undated letter; instead, she asked him to come and stay at Garsington while Philip coached him for his appearance in court. Lytton was stimulated by the prospect, now that he had Philip's support. 'I am quite ready if necessary to tell any number of lies,' he blithely informed his brother. 'But I shall tell them with my eyes open. Footpads! Footpads at the street corner! Knock them down if you can, but if you can't cut and run!'[9]

Cutting and running was out of the question, but Lytton and Philip's double act at the March hearing in Hampstead made it almost impossible for the tribunal to uphold a case for making a soldier of the bearded stick insect who stood before them. The act was less of a music-hall turn than it is often made to sound: both Philip and Lytton were acutely conscious of what they were doing. The air cushion on to which Lytton gingerly lowered himself indicated the problem of piles; the memorable declaration that he would interpose his body between his sisters and a soldier, should they be threatened, was a careful definition of the approved pacifist stance. A doctor's letter was not deemed necessary at the medical examination which followed the hearing; Lytton's etiolated form was all that was required to gain a full exemption from his tittering examiners. 'Hurrah! Hurrah!' Ottoline wrote to him on 17 March. 'I am glad – it *is* a relief. I cannot tell you how glad I am. Dearest Lytton.'

Lytton's winter visit to Garsington was far too brief to satisfy Ottoline – he made up for it by coming for three weeks in April and staying most of the summer – but it had pleased her to see him treating Philip with real respect at last. There was no talk of Carrington's overtures, but when Ottoline knocked on his door after breakfast, she could look forward to being called in to hear the latest news about his homosexual affairs. In 1911, she had been shocked by his stories; now, she cheerfully admitted to finding them 'very stimulating to my love of fantastic confessions and descriptions'. Most of all, she liked the sense of sharing his secrets. It must, she thought, mean that she was looked upon as a real friend; she told him, not for the first time, how agonising she would find it if he ever turned against her. When she left the room, Lytton resumed a letter to his brother:

> It is pretty dreary here – they're so stupid, so painfully stupid; but I suppose it's healthy. Huxley is just what you described. I really don't know what to say to him.*[10]

Aldous, visiting Garsington towards the end of January 1916, was more enthusiastic. 'The Morrell household is among the most delightful I know,' he told his brother Julian; 'always interesting people there and good talk.' Anxious to make some return of hospitality, he invited Ottoline to tea in his rooms at Balliol.

This was her first introduction to a circle who were to become a central part of Garsington society, the Oxford undergraduates; until now, all her university friendships had been through Bertie, the ex-Apostles and their complicated network of Cambridge connections. Oxford, on the other hand, had been tainted by her unpleasant memories of Black Hall visits. Aldous's friends were, she decided after meeting young Lord Harewood, Tommy Earp, and a man whose nickname of 'the Bishop' evidently owed less to his religious interest than to a weakness for ecclesiastical costume, a little too flippant and effeminate for her taste. She was unable to take their literary posturing seriously. Still, the jewelled offerings of their magazine, *The Palatine*, were vastly preferable to the latest section of *Goats and Compasses*, a tract on sex versus science, which had just reached her from Lawrence's Cornish cottage. Reading it with a heavy heart, she wondered how a man 'so kind and understanding and essentially full of tenderness, could turn round and preach this doctrine of hate'. Lawrence's letter told her that he and Frieda were 'more married than ever before'. And 'voilà leur enfant', Ottoline observed as she finished her reading. She remembered how Bertie had recently crushed the person who asked him what he thought of Lawrence's new book of poems, *Look! We Have Come Through!* 'I am glad they have come through,' he had remarked, 'but why should I look?' And why should she? She continued, however, to send the books which Lawrence said he needed, along with practical gifts of warm bedspreads and walking boots.

The only semi-permanent guest at Garsington that winter was Molly MacCarthy, suffering from a bout of depression. Her marriage,

---

* 'Can you – will you – come on Wednesday to meet Aldous, oh *do, do*,' Ottoline had urged him in an undated letter: 'I will have a lovely taxi to meet you at 6 p.m. free of all charge. I loved your visit . . .'

never an easy one, had survived Molly's brief and injudicious affair with the sandy-haired, pot-bellied Clive Bell. That relationship had not lasted beyond the evening when Molly and he were nearly hit by a bomb, leading her to think how little she wanted to die in the arms of such a man. Desmond did not forgive the lapse. The pattern begun by his wife was picked up and continued by him. After pursuing Irene Noel until she married Philip Baker, he turned his attentions to another Irene, the coldly beautiful Miss Cooper-Willis who had fascinated Ottoline and Bertie in 1915. Opening her Valentine's Day post at Garsington, Molly read these discouraging words from her husband: 'I like her *very* much. I believe she's 1916. What luck meeting her so early in the year!'[11] The letter marked the beginning of a love-affair which lasted into 1917 and provided Irene with splendid material for her only novel.*

Ottoline had been devoted to both the MacCarthys ever since their first meeting. She liked them for their quick, clever minds and their kindness; when Desmond and Molly teased her, there was never a sting in the criticism. Desmond could remark on her startling appearance in a hat apparently trimmed with knitted hedgehogs; Molly could laugh at her for stopping to straighten her stockings in a blinding snowstorm, and there was no cruelty in it. The quality the Mac-Carthys valued above any other was intuitive sympathy. They found this in Ottoline and told her so: 'it does me so much good to see the wisdom of the heart which I think you have,' Molly wrote to her in 1913.

In their whimsical way, the MacCarthys were Ottoline's most loyal friends, but they often sighed over the confusion which enveloped her life as thoroughly as one of her voluminous silk cloaks. What were they supposed to think when she told them that nobody else knew about her relationship with Russell, leaving them to discover that Lytton Strachey was under precisely the same impression? Lytton was convinced that Ottoline had drifted into the affair to escape from a miserable marriage, Desmond reported to Molly in 1913. 'He thinks Ottoline's life is wrecked by Philip. I think *not*. But we will have a talk about this and remain, shan't we? loyal, to the dear bewildered bewitched self-entangled aspiring one?'[12]

Ottoline had often been a sympathetic audience to the problems of life with the charmingly irresponsible Desmond. Now, when Molly was at a low ebb, she took her into the manor house and looked after her. By Molly's own account many years later, Philip also tried to

* *The Green-Eyed Monster*, published in 1923, appeared under the pseudonym of Althea Brook. The novel contains a faint portrait of Russell as Tom Wolfe and an unkindly identifiable one of MacCarthy as Edward Russell, a character who has all of Desmond's flaws and none of his graces.

solace her after his own fashion, but Molly was not always a reliable witness in these matters. Her claim to have also turned down Bertie Russell's advances comes into the same category of dubious second-hand report; by the time these stories were being related, every woman in Bloomsbury was claiming to have been eyed by Philip or propositioned by Bertie. Not to have received their attentions was to seem unattractive.

Ottoline saw a little of Desmond when she went to London in early March to hear the last of Russell's wartime lectures, and to entertain her friends. The shrunken quarters at Bedford Square ruled out a revival of the Thursday revels; instead, she improvised a tea-party in the front of the big double drawing-room, the inner part of which now served as her bedroom. Bertie had already been mollified by a long afternoon alone with her; Gertler, Carrington and Brett were in ebullient form; even the inscrutable Tom Eliot grew lively enough for Ottoline to think that she had been unkind to nickname him 'The Undertaker'.

Vernon Lee had been at Russell's final lecture, 'waving her hands about, with her pince-nez dangling' as she held forth, most irrelevantly, about a cigarette-case until she was asked to sit down. She was there again when Ottoline dined with the MacCarthys at the Chelsea house Molly unromantically described as 'not squalid, and yet humble'. At dinner, the conversation was about Stendhal and the loss to them all in January that year of a much-loved friend, Henry James. Meaning, perhaps, to pump Ottoline about Vernon Lee's involvement with Irene Cooper-Willis, Desmond offered to take her home by taxi. At Bedford Square, Ottoline's hip-bath was steaming gently by the drawing-room fire.* '"How comfortable it looks," he remarked. He took up my volume of Villon that I had been reading, and sat down as is his way, forgetful of time, and read poem after poem, with his special and delightful capacity of enjoyment, and on and on we drifted talking of the delights of poetry.'[13]

Spring marked the opening of the Garsington season. Lytton was staying in early April 1916, when Russell brought Eliot for his first visit. Anxious to make up for her refusal to entertain Vivien, Ottoline assured Bertie that she had thought him '*awfully* nice'; to her journal, she confessed that she still found him a dull dog. 'I felt him monotonous without and within. Where does his queer neurasthenic poetry come from, I wonder. From his New England Puritan inheritance and

---

* Hip-baths were high-backed tubs, in use before the modern bath became popular.

upbringing?' In a desperate attempt to break through the veil of his reserve, she switched to French, but Eliot spoke French just as he did English, slowly, precisely and flatly. Low though Ottoline's opinion of his wife was, she could understand her preference for Bertie's exhilarating company.

The solution to entertaining the MacCarthys seemed to be to invite them on separate occasions, but Molly's view of Ottoline's gift for causing confusion was confirmed when she arrived for Easter weekend. Among the fellow guests were her ex-lover Clive Bell, his mistress, Mary Hutchinson, and Roger Fry. The first two were awkward enough from her own point of view, but what had prompted Ottoline to ask her old enemy to Garsington? For herself, Molly was fond of Fry and grateful for the number of times he had let her use Durbins as a country refuge, but everybody knew that he and Ottoline had never patched up their differences. What was going on? Vanessa Bell, too, was puzzled and curious. So Ottoline had interviewed him in her boudoir! What had she said? Greatly to the disappointment of all parties, Fry was honest enough to admit that Ottoline had never mentioned their quarrel and that she had been both cheerful and friendly. Untempted by the charms of Molly or Maria Nys, he was unable to offer Vanessa any scandalous titbits; she had to make do with a vague account of Fry's listening 'to the doors opening and shutting all night long in the passage . . . I suppose I ought to have gone to the W.C. once or twice to keep up appearances.'[14]

The weekend's unlooked-for tranquillity – woodland picnics, long walks, a visit to a nearby village where Ottoline's favourite and somewhat eccentric gay bishop was speaking – was interrupted on the Sunday afternoon by a shrieking army of Asquiths. Weekends at The Wharf were chaotic and claustrophobic – the rooms were small and low and the walls were paper-thin – and by the end of them, the hosts were usually as eager to escape as the guests. That they might not receive a warm welcome in a pacifist household seems not to have occurred to them as they burst in, 'all talking shrilly against each other, Margot's and Violet's voices above the others'.

Asquith was in good spirits that day. A buzz of calls for his resignation had been beaten off, the King had warmly congratulated him on having weathered the storm and news of the Easter rebellion in Dublin had not yet come through. When Ottoline beckoned him up to her study to give him a piece of her mind about the way the conscientious objectors were being treated, Asquith followed with an amiable grin.

I started by saying, 'You *know* I am a rebel' [Ottoline wrote to Russell on 25 April]. He really was serious about all I said and asked a great many questions, all of which I answered to the best of my ability, about the number and status etc. of the COs and what could be done for them . . . He was *very* nice and really rather sympathetic. I told him Norton who was downstairs was one and introduced him to him afterwards. So he saw there are *some* quite respectable men among them!

Then you will also have heard [from Clive Bell] that the B[ishop] of Oxford arrived in the middle of it all – and he in his turn had a long lecture from me and from Philip and he was evidently impressed and offered to write a letter to the Papers or to speak in the House of Lords.

Philip will tell you about it if you would like to see him. I think it is important to have a definite scheme that these people can support if one hopes to get them to move at all ... I long to hear from you, my darling. Your O.

Ottoline's tenacity in pressing the pacifists' cause was considerable and when Margot Asquith sent her car over to Garsington to fetch them to tea at The Wharf the following week, she accepted with alacrity, seeing another chance to present the COs' case. But when they arrived, the Prime Minister had vanished. 'Horrid old thing,' Ottoline crossly wrote, suspecting him of having done so on purpose to escape interrogation. Instead, she was obliged to sit and listen to Margot romancing about her long-ago love-affair with Lord Henry.

Another opportunity misfired when Desmond MacCarthy was taking his turn to visit Garsington in mid-May. Violet Asquith had invited herself to stay and Ottoline, not realising how strongly she disapproved of the pacifists, saw a fresh opportunity to get a favourable account of them to the Prime Minister: Violet was nothing if not talkative. With this in mind, she asked a young CO to stay, along with Lytton and Keynes. Unfortunately for her intentions, an angry squabble broke out between Violet and Lytton within a few hours of her arrival. Violet, 'who can't be wrong' as Ottoline wearily observed on a later occasion, started abusing the pacifists for cowardice and saying that they ought all to be deported. When Lytton countered this by saying that it sounded as though there wasn't much difference between the Government, for whom he presumed she spoke, and the Prussians, Violet snatched up her bag and rushed out of the room in tears. She did not leave the house, as Ottoline rather wished she might do, but contented herself with spoiling the weekend by ostentatiously refusing to speak to Lytton. Clearly, no kind account of the pacifists would be going back to The Wharf that week. All of MacCarthy's genius for spreading oil on troubled waters was required to placate the angry visitor.

The events of the next two weekends went into everybody's diaries. Clive Bell, Brett, Carrington and Lytton were out on a picnic with Ottoline when a breathless maid arrived with the news that someone had drowned, the Prime Minister had arrived and a strange gentleman had plunged into the pond. The story, when it could be put straight, was that Lucy, the new girl-groom, had been swimming in the garden pond with the housemaids when she saw the Prime Minister crossing the lawn. In unruffled water and with several swimming medals to her credit, she had promptly staged a drowning-scene. Robbie Ross, one of the Asquith party, had gallantly plunged in to rescue her and the Prime Minister, never averse to eyeing pretty women, had had a splendid time ogling the shivering swimmers. Ross was loaned one of Philip's suits and away they all went again. The housekeeper had borne the brunt of it, for Mrs George Keppel* had 'lost her head and berated my poor Millie like a fishwife. The story went the rounds of London. "Lucy the groom drowning in Garsington pond" – and for years the Prime Minister's first question to me was, "How is Lucy?"'[15]

Lytton, who had been raging with boredom at the prospect of spending the following weekend at Garsington with Philip Snowden, the elderly leader of the Independent Labour Party, brightened up considerably when Asquith appeared for what was becoming the habitual invasion from The Wharf. It was an opportunity he had not been given since Ottoline had introduced him to the Prime Minister at Bedford Square two years earlier. Lytton's impression on this occasion was of a likeable old lecher with a disarming zest in his pursuit of carnal pleasure. 'You should have seen him making towards Carrington,' he reported to his brother, '– cutting her off at an angle as she crossed the lawn. I've rarely seen anyone so obviously enjoying life; so obviously, I thought, *out* to enjoy it; almost, really, as if he'd deliberately decided that he *would*, and let all the rest go hang. Cynical, yes, it's hardly possible to doubt it; or perhaps one should say just "case-hardened." Tiens! One looks at him and thinks of the War . . .'[16] Perhaps, Lytton decided as he watched Asquith's little pointed tongue flicking over his lips, more of an artful dodger than the fleshy medieval abbot he had at first selected as the best analogy.

With Russell's trial only a week away, one might suppose it was to discuss this that Ottoline called Asquith up to her study again that afternoon. Bertie was well able to take care of himself in court; he had indeed invited himself to be tried by publicly declaring his authorship of a pro-pacifist leaflet, the distributors of which had been imprisoned. In fact, Asquith had been summoned to explain the Irish situation. Ottoline's mind had been stirred by the news of the Easter Rising and of the fifteen executions which followed it when the military were given a free hand; she had also heard that Sir Roger Casement was going to be tried for treason after being discovered landing in Kerry from a German submarine. Ottoline, who prided herself on her Irish blood, was in no doubt about where her loyalties lay: it shocked her

---

* Alice Keppel, who sometimes stayed at The Wharf, had been the mistress of Edward VII; her daughter was Violet Trefusis.

that friends like Lytton were indifferent both to the brutal suppression of the Sinn Fein movement and to Casement's fate.[17]

Asquith was less antagonistic to her views than she had expected. The poverty he had seen on his recent visit to Dublin (11 May) had convinced him that there, rather than in British intervention, lay the true reason for the rebellion; the Sinn Fein movement was, he told Ottoline, more poetical than revolutionary. On Ireland, he was accommodating and even sympathetic; on the question of Casement's trial, however, he was immovable.

The Casement trial was an ugly business and one which badly damaged Asquith's credibility in his own party. Ottoline had met and been impressed by Roger Casement when he was gathering support for his courageous investigation of the brutalities in the Congo. It was inconceivable to her that the Government would hang a man who had made his name as an humanitarian and an idealist. At a time when fifty COs had been deported to France and thirty of them sentenced to death, this judgement seemed to be the ultimate atrocity. The discovery of a diary, allegedly written by Casement and showing that he was homosexual, was announced early in June, before the trial. Notice of its contents was given to the London news editors and reports of the details were allowed to circulate. By the time Casement was brought to court on 28 June, he was being tried not simply as a traitor, but for his sexual preferences.

Ottoline was in London on the day of the trial. Bedford Square had been fully rented out and she was staying in a dreary bed-sitting-room around the corner in Bloomsbury Street. In the middle of this room was a large bunch of peonies that one of the cottage women at Garsington had given her as she was leaving for London. 'I cannot tell why,' she wrote, 'but that bunch of peonies will always remain in my life. I feel as if I could say, "I once had a bunch of sweet-scented, pale pink peonies in a dark room. It was when Roger Casement was condemned to death."'[18] She did all she could. She suggested to Eva Gore-Booth that they should start a petition. She wrote to all the influential people she knew, including Asquith and Violet; the latter sent back a cool note to say that she saw no reason to seek a reprieve for a traitor who indulged in homosexual activity. An attempt by Philip and Casement's cousin to persuade the King to grant a pardon got no further than a visit to Buckingham Palace where they spoke to his private secretary, Lord Stamfordham. On 3 August, Casement was hanged.

Asquith continued to visit Garsington and his family to gush over Ottoline's '"so beautiful, too adorable"' home, but his indifference had left a chill. In her diary, she wrote that he was no better than a murderer. 'I feel that he is always a spectator in life and doesn't really feel the war or anything else very deeply,' she added, but she was still fond enough of him to feel sorry when Aldous Huxley put him into *Crome Yellow* a few years later as 'a ci-devant Prime Minister, an old man, feebly toddling across the lawn after any pretty girl . . .' She had no wish to see him robbed of his dignity.

In April of 1916, when Maria Nys came back from her second term at Cambridge, she brought with her a girlfriend from Newnham called Naomi Bentwich. It was the weekend when Russell brought Eliot to stay at Garsington and Miss Bentwich had heard enough about Bertie's relationship with Ottoline from Maria to be eager to judge it for herself. She was a sharp-eyed observer and the impression made on her was that their passion had now been channelled into politics. Their conversations were all about conscription and she was struck by the spirit of friendly collaboration which seemed to exist between Russell and Ottoline's husband, 'a typical Liberal, very pleased with life, very fond of his wife, tall, handsome, jolly, not stupid'. When a dispute broke out over the right of COs to resist taking up farm-work instead of fighting, she noted that Russell and Philip instantly united in saying that they should do the work. She noted, too, that when Russell, Eliot and Ottoline went out for an evening stroll, it was Russell who came back first and alone. He did seem to go very freely into her bedroom, and she into his, but not, she thought, in the way of lovers, although Ottoline had seemed very excited before his arrival and had taken particular care with her appearance.[19]

Miss Bentwich decided that the relationship had become of a brother-and-sisterly kind. Russell, anxious to exonerate himself in his memoirs from the charge of frivolous behaviour (he was still involved with Vivien Eliot and was about to embark on a more serious affair with Lady Constance Malleson), did not hesitate to lay the blame for his change of heart at Ottoline's door, and in a fairly unchivalrous fashion. According to him, 'She gave me less and less while at the same time she gave more and more to others. For instance, I was never allowed to enter her bedroom but Aldous Huxley was habitually present while she undressed. (I do not think that she ever had physical relations with him.) In the end I rebelled and decided that the pain and frustration were more than I could endure.'[20]

How much should we believe of Bertie's sulky account? Miss Bentwich's letter suggests that he had liberal access to Ottoline's bedroom. His letters of this time show no sign of discontent. In earlier stages of the affair, he had seldom wasted time in expressing his frustration or his desire but there is no trace of complaint in the letters of this period. The most that Bertie could accuse Ottoline of was taking his love for granted.

Her loyalty to him was absolute. June 6 was the date of the trial which Russell had deliberately courted. Philip was unable to attend and stand bail as Bertie had expected him to do. Ottoline promptly made alternative arrangements. 'I am so very glad that you don't mind me coming up,' she wrote to him on 4 June. 'It is very good of you. I am so glad you will let me . . . Lytton wants to come with me [and] will stand bail for you as Philip's deputy.' The court, dazzled by the elegance and force of Russell's speech, was occasionally distracted by the spectacle in the public gallery of a tall and splendidly dressed woman with her titian hair caught up in a chignon and her blue-green eyes fixed intently on Russell's face.

On 29 June, Ottoline and Lytton were at the Mansion House again to attend Russell's appeal at which the fine of £100 was upheld. Afterwards, Bertie dined with her, Brett, Carrington and Gertler at a Soho restaurant before going to an NCF meeting; the rest of the party decamped to a music hall where Ottoline, resplendent in her favourite purple-feathered hat, swayed happily to the strains of 'If you were the only girl in the world . . .'

Elated though she had been by Russell's performance, Ottoline's enthusiasm was modified by the knowledge that he was still in Vivien Eliot's toils. 'It seems odd that such a frivolous, silly little woman should affect him so much . . .' she wrote in her journal; 'she looks up to him as a rich god, for he lavishes presents on her of silk underclothes and all sorts of silly things, and pays for her dancing lessons. It takes all of his money and now he expects us to raise a fund to pay the £100 fine.'*

Call it jealousy or pique, but it does not sound as though Ottoline was so indifferent to Russell as he was to claim in later years. Yet it is clear, too, that she still clung to her ideal of him, an ideal which she had now seen realised in his heroic work for the pacifists. The continuing infatuation with Vivien Eliot was a painful reminder that he was all too fallibly human. Disillusioned, she reverted to introspective brooding. 'I must live life up to the hilt,' she wrote passionately. 'I want to. I envy Casement, and I entreat of fate to let me live finely.'

Fate was ready to put that plea to the test.

---

* She did him an injustice; Russell was vigorously opposed to the idea of a fund.

16

A TIME OF SADNESS
1916–17

'I find it so difficult to reconcile acceptance of facts about Philip with the same feelings I had towards him. It is so difficult not to let them chill me. Of course he is the same as he was, but not really so, for the "something" that I now see was hid from me before . . .'

OM, *Journal*, 30 March 1917

It was in the summer of 1916 that Garsington settled into its dual role, as a refuge for the conscientious objectors and as an open hotel to all those of Ottoline's friends who sympathised with the pacifist cause. Russell spent much of the summer at his rooms in the Bailiff's House, but among those who became semi-permanent residents at the manor house were Aldous Huxley, Carrington, Lytton and Brett. Mark Gertler, Murry and Katherine Mansfield paid frequent visits. Maynard Keynes came for long weekends as did Goldie Lowes Dickinson, the Cambridge don who Ottoline thought of as 'a rare and gentle pagan saint'.

Among the crowd of visitors who trooped in and out of the house between June and September were Eva Gore-Booth, Clifford Allen, Miles and Lady Constance Malleson, the Sangers, Ramsay MacDonald and his mistress, Lady Margaret Sackville, Robbie Ross and H. W. Nevinson. Of these, Eva Gore-Booth and Nevinson were welcomed with particular warmth. In Eva, Ottoline found a friend who shared her concern for Casement and her indignation at the treatment of the Irish nationalists; Nevinson commanded her respect as the most compassionate of the war correspondents, as a poet and as the most powerful crusading journalist of his day. Allen was asked only as a favour to Russell; much though Ottoline admired his dedication to alleviating the hardship of the pacifists, she secretly agreed with Lytton's verdict on him as a dismal character whose voice and manner grated on his nerves. She could not quite bring herself to acknowledge, as Lytton bluntly did, that it was Allen's lower-middle-class background which made him so uncongenial. Ottoline liked the Mallesons on their only visit. Bertie had not yet evinced any interest in Lady Constance, a beautiful auburn-haired actress of twenty, but Ottoline was ready to admire a girl who had had the courage to exact a promise to be trained as an actress in exchange for being a debutante (she took the stage name of Colette O'Neil) before joining the Independent Labour Party and then the NCF. Even her marriage was unorthodox: Miles and she had agreed that they should each be free to form other relationships. A more frequent visitor, Ramsay MacDonald, who Ottoline had known since the early days of the Union for Democratic Control meetings at Bedford Square in 1914, continued to strike her as dully self-important and insincere; her feelings towards his mistress were ambivalent. In her published writings, she dismissed her as pretentious and uninteresting; to herself, she admitted that she always felt that Lady Margaret was 'more attractive and interesting than myself', and, just to make matters worse, 'so nice'.

One reason for her ambivalence was that Lady Margaret was beginning to be praised as a poet and Ottoline was becoming painfully aware of her own literary failings as she started to show her endeavours to a few friends. Fredegond Shove, an accomplished poet, had praised her visionary imagination, but Katherine Mansfield had been more professional in warning her, as Virginia Woolf would do later, against an over-ornate and self-conscious style: 'one wishes that you would be a million times more intimate – a million times more revealing, more absolutely, unmistakably you,' she told her. Writing had only come easily to Ottoline when she was collaborating with Bertie; now, she could not help envying the apparent ease of Margaret Sackville's accomplishment.

Further afield, Ottoline was still in friendly communication with Lawrence in Cornwall and sending him background reading from the London Library for his new novel. Katherine and Murry had provided her with detailed reports of their two-month experiment in living as the Lawrences' next-door neighbours and it comforted her to think that their experiences justified her own view of Frieda.

Retrospectively, it is clear that much of the tension in the adjoining Cornish households emanated from Lawrence's obsession with Murry, an obsession which was never discussed between the four of them and which Katherine did not fully understand. To her, appalled by the violence of a marriage which could veer in an hour from giggling sentimentality to screams and beatings, the fault seemed to lie with the provocative Frieda. Even when Lawrence rushed at her with a knife, roaring, 'I'll cut your throat, you bitch,' Frieda appeared to revel in the drama. Katherine found it impossible to work; she could write nothing but letters in such traumatic circumstances. The

Lawrence they loved had vanished, she told Ottoline in May, swallowed up like a little gold ring in the wife she compared to a huge Christmas pudding. All they could do, she went on, was to wait for somebody to slice the pudding up so that Lawrence could escape. Here, in language as strong as her own, Ottoline found the confirmation she wanted. Frieda was and had always been the villain of the piece, but Lawrence was still her friend. Cheerful and unsuspecting, she sent off another package of books to Cornwall.

A long hot summer and a crowded house at Garsington allowed for little formality and almost no privacy. Ottoline, who was in the habit of reading the more interesting snippets of her morning post out loud, was hurt and suspicious when her guests proved more reticent, and particularly so when the handwriting on an envelope was clearly recognisable. Looking down the table, she could see that Lytton was reading a letter from Carrington, but he was under instructions: 'Do not show my letter, as is your wont, to the whole of the company at the Breakfast Table . . . I trust you so little sometimes.' In the upper part of the house, airless rooms and thin walls drove the younger guests up to sit on the roof-leads when they had secrets to discuss. In the garden, high hedges and terraces seemed designed for scenes of Shakespearean intrigue in which every exchange was in danger of being overheard or observed. Here is Carrington writing again, on 19 June, to Lytton: 'Now I know from Brett *what was said* when I sat enthralled beside you on the lawn. And when we came back glowing from the Clumps!'* Confusion thickened. Huxley's habit of lying on the roof with Carrington suggested the beginnings of a liaison; in fact, his attention had been caught by Maria Nys, back from her third term at Cambridge. Two years in England had transformed the chubby adolescent into a pale beauty with huge, vulnerable eyes; even Lytton was tempted to wonder if he could get away with kissing her while pretending to teach her Latin. Too risky, he decided. 'Auntie' Ottoline would be sure to hear about it.

Grateful though Lytton still was for Philip's assistance at his tribunal, he was a hard guest to please and one of the things that irritated him most was Ottoline's munificence with her invitations. Did old Vernon Lee really have to be encouraged to stay for quite so long, and how was he expected to write about Dr Arnold with pugs crawling over his knees and to a thundering background of ragtime music? In June, he took himself off to stay with Vanessa, Grant and Garnett at Wissett Lodge; when he returned in July, it was to find that he had lost his bedroom and would have to sleep in one of the

---

* Wittenham Clumps was a pretty hilltop copse, much used for picnics and as a walking-point, about two miles across the fields from Garsington.

cottages while Gertler and Carrington stayed in comfort at the manor house. He decided to move on again.

The artists did not feel the same desperate need for peace as Lytton. Gertler, who was working on a view of the house from below the pond in May, July and August, was also completing his most ambitious painting. 'The Merry-Go-Round' was hailed by Lawrence when it was exhibited in London that autumn as 'the best *modern* picture I have ever seen . . . great and true . . . horrible and terrifying'. It can most easily be interpreted as an allegory of the war with the roundabout as the machine from which there is no escape, only an endless and pointless circular progression. On another level, the grouping of each set of riders into trios suggests the complicated pattern of Gertler's own life that summer. As always, he was pursuing Carrington and begging her to enter a physical relationship with him. Lytton, meanwhile, continued to express an interest in him which Gertler found both awkward and embarrassing. Yet Carrington appeared to be pressing Lytton's suit. 'Lytton sends *his* love,' she told Mark in the same letter which assured him that only their own relationship was real to her. 'You must like him, because I do, so very much.' A few days later, she reproached him because 'I do feel that you do not appreciate Lytton very much'.[1] Perhaps one should blame Gertler for naïvety, but it did not occur to him that she was asking for approval of her own feelings; her letters were never so direct as to make that clear. 'Oh, you are an artful devil!' he wrote back. 'How cleverly you evade all the important questions in my letters . . . Cold, cold girl!'

To the observant and well-meaning hostess, it was irresistible to interfere. Ottoline's sympathies were all with Gertler; it was inconceivable that Carrington should prefer Lytton to a handsome young man whose devotion made such a harrowing spectacle. Lytton left Garsington at the end of July, but Gertler and Carrington remained in the house. From Carrington, Ottoline could get nothing but evasive smiles, but Gertler was grateful for a confidante. All would be well, he was sure, if Carrington could only be persuaded to go to bed with him. The unfortunate result of that conversation was promptly reported to Lytton: it had been, Carrington informed him with her usual flair for drama, 'like the worst Verdun on-slaughter'. First of all, she had been led into the garden by Philip and marched around the pond while he told her off for being a virgin and for being 'wrong' in her attitude to Mark; then, as soon as they returned to the house, she had been taken out again by Ottoline to sit on the asparagus bed for an hour and a half, discussing it all over again. 'Only she was human and did see something of what I meant. And also suddenly forgot herself, and told me truthfully about herself and Bertie.'[2]

The letter was full of indignation, but one wonders whether Carrington really minded being forced to discuss her sexuality. The incident did, after all, provide her with a golden opportunity to reassure Lytton that she was not interested in physical relationships at a time when he was still nervous about what she might expect from him. She was, however, genuinely displeased when Gertler told her what Ottoline had said about her the following week. 'Carrington,' Ottoline incautiously wrote to him on 8 August, 'is like some strange wild beast – greedy of life and of tasting all the different "worms" that she can find without giving herself to any mate . . . I wish she would concentrate more on her work . . . nothing is so important as that.'[3]

Carrington was working, but not on her painting. The task confronting her that summer was how to make herself indispensable to Lytton. It took her a while to discover the answer. In her early letters, she had naïvely assumed that Lytton would like to hear agreeable accounts of Garsington life in his absence; by late July, she had realised that what her 'chère grandpère' most enjoyed was malice and gossip. Accuracy could be sacrificed to entertainment. So, she changed her style. Garsington became Shandygaff or Lollipop Hall and the stories grew as lurid as she could make them. Imagine what she was enduring! 'Ottoline . . . made me practically share a bedroom with [Harry] Norton!! And Poor Brett got sent out four times in one morning with Bertie for long walks across remote fields by her Ladyship!! . . . Philip plays the missionary and recites Shelley through his hairy nostrils. This is a poor letter but I lie exhausted, in the sun after swimming in that cess-pool of slime.' Weakening into sentiment at the last moment, she added that a nightingale had sung outside her window in the starlight.[4] A little weakness was forgiven and the letter was well received. She improved on it in her next effort, a spoof announcement of the forthcoming *Garsington Chronicle*, written in a very passable imitation of Ottoline's most flowery style. Lytton, while amused, declined to make a contribution. Another letter treated him to an account of Ottoline 'in high wrath' because his latest letter to her had 'told her no scandal! She makes me steeped in debt by giving me *all* her letters to read . . . I did a Goyaesque portrait of our Lady of mystery which gave me some pleasure. But as I made her look like a pole-cat it had to be suppressed from the public eye.' He need not worry about absenting himself from their new chronicle, she added; 'it will be plentifully filled with a long discourse by her Ladyship and essays by Mademoiselle and Maria . . . Goodbye chère grandpère, votre grosse bébé Carrington.'[5]

It seems unlikely that Brett would have gone out on four walks in a morning with Russell, of whom she was in awe, but Carrington's report was true to the extent that Ottoline was anxious to see that her favourite protégé was made to feel welcome by her other guests. Brett had finished her course at the Slade and, finding life at Garsington to be cheap and cheerful, she moved in. 'From July 1916 she came to stay on a visit that lasted three years,' Ottoline wrote; it was only a slight exaggeration.

Garsington suited Brett perfectly. She liked having her own quarters in the studio over the cowshed (the monastic building which had been offered to the Lawrences) and she particularly liked the fact that she could see her friends while enjoying the luxury of being able to shut herself away from them. During the mornings, she went on walks, swam in the pond or lounged on the roof with Carrington, Huxley and Gertler; after lunch, she climbed the ladder to her studio and worked on her 'Umbrellas' painting and her portrait of Ottoline. In the evenings, snugly kitted out in her new tailor-made breeches and clasping her pipe and Toby the ear trumpet, she joined the house party for dinner and waited eagerly for the moment, late into the night, when she could creep into Ottoline's room and perch on the end of the bed for long and, to both women, fascinating discussions about life, love – and the other guests.

The story of the Brett portrait is a mournful one. She adored Ottoline. 'I love you so much that I turn to stone or else babble weakly,' she wrote in one letter, and in another, 'I love you I love you, for the song you sing, for your own courageous self =and the joy and happiness of having you to race through life with and challenge the world . . .' Despite the suggestive language there seems to have been no thought of an affair in Brett's mind. She was as horrified as Ottoline when she heard in 1917 that the gossips were talking of a lesbian relationship. 'I have no real perversion: My love for you is as clean and clear as Crystal and fresh as the Wind,' she wrote in her own defence. Her portrait of Ottoline was intended as a tribute to her love, a celebration of the 'intense enjoyment a beautifully shaped head and beautiful form give to anyone who loves form and shapes'. She started work on it in January 1916. By August, the picture had doubled its height to nine feet and Brett was balancing on a stepladder to work on the head while Ottoline, done up as requested in purple hat, orange dress and pink silk harem trousers, sat patiently in the studio, smoking and, when she was permitted, reading a book. Julian climbed the ladder to the studio one afternoon and looked up at the monstrous head. 'It's no good your painting Mummy,' she said kindly. 'You can't ever make her as beautiful as she is.' When Brett returned to London in September, the portrait went with her. She was still working on it in 1919, but by that time she had slashed off the torso with an open razor and burned it; the famous purple hat with the ostrich-feather plume had been painted out. After failing to sell or even to exhibit her finished head-and-shoulder portrait, she gave it to Ottoline, who is thought to have passed it on to Lord Henry. It is not known to the author whether it survives.

Of those who were allowed to see this ill-fated work, only Juliette Baillot was admiring. It was, as she recollects it, an intensely imaginative painting, very powerful, showing Ottoline with huge aquamarine eyes and a flaming aura of hair. Ottoline hated it. The first time she saw the head, she burst into tears; later, she accused Brett of making her look like a streetwalker. 'I am really miserable at having hurt you over the portrait,' Brett wrote to her in April 1917; 'I have not made a prostitute of you – I swear I haven't.' But such assurances were of no comfort at a time when Ottoline had begun to learn how viciously she was being slandered by her friends; how they laughed at her looks and twisted her words. When she looked at Brett's portrait, she saw not herself, but the ugly mockery that had begun to pass for truth.

Neither Katherine Mansfield nor Ottoline enjoyed the young writer's first visit to Garsington in July 1916 so much as they had anticipated and neither of them chose to leave an account of it. The only recollection we have of the occasion comes from Brett, but it was written many years later when she and Ottoline were no longer friends and there is a malicious edge to it. Her description begins with Katherine arriving, 'strangely dark in her black and white clothes' in the scarlets, yellows and oranges of the Red Room before being put next to Brett at the lunch-table. 'I sat in agonies of shyness,' Brett recalled, 'she sat watchful, cold, withdrawn into herself. Conversation roared up and down the table, Bertrand Russell's horse-like laugh exploding at intervals, while Ottoline glowered at me, from her seat bang opposite, for my silence.' For some reason which Brett could not explain, she decided to spend the rest of the lunch in dropping pellets of bread into Katherine Mansfield's pocket. After lunch, there was a walk; in the evening, after much coaxing, Katherine fetched her guitar and sang folk songs and ballads, seeming quite relaxed until she 'felt something or thought she felt an antagonistic criticism and abruptly stopped'. Nothing would persuade her to sing again: 'the guard was up, the face became a mask, the eyes watchful, and a sort of discomfort fell upon us all.' Later in the evening, according to Brett, Katherine came into her room and said that she had discovered the breadcrumbs. 'It was then she realised she had one friend in the house. We made a secret pact of friendship which was never broken for the rest of her life.'[6]

Inaccurate though Brett's memory was (her 'unbroken' friendship with Katherine was in shreds two months after the meeting and another version of the encounter has the breadcrumbs being dropped into the pocket of a different jacket), Katherine's first visit to Garsington was clearly a failure. Ottoline's own impression was that she regarded them all with a novelist's eye, as potential material, and that she herself was being recorded as 'a grand lady patronising artists for my own glory'.

It took a second visit at the end of July to thaw the ice. Again, there was a large house party (this was the weekend which drove Lytton to take flight), but Katherine was more at her ease, perhaps because she had Murry with her. Ottoline warmed to her when she saw how scornful she looked when Clive Bell started telling one of the stories in which, somehow, he always appeared to advantage; Ottoline, too, found Bell a trying companion, so busily self-praising, 'so superficial and spluttering'. On this visit, Katherine came upstairs to sit in her study and here, for the first time, she started to talk about herself. As she talked, her mask dropped; her face grew animated, her hands flickered with quick, expressive gestures. Ottoline was fascinated, both by her and by her story, of growing up in New Zealand, of going to Queen's College in London where she had been taught by Ottoline's old friend John Cramb, of her brief marriage to George Bowden ('she said that he took advantage of her, and wanted to live with her which she had not bargained for') and of her adventurous life with Murry, of wild days in Paris and of a big country house where they had played the roles of grandees before doing a moonlight flit with the servants, tradesmen and rent all unpaid.[7]

Ottoline was absorbed by Katherine's stories, but she did not feel ready to trust her. There was something in her presentation which rang a false note. It irritated her to hear Katherine speaking of herself and Murry as 'artists', as if they belonged to some sacred and superior order; no artist she had known talked in that way. And why was she so evasive about her friendship with Murry? When pressed, she described it as an open relationship to which she was not ready to commit herself, but she also said Murry had given up his Oxford career to be with her, 'feeling that no sacrifice could be too great for the joy of her companionship'. (She did not tell her hostess that she had been toying with the idea of setting up a relationship with Gertler on her first visit to Garsington.) She was certainly brilliant, Ottoline decided, but there was malice and a lack of generosity in her character which chilled her. 'I should love to have known this beautiful, secretive but impulsive and emotional woman before she had been hurt and bruised by life, or perhaps before the ambition of being an artist, and of using people for that end, had become such an absorbing game.'[8]

Ottoline enjoyed the company of women but, having been the only girl in a male family, she was always more at her ease with men. She found it difficult to discuss the things she really cared about with women; the conversation seemed always to swerve away into gossip or self-revelation. 'They are too personal,' she complained; 'they don't really feel the fundamental things as strongly as a man does. They are always bored by them and relapse into pleasure, into something petty and personal...'[9] Philip, she admitted, was not fond of discussing these fundamental things; there were a great many subjects and ideas which fascinated her but which he found boring. In the past, she had been able to satisfy this questioning, intellectual side of her nature with Bertie, but she was finding him remote now. His mind, she supposed, was fully taken up with his pacifist work and with Vivien Eliot. She was still anxious about that relationship; hoping to divert him from it, she made an awkward effort to interest him in Iris Tree. Young, pretty and clever – she was a published poet – Iris was one of the gang who came to Garsington for Clive Bell's birthday weekend. 'I think you would enjoy investigating her and I should enjoy watching you do it!' Ottoline told Russell on 14 September. '... I will try and keep her until you come.' She did not tell him that she was also being visited by a young man who made her think it 'a great joy to be with anyone so human and aware of ordinary life, after the intellectuals who walk along half-blind'.[10] This was Siegfried Sassoon.

Sassoon had been invalided home from the Somme in August 1916, two months after being awarded the Military Cross for conspicuous bravery. He was convalescing at Somerville College in Oxford when he remembered having received a couple of enthusiastic letters about one of his first poems to appear in print. The letters had been all arabesques, dots and flourishes on beautiful hand-made paper, written from an Oxford address at the beginning of the year. The style suggested that their author was an intense young lady; when he idly asked his friend Robbie Ross if he knew anything about her, he learned that Lady Ottoline Morrell, a woman of fabulous kindness and charm, was 'frightfully well known in the literary and artistic world'. If Sassoon felt up to it, they could go and visit her from Somerville that day; no warning was required; Garsington was very informal. Sure enough, when they turned up at the door, they were welcomed in by a maid and taken across to the Monastery studio where Ottoline was sitting for Brett.

The reader in search of a full description of this occasion and

Sassoon's subsequent visit will find it in *Siegfried's Journey*; the following is an abridged account.

Robbie having hailed Lady Ottoline by name, he was answered in tones of pleased surprise and our hostess came down to us. Let me say at once that for more than twenty years afterwards Lady Ottoline was one of my best friends. I have been indebted to her for innumerable acts of generosity and affection. But it must be confessed that my first view of her was somewhat disconcerting. Always original in her style of dress – which was often extremely beautiful – she happened on this occasion to be wearing voluminous pale-pink Turkish trousers; and these garments, as she descended the ladder backwards, were – unavoidably – the first part of her that I beheld. She was very tall, so it seemed a long time before her head became visible . . . I had seldom seen anyone quite so extraordinary. In fact I must admit that it wasn't until about a year later that I began to feel at all comfortable with her . . . It would have made all the difference to me if she had managed to look a bit more like Rossetti's Blessed Damozel.

After an awkward visit to the studio, where the garishness of the portrait and Brett's deafness reduced the visitors to embarrassed murmurs, they went out into the garden.

I found myself pacing to and fro with Lady Ottoline on a grass walk above the swimming pool, which was shadowed by an enormous ilex. Bemused with shyness I replied to her questions about my recent battle experiences, what I thought about the war, and whether I had written any more poetry lately . . . I began to feel that I liked her, and she put me still more at my ease by telling me how he [Ross] had once jumped into the swimming-pool with all his clothes on, to rescue a girl who had decided that she was drowning in four feet of water . . . 'He's always jumping into the water to pull people out, isn't he?' she said, with that curious slow enunciation which seemed to come from half-closed lips.
   . . . On the way back to the hospital he [Ross] informed me that I had been a huge success, and urged me to be very nice to Lady Ottoline as she could be of the greatest help to me when my poems were published . . . He added that he himself was deeply indebted to her generous friendship in his times of trouble.[11]

Sassoon returned to spend a week at Garsington in September. It was long enough for Ottoline to fall completely under his spell. She could see that he was happiest in the company of Ross and his closest friend, Robert Graves; that did not trouble her much. There was only a small physical element in this new passion. What she saw in Sassoon was her ideal. Here was a young man who was both brave and imaginative, who loved nature almost as much as she did and who had no ruthless philosophy to impose on her; surely this was the kindred spirit she had been seeking all her life. A little shyly, she gave him first a vellum-bound manuscript book* and then, more shyly still, the paper on which she had drafted out her dream for Garsington. 'Come then,' she had written earnestly, 'gather here – all who have passion and who desire to create new conditions of life – new visions of art and literature and new magic worlds of poetry and music. If I could but feel that days at Garsington had strengthened your efforts to live the noble life: to live freely, recklessly, with clear Reason released from convention – no longer absorbed in small personal events but valuing personal affairs as part of a great whole – above all to live with passionate desire for Truth and Love and Understanding and Imagination.'[12]

Sassoon took this document off to his room, read it while smoking his pipe, and wondered if he could ever live up to Ottoline's aspirations. He doubted it. He had enjoyed his stay at Garsington and the respect he was accorded as living evidence from the Front. He had liked watching his dog skirmish with the pugs while Ottoline, magnificently dressed in a Velázquez gown of rich brocade, stitched on her embroidery frame; he had been enchanted when Jelly d'Aranyi came into the Red Room to play Bach's Chaconne to them. He enjoyed all this and yet, he was uncomfortable. Much though he liked and admired Ottoline, he felt artificial with her, as if he was all the time striving to be what she expected. Her expectations were high. She seemed to imagine that he thought only of his poetry, that a pleasant life and creature comforts meant nothing to him. She talked of living freely and recklessly when he had no greater freedom than a few weeks' respite from the fighting. She saw a man who was not him.

Here I sat, in this perfect bedroom with its old mullioned windows looking across the green forecourt to the tall wrought-iron gates. The moted sunlight of a sweet September evening was touching the tops of the high yew hedges; on the paved path below, the little Morrell girl was playing with the pug Socrates, and a peacock was parading with tail outspread. I desired only to enjoy this comfort and security while it lasted. On the table by the bed was a thin-paper copy of the *Oxford Book of Verse* which Lady Ottoline had given me. The bed was a creaky four-poster which looked antique and valuable enough to be in a museum, and the book was delectably bound in pale green vellum . . . Garsington was just about the pleasantest house I had ever stayed in – so pleasant that it wouldn't be safe to think about it when I was back at the Front. In the meantime the maid had knocked at the door with my

---

* Sassoon was a talented painter. When he returned the book to Ottoline some years later, he had dedicated it to her and had copied into it the poems which he regarded as his best, illustrating each one with a full-page pen-and-ink drawing, coloured in with a black and grey wash. The first of the poems, 'The Mystic as Soldier', was one which he knew would appeal to her; the drawings showed a naked young man stretching up to the sky, towards woods or towards a naked female figure. One of the inscriptions read: 'My body is the magic of the world.'

can of hot water and I must get ready for another simple but delicious dinner.[13]

Ottoline had been ecstatically happy during Sassoon's visit; as soon as he left, doubts began to plague her. Scanning the post each day, she found nothing from Sassoon but a photograph of himself which seemed to taunt her with its withdrawn stare. How could she ever have let herself dream of their being twin souls? she wrote in her journal as she sat up in bed on a cold night, shivering under the coverlet. She wallowed in self-pity. Nobody loved her. Nobody cared. She was doomed to be a tragic personality. She might as well accept the truth: 'I am really not attractive to men and never was – unless they get into my inner self.'

Terrified that Sassoon would slip out of her life as easily as he had drifted into it, Ottoline tried to connect herself to him by a stream of letters and presents. A drab two months in the regimental depot at Litherland near Liverpool were enlivened by her zealous attention to his comfort. One day brought a crocheted rug, liberally doused with scent; another, a letter of passionate gratitude for some poems he had sent. If her spirit could be a wind, she told him, it would be blowing softly around him, now and always. 'My dear Lady Garsington, you are much too kind to me,' he wrote on 6 December after the arrival of a pretty sandalwood box. It was not much of a letter, but it was all the encouragement she needed. A few nights later, she called Juliette Baillot down from her room to read to her while she struggled to finish a petit-point embroidery for Sassoon's hut. It was 'a charming vision of deer and hounds followed by a young hunter through an open forest, designed by Brett. It had to be done by morning. I read the whole of Molière's *Tartuffe* into the small hours while her fingers stitched the bright scene. It was wonderful.'[14] This, along with a print of 'The Polish Rider', was followed up by several volumes of carefully chosen poetry. Sassoon was grateful but uneasy. Writing back, he decided it would be prudent to treat the gifts as joint offerings to himself and Robert Graves, who was sharing his hut at the depot. 'Robert and I are simply delighted with your pictures . . .' he wrote on 16 December, 'and the needlework is exquisite . . . it delights our eyes every moment we spend in the hut. And then the delightful good books came . . . I was reading Drayton's Fairy Court last night and it pleased us both greatly.' It was an appreciative letter, but it was far from the intimacy that Ottoline craved.

Her hopes were to be raised the following spring when a telegram arrived from Sassoon, proposing that they should lunch together in London. She agreed at once and hurried up to her usual lodgings at 38 Bloomsbury Street, full of an ebullience which was dashed by the news that he had been recalled to the Front. Sassoon was pale but cheerful; she did her best to match his mood and tried to laugh when he played the fool for her benefit while they wandered around the National Gallery. Before he left, she gave him a piece of opal on a gilt chain. Watching from the window of her lodgings, she waited for him to turn and wave or to make any small signal of friendship. He walked on and she thought that she had probably seen him for the last time.

For Sassoon, too, it had been a painful day. It tortured him with self-consciousness to be seen in public with her in her old-fashioned clothes and huge feathered hat, even though he realised that she 'was a noble and distinguished figure among the drably-dressed nobodies who gaped at her so uncomprehendingly'. Kind though she had been, he longed for her to be less anxious and more like his mother, who was making the best of his departure by saying as little as possible about it. To him, the moment when he rose to say goodbye had come as a relief.[15]

Mercifully for Ottoline, her infatuation with Sassoon had escaped the sharp-eyed tribe at Garsington, but only because they were looking in another direction. 'O. is trying to get up an affair with Murry,' Clive Bell gleefully reported to Vanessa in December. 'She writes to him and he leaves her letters about.'

Murry visited Garsington without Katherine on 18 August; he was there again with Katherine before the end of the month. 'I love him and get on with Katherine very well,' Ottoline wrote, but nowhere in her journals for 1916 was there any indication of an affair. Her thoughts were all of Sassoon. Clive Bell had got the wrong end of the stick. It was Murry who was idly pursuing Ottoline. 'I have at times a queer suspicion that I must be in love with you,' he wrote to her either on 31 August or on 22 September (Katherine Mansfield's biographers disagree about the date):

I don't know. It's very hard to get at what I feel; so rarely do I feel towards persons any emotion more intimate than amusement or blank terror. But when I try to find a name for my feeling towards you, – then it is that I begin to suspect that I am in love with you.

What was Murry thinking of? That 'I begin to suspect' and 'queer suspicion' sound too cautious for us to see this letter as more than a preliminary dabble, to test Ottoline's reaction. Careful though he was to destroy all the correspondence of this period, it is inconceivable that Ottoline was writing him passionate letters at a time when every page of her journal was dominated by her love for Sassoon. She liked Murry; she was certainly not in love with him.

Clive Bell has emerged as one of the chief mischief-makers of

Bloomsbury, but he can hardly be blamed for his confusion; the antics of Ottoline's friends were never more bewildering than in the autumn of 1916 when Maynard Keynes agreed to rent out his home in Gower Street to Brett, Carrington, Katherine and Murry. The new tenants moved in during October: it took less than a month for 'The Ark', as they blithely christened the house, to turn into a hotbed of espionage.

Ottoline, meanwhile, was paying the usual price for excessive sociability. She collapsed with influenza at the end of September; in October, the doctor prescribed a month of rest and medical treatment at Harrogate in north Yorkshire. From Garsington, where Aldous was still busy chopping wood and writing poems, she heard that Boris Anrep had visited and made himself very charming to Maria. Huxley's next letter told her that Maria, encouraged by Brett, had run away to London where she was planning to work for Anrep. Knowing Anrep's reputation, Ottoline shuddered to think what would become of her young charge. It was not easy to organise other people's lives from Harrogate, but she did her best. Brett was ordered to take Maria into The Ark and keep a close eye on her; Aldous, who admitted to feeling a 'doggy devotion' to Maria, was sent to London to find out what was going on.

Nothing of consequence, was Huxley's view; did Ottoline really have to make such a fuss? To him, it was becoming clearer every day that his future lay with Maria; in the circumstances, he found it most offensive of his hostess to suggest that she had fallen for an ageing womaniser. His letter to Harrogate was politely defiant. 'Maria has a good deal of sense,' he told her; 'and whatever the irresistibility of Anrep, it does, after all, take two to work a seduction smoothly . . . Maria seems to be very very happy; the only fly in the ointment being your terror of Anrep and consequent disapproval of her. I think she almost wept over your letter.'[16] Maria added to the confusion with an anguished letter of her own. Everyone was against her, she wrote. 'Do you know it never seemed to me before tonight that it was possible I should be what I so detest in other women . . . I recall all the many times you told me how you hated it – what a flirt this or that person was, etc. . . . Do you think me so, does everyone . . . ?'[17] A little wearily, Ottoline wrote to reassure her and to promise that she was not going to be thrown out of Garsington.

Maria ('old red flannel petticoat' to the disdainful Brett, who soon grew bored of looking after her) was only one of the complicated elements of life in the Gower Street Ark. Brett took it upon herself to keep Ottoline as well-informed as her ear trumpet would allow. Carrington had quarrelled with Katherine, Murry was flirting with Brett and Katherine lay like a spider in her room, luring all visitors into her web for long private conversations. 'Bertie, Lytton, etc. all disappear like magic . . .' Brett reported at the end of October. 'I have my little instrument trained on the cracks in the floor.' Train it as closely as she might, she could not discover who the man was who 'has arisen like the dawn on her [Katherine's] horizon, like they will all her life . . .'

It would have startled Ottoline to learn who this unknown man was. Bertie had been full of affection since discreetly embarking on his affair with Colette Malleson in late September. In October, he joined her in Harrogate for 'a very very happy time. I felt we were *very* much one – I loved it.' There was no hint of another involvement when he came to Garsington with Murry and Katherine at the end of October. In November, evidence surfaces of a dalliance of which neither Ottoline nor Colette was aware. There was, by Russell's own account, no affair, but Katherine's letters strongly suggest that they were planning to have one. Early in December, she told Bertie that she was aching with excitement after reading his letter, that it thrilled her to think of all the things that they would be doing together and that she was looking forward to asking him all about his life when they met for dinner. Later that month, Katherine was looking forward to another dinner alone with Bertie and telling him that her feelings for him were even deeper than they had been before. This does not have the ring of casual friendship.

Ottoline, while spared the knowledge of Bertie's philandering, was having a miserable autumn. She was worried about Maria. She was despondent about Sassoon's failure to answer her letters. She was also puzzled and alarmed by Philip's increasing remoteness. He rarely now returned to Garsington at weekends from the bachelor rooms he rented at 20 Bedford Square; when she wanted to talk to him, he was always ready with the excuse of farm management. While at Harrogate, she barely heard from him. If he missed her, he gave no sign of it; it was left to Aldous to tell her how empty and quiet the manor house seemed in her absence. When Philip did finally write, it was to give her the grim news that their cowman had committed suicide. He had drowned himself in the garden pond. None of the farmworkers had been able to suggest why a jovial old man should suddenly decide to take his life. 'Philip went to the inquest. They sat round a table in silence. The coroner asked each of his fellows if he had said or complained of anything. "Noo, noo, he did say as he didn't like this milking." That was all they could tell. It was all very terrible and upsetting . . .'[18]

Superstitious as she was, Ottoline could not help feeling that it was an evil presentiment, but she tried to shake gloomy thoughts off with a lively week in London on her return from the north. After a night at the opera with Brett and Ethel Sands, a cheerful afternoon at The Ark and tea with old Augustine Birrell, she took Aldous and a subdued Maria home to Garsington.

The house was full up for Christmas 1916 and, despite the fact that Philip was irritable and distracted, everyone was determined to have a good time and to put the war out of their minds for a few days. Brett arrived early to decorate the house with Chinese lanterns and garlands, Katherine brought not only armfuls of presents but a play, *The Laurels*, in which Murry consented to appear as a Dostoevsky character while Lytton stamped about as old Dr Kite in a red beard knitted for the occasion by Carrington. The Shoves arranged a fancy-dress dinner, and Murry, after throwing Brett into a state of great excitement by announcing that he wished to spend all of his Christmases with her for as long as she was ready to be kissed by him, informed Ottoline that his love for her would never die. Katherine retaliated by sitting up with Bertie in the Red Room, long after everyone else was in bed; Ottoline, in the room above, wondered what they were talking about, never supposing that Katherine was maligning her.

Lytton had enjoyed his visit; he signed himself as Dr Kite in the Visitors' Book and told Ottoline that not even fog, a missed train and the fact that he had left most of his possessions behind could dampen the memory of a perfect Christmas. True to form, he made up for his gratitude by telling Virginia Woolf that poor 'Lady Omega Muddle' had become ill, bad-tempered and infinitely old. (She was forty-six.)

Shortly before Christmas, Ottoline heard from Mark Gertler that he was distressed by the publication of *Mendel*, a novel by Gilbert Cannan which, while offering a reasonably accurate account of the artist's life, unkindly caricatured some of Gertler's closest friends. William Rothenstein, his first benefactor, appeared in a viciously unpleasant light; Carrington was unflatteringly recognisable as the tough and heartless Greta Morrison. Ottoline, who was only faintly discernible as Mary Tutness, was inclined to think that Gertler was making a fuss about nothing. A month later, she learned how painful such an experience could be.

It was probably Murry, visiting Garsington in October 1916, who first advised her to get hold of the manuscript of Lawrence's new novel. On 26 November, Ottoline wrote to Lawrence to tell him that she had heard he was portraying her as the villainess. 'It is very strange how rumours go round,' Lawrence wrote to his friend Catherine Carswell. '... Don't talk too much about my novel, will you? And above all, don't give it to anybody to read, but Don [Donald Carswell]. I feel it won't be published yet, so I would rather nobody read it. I hope Ottoline Morrell won't want the MS.'[19] His forebodings were well-founded. Ottoline was not the only person to be outraged and to demand revisions (Philip Heseltine threatened his former friend with a libel suit for depicting him as the dissolute Julius Halliday.) *Women in Love* had to wait four years to find a willing publisher.

To Ottoline, the representation of herself as Hermione Roddice was a shocking betrayal of affection and trust. To the dispassionate reader, it is apparent that Hermione has some redeeming features and that Lawrence's observations were perceptive. Like Ottoline, Hermione is a lavish bestower of presents on those she loves; like her, she is intelligent and formidably well-read. There is no cruelty in the description of her readiness to love nature as it is, without wanting to analyse it; the account of Hermione's maid at Breadalby bringing out an exotic collection of shawls and robes for the women to wear when they dance is no more objectionable than the instantly identifiable portrait of Philip as Alexander Roddice, rattling out Hungarian music on a pianola. Hermione's background was the one Ottoline had often described to Lawrence: the lonely unhappy girlhood, the mother who almost died in Florence, the passionate love of Italy, the visits to a remarkable doctor who had taught her how to control her emotions. The only objection she could make to the depiction of her little study as 'a remote and very cushiony place' was that it had never entered her head to try and hit anybody on the head there with a paperweight, as Hermione did in her most famous scene.

The paperweight scene was irritating, but it could hardly be described as offensive, and it was such aspects of the book which Lawrence had in mind when he complained that Ottoline was being absurdly oversensitive. Was she? Hermione's appearance, while sometimes allowed to be exotic and even beautiful, is also described as 'macabre', 'ghastly' and 'repulsive'. In her first appearance, she is given 'the face of an almost demoniacal ecstatic'. Her expression is 'almost drugged, as if a strange mass of thought coiled in the darkness within her . . .' When she speaks, in the seductive singsong drawl for which Ottoline was famous, she utters earnest platitudes: 'To me the pleasure of knowing is *so* great, so *wonderful* . . . one thing was the stars, when I really understood something about the stars. One feels so *uplifted*, so *unbounded* . . .' The criticism which Lawrence had frequently levelled at Ottoline – of imposing her will to get what she wanted – is richly developed in the creation of Hermione. Her guests are forced out on walks 'like prisoners marshalled for exercise'; they must start the day early because Hermione needs 'to grip the hours by the throat, to force her life from them'. When she speaks, however gently, 'under the straying voice, what a persistent, almost insane *will*!' She cannot be wrong. 'She lived in and by her own self-esteem, conviction of her own righteousness of spirit.'

It is impossible to believe that Lawrence was unaware of what he was doing. The triangle of Hermione, Rupert Birkin and Ursula

Brangwen reproduces that of Ottoline, Lawrence and Frieda. The chapters 'Woman to Woman' and 'Excurse' show Lawrence exchanging the spiritual, sexless passion of Ottoline for the robust and physical world of Frieda. In 'Woman to Woman' we can see Lawrence and Ottoline at Garsington, through the resentful eyes of Frieda.

> Tea was brought in and Birkin poured out for them. It was strange how inviolable was the intimacy which existed between him and Hermione. Ursula felt that she was an outsider. The very tea-cups and the old silver was a bond between Hermione and Birkin. It seemed to belong to an old, past world which they had inhabited together . . . And she, Ursula, was an intruder. So they always made her feel.[20]

What we are hearing in this passage is the echo of those conversations dear to both Ottoline and Lawrence about Welbeck and old Nottinghamshire, a world to which Frieda, who had seen it only from the limited perspective of a professor's foreign wife living in the city, had no entry. In the next chapter, however, Ursula strikes back, and wins. The chapter starts, ominously enough, just outside the Welbeck estate.

> Suddenly a flame ran over her, and she stamped her foot madly on the road, and he winced, afraid that she would strike him. 'And *I*, *I'm* not spiritual enough, *I'm* not as spiritual as that Hermione –!' Her brows knitted, her eyes blazed like a tiger's. 'Then *go* to her, that's all I say, go to her, go. Ha, she spiritual – *spiritual*, she! A dirty materialist as she is . . . Is *that* spiritual, her bullying, her conceit, her sordid materialism? She's a fishwife, a fishwife, she is such a materialist. And all so sordid. What does she work out to, in the end, with all her social passion, as you call it. Social passion – what social passion has she? – show it me! – where is it? She wants petty, immediate *power*, she wants the illusion that she is a great woman, that is all . . . In her soul she's a devilish unbeliever, common as dirt . . .'[21]

Shocked though Ottoline was, she had loved Lawrence too much to be able to believe that he alone was responsible for such a piece of character-assassination. It was easier to assume that his wife was behind it: 'all the worst parts were in Frieda's handwriting.' It has never been possible to demonstrate that Frieda composed any part of the novel, although she did hand-correct the pages which Ottoline saw. But the victim had a point. The most vicious attacks on Hermione are made by Ursula, and they sound uncannily like the letter which Frieda had written to Cynthia Asquith in which she accused Ottoline of being a cheap and vulgar fraud.[22] Lawrence had not seen Ottoline for a year; he had spent that year living in almost uninterrupted seclusion with a woman who strongly resented her attraction for him. Hermione Roddice had started life as a portrait of a very different woman, Jessie Chambers; Frieda's influence must not be underestimated in considering the character's dramatic metamorphosis.

The quarrel resulted in a ten-year rift. Ottoline demanded the return of the opal she had given Lawrence (it had reappeared in the novel as Birkin's gift to Ursula). Lawrence complained that she was 'full of malice' and referred to her as 'that old carrion'. When, late in 1918, he used Mark Gertler to sound out the possibility of an invitation to Garsington, Gertler told him that a visit was out of the question. The breach was not healed until 1928, when Lawrence, fighting against tuberculosis in Italy, heard from Aldous Huxley that Ottoline had been treated for bone cancer. It was time for him to offer his apology for Hermione.

It doesn't matter what sort of vision comes out of a man's imagination, his vision of Ottoline. Any more than a photograph of me is me, or even 'like me'. The so-called portraits of Ottoline can't possibly be Ottoline – no-one knows that better than an artist. But Ottoline has moved men's imagination, deeply, and that's perhaps the most a woman can do.[23]

Bloomsbury heard from Clive Bell that Ottoline was wild with grief and rage and that she could talk of nothing but Lawrence's book. It was untrue. Her journals show that, after the initial shock, she put *Women in Love* out of her mind. She had other things to worry about. In London, Brett was writing furious letters about the restored presence of 'old red flannel petticoat' in The Ark. Katherine Mansfield was looking for new lodgings and Carrington firmly eschewed responsibility for Maria; the prospect of being left in sole charge of the girl filled Brett with horror. Maria must be got rid of at once, she wrote; she was treacherous, odious. Ottoline remained fond of 'that oriental sensuous child', but Philip, who claimed that Maria had done her best to seduce him during the autumn, did not want her to live with them any longer. Aldous was now deeply in love with her, but Maria did not appear to return his feelings. In the end, Ottoline decided to write to Madame Nys and, on 23 January, a tearful Maria was packed off to join her family in Florence. The following month, Aldous left Garsington to start a London job at the Food Control office and then the Air Board; in September 1917, he found a more congenial post as a master at Eton.

Russell was another cause for distress. Shortly after Christmas, he wrote to tell Ottoline that she had a dangerous friend in Katherine Mansfield, who had spoken very maliciously about her. (His brief interest in Katherine had evidently waned.) As for himself, he felt the time had come when he needed to be free to form new relationships. Nothing would ever affect the bond between them, but he could not do his best work when she was always so critical. He did not dare to mention Colette. Ottoline was hurt. It was, she wrote in her journal, 'a garden-party parting, polite and formal'. Brett tried to reassure her and offered her own interpretation. 'His cry for freedom was the cry for help that creative people give to keep from losing themselves in one another,' she wrote to Ottoline on 15 January, 'and it is very easy to lose oneself in you and it's a thing you have no control over. It is the subconscious effect of personality . . . it's what made Lamb turn on you and stamp on you.' There was a good deal of truth in this, but Ottoline was too depressed to agree that Russell still needed her. If he did, it was only on a spiritual level and what she longed for now was love and companionship. It was, she told him, a *great* loss to her; on a more practical plane, she asked him to have her suitcase sent round to Philip's London flat from Russell Chambers.

Ottoline had taken Philip's word for it when he told her that it was political business which required him to spend so much time in London during the summer and autumn of 1916. She had thought nothing of it when he brought his London secretary to stay for a weekend. Alice Jones was a slight, pretty, auburn-haired woman, a skilled calligrapher and an excellent professional typist who did some work for Ottoline as well as for Philip in her spare time from her main job as secretary to H. W. Massingham, the editor of *The Nation*. Neither had she drawn any sinister conclusion from the sudden departure at Christmas of her personal maid, Eva Merrifield. Unlike almost every woman who worked for her, Eva had never become a friend. 'She is an odd girl,' Ottoline had written in her journal on 15 October 1916, when Eva was with her at Harrogate. 'She has the honey-coloured eyes that I never trust. I do all I can to make her happy, but she really is very unkind to me. I don't know why.'

The first hint of what had been going on comes in a letter which Aldous Huxley wrote to Carrington at the beginning of March 1917, when Ottoline was undergoing one of her cures in a nursing home in Royal Avenue, Chelsea. On 28 February, Aldous and Carrington went to a show at the Palladium and caught sight of Philip with a young woman. When Aldous questioned him about her a few days later, Philip denied that he had been there but changed the subject after hearing that Carrington had been sketching members of the audience. Most interesting, Aldous wrote with glee, particularly since Ottoline's former maid Eva was now living in London, 'where the pug bitch presented to her on leaving has just died in giving birth to a child begotten incestuously by her Borgia-esque brother, Gobbo. All fits well – and all the time Philip is suffering from a bronchitic cold, which forbids his going out at nights!'[24]

It may have been this unlucky sighting which caused Philip to decide that Ottoline must be told what was going on; on the evening of 7 March, he went to the nursing home. Sitting up in bed in an uncurtained room while a bright moon glared in on their faces, Ottoline heard that he had two mistresses and that both of them were pregnant. Alice Jones's child was expected in August, Eva's in mid-June. Miss Jones, an admirably independent woman, had already resolved to do everything she could to support herself and the child, but Eva, whose resentment of her situation was wholly understandable, was threatening to disclose what had happened if she was not adequately supported. Philip was terrified that a journalist might get hold of what would, after all, make a sensational story. If it came out, he said, he would be ruined. The pacifist cause, with which he had strongly identified himself, would be tainted by the scandal; he would almost certainly have to resign from politics.* Ottoline tried to persuade him to talk the whole matter through with her, but Philip was not in a state to listen. Instead, he insisted on going straight to the House of Commons, where his agitated condition caused such alarm that he had to be taken back to his flat in Bedford Square. A doctor was called, but Philip dismissed him and rushed back to the nursing home. It was by then very late, and he was refused admission. The letter he left for his wife was painfully brief: 'Darling O, I love you and *only* you. Forgive me, oh forgive me. I am dying of grief. Your P.'

The following day, Philip went to Garsington. Fredegond and Gerald Shove were called into his room. He said that he had important information which they must write down. He was an intelligent man. They all thought Ottoline was the clever one, but it was he who had made her so. When he had repeated this many times, always insisting that it should be recorded, Gerald Shove decided that help was needed, but not, unfortunately, before he had confided in Clive Bell, who duly passed news of Philip's breakdown on to Lytton and Carrington. Ottoline, accompanied by her brother Henry, returned to take charge and to arrange for Philip to enter a nursing home. A mental home was discussed, but Philip made a rapid recovery which rendered this step unnecessary. Violent 'nerve-attacks', as Ottoline continued to call them, were a regular feature of the next two years.

Rewriting parts of her journals for her memoirs several years later, Ottoline compressed this part of them to make it look as though both she and Philip had been quick to overcome what she was only prepared to describe as a time of trial. No more could be said. Discretion remained essential. Besides, 'it does not do to show that one is unhappy', she wrote in one of her most poignant entries in May 1917. 'People don't like one.'

---

* The scandal was hushed up successfully, but Philip Morrell lost his Burnley seat in the general election of 1918, and left politics.

'Don't, don't, oh don't ever again deceive me, I beg and entreat that,' Ottoline wrote to Philip the day after his revelation in a long and bitter letter which he later admitted that he had been unable to bring himself to open until years afterwards. It was the duplicity which hurt her. From the earliest years of their marriage, she had been allowed to suppose that Philip's lack of desire for her meant that he did not have any strong sexual urges. She had heard his shocked account of Maria's attempt to seduce him. What had really happened? It had never occurred to her that, while she was unwanted, his interest in other women could be strong and general. (Eva and Alice were, as she learned in 1917, part of a chain of flirtations and infidelities which had begun in 1906.) Ottoline's own passions always meant more to her as spiritual and mental affinities than as physical adventures and this side of Philip's nature was a foreign country to her, primitive and incomprehensible. In her journals, she offered earnest prayers that his sexual desires would decrease; in everyday life, she had to learn to face his weakness and deal with it. Any show of grief or resentment brought on one of the nervous attacks; if she wanted to preserve his sanity, she would have to ask no questions, make no complaints and allow him to lead his other, private life. It was a hard part to play. 'I have to smile and smile and pretend that I am so happy,' she wrote in her journal late in March, 'and underneath there is the longing for that tenderness and I don't know what quite, that doesn't exist. I have now to manage him and hide my inner solitude from him. It can't be helped.' She had never felt so utterly alone.

Help came from an unexpected quarter. At Garsington, Millie Ellis quietly stepped into the role of nurse-companion that she was to fulfil with tact and discretion for the rest of Philip Morrell's life. She performed it so well that many of his friends remained unaware of his collapses. Millie's letters to Ottoline were calm and reassuring, but they suggest that one of the chief worries with Philip was that he would take his life, as his brother Hugh had done. Millie spoke, for example, in March 1917, of having decided to sit up through the night and to sleep on the same landing, 'as I know Mr Morrell is always rather nervous of himself'.

The other person who came to Ottoline's rescue was her former maid, Brenty. Still living at Peppard, she had kept in close touch with Eva; now, she was anxious to do whatever she could to help Ottoline. 'I tried from the first to make her [Eva] see that the thing she was doing spelt disaster,' she wrote on 15 March 1917, 'but Mr Morrell's influence over her was greater than mine, and I had no chance. The inevitable happened, and then all seemed lost . . . The thing is, My

Lady, she *must* not see him. She *must* not know where he is and she must not have any assistance from him. *We* must help her . . . it is the only way.' Ottoline took Brenty's advice literally; her account books from Drummonds Bank show that, along with Philip's clothes, his club bill at the Savile and the wages for four maids, the cook and Millie, she made regular payments to Eva from 1917 until her marriage in 1922. Eva worked for a London dressmaker during this period.

Ottoline's first instinct had been to turn to Bertie for help. On 17 March, she wrote begging him to come and advise her in London on 'very unhappy news about Philip . . . *very private* – don't mention it to anyone'. We do not know what Bertie said, but he may have suggested that a mental home would be the best option. 'I *do want* to save Philip for all reasons,' Ottoline told him on 18 March, with an emphasis which sounds as though she felt a need to defend her decision; later in the month, she thanked Bertie for giving her a book on the treatment of insanity. But Russell had his own life to think about. When he visited Ottoline at Garsington in April, he told her that, while he never wanted to break the bond between them, he had become involved with another woman; he still did not mention Colette Malleson by name. His parting shot, delivered as she was climbing over a stile, almost made Ottoline laugh, so insignificant did it seem in the trauma of her life. 'What a pity it is,' he remarked, 'that your hair is going grey.' Ottoline had not lost her sense of humour: Bertie was given a new lodging for his next visit. Its name was Conscience Cottage.

'Do please get out of your mind that my life is empty or purposeless . . . never have I felt younger or more full of hope,' Ottoline wrote to Bertie on 15 July 1917, a month after the birth of Eva's son. It was bravely said. The heaviest price Ottoline paid for her new knowledge of Philip was a corroding loss of belief in herself which betrayed itself in the journals of the next two years. All her confidence had gone; smothering her face in make-up with smudged lines of kohl around her eyes, she made herself look as grotesque as she felt. Old friends were shocked by the change: 'Ottoline has become very ugly and careless in her dress and makeup,' Arthur Ponsonby's wife noted disapprovingly after meeting her in London in the summer of 1918, although she added that Ottoline had still been 'quite amusing'.[25]

It hurt Ottoline to know that Bertie had found a new love and it continued to pain her that Sassoon was so casual about her feelings for him, but the main cause of Ottoline's misery was Philip. Remembering how upset he had been by the loss of their own baby boy, it tormented her to think that both Eva and Alice Jones had now become the mothers of Philip's sons. She sent them christening presents of books, but she admitted in her journal that she was haunted by the thought of these other families. 'It is an awful obsession this ghosthauntedness . . . the ghosts of their children,' she wrote. 'I must occupy my intellect so as to have ideas and other images, for if not they will kill me – they will kill me.' More distressing still was the fact that she seemed to have lost Philip's affection. On Valentine's Day, 1918, she wrote sadly of 'that dreadful feeling of his want of warmth for me'; a few months later, when they were on a driving tour in Berkshire, she saw the ominous signals for one of his nerve-attacks and, feeling unable to cope without Millie to help, she shut herself in the bedroom of the hotel and 'sobbed and sobbed with the appalling loneliness of life, and I longed for P. to be really loving – longed for some warmth in his love'.

It is not easy to say how much of the situation was Ottoline's fault. Some parts of the story are unlikely ever to be revealed. We do not know the exact degree of Philip's nervous instability before he married, only that he had suffered at least two nervous breakdowns and that he was severely affected by the fact that his brother had shot himself. We do not know what the conditions were which Ottoline laid down when she agreed to marry him, only that she was shaken to discover that she held no physical attraction for him. On the other hand, we do know that Philip suffered from living in his wife's shadow. Eva Merrifield told her son that Philip ascribed his later breakdown to the shock of discovering that Ottoline's relationship with Bertie Russell had developed into a consummated love-affair (but Eva might have used this excuse to justify her own behaviour). Virginia Woolf received a pathetic letter from him in 1938, shortly before Ottoline's death, thanking her for the fact that she had, the previous year, invited Philip to stay on his own, 'as if you really liked me for my own sake, and not merely as O's husband, being the only person for these last 36 years (since the date of my marriage) who has ever made so brave an experiment'.[26] If it is hard not to feel sympathy for Philip, it is impossible not to pity and admire his wife, bleakly writing in her journal at the end of 1917: 'The precise truth is that I am a widow with a child and a brother.'

17

THE END OF AN ERA
1917–18

'And here we all sit: Brett, Aldous, Gertler, Clive Bell and the Shoves, and talk and talk, and we all remain outside each other.'

OM, *Ottoline at Garsington*

News of the Morrells' domestic dramas was quick to spread. Lytton, visiting Garsington at the end of April 1917 with a view to enlisting Philip's support for his appearance at a second military tribunal in May, was inclined to wish that he had stayed away. Her Ladyship was 'more fevered, jumpy and neurasthenic than ever', he told Carrington, and 'Philip is fearful – a ghost masquerading as a husband, and knowing that it takes nobody in – visibly worse, I think, since the lunacy.'[1] Virginia, who had been invited for a summer visit, was warned against it. 'I am told that she [Ottoline] is deserted and despised, and claws you like a famished tigress to go to Garsington, where no one will now stay, save the COs, who have to . . .'[2] Ottoline, terrified that gossip was leaking out about Eva and Alice Jones, suspected Clive Bell of being the culprit. 'I hear Clive visited you: did he make mischief?' she asked Virginia. 'I always hear that he gains the "Champion" rosette for it. He seems so innocent, but –'[3] Virginia, who had indeed heard a good deal from Clive Bell, but only about Philip's breakdown, was sufficiently familiar with the strain that mental illness imposed on families to be sympathetic. When Ottoline went to London for a week in April, staying at The Ark with Brett, Virginia made a special point of going to see her and telling her how much everyone in London had missed her. Well! Roger Fry wrote to Vanessa. So Virginia and Ottoline were in each other's arms, flattering to the top of their bents. How delightful. 'I suppose it'll cut me off from Virginia, and Ott. will get in some fine whacks at you too. But it won't last long.'

The Bloomsberries tended to assume that if they were not at

Garsington, the place must be deserted, but the house was full all summer; Ottoline had always put her function as a hostess before her private life, and she did not intend to change her ways: visitors included Robert Graves, Augustine Birrell, Jack Sheppard (an ex-Apostle who later became Provost of King's College), Julian and Aldous Huxley, the artist Chile Guevara, Lucy Silcox, Katherine and Murry, H. W. Massingham, Carrington and Gertler, Boris Anrep and Ottoline's old nanny from East Court, Jane Powell.

Sassoon came back into Ottoline's life in June. Invalided home from France in April, he had reached the conclusion that the war was being unjustifiably prolonged and that he could no longer take part in it. Walking out to Wittenham Clumps with Ottoline on the evening of 10 June, he asked what she would think of his making a public statement of his feelings. Bertie would know how he could make a protest effectively; would she give him an introduction?

In her memoirs, Ottoline loyally gave all the credit to her husband for encouraging Sassoon to take action; *Siegfried's Journey*, published after Philip's death, offers a very different account while providing a vivid portrait of Philip during what was undoubtedly one of the most difficult years of his life. Philip had advised him against the project, Sassoon wrote, pointing out the hopelessness of one second lieutenant denouncing 'the architects of a world conflict'.

Staring at the sunset as he leant on a farm gate, he himself – in his wide-brimmed black hat – had looked somehow defeated and ineffective, a compromising pacifist who had lost hope of dissuading mankind from its madness. It was the face of a man with fine aspirations, but his handsome features had no potency behind them. Kind and magnanimous, he lacked intellectual toughness.[4]

Ottoline's enthusiasm made up for her husband's conspicuous lack of it. 'It is *tremendously fine* of you doing it,' she wrote to Sassoon after enlisting Bertie's help. 'You will have a hard time of it, and people are sure to say all sorts of foolish things. They always do – nothing of that sort can really tarnish or dim the value and splendour of such a true act.'[5]

Bertie's readiness to help had a little to do with a feeling of guilt about Ottoline. He had told her that he was involved with another woman but, perhaps because he knew what she was suffering already, he had not indicated that his feelings towards Ottoline might have changed. As the summer went on, Ottoline's letters began to sound more cheerful and he decided that she was strong enough to take the truth. On 25 July, for the first time, he gave her a frank answer to a direct question: 'It is true that I am not in love with you now.'

It was true, but only in the degree of intensity. Bertie's feelings of love for Ottoline long outlasted his passion for Colette Malleson, and he was almost ready to love her again on the instant for being so graceful and telling him on 27 July that 'there is *nothing* to forgive'. 'You wrote "don't let me go,"' he told her gratefully a month later, quoting the frantic letter she had written after Philip's collapse in March. 'I *won't*. Goodnight dearest. I love you always.' But 'always', in this case, lasted only until the end of August when Ottoline grew impatient of dealing with Bertie's old habit of criticising her. Communications were severed – for three months.

'Of course it is *not true* about Lady Ottoline and Murry,' Mark Gertler wrote to an inquisitive Koteliansky in the autumn of 1917. The gossips had been busy again. Drawing up her lists of loyal friends became something of an obsession with Ottoline after the rift with Lawrence: Murry and Katherine Mansfield were at the top of it in the summer of 1917. She had seen them on her April visit to London and, puzzling though she found their relationship – Katherine was living in a studio flat on her own and insisting that she was independent – she was full of affection for them both. She had already started to make plans to set Mark Gertler up in a little cottage in the village for which he would pay a peppercorn rent;* now, having returned to Garsington 'full of beans and fight', she promised to do the same for Katherine. Murry's young brother Arthur joined the pacifist farmworkers in July. He was only fifteen and desperately shy, and Katherine and Murry made several visits in order to keep a friendly eye on him.

Sitting out in the garden with Katherine in the hot days of late July, Ottoline continued to puzzle over her relationship with Murry. She probed for an answer and was shocked when Katherine jeered at him. What Murry needed in life, she said, was 'a sweet, gentle "Muriel" ' who would give him no trouble and look after his clothes. Murry reminded her, she added, of ' "a little mole hung out on a string to dry" '.[6] Ottoline had yet to learn that Katherine often went to extraordinary lengths to hide her true feelings. Supposing that she was telling the truth, Ottoline could not help feeling sorry for Murry who, for all his flirtatious declarations, was so obviously in love with Katherine. When he came to stay at Garsington on his own a month later, she decided to make a last attempt to get at the truth of their feelings for each other.

Murry, as we know, destroyed his letters during this period. Ottoline's own account makes it apparent that he was being

---

* This arrangement only lasted until the autumn of 1919, when Brett left Garsington and Mark Gertler took over the Monastery studio. Brett had already acquired a new London home in Hampstead, in which she gave Gertler a rent-free room.

exceptionally charming. On the first night, after a long and engrossing conversation about Lawrence, he asked if he might 'come into her heart'. She told him that she would rather he did not. On the second day, Ottoline was so enchanted by his conversation that she called up to his bedroom window and asked if they could continue it in the garden. He came down and they talked for two hours, 'not of love but of life . . . It was heavenly but don't run off and think it is a love affair,' Ottoline told herself. 'All his love is Katherine's. It is only an affectionate friendship.'

Life was never allowed to be so uncomplicated. A few days later, Katherine sent a brief note to say that the tiny rent for the cottage would be beyond her means and that she had decided against it. No word came from Murry. Puzzled though she was by their odd capriciousness, Ottoline reluctantly agreed when Katherine wrote again in November, asking her to have Murry to stay for a week as he had been very ill and they were afraid that he had caught tuberculosis. (It was a false alarm and Katherine, not Murry, was diagnosed as the victim before the end of the year.) Murry made his visit and Katherine joined them for two days, but the old ease had gone. Ottoline had to wait another two months to learn the truth from Katherine; she had rejected the cottage only because Murry had reported to her that Ottoline had done her best to seduce him as soon as he was alone at Garsington. Bloomsbury had heard once again that Ottoline was on the hunt for a young lover. 'It was in my mind a low and wretched thing to do, such a fabrication of his mind,' Ottoline wrote in her journal but her anger was, as always, short-lived. It was Murry who maintained his grudge against her, while never giving a reason; when he published Katherine Mansfield's letters in a carefully selected edition after her death in 1923, he excised from it every affectionate reference to Ottoline or to Garsington.

Murry's unchivalrous behaviour came at a bad time for Ottoline. The house was empty. Julian, now a sturdy eleven-year-old, had gone to Suffolk for her first term at Lucy Silcox's school in Southwold; Juliette had left to look after the Ranee of Sarawak's daughters; Mark Gertler and Brett were only occasionally in residence and Philip was in an unusually cold mood after a weekend visit to the Woolfs. In her journal, Ottoline wrote that the ghosts of fear and disillusionment followed her wherever she went. Making what was meant to be a comforting visit to Julian at school, she found herself in such a state of misery that she could hardly speak. Neither Mark Gertler's gratitude for her friendship nor a kind letter from Virginia Woolf could raise her spirits. 'No, I don't realise that it is nice to see me . . .' she wrote to Virginia on 22 October. 'I get so self-conscious of being a leaden weight.' She must have been very unhappy; pride usually kept her from making any admission of despair.

THE END OF AN ERA

At the beginning of November, Ottoline decided to make a journey to Scotland to see Sassoon. The court-martial that he hoped would publicise his protest had been averted by the hasty intervention of Robert Graves; instead, he had been sent to a war hospital near Edinburgh, specialising in cases of nervous breakdown. His doctor, Sassoon told Ottoline, was an eminent psychologist who was doing his best to alter his patient's attitude to the war, without success. However, the letters made it clear that Sassoon had been persuaded to change his mind. In the summer, when Ottoline had last seen him, he had been resolutely opposed to taking any further part in it; now, locked away from action in the place he irreverently called 'Dottyville', he was eager to get back to his regiment in France. 'Oh, I wish I could talk to you about it,' he wrote to Ottoline on 17 October. 'It's so hard to say what one means ... You *must* see how futile it would be for me to let them keep me here in these intolerable surroundings ... Let me know what you think, and if you are angry with me – say so.' With his letter, he sent her his most recent poem, 'Death's Brotherhood'. The last lines expressed all the frustration he felt, and the guilt.

> In bitter safety I awake, unfriended;
> And while the dawn begins with slashing rain
> I think of the Battalion in the mud.
> 'When are you going out to them again?
> Are they not still your brothers through our blood?'*

Moved though Ottoline was by the poem, Sassoon's declared intentions dismayed her. Unlike Russell, who had been quick to see that he was in no way a committed pacifist, she had assumed that Sassoon's protest meant that he was ready to dedicate himself to peace. It horrified her to read of his plans to go back to the Front, but she took hope from the fact that he was still anxious to know what she thought. He wrote again, urging her to come. It was an expensive journey and Garsington was eating up her resources at an alarming rate, but she did not want to disappoint him. On 9 November, she packed a case and started off, 'very anxious and nervous'. Her departure was thoughtfully recorded for posterity by the ubiquitous Clive Bell. What a pathetic sight, he observed, this haggard old wreck in her dirty finery, plastered with badly-applied make-up, stumbling on her high heels, weighed down with gimcrack jewels as she tottered away in search of young love with a rampant homosexual. One felt

---

* 'Death's Brotherhood' was published in January 1918 in *The English Review* and later that year in *Counter-Attack* under the new title 'Sick Leave'.

almost sorry for her – hadn't he seen her a few weeks earlier, underwear exposed for everyone to see as she sprawled over the high rail of a capsized pony-trap? (Clive had been driving it but the fault, naturally, was all Ottoline's for having an old and unsteady horse.) He had taken a good look at the underwear – dyed lilac to match her hair, he supposed. Why waste valuable sympathy on such a creature?*

It was an eight-hour journey from Oxford to Edinburgh by train. When Ottoline arrived, Sassoon was out playing golf. He had, however, engaged the best hotel rooms in Edinburgh for her, although she had told him that she and Philip were becoming desperately short of money. He came to dinner that night and joined her for a long walk the following afternoon. He did not discuss his plans; his mind was already made up. Instead, he devoted his time on their walk to telling Ottoline that it was impossible to talk seriously to anybody who was so artificial. 'I remember after he had gone, as I leant up against the mantelpiece, feeling very chilled and desolate that he should not show me any sign of friendliness after having asked me to come all this long way.'[7] Sassoon went off for a morning round of golf without coming to thank her or say goodbye; sitting in her corner seat of a third-class carriage, Ottoline broke down in tears: 'I think the tension of my nerves must have given way at last.'

It had, but she needed to put on a cheerful face for the coming weekend: the Woolfs were paying their first visit to Garsington and a good show must be made, the semblance of happiness propped up. The weekend was a success and Virginia urged Ottoline to treat her as an old friend and confide in her. Ottoline decided against it, fearing that anything she said would instantly be woven into a story for the entertainment of Virginia's next correspondent. 'She does not seem to realise human beings as they are,' she wrote after her guests had gone, 'but has a fantastic vision of them as strange birds or fishes living in air or water . . .' She liked and admired Virginia, but there was something about her which reminded Ottoline of a predatory bird. As with Katherine Mansfield, she had the uneasy feeling that she was being watched from behind a mask.

We may recall that years earlier Ottoline had playfully spoken of herself as being like one of the masked observers 'laughing from behind the trees' at a Watteau *fête galante*. In January 1918, she made

---

* The account formed part of a speech Bell was preparing for the Memoir Club many years after Ottoline and Philip were dead. I am indebted to Professor Quentin Bell for showing it to me.

the painful discovery that the figures laughing behind the trees were her Bloomsbury friends and that the object of ridicule was herself.

It was Mark Gertler who revealed that her effort to turn Garsington into a refuge for artists and pacifists was being interpreted in Bloomsbury circles as a ruthless egotist's last bid for power and attention. Full of bitterness himself now that Carrington had taken the decisive step of moving into a country house with Lytton, Mark was sick of Ottoline's creed of forgiveness and understanding. It was time, he thought, after hearing the latest gossip in London, for her to see her supposed friends as they really were.

Murry had already hinted to Ottoline that she was being reviled behind her back. She had not believed him, but she knew that Mark Gertler was utterly truthful and had no personal interest in hurting her. His revelations shattered her. One of her few comforts in the aftermath of her new knowledge of Philip had been the thought of her friends and the fact that she had, through Garsington, been of some use to them. It seemed that she was wrong. 'I am,' she wrote after her talk with Mark, 'known as a dangerous and designing woman, immoral and unclean . . . nobody likes me . . . Everything I lived for has been knocked over . . . what I imagined one was giving to others lived only in my breast. It was *not* wonderful to them. If I could leave Philip I should certainly go away and begin life somewhere else – but I cannot do that.' (January 1918)

Ottoline had never lacked courage or the ability to discipline herself; when the first shock was over, she sat down to examine herself with an objective eye and to ask if others had cause to damn her. She did, she decided, have many faults, but they were superficial, 'external ones, of binding'. She could not convict herself of being immoral, wicked or designing, and she could not shake off the horror of being expected to go on entertaining and mixing with people who regarded her as a monster. How could it be designing to want to help people? she asked herself.

In February, Ottoline followed her instinct to stay away from her detractors; the only friends from Bloomsbury she would have in the house were the MacCarthys and Maynard Keynes, none of whom ever participated in the game of ridiculing her. At the beginning of March, she went with Brett to watch the flying exercises nearby at Port Meadow. The best pilot in the display went up just before they left and the young airmen who were escorting them said that they should stay to watch. As the flimsy machine soared up to loop the loop, one of the wings doubled under and snapped. For a fraction of time, the plane seemed to hang still. 'It was still an enormous distance up, and that made me feel horror floundering there,' Ottoline wrote. Then it plunged and 'we saw each other quite flatly, seeing it in our faces, the sudden rush to death'. As the wreck burst into flames, the next pilots climbed into their machines and took off.

The memory of this horrible incident dominated Ottoline's thoughts when she started writing her journal again a week later. It had, she thought, offered her a lesson in how to behave. She had always said that there was nothing she despised so much as cowardice; she compared her own behaviour to the matter-of-fact courage of the pilots, and resolved to put her fear of further ridicule behind her. 'Courage is the only thing,' she wrote. 'Courage to go on and see more . . .'

When Ottoline first came to Garsington, she imagined that she would always be happy there. She stood on the brink of an ideal world, full of friends whose talents would flourish in such a tranquil setting, full of happiness for her in watching them create. She saw the beauty of the setting still, but she had been robbed of a large part of the joy. She was glad to escape when Philip suggested a country driving tour in May. There was the bad moment when one of Philip's nerve-attacks started to develop but it passed and he was well enough to join her in calling on Asquith at The Wharf on the way home. The former Prime Minister had been 'quite nice and platonic' on this occasion, Ottoline noticed with relief, but two years out of office had blunted his wits. He had got into the terrible habit of telling nothing but anecdotes, she noted disapprovingly: 'so boring, and lazy-minded'. Talking about him with Augustine Birrell some years later, she was not surprised when Birrell said that he could not remember a single interesting thing that Asquith had ever said.

The excursion did Ottoline good and her spirits were raised still higher when she found a long letter from Sassoon waiting for her at Garsington, together with his pocket journal. She was pleased to discover that she could read the letter, written on his way from Egypt to Marseilles, without the usual sense of hurt. 'He *is* a very very fine character . . .' she wrote in her journal. 'No love for me – only confidence.' Confidence was a good enough foundation for the enduring friendship that she still hoped to achieve.

The summer season had come again and, if Bloomsbury visitors had thinned to a trickle, there were plenty of others to swell the stream. Parties of wounded officers came every weekend: columns of their tidy signatures filled the Visitors' Book from May to September, while a brilliant young friend of Aldous Huxley's, John (J. W. N.) Sullivan the scientist, came with his wife to join the COs who were living opposite the manor house. Sylvia Sullivan's habit of sitting out in the garden and stroking the soldiers' legs caused

Ottoline to raise her eyebrows, but she was glad of a chance to help Aldous's friend. (Already seriously ill, Sullivan later became paralysed.) The Woolfs made a second visit in July and Virginia wryly noted that the villagers showed none of Bloomsbury's inclination to mock Ottoline. Making her diary entry for 29 July 1918, she remarked that 'the dazzling appearance of Ott. & her pearls [seemed] to strike the agricultural labourer neither as wrong nor ridiculous, but as part of the aristocratic show that he'd paid for. No one laughed . . . They seemed all a little excited & very anxious to please. "Very nice people, aren't they?" she said when we came in.' Very, Virginia agreed, but she was disappointed. This was not what Clive Bell's latest accounts had led her to expect.

Bertie had made his peace with Ottoline over a Christmas visit to Garsington. During his stay, he made the flippant proposal that the American troops, who had been successfully used to break strikes at home, might be put to the same use in Britain; in early January 1918, he introduced this notion into an article for *The Tribunal*. Unlikely though it seems now, his remark was seen as a serious enough threat to Anglo-American relations for Russell to be sentenced to prison for six months. An appeal for a reduced sentence in April failed but the intervention of the Foreign Secretary, Arthur Balfour, and of Russell's older brother Frank, resulted in his being allowed to serve his time in the First Division of Brixton Prison and he was eventually released early.

Sentence to the First Division was a reasonably comfortable form of imprisonment, a little too comfortable for Ottoline's romantic soul. Bertie, while eager for prison visits, had already disappointed her by refusing to sound distressed by his fate; having imagined what the effect on her feelings would be if she was visiting a real criminal, she was unable to keep such picturesque conjectures in her head while travelling on the train to Brixton in the company of the pink-cheeked, roving-eyed Frank Russell, invariably puffing a large cigar. Envisaging her encounters with grim-faced warders, it was not altogether pleasing to see the Brixton employees rushing forward to shake her companion's hand. (Lord Russell was a popular figure at Brixton, the prison where he had once done time for bigamy.) Solitary interviews were not permitted; instead, Ottoline was obliged to put up with the company of the affable Frank or, which she liked a good deal less, of his new wife Elizabeth, the irritating author of *Elizabeth and her German Garden* and an enthusiastic supporter of Colette Malleson's relationship with Russell.

Restrictions on correspondence, however, provided ample scope for adventurous behaviour. Bunches of flowers were, as Ottoline soon discovered, a splendid way of smuggling in letters and there was a new excitement in reading Bertie's when they were written on sheets of flimsy India paper hidden between the uncut pages of books. This device, thought up by Russell, soon became their chief form of communication.

Reading the prison letters, it is tempting to argue that this was a relationship which was always at its best in correspondence. Away from Bertie's physical presence, Ottoline became relaxed and spontaneous. She told him about the intensity of her feelings for Sassoon and groaned over her daughter's argumentative nature, which 'is healthy and good and all right but oh! dear, it is so exhausting', promising to be patient when Bertie responded that Julian was only behaving like any other twelve-year-old. To please him, she wrote kindly about Colette; to cheer him up, she offered him images of a mind which could never be imprisoned, 'a mind powerful and creative which never rests but ranges far and wide with steel-like wings reaping into itself subject after subject, creating out of chaos an edifice illumined by reason and light – and that is you'. (28–30 May 1918)

Years had passed since they had felt so close to each other: Ottoline was Bertie's beloved confidante again. He told her of his determination to become an unofficial leader at Cambridge after the war '(I would not return as an official leader however much they asked me to),'* and of the fear of her own influence over him which had kept him from mentioning Colette for so long because 'if I spoke, even if you said nothing, my growing feeling for her would wither and die, and I didn't want it to'. Touched though she was by that letter, in which he asked her, if she died before him, to leave him the painting of a dove which Mother Julian had given her, it was another, dated 11 August, which moved her to write: 'This is wonderful.' In it, Bertie seemed to have expressed not only his own feelings about religion, but hers as well.

Even when one feels nearest to people, something in one seems obstinately to belong to God – it is odd, isn't it? I care passionately for this world, and many things and people in it, and yet ... what is it all? There *must* be something more important, one feels, although I don't *believe* there is. I am haunted – some ghost, from some extra-mundane region, seems always trying to tell me something that I am to repeat to the world, but I cannot understand the message. But it is from listening to the ghost that one comes to feel oneself a ghost.[8]

Ottoline's generous and warm-hearted letters lacked the fluent beauty of his, but they meant much to Russell. Perhaps for the first

---

* The Council of Trinity had dismissed Russell from his lectureship in the summer of 1916, following his first court case.

time, he realised how incapable she was of resentful behaviour; he wished he could be equally compassionate. 'You are so right not to pollute your soul with hatred, as you say,' he told her, 'and I *do* try not to hate. But it is difficult . . .' He remembered now how much she had done to help him to accept the two sides of his nature, the romantic and the rational, and told her how free he felt as a result. 'You began that, and the war completed it.' He longed to make some return for all the unhappiness he had caused her: 'I can be more use to you in future than I have been these last two years – if you will let me. I *want* to be, and it means a great deal to me.' (4 September)

Bertie had no plan to transfer his affections entirely back to Ottoline, but Colette was being flighty and prison magnified the image he had of her as surrounded by adoring lovers, an image which her sensual letters failed to dispel. Guarding himself against the possibility of disappointment, he proposed a holiday with Ottoline at Lulworth, near Studland where they had spent their first three days alone together in 1911. 'Say for a week?' he pleaded on 4 September. 'Oh *do*. It would be so heavenly . . . It is a *very* warm place – Oh I do *long* for talk and freedom – think of the wind off the sea blowing through one's hair, and the smell of the sea and the sound of the sea and the great sky . . .' A day together in Richmond Park after his release only increased his desire to spend more time alone with her: 'it is a great joy to find things so imperishable,' he told her. But Philip did not respond well to the idea of their going on holiday alone. Fearing another of his nerve-attacks, Ottoline regretfully told Bertie that they would have to give up the idea.

A free man again, Bertie did not take long to decide that Colette's adherence to her policy of sexual freedom was bad for his work: 'I cannot get any rest except away from her,' he wrote to Ottoline on 20 November. He did not wish to give Colette up, but he proposed to cut his time with her down to two days a week and to spend the rest at one of the Garsington cottages. 'I don't want emotions,' he added nervously, 'but I want quiet companionship and good air and exercise.' Nothing could have been more congenial to Ottoline in her mood of renewed affection for him. A cottage was prepared and arrangements made for Bertie to have all his meals at the manor house. He remained as a semi-resident until late in 1919 when he fell in love with Dora Black, who became his second wife.

Much of Ottoline's prison correspondence with Bertie revolved around the books which she sent him; among them was the one which brought Lytton Strachey the fame he had craved for so long. From

Ottoline, Lytton learned only that Bertie had laughed out loud when he read *Eminent Victorians*: tactfully, she withheld their less flattering comments.

It was not so surprising that they should have disliked the book; they were products of a Victorian society and the men and women described by Lytton with feline wit and with the clear intention of demythologising them had been among their early idols. Russell, while full of praise for Lytton's erudition, was repelled by his willingness to show Dr Arnold and Cardinal Manning as neurotic egotists to be exhibited for public merriment; Ottoline was in wholehearted agreement. 'I admire it and think it very good,' she wrote to him on 29–30 May, 'but it *hurts* me, hurts me . . . It is a book that just suits the ordinary clever men of today who are not thinking of risking anything for Faith . . .' The essay on General Gordon was, they agreed, superb, but it depressed them to think of the gossips of Bloomsbury giggling over the toppled figures of the giants they had revered.

Lytton was never allowed to know that they had not liked the book; Ottoline loyally did all she could to promote it. She sent a copy to Asquith with a note of recommendation and seemed as pleased as the author, who was sitting beside her, when Asquith opened a lecture on the Victorian age with a tribute to '"the most trenchant and brilliant series of biographical studies I have read for a long time . . ."'

Eminent Victorians was in its third impression by the beginning of July 1918 (bringing the printed total to 3,000 copies) and Lytton was transformed into an unlikely darling of society. The new Duchess of Marlborough and Lady Cunard were as eager to entertain him as Ottoline's old friends, Lady Desborough and Lady Horner; he even made an August visit to the Asquiths at The Wharf. 'It amused me to hear of it,' Ottoline wrote, 'he who was always so "superior".' She was a little hurt that he should stay so near to Garsington and yet find no time to visit her.

Grateful though Lytton was for her support, he no longer thought of Ottoline as one of his closest friends. She had never again amused and fascinated him so much as in the years when they were both involved with Henry Lamb; he had finally outgrown his need for a sympathetic friend and a free bed, and she had begun to irritate him. (He had, of course, been saying as much to friends for years, but it was only now that his feelings began to tie in with his words.) Doubtless, Ottoline had intended to be kind when she wrote (on 14 June) that he had 'done a wonderful work on Carrington . . . your creation of a happy calm and very fine woman is almost equal to your creation of E[minent] V[ictorians]', but he did not like to hear Carrington being patronised, and he found it hard to forgive Ottoline when she issued her next invitation to him, on 10 July, with a request that Carrington might be left behind, because 'there is Gertler at the cottage'.*

Following his literary success, other and grander doors than Garsington's had opened to Lytton during 1918 and the society behind them glittered, however superficially, with great brilliance. The Marquise had already failed to live up to his expectations; now, with Carrington as his devoted companion and a pleasant country home of his own, he had no further need of her friendship. He was not cruel to her. He simply – and gradually – withdrew from her life until, by moving to a small house in Gower Street, she made herself into a social embarrassment.

The other literary topic of Ottoline's letters that summer concerned a slighter event, but one which exposed the Morrells to much mockery and anger.

It had been Ottoline's idea to ask Murry to review *Counter-Attack*, Sassoon's new volume of poems. No reviewer likes to be buttonholed and it was silly of Ottoline to imagine that either guilt or gratitude would oblige Murry to speak well of her friend's work. Still, he had said how much he admired Sassoon and the poems were very fine: she was astonished to see them described in Murry's anonymous review for *The Nation* as incoherent cries which left the imagination untouched. Sassoon was, in his own words, 'lacerated', but he had no wish to pursue the matter; he had been highly praised by several other critics. The Morrells were less forgiving. 'We were very outraged by the review,' Ottoline told Bertie in July. '. . . A mighty quarrel is raging between JMM and myself.' Sassoon was convalescing after a head wound and could not be expected to protect his own interests, so Philip sent off a thundering letter to *The Nation*, reproaching the editors for allowing their reviewer to insult 'a gallant and distinguished author'. When the Woolfs made a July visit to Garsington, Virginia was treated to a reading of the review, Philip's letter of protest and Sassoon's letter of thanks, 'three times over, so I thought, emphasising his points, & lifting his finger to make us attend . . . I think Ott. was a little bored.'[9] As a guest, it was necessary to look approving; privately, Virginia thought they had been rather absurd. Ottoline lavished armfuls of flowers on Katherine (now Mrs Murry) to show that she bore no ill will, but the reviewer was not to be won. 'Murry will never forgive either P or me . . .' she told Bertie, and she was right.

Virginia's reaction to Ottoline on her second visit to Garsington had been, on the whole, a favourable one. She was sceptical of her

---

* Carrington was invited again, but not until two years later, in 1920.

hostess's habit of standing in dreamy contemplation of the beauties of nature and she was tempted to scoff at Ottoline's enthusiasm for improving the lives of the villagers, but these were minor faults in a woman Virginia now perceived as having 'an element of the superb'. While Ottoline was beginning to notice that Virginia, however satirical, was 'faithful and lenient to her old familiars', Mrs Woolf was feeling touched by her unshakeable faith in her friends. She expected too much of them, she wrote to Ottoline on 18 August, but it was wonderful that she should continue to do so: 'it is superb that you should go on trying to make us out more beautiful and brilliant and humane than we can ever possibly be.' What she could not say without hurting Ottoline's feelings was that it was not altogether pleasant to be always made aware of the gap between expectation and achievement. What, the Bloomsberries might ask, had Ottoline herself achieved that gave her the right to judge her intellectual superiors, however kindly?

The 'element of the superb' was in evidence in the autumn of 1918 when Ottoline went to London to help welcome back the Russian Ballet. It was not a glorious return (their performances were sandwiched between circus turns and comedians at the London Coliseum), but it was all that was available in a country that had taken refuge in the music halls from the horrors of war. Ballet-lovers struggled to make up for a conspicuously tepid welcome from the public.

Ottoline installed herself in her Bloomsbury Street lodgings until Philip joined her at the end of October, when they moved to Garland's Hotel in St James's. Every morning, she went for an hour to Mr Alexander,* founder of the celebrated technique for posture, before calling in on Harold and Alida Monro, owners of the Poetry Bookshop in Devonshire Street. In the late afternoons, she held open house for the ballerinas who came for Russian-style teas. The new star, Lydia Lopokova, was brought round by Diaghilev and Ottoline was enchanted by her. 'She is a most charming and perfect little woman,' she wrote on 14 October, 'full of spirit and affection and intellect and enthusiasm – so different from the English sticks who keep and guard themselves so well – I love her.'

Diaghilev's expectation of glittering entertainments of the kind which had been arranged by the late Lady Ripon left Ottoline in a state of alarmed despair, but she did her best to amuse him and Léonide Massine, with whom the ebullient impresario was now as

---

* Ottoline, like Aldous Huxley, to whom she passed on her discovery, found the Alexander technique helpful to her as a person of unusual height.

much in love as he had formerly been with Nijinsky. They were invited to Garsington, where Diaghilev's hunger for fine titles was partially assuaged by the news that Dorothy Brett's sister was a queen (a mere Ranee would never have satisfied him). Judging dead royalty to be better for him than none at all, Ottoline took the two men off with Aldous Huxley to admire Tudor monarchs at Hampton Court. Diaghilev, whose energy made him rather an exhausting companion, divided his enthusiasm between the pictures and his lunch, for which he showed an appetite which left Ottoline and Aldous gazing in astonishment. Massine, while always courteous and charming, neither looked at the paintings nor ate his lunch: 'if we got him away from D. he might be quite young and gay,' Ottoline noted with maternal interest. 'He is terribly overworked, poor boy.' (5 October)

Night after night, she went to the ballet, surrounded by a clique of friends: Sassoon, Gertler, Brett and Aldous, whose reward was to be taken backstage with her to talk to Massine and Lopokova. It was expected. The dancer had become a friend and when Lydia wanted advice on where to buy cosmetics or clothes, Ottoline was eagerly consulted. They were kind to her in this world, and she felt at home in it.

She looked it. Osbert Sitwell, a fascinated observer of her nightly appearances as well as of the dancers', thought she bore a striking resemblance to her remarkable ancestress, the Duchess of Newcastle. The thick and glossy chestnut hair which, when unpinned, still reached to her waist, was dressed high to fall in clusters of curls on either side of her pale, heavily powdered face; rakish black patches hid the facial rashes which had plagued her for two years; rows of pearls lay against the scooped bodice of a dress in the vivid Chinese yellow she loved to wear. Half-moon lids drooped over her extraordinary eyes, both pensive and penetrating, clear as a nun's. She could easily have been a Spanish Infanta, Sitwell reflected, looking at the long neck, the straight proud back. It was interesting to observe her and even to produce her at parties as an object of curiosity, but it was not fashionable to seem too enthusiastic about Ottoline, and the Sitwells could not afford to be laughed at. 'And then there was the Sitwells' party,' Virginia Woolf wrote of a Chelsea soirée, 'at which it was proposed to read aloud a sentence of banishment upon Ottoline.' The resolution collapsed at the first rustle of yellow silk across the drawing-room floor.

The war was only a month from its end, but nobody would have guessed it. The crimsons and vermilions of the Russian Ballet were the colours in which the whole world seemed to be drowning. Chaperoned by Mark Gertler, Ottoline wandered through the night streets. One evening, she saw two drunk men trying to prop a crippled schoolboy in uniform back on his crutches before they gave up and dropped him, laughed, and dragged him away down the pavement on his back. 'War, war, that is what you make of a human being, you maim him in body and you ruin his soul,' she wrote in her journal afterwards. Sassoon, out of hospital and enjoying his role as London's pet soldier-poet, seemed bent on maiming her. He had already turned down her offer of one of the cottages at Garsington and some farm-work, saying that looking after carthorses was 'much too alluring' to be good for him. He was friendly enough when she lunched with him and Robbie Ross, but Ottoline was astonished to be told once again that her artificial manner made it impossible for him to talk to her. Caring about him as much as she did, she could not believe that he would be so unperceptive, or so unkind. 'He does not know anything about me . . .' she wrote on 5 October. 'If he troubled to know the fundamental self in me, he *never* could for one moment say that I was artificial.'

Most unwisely, Ottoline shared her unhappiness about Sassoon with her friends. After pouring her disappointment out to Katherine Mansfield (who promptly passed the conversation on to Virginia Woolf), she put a mask of colour on her face to go to the Sitwells' party, where Virginia marked her down as 'brilliantly painted, as garish as a strumpet'. A day or two later, she called on Duncan Grant and the heavily pregnant Vanessa at Gordon Square and was said by Virginia, writing to Roger Fry, to have left the house looking 'like a foundered cab horse'. On her last night in London, she went with Mark Gertler to a party given by his hospitable patron Monty Shearman, whose open-house evenings of drinking and dancing were a highlight of the last months of the war. 'I danced madly,' Ottoline wrote. 'I was very unhappy about S.S. It was the day I had seen him and I danced and danced to forget it all – and succeeded.' She also succeeded in attracting Virginia's attention once again; she went into the October letter as 'utterly clandestine and nefarious', by which Virginia meant only to convey that she was not in the company of her husband.

While Sassoon was convalescing in the summer of 1918, he had made friends with a fellow invalid, a handsome, fair-haired, moody young Canadian called Frank Prewett, known to his friends as 'Toronto'. He had in common with Sassoon a robust love of the countryside, a sense of bitter disillusion about the war and a desire, not yet fulfilled in his case, to make his mark as a poet. Sassoon thought his work good and was sufficiently attracted to be eager to help him. After leaving the nursing home Toronto went to Christchurch, Oxford, and when Sassoon visited Garsington in November, he decided to take his new friend along. He knew Ottoline had a special affection for poets; he may also have thought that a companion would help to protect him from any awkward moments of intimate conversation with his hostess.

Sassoon had just returned from a two-day visit to Thomas Hardy; now, he heard that Ottoline had arranged for him to meet another poet, John Masefield, who was willing to introduce him to the Poet Laureate, Robert Bridges. The visit was not an unqualified success – Bridges shattered his composure by firmly addressing him as Siegfried Digweed – but it marked the start of a ten-year friendship between a forgivably vain young man and a genial old master-craftsman. The day ended with a perfect evening at the manor house. Aldous Huxley was there; another guest played the piano; Ottoline, busy as always on her enormous embroidered quilt of tangled flowers, was full of the news of the Kaiser's abdication, having heard that he was off to stay with her Bentinck cousins in Holland. (The Dutch and German families were close friends.) Toronto, shy to the point of gaucheness, sat quietly by the fire, drinking it all in. It had, for Sassoon, been an unusually happy day. He could not give Ottoline the kind of love she needed, but he did feel increasingly ashamed of his callousness. Her kindness, her obvious pleasure in helping him, were slowly winning her the friendship she longed to achieve.

Sassoon was walking in the water meadows near Garsington on 11 November when he heard a peal of bells from the village church, a clamour of joy for the news of peace. To him, as to Ottoline, it seemed horribly inappropriate to start rejoicing at the end of a four-year massacre. 'I felt as if I *must* talk to you,' Ottoline wrote to Bertie on the following day, 'must share with you all the overwhelming sadness and yet relief and peace – I feel as if it came and found us all like ghosts looking out from a hill on to those devastated fields . . .' On Armistice night, she dutifully lit a candle at each window, but the spectacle had no more significance for her than lights on a Christmas tree. Mourning, she thought, would have been more fitting than the drunken three-day orgy of celebration into which London plunged itself. She stayed away, but it pleased her to receive a letter from Katherine Mansfield, to say that 'I shall always feel that you understood all that this war has meant to the world in a way nobody has'. It was the nearest she got to a letter of thanks for all Ottoline had done for the pacifists.

The end of the war brought an end to Garsington's use as a working refuge. Graceless to the last, the COs left without gratitude and with a sackful of stories of how they had been patronised and exploited. (The Shoves, to be fair to them, resisted the temptation to talk about their experiences until 1920, when Virginia Woolf was treated at last to a full account of Philip's infidelities and breakdown by her cousin

Fredegond.) Only Clive Bell was still living in the village when Aldous Huxley, Gertler and the MacCarthys arrived for Christmas 1918. On Boxing Day, Ottoline was given a kindly lecture by Philip and Clive. The trouble with her, they said, just as Virginia had done earlier in the year, was that she wanted people to behave like paragons when they were only human and bound to err; high expectations would lose her the few friends she had. Ottoline refrained from pointing out that their own behaviour towards her put them in a weak position to sermonise; she was well aware that Clive Bell had been one of the ringleaders in the game of ridiculing her. Instead, she thanked the two men for their advice with suitable gravity, while resolving to continue to expect the best of those she loved, even Clive Bell. For all his mischief-making propensity, she thought she would miss him when he left in the New Year. By 1932, she was ready to think that Henry James had been right to call Clive 'that sullied little piece of humanity'; in 1918, she was able to say that, for all his love of scandal and the harm he had done her, she had enjoyed his presence at Garsington.

18

DUBLIN, TORONTO AND TIGER
1919–22

'I used to call for a lover, and now God has sent him . . . I have loved to give – now I am allowed to receive. It is a miracle.'

OM, *Journal*, November 1921

Confronted with a background of spectacular wealth in Ottoline's family, a big, well-furnished house and constant hospitality, friends and acquaintances could not be blamed for supposing that money presented no problems to the Morrells. Ottoline's striking clothes were home-made from the materials she found on her travels, but Philip's suits (paid for by his wife) were always new and as unobtrusively elegant as only the best could be. If there was a shortage of food on the table, the guests put it down to meanness or bad housekeeping; a shortage of bathrooms suggested eccentricity rather than a need to economise. They had no cause to draw any other conclusions: Ottoline had never talked about the fact she had been excluded from her mother's legacy, and Philip would not have dreamed of embarrassing his mother by revealing that his father had left everything to her rather than to his children. Pride, which Ottoline recognised as being a fault in her character, forbade any admission of poverty, but poor they were by 1918, and the spectre of debt and even ruin haunted their last ten years at Garsington.

The root of the problem lay in the farm. A good many gentlemen farmers were severely impoverished by the war. Rents and livestock value dropped along with the pound, which in 1918 had fallen to half of its 1914 value; good agricultural labour had become almost impossible to find. Philip, lacking in practical experience and ill-suited by nature to a career requiring steadiness, knowledge and plenty of common sense, was made to pay the price of his idealism. He had spent almost three years employing men who knew more about sonnet-writing than ploughing fields. The only area in which he had enjoyed a modest success was pig-keeping and two devastating attacks of swine-fever wiped out any hopes of making a profit from this.

Ottoline had been conscious of an impending financial crisis since 1917, when Philip was forced to admit that he had no means of helping with the upkeep of his baby sons. Such discussions were rare after this time; both Ottoline and Millie were constantly on guard to prevent him from entering the worried state of guilt and anxiety which invariably led to hysteria and nervous crisis. Perhaps he should have been encouraged to discuss his worries earlier, but by 1919 the situation was out in the open. 'Philip says we are ruined,' Ottoline wrote on 7 April: it was up to her to see what could be done. After trying to reassure him that there was no disgrace in his failure ('everyone has lost money farming'), she suggested cutting the running of the farm down to the bare necessities before looking for ways in which she could help to economise. Her natural generosity rebelled against pruning the list of refugees and homeless women to whom she had been making small monthly payments throughout the war and she could not bring herself to tell Mark Gertler and Brett that their modest contributions to the housekeeping did not begin to cover the cost of feeding and looking after them. She did, however, resolve to start encouraging some of her regular guests to consider renting the Garsington cottages, while not admitting that she needed the money. Secretly, she hoped that her brother Henry would come to their assistance, but she failed to make it clear how desperate their plight was and received nothing more substantial than a tip that there was money to be made from growing blackcurrants. The duke sent £50 to help with the farm. There was little to be got from selling modern art just after the war; instead, Ottoline sadly decided to sell her most precious piece of jewellery, the pearl necklace belonging to Marie Antoinette for which her mother had paid £500 in 1892. The £1,300 it raised in the summer of 1919 (£650 in pre-war terms) was a drop in the ocean of their debts.

Financial worries aggravated the depression which Ottoline was finding it impossible to shake off. Her determination to suppress the pain which Philip had caused her was brave but unwise; however deeply she buried the sense of hurt and rejection, the memory of it kept seeping out again, poisoning her life. The eczema attacks returned, her head ached until she wanted to scream with pain, everything she saw took on the quality of a nightmare. When Philip's niece, Dorothy Warren, said that she was only getting married in order to escape from her mother, Ottoline was in a bad enough state to see it as a prophecy that Julian would soon come to feel the same hatred of her.

Only the sinister rashes on her face indicated to her friends that she was not cheerful and contented. Her diary was full of social events. Dorothy Warren's impetuous engagement to an American antiques-dealer was followed by two Huxley weddings. The brothers had, as Aldous observed, made a clean sweep of the Garsington girls, leaving only the virginal Brett to keep Gertler company: his marriage to Maria in July 1919 came three months after his brother Julian had married Juliette Baillot.

Aldous had always been Ottoline's favourite of the Huxleys, and she urged him and Maria to take one of the cottages for a weekend lodging in the first year of their marriage, but it was his brother who most needed her help that year. Always highly-strung, Julian collapsed with a nervous breakdown shortly after the honeymoon; after sending him to Dr Vittoz, whose eliminating exercises once again proved therapeutic, Ottoline arranged for them to spend the rest of the summer in another of the cottages. Money was short, and Juliette decided to open a dress shop in Oxford the following year. Ottoline became a regular client but not, Juliette suspected, because she liked the clothes. 'We had very little money. She bought to help us. I am absolutely sure she gave away all those clothes again.'[1]

In the spring of 1919, in a sudden fit of recklessness, Ottoline decided on a change of appearance and went to London to have her hair cut quite short, free of her sloping shoulders. She also had it dyed bright red before going to inspect Hogarth House, Virginia's new home in Richmond. Virginia approved of the change, noting that she had looked remarkably young and cheerful: both she and Leonard had been impressed by the shrewdness of her observations and the generosity of her wish to forget the malice of her friends in the past year. For the first time, Leonard was prepared to say that Ottoline was rather nice.

The change of appearance and the arrival of summer had a restorative effect; by the end of May, Ottoline was ready to enjoy a rare visit from Lytton and another from the Eliots, who seemed miraculously transformed, he positively jocular, Vivien so friendly that she was added to the list of women Ottoline liked best. Virginia, too, was high in favour after she, together with Goldie Lowes Dickinson, came to stay in late June. Sitting in deck-chairs on the lawn, they took turns in reading out passages of *The Young Visiters* and guessing who the real author could be. One thought Barrie; another thought Beerbohm; the one point on which they could all mistakenly agree was that it could not possibly be by nine-year-old Daisy Ashford. 'This hot weather makes me happy,' Ottoline wrote in her journal on 20 May; 'so long we have been in darkness and cold and censored by people. Now I wake up to find that friends exist and are wonderful.' In between entertaining Virginia and arranging a fancy-dress pageant for the village children as a reward for helping to water the garden, she delighted Aldous and Maria by asking them to stay to meet the Picassos, Massine and Diaghilev at the end of July, following their triumphant presentation in London of Manuel de Falla's ballet, *The Three-Cornered Hat*.

There was far too much socialising that summer for the taste of Mark Gertler, who liked being with Ottoline best when they were alone. His letters to his friend Kot were full of complaints. He had been dragged to London to see the Sitwells' *Façade* and told off for getting drunk before dinner. He had endured a dreadful day at Garsington when André Gide and a 'nephew' had come and they had all talked French; the last straw had been the intrusion of W. B. Yeats when he was trying to get on with some painting in the garden. 'I have never met a more pompous and theatrical humbug of an Irishman,' he grumbled, furious at having been obliged to listen to Yeats in full flow on mysticism, a subject which Mark detested. He had never quarrelled with Ottoline in his life, but he came near to doing so when Yeats's visit was followed by her announcement that she was going to visit Lytton and Carrington at their new home at Tidmarsh. To Mark, still smarting with the sense of rejection, this was as good as saying that she condoned the relationship which had destroyed his hopes. He begged her not to go. Ottoline ignored him and went, only to shudder with horror. The house had been dark and damp; Lytton had talked of nothing but social visits, and Carrington, who she had thought so friendly and grown-up on her last visit to Garsington, was like 'a mere snobbish echo of the Bloomsburyites, always thinking of who is important'. Regretfully, she decided that Lytton's new fame had gone to both of their heads.

It had been a glorious summer. Coming back from the dank Mill House, Ottoline thought that, for all their money worries, there was nowhere in the world she would rather be than at Garsington, where apricot-coloured roses smothered the walls and where the fields fell away beyond the garden in long lapping folds, where she could lie behind the yellow curtains of her study in the cool shade, listening to the drone of bees while she read or wrote.

Sassoon's friend Toronto Prewett was partly responsible for this new mood of contentment. Having been told by Sassoon that he was talented and very poor, she had installed him in one of the cottages and tactfully suggested that he might like to come and eat his meals at the manor house. The invitation was readily accepted. Philip, suffering one of his worst brainstorms, brought on by worries both about the farm and Virginia Woolf's rebuff to the first of three timid overtures, rarely emerged from his bedroom; Toronto took his place in the family circle which consisted of Gertler, Brett, the Julian Huxleys, Ottoline and Julian.

Julian, like most schoolgirls, was a keeper of secret diaries. In 1917, the year of her father's revelations, she filled the pages with pictures of sinister men in black masks. The following summer, she reverted to childhood with drawings of her schoolteachers and Socrates (Soey), her favourite of the pugs. In the summer of 1919, on page after page, she entwined her own initials with those of Frank Prewett. On one or two, she interlaced a J with a P, to see how Julian Prewett would look.

Ottoline, too, was allowing Toronto's name to appear on almost every page of her journals. He was unlike the other undergraduates who came from Oxford to visit her and were so painfully shy that they could only stand and glower in silence, smoking cigarettes with furious determination: Toronto Prewett reminded her more of the young Etonians she had met in June when she took her nephew Morven Bentinck out with some friends for an afternoon from the school. She had been charmed by Morven, a tall, affectionate, dreamy boy, and she had thought how pleasant it would be when he, Eddy Sackville-West and David Cecil came to Oxford the following year. In the meantime she had Toronto, who shared her love of music and poetry; his feeling for the countryside and his evident homesickness increased her fondness for him. She was forty-six to his twenty-five, old enough to be his mother; in the pattern that was to repeat itself many times after the birth of Philip's two sons, she started to look on him as her child, and to plan ways of helping him.

Toronto had been living in the village for a month when, one night in early August, he asked Ottoline to come out into the stableyard of the manor house to look at the beautiful moon. Then he pounced. 'I thought I meant something to him,' she noted with disgust, 'but I see *I* meant nothing, only a physical want.' (August 1919) Nothing could have pleased her less; her dislike of sexual contact had become even stronger after Philip's confessions of 1917 (in one curious journal entry, she had compared the ugliness of the human act to the peacock's modesty as he wrapped the hen in a cloak of feathers). Stung by her rejection, Toronto made it clear that anybody with a husband like Philip ought to welcome the chance of an affair.

'The agony of that time will never leave me, the castigation that his rudeness gave my spirit,' Ottoline wrote in her journal at the end of the month when Toronto was preparing to return to Canada. As with Sassoon, she had allowed herself to dream of an ideal love; as with Sassoon, she plunged from ecstatic expectation into a despair in which all her suppressed grief about Philip found an easy outlet. It was, she told Katherine Mansfield, as though she had seen a lantern being held up at the end of a dark path and then an unseen hand had suddenly extinguished it. Katherine was sympathetic and so was Brett, but she could not shake off the feeling of disappointment. '*Everyone* has let me down, including my loved one, Philip,' she wrote on 24 August. She was depressed enough to think that she had only ever known happiness once, in the long-ago summer when she had stayed in Capri with Axel Munthe.

At the beginning of September 1919, Ottoline fulfilled a long-cherished ambition and visited her mother's country for the first time, taking Millie with her. It was the first time for years that she had not spent September with Henry and Birdie Bentinck at Underley, and, devoted though she was to Henry, it was a relief not to be seeing her sister-in-law: she could never forgive Birdie or her mother, Lady Bective, for their undisguised hostility to Philip. She was thankful to exchange the quiet, almost bland luxury of Underley for the shabby comfort of the Hotel Russell in Dublin.

The city was everything she had hoped for, raffish, unexpected, exuberant: it seemed clear why her mother had always talked of it with such longing. Ottoline was childishly pleased when she heard that she was known as 'the French lady' in the hotel because nobody could believe that such an exotic personage could be English; when she proudly said that she was half-Irish, she was treated like a queen. And properly so, they told her, for had her grandmother not been known as the queen of Ireland for her beauty, and had not her own mother been one of the loveliest girls in Dublin? There may have been a dash of Irish flattery in these observations, but they were very pleasing both to Ottoline and to Millie, who had worshipped Lady Bolsover.

Desmond MacCarthy had provided a list of introductions. She went to see George Russell (the writer known as Æ) in a big shabby office suitably papered with dancing elves and fairies, to a new play of Lady Gregory's at the Abbey Theatre* and to a party given by Maud Gonne. Katherine Mansfield's friend Beatrice Glenavy was there with her husband and eager to show her around. She went to Connemara, Galway and Achille Island, where she and Millie rolled up their sleeves and went digging for a fortune because, it was said, the ground was full of amethysts.

---

* This was probably *The Dragon*, first performed at The Abbey in April 1919.

'James Stephens is the man I like best . . . a little hideous dwarf with a huge head,' she wrote to Philip on 9 September. Stephens was a fine poet with a fund of knowledge about Irish myths and folklore. Much underrated outside his own country, he played a significant part in the Celtic renaissance, taking his subject-matter from the great Irish epics. He showed, from the first time they met, an instinctive understanding of the kind of woman Ottoline was, of her loneliness, her unwavering religious belief, and her capacity for loyal, enduring friendship. Stephens and his wife came to live in London in the later 1920s; ill at ease in a city which had none of the Irish enthusiasm for conversation, only for celebrities, he settled into Ottoline's weekly tea-parties as if they had been made for him. Good talk was what those parties existed for and Irish visitors often told their hostess that she had recaptured the quicksilver brilliance of Dublin salons at the turn of the century. But in Dublin, it had been Ottoline who was in need of friends, and who found one in this passionate, ugly little man who seemed transfigured when he started to speak. 'I will try and remember it as I go along,' Ottoline promised herself on 1 October, but like many of Stephens's admirers, she found it hard to convey even a shadow of his eloquence. She could only remember that he had told her that the best way to deal with any sense of rejected love was to give it again, quickly, 'fourfold, to something else'.

She felt as if she had come home, to a place where she had no cause to feel self-conscious or fear censure. The Irish looked upon her as one of themselves in a way that the English never had. Even the annoyance of being confined to a nursing home after gallantly hobbling around Dublin on a sprained ankle for four days did not diminish her pleasure. If she was on her own, she wrote, this would be where she would live, but Philip could never be abandoned.

The news from England cast a pall over the last days of her trip. Philip announced that he was going to spend a week at Torquay; since Julian was far too young at thirteen to be left on her own at Garsington, Ottoline wrote to ask Brett to have her to stay in her new London home for a few days. It was not, as she bitterly remarked afterwards to Gertler, as though she had ever asked a single favour of Brett, whose first lame excuse was that there had been a rise in crime and that Julian would be exposed to danger. From the first day of her charge's arrival, a screed of grievances began to be drawn up. Philip, who cut short his West Country holiday to come to London, made matters worse when he tried to arrange an excursion and lost Julian in the men's lavatory at the 1917 Club, leaving Brett to retrieve her. 'I'll never travel with Philip,' Brett wrote on 8 September. 'If we go Ottoline darling for heaven's sake let us leave him behind for he doesn't travel well.' Whatever the truth of that observation might have been, Ottoline did not feel it was for Brett to make it, and she was made still angrier by the list of complaints about 'your wretched child'. At Garsington, Brett had never stopped saying how much she adored Julian and how cruel Ottoline was to her – what a hypocrite she now seemed! Gertler, thrust into the role of go-between, pleaded for peace between his two closest women-friends: 'You really oughtn't to worry yourself about Brett and her letters,' he told Ottoline. 'It isn't worth it. You *must* learn to take her for what she is . . .' (17 September) Ottoline reasonably inquired how else she was supposed to take her than by what she herself said. It did not make her mind any more at ease to hear that Gertler was also staying at Thurlow Road, Hampstead, in the house which Brett dreamed of turning into a version of the Gower Street Ark, and that he 'would always like to have her (Julian) near me'. She began to wish that she had ignored Julian's protests and packed her off for a quiet week in the country with her old nanny, Billy Townshend.

Ottoline was already feeling hostile towards Brett; her feelings were hardened by the news that Toronto was deluging her with loving letters from Canada. So Brett claimed, and rubbed it in by lamenting that she was having to work so hard to keep up with him. 'She says she is writing to him every four hours as requested,' Ottoline noted in October, and added with uncharacteristic savagery: 'I wish to God she would go to Borneo and stay there.'

Brett had already long outstayed her welcome at Garsington, which she continued to regard as her chief home. Her eagerness to proclaim Toronto as her property, together with her unpleasantness about Julian, led Ottoline to decide that she was not worth the trouble she delighted in provoking. Shortly after her return from Ireland, she told Brett to pack up her canvases and leave for good.

It was not quite the end of their friendship; Gertler pleaded eloquently in Brett's favour and she made a few more visits to the manor house as a guest. But Ottoline had ceased to trust her and she had had enough of Brett's impulse to interfere with her life. She was given another taste of it in the summer of 1921 when Brett ordered her to ignore Mark Gertler's pleas that Carrington should not be asked to Garsington when he was there; the last straw came in 1923, when Julian, bewailing her fate at having been sent for the final stage of her education to a Roman Catholic convent school, was sent a rope-ladder, together with Brett's detailed plans for her escape. The ladder was discovered and Ottoline was held responsible by her mother-in-law, who had selected the school in the hope of converting Julian to Catholicism. Until this point, Ottoline had been prepared to dismiss Brett as 'a fool with the brain of a hen': after this, she was usually described as a poisonous insect.* Even when Brett asked to visit her in 1938, when Ottoline was dying, she was refused. 'Never!' Ottoline wrote in her journal. Julian, however, had appreciated the kindly intention behind the gift of the ladder and she maintained the friendship. One of Brett's last letters to her was beside her bed when she died in 1989; in it, she had written of Garsington as 'the spotlight of our lives ... the haven from the continual strain of poverty, worry, problems ... What truly mattered was the gesture, the endeavour, the generosity to bring happiness into the lives of creative people ... I know the importance of what Ottoline tried to do, did do, on a very small income ... and I think of Garsington ... always with admiration and love for the ardent spirit who created it.'[2]

Ottoline's visit to Ireland meant much to her. From then on, she took a particular pride in her Irish blood and made a point of seeking out Irish friends. Writing of her affection for Vivien Eliot early in 1920, the highest compliment that she could pay her was that she was Irish in her charm; when she visited Rome the following year, she proudly recorded that the Pope had promised her that he would give his special blessing to Ireland. Yeats became her hero and one of her most valued friends: 'such a relief to me after these dry English ... we talked by the hour and I enjoyed him enormously.' (17 December 1919) She went to Sinn Fein meetings in London and followed the troubled course of the Irish Nationalists with passionate interest. She was outraged by the arbitrary imprisonment in Dublin of friends like Margaret Llewelyn Davies. 'Most people I met when I was in Ireland are now in prison,' she told Russell on 30 May 1921. 'A *very* charming gent I saw a good deal of is sentenced to four years penal servitude.' There was no doubt where her sympathies lay.

Back in England, she was obliged to turn her mind to new ways of saving money, since Philip was determined to continue with the farm. One of the first sacrifices to be made was 44 Bedford Square, together with most of its contents. It was with considerable sadness that she recorded on 30 November 1919 that she was going up to London to sort out the contents of 'our darling old house'. Its party days were over but she was pleased by the number of friends who came to express their sympathy. It was Ethel Sands, usually so restrained,

---

* Although several reasons have been suggested, it has never been possible to establish precisely what it was that made Ottoline so bitter about Brett's behaviour. An additional reason may have been that Brett mischievously decided to employ Eva Merrifield as a cook until 1922, when she left Hampstead to get married. If Brett's servant, Eva, and Eva Merrifield were indeed one and the same person, Ottoline would have been likely to think that her friend had behaved treacherously.

who touched Ottoline most with the tender eloquence of her memories of all that Bedford Square had meant to her. Ottoline had known it for almost the whole of her married life and she was bereft at the thought that the doors would soon be closed to her, as to a stranger. The house was eventually sold to the Asquiths; Lytton, on whose advice she had often relied about what to read, was among the bidders for Ottoline's library.

She was still trying to come to terms with the loss of her old home when Bertie wrote to say that he thought he had found happiness at last, with Dora Black, a strong-minded young woman he had met in the summer.* Ottoline was genuinely delighted for him. 'I feel *very very* glad my dearest B. at your own news,' she wrote on 23 December, 'very glad, for I feel she may be the ideal you have been seeking and it gives me such real happiness to think and hope that you may have found her ... I have a very happy instinct about it. I do so hope it won't be a barrier between our friendship. I don't think it will – do you? After all it has survived a good deal!'

The friendship did survive and Russell continued to depend on Ottoline for advice while providing a steady glow of affection which meant more to her than his desire had ever done. Nevertheless, his new relationship and his failure to shake off the old one with Colette kept him busily occupied; for everyday friendship, Ottoline was obliged to look elsewhere.

Her liking for the Eliots had been slow to develop, but she had noted on their last visit to her that Vivien had been so affectionate and beguiling that she could understand why some women fell in love with their own sex. Her husband was harder to know. Ottoline never considered him to be a genius as a poet; she admired him as a critic, but it was a love of Dante that drew them together. In religion, Eliot's punitive God and hell-fire flames were far removed from Ottoline's dulcet pantheism; in Dante, whom they both thought of as the noblest voice in Christian civilisation, they found their common ground.

A shared devotion did not make communication much easier. The gently discursive Ottoline was ill at ease with the orderly, jigsaw-making aspect of Eliot's mind. Tom 'makes me feel very shy', she admitted to her journal on 17 December 1919; 'his mind is so accurate and dissecting and fits in every idea like a Chinese puzzle, and my mind is so vague and floating and I feel he must think me such an ass.' She underrated his interest; a month or two later, she recorded that they had been to dinner and the theatre several times alone (he shared her taste for music halls, she his for Restoration comedy), and that these evenings had been intimate and enjoyable enough to remind

---

* He had met Dora already, but briefly, in 1917.

her that she did not want Vivien to become resentful of their friendship.

The loss of Bedford Square left Ottoline dependent on the kindness of her friends during visits to London until the Morrells moved to Gower Street in 1928. (The lodgings at 38 Bloomsbury Street were too small and drab to be used beyond an occasional night.) Gertler had found himself a kind old patron in Bayswater called Walter Taylor whose large cold house in Oxford Square had plenty of spare bedrooms, and she was always welcome in the Portman Square home of Ena Mathias, a generous and warm-hearted friend since the first years of her marriage. At the beginning of 1920, however, with the great Bedford Square parties still fresh in her memory, Ethel Sands gave Ottoline the chance to enjoy being stylishly hospitable by lending 15 Vale Avenue, her big Chelsea house, at a nominal rent for six weeks.

Parties of the sort Ethel had in mind were too expensive an indulgence, and it was at Vale Avenue that Ottoline discovered that tea-parties were the best way to entertain on a shoestring. Maynard Keynes, Duncan Grant, Ezra and Dorothy Pound, Wyndham Lewis, Walter Sickert and Clifford Allen were among the vast number of guests who came to tea in January and February; when Virginia Woolf went there, she met Edith Sitwell, the Eliots, E. M. Forster and *Façade*'s young composer, William Walton.

The Johns were also often to be found there. Ottoline was sitting to Augustus once again for the portrait he had begun years before,[*] but she preferred her outings with Dorelia, to view the new Duncan Grants, to eat oysters (a mutual passion) in the City and to order new clothes. Dorelia bought pretty shoes; Ottoline, tired of being economical, picked out a rich yellow material for a new dress and a crimson satin skirt with a top cut like a Tudor king's jacket. 'I love being really rather gorgeous,' she admitted after this uncustomary act of extravagance. (February 1920) She had enjoyed her time in London, her lunches with Wyndham Lewis, her visit with Russell to a Sinn Fein rally, her leisurely pilgrimages with Dorelia; she was glad that she had not allowed Philip to bully her into giving up too many of her evenings to entertaining bridge-players.

---

[*] Ottoline did not see the picture until it went on exhibition in the spring; the upper part of the face, she reported, was fine and tragic, 'but the mouth is too open and indefinite, as if I was washing my teeth and all the foam was on my mouth. He is asking £600 for it.' (4 April 1920) The journalists who described the picture they saw hanging at the Alpine Club as 'snake-like', 'witch-like' and 'snarling' were rather disappointed at Ottoline's refusal to be upset. John, when interviewed, said that he had certainly not meant to be cruel but that it was 'the aspect he had been unfortunate enough to get'. (*Weekly Despatch*, 11 March 1920) Ottoline subsequently bought the painting, but not for the price John wanted.

She was called back to Garsington by the news that Julian had whooping cough and could not remain at Southwold. Her health was still a source of anxiety and she had not settled well into Lucy Silcox's school, so it was decided to keep her at home with governesses for the rest of the summer. Remembering her own visits to Italy with her mother at approximately the age Julian was now, Ottoline resolved to give her daughter the same experience later that year. It could hardly make the relationship between them worse than it already seemed to be; she was optimistic enough to hope that an encounter with Europe might work a miraculous transformation on her resolutely philistine child.

Ottoline was at Garsington throughout the spring and summer of 1920. She saw little of her husband, whose days were spent on the farm or the golf course and whose evenings were passed in playing bridge with friends in Oxford. Ottoline occupied herself by teaching Julian and writing the autobiography which she had tentatively started to compose the previous August. Every fortnight, she sat at her desk to write a long letter of advice in the role of worldly godmother which Russell had assigned to her as he dithered between the charm of Colette and the intelligence of Dora. Ottoline had still not met Bertie's new love, but she was sure that he could not be lastingly happy with a woman like Colette, who could not keep up with his ideas. Dora Black had the additional merit of being unencumbered by a husband; marriage and children, Ottoline thought, would give him the happiness he craved.

Ottoline's own marriage had been empty for so long that she had grown used to it. Philip had little to say to her. There was no physical contact, not even an occasional kiss on the cheek. She slept alone, in a narrow white bed as plain as a nun's. In her journal, she wrote that her husband had become completely indifferent to her, if not to other women.

It would be easy to sneer at the next episode in Ottoline's life if it had not made her so happy. She expected that it would be known about one day. With that thought in her mind, she wrote: 'Whoever reads in the years to come, don't laugh or mock or be pained. Nothing can alter my absolute devotion to Philip . . . but he knows that I have hungered for simple love.' (November 1921)

Lionel Gomme, always known in the journals as Tiger, came to Garsington in June 1920, to work on some plinths in the garden, and to begin laying a terrace on the east side of the house. His history is obscure; all we know is that he lived in the village with his fostermother and that Ottoline's initial, startled impression was that she was seeing a ghost. He appeared 'as if my baby son had come to life', she wrote in July 1928, 'as if he was a child of my own self and my spirit'. She was too afraid of destroying the illusion to speak to him at first; instead, she found pretexts for being near to him while he worked. 'I am out painting a seat blue-green, on the lawn,' she wrote on 9 June; 'my beautiful boy making a base for the sitting statue . . . I would give anything to know him.'

Caution was necessary. Millie Ellis, who already knew the boy and may have been responsible for bringing him to work at the manor, warned Ottoline that Mrs Gomme was a jealous foster-mother; Tiger himself, as highly-strung as his expressive face suggested, was both proud and shy. Quietly, Ottoline set out to win his trust. At the end of June, she took him on a tour of the Oxford colleges, which he appeared to enjoy, and gave him tea. Her natural gift for sympathy and understanding did the rest. A week later, he knocked on the door of her study, asked to shake hands with her and said that he thought of her as his friend. They saw a good deal of each other over the next few weeks; by the end of the summer, they had become lovers. At last, Ottoline was able to enjoy the physical act of love. 'The purity of it carried away the doubts,' she wrote retrospectively in November 1921.

I saw that having at last found the ideal companion, the one perhaps on earth who could love me, as my ideal, that it was denying good to cast it away. Conventions exist for the world . . . It is not an easy thing to have met across the great gulf of the world, conventions and positions, etc. But – I jumped and he jumped and we both stand on an island of the soul. I used to call for a lover, and now God has sent him . . . I have loved to give – now I am allowed to receive. It is a miracle.

It is, of course, tempting to draw parallels with the novel by Lawrence which both Ottoline and Russell thought true to life and beautifully written when they read and discussed it in 1928. Was Lawrence thinking of Ottoline when he described Lady Chatterley's passionate affair with the gamekeeper? A small number of friends, including Yeats and Mark Gertler, knew about Ottoline's secret love-affair; Gertler, who was hopelessly indiscreet, was in frequent contact with Dorothy Brett, who wrote regularly to Lawrence. Constance Chatterley is a woman in her early twenties, but she is said on the first page to be 'one of those very modern, brooding women who ponder all the time persistently and laboriously'; she lives in an isolated old country house on an inadequate income with an invalid husband with whom it is difficult for her to communicate. There is certainly some resemblance here, and we should not overlook the matter of the gamekeeper's name. Lawrence, Ottoline and Frieda all spoke of the conversations that had taken place between them about Ottoline's childhood. Among the stories Lawrence must have heard was one about her mother's fondness for the gamekeeper at Bolsover, who is mentioned regularly in her diaries for the occasions when she visited him privately and took him presents of art books. His name was Mellors.

The conventional view is that Constance Chatterley was loosely based on Frieda. Lawrence had not been in touch with Ottoline since their quarrel over *Women in Love*; Brett and Gertler's gossip would hardly have been enough to inspire the wealth of passion he poured into the book which he started writing in Italy in 1926. That said, nobody else would have understood the affair so well or done more justice to the shock of its ending, or to the problems Ottoline had with accepting that she could know sexual happiness with a man all of her friends would have described as her inferior. She did not care about their social differences; she did find herself minding about the intellectual gap. Tiger, despite his poet's face, preferred talking about football and cars to books; Ottoline was too kind-hearted to tell him that she had little interest in how a car worked, so long as it went. Fortunately, he shared her love of the English landscape (he had Lawrence's ability to identify any flower, beetle or butterfly on sight); in this respect, Ottoline could truthfully say that he 'was an echo of my own spirit'. But most of all, she thought of him as her 'life-giver'. By giving his love to her with absolute trust, he drove away the ghosts of disillusion and failure which had haunted her for so long.

Her trip to Europe with Julian had already been planned, the letters to her friends in France and Italy had been sent; now, she regretted having inadvertently arranged a means of keeping Tiger apart from her for half a year. Even on a brief autumn expedition to visit Sickert at Dieppe (her brother Henry had asked her to go with him to help choose some additions for his collection of paintings), she found herself longing to get back. Fond though she was of old Sickert, she did not enjoy the visit or the embarrassment of trying to translate a stream of unsuitable anecdotes to her puzzled brother. When she arrived home, she wrote out a long list of European addresses and made Tiger promise to write as often as he could.

His letters were, she recorded, 'wonderful': it was more than could be said for most of her correspondence. From Marseilles to Paris to the Riviera and Rome, the bad news poured steadily in as letters from Millie reporting the return of the nerve-attacks alternated with frantic missives from Philip to say that the farm was going from bad to worse and that ruin was inevitable. Never had he been so desperate for reassurance as he contemplated the loss of face, the humiliation; Ottoline did what she could, which was to suggest that they should let Garsington and try to sell their best Johns and Gertlers to Henry, and to beg Philip to take some time off and try to join her for Christmas in Rome.

The tour lasted from November 1920 to May 1921. It was Ottoline's first return to Europe since before the war and she was determined that shortage of money should not stand in the way of Julian's exposure to culture. By staying in small pensions or with friends, and travelling on buses, they were able to live more cheaply than they would have done at home. They started at Marseilles 'in a grubby nice feckless hotel' and progressed to Paris, where Julian went to the theatre with André Gide and spent a morning visiting Picasso; in Monte Carlo, she was taken to the Russian Ballet and given dancing lessons. Unsurprisingly, she was far more interested in the notorious casino, where they found Gilbert Cannan's wife Mary (now divorced) among the gamblers. Philip was informed in a letter from his enthralled daughter on 6 December that Mary had seen 'four suicides, which is very exciting . . . If you are ruined, they pay your hotel bill and fare back home, if you don't commit suicide! Outwardly they are *tremendously* decorous and proper.'

Discovering the pleasures of gambling with Mrs Cannan had not been part of Ottoline's grand design; her dreams of turning her daughter into the mirror-image of herself as a young girl were doomed to failure. Julian was no sighing maiden and this was 1920; who could expect a lively fourteen-year-old not to prefer seeing the casino to going to tea with Katherine Mansfield in Menton (Murry was in London)? She refused to go and Ottoline was obliged to make the visit alone. There was an angry scene afterwards, the first of many, in which Ottoline's accusations of selfish ingratitude were met with justifiable indignation by Julian, who now perceived that what had been presented to her as a glorious holiday was only to be a new form of education, masquerading as fun.

It was fortunate that Philip decided to join them for the Christmas week in Rome. He was easily able to understand, as his wife did not, that a young girl whose chief passion was for dancing was unwilling to devote her first visit to Italy to gazing at frescoes and altar-pieces. While Ottoline went to evening lectures (and was mortified to discover that the Roman ladies did so in dazzling *décolletée* dresses while she had only put on a wool coat and skirt), Julian was taken off for jolly suppers with the Huxleys, whom she adored. It was, for her, far more fun to hear Maria chattering about clothes and scandal than to be force-fed with culture, or to hear about her mother's audience with the Pope.

Everybody they knew seemed to be in Italy that winter; travelling around the Tuscan hill-towns, Ottoline and Julian encountered Diaghilev, Harry Norton, Clifford Allen, Eric Gill and, rather to Ottoline's embarrassment, Colette Malleson, who had come to Italy with her mother. Colette went out of her way to be friendly; Ottoline was not so kind. 'I don't find her very interesting, too affected, and not clever,' she wrote in her journal. 'However, she isn't bad and is rather a pathetic exhibition having been dropped by B.R.'

Julian was beginning to enjoy herself at last. The Huxleys were on hand again to entertain them when they arrived in Florence; her letters to her father were full of accounts of parties and outings. Ottoline told him that she had smartened up an old blue muslin dress for Julian to go to a dance in, looking 'slightly puddingy' but '*very nice* her old mother thinks. I do hope,' she added with emphasis, 'you feel *happier.*' (30 March 1921)

For herself, Ottoline was feeling increasingly ill. By April, unable to see well enough to write or read, she decided to go back to the Lausanne doctors. She had always disliked the town and never hated it more than on this visit with a bored, resentful daughter and the worry of knowing how much of their depleted resources were being eaten up by medical treatment. There was one pleasant surprise at Lausanne, however, in the form of Marion Colomb, the young Swiss woman who had once acted as Julian's nurse in England and who had now just completed a thesis on a mystical aspect of philosophy. Ottoline thought her as pretty as ever and much livelier than she had been before. 'She is to be married in a few months time,' she wrote to Bertie in China on 27 April. 'I feel sorry she is to be hidden away in this dull country but there it is – now if only Aldous had married her instead of that tiresome Maria, how nice it would have been.'*

Ottoline and Bertie had been in almost daily communication during her visit to Europe and his with Dora – not yet his wife – to China. Ottoline, assisted by Lytton, had chosen the books he took with him and she enjoyed earning his reaction to them as much as hearing about his experiences. But in April, to her alarm, the letters suddenly stopped. When she arrived back in England in May, she was horrified to receive a letter from Frank Russell asking if she had any news about his brother's death. A report to this effect had begun to spread and one brief obituary had already been printed: 'Missionaries may be pardoned for heaving a sigh of relief at the news of Mr Bertrand Russell's death.'[3] Ottoline's grief was short-lived; he had only very nearly died of double pneumonia. On 28 April, the first day of his recovery, Bertie's first action was to write to her. 'I want to tell you how profoundly you have been in my thoughts all this strange time,'

---

* Marion Colomb married Jean Reymond in 1921, the year in which she also began to write novels. (As Catherine Colomb, she became a widely-admired writer in Switzerland.) The friendship between Marion and Ottoline became close after their reunion and the Morrells made several visits to the Reymonds' Swiss home. Ottoline, who kept up a steady flow of presents of books, became the godmother to Marion's second son. About three hundred French works from her collection were sent to Marion after Ottoline's death. The two families remain close friends today.

he said. 'I am told I tried to write to you during my delirium ... I kept thinking of you. I am nearly well now, very grateful for your letters, which are an *immense* joy to me ...' The letter was accompanied by an account of a dream which he rightly thought would please her with its vision of the world as an earthly paradise, governed by wisdom and gentleness. Reading it, she rejoiced to think that the mystical side of his nature remained so strong. Writing to Lytton, she had laughingly described Bertie as 'an old rip' for going off to China with 'a lady secretary', but she still longed to see him as the man who had told her that he dreamed of finding a bridge between intellect and vision. It sounded as though there was still cause for hope.

It was largely due to the joy of her continuing relationship with the young stonemason that Ottoline recovered her health so quickly after her return to Garsington. Toronto Prewett had arrived back and was confident that he could make money for the farm by selling cheeses. He was as surly as ever, but Ottoline was too happy for his moods to affect her. Tiger's love made it easier, too, for her to bear the sense of her husband's indifference; she did, however, mind intensely when Philip forbade her to attend a memorial service for young Michael Llewelyn Davies, drowned in what seemed to have been a suicide pact with his lover, Rupert Buxton, in May 1921. Michael, one of the five brothers brought up by the playwright J. M. Barrie after the deaths of their parents, had been a regular visitor to Garsington, but the whiff of scandal made Philip anxious to keep at a careful distance after the tragedy.

Ottoline had never been most at her ease in what she called 'smart' society, by which she meant the people who cared only about making an impression. Under the influence of her relationship with Tiger, she drew still further away from it. The friends she most enjoyed seeing after her return to England were Mark Gertler, who was glad to have some motherly attention after spending several months in a sanatorium for tubercular cases, and the Spencer brothers, who both arrived to set up their easels at Garsington that summer. Stanley had Ottoline's unqualified admiration as a painter of genius, but she was fonder of Gilbert, with his mixture of tomfoolery and mysticism and his refusal to be intimidated by snobbery. She was delighted when, a couple of years later, Gilbert burst in on a lunch-party at Garsington for the composer and painter, Lord Berners, and reduced that suave dilettante to a state of baffled displeasure; she was vehemently on Gilbert's side in 1924 when his adored mistress, Hilda Harrisson, suddenly left him to be with Asquith. Gilbert returned Ottoline's affection in kind; he rented one of the village cottages in the 1920s and was, until her death, one of her most loyal friends.

Ottoline did not thirst for other company, but curiosity prompted her to accept an invitation to lunch at Blenheim to meet the new

Duchess of Marlborough. Her lovely face still unravaged by the wax injections with which she tried to improve on perfection, the former Gladys Deacon came across as a likeable adventuress, full of charm and wit. She had not yet been socially accepted, but Ottoline did not doubt that it was only a matter of time. 'I expect she will climb up and get into the top set and then she will drop us – but we shall see.' (26 September 1921) Gladys was almost too friendly, insisting on presenting Ottoline with a Siamese kitten as a solace for the recent deaths of two of the pugs (not a good present for a woman who disliked Siamese cats), but there was a wildness about her which made Ottoline uneasy. It was kind of Gladys to speak of her as the most intelligent woman in Oxfordshire, but who, she wondered, was Gladys to judge? Meeting her again in 1922, Ottoline decided that the duchess's tirades against society were always most vehement when she had a good audience; on her last visit in 1926, when Gladys rushed her around the park in a curious miniature car, talking incessantly until she and it broke down, Ottoline concluded that she was well-meaning but not quite right in the head.

In October 1921, shortly after her first lunch at Blenheim, Ottoline was finally allowed to meet the model of sanity, now eight months' pregnant, who had just become the second Mrs Russell. Colette was devastated by the marriage; Ottoline, who had offered to have them to stay and to look after Dora 'as well as I could' during the last weeks of her confinement, was overjoyed. On 8 October, she went to spend a day at the cottage the Russells had been loaned in Sussex, and noted that Dora, while no beauty, was evidently going to make Bertie immensely happy. She told Bertie so in a letter the following day, describing her as the most perfect wife he could have wished to find for himself. A month later, she wrote to congratulate them on the birth of John: 'I hail the little fellow with great delight. May he work wonders in his time.' (17 November)

It was a long time since Ottoline had given Virginia a chance to have some fun at her expense; a perfect opportunity offered itself that autumn and Virginia gleefully reported that Ottoline had made a complete fool of herself by gate-crashing a party given by H. G. Wells in a desperate attempt to meet Charlie Chaplin, her film hero. Arrestingly garbed in a vast green silk crinoline and flourishing an ivory parasol, she had struck the room dumb with her loud demands to be introduced to him. But she encountered Chaplin only as she left and, for some reason best known to herself, smartly opened her parasol in his face.

It made a good story. The truth was not so exotic. 'I went to a queer party at H. G. Wells' with Brett and Gertler and (Sidney) Waterlow,' Ottoline told Bertie on 9 October. 'I was in a coat and skirt and all the rest in *very* low dresses.' The invasion was Waterlow's idea; having heard that his aunt, Lady Russell, was dining with Wells to meet Chaplin, he had used her to secure a general after-dinner invitation from the host. The evening, so far as Ottoline was concerned, had been a boring failure; Chaplin never appeared and she spent the whole evening being interrogated about Dora by Lady Russell. The parasol, the green crinoline, the credit for arranging the invasion and the last-minute encounter with Chaplin, all were the work of an exuberant imagination.

However gleefully treacherous Virginia became in her letters and diaries, she never intended her Ottoline-extravaganzas to be for public consumption, but Ottoline had, by the end of 1921, been put to more upsetting use by two writers she trusted as her friends. Gilbert Cannan's description of the well-meaning Lady Rusholme in *Pugs and Peacocks* wounded her with its snide tone; Huxley's *Crome Yellow* was a more serious embarrassment. He had been almost an adopted son of the house at Garsington; Ottoline cared a good deal less about any faint resemblance his Priscilla and Henry Wimbush might bear to herself and Philip than the fact that the novel was crowded with caricatures of her friends and wartime guests. Gertler, Carrington, Brett, Russell: there they all were, recognisable and ludicrous. In the copy of the book which he sent her, Aldous wrote: 'Ottoline Morrell – with apologies for having borrowed some of her architecture and trees'; his claims that the characters were pure invention were singularly unconvincing. 'It is incredible that he can think it is creation,' Ottoline wrote after a brisk exchange of letters with the impenitent culprit. 'It is simply photography and poor ragged photography at that.' (December 1921)

Caricature though *Crome Yellow* was, Ottoline was hurt by it. She could shrug off Osbert Sitwell's 1924 parody of her in *Triple Fugue* as Lady Septugesima Goodley, easily identifiable by her red hair, long nose, sharp chin and by 'a height that was over life-size for a woman, so that without looking a giantess she might seem an animated public monument'. Sitwell's sketch was unflattering, but he had never been a close friend and he was not to know how badly she still felt betrayed by Lawrence's portrait of her as Hermione, 'a sort of awful aesthetic Grosvenor Gallery woman'. (6 November 1932) But Aldous did know, and it was not pleasant to think that he had begun his Garsington novel only a month after they had all been together in Florence. She had no wish to make an enemy of her old friend. Instead, she decided, as with Frieda Lawrence, to blame Maria. There had, she remembered, been an unpleasant scene in Italy after Clifford Allen told Maria that Ottoline had spoken of her as a liar; could Maria's resentment have made her encourage the lampooning of Garsington? Ottoline appears to have convinced herself that this was what had happened. She resumed her friendship with Aldous in 1927, but her observations on Maria became cold and uncharitable.*

Ottoline's journals show that she was in a depression which she called 'my pit' at the beginning of 1922. However, it had more to do with her family than with *Crome Yellow*, and with the feeling that Philip and Julian were conspiring to exclude her from their lives. 'They are Morrells,' she wrote, and meant it as no compliment. Outwardly, as always, she maintained an appearance of cheerfulness for the benefit of her visitors. The young had begun to filter out from Oxford for weekend forays to the manor house. The surprise, for David Cecil, a shy pink-faced student with a passion for literature, was in finding such eminent people as Yeats and Sassoon behaving exactly as if they were at home. 'The lions were there there all right,' he wrote, '– Yeats, Sassoon, and the rest – but they were not on show, not caged. Rather I saw them in their natural haunts, relaxed, unobserved, at play; or, if they wanted to work, free to go and do so.' Ottoline, he went on, 'far from being a lion-huntress . . . was a lion herself, a creative artist of the private life . . . In the company of her distinguished friends she seemed of their spiritual kin, and in force and originality of personality wholly their equal. One looked at her and listened to her and remembered her as much as them.'[4]

David Cecil was recalling his impressions as a very young man; Virginia Woolf felt no similar need for reverence when she visited Garsington with Jack Sheppard and Walter Taylor, Gertler's patron, on 15 July 1922. Julian, a sulky sixteen-year-old, got on her nerves by grumbling about her boredom with country life and the lack of hot baths but she redeemed herself with a word-perfect recital of 'Prufrock' when Ottoline introduced the idea of a fund to rescue Tom Eliot from the drudgery of his job at the bank. Ottoline was in an unusually subdued mood, but Virginia enjoyed the visit. After two days, she returned to Hogarth House longing for a bath and thinking that young Julian was justified in at least one of her complaints about Garsington.

Sharp-eyed though Virginia was, she retained the view of an out-

---

* Huxley had not finished with Ottoline as a source of inspiration. In *Those Barren Leaves*, he borrowed some aspects of her – but not all – for Mrs Aldwinkle; in *Point Counter Point* he mocked Dorothy Brett's pathetic obsession with Middleton Murry in the relationship between Beatrice Gilray and the appalling Burlap, and introduced Ottoline in the guise of Mrs Bidlake, a tall and imposing lady of fifty, keeper of a pack of Pekineses. Mrs Bidlake has 'a face like a saint's'; drifting through her garden in a veiled hat, she indulges in 'vague, unending meditations' on 'God, Pinturicchio, dandelions, eternity, the sky, the clouds, the early Venetians, dandelions . . .' (Granada edn, 1978, pp. 190–1)

sider. Ignorant of the financial problems and of Philip's continuing instability, she remained more intrigued than shocked by what she had gleaned from the Shoves and Clive about his liaisons. Having rejected his suit to her in 1919, she continued to feel a little sorry for him, 'an amorous man, a man of a different generation & tradition, in cross over waistcoat & jewels, half man of the world, half aesthete, appreciating furniture that is, but living my word! among what humbugs, & palming them off on us plausibly enough – Ottoline & &c.'[5] Intent, as so many of the Morrells' friends were, on seeing Philip as the victim of an overpowering wife, Virginia's portrait of him was less perceptive than that of the young son of Marion Reymond who was only thirteen when he watched Philip 'slowly going down the staircase leading to the dining room at my parents' house, in a splendid dinner jacket, smiling and obviously very pleased with himself. I had a sudden reaction that I did not understand at the time but that I discovered years later to be the reaction of a man against what we call in French "un homme à bonnes fortunes".'[6] (The phrase means 'a lady-killer'.)

What would Virginia have thought if she had been allowed to look below the surface of her agreeable weekend: would she have been disgusted or sympathetic? It had taken all of Ottoline's courage to maintain a serene manner after the horror of that week's events; how well she succeeded is indicated by the fact that she was only thought to be 'subdued'. She had gone to London for a minor operation when a telegram arrived from Tiger's foster-mother to say that he was seriously ill. Ottoline telephoned to ask the local doctor to go directly to the manor house and took the first train home. She arrived to find him lying in the stableyard after a second massive brain haemorrhage. He was already unconscious. Half an hour later, he died in her arms.

It was a devastating loss. Crying in the privacy of her room, Ottoline began the terrible, unrewarding lament of the bereaved: if only. If only she had not gone abroad with Julian; if only she had not laughed at Tiger for preferring cars to poetry; if only she had done more for him, spent more of her time with him. Mark Gertler, almost the only person in whom she felt able to confide some of her feelings, sent a kind letter, urging her not to feel too conscience-stricken. 'As for your not having given him enough, that I feel sure you need not reproach yourself with,' he told her, 'because even from the little I know of it I don't feel that to be so for a moment. You must remember that for him you were a unique experience ... Well, I will not write more in this letter. I only wanted to tell you how much I feel for you and to ask you not to worry yourself too much.'[7]

The letter was typical of Gertler's warm-hearted affection for Ottoline (oddly, it was he, of all Ottoline's younger friends, who the dead boy had physically most resembled), but she could not act on his advice. She was heartbroken. Thirteen years later, she wrote in her journal that Tiger was the only man she had been able to love sexually as well as emotionally. It was a double blow, for while the relationship was that of lovers, she had also found a substitute for her lost son.

Séances were popular in the post-war years when grieving families were desperately seeking comfort in spiritual communication. When Gertler, who hated mediums, returned to Garsington in the autumn, he was dismayed to find that Ottoline, vigorously encouraged by Yeats and his wife, had been visiting clairvoyants and claiming to have received messages from Tiger. The homely evenings of backgammon, poker and chat were replaced by the feverish shuffling of the Tarot pack; even Millie had succumbed to the general mood and was receiving messages for Ottoline 'from the other side'. 'The only comfort is that I have a spirit companion and I think too my little son Hugh,' Ottoline wrote on 6 November 1922; two days later, she reported that 'I feel Tiger's spirit all the time with me'.

One unexpected outcome of Tiger's death was that it brought Ottoline and Philip together more closely than they had been for years. We have no clue as to what Philip may have thought about the relationship; we can assume that he knew about it from the fact that he did not feel any need to annotate the entries about Tiger in Ottoline's journal, as he did after her death whenever he read something which came as a surprise to him. It seems reasonable to suppose that he also knew how agonising the loss would be to her and was terrified of what it might lead her to do. Late on the afternoon of the tragedy, he came into her bedroom, burst into tears and begged her never to leave him. Nobody, Ottoline wrote, could have been more understanding of her pain that day than Philip.

19

THE TRIALS OF MOTHERHOOD
1922–25

*'I who never wished for children find I am just one universal mother
... to all the young men and women that I know.'*
OM, *Journal*, January 1926

Lionel Gomme's death marked the opening of a new phase in the Morrells' marriage. Philip continued to stray and Ottoline to feel humiliated in a relationship which was made more difficult by his lack of perception and her pride, but the troubles which they had shared since 1917 bred a new and fierce loyalty, especially on Ottoline's side. Julian's Austrian governess was sacked for gossiping about Philip's love-affairs; when Ottoline was invited alone to visit the Conrads, she took Philip with her and made sure that he was included in all the conversations. She tried to keep his spirits up as swine-fever brought the farm's finances to a new level of crisis and she wrote him loving daily letters when he went off to Denmark in the autumn of 1922 to learn about co-operative farming. In the past, she had tended to impose her friends on Philip without much consideration for his feelings; now, she waited until his absence to ask Bertie to bring Dora, who was just the modern-minded sort of woman Philip hated, to Garsington, and to invite Hilda Douglas-Pennant, who had never attempted to conceal her scorn for Ottoline's husband. As a last gesture of grace, she submitted to Harriette Morrell's wish to see her grand-daughter become a Catholic and sent Julian to the Convent of the Sacred Heart at Roehampton. (Julian endured this grim establishment for two terms before rebelling: she never forgave Harriette.)

A dramatic test of the Morrells' new-found affection came early in 1923. Sassoon, Gertler and Toronto Prewett had spent a quiet

Christmas at the manor house. Shortly afterwards, Sassoon forwarded to Philip a postcard from Toronto, who had been running the dairy side of the farm for almost a year. The reason for the dairy's failure to show a profit was instantly apparent. The postcard declared: 'I have swindled Philip beyond the dreams of avarice.'

Philip, although horrified, could not face the thought of a confrontation; it was Ottoline who reluctantly summoned Toronto to explain himself. He did not deny what he had done; on the contrary, he asserted that a man who treated his wife so badly deserved to be robbed. There was a harrowing scene during which Ottoline passionately defended her husband; at the end of it, she told Toronto to pack his bags and leave. A few months later, still smarting from the whiplash of her anger, Toronto tried to defend his behaviour to Sassoon. 'I suppose I shall bear the brand of brute now forever,' he wrote, 'but it was a brutality to counter an equal and long-standing oppression. I think I do not exaggerate if I say my pity and admiration of Ottoline amount to love, but reason and experience told me that a husband and wife, however little they have in common with one another, combine to the death if either is attacked. So friendship, or at least, intimacy with Ottoline was part of the price . . .'[1]

If Toronto hoped to regain Sassoon's esteem with this explanation, he was disappointed: Sassoon had become one of Ottoline's most devoted supporters and he would hear nothing said against her or her husband. Staying at Garsington in the summer of 1922, he had thought that 'Ottoline was, if possible, nicer than ever before'; when Robert Graves's wife announced that she wasn't going to have a woman like Ottoline anywhere near her, he warned her that such silly behaviour would only lose her his own friendship. Touring Europe in the autumn of 1922 with Gerald Berners and Prince Philip of Hesse, Sassoon was always on the lookout for little presents to amuse Ottoline; when a bad hunting accident immobilised him for three weeks in the spring of 1923, his only comfort was that it allowed him to spend three weeks convalescing at Garsington.

Sassoon was one of the few guests to come who had been at the manor house during the war. The MacCarthys and the Woolfs made occasional visits, but Aldous and Maria were in Italy, as were the Lawrences; Katherine Mansfield died of tuberculosis at the beginning of 1923; Brett had been banished; and Mark Gertler was doing most of his work in his London studio. Ottoline's friendship with the Eliots continued to thrive, with Tom taking her increasingly into his confidence about Vivien's signs of mental instability after his own visit to Roger Vittoz on Ottoline's recommendation, but it was Sassoon she had to thank for introducing her to a new circle of poets and critics. Vivien de Sola Pinto, Sassoon's second-in-command on the Western Front, was a poet and essayist who made several visits to Garsington;

Lord Berners, the owner of Faringdon, a handsome eighteenth-century house not far from Oxford, was introduced in 1924 when Sassoon took Ottoline there for her first visit. She liked the house, while finding its owner 'very restrained and nervous'. There was a coldness in his character which unnerved her and she was never entirely at ease with his odd blend of frivolity and erudition; pigeons with brightly-dyed tails, emerald-tinted sunglasses and beer infused with red cabbage to resemble *vin rosé*, were all a shade too whimsical for her more rollicking sense of humour.

Sassoon's introductions to Walter de la Mare, Edmund Blunden and Walter Turner were more successful. Ottoline had been longing to meet de la Mare after reading *Memoirs of a Midget* and she was quick to decide that he was 'the very nicest man I know', sympathetic, modest and a spell-binding conversationalist who she and Philip often went to visit at his family home at Taplow. (Unlike Sassoon, she seems to have remained unaware of de la Mare's division of his time between his country wife and his London mistress.) Edmund Blunden, Sassoon's favourite protégé at that time, visited Garsington several times in the early 1920s. Ottoline liked his poetry enough to try to further his career with useful introductions: in 1920, Murry, then the editor of *The Athenaeum*, wrote to tell Blunden that he was willing to help him on the recommendation of 'our kindest of friends, Lady Ottoline Morrell'. Less wisely, Ottoline sought to intervene in a marriage which she had opposed from the start. Mary Blunden was noted down on her first visit to Garsington as a vapid woman with an infuriating habit of fluttering her eyelashes and smirking whenever she was addressed; when Blunden revealed that his wife had been bullying him, Ottoline jumped at the chance to write and give Mrs Blunden a piece of her mind. Mary was reported to have mended her ways after this, but she did not forgive the reproof. When Ottoline interfered once again, this time on Mary's behalf, to remonstrate with Blunden for bringing a Japanese mistress to England, he made it clear that her sympathy would not be well-received by his wife, who had been busy slandering her for the past seven years.

Ottoline was sucked into another marital whirlpool through her friendship with Walter and Delphine Turner, Sassoon's London landlords. Turner, an Australian poet and journalist who had settled in England, was talented, poor and unscrupulous; he had been visiting Garsington for almost five years when he suddenly appeared for a weekend with a young lady called Cynthia Noble instead of his wife. Ottoline was outraged, and Sassoon even more so, when Turner showed him a vicious skit about Ottoline which he had written and was hoping to publish. Deep in consultation on behalf of Delphine, whom they greatly preferred to her husband, Ottoline and Sassoon decided that he was only interested in Miss Noble's fortune, a suspicion which looked to have been well-founded when Turner was seen to blanch at the news, offered by a demure Ottoline, that Cynthia's father had promised to disinherit her if she didn't behave herself.

What began as a drama rapidly deteriorated into farce. Cynthia insisted on going to explain herself to Delphine, accompanied by a reluctant Ottoline; Turner asked Ottoline to tell Cynthia Noble what a wonderful woman his wife was; Delphine continued to assert that it was all a terrible misunderstanding and that Walter had never suggested leaving her. It was, she said, all the fault of Cynthia Noble.

In 1925, Ottoline was still prepared to like Turner, shocked though she was by his treatment of Delphine. He had a kind side to his nature and she was touched on her return from a spring visit to Holland with Philip to find Walter Turner standing on the station ready to welcome them home. But in 1927, Turner published the skit he had already shown to Sassoon. *The Aesthetes* (discussed in the following chapter) was the most vicious of the works in which Ottoline was made to cut a ridiculous figure during her lifetime by writers she had liked and trusted. She read it, and never spoke to Walter Turner again.

Garsington in the twenties, although run on a shoestring, was even livelier than it had been in the years of pacifist occupation. The arrival at Oxford of Ottoline's agreeable, musical nephew Morven, together with a group of Etonian contemporaries, heralded the manor house's post-Bloomsbury renaissance. Morven's particular friends were Lord David Cecil, Eddy Sackville-West (Vita's intensely musical cousin, the heir to Knole), and Robert Gathorne-Hardy. These four were regular visitors and word soon got out in Oxford that kind, eccentric Lady Ottoline was ready to welcome any students who cared for literature, art or music. To visit Garsington and, better still, to be invited to return, became the acme of social achievement for young intellectuals – and snobs: it was of this period that Evelyn Waugh was thinking when, in *Brideshead Revisited*, he allowed Anthony Blanche to wonder aloud to Charles Ryder whether or not he should accept his Sunday invitation to Garsington and whether it would be dreadfully unchic to be truthful and admit there that he hadn't yet read Huxley's latest novel. Ottoline's by now very bizarre appearance only added to the fascination. Most students had caught sight of a tall, unusually slender woman, her face hidden by a broad-brimmed hat swathed in chiffon, her high scarlet shoes peeping out from the billowing skirts of a long summer dress, clipping briskly through the city streets in a phaeton with a whip in one white-gloved hand. They had stared in 1899, when Philip Morrell first saw her bicycling along The Broad, and they stared even more in 1923.

In the mass of recollections which have been written of visits to Garsington in the 1920s, there are few which do not dwell on the terror of the first occasion. Ottoline went out of her way to make new guests feel at home, but not all of them had the *savoir-faire* of the fictitious Anthony Blanche and not even Ottoline could rescue one wretched, anonymous young man mentioned by Gathorne-Hardy who, too shy to speak, finally contributed to the conversation with 'that sound which of all sounds is the most embarrassing to emit in company. Talk ceased for a moment, and then "Ye-e-e-es," desperately, fruitlessly, sighed Ottoline.' A shy student who was not used to being interrogated about his interests and beliefs could easily be disconcerted by her probing solicitude, but there was a greater risk in claiming too much. Should the visitor mention an interest in art, as Gathorne-Hardy did, he might face being instantly subjected to a brisk course in critical appreciation of the genius of the Spencer brothers. (This was mutely received in the case of Gathorne-Hardy, who did not want to admit that he had never heard of Stanley or Gilbert Spencer.) Another undergraduate, L. A. G. Strong, remembered sitting in anguished silence after Ottoline had led him across the lawn to talk to Eliot and the Woolfs; others were reduced to jellies of nerves as they were inexorably propelled into the orbit of Yeats, E. M. Forster or Sassoon. To come and gaze at one's heroes was one thing; to be expected to spend half an hour walking round the garden in discussion with them was quite another. The less ambitious of the visitors were thankful to escape into a round of croquet with Julian and old Walter Taylor, or a game of bridge or whist with Philip.

Visiting Garsington became part of the experience of being at Oxford, to be endured and, with luck, enjoyed: the undergraduates arrived in scores. Virginia, visiting in May 1923, claimed to have been appalled to find herself sharing the lawn with thirty-seven students, 'mostly the sons of Marquises', as she could not resist the opportunity to boast before distancing herself with a few groans about the 'drawl and crawl and smell' of Ottoline, 'which might be harmless in the stir of normal sunlight. Only is the sunlight ever normal at Garsington? No, I think even the sky is done up in pale yellow silk, and certainly the cabbages are scented. But this is all great rubbish.'[2] Rubbish it certainly was, of the hyperbolical kind in which Virginia loved to indulge; in the same month, she was passing on Eddy Sackville-West's praises to Ottoline and begging her to invite Sebastian Sprott, a young friend of Lytton's who had said that he was pining to see Garsington.

There may have been a future marquis or two among the guests, but Ottoline paid them no special attention. It was Sassoon, not she, who thrilled to the thought of David Cecil's illustrious family; Ottoline was more excited by the fact that they had just been visited by A. L. Rowse, whom she described to Bertie as 'a wonderful young man, the son of a stonemason in Cornwall... P[hilip] and I were enchanted with him' (18 February 1926).

Ottoline had no trace of snobbery in her character, but she did, as she grew older, mind increasingly about what she considered to be good manners. She noted with disapproval that L. P. Hartley, his own name still unknown, would always push himself forward when there was anybody famous to be met; she was furious with Eddy Sackville-West when he sat next to Yeats at dinner and never said a word to him. She wrote in jest of holding her Sunday court; it was not for herself that she required homage, but for the eminent older guests she loved and admired, and to whom she felt that a proper degree of courtesy was due.

'Appalling! A fatal error to have come, I see now only too clearly,' Lytton wrote to Carrington on 3 June 1923. He was on one of his increasingly rare visits to Garsington and, perhaps because he did not want Carrington to feel that she was missing anything, he omitted to tell her that the Woolfs were his fellow guests.* A fib, in these circumstances, could be construed as kindness; and so Lytton chose only to own up to the presence of 'a miserable German doctor – a "psycho-analyst" of Freiburg' who bored him to death with lectures on mysticism whenever Philip was not forcing him to listen to the article he had written for *The Spectator*.

The German in question was a Dr Marten and Lytton's scepticism was not misplaced; Ottoline was once more convinced that she was about to be cured. Always ready to endure discomfort for any doctor who promised a miracle, she put herself into Marten's hands when she went to Freiburg in the autumn of 1923. He was, she told Russell, 'a real saint, besides being very able'; Eliot was urged to let Vivien be seen by him; Bob Gathorne-Hardy was encouraged to follow her to Germany in order that his lover, Kyrle Leng, could be treated; only Dora Russell had the good sense to resist Ottoline's entreaties that Marten should be allowed to cure her sciatica with injections of bees' stings. A little superficial analysis was provided with the treatment; Ottoline left Freiburg firmly convinced that her love of costume could be traced to a doting mother's love of seeing her little girl in elaborate party-dresses, and that her longing to be loved stemmed

---

* Mark Gertler had written to Carrington after her marriage to Ralph Partridge in 1921, telling her that she was no longer welcome at Garsington. Assuming that he wrote on Ottoline's behalf, Carrington made no further visits until 1926.

from an excessive affection for her handsome brothers and the sense that they had rejected her.

There was a measure of truth in this, and it certainly did not harm Ottoline's health to be made to think about it. It may even have done her good; certainly, she began to write about her feelings towards her family with greater freedom after 1923. It was as a doctor, not as an analyst, that Marten was an unfortunate choice. 'He thinks he has found out my trouble – some old germ left from typhoid years ago,' Ottoline reported to Bertie in November 1923, 'and now he is injecting me with all sorts of injections of milk and other things quite in advance of England.' The milk injections did her no good; Marten's belief in starvation diets, dutifully followed by Ottoline over the next ten years whenever she felt ill, did her considerable harm. No woman of her age and complicated medical history should have expected an improvement in health from fortnightly regimes of fruit and water which left her so weak that she could scarcely sit up, but this was Dr Marten's panacea for all ailments, and Ottoline never argued with doctors. When, in 1932, she finally left Marten for the equally unsatisfactory Dr Cameron, it was only because she was horrified by Marten's anti-Semitism.

Fortunately for Bertie, Ottoline had more interesting things to write about than her medical agenda. She had been on a visit to the Russells during the summer, spending a miserable five days sitting among heaps of nappies and struggling to wean the conversation away from the all-absorbing topic of baby John. At the time, she had been bored and depressed by the degree of Dora's influence over Bertie; wandering through the streets of poverty-stricken Freiburg – these were the years of the French occupation of the Ruhr and the collapse of the German economy – she kept thinking what a waste it was that Russell should be hanging over a cradle when he could be helping the young mathematicians and philosophers who spoke of him so highly. Surrounded by evidence of their despair, she tried to fire him with her own sense of their need:

I have seen several people here. Mathematicians who are *very* interested in your work and in you and I wonder if it is possible to get some of your books to give to the university here – for they cannot as you know afford any books – I wondered if Cambridge ever gives grants of books such as your big opus, *Principia Mathematica*. Do they? I should like to give them some of the others too but we had better wait and talk about it when we meet. They are such wonderful people here and so keen and full of intellectual life and activity . . . I long to get books for their poor people. They are starving. (9 December 1923)

The highlight of Ottoline's visit to Freiburg was her meeting with Maxim Gorky and his beautiful, fascinating companion, the Baroness Budberg. Bertie had already praised Gorky to her after meeting him in Russia, describing him as Milton to Lenin's Cromwell. Ottoline wrote to beg him for a letter of introduction and ended, 'with my usual audacity', by introducing herself before it arrived.

The encounter with Gorky came close to matching the excitement she had felt at her first meeting with Joseph Conrad. More flirtatious than Conrad, Gorky was delighted to be admired for his beautiful eyes, a tribute which was accepted with many bows and smiles; overwhelmed by his charm, Ottoline thought he was probably telling the truth when he laughed and told her not to invite him to England, because '"I am more dangerous than anyone"'. But most of their talk was about books. After they had agreed on the magnificence of Constance Garnett's translations from the Russian, Ottoline asked him which novelists he thought wrote best about women: 'He said that if one reads *Anna Karenina*, *Madame Bovary* and *Tess of the d'Urbervilles* in sequence you get all you want to know about women,' she reported to Bertie on 19 November. 'I think myself there is more to know for there are other types of women than come into those books. Meredith's Diana for instance.'*

Gorky evidently enjoyed Ottoline's company, for he urged her to come back a few days later and asked for a present of her rose-coloured writing-paper. 'He is a fascinating man,' she wrote in a postscript, '*so* alive, alert and forcible, intelligent and yet with such immense primitive force and humour.' She was not quite so sure about the baroness, the interpreter at their meetings. 'What a clever woman she is. Cruel I think at bottom but very attractive too – so immensely well read up on everything.' Still, she liked Moura well enough to lend her her own copy of *The Waste Land* and to promise that she would introduce her to Russell if she ever came to England. When Gorky and Moura Budberg left Freiburg at the end of November, Ottoline went to the station to see them off, 'all packed into a 4th class carriage in truly Russian style on the way to Berlin and then Italy . . .'

The town felt as though a light had been turned off when the Russians had left, but Kyrle Leng and Bob Gathorne-Hardy came out to join Ottoline for a fortnight – Kyrle had agreed to place himself in the care of Dr Marten – and to see for themselves why she was becoming known in Freiberg as '"die komische Engländerin". Certainly I had the impression that the university students when we passed them tried to barge one another into me, and me thus into her,' Gathorne-Hardy observed in his introduction to Ottoline's memoirs after telling some tales of life in the Freiburg hotel:†

---

* *Diana of the Crossways*, George Meredith's immensely popular novel of 1885 about a witty and emancipated Irish beauty.

† The best of them described Ottoline's wrath with a fellow guest, a German countess so poor that she tried to sell Ottoline her box camera, but not so poor that she did not insist, to Ottoline's disgust, on ordering her pug dog a full three-course dinner in the dining-room every day. ('"*Poor* dog! *Poor* dog!" screamed Ottoline . . .')

I had a horrid fear that if they should succeed in toppling us over, I should be forced in honour to challenge one of them to a duel. I think that Ottoline was aware of the effect she was creating. I seemed to discern in her face something of an amused tolerance ... although the strange mode of dress was natural to her, she knew quite happily that to some people it was comic. She loved going out into gay crowds, and often alone. At the time of George V's jubilee, I saw her after one of these excursions. 'Do you know,' she said, 'they mistook me for a maypole. They tried to dance round me.'

Away from Philip, Gathorne-Hardy was struck by Ottoline's zest for an independent life. By the time the two young men arrived, she was utterly at home. Her hotel room had been turned into an extension of Garsington, full of pretty objects and delicious scents; she had been to all the musical events, seen and formed her views about the superb Gothic cathedral, met and made friends with Gorky; the young men were impressed, and Gathorne-Hardy was thrilled when Ottoline said casually that she would be delighted to have him at Garsington after Christmas as a paying guest while he prepared his thesis on eighteenth-century literature. The payment was, he imagined, a mere formality for her; it was impossible to guess from Ottoline's manner how pleased she was by the prospect of this new way of increasing her income.

When Julian's schooling at the Roehampton convent came to an abrupt end in the early summer of 1923, Ottoline was forced to realise that she was never going to make an academic or an artist out of a lively girl whose school reports had always praised her enthusiasm above her aptitude and who made no secret of the fact that she preferred pug dogs to painting, and dancing to Dante. Faced with the prospect of sitting at Garsington with only Bob Gathorne-Hardy and Gilbert Spencer to amuse her, Julian expressed a wish to become a debutante the following year. Charlie Bentinck's daughters were going to be given seasons in London, and it seemed only fair that she should enjoy the same privilege.

The Morrells' finances had improved a little since the post-war years, but not very much; the life of a debutante had never been cheap. Looking at her account-books in the summer of 1923, Ottoline decided that it was time to make peace with her family in the hope that they might come to her assistance. So they might have done if Ottoline had been able to swallow her pride and admit that she was short of money; instead, as she had in 1919, she gave them the impression that they were being informed of her plans only as a matter of general interest. The duke and duchess had already committed themselves to bringing out Charlie's two girls, but Ottoline and Julian were invited to stay with them at Langwell, their home in Scotland, where Julian could make friends with her young cousins. The visit was made but Julian, bored and shy, failed to charm and Ottoline was aware of a tense silence whenever she mentioned Philip. Not daring to ask what he had done to offend them again, she wondered if somebody had told them about his illegitimate children. (Her suspicion had no basis; they knew nothing about Philip's infidelities.)

It was a shrewd instinct which led Ottoline to seek help at the same time from her cousin, Lord Howard de Walden. Having spent much of his early life as a poor young relation at Welbeck, he had inherited what had once been the Fifth Duke of Portland's London estate and become a very rich man.* It now gave him some pleasure occasionally to be able to outshine Ottoline's family; and in this, he had the support of his handsome, strong-willed wife, Margherita. He was delighted to be asked to make sure that Julian was not neglected.

Grateful though Ottoline was, she found it hard to reconcile herself to her distant cousins' mode of life. 'Wealth, wealth, all the manservants so large they might have made 3 ordinary men,' she wrote on 29 June 1923 when she was staying with them at Seaford House, their home in Belgrave Square, and getting ready for one of Margot Howard de Walden's grand evenings, for the Infanta of Spain on this occasion. Always shy at formal parties, she dreaded the moment of leaving her bedroom to walk down the great green malachite staircase which, her host gaily told her, probably for the fun of watching her expression, had been replaced after he christened it by sliding down the balustrade with his tiepin undone, scoring the surface from top to bottom. Ottoline laughed, as she was intended to do, but the extravagance horrified her.

The Howard de Waldens were overwhelmingly kind. Knowing that Ottoline was homeless in London, they urged her to bring Julian to stay with them whenever she wished and to visit Chirk, the Welsh castle which they had leased from the Myddelton family and which they were in the process of restoring. Most importantly, they promised to give a dance for Julian.

The death of Soey, her favourite of the pugs, and the news that she would be having all her ballgowns made at home by Ivy Green, the young lady's maid Ottoline had engaged for her, did not put Julian in the best of spirits for her debutante year, but she had recovered her good cheer by the late summer when her mother chaperoned her around the disappointingly small number of dances to which she had been invited. Julian danced; Ottoline sat yawning by the wall,

---

* His grandmother, Lucy Howard de Walden, was the Fifth Duke's sister; the bestowing of the London estate on her after the Fifth Duke's death was arranged by their father, the Fourth Duke of Portland.

wondering if she was obliged to talk to the other mothers or if she could risk striking up a conversation with a friendly-looking saxophonist. Convention won the day, but she could not remember when she had last enjoyed herself so little.

Ottoline's family were pleased to see that she was at last showing signs of becoming a conventional mother. Julian was invited to Underley and given a dinner-dance at Claridge's by Henry and Birdie, her childless uncle and aunt; the duke showed his approval by asking himself to Garsington for a weekend. It was an exhausting experience for his hostess, ominously heralded by the appearance of a chauffeur and a luggage-laden car (the duke had been staying at Windsor, where many elaborate changes of clothes were required), and ending with an intensely embarrassing impromptu visit to Blenheim where a truculent gatekeeper only unbarred the entrance after being rebuked by Philip for failing to recognise their companion. It was, in Ottoline's view, typical of her brother to want to visit the most ostentatious house in Oxfordshire and to expect them to sound forth his name to secure a ducal welcome. She preferred it when his oldest son visited them a few months later. Kind, unassuming and funny, Arthur Titchfield ('Sonnie' to his family and friends) won his aunt's heart immediately. 'He seemed very well read and very intelligent,' she noted approvingly. 'I liked him enormously. He has charming looks and the long Hapsburg under jaw which we all have. He is like Henry and myself.' (9 October 1924)

It was her nephew Sonnie who persuaded Ottoline to make a visit to Welbeck the following autumn; much to her surprise, she enjoyed herself. Maurice Baring, whose company she always liked, was in the house party, and the duke took her off to his dressing-room to entertain her with scandalous tales (one was of a house party – not at Welbeck – where a female guest had been caught rolling a male corpse out of her room in the middle of the night after an over-exuberant encounter), and with a riveting account of his own youthful flings. These confidences put her brother in quite a new light, and Ottoline liked him the better for admitting that he had known what it was like to be recklessly in love. But the atmosphere at Welbeck remained oppressively formal, and she would not have been Ottoline if she had not jumped out of the train at Sheffield on her way back to London with a happy cry of: 'Oh, the joy of populace!' What the populace thought of this is not recorded.

Neither Julian's dances nor a driving tour through the south of England to visit the Johns, Thomas Hardy, David Cecil and, after ten years of estrangement, Henry Lamb, could banish the terror of debt.

'I would give anything to make money,' Ottoline wrote in September 1924, after a visit to Chirk where the friendly Howard de Waldens struck her as being like two rich children at play, blissfully unaware of what it was like to have to reckon the cost of replacing a run-down motorcar or the price of a new winter coat. Philip sold some land and they took in a French student, Jean de Menasce, as a paying guest for a month, but these were short-term remedies and de Menasce upset Ottoline with accounts of all the friends he had heard telling malicious stories about her behind her back. Lytton's sister, Pippa, had warned him that she was as wicked as she was cruel; the Sitwells fed their guests on Ottoline-jokes; Roger Fry was still telling everyone he met that she was a venomous, dangerous woman. What, Ottoline wondered again, had she done to deserve such slander? 'My chief mistake has been to be too kind to people who have abused it and have tried to live on us,' she wrote with understandable bitterness on 18 October. She had loved Garsington more than anywhere except Bolsover, the home of her dreams, but now, she began to think of it as the source of all unhappiness – the house where her lover had died and where envious friends learned to hate her. There were still times when the sweet-smelling garden and the quiet landscape could make her shiver with pleasure, but it was, increasingly, feeling like a millstone under which she and Philip were being stealthily crushed.

An outside event which brought them a year of financial ease and the chance to modernise and improve the house was the death of pneumonia, in November 1924, of Philip's mother. He had, despite many quarrels and difficulties, been a devoted son; Ottoline did her best to summon up a show of grief for a woman she had admired without love. Knowing that Philip had always adored Black Hall, she waited with dread for him to make the obvious suggestion, that they should sell Garsington and move to the Oxford house which the Morrells leased from the university. She did not have to wait long; at Christmas, Philip put forward the suggestion that they should at least try living there for a few months. It would, he said, be an excellent opportunity for them to arrange an exhibition of his mother's needlework, the screens, fans and chairs which had been worked in seventeenth-century designs with the consummate skill of a brilliant craftswoman.

They moved in January. Ottoline dutifully arranged the exhibition and did her best to defend Philip from his sisters as the squabbles began as to who was going to have which piece from Mrs Morrell's magnificent collection of furniture. Margaret Warren and Frederica Peel wanted to sell their share; determined to keep the collection together, Philip used a considerable part of his legacy to buy it back when it was sold by public auction in March.

Living at Garsington, Ottoline could describe Oxford as 'the loveliest town in the world': living at Black Hall, surrounded by Harriette's needlework and Harriette's possessions, she felt she hated it. Now, temporarily removed from the home she had created with so much care and imagination, she found herself longing to be back there. She could not bear it when Sassoon, who had shown such sensitivity when she took him to see Harriette's body laid out (he used the occasion for one of his most moving poems), callously observed that he was looking forward to seeing '"what awful things your successors make of it [Garsington]." How would he like his poems altered and parodied?' (17 February 1925)

It was Julian who unexpectedly came to the rescue. She hated the Oxford house and she had not forgiven her grandmother for getting her sent to a convent school which she had loathed. She refused to attend the laying-out and greeted the notion of a permanent move to Black Hall with such screams of anger that Ottoline, alarmed, took her to an Oxford doctor for nerve treatment. In March, the three-month experiment was declared a failure and they returned to the manor house.

Relieved though Ottoline was at what she felt to have been a narrow escape, she was still uncertain about their future at Garsington. Guilty about the way Philip's feelings had been overridden, she promised herself that any money they had to spare should be used to improve the house. She had started, nevertheless, to make the first moves towards finding them a home in London: Garsington, she thought, could easily be rented out and used for an occasional holiday. This plan appears to have been triggered by a February visit to Molly MacCarthy in Wellington Square. The following day, Ottoline went to Chelsea again and found what seemed to her the ideal home in St Leonard's Terrace, just south of the King's Road, where Violet Hammersley had a house which she was willing to rent. Ecstatic, Ottoline hurried home to outline the new life she had planned for them. A few days later, she received an embarrassed letter from Violet Hammersley to say that the house would not, after all, be available. When Ottoline called on her to ask what had gone wrong, she was coldly informed that Mrs Hammersley would not be able to discuss the matter with her. Ottoline was baffled; it was Philip who discovered what had happened. Unknown to Ottoline, Logan Pearsall Smith and Alys Russell were also living in St Leonard's Terrace. When Logan heard the news, he was infuriated by what he felt to be a piece of deliberate provocation by his sister's enemy and hurried along to tell Mrs Hammersley that Ottoline would be highly undesirable as a member of their community. 'What spite and vengeance after sixteen years . . .' Ottoline wrote in her journal, pondering the destruction her relationship with Bertie had caused in her life. Had it really been worth it? On the whole, she was inclined to think it had, but the words she chose were hardly romantic. 'I believe really the education that B has given me is worth paying for,' she wrote, 'altho' he himself has never given me happiness. I did not care enough for him . . .' (4 March 1925)

Julian's love of dancing and a promise from Ivy Titchfield, Sonnie's wife, to present her at court encouraged her to beg for a second London season in 1925. Two of her friends were engaged already and a London season offered the chance of an escape into marriage from a home life which she was finding increasingly claustrophobic. Vale Avenue was rented from Ethel Sands for the summer and visiting cards were left at all the appropriate addresses, but the response, which had been tepid in 1924, was now pointedly cool. Ottoline had chosen to turn her back on her old friends and their world; they saw no reason why they should now welcome her back into it as an embarrassing misfit with a daughter to be married off. 'I felt rather crushed and disappointed that no invitations came from all the grand people for balls for Julian,' Ottoline wrote sadly. 'I don't know what to do as I have left cards and asked them to tea etc. and after all Julian is beautiful and attractive.' (1 May 1925) Julian, raging at the injustice of being made to suffer for her mother's unconventionality when all she had ever asked of life was to be allowed to be normal, lost her temper. Why could she not be ordinary? Why, when Lady Desborough asked them to stay, did her mother have to go rushing off at tea-time to see the de la Mares and look so rude and unfriendly? Why was it so much more wonderful to go off to music halls with Bob and Kyrle than to go to dances? Of course it was nice that Uncle Henry had asked them to dinner in London with their cousin, the Duchess of York, but how was she supposed to feel about the fact that Lady Hambleden, the mother of her two closest men-friends, Billy and Jimmie Smith, refused to ask her to a dance?* It was all her mother's fault. 'She is so cruel to me,' Ottoline lamented, but it is easy to sympathise with Julian's sense of injustice.

Fearing that no more invitations were going to come, Ottoline decided that Julian should accompany her parents on a visit to Holland to meet their Bentinck relations and see that they were not, after all, quite the outcasts from society that she imagined. It was, from the sound of it, a fairly grand holiday and the highlight of the visit

---

* Lady Hambleden later relented and issued an invitation. Ottoline, fairly predictably, shirked her duties as a chaperone and slipped away during the dance to attend a more bohemian gathering at Viola Tree's before she returned to escort Julian home.

was a dinner-party at which the Kaiser was Godard Bentinck's guest of honour at Amerongen.* The night of his visit was gloriously warm and they sat out on the terrace with Ottoline next to the guest, making mental notes for her journal of his unexpectedly handsome head and sailor-like body. 'It was like a visit to Napoleon at Elba,' she told Russell. 'He is very full of vitality and superficial intelligence but no judgement and of course very undemocratic ... His vanity is still extreme and he is very histrionic, but so alert and vital that he has charm.' (15 August 1925) Twice, she had to suppress an urge to giggle, once when he praised Lytton's life of 'grandmama' and asked how many years the author had spent at court, and again at his expression of horror when she told him that her relation, Lady Diana Cooper, had started acting for the cinema. '"Grandmama wouldn't have allowed that,"' was the Kaiser's shocked response. (28 May 1925) It was, in Ottoline's view, a typically pompous reaction; she thought it absurd to suppose that Queen Victoria would have objected to anything done by a young woman who was not only beautiful, but 'incredibly polite and cheerful: if you suggested walking to London at midnight, she would say, "Do let's."' (7 October 1925)

A second sojourn at Vale Avenue was ruled out by Ethel Sands, who complained that Julian's friends had made a pigsty of her immaculate home. Deprived of a roosting-place in London, Julian came back to spend the remainder of the autumn at Garsington, where her mother was supervising some long-planned improvements. Thanks to Harriette Morrell's legacy, they were at last able to add a loggia to the garden's stone terrace (it was copied from the south portico at Cranborne Manor, the home of David Cecil's parents, and the architect was Philip Tilden). After ten years of oil lamps, the house was finally converted to electricity. 'It is a huge excitement and we all run about looking at it,' Ottoline noted on 16 October, but a few days later a letter arrived to draw the Morrells' attention to a sizeable overdraft. The improvements stopped.

The house was full of Julian's friends, and Ottoline realised that she was beginning to feel old for the first time, since 'they do seem *young* to me now'. Of her contemporaries, only Bertie still managed an occasional visit, but he was too wrapped up in his plans for the school which he and Dora wanted to start to take more than a perfunctory interest in Ottoline's worries about money and her headstrong daughter. The last of the friends who had lived at Garsington, either in the house or the village, were starting to drift away. The Julian Huxleys were moving to London; Gilbert Spencer was leaving his cottage; Mark Gertler was again being treated for tuberculosis in a

* The Kaiser lived in Holland from November 1918 until his death in 1941.

distant sanatorium. Once, Ottoline had looked on all these friends as if they were children; it was a shock to realise that they were approaching middle age.

PART FIVE

No. 10 Gower Street

'It is very like conducting an orchestra where each player plays his own tune and I have to induce them at whatever cost to play in harmony.'

OM, *Journal*, 16 July 1931

20

MEMOIRS AND A TEST OF COURAGE
1925–28

'After all, there's only one Ottoline. And she has moved one's imagination.'

D. H. Lawrence to OM, 24 May 1928

'I sat in my window-sill with my back in the sun and began to write "My Life", sketches of my past,' she wrote on 28 September 1925. 'It is difficult to begin . . .'

Ottoline did not often think about her age, but the realisation that even her younger friends from the early days at Garsington were now middle-aged made her reflective. Looking back, it seemed to her that she had lived most of her life on a stage (an image which dominated her memoirs to a quite remarkable degree), as an actress whose skills had proved hopelessly inadequate in aristocratic society, but who had found her role as a stage-manager and producer first at Bedford Square and then at Garsington, 'a romantic theatre', as she would describe it, 'where week after week a new company would arrive, unpack, shake out their frills and improvise a new scene in life.' Gradually, over the years, she had seen the younger actors beginning to mingle with 'the old stagers' who lived at the theatre: 'they would lose their shyness and wander about together and I would watch them playing most unexpected parts.' Her job now was to write a history of that theatre – and of herself.

She had started to toy with the idea of writing an autobiography in 1919; now, she began to apply herself to it with zeal and to push her memory back towards the early years at East Court and at Welbeck. Dominating everything else after her talks with Dr Marten was the memory of her terror of her brothers, of her sense of their glamour and good-looks, and of their contempt. They had treated her, she wrote in her October diary, as if she had been 'a stupid dog . . . they were brutal to me'. Only of William, dead for more than twenty years, could she say that she remembered nothing but kindness; in her lists of the people she had loved most, she now added his name to those of her mother, Tiger, and Mother Julian. She was reluctant to look too closely at the way her love for her brothers had affected all of her other male relationships, but she wrote that she was having dreams in which William turned into a girl, and kissed her.

By the end of the autumn, she had written the first section which ended with the move to Welbeck; a little nervously, she began to show her work to a few friends. Walter Turner was full of enthusiasm, but Sassoon alarmed her by saying she had been too effusive, while Mark Gertler urged her to show more of her own feelings. Philip confined his comments to style. Virginia Woolf, hearing about the project from Sassoon, wrote to urge her to go on, for 'it is one of the things you owe the world:

Then let me have them, and publish them, and write a character of you, to supplement the works of Lawrence, Sitwell, and Aldous and Cannan – what a tribe, to be sure! Write everything as fast as you can, as it comes into your head, and it will be a masterpiece. Pick us all to pieces. Throw us to the dogs. It is high time you came off your heights and did a little dusting in a high minded manner.[1]

Picking people to pieces was just what Ottoline hated the idea of doing. She was perfectly capable of being malicious about anybody she considered second-rate or pretentious, but she was planning to write about the people she admired and loved; the idea of using her memoirs as a way of getting her own back was as distasteful as the prospect of exposing her own private thoughts to the unknown reader. 'I have,' she wrote in April 1927, 'a horror of opening myself to the world.'

Ottoline continued to work on her memoirs for the rest of her life. When asked about their publication, she told an astonished Margot Asquith in 1936 that she would certainly not allow this until after her death. But to Koteliansky she said she might consider it if the duke predeceased her. (Her portrait of Welbeck life was, as she was well aware, far from flattering and she had no wish to cause him unnecessary unhappiness.) The unfortunate result of her discretion will have been apparent to anyone who has read the two volumes, *The Early Memoirs of Ottoline Morrell* and *Ottoline at Garsington*. They are not as she wrote them – Philip's improving hand went very thoroughly over the manuscripts after her death, weeding out adjectives, adding commas to replace Ottoline's hectic dashes. In many instances, he succeeded in turning a fresh and original image or idea into something more staidly correct. Lacking his wife's spontaneity, he worried about the odd punctuation and leaps of thought which were part of the charm of Ottoline's idiosyncratic prose; for a man who revised the first six chapters of his own never-to-be-completed memoirs at least eight times between 1938 and 1943, it must have seemed his bounden duty to offer the same service to his late wife. Ottoline had already decided to restrict herself to a few graceful hints about Axel Munthe and Augustus John, while excluding John Cramb altogether; Philip made it his business to cut Henry Lamb's part in her life down to a bare minimum. Anxious to comply with the urgent pleas from Ottoline's family to make the book tasteful rather than truthful, he gave Russell a pseudonym and finally excluded him. Julian, who took the decision to restore Russell's place in the story, if only in an appendix which is full of misprints and inaccuracies due to poor editing, was astonished by the difficulties which were put in her way when she tried to carry out her mother's wish to include the letters of her friends. Lamb's refusal was understandable, but why should James Strachey have refused to allow her to print even one extract from Lytton's hundreds of playful, affectionate, grateful letters to her mother, on the grounds that they did not show his true character?*

Ottoline's memoirs are, in many ways, infuriating. While warm-hearted and amusing, the introductions by the editor, Robert Gathorne-Hardy, are an uneasy blend of affection and archness; the editing has been done in such a way as to make the chronology a triumph of obscurity; the unwearying emphasis put by Ottoline herself on her devotion to Philip, while poignant in what it seeks to hide, falsifies the picture. A less vain man than her husband would have deleted at least half of the references to his own perfection, but Philip altered only what displeased him. The memoirs are at their best when Ottoline applies herself to describing the appearance and mannerisms of the artists and writers she admired and loved. Ottoline was perceptive and observant. She excels in the shrewd selection of a memorable image or attitude which sets the subject as clearly before the reader as her remarkable collection of photographs. She shows us the young Augustus John looking like a Renaissance boy with pale grey-green eyes 'expanding like a sea-anemone'; Conrad, 'this super-subtle Pole' whose 'apparent frankness hid a great reserve' and whose profound, compassionate eyes could become suddenly and devastatingly flirtatious; Virginia Woolf, with the hard, lidded eyes of a falcon and the remoteness of a person who has to preserve her sanity by withdrawing

---

* The first volume of Ottoline's memoirs appeared, without James Strachey's permission to quote from his brother's letters to her, in 1963: Michael Holroyd's two-volume biography of Lytton Strachey, for which the necessary permission was granted, was published in 1967 and 1968.

from emotional situations, and who 'seems to come at full sail up to a subject one expects her to tackle, and to combat and conquer the problem, but generally she evades the crucial moment'. She gives us Aldous Huxley, lying back in a chair and rolling a magnifying glass between long delicate fingers or drawing grotesque heads on a sheet of paper. Lytton Strachey is first glimpsed, memorably and delightfully, as if he had emerged from the mind of Edward Lear, his small voice appearing 'to come from very far away, for his delicate body was raised on legs so immensely long that they seemed endless, and his fingers equally long, like antennae'. Even Clive Bell was allowed to appear, not as a fat, ungrateful mischief-maker, but as a happy, flattering, good-tempered Autolycus.

Ottoline was hard at work on her memoirs when she went into a nursing home at Ruthin Castle in Wales for treatment at the beginning of 1926. Anxiety about Garsington and about her intransigent daughter had affected her health. She had been suffering from acute back pains all autumn; according to Virginia Woolf's unreliable account to Lytton Strachey, a course of X-rays now revealed that her body was swimming in sour milk from Dr Marten's injections. But it was a relief to get away; she made friends with her Irish nurse, worked on the magnificent description of her family's arrival at Welbeck, and reread Proust, the writer she most admired.

In March, after a brief visit to the Howard de Waldens at Chirk Castle, she went to do a little more London house-hunting from Vale Avenue, where Ethel Sands had invited her to spend a quiet two weeks. No satisfactory house was for rent, and, despite Ethel's good intentions, there were parties almost every night, of the Sybil Colefax kind which Ottoline most disliked, a parading of embarrassed celebrities before lesser mortals. Ottoline looked forward to escaping for a quiet tea with the Eliots, but Vivien was in no mood for tranquil gossip. It was, Ottoline wrote, a nightmarish visit. Vivien announced in the first minute that she was going to sue Tom because he had tricked her into going into a mental home, in the second that she had loved it and wished she was back there, and in the third that she had met a wonderful young man, a Mr Haden Guest, who appreciated her in a way her husband never had. And all this in a high, fast, hysterical voice: no wonder, thought Ottoline, that Tom had taken to the whisky bottle and that he watched his wife all the time with such a frightened look in his eyes. She went away feeling desperately sorry for him and worried about Vivien.

The mournful drama of the Eliots' marriage was forgotten in her difficulties with Julian that spring. Philip was in despair about her and Ottoline found it impossible to have any conversation with her daughter which did not lead to a quarrel: every day seemed to end with slammed doors, tears, and outbursts of rage. Searching for explanations, Ottoline decided that she must be having an unhappy love-affair; when Julian reacted violently to the news that Mark Gertler was to come and stay for Easter, she thought she had found the answer.

Mark had always been fond of Julian and, if it had not been for his passionate attachment to Carrington, Ottoline might have started to worry earlier about the fact that his favourite nude model, Alice Edwards, bore a striking resemblance to her daughter. Mark corresponded regularly with Julian and often took her side against her parents. He had taken her dancing in Brighton and to dinners and parties in London; they had spent whole days closeted in the Monastery studio while he painted her. Fond though Ottoline was of him, she knew him to be sensuous and volatile. 'I have made up my mind I *must* have a woman once a week,' Mark had written to her on 3 December 1917, before going on to plot an imaginary assault on Brett: 'Beware Oh! Brett at last, at last, will I sever your long cherished virginity from your fragile body, the time has come, I come prepared. Vessels of blood will flow and the pain! Oh! the pain ...' It was not the sort of letter to make her feel at ease about his intentions now towards Julian. Frankness, she decided, was the best policy. She wrote to him, and received by return of post an indignant denial of anything more than brotherly affection: 'Even if such feelings could have cropped up in me,' Mark wrote, 'I would have nipped them in the bud, knowing as I do, how very inappropriate and entirely out of place such feelings would be, in the particular setting that we are placed – now we had better drop the subject once and for always – because it is really a little unpleasant...'*[2] Nevertheless, he came to stay for Easter. So, too, did the Turners, Gilbert Spencer and Igor Vinogradoff.

Igor was a fair-haired, burly young man of enormous charm. The son of an eminent Russian, Sir Paul Vinogradoff, Professor of Jurisprudence at Oxford, he was Ottoline's favourite of all the young men who flocked out to Garsington each summer. He had made his first visit early in 1924, and the rapport between them had been immediate: in her journal, Ottoline wrote of him as a delightful companion and of his being 'far and away the cleverest young man I know up here'. At

---

* Ottoline's fears were well-founded, according to her daughter, who told the author in December 1988 that she had been too frightened to admit that Mark had tried to seduce her in the Monastery studio before swearing her to secrecy. This makes it likely, but not certain. Julian also claimed in this interview to have been the sole object of Toronto Prewett's interest.

Easter, he was as charming and affectionate as ever. Ten days later, the bombshell exploded: Julian told her parents that Igor had asked her to marry him.

Julian, years later, was convinced that her mother opposed the marriage because of jealousy. Certainly, Ottoline's reaction was violent. She wrote to tell Bertie that she disliked Igor, that he was only superficially intelligent ('not a true mind') and that he was after Julian's money. (Julian knew, and talked about, the fact that her childless Uncle Henry had promised to make her his heir as a compensation for Lady Bolsover's neglect of Ottoline in her will.) She added, for good measure, that it was the urge to have children which had made Julian accept him. In her journal, she wrote that Igor was self-indulgent, drank too much and lacked any merit. She gave away her own feelings in the same entry: 'I do resent his behaviour ... pretending to be so fond of me and then stealing Julian away without a word to me.' (18 April 1926) It was this that she could not forgive, the fact that he had never allowed her to guess that it was Julian he came to see, not her. She felt betrayed, and both Philip and she flatly refused to agree to the marriage.

The gossip was quick to spread. Sympathy was, on the whole, with Julian. 'You will be delighted to hear that Ottoline and Philip are behaving scandalously,' Virginia reported to her sister; '[they] refuse to consent; dislike the young man who is penniless; and ignore the whole affair. Julian is behaving with great spirit, and it is said that Garsington presents a scene of unparalleled horror. Needless to say, I am going to stay there.'[3] The news that Ottoline had at last found a house in Gower Street and taken it on a six-year lease seemed insignificant beside such enthralling dramas.

Gertler, still smarting from the letter Ottoline had sent him, sided with Julian; Sassoon, to Ottoline's relief, was ready to support her. Julian, he agreed, was far too young at nineteen to know what she wanted; it must be dreadful to have to deal with a daughter who said she hated you. Of course nobody thought of her as a bad mother. Somewhat mollified, Ottoline began to calm down. After a long private conversation with Igor, she persuaded him to agree to wait for a year before becoming engaged. Sassoon took the view that the more Julian had to do during that year, the less she would think about marriage; Ottoline gratefully accepted his proposal that they should begin the diversions at once with a visit to Ettie Desborough at Panshanger, her family's home.

The idea was a happy one. Ottoline liked the house and was amused by the guests; no French eighteenth-century gathering could, she thought, have been more decoratively artificial. There was added spice in the fact that Sassoon, initially assumed to be her lover, became wildly excited by a young girl who appeared at dinner in men's clothes. We do not know what Julian thought of the weekend, but shortly after their return to Garsington, she came into Ottoline's room and said that she had decided not to marry Igor; all she wanted now was to be taken out of England on a long holiday and to put it all behind her. 'Poor Vino,' Ottoline wrote, 'unhappy and desperate.' But she had no regret about the part she had played in preventing the marriage.

The tour started at the end of July with Philip, Bob Gathorne-Hardy and Sassoon travelling in the Morrells' cantankerous Overland car with Ottoline at the wheel* and Julian and Kyrle Leng, Gathorne-Hardy's lover, in a Buick. Sassoon, in love with Glen Byam Shaw, a young actor,† and in the swirl of a furiously sociable summer, had been reluctant to come, but the prospect of a luxurious free holiday – Ottoline had offered to pay all his expenses – and the company of Bob, whom he liked, proved irresistible. Foreseeing a good deal of family squabbling along the route, he took a large number of books and prayed for peace.

It began as a charming holiday, with visits to the ninety-six-year-old Monet at Giverny, to Chartres Cathedral by moonlight and the gardens of Versailles at dusk. The fault was not in the places visited, but in the travellers. Bob Gathorne-Hardy and Kyrle Leng resented having to confine themselves to single beds and slipped back to England after four days; Sassoon, missing his actor, thought wistfully of other, more congenial holidays, of travelling in the hedonistic comfort of Gerald Berners's Rolls with a clavichord – so the story goes – strapped between the seats as they purred gently along from one delectable meal to the next. The Overland, by contrast, never stopped breaking down; they had only reached Paris when it needed its first overhaul, and there were many more. Ottoline was determined not to let mechanical hitches interfere with their enjoyment. Sassoon's spirits sank as he saw his hostess poring over a map of Italy, and talking of Vicenza, Mantua, Padua, Bergamo, Rimini, Ravenna, Siena, and on, and on; he began to wonder if they would ever return home.

At the beginning of the journey, Sassoon's sympathies were all with Ottoline. Julian, still depressed and angry, was a truculent companion, seeming only to care for driving very fast and for playing

---

* 'In those days it was necessary to pass a test in order to get an international driving licence. Ottoline duly took hers in Oxford. Being told to turn to the left she ran into a lamp post. However, the examiner passed her, saying, "I could see you were nervous." She used to tell this story with roars of laughter.' *The Early Memoirs of Ottoline Morrell* 1873–1915, ed. Robert Gathorne-Hardy (Faber, London, 1963), p. 46.

† Glen Byam Shaw did not begin his better-known career as a director until after the Second World War.

interminable games of bridge. She frowned when Ottoline stopped to buy apricots from a barrow; she grumbled when her mother wanted to sit in a village square and listen to the little local orchestra playing under the trees. Torn between pleasing Ottoline and placating Julian, he wondered at the chasm between them. Ottoline wanted to stay in a pretty old-fashioned hotel; Julian only liked modern ones. Ottoline wanted to look at cathedrals; Julian grew more cheerful when she found a band which played Charlestons and a motor-launch owner who was willing to take her at top speed across Lake Como.

At the end of thirty-two days on the road, family hostilities had robbed Sassoon of all pleasure in the holiday. Writing his daily journal in Milan, he noted that Julian was being thoroughly disagreeable and that every day he and Ottoline found themselves having a long and inconclusive discussion of her character. A week later, the Overland wheezed and boiled its way back over the Alps, with halts every half-mile while water was poured into the steaming radiator. Ottoline's temper matched it and Sassoon was beginning to lose sympathy with her. He was impressed when Julian, finding that they had lost the other car during a night drive over a mountain pass, insisted on turning back and rescuing her parents, convinced that they had met with an accident. At the end of a twenty-five-mile drive, they found Ottoline complaining about the lack of Vichy water in a small inn where they had taken refuge when the car lights fused. She did not seem to be touched by Julian's gallant endeavour. The following day, hearing Julian talking about a pâtisserie which they had passed, she casually observed that her daughter had a nose for cake shops, just like a pig grubbing up truffles. Julian said nothing, but Sassoon winced for her.

Sassoon's first loyalty was always to Ottoline but, by the end of the tour, he had decided that, generous and brave though she was (she had paid for everything and refused to let her evident ill-health disrupt the agenda), she expected too much of her daughter. It was, he thought, unfair to impose an image of the perfect Victorian daughter on Julian and to reproach her for failing to match up to it. After two months with the Morrells, he was glad to get back to his actor and to have Osbert Sitwell on hand to entertain him with stories of the furore over the broadcasting of *Façade*. He did not think he would go on a family vacation again.

The tour did not improve the situation between Julian and her parents; by mid-September, the atmosphere at Garsington had become so tense that Ottoline sent her to stay with Juliette Huxley in London for three months while taking a domestic science course.

Juliette was a calming influence; by the beginning of 1927, Julian was prepared to come home, bringing with her a mass of young friends who included Bryan Guinness, Christopher Sykes and David Cecil's cousins, the Smith brothers. After drily noting that she ought to keep a toy-cupboard ready for such playful visitors, Ottoline decided that she liked Bryan Guinness best, but her hopes for Julian's future were pinned on David Tennant. She was amused by the airs, postures and scent-obsessions of his younger brother, Stephen, but it was David who charmed her and who seemed to be fond of Julian. 'How I wish J. could marry David,' she wrote on 25 April 1927 after a long talk with one of his relations: 'I wish and wish.' He came to Julian's twenty-first birthday party at Garsington that May, but the following year he married a young actress, Hermione Baddeley.

The summer of 1927 promised to be an agreeable one. Philip, who had been underemployed since leaving politics in 1918, was enjoying his new responsibility as a local magistrate and drawing up plans for a rose-garden. Ottoline, pleased with the way work was going on her memoirs, was happily renewing an old friendship during Aldous and Maria's brief visit to England. Maria was still in Ottoline's bad books for having, she believed, influenced the presentation of Garsington in *Crome Yellow*, but Aldous was as natural and engaging as he had been in his Balliol days, lolling back in his chair like a graceful grasshopper and telling stories which always had an unexpected twist or reversal: 'he has a *dear*, serious character,' Ottoline wrote after seeing him in London. Walter de la Mare thought he had found a perfect tenant for the manor house; Julian's sullenness seemed to be evaporating. All augured well for the move to London and a new life, and then, just when she had assumed that her days of being pilloried by her friends were over, Walter Turner published *The Aesthetes*.

Turner had written to her in April, describing the book as a philosophical dialogue modelled on Plato and asking if he might dedicate it to her. He added that it was possible that she might find a faint likeness to herself in one of the characters, but he urged her not to be alarmed. The central figure and the dialogues were all the creations of 'individual imaginations' in the book and he was confident that there would be no misunderstanding on her part.[4]

It was the letter of a nervous man, and Ottoline did not like the reference to a central figure. Declining the honour of a dedication, she asked to see a copy. Turner did not answer: when the book was published in May, he was safely out of the country. On 13 May, a letter arrived from Austria to say how sorry he was that she had refused to let the book be dedicated to her. There had, he wrote, been a good reason for asking her to permit it, 'and one day I will tell you why'.

The day never came, for *The Aesthetes* killed Ottoline's wish ever to hear of Walter Turner again. She despised him above all for not having dared to send her the book; if he did so now, she wrote after buying it herself, she would crucify him, 'with ice'.

Turner did not send it, and Ottoline's friends hardly dared to mention the book to her. The reviews had been cool; it was better not to be aware of its existence. Virginia was the only friend bold enough to ask if she could borrow Ottoline's copy to take on holiday that summer; she got the book, but not the reaction to its contents that she had hoped for.

Ottoline's distress was understandable. What Walter Turner had done was to parody the kind of character-assassination indulged in by the Bloomsbury Group, to incorporate characters based on Lytton, Virginia and Desmond MacCarthy, and to give them Ottoline, represented as Lady Caraway, for their target. One character describes her as 'a masculine libido, unable to express itself in direct creation, but which is, nevertheless, active ... normal males have invariably fled before her eagerly offered embraces.' Another wonders if there is a human face 'underneath that chalky mask, with its withered lip-salved gash'.[5] An account is given of Lady Caraway, crooked as the Tower of Pisa, coming downstairs to lunch with her pack of fifteen pugs and with her head swathed in bandages against neuralgia. Even the colours of Ottoline's embroidery silks are identified, the scarlets and oranges she loved, clutched to Lady Caraway's withered breast as she sits in her closet of green and gold (the colours of Ottoline's study), looking over a sombre garden with low yew hedges, surrounded by the collected novels of Henry James and paintings by Conder and John. Lawrence's Hermione Roddice had, by contrast with this, been a masterpiece of discreet allusion.

Ottoline's first reaction was of outrage; her second was to draw up a new list of the traitors in her life: Roger Fry, Logan, Lawrence, Sitwell, Aldous, Toronto Prewett and now Turner. Amending the list, she decided that it was unfair to include Aldous and that there had never been a friendship for Osbert Sitwell to betray with his parody of her in *Triple Fugue*. But Turner had been a friend and she knew by this time that Sassoon had begged him not to publish the book. 'I will *never* forgive him – little cad,' she wrote in her May journal, and she never did.

Thoughts of duplicitous friendships drew her towards the memory of Katherine Mansfield. Once, she would have wanted to add her name to the list for helping to spread the story that Ottoline was pursuing Murry; now, she laid all the blame on Murry and bitterly regretted the estrangement. Looking again at Katherine's letters, Ottoline thought that only she of their London friends had loved Garsington without envy or spite; if the clock could have been turned back to the war years when Katherine was living in The Ark, she would have been her closest neighbour in Gower Street. 'I would give much to have her back,' she wrote in July 1927, on the eve of the move back to London.

Had Ottoline known what her husband was about while she was recovering from the shock of Turner's book, she would have been tempted to add his name to the list of men who had betrayed her. While she was writing nostalgically about Katherine, Philip was again urging Virginia Woolf to have an affair with him. Terrified of being found out, he begged her to burn his letters. Virginia, mildly astonished by this second assault by a man who professed to be terrified of her, wrote in her diary of 'the amorous Philip – coarse as an old ram', kept the letters and spread the tale. Ethel Sands was allowed to suppose that she might respond: 'How nice, at my age, to have a little love,' Virginia sighed, tongue in cheek. Vita Sackville-West was informed that she had a handsome married suitor whose proposals had made her blush 'like a girl of fifteen'. But Virginia had no intention of becoming involved with Philip, and she went out of her way to be especially affectionate to Ottoline, telling her that 'you made my head swim with beauty' when they met, and urging her to hurry to Gower Street so that they could see each other every week instead of three or four times a year. In 1922, the weekend after Tiger's death, Virginia had been willing to see Philip as a weak, good-natured martyr, imposed on by Ottoline's social inclinations. Now, however, she was astonished that Ottoline should have remained so loyal and loving to such a determined philanderer. If Philip's second pursuit had any effect at all, it was to strengthen Virginia's feelings for his wife.

Why, with her love of beauty and originality, did Ottoline decide to make their London home in a road which Ruskin called one of the ugliest examples of street architecture in all London? How could she have chosen to live in a house which sat so drably in the shadow of Bedford Square while Margot Asquith gave glittering evenings in her own old home at No. 44? The answer was, in part, an economical one: 10 Gower Street was available at a very low rent. The other and more interesting answer is that Gower Street was a deliberate rejection of the kind of setting which she felt had kept her apart from the friends she loved. At Garsington, as at Bedford Square, it had been a hopeless dream to think that they would come to regard her as an equal; she had always been cast in the role of the generous patron, the grand hostess, envied and mocked. 'It is indeed a damnably difficult thing to live fully, richly, gorgeously and yet courageously. To live on the grand scale,' she wrote shortly after deciding to take the Gower Street house. She had not given up her wish to live gorgeously, but she no longer wished to be seen as a hostess and benefactress. In Gower Street, she hoped, her friends would learn at last to treat her as one of themselves. It is, ironically, only at Gower Street that a blue commemorative plaque has been put up, announcing that this was the home of Lady Ottoline Morrell, literary hostess.

Gower Street could never achieve the spacious ease of No. 44 Bedford Square, but Ottoline, Millie and Ivy Green worked hard to make the new house habitable. Philip was persuaded to design mock-Georgian bookcases for the first-floor library; pink and silver curtains obscured a dreary view from the dining-room across the street; unremarkable cornices and a dull entrance faded into the background when the prints and silver sconces were placed to catch the eye. The communal gardens were never used by their neighbours; after a year, Ottoline discreetly signalled her sense of ownership by the introduction of her three favourite statues from Garsington.

Not everybody approved of the move. Lytton painted harrowing prose-portraits of the tragic ruin of a former friend, crouched in wait in rooms of a most wretched pokiness: Gower Street probably did seem a little on the simple side after his weekends at Blenheim. But the general response was encouraging. Virginia, who had spent years urging Ottoline to return to London, started by coming to help arrange furniture (a task at which, Ottoline mildly observed, she was, for once, able to say that Virginia was less clever than herself), and ended by making a regular habit of 'owling' visits before dinner; Tom Eliot came for longer, staying to pour out his worries about Vivien; old Augustine Birrell came to sit by the fire and reminisce, Margot to bully Ottoline into remembering her duties as a hostess, Maurice Baring, 'that old society warhorse', backing her up with a few questions of his own. When, they wanted to know, were the parties going to start?

Ottoline's heart sank at the prospect. Virginia and Tom Eliot both told her that what they really liked was being able to wander in for long, cosy conversations. When she was alone with them, she could hear every word, but deafness was becoming a problem and she dreaded the prospect of trying to deal with a room full of shouting strangers. A spate of visits to the Chelsea home of Lady Colefax (Sybil's invitations had been almost the first and were certainly the most persistent to arrive at Gower Street) temporarily weakened her resolution to renounce party-giving; she was honest enough to admit that she even felt a bit envious of the redoubtable Sybil's ability to lay on an all-star cast of performers for her guests. The organisation was superb, the house beautiful if showy, the food always delicious and none of the guests seemed to mind the presence of their poor, silly hostess, chattering away at them like an over-wound mechanical doll. 'I should like to do it too,' Ottoline mused after a Colefax party in February 1928; 'but then if one *did* do it – does it do them [the celebrity guests] or the young guests who have to look on and meet them any good?' If the only real purpose of the parties was to make Sybil feel important, then they couldn't be applauded. '... There is something in me that tells me that it isn't right,' Ottoline concluded. Writing it down had brought her back to her senses; she returned to her original idea, to hold a well-planned weekly tea-party in the drawing-room overlooking the gardens, at which the guests would be encouraged to join in general discussion and the only rule would be that nobody, however important, should be allowed to dominate. In such a small gathering she could continue to do what she most enjoyed, helping the young by providing a setting in which they could talk as equals to the men and women they most admired.

Julian had been in high spirits during the first autumn in Gower Street, having recently spent a holiday with the Grenfell family at Schloss Tollet in Austria. The reason for her good humour emerged in October. She was not, she said, entirely sure if her love was returned, but she had become very fond of Victor Goodman, one of her fellow guests in Austria. He proposed a few days later and was accepted. Julian's friends, when questioned, said that Victor was quiet, friendly and agreeable; they all seemed to think he could make Julian happy. He did not have much money, but Julian was prepared to live modestly in the comfortable knowledge that she was her Uncle Henry's heir. It was not the marriage Ottoline would have chosen for her daughter, but Julian had a set to her strong jaw which indicated that she did not mean to be crossed a second time. The wedding took place in London at St Martin-in-the-Fields on 24 January 1928, and was followed by a reception at Ena Mathias's home in Portman Square. The Goodmans moved to a house in Draycott Place, Chelsea, and, a year later, Ottoline became a grandmother with the birth of Anne Arianna. She behaved with exquisite correctness – the christening party was held at Gower Street with a cake baked by Millie, and with Ethel Sands, Hilda Douglas-Pennant and Ena Mathias joining the family party, but it is worth noting that Victor Goodman was still being obliged to address his mother-in-law as Lady Ottoline in letters written in 1930. Ottoline was prepared to be cordial, but it cannot be said that she was much more affectionate to him than her own mother-in-law had been to her.

It was on the evening in October 1927 when Philip and Ottoline sat by the fire discussing Julian's engagement to Victor that they finally made up their minds to let Garsington go. 'Its charm had gone,' Philip wrote in one of the drafts for his memoirs. 'In war it had been a refuge from the storm – now it had become for us almost a prison. Its beauty grew. It became almost like a museum.* People came to see us . . . But there was a weariness about it. No one wants to be known only as the owner of a beautiful house. At last we decided to leave it, and not only to leave but to sell . . .'

Ottoline had often imagined that she would be relieved when the decision was made; to her surprise, she found herself close to tears. Putting photographs between the pages of her journals, she added a picture of an unruly pyramid of Garsington village children, giggling and waving as they toppled towards her camera. She thought of the garden she had created with so much love, of the silver-green shade of the ilex, the fragrant lavender hedges, the glow of colour in the flower-beds, the summer scents of phlox and lemon verbena. 'Something has gone out of me into them, and I will remain in them for ever,' she wrote that night. A week or two later, Bob Gathorne-Hardy was lunching at Gower Street when news arrived from Garsington that a massive branch had broken off the old ilex tree. Philip, after making a few soothing noises, continued eating his lunch. And then, Gathorne-Hardy wrote in his introduction to the memoirs, for the only time in his life, he saw Ottoline lose her temper. '"You drive me mad," she said suddenly and fiercely, "taking it so calmly."'

The house was sold the following summer and the crowds of villagers and neighbours who came to buy the contents on 11 and 12 July 1928, saw Philip and Ottoline walking alone in the garden, their heads bent. To Ottoline, there was a sense that they were walking among a crowd of ghosts from the past, cold-faced and unforgiving. 'I don't really yet see what was wrong,' she wrote sadly, 'why it aroused so much venom in others and why so many people turned against us.' Their first impulse had been to rid themselves of every memory of the house by selling everything. When it came to the day of the auction, they found it unbearable to go through with such a rigid policy and half of the 1200 lots found their way back to Gower Street; old friends who came along in the hope of cheaply acquiring some of Ottoline's superb collection of paintings and books went away with downcast faces.

Ottoline scarcely ever mentioned Garsington again after the sale. In her journal, she admitted that she continued to feel miserable about it and never more so than in the spring when she looked out at the sooty communal gardens and thought of the pink pear blossom curling round the window of her green-and-gold study and the quiet Oxfordshire landscape. To her friends, she spoke of the relief it was to see Philip so relaxed and cheerful now that he was free of the

---

* The museum atmosphere came with the arrival of Harriette Morrell's magnificent collection of furniture from Black Hall in 1925.

burden of the farm. Occasionally, she allowed herself a joke at the expense of her own nostalgia; Lytton Strachey was sent a postcard with a drawing of the garden pond and a large ink blot which, she teasingly informed him, represented the tear which had splashed on the paper as she thought of it. Lytton's reply was cool; he could not get over her folly in abandoning her only chance of distinction for a dreary London home to which nothing but pity would ever draw him. 'This was the last and dingiest phase in her career as patroness of the arts,' his biographer has said on his subject's behalf, 'and not even the presence of W. B. Yeats . . . could quite dispel the atmosphere of mediocrity.'[6]

Ottoline had long since recovered from the annoyance she felt on hearing that her old friend Asquith was to call himself the Earl of Oxford and Asquith (the eighteenth-century Countess of Oxford was among her own ancestresses, and one for whom she had a warm regard); she had reluctantly forgiven him for annexing Gilbert Spencer's chosen wife, Hilda Harrisson, for his last romance (an event which had a good deal to do with poor Gilbert's eagerness to get away from Garsington). She had come to prefer Margot, infuriating though she could be, to her husband, but she was genuinely saddened when the old man died in February 1928, after a four-month illness. Her thoughts went back to one of the first times she had seen him, flushed with desire as he clutched the hand of a beautiful girl at one of the Duchess of Sutherland's balls; she felt she could see him now, fondling the wing of a pretty angel as he urged her to consider her potential for flight. She smiled as she remembered how innocent she had been when she had first met him and how grateful for his offer to act as her unofficial tutor until the roué's eyes looked out of the rosy, avuncular mask. The memorial service was impressive, too impressive, she thought, for a man whose only real nobility had been in his passion for the classics.

Standing at Asquith's funeral service in February, Ottoline was aware of nothing more sinister than the familiar stab of a headache. Four months later, she was thanking God she was still alive. 'I have been,' she wrote, 'on a long and horrible journey down into hell . . .'

The first sign of trouble had been absurdly slight. She had been giving a tea-party for the Huxleys, Eliot and her Irish friend, James Stephens, when one of the guests commented on a curious mark on her face. It was even more noticeable the following day and a net of red lines had spread over her cheeks, but she covered them with powder and set off to a party at Seaford House where Hilaire Belloc and the Sitwells were to read a selection of their poems. The pain began the next day; by the end of the week, it was so extreme that a surgeon was called in. Gordon Taylor sent her straight to hospital in Fitzroy Square, where Dr Rau, a friend of Julian Huxley's, told her that she was suffering from an advanced stage of necrosis of the jaw, a localised form of cancer. Her only chance of survival was to have all her lower teeth extracted and the jawbone partly removed. After the operation, she would be kept in hospital for two months while tubes were used to drain the infected area.

By May, Ottoline was well enough to sit up for the first time in nine weeks and to ask if she could see the extent of the damage. The change was great. The wound had healed, but the loss of flesh and bone had left her with a chin that was 'so disfigured and repulsive that no eye could look on it without turning away in disgust'. Her first instinct was to hide herself away, but gradually, as her health improved, so did her spirits. She had always liked wearing big hats with veils tied or swathed under the chin; now, she practised drawing the material a little higher than before and told herself that a disfigured face was no harder to bear than the physical pain she had endured for almost forty years. A year later, she was able to laugh when Augustine Birrell praised her for being so gallant about her scars: 'I said what can one do – it was no use screaming and howling ... They little know what bravery I have had to exercise all these years to carry on at all ... the less said about that the better.' (19 November 1929)

Of all Ottoline's friends, only Russell had ever known how real her suffering had been. Some, like Sassoon, Juliette Huxley and Mark Gertler, had seen and admired the way she made light of her ill-health and did her best to conceal it; a much larger number, including most of the Bloomsberries, had written off the headaches and nursing-home visits and special diets as symptoms of a rich woman's hypochondria. The discovery of their misjudgement resulted in alarm and a little shame. Roger Fry insisted on being let into her room to make his peace. Lytton arrived, bearing books and flowers. Duncan Grant, who had always been fond of Ottoline, sent a letter which, Virginia informed him, was so treasured by the invalid that she kept it beside her bed. To Duncan, Virginia made light of her own concern with a jocular reference to Ottoline's having had her jaw tied up 'in a nosebag like an old horse'; like Lytton, she had an extraordinary reluctance to expose her true feelings to a third party. The letter that she wrote to Ottoline on 30 May read as though she was trying to make an oblique apology for all she had said about her in the past. 'I have thought of you and wanted to tell you how sorry I was about your illness and how fond of you,' she wrote.

But it's just these words one can't say. I think perhaps if one had never written a word one would then be able to say what one meant. I dread so getting tangled in a mass of words that when I want most to write, I don't. So you must write all my affection for me; and make it very strong and also the real odd, recurring discomfort it is to me to think of you in pain. How horrible it is that this should have happened to you. I have this silly romantic but impossible to avoid sense of your beauty; and then to combine this with the idea of you in pain – but you'll say I don't really know you.[7]

So she would, for Ottoline had always felt that Virginia was more observant than perceptive, stronger in intelligence than understanding. But this letter was so obviously heartfelt that she could not resist it. 'I really do love her,' she wrote after a visit from Virginia a few months later, and Virginia in turn, while slow to give up the habit of concocting Ottoline-stories for her letters, became increasingly conscious of the division between the caricature she joked about when writing to her old Bloomsbury friends and the woman she loved and admired. There was a grisly bond in finding that they were sharing the sad honour of being supposed by poor, mad Vivien Eliot to be Tom's secret mistresses; more to the point, she had learned to appreciate Ottoline's courage, her undemanding kindness and her unfailing loyalty to Philip. She had always been suspicious of what Ottoline was trying to do at Garsington; now, as she watched her presiding over her tea-parties in Gower Street, a hideous black trumpet held up to her ear as Yeats and de la Mare leaned towards each other across the fire, talking of dreams, the soul, art and Ireland while Ottoline nodded and smiled, she saw only the courage and the sincerity. This new and more generous attitude was reflected in the lines which she and Tom Eliot drafted for a memorial tablet to Ottoline ten years later (sadly, Philip rejected them in favour of his own tribute):

> Faithful and courageous
> Most generous most gentle
> In the weakness of her body
> She preserved, nevertheless
> A brave spirit, unbroken,
> Delighting in beauty and goodness
> And the love of her friends.[8]

Virginia's concern was heart-warming, but the letters which pleased Ottoline most when she was lying in hospital came from D. H. Lawrence, informed by Aldous and Maria of her illness. His first note was cautious, for he was not sure whether she had yet forgiven him for publishing *Women in Love*. Ottoline had heard that he was dying of tuberculosis; she wrote back at once to tell him that she, too, was ready to laugh at their old quarrels and eager to hear his plans, if he had any, for a new Rananim. His second letter of 24 May was written with all his old affection. More perceptive than Virginia, he had guessed how sad she would feel about the loss of Garsington; he, too, was grieved to think that it had gone, he told her: 'While you still had it I always felt in some way I still had it.' She had told him that her illness made her think about the past, and of how little she had ever managed to achieve: 'Don't say you feel you're not important in life,' he urged her. 'You've been an important influence in lots of lives, as you have in mine: through being fundamentally generous, and through being Ottoline. After all, there's only one Ottoline . . .'[9]

It pleased them both to find how easy it was to pick up their friendship where they had left it in 1916. Ottoline's heart sank when he told her that his new book dealt with phallic awareness and, when she discussed *Lady Chatterley's Lover* with Bertie over a lunch at Gower Street in December 1928, she was surprised that he thought it a masterpiece. To her, while she admired its vitality and honesty, the book seemed to be an argument for perpetual sex. If she was struck by the similarity to her own relationship with Lionel, she kept her thoughts to herself; it amused her when Lawrence wrote to suggest that a little robust sex in her own early life would have done her nothing but good. 'Nothing nauseates me more than promiscuous sex,' he told her, but '. . . if a man had been able to say to you when you were young and in love: an' if tha shits, an' if tha pisses, I'm glad, I shouldna want a woman who couldna shit nor piss – surely it would have been a liberation to you . . .'[10] She laughed, but it relieved her when Lawrence sent his most recent poems and she was able to tell him that they were among the finest things he had ever done.

Their letters were not all about books. Ottoline sent him news of Bertie's marriage and of the school which he and Dora were running; Lawrence gave her accounts of sitting peacefully by the sea as he watched the fishermen unloading their lobster pots, and of waking to the sight of the morning sun rising behind the eucalyptus trees. He confided in her about his frustration when *Lady Chatterley's Lover* was pirated while he was under threat of prosecution and admitted that, fond though he was of Aldous and Maria, he could not like Huxley's novels, 'even if I admire a sort of desperate courage of repulsion and repudiation in them'. Weak, gaunt, and in constant pain, he was happier now in a friendship of letters than with the strain of conversation. 'I agree with you,' he told her on 8 February 1929; 'people are most exhausting. I like them all right at a little distance, if they will leave me alone – but I don't want to talk to them any more.'

Ottoline had a chance to demonstrate her friendship later that year when Philip's niece, Dorothy Warren, organised an exhibition of

Lawrence's paintings at her London gallery. The gallery was raided and a court case was held in August to decide whether the confiscated paintings should be burned. Proceedings had already begun when Ottoline, always a striking figure, made her entrance and, after some confusion, was found a seat. The speaker had scarcely resumed the case for the prosecution when, to the delight of all Lawrence's friends who had rallied to his support, she rose to her full – and considerable – height, pointed an accusing finger at the magistrate and declared that he, not the paintings, deserved to be burned. Seven months later, Aldous Huxley came to tell her that Lawrence was dead: 'It fell on me,' she wrote with bleak understatement, 'as a great blow.' (4 March 1930)

21

FRIENDSHIPS AND RENEWALS
I

*'Oh let not these last few years be stagnation of folly or self-indulgence;
let me see what is the true value.'*

OM, *Journal*, August 1928

In the first years of her marriage, Ottoline made homily-books of her diaries, filling them with religious quotations and prayers for Philip and herself in a way that she later thought embarrassingly prudish. In middle age, she used them as a confessional box. The years at Garsington had taught her the danger of entrusting confidences to her friends; after the move to Gower Street, the journals were her only emotional outlet.

Examining his wife's papers after her death, Philip was shaken to discover how much he had never been allowed to know in the last twenty years of her life, when she stopped showing him her diaries. If only, he wrote in the margin of a page where she had spoken of his lack of desire for her and his indifference, she could have known how often he had longed to talk intimately with her and been checked by her withdrawn expression. Now, he learned how painfully aware his wife was of her reserved nature. 'It is very sad in life the want of frankness and it may be my fault,' she had written on 26 July 1935, and earlier, on 28 June 1931: 'It is no fun being an oddity for it makes one eternally lonely. Unfortunately, I combine being an oddity with being very proud, and that makes one aloof.' For the first time, he saw how much she had longed for his success – every article he wrote, every book he reviewed, had been proudly recorded: he saw, too, what an effort it had been for her to keep up the semblance of a normal life. 'The spirit *can* conquer – I know it can,' she wrote after one of her physical collapses. Until late in 1936, she had walked three times a week to the hostel in Holborn run by the Cecil Houses Trust where she helped to look after and counsel prostitutes and unemployed women who had fallen on hard times. In the last few months of her life, she was still angrily reproaching herself for having allowed illness to prevent her from doing more to help them. It was bitter for Philip to discover how terrified she had been of dying before him. 'These are the two desires in my heart,' she wrote in October 1936, 'that Philip should finish his book; that I may live to help him die.' She had never doubted that she was the better equipped to survive alone.

Ottoline's journals were an intensely personal record, but exceptions were made for events of national importance. In October 1930, she went out to join the silent crowds mourning the R101 airship's explosion over France on its maiden voyage, killing all but a handful of its eminent passengers, but she had been far less interested in the Labour Party's election victory the previous summer than by her brother Henry's loss of his South Nottinghamshire seat. Better informed than many women of her circle, she was predicting a second world war by 1931 and showing none of the upper-class English enthusiasm for Hitler. He was, she wrote, a clever lunatic with 'the mania of race . . . a wretched little specimen who is obviously degenerate and admires the great blond beast nordic race . . . They bully, beat and torment any pacifist, any Jew, or any advanced mind – even *Einstein*. They would certainly crucify Christ if he was there now.' (April 1933) Her presentiments grew stronger, but in 1936 they briefly gave way to the enthralling spectacle of the monarchy in crisis. George V was buried on 23 January and Ottoline's impression as she looked at his son's weak, lined little face was that he would never be up to the job of ruling. Mrs Simpson was already in the wings and, knowing that Margot Asquith was friendly with her, Ottoline suggested a lunch for the three of them and Virginia, who was avidly following the trail of royal gossip. Margot refused to gratify them – '"You must be mad, darling. She has never opened a book in her life"' – and Ottoline was forced to make do with first-hand gossip from Sonnie Titchfield's mother-in-law, Blanche Gordon-Lennox. Ten months later, the uncrowned King's relationship with Mrs Simpson was the only subject in the country: 'All England and the Empire live in terror that he will marry her,' Ottoline reported. 'She isn't a bad sort, I hear, but very common . . .' (8 November 1936) Too common for Queen Mary to consider allowing her to become a royal consort; too necessary for Edward to renounce, whatever the price. 'It is said that he is very nearly mad,' Ottoline wrote in December 1936 after lunching with Blanche. 'He had injections to make himself more virile and they affected his head and have made him very violent. He has remained shut up at Fort Belvedere . . . Poor little fellow –

they also say he has been drinking all these last weeks and has signed two abdications and torn them up.' Virginia and she had followed every stage of the short journey from Coronation to renunciation. On the day the abdication statement was made, they went to Parliament Square to join the crowds and then, at Ottoline's suggestion, walked up Whitehall to the Banqueting Hall where another monarch had met a grimmer end. Charles I, she was forced to explain as Virginia looked blank. 'This excited her very much.' (December 1936)

Strong though the evidence is in Ottoline's later journals of her affection for her husband, there must have been a good many occasions when Philip wished that he had never opened them. In his presence, she had always been careful to show no sign of concern or unease; only now did he realise how anxiously she and Millie had watched over him. 'I really like going out alone with Philip. He's much quieter,' she wrote in November 1928, when she believed that the sale of Garsington had cured him. Two months later, she was sadly noting that there had been a relapse; there were references to Philip's 'rages' when she had visitors; in 1933, she recorded that he had been growing 'excitable' again. There was probably no surprise in learning of the small moments of social embarrassment he had caused her, the lunch-party at which he had failed to realise that he was sitting next to the well-known American writer, Anita Loos, the evening when he had fallen asleep while Charlie Chaplin was talking about his boyhood in the East End, but he had never known about the occasion when Ottoline called in at his club (in 1929) and was handed a letter for Philip from Eva Merrifield. She had never mentioned the humiliation she felt when Molly MacCarthy took her out to lunch in November 1932 and calmly told her that she had had an affair with Philip. 'A gross exaggeration of Molly's . . .' Philip wrote in the margin. 'She merely said it to be spiteful to poor O. The advances all came from Molly; I merely tried not to be priggish and cold. She never interested me at all. The little spitfire! What unspeakable treachery after I had tried to befriend her!'*

If this made for some mortifying moments for Philip as he pored over his wife's papers, he could comfort himself with the entries which spoke of Ottoline's respect for his judgement. He could feel flattered to see how often she had deferred to his opinions, dropping the Kenneth Clarks when he expressed dislike of the young art historian, rewriting whole chapters of her memoirs because he had raised objec-

---

* Ottoline guessed that this affair had taken place in 1916, when Molly was staying at Garsington. It has to be borne in mind that Philip was having her journals typed out, with his pencilled comments, by Alice Jones, the mother of one of his sons, with whom he had been involved that year. He would not have wanted Alice Jones to think that he could also have been having a liaison with Molly MacCarthy, and this might explain his pencilled denial.

tions to the style. She continued to say that Bertie was the only person with whom she felt completely at home, but it had been to Philip that she turned when there was a difficult letter to be written. It had been his approval that she sought when she wanted to refuse a party to be given at the Café Royal in her honour.* There was no doubt in his mind that when the world looked at the two of them they saw a remarkable woman and a shy, dull man, but the journals told him that he had never entirely lost the esteem of his wife.

Ottoline had always known that her husband was uneasy with her more intellectual friends. He could happily spend an evening chatting with one of the Spencer brothers or Mark Gertler, but when the conversation grew abstract, his discomfort was evident. His spirits could easily be revived by a tactful suggestion that he should read the guests one of his contributions to *The Nation*, but even the kindest of guests could not be expected to submit to this test of good manners more than twice. At Garsington, he had always been able to escape with the excuse of the farm; at Gower Street, there was nothing to engage him other than long lunches at the Savile Club and the evenings of bridge which he loved. Ottoline did her best to ensure that there was an old friend like Augustine Birrell present at the weekly teas, with whom Philip could comfortably retire into a corner, but her plans did not always work and it spoilt her own enjoyment to see her husband looking stiff and miserable or, on one of his anxious days, launching into a diatribe which reduced the guests to silence. What Philip needed was an occupation, a diversion which would give him the sense of purpose he had lost. (The idea of writing his own memoirs came later, after Ottoline's death.)

In 1927, Ottoline's eye had been caught by a letter from Lytton Strachey to *The Times* complaining about a newly-published and bowdlerised edition of the diaries of one of her ancestors, Charles Greville. (His wife was a sister of the Fourth Duke of Portland.) What was needed now, he wrote, was a new and full edition of Greville's diaries, which were held at the British Museum. Not knowing that Lytton himself was planning to produce just that, Ottoline pointed out the letter to Philip. He had always loved diaries; he was fascinated by her ancestors; the museum was a minute's walk from Gower Street. The idea took his fancy; in 1929, Ottoline was proudly presented with a one-volume abridgement which she despatched to all her closest

---

* In June 1933, Clive Bell, Maynard Keynes and Boris Anrep decided that a lunch should be given for Ottoline at the Café Royal. While grateful, Ottoline was quick to put a stop to the scheme, saying that she would be delighted to be at a party where everybody toasted each other but she did not like the idea of being publicly thanked. 'I don't think private friendship can be ever acknowledged en masse,' she wrote to Virginia Woolf on 12 June 1933. Virginia agreed with her that the lunch project had sounded like 'a raving nightmare – still the will was better than the deed'.

friends. Lawrence was courteous – 'Quite a job worth doing, to make such a book accessible' – and Lytton was tactfully ambiguous; reading Philip's delightful work, he said, had made him even more conscious that a full edition was required. *Of course*, he understood that they had acted in ignorance of his own plans; he would not dream of taking offence.

Arranging to keep Philip busy with a second work was not quite so easily achieved. He had chosen another of Ottoline's family for his subject, Lord William Bentinck, the Governor-General of India best known for his efforts to abolish suttee. Knowing how coolly the family regarded her husband and that the papers were all at Welbeck, Ottoline rather wished he had picked another figure to write about, but nevertheless, she asked the duke to tea and mentioned Philip's interest. Her brother grew evasive. No difficulty in granting permission, he said, but that was all he could do. The papers were in a fearful muddle; nothing could be looked at until there was a new librarian. Asked when that would be, he grew vaguer still. Ottoline persisted; as a matter of fact, she said, she knew a charming young man, Francis Needham, who would be ideal for the job. She had her way; by the summer of 1931, Philip was happily engaged in researching the background for the book on which he was still working when he died.

Ottoline's second project for Philip's happiness was a little less altruistic, since she shared his love of travel. For three to four months of every year, the tea-parties stopped and the house was closed down while the Morrells set off on a tour in their latest acquisition, a second-hand Rolls which roared, according to Ottoline, like a menagerie of lions.

Spring and autumn were their favourite times for seeing England and they usually drove south to stay with the Russells in the hospitable chaos of Telegraph House in West Sussex or to visit Ottoline's favourite stretch of the Dorset coast where her love-affair with Bertie had begun. They knew what they liked and errors in judgement were rare: they fled from the chirpy vulgarity of Brighton in the thirties, where smart young women foxtrotted with their lovers in the ballroom of the Metropole, preferring to go and visit old friends in more tranquil surroundings. Theodore Powys (T.F., one of the three Dorset-based novelist brothers) and Thomas Hardy's widow were on their list of annual pilgrimages, as were Gilbert Spencer and Mark Gertler and his wife (he finally married Marjorie Hodgkinson, a Slade graduate, in 1930), who sometimes joined the tour for a few days; occasionally, they would incorporate a visit to old friends like Lady Desborough at Panshanger or Taplow, her husband's home, and Ena Mathias, whose country home was near Bury St Edmunds. In the summer of 1936, they went to Ireland to stay with the Hacketts, at their home in County Wicklow. Francis, a kind and round-faced man who was trying to make a career as a screenwriter, and Signe, author of a life of her Danish kinsman, Hans Christian Andersen, had become very fond of the Morrells in the two years they had known them, but they found Ottoline an exhausting guest whose hunger to know Ireland better made her want to be shown something new every day. (She made it up to them in the autumn, when she took care to see that they were introduced to every English writer in whom they had expressed an interest.)

Shortage of money, although still a problem, never prevented Ottoline and Philip from travelling; European trips were so cheap in those days that Lord Kinross was able to go to Hamburg on a luxury liner, with everything included, for only £3. In April 1931, the Morrells went to Rome, despite gloomy warnings from Lytton. 'It is no longer that vague, dreamy, half-collapsed town we used to wander in,' he told Ottoline on 8 April; 'motor-buses pursue you round the fountain of tortoises.' Ottoline was rather in favour of motor-buses, and both she and Philip hugely enjoyed their visit. Alberto Moravia, whom Ottoline had already met and liked enough to introduce to Russell, Yeats and Wells, judging him 'more fundamentally interesting than a modern English youth', was there and Mussolini was to be seen and photographed if not to be spoken to. Best of all, Duncan Grant was visiting Rome with his intrepid and vivacious Aunt Daisy, a splendid old lady who appointed herself as their chauffeur and chattered nonstop while Duncan, always charming, always good-tempered, flattered Ottoline by asking her to open his new exhibition the following month.*

Later in the same summer, the Morrells made a second visit to Holland and Ottoline whisked out her camera to photograph Godard Bentinck and the Kaiser arm-in-arm, looking like twins with their bushy white moustaches, naval blazers and bright badgers' eyes twinkling with pleasure. The Kaiser was always relaxed and good-tempered in the company of his old friends and Ottoline was not so shy of him as she had been on her earlier visit. Endearingly vain, he was ever ready for another photograph; at dinner, he confided that he hated nothing so much as the new women's fashion for going about without stockings and roared with Teutonic mirth when Ottoline pointed out that it depended on the shape of the legs.

From Philip's point of view, this was the ideal holiday, luxurious and undemanding; he looked back on it with longing when Ottoline arranged a grand tour of Sicily and southern Italy two years later.

---

* She did so, and it was a great success; afterwards, she noted that even Virginia had seemed to be quite moved by her speech and that Leonard Woolf, who never had a kind word to say to her, actually came up and complimented her on her eloquence.

Philip, in his sixties, had lost his youthful enthusiasm for sightseeing, but his wife had not. 'I am not a very conscientious traveller, and can never see the necessity of seeing every town and church and gallery that happens to find a place in Baedeker,' he wrote to Julian at the end of a long hot afternoon spent walking in Naples; 'but YM [your mother] is very different and will never give up any sight on which she has once set her heart. You may sometimes *think* she has forgotten about it, but you will be wrong; she never does . . .'[1]

In the summer of 1934, fired by Virginia Woolf's accounts of ravishing landscapes and bug-free beds, the Morrells went to Greece, driving south from Athens through the Peloponnese – little fun in the days when roads south of the Corinth isthmus were hardly more than cattle tracks – and travelling on by boat to Crete, where Sir Arthur Evans was in the last stages of recovering the Bronze Age city of Knossos. Philip, exhausted, returned home; Ottoline set off for Venice to spend a fortnight with L. P. Hartley. She had long ago forgiven Hartley for his youthful snobbery at Garsington; since his move to Italy, he had become one of her favourite correspondents, keeping her dressing-table stocked with the exotic scents she adored and could not get in England, making her laugh with such stories as the one of the time he had bravely owned up to his ignorance of Proust at a tea-party given by Ethel Sands: 'The silence that followed my admission was broken by someone saying almost hopefully, "Is that an attitude?"'[2] Hartley evidently enjoyed the 1934 visit quite as much as his visitor: 'You are the most constructive, creative, considerate and life-giving of guests,' he wrote; 'promise to come again, and very soon.'

Ottoline did not have all of the trips her own way. As Philip delved deeper into the life of Lord William Bentinck, it became clear that the book could not be written without going to India. 'I don't look forward to it . . . I have a horror of India,' Ottoline confided to her diary on 18 July 1934; despite her fears, she loved almost every moment of the three months that she spent there. Had it not been for the fact that the death of Philip's favourite aunt, Helen, obliged them to return for the funeral, she would happily have extended the visit.

A trunk still filled with brightly-coloured silk blouses of the type worn under saris bears witness to the many mornings when Ottoline left Philip to his research and went off alone to explore the bazaars, to peer into temples and, on occasion, synagogues, and even to join in a wedding feast. It was this that she enjoyed rather than the state banquets for which she was obliged to abide by such trifling points of etiquette as 'Mama says carry gloves tonight' and to feign an interest in sport and local scandal. In Bombay, where she was disgusted by the sight of spoilt little girls flirting with all the cold aptitude of film stars and bejewelled young boys rapping out their orders like drill commanders, she met the notoriously mean Nizam of Hyderabad who dressed his court ladies in department-store rejects, and Ross Masood, the once beautiful young Punjabi with whom Forster fell in love while teaching him Latin and on whom he modelled Dr Aziz. Masood had since become the vice-chancellor of the university founded by his grandfather, Sir Syed Ahmed Khan, and was now Bhopal's Minister of Education. Ottoline loathed him. He was sly, oily and corrupt, she wrote; she also decided that he was a prize liar.

Delhi depressed her. It was impossible to escape from Viceregal Lodge, which she found dismally cold and formal with its huge floodlit statues of King George V and Queen Mary looking like staring ghosts under the moon. Calcutta, however, was a great success. Government House was 'very eighteenth-century and English and unpretentious – spacious and aristocratic', and she was enchanted by the open maidan and the tropical atmosphere of a city surrounded by jungles of palms. She found new friends here in the form of Boshi and Gertrude Emerson Sen, a clever, genial couple with a refreshingly open attitude to religion; they had never, they said, seen any reason why Christ and Buddha should not be worshipped in the same house. Gertrude Sen shared Ottoline's love of bazaars and there were many agreeable expeditions on foot and one, rather guiltily, in a rickshaw.

Jaipur was next on the agenda, dazzling them with its rose-coloured palaces, but their pleasure in staying with the young Maharajah and hearing about his passionate love for an Irish doctor's wife was marred by the fact that their fellow guests were the Swiss jeweller, Cartier, and his eagerly snobbish wife who paraded his wares like a shop window while he spread collections of necklaces and bracelets on a carpet. They were not congenial companions, but they strove to charm. 'Ah, you have so much chic!' Madame Cartier screamed as she swept past Ottoline's elephant in a vast limousine, smothering her in dust. How clever to be so original in her dress! How brave to go out alone! Ottoline did not record her replies, but she noted that she would be happy never to see either of the Cartiers again.

The Morrells' last hosts were the Maharajah of Indore and his wife; they were also the most intriguing. The Maharajah's father had disgraced himself by marrying an actress with whom he lived in Paris where, according to his son, he passed the time by flying elaborate kites from the roof. Life in Indore had not been improved by his absence. The Maharani, a sallow, greedy woman, was interested in nothing but her *Vogue* magazines, her vast array of Elizabeth Arden products and her floodlit collection of jewellery. Both she and her husband were completely in the power of a Swiss-German couple, who made it clear that they, not the Maharajah, controlled Indore and that they did not welcome guests who asked awkward questions. Ottoline was half-relieved that the news of Aunt Helen's death obliged them to cut short their stay.

The move to Gower Street heralded a surprising renewal of friendship between Ottoline and her half-brother, the duke. It was greatly strengthened by two losses in 1931. Major George Baker-Carr, who had met the Portlands en route to Delhi and came to live with them at Welbeck for almost thirty years, died and deprived the duke of his favourite companion. Everybody had loved him, Ottoline wrote in her journal, the wonderful 'B' Carr who rode with the duke every morning, drove with the duchess in the afternoon and danced with their daughter in the evenings. The duke was almost inconsolable, but a loss which was far harder for Ottoline to bear was that of her own oldest brother, Henry, her only unfailing supporter and friend in the family since the early years.

She was staying with the Mathias family in the country when a telegram came from Charlie Bentinck: Henry had congestion of the lungs and was not expected to survive. Ottoline left for Underley at once. Henry gave no sign of knowing her, but she was comforted to find that her own trusted Dr Cameron was looking after him. Neither she nor Charlie could bear to sit waiting in the grim silence of the house with Henry's wife; instead, they went for long walks across the fells in the rain, Ottoline half-running to keep up with her brother's long stride, just as she had always done, she remembered, in the old days at Welbeck.

The whole family came north for the funeral at the beginning of October, but it was Ottoline who stayed on at Underley with the widow, helplessly watching as Birdie methodically destroyed the packets of letters from Charlie, from Augustus John, Henry Lamb, Walter Sickert, Epstein, Ottoline herself . . . 'It makes me want to scream,' she admitted on 9 October to Bertie, but she did not dare to protest.

There was a little self-interest in Ottoline's kindness to her sister-in-law. Henry had promised that Julian would be his heir, to make up for the odd injustice of Lady Bolsover's exclusion of Ottoline from her will. But now, when she dared to broach the subject, Birdie gave her the bleak news that Henry had been in debt for years. Collecting had become his obsession. Their London home had been turned into a vast warehouse, crammed with paintings, busts and boxes of Chinese porcelain which had never been unpacked. There was no money to leave to anybody, but Ottoline might, if she liked, choose something for herself. Wondering how to break the news to Victor and Julian, who were eagerly waiting in London for news of their legacy (and who were understandably devastated by this blow to their expectations) Ottoline murmured her sympathy. She chose to take her brother's pocket Wordsworth, his favourite reading when he was off on one of the walking expeditions he loved, and his gold-rimmed spectacles.

Of her three sisters-in-law, Ottoline had always found it hardest to get on with Birdie, mostly because it hurt her to see how often Henry's wishes were overruled by his wife. Travelling back to London, she remembered a time, not so long before, when she had spent some nights at the Bentincks' home in Queen Anne's Gate and was asked by Birdie to go out because they were having a dinner-party. Coming back from a solitary supper at an ABC restaurant, she had just started to climb the stairs when Birdie led the ladies out of the dining-room. No introductions were made, no friendly nod given; she had been made to feel as invisible as a servant. The memory was still like a wound. She pitied Henry's widow now, but she could not love her.

The duke had always been a sociable man. His marriage, seen as a model of harmony and mutual understanding by his friends, was less fulfilling than it looked. The duchess had not changed much in thirty-five years of marriage; she remained a superb hostess who was unflagging in her zeal for good causes and her pride in Welbeck. The duke respected and admired her, but they were not very close. With Henry and his kindest, easiest comrade gone, he turned for comfort and for reassuring love to his half-sister.

He had not always understood her; only now, in his seventies, did the duke begin to appreciate how much Ottoline must have minded his hostility to Philip, how little she had complained about her troubles and how bravely she had endured years of physical pain. In the past, he had usually been ready to share his wife's views on the absurdity of Ottoline's wish to surround herself with ungrateful bohemians, although he had enjoyed his two visits to Garsington (Ottoline had been careful to see that the house was empty on both occasions). He had always respected her intelligence; now, as he heard old friends like Ettie Desborough praising Ottoline for the help she had given to young artists and writers, he began to change his mind about her way of life. His older son brought back glowing accounts of a lunch at Gower Street with Lytton Strachey; a few weeks later, the duke startled himself with the pleasure he felt when he went there to meet Madame Nijinksy. (Hardly surprising, Ottoline drily noted, since Romola Nijinsky had behaved as if she was in the presence of the Sun King.) But the duke preferred to be alone with his sister, and visitors to Gower Street often saw him, handsome and white-haired, sitting patiently in the back of his Rolls-Royce outside the door, waiting for them to leave. Later in the evening, the two of them would go to a film or a play, Ottoline wearing one of the duchess's elegant dresses from Grosvenor Square to please her brother.

January 1932 marked the beginning of a correspondence which, in its copiousness, if not in its eloquence, can be compared to Bertie

Russell's in the first flush of his love for Ottoline. Not a letter went off without some reminder to her of the strength of the duke's affection. 'The more I know you, the more *I love you*,' he told her on 23 November 1932; a month later, he urged her: 'Do make some plans for *us* and let me know.' Sending her a present of a watch, he said that he would never be able to see her (as she had cheerfully described herself) as 'an old and dilapidated Granny but a *most attractive* and delicious O. Mind you think of me whenever you look at your watch,' he added, before asking her to thank him *'very very* nicely when next we meet. Bless you darlingest love.' Lamenting that she had been forced to cut short a four-day holiday alone with him in Scotland, he complained that the St Enoch's Hotel was 'oh!! so lonely and drab without a lovely figure to greet me'. (5 July 1935)

It was a remarkable transformation; disapproval had been replaced by an absolute and uncritical devotion; understandably, Ottoline was astonished by the feelings she seemed to have inspired, but she could not help being touched by such total love. The duke told her that he was only happy when she was with him; he consulted doctors about her health and tried to pay for her treatment; he lavished presents on her and went to endless trouble to arrange treats which he thought would please her. Ottoline mentioned that she had always longed to see inside Bramshill, 'the first beautiful house I ever saw', and was instantly swept off to look at the Jacobean manor and to make a sentimental return to East Court, her childhood home. When she said that she had never been to Ely Cathedral, the duke suggested that they should go there together and then, if Ottoline did not mind, perhaps she would take him to meet some of her Cambridge friends. They lunched with Steven Runciman – gratifyingly riveted by the duke's recollections of Queen Victoria – before going to tea with Jack Sheppard, one of Ottoline's favourite eccentrics, and Maynard and Lydia Keynes (where the duke caused a blush and a giggle by mistaking the celibate provost of King's for the dancer's husband).* They drove back to London by the light of a full moon after attending Evensong with Sheppard in King's College Chapel.

The duke enjoyed his Cambridge expedition so much that he insisted on another the following year, 1936. He wanted to drive them there himself; arriving at Grosvenor Square, Ottoline was touched to learn that he had been waiting eagerly at the window for a first glimpse of her, just as Bertie used to do at the Bury Place flat, she

---

* Despite his well-known preference for men, Keynes had been married to Lydia for ten years. Virginia Woolf, writing to her niece Angelica on 18 November 1935, told her that the duke, never having heard of Keynes, had asked Ottoline if he was related to '"the Miss Maynard who married Lord Warwick?" So you see Bloomsbury is still very very obscure.' Virginia Woolf, *Letters*, 5 (Hogarth Press, London, 1979), p. 445.

observed; she was more impressed by his announcing that he wanted her to show him round the Fitzwilliam Museum and to educate his eyes. In the past, she could not remember his ever having bothered to consult her views or to look at any work of art that did not feature a house, a field sport or a handsome woman. She laughed when he told her that it was all thanks to her good influence: 'Still, it is very remarkable that he has *grown* so much.' (8 November 1936)

For both of them, it was an opportunity of the kind which is rarely given to cancel hurt and misunderstanding with love. They wrote to each other nearly every day for the last six years of Ottoline's life. When she died, the duke went into his room and kept the door closed for three days. He had no words for the loss. 'As time went on I loved her more and more and that is all I have to say,' he wrote in his huge sprawling hand to Julian in April 1938. 'I know what you are suffering and you know what I am suffering too.'[3] But it is unlikely that either Julian or her father knew quite how much grief he was trying to express.

Ottoline did not find it so easy as she had anticipated to come to terms with Russell's marriage to Dora Black in 1921; comments on her first visits to the Cornish seaside house where they spent their summers in the 1920s were dour and grudging. She had always known that Bertie longed for children and she was greatly taken by his little boy, but it exasperated her to hear him blandly disowning all his old interest in nature, poetry and religion. However much they might have disagreed in the past, their conversations had been full of excitement. Now, he seemed ready to agree with everything that Dora said, and Ottoline felt that she had been robbed. 'I cannot recognise Bertie who used to be so fine and critical . . .' she wrote on 31 June 1923; 'I could have howled with boredom.'

The sense of alienation did not last long; it would have taken more than a marriage to break a friendship which Russell valued quite as highly as Ottoline did. With, and more often without Dora, he continued to visit her both at Garsington and at Gower Street; by 1927, when he was jokingly comparing them to two shipwrecked Victorian mariners adrift in the twentieth century, they were, according to Ottoline's journal, lunching together almost every week and airing their views with a frankness that was not possible when either Dora or Philip was present. On one occasion, after debating the merits of a marriage as open as H. G. Wells's, Ottoline staggered Bertie by blandly telling him that Philip had always been disgusted by the idea of adultery. On another day, when Russell came to tea with Thomas Sturge Moore, the philosopher's brother, he delighted Ottoline by saying how much he still loved Wittgenstein: 'I was so pleased to hear [it] ... for he used to but turned against him when he was religious.' (November 1932)

Bertie had always said that seven years was the outer limit for a sexual relationship; by 1930, he had been married to Dora for nine years. In July, the month Dora's daughter by Griffin Barry was born, he told Ottoline that he was no longer in love with his wife. A year later, just before his departure on an American lecture tour, he decided to take Ottoline into his confidence about his new relationship with Patricia (Peter) Spence, a striking Oxford undergraduate who had been engaged to look after John and Kate, his children, during the previous summer.

Bertie wrote and told me that a young woman whom he had been in love with was going to have a child by him and that as she was poor she was going to live at Telegraph House – this shocks me dreadfully ... It shows such extraordinary want of respect and *deference* to Dora or to this girl. I am to see her so I shall see what she is like ... I am sorry for her ... Since writing this, I have heard that she has had a miscarriage ... (26 October 1931)

Shocked though she was, Ottoline was still too upset by her brother's death the previous month to relish embarking on a quarrel about the ethics of Bertie's behaviour; instead, she sent a tactful letter, suggesting that he would probably always need to have two women in his life, one to satisfy his mind and one his body.

Peter Spence had told Russell that she wanted to meet Ottoline, perhaps because she had heard him say that she was not wholly devoted to Dora. And so it was that Ottoline, twenty years on, found herself playing Evelyn Whitehead's role and being asked to approve of Bertie's mistress. She did not need so much persuading as Mrs Whitehead had done. One meeting was enough to convince her that he would be happy with this attractive and seemingly unambitious young woman; in her journal, she approvingly noted that Peter Spence was very much aware of the mystical side of Bertie's nature which Dora had wanted to erode. 'She was very shy poor thing at first,' she wrote to him on 18 November 1932, 'and I was shy, but after a bit we got on very well and I liked her immensely, and indeed she is a dear and has so much in her that would suit you.' Later, she would persuade herself that she had been very sorry for Dora; at the time, she did all she could to encourage him to leave her.

Bertie was delighted by such a warm response. A couple of months later, he asked himself to Gower Street to hear more of her praises of Peter Spence and to unburden himself on the subject of Dora, who was being unexpectedly firm on the matter of alimony for herself and the children. As he rose to go, he casually let drop the news that he had just finished writing his memoirs and would be sending them for her inspection.

The timing should have been perfect. Ottoline had just finished reading his early letters and wondering how she had managed to resist such a passionate assault on her marriage. It astonished her to see what dramas had been created from ludicrously small events: could he really have thought that the whole relationship was doomed because she spent one extra day away from him in Paris? Had he always lived in such a storm of emotion as the letters suggested? Reading them again brought home to her how passionately he had loved her; it was natural enough that she should feel a moment of regret as she thought of the life which might, had she been ruthless enough to leave Philip, have been hers. Now, she wrote in her journal, she would behave very differently. She was impatient to read Bertie's own account of the early years of their love.

The manuscript reached Gower Street in mid-January 1932 and was promptly scanned for its references to herself. They were not pleasing. Bertie had on the one hand managed to find space for a remark about his bad breath which she deeply regretted and had certainly never wished to see in print, and on the other had said nothing at all about the part that Garsington had played in his life during and after the war. As for his descriptions of herself, she could hardly believe her eyes. 'He describes me ... as using too much powder and scent and [says] that I had a face like a horse! I whom he said would always remain beautiful even as a very old woman!' (22 January) Learning that he hoped to publish it, she told him to take out every mention of her and showed no sign of relenting when Bertie sent her a pathetic letter saying he was miserable at the thought that he had hurt her. At the end of the year, he came to Gower Street to throw himself on her mercy. He had done as she asked and she could congratulate herself on having ruined the book since 'I was really the centre of his life and that out of my influence all his later life flowed'. Ottoline was not able to resist this heart-rending declaration; she told him to put her in again and they promised to publish nothing personal during each other's lifetime.

The dispute was resumed the following year, but this time it was Ottoline who was seeking permission to include some of Bertie's letters in her own memoirs. He had been ready to accept the idea of a posthumous publication but now, to Ottoline's considerable irritation, young Peter Spence announced that she would rather they were only published after her death. 'Bertie is entirely under her thumb ...' Ottoline wrote on 7 April 1933, and added a few days later that 'the Peter minx does not want me to let his letters to me ever see the light. It is very foolish as they were written when she was one year old.' Foolish or not, Peter was determined to have her way and Ottoline ceased to look on her with a friendly eye. At their meetings in London, she jeered at Peter for insisting they all have dinner in evening dress when it was only Ottoline, Bertie and herself; on a rare visit to Telegraph House, while conceding that Peter had made it a good deal cleaner and more agreeable, she complained of the dullness of her mind and of her drawling, affected voice. Forgetting how ready she had been to advise Bertie to leave Dora, she now began to refer to 'poor Dora' and to find it disgraceful that Peter Spence should show her so little sympathy.

The storms between Peter Spence and Ottoline never undermined her relationship with Bertie: 'He is the one real friend I have. We talk the same language . . .' she wrote when he came to visit her in a nursing home near Bristol. 'He and I know what we mean.' (28 November 1934) A week or so later, when she was back in London, they paid a visit to Virginia Woolf together, strolling through the door arm-in-arm, 'two old friends . . . He is *human*,' she added, comparing him to the lovely but always slightly remote Virginia.

Ottoline's health grew steadily worse in the last years of her life: Bertie continued to be one of her most regular and welcome visitors. He stayed away from the memorial service and the letter he wrote to Philip, while sad, was brief and personal only in its reference to her 'gay courage' and to the length of time that they had known each other. Theirs had always been a private relationship.

The fault, she felt sure, was hers for being old and unfashionable, but Ottoline could not help feeling hurt by the way Lytton had dropped her after the move to Gower Street. His excuse was that he could never tear himself away from Ham Spray, the country house to which he and Carrington moved from Tidmarsh; she heard from other friends that he had a diary full of London engagements. She did her best to be forgiving. 'It is the happiness of success,' she wrote on 15 July 1931, 'of what he did not get when he was younger. He must drink his champagne and I doubt if he will ever return to our modest cups of tea.'

Ottoline was far too fond of Lytton to give up asking him to visit her at Gower Street; the letters and journals show that she tried only to invite him to those occasions which he would find irresistible. One was a lunch with her nephew Sonnie Titchfield and his wife; Lytton, who seldom refused a chance to talk to an aristocrat, came and behaved with unusually sedate charm. Another was a tea for Charlie Chaplin. Chaplin's first visit had been a huge success, ending up with him and Mark Gertler swapping East End stories and doing imitations, Gertler of a pompous colonel, Chaplin of Ascot ladies trying to catch the royal eye. The second was less satisfactory. The actor had asked to meet Lytton and Augustus John and was disappointed by both. John arrived considerably the worse for drink and failed to make sense; Lytton, overcome with shyness, conveyed the impression of a snobbish bore. Chaplin only cheered up when the guests had gone and he could sit and talk to Ottoline about himself while Philip gently nodded off by the fire.

That visit, made in November 1931, was the last time Ottoline saw Lytton. Two months later, she recorded that he had become seriously ill: 'I feel it very much, for he is a dear old friend, twenty-one years now.' (1 January 1932) She did what she could to help, recommending specialists, writing affectionate letters and sending bottles of specially blended toilet water when she heard that he liked having it dabbed on his face and to know that it was she who had sent it. Three weeks later, she wrote in her diary that he was dead: 'dear dear Lytton ... the fuse of the French and the ... rollicking life of the English – all this in the exterior of a nineteenth-century tutor.' (22 January 1932) Carrington, who had kept her informed during the last weeks, sent her some photographs and a short, touching letter thanking her 'for those days at Garsington, when I grew to love him'. Two months later, Virginia sent the news that Carrington had shot herself, unable to bear the prospect of life without the only man with whom she had ever felt totally happy. Ottoline had not spoken to Carrington since 1926 (when she visited Garsington with great reluctance) but she was horrified by her death. Carrington had seemed so young, so childlike. She remembered how she had loved to sleep out on the roof at Garsington on summer nights with Aldous and, later, to sit curled like a cat at the side of Lytton's deck-chair, watching, adoring. It was difficult to stem the flow of words that rushed out when she began to describe Lytton for her memoirs, but she found it almost impossible to conjure up the elusive, wayward charm of Carrington. 'She was an original,' she wrote in the end. 'I have never known anyone else like her.' (27 March 1932)

To Ottoline's old friends, knowing how cruelly Lytton had jeered at her for the past twenty years, it was embarrassing to see her in such distress about his death. Had she really not known what he thought of her? Surely she could not have cherished an illusion that he liked her? It seemed that she did. Virginia, having proudly exhibited all Lytton's letters to her, was torn between embarrassment and curiosity when Ottoline offered to return the compliment. It was a shock to discover that, at the very time when Lytton had been most eloquently vitriolic on the subject of Garsington, he had been pouring out letters to Ottoline of abject adoration, begging for invitations and praising her as his adored Marquise without whom he pined. There was no longer any need to wonder why Ottoline had been so loyal, but what should the Bloomsberries now think of him? Integrity and sincerity were the words they had always reserved for Lytton; it now began to look as though duplicity would have been the more accurate one. Virginia had come to Gower Street to see the letters with the intention of being kind and tactful; it was mortifying to find that Ottoline thought it was she who needed to be reassured that Lytton had always loved her. 'She was astonished that he wrote so warmly and affectionately to me . . .' Ottoline noted on 23 November 1932; 'I was very much afraid that she would be slightly jealous, so I said all I could about Lytton's devotion to her.' Their conversation grew more general. Ottoline thought that he must have modelled his letters on Walpole's; Virginia thought he had done so far too much. It was a tragedy, they agreed, that such a mind should never have produced what they could call 'a real book'. Gracefully, watchfully, they skirted the subject which was on both of their minds: had these letters been Lytton's real bid for posterity? And, if so, what should be done about them?

Ottoline had never forgotten how kind the Irish poet James Stephens had been to her on her first visit to his country. When he and his wife moved to London, where they had few friends, she took them under her wing.

Looking through the Gower Street Visitors' Book, it is clear that Stephens made himself at home; there is hardly a tea-party to be found at which he was not present; it was, he told Ottoline, almost like being back in Dublin, where people cared about the art of conversation.

Unfortunately for Ottoline and her guests, Stephens's love of good talk encompassed an enormous amount of rubbish; it was not unusual for a visitor to find, say, Yeats, de la Mare and Eliot sitting in polite silence while Stephens told tales of leprechauns and, far too often, of his poverty-stricken childhood. (He was particularly fond of telling his audience that he had often had to fight with swans for a piece of bread, a tale which smacked of Mr Bounderby's famous nights in an egg-box.*)

Year by year, Ottoline grew more painfully conscious of Stephens's ability to kill a party stone dead with boredom; even Philip said that Stephens was the most tedious man he had ever known. But, having chosen her cross, she was determined to carry it with resignation, if not with total grace. It was not easy; she had to remind herself on

---

* '. . . in an egg-box. That was the cot of *my* infancy; an old egg-box.' (Charles Dickens, *Hard Times*, ch. IV)

several occasions that it would hurt Stephens's feelings if she asked him not to repeat the same stories every time he came. A hint of what she was enduring can be found late in 1933, when her journal ruefully described Stephens as asking who Rimbaud was before going on to announce that Shakespeare wrote like a peasant and that he himself had conceived a poem 'that would make Dante look like a midge'.

For all his silliness, Stephens was a good and generous man and Ottoline continued to support him and to rebuke the younger poets who visited her, when they fawned on Yeats and ignored Stephens. She admired him for his unworldliness and, despite the remark about Dante, his modesty about his work. It delighted her when James Joyce told her that he was planning to commission a twin-headed bust of Stephens and himself; she was glad to think that she was not alone in feeling affection for him.

Another man who had cause to be grateful for what Ottoline lightly referred to as 'a sort of extended maternal instinct' in her nature was Koteliansky, the Russian translator she had first met through the Lawrences in the early war years. Although they had seen little of each other in the 1920s, they had followed each other's careers through their mutual friends, Mark Gertler and Beatrice Glenavy, but it was the discovery of Kot's profound love for Katherine Mansfield that made Ottoline decide they should get to know each other better.

Kot was, in his singular way, as tricky a friend as James Stephens. Fond though Ottoline became of 'dear old Kot', she often found him infuriating. He was, she wrote, used to being humoured and allowed to get away with parading bombast as sense; she was exasperated when she saw him lumber up to Tom Eliot, wring his hand and boom for all the room to hear of the pleasure he felt in being able to tell him that he couldn't stand any of his poetry. She knew how much he enjoyed posing as a philistine, but it was going too far, she thought, when she had taken him out for an evening to see *Così*, her favourite opera, only to be thanked with the observation that it had been quite pleasant. 'Quite pleasant!' she repeated. 'I could have hit him.' But she had already learned that there was no point in quarrelling with Kot. 'I cannot argue with a nice dear old charming bull who just rushes at anything one says like a red cloth . . .' (May 1931)

Kot did not have many friends in the 1930s; he knew that his black depressions made him a trying companion and he often allowed weeks to pass without leaving his drab flat in north London. Ottoline was one of the few who were allowed to visit him and for whom he was prepared to go out; her photograph albums are full of pictures of

Stephens and Kot, who got on well together, sitting in the garden behind Gower Street. At the times when he could not be persuaded to come, she wrote him long, charming letters about writers they both admired and people who she thought might interest him; without being flirtatious, she encouraged him to think that he occupied a privileged place in her life. When, for example, she arrived home from India, off went a letter to Kot on the first day, telling him to come and visit and not to tell anybody else that she was back.

In 1936, most probably in reaction to the horrifying news that Gertler had tried to cut his throat with a razor, Kot had a breakdown. 'I feel haunted by that poor old bear,' Ottoline wrote on 22 August after she had been to visit Mark's wife and to reassure Kot that he would survive. (In fact, Gertler took his life in 1939.) She herself was being treated in a nursing home that summer, but she was more worried about Kot's state of mind than her own welfare. Hearing that he was reluctantly undergoing treatment for depression, she tried to raise his spirits by promising to come and abduct him: 'I will bring a complete disguise and a long black cape and a large flowery hat – but how shall we manage about your feet, for high-heeled shoes must be worn . . . Don't lose use of legs – keep them in good shape for the escape.'[4] It is a pity that we only have her side of this engaging correspondence, but Kot was evidently very attached to Ottoline, while retaining a good sense of humour about her hopes of bringing him into a proper relation with God. Beatrice Glenavy, in her memoirs, tells the story of Ottoline escorting Kot to St Paul's and being rewarded with the disconcerting observation that it was all very Jewish. Ottoline took the comment in good part, but she made no more attempts to convert her friend.[5]

Frieda Lawrence was another figure who reappeared in the Gower Street years. She arrived in London in March 1930, shortly after Lawrence's death. At the end of the month, splendidly arrayed in shades of fuchsia pink and crimson – she had worn bright red for her husband's funeral – she turned up at Gower Street, 'and stayed for hours. I feel so sorry for her,' Ottoline wrote on 28 March after an uncharacteristically humble Frieda told her that she had always been jealous of her relationship with Lawrence and that she had always felt that they could, as she vaguely put it, 'do something together for England'.

The two women saw a good deal of each other over the next two years and Ottoline, while never able to forget the difficulties she had endured with Frieda in the past, could not help admiring the energy and enterprise she showed. Lawrence had taken the image of the phoenix for himself, but Frieda needed no symbol to emphasise her indestructibility as she rose from her husband's ashes, a buxom, middle-aged Valkyrie who cheerfully admitted that she was sleeping with Murry while waiting for her young Italian lover to get a divorce. Other visitors to Gower Street might sign their names with neat precision; Frieda recorded her return with typical bravura: 'Here's Frieda – yet again!'

True to form, Frieda brought havoc to Gower Street. She sulked when Ottoline told her off for trying to enliven her daughter Barbara's existence by arranging a quick course of sexual encounters; Philip was coaxed into negotiating with Lawrence's family over his estate on Frieda's behalf, only to be undermined by Frieda's revelation of his strategy when she began to suspect that he was giving away what was rightfully hers. Eager to please and placate, she assured Ottoline that Lawrence had always loved her and that Hermione Roddice had been a heartfelt tribute to her finest qualities, a view which Ottoline found it impossible to share. She was doing her best to be impartial in the account of Lawrence which she planned to use in her memoirs, but she admitted to Virginia that her hostility to Frieda was unbalancing her writing. Frieda without Lawrence was more tolerable than she had been with him, but only just. It came as a relief when she made her last visit in 1933 to announce that she was off to live in Taos with Angelo Ravagli.

Of the three men who had been emotionally involved with Ottoline and who she saw again after her move to London, the least welcome was Axel Munthe. He had made one brief visit to Garsington in 1925. In 1929, *The Story of San Michele* was published and its author came to England to ensure that it had a proper reception. Ottoline leafed through it with alarm, dreading an account of her girlish infatuation. She had not been mentioned but that was not, she suspected, because he cared about her feelings but because it would have been difficult to show himself in a good light. Reading the book, she found it hard to imagine what had charmed her; certainly, there was little about him to charm her now. Munthe had written from Rome to announce his arrival in England; his messages were as mixed as they had always been. On the one hand, he begged her to find a kind reader to sit with him now that he was old (he was seventy-two) and blind; on the other, he proposed to appoint himself as her European agent for any furniture she might like to buy. It was not clear how he intended to do this job without his sight, but Ottoline sent a courteous letter, agreeing to see him one afternoon. He came, flattering and silver-tongued as when they had first met; sorry though she was for his loss of sight, Ottoline could only wonder that love had once so blinded her to his imperfections.*

The coda came shortly after Ottoline's death, when Philip was startled to receive, not a letter of condolence, but a request to return a gold watch. Ottoline had, Munthe explained, given him one in exchange belonging to her father, but since that had now been lost, he would be glad to have his own back. To his credit, Philip sent a polite reply, promising to return the watch if it was possible to identify it.†

Ottoline had already made her peace with Henry Lamb, visiting him in Dorset and attending his London exhibitions. The extraordinary beauty of his youth had gone and the graceful figure had become spare and stooped, but she still thought of him as one of the most fascinating personalities she had ever encountered; reading his letters in 1929, she was overwhelmed by nostalgia. An objective reader might conclude from Lamb's correspondence that he had treated Ottoline atrociously, but that was not how she remembered it. The fault, in her memory, had all been hers for not softening the blow to his self-esteem of her relationship with Russell. 'The moment in my life that I most regret was when poor Henry came over from Brittany and found Bertie at Peppard,' she wrote in her journal twenty years later.

Ottoline had just finished describing her relationship with Lamb for her memoirs in the spring of 1929, when he rang and asked if he could bring to tea a young woman who he only admitted was his wife after Ottoline had expressed her approval. His fears were excessive (he told his wife that Ottoline was unable to bear the thought of any man she knew getting married, let alone an ex-lover). Ottoline was delighted to see him looking so in love and 'dancing with happiness' while Lady Pansy (a sister of the present Lord Longford) was 'like a succulent plum, very nice as far as I could see ... very devoted to him obviously, always looking at him and passing telegraphic messages ... She is fair, *lovely* skin, and amiable.' (14 February 1929) The Lambs made several visits to Gower Street in the thirties; later, noticing that Lady Pansy continued to bloom while Lamb looked more exhausted on every occasion, Ottoline decided that he might have made a mistake in marrying a girl twenty years younger than himself.

Seeing Lamb again caused Ottoline to grow reflective about the value of some of her more passionate relationships and to ask herself

---

* An operation in 1934 restored Munthe's vision.

† Privately, Philip was outraged, describing Munthe as 'that most odious of calculators' to his daughter, who prudently put the gold watch away in order that conscience should not oblige him to return what had, after all, been a gift.

if she could justify them. 'I have not sought "love affairs",' she wrote a few months after his first visit. 'They are false if sought. Instinctively I have given encouragement to the intellect and to the spirit and to generosity, and have shown enthusiasm for what is courageous and fine in life . . . I know I have given love, affection, interest and sympathy. It has often been trampled on, abused or misunderstood and derided, but that doesn't matter.' (November 1929) What did matter, she wrote later, was that she had used the power she possessed to stir people's imaginations, even though she had often been hurt in the process: 'après tout I should never want to have a soothing quality.' (16 July 1931)

Enchanted though Augustus John had once been by Ottoline and devoted to her though he remained, he had risked his friendship with a painting of her which left no sense of a soothing quality in the viewer's mind. It had not pleased Ottoline to find herself the subject of several newspaper articles speculating on her reaction to John's portrait of her in 1920, but it was the journalists, not she, who accused John of using his brush too cruelly. She showed the same detachment in November 1928 when she calmly recorded having seen 'a very ugly and queer portrait of myself' by John at Tooth's Gallery; it made her laugh to think that it had been done by a man who used never to tire of telling her how beautiful she was. As for the first picture, she took great satisfaction in hanging it over the fireplace in the Gower Street dining-room and waiting to see what the guests would say.

Ottoline had never lost touch with John and Dorelia and, while she shared the general view that drink had subdued his early brilliance, she continued to support his work and to encourage her brother Henry to do the same. Her fears about John's decline were confirmed in the spring of 1930 when he wrote to ask if she knew of a doctor who could cure what he preferred to call a nervous condition. The appeal was well timed. Ottoline was about to make her second visit to Preston Deanery, a fashionable and hideous nursing home in Northamptonshire where drugs and vitamins were reportedly handed out on silver salvers by footmen.* Ottoline disliked the place, but she had great faith in the man in charge of it, a society quack with an ugly record of alcoholism and a jail sentence for running over a child. Unaware of his past, Ottoline had become one of his most enthusiastic admirers.

---

* Ugly outside, it was uglier still within, according to Eddy Sackville-West, who was appalled to find 'fumed oak, leatherette, beaten copper and suburban mauve everywhere'. (ES-W to Raymond Mortimer, 3 November 1930, quoted in Michael Dela-Noy, *Eddy: The Life of Edward Sackville-West* (Bodley Head, London, 1988), p. 138.

Nothing could have pleased her more than the thought that her own dear Dr Cameron should have the honour of curing John's 'nerves'.

In April 1930, Ottoline arrived at Preston Deanery and found John already ensconced. Cameron had been artful enough to suggest that abstinence would have the best possible effect on his nerves and John was claiming to feel himself 'like a giant refreshed', but he was not enjoying an existence in which the highlights of the week were a feast of tea and toast, a walk to the local church and an occasional tantalising glimpse of a pretty chambermaid. Ottoline was ordered to come and sit by his bed every day, to photograph his newly etherealised form and to entertain him with stories. She did her best, chatting away about her recent encounters with Stanley and Hilda Spencer, and with Jacob Epstein, to whose work John had introduced her when he was living in one room and desperately in need of commissions and who was now admired and sought-after but just as friendly and unaffected as ever. Talking about Epstein, Ottoline could not help drawing a comparison with John, who had then been at the height of his career and who now seemed as if life had used him up and drained his power. 'How like he has become to Asquith, who had his two failings, drink and women,' she noted disapprovingly, but she was touched by his evident pleasure at being with her and his entreaties to her to stay on and keep him company. Philip arrived to collect her and John came down to the door to wave her off. He looked, she said, like the boy who had been left behind at the school gate, but a few weeks later, she had an ecstatic letter, blessing her for the introduction to Cameron and assuring her that he had never felt better. Dorelia, too, sent a grateful note, although she did not hold out much hope that the cure would last. It would only take one meeting with an old drinking friend, she predicted; and so it did.

Ottoline's last meeting with John took place in 1936 when she and Philip dropped in on him on a summer afternoon on the way to Ashcombe where Ottoline was to be photographed in Cecil Beaton's country garden. She looked particularly splendid that day in a magnificent dress with a black bodice and a vast canary-coloured skirt encrusted with serpentine embroidery; she was carrying a silk parasol. Nobody except, perhaps, the glorious Marchesa Casati had offered John such a dramatic subject as Ottoline and John clearly felt a stirring of some half-forgotten impulse towards her. ' "More paintable than ever," ' he murmured, but Ottoline recoiled. It was too late. ' "I *couldn't* face it." ' (July 1936)

Julian and Juliette Huxley had never been out of favour and Aldous and Maria were restored to it by the time Ottoline arrived in Gower

Street. The Huxleys, as she and Juliette agreed in a long and frank discussion of Julian's dalliances, could not be judged by ordinary rules; it was no more possible to make Julian see why he shouldn't boast about the fact that his mistress had just been proposed to by the Aly Khan (as he did, with great pride, when he visited Ottoline in March 1932) than it was to make Aldous understand how hard it was for his friends to forgive his habit of caricaturing them. He did not do it to be cruel, Ottoline decided; he simply failed to calculate the impact it was likely to have. Lawrence had guessed at the pain it must have caused Maria Huxley to read in *Point Counter Point* about the death of a child who was easily identifiable as their own, living son, Matthew; Aldous did not. But Lawrence had loved Aldous and Maria and it was Frieda's accounts of her husband's last days, when they had all been together, followed by Aldous's sensitive and warm-hearted introduction to Lawrence's *Selected Letters* in 1932, which made Ottoline think how much she missed him and longed for them to settle in London. She saw them whenever they came to England, it was true, and delighted in saving up little presents for Matthew ('I like to be the old lady with a present for every child,' she wrote in January 1929), but their encounters were frustratingly brief.

Ottoline's wish was granted in 1934 when the Huxleys moved back to London, taking rooms in Albany where Sybille Bedford remembered seeing Ottoline standing, quite unruffled, while the guests crawled about the floor gathering pearls from her broken necklace which she eventually took away with her in a paper bag. And she didn't even bother to count them, Miss Bedford noticed with considerable respect for such panache. (It is a shame that she was not present to record the other, better-known occasion when Ottoline, who loved sticky buns, was seen retrieving one from the floor at an exhibition with the gleeful declaration that she loved eating buns off the ground.)

Ottoline had been in Gower Street for six years by the time the Huxleys returned to England. While standing lower than the Tower of London and Kew Gardens, she had become a high-ranking attraction for visitors to the capital. It was all very well being treated as a relic in a shrine, she plaintively told Aldous, but the old relic did occasionally like to be able to go adventuring instead of being gawped at by young poets. The Huxleys took the hint, taking her off to Albert Schweitzer's lectures, inviting her to their parties in the Albany rooms and urging her to come and have her palm read by their new discovery, a Frenchwoman called Charlotte Wolff, a palmist who rapidly fell in love with Ottoline and showered her with passionate notes ('Je pense à vous tous le temps, tous le temps') and bouquets of roses.

The Huxleys' names feature at almost every social event that Ottoline attended in 1935, but she was always happiest to see them on their own or with a mutual friend such as Anita Loos, who came to spend a part of each year at the Savoy Hotel and who helped to persuade Aldous and Maria to make the move to America in 1936. Ottoline dreaded their departure. There was almost nobody, she wrote in her journal, who gave her such pleasure whenever she saw him as Aldous or who made her laugh so much: who else would have irreverently characterised Virginia Woolf as 'ashes in a glass case', a description with which, feeling terribly guilty at her disloyalty, she agreed? It seemed particularly cruel that they should be leaving just as Aldous was showing signs of becoming religious. It pleased her to think that she might have helped to work the change.

The Eliots' marriage was in decline by the time Ottoline moved to Gower Street. Vivien, who now called herself Vivienne, had become deranged. Her elegant appearance and good-looks had gone; photographs show an emaciated, elderly-looking woman with hollow cheeks and anxious eyes. A form of persecution mania had convinced her that there was a secret plot against Tom. While she took refuge from reality in ether and – so the Morrells heard – an unhappy relationship with Prince Dimitri Mirsky, regarded by Ottoline as 'a dreadful man . . . a fraud . . . a brute', Tom found solace in religion (he secretly joined the Church of England in 1926) and in drink. (Ottoline, a teetotaller, often found it unbearable to be near him.) As time went on and Vivien's condition grew worse, he spent an increasing amount of his time with Alida Monro, the only woman, according to Vivien, who thoroughly understood him.*

Few friends were willing to spend much time with Vivien after the deterioration began in the mid-twenties. Ottoline remained loyal and Vivien responded with touching devotion, describing her in one of her strange, disjointed letters as 'the only real friend we have, and perhaps the only *real person* we know'. There were many difficult periods with Tom, but Ottoline never quarrelled with Vivien, even when she had been accused, along with Virginia, of seducing her husband. Tom preferred to visit Gower Street on his own, usually to discuss what he should do about his wife, but when they came together, Ottoline always took care to sit beside Vivien and look after her, keeping her away from the other guests while she whispered and muttered and plucked at her clothes with nervous fingers. This, Ottoline frequently thought, was how she herself might have ended up if she had not forced herself to be rigidly self-controlled about her emotions. Being kind to Vivien felt like being kind to a ghost of herself.

If being visited by the Eliots was an uncomfortable experience, with

---

* Alida Monro was the wife of Harold Monro, publisher of the highly regarded *Georgian Poetry* series and founder of the *Poetry Review*. Vivien's suspicions of her relationship with Eliot seem to have been as groundless as the talk of her own affair with Mirsky.

Tom seeking support for his plans to have his wife locked up and Vivien talking about strange men who were planning to kidnap her husband, visiting them was equally unnerving. Suspecting that Vivien was desperately lonely, Ottoline went regularly, but it was not an experience that she enjoyed. On one occasion, she was embarrassed to find herself there with Prince Mirsky; on another, in November 1930, Mrs Haigh Wood was lurking in the background while her daughter prowled in and out of the room, reeking of ether, shouting and banging the door if anybody failed to speak to her. Tom was there, looking 'grim and fat; horrid', but who could wonder, Ottoline thought, when his wife was in this mood? Despite her affection for Vivien, she was shocked. 'She spoke to him as if he was a dog.'

Vivien was in a disruptive mood again when Ottoline went to a poetry evening arranged by Tom. The guests, uncomfortably arranged in rows on small chairs as if for a prayer meeting, struggled to pay attention to the calm, flat voice of their host while, out in the street, the voice of Vivien was equally audible, high, insistent and frantic with rage. One good thing came out of this awkward occasion; Ottoline found herself exchanging looks of mutual sympathy with John Hayward, a caustic young writer confined to a wheelchair, who became for a time one of her closest friends and confidants.

A more successful visit to the Eliots took place in July 1931 when they asked her to come and have tea to meet James Joyce.

I was nervous as I never know what I may say that might offend them and Tom is odd. I feel I don't know him now or what he thinks. I talked of being inhuman . . . I was so afraid he would think I was talking *at* him that I had to drag in people like Lytton . . . Mrs Joyce came and sat like an image – hardly talked at all, like most women. Fat, placid and I expect a good manager. We waited and waited . . . But at last the bell rang and T and V ran out and opened the door and looked at me as if the king was entering with a look as much as to say: 'Arise and meet his Majesty.'

Amused though she was by the Eliots' anxious reverence, Ottoline was moved when they carefully led a slight, very graceful figure into the room: she had not known that Joyce was almost blind. Tom and he talked for a while and then, much to her delight, Joyce produced a recording that he had made of 'Anna Livia Plurabelle' (she had read and loved it two years earlier) which they played while Joyce sat with his head bowed. He had, she noticed, extraordinarily white and beautiful hands.

She had enjoyed the afternoon. Late that evening, she contrasted it with the noisy cocktail party she had briefly visited on her way home, given by Duncan Grant and his new lover George Bergen, while Vanessa sat in the next-door room. People might talk about the oddness of the Eliots' marriage, she thought, but could anything be half so odd as the Bell, Bergen and Grant ménage? Vanessa 'seemed absurdly matronly and old compared to them . . . so staid'. Still, 'Duncan is very fond of her and it is nice of him to be so . . .'

In the summer of 1932, the Eliots made their last appearances together, one of these at Gower Street when Ottoline wanted to introduce them to Alberto Moravia. In September, when Eliot left alone for a tour of the United States, Ottoline was instructed to keep an eye on Vivien and to send him reports on her; in February 1933, she received a tart reproach for failing in her duty. If she did so, it was because Vivien was becoming almost impossible to be with as she grew increasingly alarmed by Eliot's absence. It was not, according to the testimony of Virginia and Ottoline, until July 1933 that she received the letter announcing that he had left her for good.

Eliot continued to visit Ottoline at Gower Street during the midthirties, but the old ease of their friendship had gone. Vivien, even in her worst moments, was always able to show her feelings; Eliot, even with his closest friends, kept his hidden. It was very kind of him to send her huge bunches of lilac, Ottoline wrote despairingly in the spring of 1934, and she was touched that he should still want to come and have long talks with her, but she felt uneasy with a man who was so cool and critical. He had become rigid in his views. Everything had to be black and white. D. H. Lawrence was evil. Ottoline's photographs of Greek statues were images of serpent-worship. When he announced that only the Church's view was right, he reminded her of Vava Bentinck, still unmarried, still busy with her tracts and homilies. His new work depressed her. She went with Charlotte Wolff to see *Murder in the Cathedral* and wondered that such human history could be made so cold. Try though she did to like the American woman who was now Eliot's constant companion, she could not understand what he saw in her. By their second meeting, she had become 'that *awful* American woman Miss Hale. She is like a sergeant major, quite intolerable. However Tom takes her about everywhere . . .' (22 October 1935) Only rarely now did she catch sight of the old Tom Eliot she had loved; in 1936, when they were both trying to raise funds for one of his most talented young protégés, George Barker, she observed that Eliot, for all his odd fits of meanness – who else would send out printed Christmas cards to avoid signing them and giving the card a commercial value? – was a good deal more generous than Sassoon, who could so easily have helped the young poet, and would not. It would have pleased her to know that, years after her death, Eliot found time to give a speech on behalf of her favourite charity, the Cecil Houses Trust, and that he helped to write the verse for her memorial tablet in which he and Virginia praised her brave spirit and her gift for friendship.

The last of Ottoline's old friendships to flower into something close to love was with Virginia Woolf. 'I feel you are my guardian angel,' Ottoline had told her on the eve of the move to Gower Street, but Virginia was not ready to become so saintly. In 1928, she was still describing Ottoline in fairly uncomplimentary terms as 'out hawking the streets' after having 'befouled the twigs' of a few homes; a year later, after they had met at a party given by Samuel Courtauld at 20 Portman Square,* she told Vita Sackville-West that she had been indulging in 'those labyrinthine antics which is called being intimate with Ottoline; I succumb: I lie; I flatter; I accept flattery; I stretch and sleek, and all the time she is watchful and vengeful and mendacious and unhappy and ready to break every rib in my body if it were worth her while.'[7] There is no evidence that Ottoline had done anything to deserve such a description; the mendacity of which Virginia most regularly accused her might more properly be described as the prudence of having refused to disclose to Bloomsbury any precise details of her personal life. Integrity, to Virginia and her friends, still meant total candour; they could not forgive Ottoline for her enraging willingness to spread gossip while remaining discreet about herself.

It is tempting to see a flicker of guilt in the letter Virginia sent Ottoline a couple of months later in which she acknowledged her passion for making up stories about her, 'the wilder the better'; certainly, 1930 marked a sea change in their friendship. There would still be betrayals – Ottoline was horrified when David Cecil told her that Virginia had whispered that he was lucky never to have seen her real character – but they were rare enough to be forgiven.

Virginia, more than most, judged people by their settings and backgrounds. She had heard about Welbeck; she had seen Ottoline at Bedford Square and at Garsington; it all seemed very grand to her curious eyes, grand and artificial. It was not until she had become familiar with Ottoline in her new Gower Street surroundings that she began to see how little the background had ever mattered. Vita Sackville-West flourished best, she felt, when placed in the romantic setting of Knole; Ottoline, by contrast, continued to be as vivid, as idiosyncratic and as unselfconsciously bizarre whether you put her in a Lyons Corner Shop or in Windsor Castle. And so, while Lytton had

---

* Samuel Courtauld (1876–1947) was one of the first British collectors of Impressionist and Post-Impressionist art. He funded the Tate Gallery's French collection in 1923 and gave his own collection, and his home, to the University of London, endowing it as the Courtauld Institute of Art. Ottoline went to many of his parties.

hurried to spread the word of tragic decay and fallen grandeur, Virginia looked with her own eyes for the first time and saw that he had been talking nonsense. Nothing had changed, except, in her view, for the better; stripped of the trappings of a more ostentatious life, Ottoline's character emerged more clearly, and Virginia decided to revise the vocabulary in which she sought to contain her. In the past, she had described her as garish, mendacious, intriguing, outrageous; now, in the 1930s, she became fascinating, shabby, humorous and brave.

If we were to look for a single occasion on which Virginia changed her mind about Ottoline, it was probably a tea-party in November 1930 when Ottoline asked her to come and meet Yeats and de la Mare, described by her in two long and unusually enthusiastic letters. Virginia, who shared Ottoline's belief that Yeats was their greatest contemporary poet, was thrilled to be asked, but it was an almost irrelevant incident which left its mark on her. Ottoline had been sitting quietly over her embroidery while the three guests talked about Milton:

Then, as the talk got more and more rapt, refined and erratic, I saw Ottoline stoop her hand to what seemed a coal scuttle and apply it to her ear: An ordinary black ear trumpet it was, ungilt unfunnelled, and the apparition of this bare and ghastly object had somehow a sepulchral effect – and I cried out, in the midst of all the poetry. Heavens Ottoline, are you deaf? And she replied with a sort of noble negligence which struck me very much 'Yes, yes, quite deaf – ' and then lifted the trumpet and listened. Does that touch you? Well it did me, and I saw in a flash all I admire her for; and think what people overlook . . .[8]

The meeting with Yeats marked the beginning of what might, if only comparatively, be called the golden period of their friendship, but it was still capable of disruption. Virginia's account of the afternoon was rounded off with a reference to her hostess's 'obvious tortuousness and hypocrisy', while Ottoline's journal entry that evening carried the terse observation that Virginia had made a complete fool of herself in front of Yeats. Angry words were exchanged two years later when Virginia was rash enough to declare that no aristocrat was capable of writing decently and that any who did write ought to study her own books. Ottoline could hardly be expected not to see this as a direct criticism of the memoirs which Virginia was reading and helping to supervise, and she was almost as irritated when Virginia dismissed David Cecil's work as 'very frothy'. But it was the insult to herself which rankled most: 'For all my humility I am not a woman that can be patronised,' Ottoline wrote that evening. (3 February 1932) But Virginia apologised profusely the next day, saying she had been overcome by the fumes of aristocracy in Gower Street, and was forgiven entirely when she came to tea at the end of the month and gave Ottoline an exact description of her own writing method. From then on, they visited each other regularly, Virginia coming to tea to meet Elizabeth Bowen (a great success), Ottoline going to meet Edith Sitwell (less of one), Virginia coming to meet David Cecil's sister, Lady Hartington ('charming'), and Ottoline to join an old Bloomsbury gathering at the Woolfs' where they played a game in which each person had to name their secret desire. Ottoline did not disclose what her own had been, but she was much amused that flirtatious Mary Hutchinson should want to go and look at trees in South America. It would, Ottoline mused, be a charming subject for an embroidery picture, Mary at the window, with a young man scrambling up a tree to present her with some particularly luscious fruit . . .

By the end of 1932, Ottoline felt that she could truthfully describe Virginia as one of her closest women-friends. 'She has been much more affectionate and kind to me,' she wrote. 'She is critical, but is she more critical than I am myself?' (6 November 1932) The bond had been strengthened by Virginia's new sense that Ottoline had been extraordinarily ill-used by D. H. Lawrence. She had been reading Aldous Huxley's new edition of his letters and listening to Vita Sackville-West praising him to the skies on the wireless; although she had only ever heard him described in the most affectionate way by Ottoline, it seemed to Virginia that he had exploited her from the first. 'My word, what a cheap little bounder he was,' she wrote to Vita, 'taking her money, books, food, lodging and then writing that book.'[9] A cad, she thought, was the only word for him. But Virginia had never been fond of Lawrence and, now that she had begun to feel guilty about the way they had all treated Ottoline in the past, he, who had never been one of her circle, was an easy scapegoat.

Another bond was forged at that time when Ottoline's old enemy Logan Pearsall Smith suddenly started persecuting Virginia for failing to invite him to her parties. Briskly informed that she preferred not to have guests with a taste for slander, Logan grew venomous, and made an enemy as sharp-tongued as himself. To Ottoline, who had been mortified when one of her closest friends, Bob Gathorne-Hardy, took up the post of Logan's personal assistant, it was a joy to hear Virginia describing him as 'coarse and rank' and adding that he 'would, if he were a fish, stink, to put it plainly'. She could not have put it better herself.

Looking at each other with newly affectionate eyes, each woman saw the other as born out of her time. Virginia thought that Ottoline would have been most at home in the Carolean age of her playwright ancestress, the Duchess of Newcastle. Ottoline, who had just read what Virginia had to say about the duchess in *The Common Reader* and thought it 'superlatively good', felt that Virginia only became her real self when discussing the writers she most admired. That, she thought, was 'the set where Virginia is really at home ... Fanny Burney – Donne – Christina Rossetti. She moves among them with great ease and unselfconsciousness, happy, with lovely careless ease and grace ...' (9 November 1932) Virginia had confided in her that month about her traumatic experiences as a child, when Gerald Duckworth 'used to come into the bedroom after a party at night and help her undress and pawed her all over. "He sent me mad,"' Virginia told her and Ottoline readily accepted that this was the root, not only of Virginia's periods of insanity, but also of her manner. 'I rather fancy that the foolish things she says about people – spiteful things – are said from nervous shyness,' she wrote after agreeing with Virginia about the likely effect of Gerald's behaviour on a young and innocent girl. (9 November 1932)

If anything further was required to cement the friendship, it was provided in abundance by the redoubtable Dame Ethel Smyth, who bounced into Virginia's life in 1930 and into Ottoline's a couple of years later, falling extravagantly in love with both of them.

Dame Ethel, the best-known female composer of her time, was a law unto herself. You might love her or loathe her; you could not possibly ignore her. Ottoline had known about her for years (the only man Dame Ethel had ever loved, Harry Brewster, had competed with Philip for her attention at the dinner-party given by Arthur and Eugenie Strong in 1901; Brewster's sister, Clothilde, had married one of Philip's closest friends, Percy Feilding). She had listened to Dame Ethel's Mass in D and her most famous operatic work, *The Wreckers*; she must have been familiar with the stories of Dame Ethel at Holloway Prison, where she conducted concerts with a toothbrush. Dame Ethel, a fearful snob, longed to know Ottoline, but it was on Virginia that she first descended, coming down, in Virginia's description, like a wolf on the fold, shouting, singing, shabby as a washerwoman and listening to nobody but herself. Having won Virginia, she felt ready to advance on Ottoline, but their first meeting, arranged by Virginia at Dame Ethel's suggestion, was doomed by the presence of Cyril Connolly, whom Ottoline hated so much that she would run away down a street to avoid being forced to invite him into her home. It was a bad start, but Dame Ethel was a determined old lady and by 1933 she had got what she wanted. 'You have made a complete conquest of old Ethel,' Virginia told Ottoline on 7 October 1933, and added, thankfully, 'All her love is transferred to you.'

Ethel's love was a gift which Ottoline often felt she could gladly have done without, but she, like Virginia, found it impossible to resist the great gale of affection which now blew with equal force upon them both. Writing to each other about Ethel, they described her as a buccaneer, a pirate and sea dog; for all their groans, it is clear that they were very fond of her. 'I had an invasion today from our old buccaneer,' Ottoline wrote to Virginia in 1933. 'She seemed as if she turned the room into a raging sea, she at the helm of a tempest-tossed boat – I felt as if I had been wrecked after she had gone. But I like her. I think she has the kindest heart under all the bluff Sea Captain manner . . .'[10] It was not her emotions but her way of showing them which was so exhausting to her friends. 'Are you drunk?' Ottoline asked her one evening in 1934 when Dame Ethel swept into the drawing-room like a tornado, singing and roaring, 'egotistical as a storm'. No offence was taken; the guest only gave another shout of laughter and said that she was drunk with praise before volleying off a round of extravagant compliments. She had her reward a few months later when Virginia was able to tell her that Ottoline had just described her as a trump, a magnificent Englishwoman, and her 'ideal of a great and noble nature'. They were sentiments which were cordially reciprocated; writing to Philip shortly after Ottoline's death, Dame Ethel told him that it would be complete truth, not sickly sentiment, to say, 'I worshipped her.'[11]

Worship is not the word that best describes Virginia's and Ottoline's feelings for each other. What they had achieved by the time Dame Ethel burst into their lives was mutual respect, tolerance and an affection which bordered on love. Virginia, who was not always considerate, took trouble to please. When she brought her niece Angelica to visit Ottoline and to meet Yeats, she nagged Vanessa into making sure that a letter of thanks was written while sending a grateful note of her own to exclaim: 'What a born giver you are!'* On another occasion, when Ottoline was about to visit India, she went out of her way to find people who knew it and who could give helpful advice. If she teased her and threatened to put Lady Ottolilia Morrett into her next work, it was with good humour and received in the same spirit. She had, after all, been making that threat for over ten years.

The letters which Ottoline wrote to Virginia in the 1930s are among the most spontaneous and revealing of all her correspondence. 'I came back so happy from my visit yesterday and I kept murmuring to myself all the way home, "I do love Virginia,"'[12] she told her after a tea to which she had come, said Virginia, looking like a weeping willow strung with pearls and exuding 'truth, humanity and loving kindness'. Ottoline brought with her the promise of the latest batch of her memoirs, on which Virginia had become her chief adviser. The new chapters were perused with breathless interest: 'Bertie, Lytton,

---

* Virginia had arranged an earlier visit for Angelica in 1929 when she came with her mother, two years after playing the part of the strange lady she had never met in a red wig and long black shawl for a charade at Charleston. Ottoline thought her an enchanting child. 'I loved her because she was so fond of her mother and stroked her hand in the most charming way,' she wrote after her first visit, adding that she was remarkably like her father, Duncan Grant. (January 1929)

Henry Lamb, Lawrence,' Virginia told Dame Ethel, who was itching to get her hands on the manuscript. 'Since Helen of Troy I don't think any woman can have launched so many ships.' Meanwhile, she continued to support and encourage the anxious authoress, telling her to hurry up and finish Garsington and to stop worrying about her style. 'You can't think what a joy to me your unpruned dew wet moon lit phrases are . . .'[13]

It is odd to think of such a perfectionist as Virginia Woolf admiring Ottoline's lushly romantic style, but there was nothing insincere in her praises; describing Ottoline's prose to another friend, she summarised it as top-heavy, like a flight of owls in the afternoon, yet beautifully balanced. Ottoline needed all the encouragement she could get. 'I have actually begun Garsington,' she told Virginia in 1933 ' – how the Devil can I ever do it?' And a month later, when she had been reading William Faulkner's "Mistral" and groaning at her own incompetence: 'I feel in despair about the Garsington part of the Memoirs . . . I try and try and it seems to me perfectly deadly dull, I mean the way I am doing it. I long to tear it to pieces as I do a new and unbecoming hat!'[14] We have Virginia to thank for the fact that she did not tear up what is arguably her best work, an imaginative rendering of her 1915 visit to Bolsover with Russell. 'I had wanted it to be the inner vision . . . but I *see* quite clearly it failed.' Luckily, Virginia was on hand to reassure her.

New friends such as John Hayward and Francis Hackett, both of whom regarded themselves as Ottoline's intimate confidants, received letters about the people she had known, loved and quarrelled with in the Bedford Square and Garsington years. Ottoline was writing these letters alongside her memoirs and they were for her a way of trying her impressions on a new audience. There is nothing in her letters to either which she did not intend to write about for her posthumous public. But Virginia was allowed to share her private feelings. Only to her could Ottoline admit that she really did not like women any more. Hilda Douglas-Pennant, who had done her best to wreck her marriage, had been 'queer and narrow', Ethel Sands was too worldly and cold, Margot Asquith too noisy and self-centred. (Ottoline was furious with Margot for trying to make out after Henry Bentinck's death that he had remained secretly in love with her when in fact Philip had once almost been thrown out of Henry's house for praising Margot, whom he detested.) Frieda Lawrence could be endured, but not with grace; as for Brett, 'no one was such a Judas to me as she, Iago and Judas'.[15] One wishes Virginia had asked her why, if she disliked women so much, she chose only to have women working for her; instead, she asked why she invited so few women to her parties. Ottoline had a brisk answer ready: petticoats, she said, invariably muffled good conversation.

Virginia, like Ottoline, was much courted by young men, poets and novelists, many of them homosexual, who were shrewd enough to know the value of a few famous friends. Ottoline had always loved helping the young, but she admitted to Virginia that she felt a little frightened by these youths, so skilled at masking their thoughts with a languid manner. Stephen Spender, for example, had told her that he adored Virginia, a compliment which she promptly passed on, but was he sincere? 'I don't know what goes on inside him,' Ottoline confessed when Spender was visiting her almost every day to glean information on a book about Henry James which he was planning to write; '. . . these young fellows seem to me so cold and aloof and so half-awake – probably a great deal goes on that they don't let anyone as old as I am see. They come and go like automatons with smiling superior masks and a few cynical phrases. William Plomer is just the same.'[16] Virginia agreed. The Stephens and Williams were always charming, she wrote back, but '[their] minds are refrigerators, and souls blank paper'.*[17]

Virginia's nephew, Julian Bell, died in the Spanish Civil War in the summer of 1937. Vanessa was devastated and in need of all her sister's attention. Temporarily out of touch with her friends, Virginia was shocked to hear that Ottoline had suffered a stroke that year which had temporarily paralysed her and might still kill her. 'Please don't wave your adieu just yet,' she wrote, and added that she hoped Philip might find time to send a line about her progress. That, sadly, was all the encouragement he had ever needed to return to his old dream of winning Virginia's love.

Ottoline never saw Philip's letters to Virginia, which now lie with her own in the Sussex University archives: Virginia did not want to upset her with any knowledge about what was an intensely embarrassing situation. Here was Ottoline, dying, in pain and pathetically anxious about her husband's welfare, and here was Philip assuring her that Ottoline was in the pink of good health and begging for letters from 'the most wonderful creature in the world'. She did, reluctantly, send him a friendly letter which required no answer. Back came the reply, telling her she had made him feel absurdly happy to have a letter all of his own, because she had sent it (as he asked) to his club. He went on to say how little he had to offer her before cataloguing every occasion on which they had met, a day at Garsington when he thought he had offended her, a drive they had once taken together, the three times when Leonard and she had asked him to stay on his own. If only, he concluded, they could be alone together; could she

---

* But it was Virginia who was the first to encourage Stephen Spender to think it was smart to decry her old friend: 'Lord! what a grind these Ottoline parties are,' she wrote to him in 1934.

meet him at St Paul's, or at the National Gallery? The letter ran to six full pages.[18] Prudently, Virginia decided not to give him any more encouragement.

Ottoline's death put an end to an awkward situation. Philip wrote to break the news to Virginia himself and to ask her to write an obituary. A fortnight later, he asked her to come and collect her legacy of a shawl or a ring and showed her – a tempting spectacle to an inquisitive visitor – the massive pile of Ottoline's journals laid out on a stool. He touched her hand as he gave her the ring, Virginia wrote; it made her feel uncomfortable.

She paid a last visit to Gower Street in August 1938. Philip, lying in bed in a lemon-coloured jersey, told her that he had been reading Ottoline's journals, but not what was in them. She had the impression that he had become disillusioned about Ottoline and wondered what he had discovered. Millie gave her one of Ottoline's shawls and told her that Philip was terribly lonely; nobody but the family came to see him. It was as strong a hint as Millie felt able to give, but Virginia decided not to commit herself to further visits. It was Ottoline she had loved, Ottoline whose death had left her feeling, she told Dame Ethel on 23 April 1938, 'rather lacerated . . . can't help feeling a queer loveliness departed'.

22

FRIENDSHIPS AND RENEWALS II

'I know I have given love, affection, interest and sympathy. It has often been trampled on, abused or misunderstood and derided, but that doesn't matter ... Self-satisfaction is death.'

OM, *Journal*, November 1929

In 1917, Siegfried Sassoon had been embarrassed by Ottoline's unconventional clothes and sceptical about her ill-health. At the age of forty, he fell in love with Stephen Tennant, a nineteen-year-old Narcissus whose ruling obsessions were his health and his wardrobe. The uncrowned king of the social columns, Stephen's radiant appearances in silver cloaks and made-to-measure beggar's rags, his lips rouged, his blond hair newly waved, secured him the attention he adored. Beautiful and capricious, he held Sassoon by the dangerous combination of need and cruelty which enslaved Oscar Wilde to Lord Alfred Douglas. Happily for Sassoon, the times were a little more tolerant and the passion shorter-lived.

The first that Ottoline heard of the affair was when Sassoon sent her an ecstatic postcard in the late summer of 1928, while he was taking Stephen, and Stephen's nanny, on an Italian tour. Despite the fact that his own function had been to act as chauffeur, banker and valet – he only with difficulty dissuaded his friend from wearing a pretty coral necklace out to meals – he came back to England more enraptured than ever.

The death during their tour of Stephen's adored mother and a sudden decline in his health – he was tubercular – bound Sassoon to him even more closely. Wilsford Manor, the Wiltshire house in which Stephen and his friends had posed for Cecil Beaton's camera-lens in 1927, became the exquisite retreat of an invalid, with Sassoon using his position as nurse-companion to drive younger friends away. Stephen, while grateful, was oppressed by such dogged and unamusing love.

From 1928 until 1933, Ottoline was an understanding confidante for Sassoon's obsession. He had always lived an active outdoor life, writing only after midnight; now, as Stephen's nurse, he spent his days sitting in a silver-and-white bedroom reading children's stories to the invalid or spraying the air with one of the fifty-odd scent bottles without which existence was deemed intolerable. (It was Stephen's habit, when he went to his London home in Smith Square, to have a servant spray the rooms with scent before his arrival.) It was, Sassoon admitted to Ottoline, an almost unbearable existence; he was being crushed; she could not imagine the pain of giving everything to someone who took all you did for granted. Ottoline, while ready to do what she could by lavishing presents on Stephen and singing the praises of 'Sieg', was tempted to point out that his own response when she visited him in Edinburgh in 1917 had taught her just what it felt like.

She made her first visit to the silver bedroom in Smith Square in January 1929. No stranger to the scent bottle herself, she almost fainted at the richness of the amber odour which hung in the air. Stephen, elegant as always in a pastel sweater, was at his most charming. He was amusing, gay, and even rather nice, Ottoline noted; she also thought him dispassionate, spoilt and far too rich for his own good. '*Fatal facility,*' she added sternly. 'Fortune suffocates those she spoils.' (16 January 1929) It seemed to her an undisguised blessing when he finally dropped Sassoon in 1933. Sassoon almost immediately announced his engagement to Hester Gatty, a young woman who was observed to bear an uncanny resemblance to Stephen. Ottoline kept up her friendship with the invalid, always treating him as a frivolous, precocious child. 'Do let's have a scent gossip,' he would beg, accompanying the request with a handsome bottle, but he seemed pleased when, tired of discussing the relative merits of L'Infini or Le Moment Suprême, she sent him, in 1936, three of her favourite Conrads. Stephen was thrilled: *Lord Jim*, he told her, had been such a revelation!

In the summer of 1933, Ottoline wrote that she had been to visit Sassoon's home in Teffont Magna near Salisbury and that he had taken her to meet 'a most wonderful woman'. Her name was Edith Olivier.

A rector's daughter of almost exactly Ottoline's age, Edith lived at the Daye House (less formally known as the Dog House) at Wilton. Small, dark and full of fun, Edith was the devoted friend of a group of young men who appealed to her love of the fantastic, encouraging her to dress up and play the fool as elegantly as they did themselves. Stephen Tennant advised her on make-up and clothes; Cecil Beaton photographed her; Rex Whistler illustrated her books with wispy charm; all she needed was for Evelyn Waugh to put her in a novel. It was one of Ottoline's most constant complaints that she could never find a woman who really interested her; it had occurred to Sassoon that she and Edith would have a lot in common.

It seems that they did, and Edith was entranced to meet a woman who could keep up a steady flow of appreciation of her surroundings while walking at a brisk pace in high red shoes and showing a fascinated interest in her hostess's stories of a Wiltshire childhood. It was, Edith noted approvingly, quite a feat. Ottoline was swept off to Ashcombe to be photographed by an excited Cecil Beaton the following day,* and a candlelit dinner with Sassoon rounded off what Edith thought had been an enchanting visit. Ottoline's only reservation was that Edith never stopped talking about herself; to be fair to Edith, her young men-friends had never given her the chance to do anything but listen.

An affectionate correspondence began, but it was after the Morrells came to the Daye House as paying guests for two weeks in the summer of 1936 that Edith became one of Ottoline's greatest admirers; recording the stay in her diary, she said that she had never enjoyed herself more. Ottoline made use of the visit to get on with her memoirs and one night she read them her portrait of Katherine Mansfield. 'She set her before us completely – body, soul and spirit,' Edith wrote. 'It seemed as if a little ghost-like figure had been created and was standing in the room; and at the moment when this impression was complete, all the lights suddenly went out.' Philip had found a candle, and she read on in the darkened room, 'the candlelight playing on her face till she too looked like a ghost, and her voice came from some remote distance. That is the kind of happy accident which Ottoline seems to call up wherever she is. She creates her own setting and speaks out of it.'[1] On another evening, David Cecil and his wife (he had married Desmond and Molly MacCarthy's daughter Rachel) came to dinner and David coaxed Ottoline into telling stories about the old days at Bedford Square while they all sat spellbound. 'I *could not* have enjoyed anything more,' Edith repeated. 'Talk is always good when David comes, but this was Ottoline's night.'[2]

---

* Beaton's more famous photographs of Ottoline in evening dress date from her second visit to Edith Olivier in 1936. Dramatic though the photographs are, they present an image rather than a character.

Like Sassoon, David Cecil had heard Ottoline lamenting that she had no women-friends: it was his idea that the half-Irish Ottoline would get on well with the Anglo-Irish novelist Elizabeth Bowen (Mrs Alan Cameron), then living in London. Ottoline was introduced to her in 1931, shortly after she had inherited Bowens Court and was contemplating a return to Ireland. 'I cannot tell if we shall be friends as yet,' Ottoline wrote, but she was sufficiently impressed to reread Miss Bowen's works and to introduce her to Virginia (who was charmed and visited her in Ireland). By 1932, Ottoline thought Elizabeth was one of the women she liked best. 'It's such a relief to meet a woman who has spirituality and a certain poise,' she wrote in January. 'She has the background of the aristocrat which helps us to understand each other.' Wit was something she met too rarely in women; Miss Bowen, who once described Edith Sitwell as 'a high altar on the move', was one of the delightful exceptions. Later, however, Ottoline took against her, on the odd grounds that she was obsessed with looking stylish.

The curiosity which kept Ottoline young led her to continue the search for women with whom she could establish friendship. Not all of them were so bohemian as one would suppose from the apocryphal story told by William Plomer of an old lady hissing in his ear that Ottoline had betrayed her class. (Her Majesty the Queen Mother, when the author mentioned this story to her, thought that it threw a dubious light on the status of the old lady rather than on her relation.) To old friends like Ettie Desborough and Margot Asquith, Ottoline added David Cecil's 'lovely . . . frank and unpretentious sister' Lady Hartington and, until she proved to be a steadfastly silent guest at the tea-parties, Bryan Guinness's wife, formerly Diana Mitford. (Her face hung above the table like a beautiful harvest moon, Ottoline sighed, round, perfect, silent.) But these were essentially social friendships and she longed for the sisterly, intimate exchanges that she had known for a time with Katherine Mansfield. An attempt to make friends with the poet Charlotte Mew was a failure: Miss Mew refused to speak to her after Ottoline had dared to criticise her style in one of her letters. Djuna Barnes, whose novel, *Nightwood*, had been greatly admired by Ottoline and passed on to Virginia, came to Gower Street to be inspected and interrogated, but Ottoline's inquisitiveness got the better of her good manners. 'I offended her very much by asking if she was a sapphist,' she wrote sadly in November 1936; 'it seemed a natural question as her book is about them.' Miss Barnes's irritation did not last; she was one of the few new friends who took the trouble to come and sit with Ottoline the following year when she was too ill to entertain or to go out.

Young women who showed no sign of wanting to do anything with their lives held no great interest for Ottoline. An exception was Dilys Powell, a young poet who was first noticed by Ottoline when she wrote a thoughtful appraisal of T. S. Eliot in 1931. Dilys's first visit to Gower Street went well; on the second, Millie led her aside to tell her how struck Her Ladyship was by her beautiful high cheekbones; did she by any chance have Red Indian blood? Dilys, who had a good sense of humour, gravely regretted to inform her that she did not. In the drawing-room, the conversation turned to Kot, for whom Dilys shared Ottoline's affection and concern. They agreed to keep each other informed about his state of mind. It was Ottoline's unfailing kindness to him which filled Dilys with admiration for her.

Fond though she became of Ottoline, Dilys remained baffled by her marriage; Philip's invitations to her to come and look at books or drawings in his library upstairs were relentlessly persistent and caused her to dread visits to Gower Street. Ottoline's older friends met her questions about him with shrugs and smiles, and she had the impression that something strange was being concealed. It was more comfortable to go out with Ottoline alone. The reward could be an unexpected introduction: she met Auden when they went to see the play he had written in collaboration with Christopher Isherwood, *The Dog Beneath the Skin*, and shared Ottoline's instant liking for him. The price was the embarrassment she felt whenever they went to a restaurant and found themselves being treated as an impromptu cabaret. Dilys cringed when the waiters started climbing on tables to get a better view, but Ottoline seemed oblivious, sailing forward with her head held high and her silk cloak billowing behind her.* The clothes which the young wore in the thirties were unabashedly designed to make their wearers noticed; Ottoline was stared at because she looked, as she had for the past thirty years, as if she had walked out of another age.

In 1928, knowing that the operation on her jaw had left her with a terrible facial disfigurement, Ottoline thought she would never want to show herself in public again. A year later, she was being more social than ever before. It was as if her brush with death had made her want to seize everything that life could offer.

Deafness made it hard for her to enjoy the noisy gatherings of celebrities which took place at the homes of Sybil Colefax and Samuel Courtauld; she preferred the relative calm of lunch- or dinner-parties at which she could hear what was being said. What she heard was

---

* This may be an exaggeration; when Dilys Powell told the story for a radio programme about Ottoline in 1973, the waiters only 'practically' climbed on the tables. Interviewed by the author in 1990, she was sure the waiters had actually done so.

not always welcome. She never entered Arnold Bennett's house again after he put her next to him at lunch and told her that all her friends were drunks, but she remembered him with gratitude for having introduced her to Thornton Wilder and Max Beerbohm. Wilder became her adviser on the new American novel. Tall and shy with a quick stammering voice, he urged her to stop praising his own books and start reading William Faulkner. It was good advice; it was unfortunate that Ottoline's indecipherable hand prevented her from communicating her enthusiasm to her London friends. *Which* book did she want them to read? they asked despairingly. 'The Sand and the Fairy'? 'The Sindbad Fury'?*

She was delighted to meet Wilder and his sister on their visit to England, but it was Max whom she adored. The Beerbohms had been living in England for several years by 1929 and Ottoline had often exchanged friendly words with Florence at parties, but it was not until she sat next to Max at Bennett's dinner-table that she realised why his friends were so attached to him. He was, she wrote a week or two later, 'an enchanting child but a child with immense taste'. (January 1929) The wit of Bloomsbury was often tinged with cruelty; Max, while always funny, was never unkind. If he was among her tea-guests, as he often now was, she could rely on him to see that the conversation never became vicious or dull. There was always a danger that mysticism would rear its cloudy head when James Stephens was present; talk of elves and leprechauns was never far away, and only Max could always be relied on to save the day with a joke and a deft turn of the conversation. He did it perfectly, but he never admitted to having done it deliberately. When Ottoline once thanked him and said that she really could not bear any more of Stephens's nonsense, Max only smiled and said, 'Oh, but sublime nonsense.' She felt lucky to have found such a friend.

H. G. Wells was one of the older writers who were regular visitors to Gower Street in the thirties, with and without his mistress, the fascinating Moura Budberg whom Ottoline first met when she was with Gorky; and Ottoline was often among the dinner-guests at the flat in Chiltern Court. There was, she wrote, only one occasion when she saw Wells, 'who I . . . feel such affection for', reduced to silence and that was when he made the mistake of asking Shaw to dinner. The other guests – Ottoline, the Guedallas and Rose Macaulay – had looked at their watches and prayed for peace while Wells grew redder in the face by the minute, but nothing could stop the flow of Shaw once he had started. 'His efficiency in talk is complete,' Ottoline wrote when she was at last free to creep home to bed. That was in 1931; she never asked Shaw to Gower Street, dreading a similar ordeal.

* *The Sound and the Fury* was published in 1929.

Wells was already falling out of fashion by the 1930s; the figure who drew the young like filings to the magnet of Ottoline's tea-table was Yeats. His kindness, as they soon discovered, was unfailing to any young man or woman who cared about poetry.

Ottoline had become close to both Yeats and his wife in the early 1920s when they were helping her to get over Tiger's death; she remained convinced that he, with the exception of Bertie, was the only man of genius among her friends. They 'all seem such *little* men compared to him', she wrote in May 1929, after he had visited her twice in a week. Knowing that she was offering her young protégés a treat and that Yeats was happy to bask in their admiration, she enjoyed planning who the guests should be and watching their excitement. 'WBY came when I had a group of starlings to meet him, with the one old dove Æ,' she noted in December 1933; Stephen Spender, Herbert Read, Bryan Guinness, John Sparrow and David Cecil were the lucky starlings that week who heard Yeats talking about Gerard Manley Hopkins, the Greek dramatists and then about his own first visit from James Joyce, who began by announcing: 'I have no respect for your opinion', and 'You are too old for me to do you any good', before pulling out a pocketful of poems and reading them aloud.

The young men loved it, and so did Ottoline, until the shadow of Walter Turner fell between her and her old friend. A warning shot was fired across Yeats's bow at a tea-party for Ethel Smyth in 1935 at which he was rash enough to declare his admiration for Turner's poetry. Ottoline gave him a glacial look; somebody – de la Mare, Dilys Powell and Hope Mirrlees were also present – hurriedly changed the subject. Two years later, Yeats did the unforgivable: not only did he include Turner's poetry in an anthology which excluded Wilfred Owen, but he singled out *The Aesthetes* for praise in his introduction. Clearly, he had no thought of offending Ottoline, although he knew that she was caricatured in the book. He tried to say so, but Ottoline was too angry to believe him. 'I still cannot understand what induced you to write as you did,' she told him in a letter for which Philip had been required to compose no less than three drafts. 'The book after all was not poetry. There was no need for you to mention it at all.' (10 March 1937) Yeats's attempts to repair the damage were angrily rejected. 'Yeats fini,' Ottoline scribbled on his last letter; the only public evidence left of their long friendship were two lines he had written about Garsington's garden in one of his poems: 'where the peacock strays / With delicate feet upon old terraces.'

The image of Yeats surrounded by admiring young poets at Ottoline's tea-table invites comparison with that of a typical literary hostess using her celebrity-guest as a way to hook in a cluster of younger luminaries. The analogy is false, as her friendship with one very unsuccessful young poet shows.

Walter D'Arcy Cresswell, who came from New Zealand, spent two years in London from 1929 to 1931. Jim Ede, author of a life of Gaudier-Brzeska, took him on his first visit to Gower Street in 1930; Ottoline's photograph album that year shows a small man crouched under the statues in the garden with a terrified expression. Anxious to make him feel welcome although she did not have a high opinion of his writings, Ottoline got more than she had bargained for; by December, Cresswell was feeling sufficiently at home to turn up brandishing a pot of ginger as a festive tribute to her character, telling a series of loud and embarrassingly awful jokes before, having dropped his teacup, he pulled down his paper hat and went to sleep on the sofa. On his next visit, he announced that he only came for the introductions Ottoline was able to give him and stopped tea-party conversation with a ten-minute monologue on Napoleon, his hero. 'Oh dear,' Ottoline sighed, but she did not discourage him from calling on her until, on 16 July, he wrote her a wild letter announcing that she was Circe and made a beast of every man she met, but that she had met her match in him. There were no more invitations.

Cresswell returned to New Zealand in 1931; writing to beg for news of London and the literary world, he told Ottoline that his visits to Gower Street had been the highlight of his stay in England; it was the beginning of an odd and touching friendship which lasted until her death. For him, she became not only a provider of presents – books, ties and poetry articles – but a lifeline to the glamorous world to which he longed to return; for Ottoline, he became almost an extension of her journal, a friend in whom she could confide with no fear of spreading gossip or having her words used against her. Her letters to him remind us how widely read she was – references to Gertrude Stein, Aeschylus, Santayana, Newman, Faulkner and Sean O'Faolain are among those which crop up in the correspondence – but they also often throw an illuminating sidelight on her character. Despite her ardent passion for the literary life, it is the note of sound common sense which she most often rang in these letters, telling Cresswell that there was no point in expecting to be able to live by poetry and urging him to use his knowledge to write a realistic novel about New Zealand. 'I don't say, "Commercialise your pen," which sounds so awful,' she told him, 'but . . . the more you write the better for your style, and if you have chosen the life of letters, obviously you must endeavour to live by it! Don't be cross with me.'[3] It was only in Cresswell that she confided in 1932, when Catherine Carswell painted an unflattering picture of her as an avaricious harpy in her hurriedly-written life of Lawrence. To show her distress to friends in

London would have been to risk stirring up just the kind of gossip and speculation that Ottoline feared and hated; instead, she put her own view of Lawrence into her letters to Cresswell. The essential point she had to make was that it was impossible, in Lawrence's case, and wrong, to separate the teller from the tale. 'For he is almost unique in that he had no public life . . . he and his life and his writings are all one. He always wrote about his life. There is hardly a page that doesn't tell of some experience with Frieda.'[4] Nobody, she added, could understand Lawrence's writings if they did not take his relationship with his wife into account. Drawing up a list of Lawrence's best work for Cresswell to read, she praised his stories, the last poems, parts of *The Rainbow* and of *Lady Chatterley's Lover*. But the memory of *Women in Love* still rankled; she never mentioned it.

The correspondence continued over six years with only one hitch, when Millie sent the puzzled Cresswell the *Vogue* magazines intended for Junia Anrep in Russia; Ottoline was too ill in 1937 to supervise the packaging. Cresswell was planning a return to London when he heard of Ottoline's death. 'It saddens all my return to England,' he wrote to Philip. 'She was part of my future . . .' He came, nevertheless, and ended his life in drudgery, working as a nightwatchman at Somerset House.

'The best of the *young* men is Spender,' Ottoline wrote to Cresswell, before adding that she was talking about his character rather than his poetry which seemed to her, at best, to be 'quite nice and charming'.[5]

Counting the number of visits a young man made to Gower Street is no way to ascertain how well Ottoline knew him: Christopher Hassall made at least eight visits and left no strong impression behind. Stephen Spender's frequent attendances were, however, recorded with affection and enthusiasm. William Plomer had brought him to his first tea in September 1933; two months later, he plucked up the courage to ask if he could come on his own to enlist her help with his book about Henry James. He was naïve but rather delightful, Ottoline wrote on 16 November, 'very beautiful like a tall schoolboy with starlike eyes and a happy open face – a rather entertaining way of talking but he talks a great deal'. Spender, while storing up for later use the amusing fact that his hostess's earring had fallen into her teacup and that her dress had offered him an unexpected glimpse of a naked breast, appears to have enjoyed himself. The following week, Ottoline was asked to lunch to meet his friend, Anthony Hyndman.

To Spender, Ottoline seemed such an unreal figure that he felt no qualms about making fun of her later and declaring that nothing in London was more tedious than a tea with Ottoline. He had, as he wrote in a letter to the author, been given the impression that it was fashionable to ridicule her; many years later, he regretted having done so. She had interested him then, not so much for herself as for her friends like Yeats, Eliot and de la Mare, and for the help she could give him on his book. Ottoline, too, had her reservations. To Virginia, she had admitted that she had no idea what was going on in Spender's mind behind his smile; to herself, she sighed that Spender was no better than the rest of the young poets when it came to trying to monopolise the attention of Eliot or Yeats, and that he became 'silly and giggly' when he was among his friends. She preferred it when she saw him alone or with Tony Hyndman, who 'isn't a bad youth – indeed, I rather like him'. (3 April 1934) But the real pleasure for her was in the excuse Spender's project gave her to talk about Henry James, whose affable presence she still missed. Ethel Sands and Theodora Bosanquet, James's last secretary, were invited round to contribute their recollections while Ottoline took out his books again, to wonder at 'his blest old genius ... the tremulously passionate little old wand' breathing life into every page. He was to literature, she decided, what Michelangelo had been to sculpture; none could touch him. (21 November 1934)

Ottoline was once again deep in James's novels three years later when Spender, hearing how ill she was, came to make a last visit to Gower Street and to introduce her to his wife. Ottoline, who had been feeling sadly neglected by her younger friends, was overjoyed: 'Both so very nice,' she wrote when they had gone, 'and Stephen has improved and matured and he has, I am sure, such a lovely character. We talked of Henry James who he loves as much as I do and I was so happy.' (19 October 1937)

Writing to Cresswell on 17 October 1936, Ottoline told him that she was working hard on her memoirs, but that she would never publish them in her lifetime. 'How could I write frankly about people, which is the only way I could write, and publish it? ... You see altho' I appear so good-natured and I am, it doesn't prevent my eyesight being sharp and critical and ruthless. Few people pass through the gates into intimacy.' She had always been determined to avoid malice in her memoirs, but honesty was proving to be quite as lethal a weapon.

Difficult though that critical eyesight made it to achieve a close friendship with her, the Visitors' Books reveal a breathtaking number of acquaintances who came to Gower Street on a regular basis. Henry Yorke, whose novels were written under the name of Henry Green, had known her slightly since the days when he and Anthony Powell had bicycled out from Oxford to the Garsington Sunday gatherings in 1926; from 1928 on, he became a regular attendant. Several of the young men looked upon Ottoline as a kind of understanding aunt – Sebastian Sprott, one of Lytton's protégés, spent hours telling her how difficult it was for him and for Morgan Forster only really being able to desire men who they saw as their social and mental inferiors, a syndrome which Ottoline was better able to understand after her relationship with Tiger; others made a point of saying that she had petrified them with her inquisitiveness about their love-lives. Her favourites, apart from David Cecil and Spender, were Plomer (principally for a splendid evening at his home in February 1932, when Walter Sickert and she were persuaded to sing music-hall duets) and Henry Yorke.

At a time when Graham Greene's career was only just beginning, Ottoline thought Yorke the most interesting writer of his generation. Thin and pale with a curving nose, piercing eyes and straight black hair, he had written his first dialogue-novel, *Blindness* (1926), while still at Oxford and had based the second, *Living* (1929), on his experiences of working at the family factory of which he later became managing director. He was, in Ottoline's view, very attractive, more than a little mad and wonderfully good company. She admired him in particular for his independence and his use of a broad social canvas; she shared his contempt for the way his contemporaries clustered together and puffed each other's reputations as high as the clouds. A romantic philanderer, Yorke amused her with his indignation about the way Bertie had traded in Dora for Peter Spence; it was the work of a moment for him to cast Dora as the abandoned heroine and to announce that Bertie's behaviour was typical of the way 'writers' behaved. (He refused to identify himself as a writer.) It fascinated her to listen to Yorke describing even the most mundane events; his imagination was, she wrote, extraordinary. But she liked him best when, after coming to lunch on his own one day, he suddenly hugged her and said: '"You are so nice!" That was delightful – and did me good,' she wrote. (25 January 1933)

Of Graham Greene's work, she had read only the unsuccessful *The Man Within* and been struck by what seemed to her an unusual spiritual quality in it, when she asked Greene and his wife Vivienne to tea in the autumn of 1930. She was interested enough to start a correspondence with him, but his nervousness puzzled her. 'He is afraid of something obviously,' she wrote, but she could not discover what it was and she did not believe him when he told her that he wrote only for commercial reasons. He was using cynicism as a mask, she was convinced, but she could not discover what lay behind it.

The spirit of active benevolence which had driven Ottoline all her life was as strong as ever in the last ten years. Writing to the author in the last week of his life, the poet George Barker described a visit from the unknown woman who had joined forces with T. S. Eliot to see that he was provided with a small regular income on which he could just survive.* At the time he was living in a cottage in a Dorset village.

> I looked up one morning and saw the longest of Austria's handmade Daimlers draw up at the little white gate. I saw my first historical hallucination step out of the car. This was a very tall figure garbed lavishly in grey silk . . . with what I took to be a prizewinning Cowes yacht balanced upon its marvellous auburn head. She wore pearls suspended from her fingers on little gold chains. I realised that I was being visited by a veritable vision . . . I think back with admiration and love on the enchanted spheres she inhabited. On her first visit she gave me two cups and saucers.[6]

There is no surprise in discovering that Ottoline should have wanted to help a young poet, or that she should have taken endless trouble over Eliot's crippled friend, John Hayward (until, that is, she saw Hayward leaving one of her parties in a large chauffeur-driven car and refusing to give another cripple, J. W. N. Sullivan, a lift home). A less likely object of benevolent interest was Wyndham Lewis.

Ottoline had known Lewis since the pre-war years of his quarrel with Roger Fry.† Since then, while often described as brilliant and extraordinary, Lewis had failed to gain wide recognition as a writer or an artist. In *One-Way Song* he sourly asked:

> If so you be the authenticated sage
> Of our epoch, why aren't you all the rage?

One reason was that his books, while breathtakingly clever, had an almost impenetrable style. Another was that a readiness to bite any hand which reached towards him had made him more enemies than were good for anyone still waiting to be appreciated. He made two visits to Garsington, but Ottoline had not seen him for almost ten years when he suddenly called at Gower Street in the summer of 1929. In the old days, he had struck her as a flamboyant sexual adventurer with all the swagger of a pantomime villain; that afternoon, it seemed to her that he had lost his bravura, although his mind was as sharp

---

* George Barker, who died in 1991, had only published a collection of thirty poems when Ottoline met him. He later became famous as the married man about whom Elizabeth Smart wrote in *By Grand Central Station I Sat Down and Wept*.

† In October 1913, three months after the opening of the Omega Workshops by Fry in Fitzroy Square, Wyndham Lewis, Frederick Etchells and two other artists who had done work for Omega distributed a circular to potential patrons in which they savagely attacked Fry.

as ever. She felt rather sorry for him. When he said he wanted to come to one of her teas, she readily issued an invitation.

The Visitors' Book does not reveal who the other guests were at the tea, but they did not enjoy themselves. Reporting the occasion in her journal, Ottoline wondered how anybody but Lewis could have managed to cast such gloom over the table simply by the way he devoured his bread and honey. None of the others had dared to speak, but as soon as they left, Lewis dropped his savage manner and became easy and charming, until she innocently passed on Eliot's messages of goodwill. It was, she supposed, understandable that Lewis should resent his friend's success, but Eliot had made many efforts to help Lewis in the past and she was shocked by the vindictiveness which he showed. Nevertheless, when Lewis asked her to tea in his studio and showed her some of his drawings, she found it hard to understand why he should have been denied success: they were 'superlatively good and the abstract ones I liked especially ... if *only* he hadn't such contempt, what a magnificent creature he would be.' Film, she guessed, might be his true *métier*, something like one of her own favourites, 'Caligari – slightly mad'. (November 1929) Rather to her surprise, Lewis said that he wanted to go on seeing her; she often went to the studio after that and, like many of Lewis's friends, remained baffled by the contrast between the savage public image and the courteous, friendly, private man whose only flaw was his terrible bitterness, his corrosive sense of failure.

'Charles Morgan, the author of *The Fountain*, comes now,' Ottoline told Cresswell on 12 July 1933. 'He is rather humourless and self-important, but I rather like him too . . .'

It was Koteliansky who introduced her to Morgan's books. She was not much taken by them and her reference to this visit, Morgan's third since 1929, suggests only a passing interest. It certainly does not lead one to guess that Ottoline was about to use him as the hero of an imaginary love-affair.

In the past, Ottoline had repeatedly emphasised her wish to enjoy what she had never found, a relationship in which there was no sexual element; in real life, as she now knew, she would never find it. She had been having an unusually difficult time with one of Philip's nervous phases in the summer of 1933 and, as always during these periods, she felt a desperate need to escape. Morgan made practically no visits to Gower Street, but Ottoline's journal shows that they were meeting frequently in London by the end of the summer and that she was becoming attached to him. He was twenty years younger than her and she had no illusions about his feelings; he was, she said, glad of the introductions she was able to give him, that was all. She was not sorry when he left in November to spend six months in Italy; he had, she told Kot, occupied too much of her time.

It all sounds very rational; what followed was not. It was during Morgan's absence that Ottoline conducted her strange one-sided affair. Every week, she wrote a letter to him, put it in an envelope – and clipped it into a book. 'What I feel intimate with is a sort of shadow self of you . . .' she wrote on one page: 'I have created an *unreal* CM whom I care for out of my own desires, and I feel intimate with this double, this imaginary self . . . the real CM is only a distant acquaintance. I wonder if you know you have another self?' (11 December 1933)

Morgan never did know, although he and Ottoline continued to meet after his return. We, too, are unlikely to discover what the imaginary lover learned about her. Somebody, Ottoline, or, perhaps, Philip after her death, went carefully through the little album and removed the letters, leaving only the stain of the rusty clips as evidence of this odd and secret attachment.

Ottoline's health had been frail since the operation of 1928; by the end of 1936, she was forced to admit that illness was overcoming her will-power. Her work at the hostel for the homeless now had to be abandoned; the tea-parties became increasingly irregular. The duke, who did not share her faith in Dr Cameron's miraculous powers and who was frantically worried about her, decided to take matters into his own hands, paying for Ottoline to spend three weeks being examined at Liverpool Hospital. But the doctor, Harry Cohen, thought to be one of the best diagnosticians in the country, was unable to give an encouraging account. Neither blood tests nor X-rays had revealed a specific illness; he could only say that Lady Ottoline had a bewildering variety of symptoms and that he admired her fortitude in the face of considerable pain. Ottoline, who secretly believed that no doctor could be better than her own beloved Dr Cameron, then in charge of the Sherwood Park Clinic at Tunbridge Wells, was not displeased.

Cohen made his investigation in January 1937; late in March, after her return from a visit with Aldous to see their friend John Sullivan in hospital, Ottoline suffered a form of stroke which left her unable to walk or eat. She felt, she wrote later, as though all the sinews in her body had melted. The duke wanted her to return to Liverpool; instead, Philip took her to Cameron's clinic where, she gaily told her friends, she had been brought back from the brink of death by a glass of champagne, the first alcohol she had ever tasted. Having been given a week to live, she was diagnosed as having poisoning of the nervous system (a fashionable cover-all explanation frequently employed by baffled doctors in the twenties and thirties) and diabetes. Diabetes was a new idea, and Ottoline was ready to take hope from any new suggestion. 'If it is in fact correct insulin will put me quite right and I shall not have to worry *at all at all*,' she wrote to her Irish friends, the Hacketts, on 21 April, and to Kot, a month later that, while still weak, she was 'more in the land of living and improving'.[7]

23

THE LAST YEAR: 1937–38

'I hate the safe and coward way.'
OM, *Journal*, 19 June 1913

Bertie was one of the few friends who visited Ottoline during the three months that she spent at the clinic. He was, she recorded, 'so gentle and nice – his old nice self'. Worried about his lack of money when he and Peter were expecting a child, she wrote from the clinic to ask George Santayana if he couldn't get one of his Rockefeller connections to help. Help duly came in the shape of a cheque from Santayana's nephew, George Sturgis, together with the promise of an allowance of £1,000 a year. 'I am so delighted about it and it is a great relief to me,' Ottoline wrote happily in her journal after hearing the news from Bertie in September 1937.

By August, although still very weak, Ottoline was well enough to go abroad with Philip, to Ascona and on to Lausanne, where her exotic clothes and gentle, uncondescending manner enchanted the young children of Marion Reymond. Back at Gower Street by October, she gallantly tried to revive her Thursdays, but the strain was too much for her; by November, she saw only the few old friends who were prepared to come and sit with her while she lay on a sofa. Bertie, Eliot, Juliette Huxley and Duncan Grant were regular visitors; all were dismayed to see how thin and exhausted she looked, and embarrassed by her husband's insistence that she was in far better health than he was himself. (He, as the youngest of the Reymond children had noticed, was looking rosy and confident, sauntering down to dinner in Lausanne in a splendidly frogged dinner-jacket of maroon velvet.)

Philip was determined that Ottoline was making a good recovery; the duke, who passionately wished for this, offered to pay for them to spend the winter on the French Riviera. The trip had to be postponed when Ottoline suffered another collapse. She returned to

Sherwood Park and, after being injected with a new wonder-drug called Prontosil, was ready to believe that 'dear old Dr Cameron' had found the cure at last. She was prepared to take some of the credit herself for her determination to beat off her mysterious disease and live: 'I am very self-willed as you know – obstinate one might almost call it,' she reassured an anxious Kot.[1]

At the end of February 1938, Ottoline saw a last handful of visitors – Eliot was the only old friend among them – before she and Philip set off for Cap Martin in the South of France. They had scarcely arrived before Philip began to complain of trouble with his heart. It was, in part at least, a psychosomatic illness based on a superstitious terror that he would die that year, at the same age as his father. The symptoms were alarming; at the end of the first week he could hardly move and talked of nothing but death. It was impossible to continue the holiday; instead, they returned to seek the opinion of Dr Cameron at Tunbridge Wells. 'It was a great anxiety waiting for [a] verdict and I was impatient,' she wrote in her journal, forgetting to note the date. 'I –.' And there the entries end.

Philip, although he was warned that he had 'an enlarged heart' and would be wise to lead a restful life, was quick to recover, but worry about him had put a terrible strain on Ottoline. Dr Cameron decided that she should remain at the clinic and continue to be injected with Prontosil until she showed signs of improvement. Ottoline made no objections.

Dr Cameron was not the best of doctors; it seems that he succeeded in killing his patient. Prontosil, which had only come on to the market in 1936, was still being treated with caution in 1938. It had been shown to be effective, but only as a cure for severe infections such as scarlet fever and erysipelas. It was not meant to be injected and it was strongly recommended that the treatment should be discontinued after seven days. Ottoline received daily double injections of Prontosil for four weeks.

By March 1938, serious misgivings were being expressed in the medical world about Dr Cameron's use of the drug at his clinic; on 20 April, Ottoline was told that Dr Cameron was dead. He had in fact committed suicide two days earlier.

Ottoline wrote her last letter to the duke on the evening of 20 April. She died the following morning while being injected with Prontosil by Cameron's assistant, Dr Gourliau. She was sixty-four years old. The cause of death was given as heart failure.

Ottoline was buried in the little churchyard on the Welbeck estate with only close members of the family attending the service. The memorial service was held on 26 April at St Martin-in-the-Fields, and was attended by almost all of Ottoline's friends. Virginia Woolf reluctantly wrote an obituary for *The Times*, not because she did not love Ottoline but because she disliked obituaries. David Cecil wrote a beautiful but rather florid one in which he compared her to Madame du Deffand and also to a Renaissance princess, 'her strange beauty clothed with a gorgeous fantasy that scorned fashion'. Margot Asquith wrote a dull piece on her beauty, her discerning love of art, and her kindness.

There could only be one Ottoline, as Lawrence had said; in the letters which rained down on Philip and Julian in the weeks after her death, her friends tried to express their sense of her greatness. Some described her as one of the most influential figures of her time; many spoke of the generosity she had shown and of the inspiration they had taken from her faith in their abilities; all spoke of her courage, both moral and physical, her readiness to stand up for what she believed in.

The Huxleys were living in Hollywood when they heard the news of Ottoline's death. 'I hope she did not die of unhappiness,' Maria wrote to Eddy Sackville-West after trying to explain to him how great a gap it would make in their lives. 'She gave me a complete mental reorientation,' Aldous told Philip in his letter of condolence. Julian Huxley described her simply as 'a great soul, and the finest character I know'. 'I send you all my sympathy, dear Julian,' T. S. Eliot began his letter to Julian after her mother's death, 'but I haven't much to spare; I mean that my first feeling is of the loss to myself . . . It is very difficult to think of things *without* anyone who meant so much to me.'[6] The letter which Philip kept beside his bed for many weeks came from one of Ottoline's youngest friends, Henry Yorke. It is worth quoting, for it gives a vivid impression of Ottoline's active benevolence at work. It is, I think, the letter that would have pleased her most.

Ottoline made such a difference to me, as she did to everyone she met, that I can't do anything else but write.

For an undergraduate to come over to Garsington or to be entertained as each one was in company with the older people staying there . . . was his first glimpse of the world outside and his first contact with literature and intellects not built up around dons or university life. And it came to be more than that because as one fell under Ottoline's influence she taught one for the first time to see things the way great open characters see them and one began to realise how petty one was beside her. Then, when one got to know her better still, she began to open to one her love for all things true and beautiful which she had more than anyone.

I for one have had the honour of knowing she created a standard which all my contemporaries who went there have kept as a standard from that day to this and we shall never lose it.

If it is any comfort to you and Julian at a time like this, do try and remember the good she did to literally hundreds of young men like myself who were not worth her little finger, but she took trouble over them and they went out into the world very different from what they would have been if they had not known her . . . no one can ever know the immeasurable good she did.[2]

Epilogue

Philip Morrell survived his wife by five years, continuing to live at Gower Street until bombing raids caused him to take refuge in the Connaught Hotel. By the time he died in 1943, his book on William Bentinck unfinished, he had abandoned his plan to write Ottoline's biography, although Alice Jones was still typing out the journals for him, and also his own memoirs.

From her death until now, Ottoline has been seen through the distorting lens of the letters, diaries and memoirs of the Bloomsbury Group. Her beauty was forgotten, her religious faith belittled and her generosity derided. No attempt was made to understand her, to examine her influence or to interpret her actions. When the second volume of Michael Holroyd's *Lytton Strachey* appeared in 1968, it presented a striking portrait of an untutored aristocrat of bizarre appearance whose sole ambition was 'to gate-crash her way into the secret world of the artist' and to use Lytton and his friends as the means by which to do it.[3] Judging her only from the point of view of Lytton's letters to Ottoline (hers to him were not then available), and from a selective reading of Virginia Woolf's letters and diaries, that was a reasonable conclusion for Mr Holroyd to draw. It did not, perhaps, seem to matter that the picture was incomplete: Ottoline had already sunk from being seen on her death as one of the most remarkable and influential women of her time, to the level of a grotesque caricature. Mr Holroyd was only presented with half of the story: I suspect that, if he had been able to see the papers which represented Ottoline's side of the tale, he would have altered his view of her.

I did sometimes wonder if I would find myself agreeing with the post-Bloomsbury view of Ottoline before I finished writing her biography. Certainly, she was capable of being autocratic and strong-willed – I was left in no doubt about that. She could be irritating and intimidating: I still cannot imagine without feeling a twinge of alarm what it would have been like to arrive at Garsington for the first time. But having lived with her, so to speak, for the past four years, I know that I shall miss her. I have been amused, touched, impressed, and never bored. Her sense of humour and her perceptiveness have made her a wonderful companion, but more than that, I have come to admire her brave determination never to let herself be defeated. There was so much more tragedy in her life than any of us could ever have known. To confront and overcome it as she did seems to me nothing short of heroic. It *is* a damnably difficult thing to live life fully, richly, gorgeously and courageously in such difficult circumstances as Ottoline's now prove to have been, but what mattered was her gift of that way of life to her friends. Her courage was their education.

Notes and Sources

The Portland Family Papers are held at the Nottingham County Archives and the Portland Archives at Nottingham University Library. All quotations from letters to Bertrand Russell from Ottoline are from the Russell Archives at McMaster University, Hamilton, USA, whose photocopied collection I have also used for my quotations from Russell's letters to Ottoline. (The originals are held by the Humanities Research Center [HRC], Austin, Texas.) HRC also holds the originals of letters to Ottoline from the Asquith family, Augustine Birrell, Dorothy Brett, Dora Carrington, John Cramb, Hilda Douglas-Pennant, T. S. and Vivien Eliot, Mark Gertler, Francis and Signe Hackett (the letters from Ottoline to the Hacketts are also in this collection), L. P. Hartley, John Hayward, Philip Heseltine, Aldous and Maria Huxley, Dorelia and Augustus John, Samuel Koteliansky, Henry Lamb, D. H. Lawrence, Desmond and Molly MacCarthy, William Maclagan, Katherine Mansfield, John Middleton Murry, Frank Prewett, Hester and Siegfried Sassoon, Gilbert and Sir Stanley Spencer, Lytton Strachey (exceptions are indicated in the text or source notes), Virginia Woolf, and W. B. Yeats.

There is a collection of Ottoline and Philip Morrell's letters to Virginia Woolf in the Monks House Papers at the University of Sussex. Samuel Koteliansky's letters from Ottoline and from Mark Gertler are held by the British Library, as are several letters between Lytton Strachey and Ottoline and between him and Duncan Grant which refer to Ottoline. These are indicated in the source notes.

Unless otherwise stated, all quotations from Virginia Woolf's letters are taken from the Hogarth Press six-volume edition.

Where quotations are given without a source, they have been taken from the Goodman collection of private family papers. These include the diaries of Ottoline's mother, Lady Bolsover, all of Lytton Strachey's letters from Ottoline, letters relating to Ottoline's death, the papers, journals, account-books and typescripts belonging to Ottoline, together with the memoirs and correspondence of Philip Morrell, their daughter Julian, and 'Hugh James', one of Philip's sons. The names of the two Morrell sons who are discussed in this book have been changed since they are both alive and have, indeed, been extremely co-operative and helpful in providing information.

I have banished the ampersand in my quotations. Ottoline was an enthusiastic underliner and user of the long Victorian dash as punctuation. It was not always possible to distinguish the dash from the underlining, and in these cases I have had to rely on my own judgement. I have occasionally acknowledged defeat and used the word [*illeg.*]: Ottoline's handwriting, while extraordinarily decorative, is difficult to decipher. 'My writing – ah! It is as changeable (also my spelling) as there are moods in this creature,' she told a reproachful Lytton Strachey on 13 March 1912, but with no sign of changing her ways. I have edited the spelling of Ottoline and her correspondents only where it might cause confusion. There were a few instances – one was a misreading by Sandra Jobson Darroch of Augustus John's declaration: 'let us be gay little heroes' as 'let us be gay like herpes' – where a silent correction of a published version seemed to be in order.

Abbreviations which appear in the text and source notes are as follows:

British Library (BL)
Goodman Papers (GP)
Humanities Research Center (HRC)
Monks House Papers (MHP)
Ottoline Morrell (OM)
Philip Morrell (PM)
Bertrand Russell (BR)
The Early Memoirs of Lady Ottoline Morrell 1873–1915 (*OM, I*)*
Ottoline at Garsington 1915–18 (*OAG*)*

CHAPTER 1: A PROTECTED GIRLHOOD 1873–92 [*pp. 11–28*]
1. Augusta Bentinck to the Fifth Duke of Portland, 7 July 1873 (Portland Papers, OM, PWK 437).
2. Arthur Bentinck to the Fifth Duke of Portland (Portland Papers, PWK 533).
3. *The Early Memoirs of Lady Ottoline Morrell 1873–1915*, ed. Robert Gathorne-Hardy (Faber, London, 1963), p. 70 (hereafter referred to as *OM, I*).
4. Ibid.
5. Portland Papers, PWK 1468.
6. *OM, I*, p. 284.
7. Margaret, Duchess of Newcastle, *Nature's Pictures drawn by Fancie's Pencil*, 1656, p. 387.
8. Galway Papers, GA/2 and GA 2/94 (Nottingham University Library).
9. *OM, I*, p. 84.

CHAPTER 2: FROM DAUGHTER TO WIFE 1893–1902 [*pp. 29–47*]
1. *OM, I*, p. 90.
2. Ibid., original version.
3. OM to Francis Hackett, 21 April 1937 (HRC).
4. Gladys Scott Thomson, *Mrs Arthur Strong* (Cohen & West, London, 1949), p. 47.
5. *OM, I*, p. 98.
6. OM to BR, 9–10 April 1911 (McMaster).

* The words 'original version' mean that I have quoted from the unedited version of the published memoirs. 'Original version only' indicates that I have quoted from a passage which was deleted from them.

NOTES AND SOURCES

7. OM to Francis Hackett, 21 July 1937 (HRC).
8. *OM, I*, p. 107.
9. Maud Cruttwell to OM, May 1899 (GP).
10. Vernon Lee to OM, 18 October 1899 (HRC).
11. OM—PM, 21 December 1901 (GP).
12. OM-PM, 24 December 1901.
13. OM-PM, 2 January 1902.
14. OM-PM, 7 January 1902.
15. The Duchess of Portland to Philip Morrell, 26 January 1902 (GP).

CHAPTER 3: MARRIAGE AND MOTHERHOOD 1902–7 [*pp. 51–68*]
1. *OM, I*, p. 147.
2. Ibid., p. 148.
3. Barbara Strachey, *Remarkable Relations* (Gollancz, London, 1980), pp. 197–8.
4. OM-BR, 5 August 1913.
5. *OM, I*, pp. 223–4.
6. Ibid., pp. 174–5.
7. The quotations from J. A. Cramb's letters to Ottoline are from the collection at HRC. It is a large collection and there is no clear chronological order, seasonal references being the only indication of date. It has, however, been possible to establish that the friendship began in November 1903 and ended in November 1904. Cramb's three later letters to Ottoline are clearly dated.
8. OM-BR, 11 February 1915.
9. *Ottoline* by Sandra Jobson Darroch (Chatto & Windus, London, 1976), p. 53.
10. *OM, I*, p. 148.
11. *OM, I*, p. 149.

CHAPTER 4: IMAGINATIVE IMAGES [*pp. 69–73*]
1. Miss Brenton to OM, n.d. (HRC).
2. *OM, I*, p. 181.

CHAPTER 5: BLOOMSBURY, LOVE AND ART 1907–10 [*pp. 74–91*]
1. Quentin Bell, *Virginia Woolf*, I (Hogarth Press, London, 1972), p. 124.
2. John Maynard Keynes, 'My Early Beliefs' in *Two Memoirs* (Rupert Hart-Davis, London, 1949), p. 98.

3. Ibid., p. 89.
4. Ibid., p. 103.
5. Virginia Woolf to OM, 1 January 1911, *Letters*, 1, ed. Nigel Nicolson (Hogarth Press, London, 1975).
6. Virginia Woolf to Violet Dickinson, 13? May 1909, *Letters*, 1, op. cit.
7. *Ottoline at Garsington: Memoirs of Lady Ottoline Morrell*, 1915–1918, ed. Robert Gathorne-Hardy (Faber, London, 1974), pp. 244–5 (hereafter referred to as *OAG*).
8. Roger Fry to OM, 25 March 1907 (HRC).
9. OM to Francis Hackett, 9 December 1937 (HRC).
10. Duncan Grant to OM, 5 June 1919 (HRC).
11. Lytton Strachey to Duncan Grant, 12 April 1907, quoted by Michael Holroyd in *Augustus John*, I (Penguin, Harmondsworth, rev. edn, 1976), p. 322.
12. *OM, I*, p. 141.
13. Ibid., p. 157.
14. Augustus John to OM, 30 May 1908 (HRC).
15. OM-BR, 21 February 1913 (McMaster).
16. *OM, I*, p. 178.
17. OM-BR, 27 January 1912 (McMaster).
18. Nicolette Devas, *Two Flamboyant Fathers* (Collins, London, 1966), p. 147.
19. Roger Fry, 'The Last Phase of Impressionism', *The Burlington Magazine*, March 1908.
20. Roger Fry to D. S. MacColl, 16 March 1909, *The Letters of Roger Fry*, I, ed. Denys Sutton (Chatto & Windus, London, 1972).
21. *OM, I*, p. 167.
22. Ibid., p. 191.
23. Ibid., p. 189.
24. Ibid., p. 200.

CHAPTER 6: A MAGNET FOR EGOTISTS 1909–11 [*pp. 92–107*]
1. Francis Hackett to OM, 7 May 1937 (HRC).
2. *OM, I*, p. 183.
3. Ibid., p. 184.
4. Ibid., p. 193.
5. Bertrand Russell, *Autobiography*, I

(Allen & Unwin, London, 1967), p. 202.
6. *OM*, I, p. 192.
7. Ibid., p. 186.
8. *Lytton Strachey by Himself*, ed. Michael Holroyd (Heinemann, London, 1971), pp. 119–25.
9. *OM*, I, p. 196.
10. Unless otherwise indicated, all quotations from Henry Lamb's letters to Ottoline are taken from the collection at HRC.
11. *OM*, I, p. 195.
12. Jane Harrison, *Reminiscences of a Student's Life* (L. & V. Woolf, London, 1925), p. 17.
13. *OM*, I, p. 202.
14. Ibid., original version, pp. 214–15.
15. Ibid., p. 203.
16. Lytton Strachey to Duncan Grant, 4 April 1910 (BL, Strachey add. 6288).
17. Lytton Strachey to James Strachey, 18 November 1910 (BL).
18. Lytton Strachey to James Strachey, 30 November 1910 (BL).
19. *OM*, I, p. 203.
20. Ibid., p. 207.
21. Ibid., original version, p. 211.

CHAPTER 7: AN OVERWHELMING PASSION March 1911 [*pp. 108–15*]
1. Bertrand Russell, *Autobiography*, I, op. cit., p. 203.
2. *OAG*, original version, p. 268.
3. *OAG*, appendix, original version only.

CHAPTER 8: PORTRAIT OF A RELATIONSHIP 1911–16 [*pp. 119–25*]
1. Bertrand Russell, *Autobiography*, I, op. cit., p. 70.
2. Ibid., pp. 121–2.
3. Bertrand Russell, 'The Essence of Religion', *Hibbert Journal*, 2 October 1912.

CHAPTER 9: CONFIDENCES AND INTRIGUES April 1911 [*pp. 126–36*]
1. Logan Pearsall Smith to OM, 20 April 1911 (HRC).
2. *OAG*, original version, pp. 267–8.
3. Ibid., pp. 272–3.
4. *OAG*, pp. 278–9.
5. *OAG*, original version, p. 278.

6. *OM*, I, p. 212.
7. Ibid., p. 213.
8. Ibid.
9. Virginia Woolf, *Diary*, I, ed. Anne Olivier Bell (Hogarth Press, London, 1977), 17 October 1917.
10. Logan Pearsall Smith to OM, 24 May 1911, quoted in Barbara Strachey, *Remarkable Relations*, op. cit., p. 261.
11. *OAG*, original version, p. 213.
12. Ibid., p. 276.

CHAPTER 10: THE IPSDEN CRISIS 1911–12 [*pp. 137–54*]
1. *The Collected Papers of Bertrand Russell*, 12, ed. Richard Rempel, Andrew Brink and Margaret Moran (Allen & Unwin, London, 1985), p. 105.
2. Ibid., p. 103.
3. *OM*, I, pp. 221–2.

CHAPTER 11: TRIANGULAR RELATIONSHIPS 1912–13 [*pp. 155–81*]
1. *Ludwig Wittgenstein: Personal Recollections*, ed. Rush Rhees (Rowman & Littlefield, New Jersey, USA, 1981), p. 3.
2. Bertrand Russell, *Autobiography*, II (Allen & Unwin, London, 1968), p. 57.
3. *OM*, I, p. 223.
4. *The Perplexities of John Forstice* is published in *The Collected Papers of Bertrand Russell*, 12, op. cit.
5. Russell, 6 April 1968, quoted in *Collected Papers*, 12, op. cit., p. 127.
6. *OM*, I, original version only, p. 51a.
7. *OM*, I, original version, p. 227.
8. Michael Holroyd, *Lytton Strachey*, II (Heinemann, London, 1968), p. 109.
9. *OM*, I, p. 231.
10. Ibid.
11. David Garnett, *The Flowers of the Forest* (Chatto & Windus, London, 1955), pp. 116–17.
12. *OM*, I, p. 231.
13. *OM*, I, original version, p. 232.
14. Michael Holroyd, *Lytton Strachey*, II, op. cit., p. 59.
15. PM to Lytton Strachey, 11 November 1912 (BL).
16. *OM*, I, p. 233.
17. Omitted from *OM*, I. The published version in *OAG*, p. 281,

differs radically from the original. By fusing together a visit Russell made to Churn and a later visit to Breach House, Cholsey, a much greater sense of a traumatic estrangement at Churn is suggested. The fusion was the work of the editors, Philip Morrell and/or Robert Gathorne-Hardy.
18. Lytton Strachey to Saxon Sydney-Turner, 20 November 1912, Michael Holroyd, *Lytton Strachey*, II, op. cit., p. 72.
19. *OM, I*, original version only, p. 62.
20. *OAG*, p. 123.
21. Frances Spalding, *Vanessa Bell* (Weidenfeld & Nicolson, London, 1983), p. 154.
22. *OAG*, p. 51.

CHAPTER 12: INDIAN SUMMER 1913–14 [*pp. 182–201*]
1. *OAG*, original version, p. 283.
2. Ibid., original version only.
3. Ibid., original version only.
4. *OM, I*, p. 240.
5. Ibid., p. 242.
6. *OM, I*, original version only.
7. *OM, I*, p. 244.
8. Ibid., p. 253.
9. *OM, I*, original version, p. 256.
10. *OM, I*, p. 253.
11. Ibid., p. 256.
12. Michael Holroyd, *Lytton Strachey*, II, op. cit., quoting on p. 110 an undated letter from Lytton to his brother James.
13. *H. H. Asquith: Letters to Venetia Stanley*, ed. Michael and Eleanor Brock (Oxford University Press, London, 1985), p. 94.
14. *OM, I*, p. 260.
15. Bertrand Russell, *Autobiography*, II, op. cit., p. 18.
16. *OM, I*, original version only.
17. Ibid.
18. Ibid.
19. *OM, I*, p. 288.

CHAPTER 13: NEW FRIENDS, NEW FOES 1914–15 [*pp. 202–20*]
1. *OAG*, p. 204.
2. Maria Huxley to Eddy Sackville-West, 4 May 1938, quoted by Sybille Bedford in *Aldous Huxley*, I (Chatto & Windus/Collins, London, 1973), p. 359.
3. Philip Gibbs, *Now It Can Be Told* (1920), quoted by Paul Fussell in *The Great War and Modern Memory* (Oxford University Press, London, 1975), p. 8.
4. *OM, I*, p. 277.
5. David Garnett, *The Flowers of the Forest*, op. cit., p. 22.
6. Ibid., p. 31.
7. Ibid., p. 37–8.
8. Ibid., p. 38.
9. Dora Carrington to Mark Gertler, 16 April 1915, *Carrington: Letters and Extracts from her Diaries*, ed. David Garnett (Jonathan Cape, London, 1970), p. 17.
10. Ibid., p. 21.
11. *OAG*, p. 52.
12. Dorothy Brett's unpublished memoirs, quoted by Sean Hignett in *Brett* (Hodder & Stoughton, London, 1984), p. 50.
13. *OAG*, p. 120.
14. *OM, I*, p. 272.
15. D. H. Lawrence to OM, 11? February 1915 (HRC).
16. D. H. Lawrence to Cynthia Asquith, 8 November 1915, *Letters*, II, ed. George Zytaruk and James T. Boulton (Cambridge University Press, Cambridge, 1981).
17. *OAG*, pp. 36 and 37.
18. Ibid., p. 38.
19. D. H. Lawrence to OM, 20 June 1915, *Letters*, II, op cit.
20. D. H. Lawrence to OM, 20 April 1915 (HRC).
21. *OM, I*, p. 273.
22. Ibid.
23. *OAG*, p. 65.
24. *OM, I*, p. 287.

CHAPTER 14: A PORTRAIT OF GARSINGTON 1915–28 [*pp. 223–8*]
1. L. A. G. Strong, *Green Memory* (London, Methuen, 1961), pp. 236/239.
2. *OAG*, p. 34.
3. *OM, I*, p. 101.
4. Harold Acton, *Tuscan Villas* (Thames & Hudson, London, 1973), p. 276.
5. Aldous Huxley to Frances Petersen,

7 August 1916, *Letters*, ed. Grover Smith (Chatto & Windus, London, 1969), p. 109.
6. Aldous Huxley, *Crome Yellow* (Grafton, London, 1977), p. 21.
7. Juliette Huxley, *Leaves of the Tulip Tree* (John Murray, London, 1986), p. 33.
8. *OAG*, p. 187.
9. Ibid., p. 187.
10. Ibid., pp. 255 and 256.
11. Michael Holroyd, *Lytton Strachey*, II, op. cit., p. 155.
12. Siegfried Sassoon, *Siegfried's Journey* (Faber, London, 1945), p. 21.
13. *OAG*, p. 36.
14. Ibid., p. 33.
15. Virginia Woolf, *Diary*, I, op. cit., November 1917, p. 79.
16. Juliette Huxley, *Leaves of the Tulip Tree*, op. cit., p. 43.
17. Ibid., p. 38.
18. Mrs Ada Eden, in an interview with the author, July 1990.
19. Miss Mollie Witcomb, in a letter to the author, September 1990.

CHAPTER 15: THE FIRST YEAR AT GARSINGTON 1915–16 [*pp. 239–62*]
1. *OAG*, p. 37.
2. Ibid., p. 50.
3. Ibid., pp. 46–7.
4. Ibid., p. 45.
5. Ibid., p. 96.
6. In the McMaster archive, this letter is dated as 9 September 1916, but references (not quoted here) to the Eliots being at Eastbourne and to Lawrence being in London and involved with a new magazine (*Signature*, Oct.–Dec. 1915?) suggest that the earlier date is the more plausible one.
7. *OAG*, p. 80.
8. Ibid., p. 77.
9. Lytton Strachey to James Strachey, 28 February 1916, quoted by Paul Levy in *Lytton Strachey: The Really Interesting Question* (Weidenfeld & Nicolson, London, 1972), p. 15.
10. Lytton Strachey to James Strachey, 26 January 1916, ibid., p. 8.
11. Desmond MacCarthy to Molly MacCarthy, 14 February 1916, quoted by Hugh and Mirabel Cecil in *Clever Hearts* (Gollancz, London, 1990), p. 162.
12. Desmond MacCarthy to Molly MacCarthy, 19 May 1913, ibid., p. 131.
13. *OAG*, p. 97.
14. Roger Fry to Vanessa Bell, 1916, quoted by Frances Spalding in *Roger Fry: Art and Life* (Paul Elek, London, 1980), p. 206.
15. *OAG*, p. 108.
16. Lytton Strachey to James Strachey, 31 May 1916, quoted by Michael Holroyd in *Lytton Strachey*, II, op. cit., p. 197.
17. *OAG*, p. 109.
18. Ibid., p. 116.
19. Quoted by Ronald Clark in *The Life of Bertrand Russell* (Jonathan Cape/Weidenfeld & Nicolson, London, 1975), pp. 280–1.
20. Ibid., p. 282.

CHAPTER 16: A TIME OF SADNESS 1916–17 [*pp. 263–86*]
1. Quoted by John Woodeson in *Mark Gertler* (Sidgwick & Jackson, London, 1972), pp. 217–18.
2. Dora Carrington to Lytton Strachey, 30 July 1916, quoted in *Carrington: Letters*, op. cit., p. 33.
3. Quoted by John Woodeson, *Mark Gertler*, op. cit., p. 217.
4. Dora Carrington to Lytton Strachey, 30 July 1916, *Carrington: Letters*, op. cit., pp. 32–3.
5. Dora Carrington to Lytton Strachey, 5 August 1916, ibid., p. 35.
6. Sean Hignett in *Brett*, op. cit., quoting from her unpublished papers, pp. 104–5.
7. *OAG*, p. 148, quoting a letter from Aldous Huxley to OM.
8. Ibid., pp. 149–50.
9. Ibid., p. 151.
10. Ibid., p. 152.
11. Siegfried Sassoon, *Siegfried's Journey*, op. cit., pp. 9–10.
12. Ibid., p. 23.
13. Ibid., p. 24.
14. Juliette Huxley, *Leaves of the Tulip Tree*, op. cit., p. 52.
15. Siegfried Sassoon, *Siegfried's Journey*, op. cit., pp. 47–8.
16. *OAG*, pp. 202–3.

17. Maria Nys to OM, undated (HRC).
18. *OAG*, p. 161.
19. D. H. Lawrence to Catherine Carswell, 27 November 1916, *Letters*, III, ed. James T. Boulton and A. Robertson (Cambridge University Press, Cambridge, 1984).
20. D. H. Lawrence, *Women in Love* (Penguin, Harmondsworth, 1979), p. 337.
21. Ibid., pp. 345-6.
22. Frieda Lawrence to Cynthia Asquith, 20 May 1916 (HRC).
23. D. H. Lawrence to OM, 24 May 1928, *OAG*, pp. 130-1.
24. Aldous Huxley, *Letters*, op. cit., no. 109 (undated), p. 121.
25. Dolly Ponsonby, Diary, 30 April 1918 (McMaster).
26. PM to Virginia Woolf, February 1938 (MHP).

CHAPTER 17: THE END OF AN ERA 1917–18 [*pp. 287–304*]
1. Lytton Strachey to Dora Carrington, 28 April 1917 (BL).
2. Virginia Woolf to Margaret Llewelyn Davies, 2 May 1917, *Letters*, 2, op. cit.
3. OM to Virginia Woolf, 8 August 1917 (MHP).
4. Siegfried Sassoon, *Siegfried's Journey*, op. cit., pp. 51-2.
5. OM to Siegfried Sassoon, 1917?, *Siegfried Sassoon Diaries* 1915–1918, ed. Rupert Hart-Davis (London, Faber, 1983), p. 178.
6. *OAG*, p. 188.
7. Ibid., p. 231.
8. BR–OM, 11 August 1918 (McMaster).
9. Virginia Woolf, *Diary*, I, op. cit., 29 July 1918.

CHAPTER 18: DUBLIN, TORONTO AND TIGER 1919–22 [*pp. 305–26*]
1. Lady Huxley, in an interview with the author, 19 January 1989.
2. Dorothy Brett to Julian Vinogradoff, 28 May 1969 (GP).
3. Ronald Clark, *Bertrand Russell*, op. cit., p. 392.
4. David Cecil, in his introduction to *Lady Ottoline's Album* (Michael Joseph, London, 1976), p. 10.
5. Virginia Woolf, *Diary*, II (1978), 19 February 1923. (This entry was made the day after Philip Morrell had dined alone with the Woolfs in London.)
6. Claude Reymond, in a letter to the author, 6 August 1991.
7. Mark Gertler to OM, 26 July 1922 (HRC).

CHAPTER 19: THE TRIALS OF MOTHERHOOD 1922–25 [*pp. 327–42*]
1. Frank Prewett to Siegfried Sassoon, 4 August 1923 (HRC).
2. Virginia Woolf to Barbara Bagenal, 24 June 1923, *Letters*, 3 (1977).

CHAPTER 20: MEMOIRS AND A TEST OF COURAGE 1925–28 [*pp. 345–63*]
1. Virginia Woolf to OM, January 1926 (HRC).
2. Mark Gertler to OM, 27 March 1926 (HRC).
3. Virginia Woolf to Vanessa Bell, 2 June 1926, *Letters*, 3, op. cit.
4. Walter Turner to OM, 23 April 1927 (HRC).
5. Walter Turner, *The Aesthetes* (Wishart, London, 1927), pp. 40 and 48.
6. Michael Holroyd, *Lytton Strachey*, II, op. cit., p. 573.
7. Virginia Woolf to OM, 30 May 1928, *Letters*, 3, op. cit.
8. Virginia Woolf to PM, 7 July 1939 (GP).
9. D. H. Lawrence to OM, 24 May 1928, *OAG*, pp. 130-1.
10. D. H. Lawrence to OM, 28 December 1928, *The Collected Letters of D. H. Lawrence*, II, ed. Harry T. Moore (Heinemann, London, 1962).

CHAPTER 21: FRIENDSHIPS AND RENEWALS I [*pp. 364–98*]
1. PM to Julian Goodman, 14 May 1933 (GP).
2. L. P. Hartley to OM, June 1934 (HRC).
3. The Sixth Duke of Portland to Julian Goodman, 21 April 1938 (GP).

4. OM to Samuel Koteliansky, 9 August 1936 (Koteliansky Papers, BL).
5. Beatrice Glenavy, *Today We Will Only Gossip* (Constable, London, 1964), p. 183.
6. T. S. Eliot to Julian Goodman, 21 April 1938 (GP).
7. Virginia Woolf to Vita Sackville-West, 13 November 1929, *Letters*, 4 (1978).
8. Virginia Woolf to Dame Ethel Smyth, 14 November 1930, *Letters*, 4, op. cit.
9. Virginia Woolf to Vita Sackville-West, 8 November 1932, *Letters*, 5 (1979).
10. OM to Virginia Woolf, 29 September 1933 (MHP).
11. Dame Ethel Smyth to Philip Morrell, 27 April 1938 (GP).
12. OM to Virginia Woolf, 9 November 1933 (MHP).
13. Virginia Woolf to OM, 23 February 1933, *Letters*, 5, op. cit.
14. OM to Virginia Woolf, 29 September and 16 October 1933 (MHP).
15. OM to Virginia Woolf, 10 July 1933 (MHP).
16. OM to Virginia Woolf, 22 December 1933 (MHP).
17. Virginia Woolf to OM, 31 December 1933, *Letters*, 5, op. cit.
18. PM to Virginia Woolf, February 1938 (MHP).

CHAPTER 22: FRIENDSHIP AND RENEWALS II [*pp. 399–413*]
1. Edith Olivier, *Without Knowing Mr Walkley* (Faber, London, 1938), pp. 259–60.
2. *The Journals of Edith Olivier*, ed. Penelope Middelboe (Weidenfeld & Nicolson, London, 1989), pp. 180 and 146.
3. OM to Walter D'Arcy Cresswell, 3 October 1933 (Alexander Turnbull Library, New Zealand).
4. Ibid.
5. Ibid.
6. George Barker to the author, October 1991.
7. OM to Samuel Koteliansky, 28 May 1937 (Koteliansky Papers, BL).

CHAPTER 23: THE LAST YEAR 1937–38 [*pp. 414–17*]
1. OM to Samuel Koteliansky, 18 December 1937 (Koteliansky Papers, BL).
2. Henry Yorke to PM, 22 April 1938 (GP).
3. Michael Holroyd, *Lytton Strachey*, II, op. cit., p. 5.

Appendix I

This poem by William Plomer was written on the occasion of the Book Bang, a book fair which took place in Bedford Square gardens in 1971. It is reproduced here by kind permission of Rupert Hart-Davis.

THE PLANES OF BEDFORD SQUARE

Never were the plane trees leafier, loftier
the planes of Bedford Square,
and of all that summer foliage motionless
not one leaf
had fallen yet, one afternoon
warm in the last world-peace before
the First World War.

At Number Thirty, consulate
of the very last Czar,
before a window on the tall first floor
Baron H., the consul, dreamy
with a Flor de Dindigul cigar,
saw the slow smoke
ghosting an arboreal form.

Tennis was thudding underneath the trees
on grass close-shorn.
A quick racquet flashed
the thump of a return,
and a young voice called the score
as if all was for the best
everywhere, not only on this marked-out lawn.

And all the soaring trees, a tree-of-heaven among them,
wore their enormous shawls of leaves
in full dress, over the court, over
the railed-in shade. Not one leaf,
not one, was yet to fall. On the first floor
was there yet one thought, one
forethought of compulsive and appalling war?

OTTOLINE MORRELL

Firbank had started carving hardstone
tesserae to fit his semi-precious prose,
had fondly made a bishop's daughter yearn
'Oh, I could dance for ever
to the valse from *Love Fifteen*!'
foresaw perhaps that she might burn away
without a single invitation to a ball.

In this well-ordered square the front-door yawned
of Number Forty-four,
and slowly into sunlight sailed
Lady Ottoline, *en grande tenue*, holding herself
as proudly as a rare goose swims;
she was swimming away from the grand and dull,
herself, as ever, too grand to conform.

On her right, the alertest of profiles
fronted the best of brains; her long-boned hand
rested on Bertrand Russell's arm.
On her left, poised on legs
without precedent, Nijinsky himself—
poised as if he could prance for ever
without a thought of any curtain-fall.

Nijinsky, seeing the ballet
of tennis players in white
darting between the tall, theatrical
and sepia-mottled columns of the vaulting trees,
threw out a dancer's arm, and called
in a faun's warm voice
'Ah, *quel décor!*'

The ball slapped into the net. It made the score
a dangerous deuce. A long white ash
dropped from the Baron's cigar. Peace hives
the virus of war. 'Game! And set!'
That moment under the plane trees (*quel décor!*)
was what these lines were cast to recall,
a crystal moment that seemed worth trawling for.

WILLIAM PLOMER

Appendix II

Ottoline's health continues to present a fairly insoluble mystery, but some light is thrown on her condition, or at least, on the problems her condition presented, by this letter from Bertrand Russell based on the account of Ottoline's regular physician, Dr Combe. It is printed with the kind permission of the Mills Memorial Library, McMaster University.

Bertrand Russell to Ottoline Morrell (1 June) 1912

Complicated case: 3 different troubles; what suits one is bad for the others:

(1) Arthritism
(2) Liver
(3) Nervosité

Combe fully expects to cure (1) and (2); (3) is hereditary, and can't be *cured*, tho' it will be better when the others are cured. It consists in too great sensitiveness, so that a thing which most people wouldn't feel much is felt very acutely. The headaches, which are caused by liver, come from what is physically a very small cause which would not give much pain to normal people; it is the bad nerves that make it give so much pain. He hopes in the end to get a *very great* amelioration, tho' not a complete cure. The radium is for the arthritism, and will not begin to produce its effect for two months. The full benefit will only come after eighteen months or two years from the beginning of the treatment.

There was a minor trouble that the stomach had become displaced, but this has been remedied. A quiet life, not seeing too many people, living as much as possible in the country, is very desirable; he has said nothing about it for fear of interfering or breaking up a ménage. If *Philip* will write to him, saying what is possible, he will make recommendations to you in the autumn. He would rather Philip wrote than came to see him (he might come afterwards) because he doesn't want you to guess that P. and I have been plotting about it . . .

Appendix III

All novelists draw on people they know for their characters; if libel suits had been as profitable a business as they are today, Ottoline would have stood to make a fortune from her friends. She only threatened to sue once, when she was first shown the manuscript of D. H. Lawrence's *Women in Love*, in which she appeared as Hermione Roddice. No further steps were taken. That was in 1917. By 1934, when Graham Greene portrayed her as Lady Caroline Bury in *It's a Battlefield*, she had become resilient enough to protest that his portrayal of her had been too gentle. The following is, so far as I know, a comprehensive list of the novels in which Ottoline was portrayed. Some caricatures are slighter than others – there are only hints of Ottoline in Mary Tutness, Clarissa Dalloway and Priscilla Wimbush. Mrs Aldwinkle has also been identified as Sybil Cutting, Hermione Roddice has elements in her of Jessie Chambers, Priscilla Wimbush owes something to Ida Sitwell, and Clarissa Dalloway has much more in her of Kitty Maxse than of Ottoline. Virginia Woolf, despite her frequent teasing promises to make use of Ottoline, kept her caricaturing impulses for her letters and diaries.

GILBERT CANNAN Ottoline appears as Lady Rusholme in *Pugs and Peacocks* (1921), of which the title is a direct allusion to the ménage of pugs and peacocks at Garsington; and, more faintly, as Mary Tutness in *Mendel* (1916).

JOHN CRAMB (writing under the pseudonym of J. A. Revermort) Ottoline is easily identifiable as the tall, red-haired and richly-scented Mary Fotheringham in *Cuthbert Learmont* (1910).

ALDOUS HUXLEY Ottoline was more upset by the descriptions of her friends and of life at Garsington than by the faint portrait of herself as Priscilla Wimbush in *Crome Yellow* (1921). She made no comment on the use Huxley later made of her in his portrayals of Mrs Aldwinkle in *Those Barren Leaves* (1925) and of the regal, dreamy Mrs Bidlake in *Point Counter Point* (1928).

GRAHAM GREENE Ottoline never publicly acknowledged that she had seen herself as Lady Caroline Bury in *It's a Battlefield*, but Greene later admitted that he had made use of her background.

D. H. LAWRENCE Ottoline never reconciled herself to her friend's portrayal of her as Hermione Roddice, whom she disgustedly described in her journal in 1932 as 'utterly horrible and disgusting, a Liberty mannequin, a sort of awful aesthetic Grosvenor Gallery woman'. She had, by 1918, persuaded herself that Hermione had been Frieda Lawrence's work; there are undeniable indications of Frieda's influence in this, the most famous of all literary uses of Ottoline. *Women in Love* was published in 1920.

CONSTANCE MALLESON *The Coming Back* (1933) contains a portrait of Ottoline as Magdalena de Santa Segunda.

OSBERT SITWELL Lady Septugesima Goodley, who appeared in *Triple Fugue* (1924), was described as having 'an almost masculine face', as being so tall that she looked like 'an animated public monument' and as having a voice which combined 'the peaceful lowing of cattle and the barbed drone of wasp and hornet'. The caricature was rounded off with a description of her clothes as looking like '"odd-lots" that had been bestowed upon her by a charitable theatrical costumier'. Ottoline, while irritated, decided that she did not know Osbert Sitwell well enough to be seriously upset. It was when her friends caricatured her that she felt wounded.

WALTER TURNER Ottoline had known the Turners well for several years when Turner, an Australian poet, decided to publish a skit on the Bloomsbury style of character-assassination with Ottoline appearing as its chief target as Lady Virginia Caraway. *The Aesthetes* (1927) was published while its author wisely absented himself from the country: Ottoline never forgave him.

VIRGINIA WOOLF *Mrs Dalloway* (1925) has traces of Ottoline in its main character's slightly guilt-ridden role as a giver of parties, but this is so slight that it only makes one wonder that the most observant of Ottoline's literary friends should have been so restrained about exploiting her in print.

Acknowledgements

I am most grateful to Her Majesty, Queen Elizabeth the Queen Mother, for the information and assistance she generously gave me, especially with regard to her grandmother's homes, Forbes House and the Villa Capponi, both of which played a significant role in Ottoline's early life.

It is sad that Ottoline's daughter, Julian Vinogradoff, was only able to see and approve the first two chapters of this biography before her death in 1989. I know that she felt the time had come for a new and more complete life of her mother to be written and her comments and suggestions were enormously helpful to me. I am indebted to her and to all of Ottoline's family for their kindness in allowing me unrestricted access to the private papers and for letting me see everything else that they felt might have a bearing on my subject. Their patience and enthusiasm have been tremendous and I hope that they will not feel that their time and efforts were completely wasted.

I owe a large debt of thanks, too, to all those friends and long-suffering members of my family who have been used as sounding boards for my ideas during the last three years. I received what I cannot help feeling was a most undeserved amount of tolerance and solace from my husband, Anthony Gottlieb, who merits special thanks for putting up with more hours than he can probably bear to count of discussing Ottoline's character or pondering her influence on Russell. My son, Merlin Sinclair, has been as much help as always in helping to lighten the frequent clouds of woe and despair.

Ben Zander and Lucille Kohlberg helped to make a transatlantic existence not only feasible but delightful. Writing this book would have been much harder without having such a wonderful home to go to in Cambridge, Massachusetts. The music, the walks to Harvard Square and lunches on the verandah helped to make a writer's life seem the best in the world.

Anthony Goff, Ion Trewin, John Glusman and Ellen Levine each know how much I owe them and the huge difference they have made to this book in its various stages. My grateful thanks and appreciation go also to Jane Birkett and Maggie Body and to Stephanie Darnill for her excellent index.

For interviews, the loan of letters, permission to quote from unpublished material and for help and advice, I would like to thank the following:

Brigid Allen; Elspeth and the late George Barker; Sara Beer; Quentin Bell; Anne Olivier Bell; Maria Theresa Rodriguez d'Arci de Benedetti; Lady Anne Bentinck; the Bertrand Russell Peace Foundation, Nottingham; Kenneth Blackwell, the Russell archivist; the Bodleian Library, Oxford; Lord Bonham Carter; Tony Bradshaw at the Bloomsbury Workshop; the British Library Manuscripts Room, London; Jane Brown; Sally Brown; Hart Buck; the Revd Christopher Butler; Dr William Bynum; Noel Carrington; Hugh and Mirabel Cecil; Michael De-la-Noy; His Grace, the Duke of Devonshire; Pamela Diamond; Elizabeth Divine; Carolyn Dixon; Ada Eden; Elaine Feinstein; James Fergusson; Jonathan Gathorne-Hardy; Luke Gertler; Mr and Mrs Glover at East Court; the Goodman family; Anthony Grayling; Nicholas Griffin; Rollin Hadley; Sir Rupert Hart-Davis; Anthony Hobson; Michael Holroyd; the Houghton Library, Harvard University; Anya Hurlbert; Juliette Huxley; Laura Huxley; Leonard and Rosalind Ingrams; Mary Jackson; Vivien John; King's College Library, Cambridge; Lady Pansy Lamb; the late Rosamund Lehmann; Eve Linn; the London Library; Fiona MacCarthy; Michael Maclagan; David and Kay Mathias; the Mills Memorial Library at McMaster University, Hamilton, USA (with especial thanks to Sheila Turcon); Ivan Moffatt; Ray Monk; Caroline Moorehead; Lord Moyne; Nottingham County Archives Office; Nottingham University Library (with particular thanks to Margaret Clarke); Oxfordshire County Council (with special thanks to Malcolm Graham); Gordon Partington; Frances Partridge; Lawrence Pollinger Ltd.; Dilys Powell; Anthony Powell; Peter Quennell; the Harry Ransom Humanities Research Center (with particular thanks to Cathy Henderson); the Estate of Frieda Lawrence Ravagli; Richard Rempel; Claude Reymond; the late Sir John Rothenstein; Alfred Salms Sonnenweld; Richard Sams; Jean Saxton; Major Brian Shone; the Society of Authors; Frances Spalding; Unity Spencer; Sir Stephen Spender; Barbara Strachey; the University of Sussex (with especial thanks to Elizabeth Inglis); the Tate Gallery (with particular thanks to Caroline Cuthbert); Nick Tschaikov; the Alexander Turnbull Library, Wellington, NZ; Miles Weatherall; the Wellcome Institute Library; Laurence Whistler; Harriet Whitehead; Mollie Witcomb; Fred Wolsey; the Estate of Virginia Woolf.

I must also thank a number of publishers for allowing me to quote from the following books:

Allen & Unwin Ltd (Bertrand Russell: *Autobiography*, vols I and II); Allison & Busby (Michael De-la-Noy: *The Journals of Denton Welch*); Cambridge University Press (*The Letters of D. H. Lawrence*, vol. II ed. George Zytaruk and James T. Boulton, vol. III ed. James T. Boulton and A. Robertston); Jonathan Cape Ltd (*Carrington: Letters and Extracts from her Diaries* ed. David Garnett); Chatto & Windus Ltd (Sybille

ACKNOWLEDGEMENTS

Bedford: *Aldous Huxley*; Sandra Jobson Darroch: *Ottoline*); Faber & Faber Ltd (*The Early Memoirs of Lady Ottoline Morrell 1873–1915* and *Ottoline at Garsington 1915–1928* ed. Robert Gathorne-Hardy); Siegfried Sassoon: *Siegfried's Journey*); Victor Gollancz Ltd (Barbara Strachey: *Remarkable Relations*); William Heinemann Ltd (Michael Holroyd: *Lytton Strachey*, vol. II); Hogarth Press Ltd (*The Diaries of Virginia Woolf*, vols I and II, ed. Anne Olivier Bell); *The Letters of Virginia Woolf*, vols 1, 2, 3, 4 and 5, ed. Nigel Nicolson); Methuen London (L. A. G. Strong: *Green Memory*); John Murray Ltd (Juliette Huxley: *Leaves of the Tulip Tree*); Weidenfeld & Nicolson Ltd (*The Journals of Edith Olivier 1924–48* ed. Penelope Middelboe).

Index

Note: BR stands for Bertrand Russell; OM for Ottoline Morrell; and PM for Philip Morrell

à Kempis, Thomas, 32, 157; influence on OM, 14, 25, 26, 29
Aesthetes, The (W. Turner), 330, 405; caricatures OM, 5, 353–4, 432
Alexander, F. Matthias (Alexander technique), 300
Allen, Clifford, 263–4, 315, 319
Anrep, Boris, 97, 104, 106, 129, 151, 186, 367n; invites OM to Paris, 130; Maria Nys and, 276; at Garsington, 288
Anrep, Junia, 106, 129, 213, 407
Anstruther-Thompson, Kit, 38
Apostles, the, 76, 77, 78, 121; and Wittgenstein, 173, 174
Après-midi d'un Faune, L', 167n
Ark, The (3 Gower Street), life at, 276–7; OM at, 287
Arnold, Matthew, 115
Asquith, Lady Cynthia, 212, 213, 246, 280
Asquith, Herbert, 39, 177, 182, 258–9, 298; father figure to OM, 35; infatuation with OM, 40–1, 42, 43; and PM's political career, 57, 103; and Home Rule, 192; and Gallipoli campaign, 245; attacked by Lord Alfred Douglas, 245–6; OM pleads pacifist cause to, 257–8; and Easter Rising, 259–60; caricatured in *Crome Yellow*, 261; dullness of, 294; Bedford Square sold to, 314; and Hilda Harrisson, 321; death of, 359
Asquith, Margot (née Tennant), 40, 192, 346, 355, 356, 359, 402; at Garsington, 257; and Mrs Simpson, 365; and Henry Bentinck, 258, 396; writes OM's obituary, 416
Asquith, Violet, 195, 260; OM and, 182–3, 192, 197; at Garsington, 257; quarrels with Lytton Strachey, 258
As Time Went On (Dame Ethel Smyth), 38
Auden, W. H., 403

Baddeley, Hermione, 353
Baillie-Hamilton, Griselda, 82
Baillot, Juliette, *see* Huxley, Juliette
Baker, Philip, 255
Baker-Carr, Major George, 372
Bakst, Leon, 166, 167, 169; influence on OM's clothes, 168
Balfour, Arthur, 56, 65
Baltus, George, 204
Baring, Maurice, 337, 356
Barker, George, 390, 410
Barnes, Djuna, 402
Barrie, J. M., 178, 321
Barry, Griffin, 376
Beaton, Cecil, 399, 401
Bective, Countess of, 31, 35, 40, 41, 310
Bedford, Sybille, 204, 387
Bedford Square (44), 69, 209, 345; Morrells move to, 65; birth of twins at, 66; Thursdays at, 75, 131, 166, 202q; as headquarters of CAS, 87; Nijinsky at, 167; entertaining at, 75, 131, 166, 177, 182, 205–6, 256, 427–8; Helen Dudley stays at, 197; war refugees at, 203–4; rented out, 260; sale of, 313–14; compared to 10 Gower Street, 355; William Plomer's poem on, 427–8
Beerbohm, Max, 71, 404
Beigel, Professor Fritz, 41
Bell, Angelica, 395
Bell, Clive, 78, 104, 113, 131, 132n, 172, 202, 213, 258, 282, 367n; and 'The Walker', 173–4; spreads gossip about OM, 174, 275, 281, 287, 325; at Garsington, 216n, 233, 235, 236, 241, 249, 255, 270, 271; accuses OM of superficiality, 247; affair with Molly MacCarthy, 255; describes OM as haggard wreck, 291–2; advises OM on friendship, 304; and OM's memoirs, 348
Bell, Julian, 249, 397, 398

437

Bell, Quentin, 249, 292n; describes OM in old age, 69
Bell, Vanessa, 2, 69, 75, 80, 104, 113, 204, 213, 252, 265, 389–90; and start of Bloomsbury Group, 76–7, 78; gossips about OM, 79; Fry and, 131, 132; OM's quarrel with, 133; OM visits, 168; friendship renewed with OM, 177; contempt for OM, 178, 227, 302; at OM's Thursdays, 205–6; and David Garnett, 207; at Garsington, 241, 257; death of son, 397
Belloc, Hilaire, 75, 359
Bennett, Arnold, 404
Benson, E. F., 170n
Bentinck, Lt.-Gen. Arthur (father), 11; marriages of, 12; OM's love for, 13; death of, 15
Bentinck, Arthur (later 6th Duke of Portland) (half-brother): OM's desire to impress, 12, 23; and death of father, 15; becomes 6th Duke 16–17; and Welbeck Abbey, 18, 22; marriage of, 23–4; son's christening, 27; OM's dependence on, 29; and OM's marriage, 56–7; and PM's politics, 65; rebukes OM's lifestyle, 140; financial arrangements for OM, 176n, 306; OM's visit to, 239–40; visits Garsington, 240, 337; and Julian's season, 336; and Lord William Bentinck's papers, 368; renews friendship with OM, 372, 373–5; and OM's last illness, 412, 414
Bentinck, Augusta (later Lady Bolsover) (mother), 310, 318, 346; birth of OM, 11; religious views and love of clothes, 12; admires Charles Kingsley, 14; and death of husband, 15; ill-health of, 5, 15, 24–5; and death of 5th Duke of Portland, 16; becomes Baroness Bolsover, 17; at Welbeck Abbey, 18, 19; and stepson's marriage, 23–4; takes OM to Italy, 26; illness and death of, 26–7; influence on OM, 27–8, 68; cuts OM out of will, 28, 45–6, 65, 176
Bentinck, Cecilia (later Countess of Strathmore), 26
Bentinck, Lord Charles (Charlie) (brother), 12–13, 15, 16, 17, 18, 31, 197, 335, 372; marriage of, 45; and OM's marriage, 46–7; in Gallipoli campaign, 202n

Bentinck, Rev. Charles (uncle), 26n
Bentinck, Lord Francis Morven (nephew), 197, 309, 330
Bentinck, Lord George, 17n
Bentinck, Godard, 341, 369
Bentinck, Lord Henry (brother), 12, 27, 31, 40, 47, 82, 171, 176n, 252, 306, 310, 318, 340; as MP, 56, 65, 185; loses seat, 365; as patron of modern art, 84, 86, 90, 106, 318; chairman of CAS, 87; OM as influence on, 140; as OM's favourite brother, 149–50; OM stays with, 162; in Gallipoli campaign, 202, 239; at Garsington, 249; and Margot Asquith, 258, 396; and PM's breakdown, 283; gives dance for Julian, 337; Julian as heir of, 350, 357; death of, 372
Bentinck, Hyacinth, 26
Bentinck, John, 5th Duke of Portland: and OM's name, 11; and death of General Bentinck, 15; death of, 19; and Druce–Portland case, 19–20
Bentinck, Lady Olivia ('Birdie') (sister-in-law), 31, 42, 86, 149, 162, 337; organises hospital in S. Africa, 40; and OM's marriage, 46; and death of husband, 372–3
Bentinck, Violet ('Vava'), 26, 390; good works with OM, 31, 32, 54–5; OM visits in Italy, 34; attempts reconciliation with Munthe, 37; OM distanced from, 82
Bentinck, Lord William (Bill) (brother), 12, 31; at Welbeck Abbey, 18, 19; in Florence, 26, 27; death of, 62; OM's love for, 346
Bentinck, Lord William (Governor-General of India): PM's proposed biography of, 368, 370, 417
Bentwich, Naomi, describes weekend at Garsington, 261
Berenson, Bernard, 38, 42, 52n, 60, 88
Berenson, Mary, 56, 114; describes OM in Italy, 52, 70
Bergen, George, 389, 390
Berners, Lord, 321, 328, 329, 351
Bernhardt, Sarah, 23
Birrell, Augustine, 57, 277, 288, 356, 367; on Asquith's dullness, 294; and OM's illness, 360
Black, Dora, see Russell, Dora

INDEX

Black Hall, Oxford, 44n; Morrells' home at, 40; OM's visits to, 43–4, 57, 93, 152, 153, 168–9, 183; 3-month move to, 338–9
Blindness (Henry Green), 409
Bloomsbury Group, 65–6; and OM's reputation, 2–3, 281, 293, 417; description of, 75, 76–8; OM and, 76, 77, 391, 393; character-assassination by, 78; attitude to OM, 78, 300, 360; discusses OM and Lamb, 97; condemns OM's character, 132; hears rumours of OM and Murry, 293; attitude to PM, 232, 252, 287–8
Bloomsbury Street (38), OM's lodgings at, 260, 274, 300, 315
Blunden, Edmund and Mary, 329
Blunt, Wilfrid Scawen, 73, 90
Boer War, 40, 62
Bolsover Castle, 17n; OM's love for, 20–1, 170; BR takes OM to, 220, 229
Bosanquet, Theodora, 408
Bowden, George, 270
Bowen, Elizabeth (Mrs Alan Cameron), 393, 402
Bowes-Lyon, Elizabeth (later Duchess of York; Queen Elizabeth the Queen Mother), 26n, 236n, 340, 402
Breach House, Berkshire, Morrells at, 174–5, 176, 177
Brenan, Gerald, 208
Brenton, Miss ('Brenty'), 69, 144; as OM's dressmaker, 70; and Eva Merrifield, 284–5
Brett, Dorothy, 232, 256, 262, 289, 293, 301, 306; portrait of OM, 70, 73, 268–9; OM and, 208–10, 281, 310; tears 'poor O. to pieces', 210, 247; in New Mexico, 216; paints Garsington visitors, 226; at Garsington, 227, 235, 238, 258, 263, 267–8, 276, 290, 307; and Katherine Mansfield, 269; at The Ark, 276, 287; and Maria Nys, 281; reluctant chaperone to Julian, 311–12; end of friendship with OM, 312–13, 328, 396; source of gossip, 317, 318; in *Crome Yellow*, 209, 323; in *Point Counter Point*, 324n
Brewster, Harry, 42, 394
Brideshead Revisited (E. Waugh), 330
Bridges, Robert, 303
Brooke, Margaret, Ranee of Sarawak, 210

Brooke, Rupert, 161, 166, 205
Brooke, Sylvia (née Brett), Ranee of Sarawak, 210, 290, 301; at Garsington, 232
Broughton Grange, Oxfordshire, 168; Morrells at, 169, 170–2
Browne, Katherine ('Cattie'), 23
Browne, The Very Rev. the Hon H. M., (grandfather), 12
Budberg, Baroness Moura, 333, 334, 404
Burlington Magazine, The, 60, 87
Burnley, Lancashire, 103–4, 191, 283n; PM campaigns and wins seat, 91, 99, 103–4; OM in, 103, 152–3, 177, 185–6; and PM's pacifism, 196, 252
Bury Place, BR's flat in, 152; OM at, 152–3; Helen Dudley besieges, 198
Bussy, Simon, portrait of OM, 69, 72, 182
Buxton, Rupert, 321

Cameron, Dr A. J. (OM's physician), 333, 372, 386; and OM's final illness and death, 412, 415
Campbell-Bannerman, Sir Henry, 57, 65
Cannan, Gilbert, 177, 211, 215, 319; friendship with OM, 178; and Gertler, 190, 191; OM caricatured in *Mendel*, 278, 431, and *Pugs and Peacocks*, 323, 431
Cannan, Mary, 178, 215, 319
Capri, OM visits Munthe in, 35–6
Carnaval (Schumann), 167
Carrington, Dora, 207, 256, 262, 283, 378; and Gertler, 208, 266; and OM, 210; and Garsington, 226, 234, 258, 259, 263, 288; banned from, 332n; and Lytton Strachey, 252–3, 265–7, 293, 298–9; at The Ark, 276, 281; caricatured in *Mendel*, 278, and *Crome Yellow*, 323; and PM, 282; OM visits, 308; death of, 379
Carswell, Catherine, 278, 406
Carswell, Donald, 278
Cartier, M. and Mme Jacques, 371
Casement, Sir Roger, 262; trial of, 259–60
Cavendish, Elizabeth (Bess of Hardwick), 17n
Cavendish, Sir Charles, 17n, 20
Cavendish, William, 1st Duke of Newcastle, 18, 20, 21, 220

Cavendish-Bentinck, William Henry, 3rd Duke of Portland, 12n
Cecil, Lord David, 225, 309, 337, 391, 392, 393, 401, 402, 405, 409; at Garsington, 324, 330, 331; tribute to OM, 2, 416
Cecil, Rachel (née MacCarthy), 401
Cecil Houses Trust, 365, 390
Cézanne, Paul, 86, 87; OM's interest in, 88–9; paintings in Post-Impressionist exhibition, 89, 90
Chadbourne, Emily, 163, 168; OM visits, 88, 96
Chamberlain, Joseph, 65
Chaplin, Charlie, 168, 233, 266, 322, 323; at Gower street, 378–9
Chappelow, Eric, 235
Charles I, 20, 366
Charles II, 21
Chesterton, G. K., 75
Chirk Castle, 336, 338, 348
Churchill, Winston, 131
Churn, Berkshire, 150, 171, 174; Morrells at, 172–3
Clark, Kenneth, 366
Cliff End, Studland, 68; OM at, 126; BR visits, 127–8
Codman, Ogden, 53
Cohen, Dr Harry, 412
Colefax, Lady, 356–7, 403
Colomb, Marion (later Reymond), 179, 185, 186, 320, 325, 414
Combe, Dr (physician, Lausanne), 151, 160, 166, 179
Common Reader, The (V. Woolf), portrait of Margaret Lucas in, 21, 393
Conder, Charles, 71, 75; portrait of OM, 70, 72, 73; introduces Augustus John to OM, 81; death of, 85
Conder, Stella, 73, 75
Connolly, Cyril, 394
Conrad, Joseph, 180, 327, 347; OM and, 183–4
Contemporary Art Society (CAS), 107, 133, 139, 151, 245; foundation of, 87; OM and, 88, 190
Cookie (OM's maid), 160
Cooper, Lady Diana, 22n, 341
Cooper-Willis, Irene, and BR, 200–1, 245; and Desmond MacCarthy, 255, 256
Cope, Sir William, 13
Cornford, Frances, 141, 149
Cornford, Francis, 101n

Costelloe, Karin, 114, 141
Costelloe, Ray, 114, 126
Courtauld, Samuel, 391, 403
Cox, Katherine (Ka), 161
Craig, Edward Gordon, 71
Craig, Miss (governess), 20, 22, 25, 33
Cramb, John, 64, 270, 431; infatuation with OM, 61–3
Cresswell, Walter D'Arcy, 408, 411; OM and, 406–7
Crisp, Sir Frank, 58–9
Crome Yellow (A. Huxley); OM parodied in, 204, 226, 323–4, 431; Brett in, 209; Asquith in, 261
Cruttwell, Maud, 41; as Vernon Lee *culte*, 38–9; infatuation with OM, 39
Cunard, Lady, 298
Cuthbert Learmont (J. A. Revermort) (J. Cramb), 63, 431

Dallas-Yorke, Mrs, 31
Dallas-Yorke, Winifred, *see* Portland, 6th Duchess of
d'Aranyi, Adela, 73, 205, 206
d'Aranyi, Jelly, 73, 205, 206, 273
Darroch, Sandra Jobson, 4
Darwin, Charles, 149n
Davies, Margaret Llewelyn, 313
Davies, Michael Llewelyn, 321
'Death's Brotherhood' ('Sick Leave') (S. Sassoon), 291
de Baillet Latour, Comtesse Elisalex, 239
de Chavannes, Puvis, 51, 89
de la Mare, Walter, 329, 340, 353, 361, 392, 405
de Lotbinière, Mildred, 45
de Menasce, Jean, 338
de Meyer, Baroness, 72
de Montmorency, Catherine (grandmother), 12
de Sola Pinto, Vivien, 328
Desborough, Lady, 298, 340, 350, 368, 373, 402
Diaghilev, Sergei, 6, 137, 165, 166, 182, 189, 308, 319; at Bedford Square, 167; at Garsington, 300–1
Diana of the Crossways (G. Meredith), 334n
Dickinson, Goldsworthy Lowes ('Goldie'), 90, 101, 121, 152, 203; at Garsington, 263, 307
Disraeli, Benjamin (Lord Beaconsfield), 16–17

INDEX

Dog Beneath the Skin, The (Auden/Isherwood), 403
Dormer, Ellen (OM's maid), 36, 52
Douglas, Lord Alfred, 245–6, 399
Douglas, James, 246
Douglas-Pennant, Hilda, 41, 55, 62, 82, 152, 357, 396; with OM in Italy, 33–4; infatuated with OM, 34; at St Andrews, 34–5; in Capri with OM, 35–6, and Europe, 41, 42; and PM, 45, 46, 327; and OM's marriage, 47
Druce, Thomas, 20
Druce–Portland case, 19–20
Dublin, OM visits (1919), 310–11, 313
Duckworth, Gerald, 394
Dudley, Helen, 200; BR and, 193–5, 197; OM and, 197–8, 244–5

Early Memoirs of Ottoline Morrell, The 1873–1915 (ed. R. Gathorne-Hardy), 7, 346–7
Earp, T. W., 254
East Court, Berkshire, 15, 22, 236, 374; Bentincks' life at, 13–14
Easter, rising, Dublin, 257, 259–60
Ede, James, 406
Eden, Mrs Ada, 237
Edward, Prince of Wales (later Edward VII), 22
Edward VIII and abdication crisis, 365–6
Eliot, T. S., 184, 193, 256, 315, 332, 361, 381, 408, 410, 416; BR and, 243–5; OM and, 256–7, 307, 314–15, 324, 328; marriage problems of, 348, 388–90; at Gower Street, 356; and Wyndham Lewis, 411; last visits to OM, 414, 415; tribute to OM, 2, 361
Eliot, Vivien(ne), 315, 332, 356; OM and, 243, 256, 307, 313, 314; BR and, 243–5, 261, 262, 271; mental instability of, 328, 348, 361, 388–90
Elizabeth I, 1
Elizabeth and her German Garden (Elizabeth von Arnim, later Russell), 295
Ellis (coachman), 22
Ellis, Edith (OM's cook), 205, 259
Ellis, Millie (OM's housekeeper), 205, 259, 310, 317, 326, 356, 357, 403; as PM's nurse, 284, 285, 286, 306, 318, 366, 398
Eminent Victorians (L. Strachey), 297–8
English Review, The, 211, 291n

Epstein, Jacob, 76, 84, 87, 167, 386
Esher, Lord, 208, 210, 232
'Essence of Religion, The' (B. Russell), 159; OM's influence on, 123–4
Etchells, Frederick, 167, 410n
Evans, Sir Arthur, 370

Façade (Walton/Sitwell), 308, 315, 352
Faulkner, William, 396, 404, 406
Feilding, Clothilde (née Brewster), 394
Feilding, Percy, 53, 71, 394; PM's friendship with, 42
First World War, outbreak of, 195–6; social effects of, 205; end of, 303; *see also* Gallipoli campaign
Florence, OM visits, 26–7, 34, 37–8, 51–3, 318–20
Florida, 250; D. H. Lawrence's planned commune in, 215, 246, 247, 248
Forbes House, Richmond, 26, 32, 35, 54
Ford, Ford Madox, 211
Forster, E. M., 76, 205, 214, 371, 409
Fountain, The (C. Morgan), 411
Fox, Charles James, 24
Franz Ferdinand, Archduke, 192
Frege, Gottlob, 156
Freiburg, OM visits (1923), 332–5
Fry, Helen, 79; mental instability of, 60–1; OM and, 91
Fry, Roger, 54, 72, 76, 100, 104, 107, 172, 177, 204, 354, 410; and Post-Impressionist exhibition, 6, 89–91; friendship with OM, 60–1, 75, 79; praises Cézanne, 87, 88; affair with OM, 113–14; and OM's affair with BR, 129, 140–1; quarrel with OM, 131–2, 133, 190; malicious gossip by, 152, 287, 338; at Garsington, 257; makes peace with OM, 360

Gale, Joseph, 176, 224
Gale, Miss, 177, 203
Gallipoli campaign, 202, 239, 245, 249
Galloway, Mr and Mrs, 235
Galway, Lady, 22
Garnett, Constance, 206, 334
Garnett, David ('Bunny'), 78, 214, 241, 252, 265; at OM's Thursdays, 205, 206; and OM, 207
Garsington, 6, 20, 21, 26, 54, 199, 210, 224–8, 228–30, 242–3, 249–50, 257–8, 265–72, 278, 345, 405, 418; purchased, 176–7; as refuge for

441

Garsington – *cont.*
  pacifists, 203, 235–6, 263; COs leave, 303; D. H. Lawrence and, 212, 215–16, 248–9, 362; move to, 220, 223; life at, 231–6; OM's relationship with village, 236–8; sale of, 238, 357–9; older visitors to, 240; young visitors to, 300–1; failure of farming at, 306, 327–8
Gathorne-Hardy, Robert, 340, 358; as OM's literary executor and editor of memoirs, 7, 109*n*; and Logan Pearsall Smith, 135–6, 393; at Garsington, 330, 331; and Kyrle Leng, 332; describes OM in Freiburg, 334–5; tours Europe with OM, 351
Gatty, Hester, 400
Gauguin, Paul, 89
George V, 140, 365
George VI, 26*n*, 236*n*
Georgian Poetry, 211
Gertler, Mark, 207, 209, 210, 215, 247, 256, 262, 270, 281, 289, 299, 301, 306, 308, 312, 315, 328, 360, 368, 381; painting bought by CAS, 88; first meeting with OM, 190–1; and Dora Carrington, 208, 252–3, 266; at Garsington, 233, 235, 240, 263, 288, 290, 303, 307, 327; and Cannan's *Mendel*, 278; tells OM of Bloomsbury's ridicule, 293; indiscretions of, 317, 318; tuberculosis of, 321, 341; in *Crome Yellow*, 323; and death of Tiger, 325–6; and Julian, 349, 350; and Chaplin, 378–9; attempted suicide of, 382
Gide, André, 308, 319
Gill, Eric, 90, 107, 319
Gladstone, Herbert, 57
Gladstone League, 96, 99
Glenavy, Lady (Beatrice Campbell), 250*n*, 310, 381, 382
Golden Bough, The (Sir J. G. Frazer), 101*n*
Gomme, Lionel ('Tiger'), 346; OM's affair with, 316–18, 321, 362; death of, 325, 326, 355, 404
Gomme, Mrs, 317
Gonne, Maud, 310
Goodman, Anne Arianna (OM's granddaughter), 357
Goodman, Victor, marries Julian, 357
Gordon-Lennox, Blanche, 365
Gore-Booth, Eva, 260, 263

Gorky, Maxim, 404; OM meets, 333–4, 335
Gourliau, Dr, 415
Gower Street (10), 230*nn*, 315, 355, 391; lease taken, 350; compared to Bedford Square, 355–6; Duke of Portland at, 373; Virginia Woolf's last visit to, 398; PM at, 417
Grafton Galleries, 89, 90, 91
Grant, Duncan, 65, 151, 167, 168, 175, 177, 202, 226, 230, 252, 265, 315, 389, 390, 395; portrait of OM, 69, 72, 182; lack of malice of, 80; and Lytton Strachey, 102, 171; at OM's Thursdays, 205–6, 209; and D. H. Lawrence, 211; at Garsington, 240, 241; and OM's illness, 360; in Rome, 369; tribute to OM, 2
Graves, Robert, 272, 274, 288, 291, 328
Greece, Morrells visit (1934), 370
Green, Henry, *see* Yorke, Henry
Green, Ivy (Julian's maid), 336, 356
Green-Eyed Monster, The (A. Brook) (I. Cooper-Willis), 255*n*
Greene, Graham, 409, 431
Greene, Vivienne, 409
Gregory, Augusta, 310
Grenfell, Cicely Mary, *see* Bentinck, Lady Charles
Grenfell, Fanny (Mrs Charles Kingsley), 14
Greville, Charles, PM edits diaries, 367–8
Grey, Sir Edward, 195
Grosvenor Place (13), 16, 24, 27, 45; OM at, 32, 35, 42; sale of, 176
Grosvenor Road (39), OM's first home in, 53, 54, 55, 60
Guedalla, Philip, 404
Guernsey, Lady, 202
Guevara, Alvaro ('Chile'), 288
Guinness, Bryan, 353, 402, 405
Guinness, Diana, 402

Hackett, Francis, 7*n*; OM's letters to, 29, 396, 413; on the quality of OM's friendship, 92–3; OM confesses love for Henry Lamb, 95; Morrells stay with, 368–9
Hackett, Signe, 368
Haden Guest, Mr, 348
Haigh Wood, Mrs, 389
Hale, Emily, 390
Hambleden, Lady, 340

INDEX

Hammersley, Violet, 339
Harcourt, Lord ('Loulou'), 210
Hardy, Thomas, 303, 337
Harewood, Lord, 254
Harrison, Jane, 85, 101; and BR, 138, 139, 141, 149
Harrisson, Hilda, 321, 359
Hartington, Lady, 393, 402
Hartley, L. P., 332, 370
Hassall, Christopher, 407
Hawkins-Whitshed, Elizabeth St Vincent, 12
Hawtrey, Ralph, 108, 195
Hayward, John, 389, 396, 410
Henry VIII, 20
Hermon Hodge, Sir Robert, 65
Heseltine, Philip (Peter Warlock), at Garsington, 248-9; gossips to Frieda Lawrence, 250-1; caricatured in *Women in Love*, 279
Hesse, Prince Philip of, 328
Hibbert Journal, The, 148
Hignett, Sean, 210
Hitler, Adolf, 365
Hodgkinson, Marjorie, 368
Hogarth House, Richmond, 307, 324
Holland, Morrells visit Bentinck relations, 340-1, 369
Holmes, Charles, 87
Holroyd, Michael, Lytton Strachey biography, 1, 347n, 417
Hopkins, Gerard Manley, 405
Horne, Mr (vicar, Garsington), 237
Horner, Frances, 298
Howard de Walden, Lord, 87, 192, 336, 338, 348; president of CAS, 87
Howard de Walden, Lucy, 336n
Howard de Walden, Margherita, 192, 336
Hudson, Nan, 59
Hurlbatt, Miss (tutor, St Andrews), 34
Hutchinson, Mary St John, 241, 257, 393
Huxley, Aldous, 247, 300n, 301, 303, 308, 361, 363, 412; *Crome Yellow*, Garsington caricatured in, 204, 226, 323-4, 354, 431; and Garsington, 226, 232, 235, 247-8, 263, 287; and OM, 254, 261, 353; and Maria Nys, 265, 276, 277, 281; and PM's affairs, 282; marriage of, 307; in Italy, 319, 320, 328; in OM's memoirs, 348; and Lawrence, 362, 387, 393; returns to London, 387-8; and OM's death, 416; tribute to OM, 1

Huxley, Julian, 247, 248, 254, 341, 360, 416; at Garsington, 288; marriage of 307; affairs of, 386-7; tribute to OM, 2
Huxley, Juliette (née Baillot), 248, 269, 360; and Garsington, 226-7, 229, 274; description of life at, 233-4; leaves Garsington, 290, 341; and Julian Morrell, 352-3; and Julian Huxley, 386-7; last visit to OM, 414
Huxley, Maria, *see* Nys, Maria
Huxley, Matthew, 387
Huxley, Trevenen, 248
Hyderabad, Nizam of, 370
Hyndman, Anthony, 407, 408

Il Palmerino (Vernon Lee's villa), 38, 39, 41, 53
Imitation of Christ (Thomas à Kempis), 25
Independent Labour Party (ILP), 259, 264
India, Morrells visit, 370-1
Indore, Maharajah of, 371
Ipsden, 146
Irving, Henry, 23
Isaacs, Rufus Daniel, 151
Isherwood, Christopher, 403
Italy: OM visits (1892), 26-7; (1896), 33-4, (1898-9), 37-8; (1901), 41; honeymoon in (1902), 51-3; (1913), 186-7; with Julian (1920-1), 318-20; (1931), 369; Morrells tour (1933), 369-70
It's a Battlefield (G. Greene), 431

James, Henry, 46, 54n, 131, 151, 182, 303; and Vernon Lee, 38; and Harriette Morrell, 44; friendship with OM, 59-60, 75; and Gilbert Cannan, 178; and Conrad, 183; death of, 256; Spender's projected book on, 397, 407, 408
James, William, 59, 141, 157, 180
John, Augustus, 65, 71, 72, 174, 185, 337, 379; affair with OM, 1, 7, 82-6; portrait of OM, 69, 82, 315, 387; rampant heterosexuality of, 80; meets OM, 81; 'The Smiling Woman' portrait, 87; at OM's Thursdays, 87, 206; heavy drinking of, 89, 385-6; and Lamb, 96, 97, 98; and Brett, 209; and OM's memoirs, 347; tribute to OM, 1-2
John, Dorelia (née McNeill), 174, 175, 213, 337, 385; and Augustus John, 81, 82, 84; and OM, 85, 86, 315; John's

443

John, Dorelia – *cont.*
portrait of, 87; in Paris and Provence with OM, 88, 89; introduces Lamb to OM, 95–6; affair with Lamb, 97, 100
John, Gwen, 88
Jones, Alice, 284, 287, 366, 417; has PM's child, 282–3, 285
Jourdain, Philip, 156
Joyce, James, 381, 389, 405
Julian, Mother, 41, 55, 82, 346; OM's religious fervour and, 32–3; and OM's engagement, 46; influence on OM, 61; death of, 151; and *The Perplexities of John Forstice*, 164

Karsavina, Tamara, 166
Keppel, Mrs George, 259
Keynes, Lydia, *see* Lopokova, Lydia
Keynes, Maynard, 76, 80, 121, 252, 276, 315, 367n, 374; biography of, 2; on Bloomsbury morals, 77; and the Apostles, 77, 174; OM and, 240, 293; at Garsington, 249, 263
Khan, Sir Syed Ahmed, 371
Kilmaine, Lord (great-grandfather), 12
Kingsley, Charles, 14
Koteliansky, Samuel ('Kot'), 215, 218, 308, 346, 403, 411, 413, 415; and OM, 381–2
Kramer, Franz, 180
Kuyumjian, Dikran (Michael Arlen), at Garsington, 248–9

Lady Chatterley's Lover (D. H. Lawrence), 5; OM's affair with Tiger and, 317–18; OM dislikes, 362; OM recommends, 407
Lamb, Henry, 6, 65, 79, 81, 84, 202; OM's affair with, 7, 68, 97–9, 104, 105–7, 114, 120; on OM's sense of colour, 54; portrait of OM, 69, 72, 106; egotism of, 92; OM meets, 96; Lytton Strachey and, 97, 104, 105, 126, 137, 160, 168, 170, 171, 172; moves to Peppard, 100–1, 102, 103, 107; and OM's affair with BR, 124, 129–30, 131; affair with OM renewed, 130; gossips about OM, 132, 199; as congenial companion, 143–4; seeks OM's attention, 152, 153; and PM, 161, 165; letters to OM, 163; quarrels with OM, 166; and 'The Walker', 173–4; OM visits, 337; and OM's memoirs, 347; marriage of, 384–5

Lamb, Nina, 97
Lamb, Lady Pansy, 384–5
Landmarks in French Literature (L. Strachey), 104, 141n, 160
Lausanne, OM takes cures in, 151, 160–2, 180, 320; with BR in, 162–5, 173; Julian taken to, 179; last visit to, 414
Lawrence, D. H., 83, 205, 266, 390, 416; notes OM's 'Elizabethan' quality, 1, 212; caricatures OM in *Women in Love*, 3, 278–81, 254, 432; *Lady Chatterley's Lover*, 5, 317–18; OM's first meetings with, 211; OM and, 212, 213, 254; Frieda and, 214, 240, 264–5; and Rananim project, 215–16; BR and, 217–19, 249–50, 251–2; at Garsington, 225, 226, 229, 248–9; and OM's affair with BR, 242; and banning of *The Rainbow*, 246; OM raises funds for, 246–7; hypocrisy concerning OM, 247, 393; and Aldous Huxley, 248, 387; OM's gifts to, 254; 10-year rift with OM, 281; friendship renewed, 361–3; death of, 363; OM assesses, 407
Lawrence, Frieda, 387, 396; and caricature of OM in *Women in Love*, 3, 217, 280, 323; and OM, 212, 215, 229, 249, 250–1, 382–3; quarrelsomeness of, 213–14, 240; and Lawrence, 254, 264–5; Lady Chatterley based on, 318
Lawrence and Brett: A Friendship (Dorothy Brett), 210
Leaves of a Tulip Tree (Juliette Huxley), 233
Lee, Vernon (Violet Paget), 38–9, 94, 184, 187, 200, 256, 265; influences OM on decoration, 53–4
Leng, Kyrle, 332, 334, 340, 351
Lewis, Wyndham, 182, 243, 315; OM and, 410–11
Liberal League, 56
Lind, Letty, 210
Lindsay, Violet (8th Duchess of Rutland), 22, 23–4
Living (Henry Green), 409
Look! We Have Come Through! (D. H. Lawrence), 254
Loos, Anita, 366, 387
Lopokova, Lydia, 207, 300, 301, 374
Lord Jim (J. Conrad), 400
Lucas, Margaret, *see* Newcastle, 1st Duchess of

INDEX

Lucy (groom), 'drowning' in Garsington pond, 258–9
Lytton, Judith, 73
Lytton, Neville, portrait of OM, 70, 73

Macaulay, Rose, 404
MacCarthy, Desmond, 75, 76, 94, 100, 104, 134, 182, 183, 186, 211, 310, 354; OM's friendship with, 79–80, 255, 256, 293; and OM's teacosy hat, 90, 255; at Garsington, 228–9, 258, 303, 328; affairs of, 255
MacCarthy, Molly, 174, 175, 186; OM's friendship with, 79–80, 255, 293; warlike attitude of, 202; affair with Clive Bell, 254–5; at Garsington, 303, 328; possible affair with PM, 366
MacColl, Dugald, 87, 90
MacDonald, George, 39; as OM's father figure, 32, 61
MacDonald, Louisa, 32
MacDonald, Ramsay, 196, 263, 264
Maclagan, William, Archbishop of York, and OM, 31–2, 33
Maitland, Helen, and Henry Lamb, 97, 100, 103; and Boris Anrep, 104, 106
Malleson, Lady Constance (Colette O'Neil), 263, 264; and BR, 121, 261, 277, 281, 285, 296, 297, 314, 316; and OM, 319–20; *The Coming Back*, 432
Malleson, Miles, 252, 263, 264
Man Within, The (G. Greene), 409
Manet, Edouard, 88, 89
Mansfield, Katherine, 2, 249, 250, 275, 310, 381, 401; D. H. Lawrence and, 211, 215, 264–5; BR and, 218, 243–4, 277; at Garsington, 227, 263, 269–70, 278, 288; first meeting with OM, 250n; and OM's literary style, 264; at The Ark, 276–7; gossips about OM, 281, 302; and Murry, 289–90, 299; and OM's understanding of war, 303; OM visits in Menton, 319; death of, 328; OM misses, 354–5
Marienbad, 151
Marlborough, Duchess of, 298, 322
Marsh, Edward, 191, 195, 211, 246
Marten, Dr, 334, 345; treats OM, 332–3, 348
Mary, Queen, 365
Mary, Queen of Scots, 20
Masefield, John, 303
Masood, Ross, 371
Massine, Léonide, 300, 301, 308

Massingham, H. W., 282, 288
Mathias, Ena, 60, 72n, 82, 315, 357, 368
Matisse, Henri, 88
McNeill, Dorelia, *see* John, Dorelia
McNeill, Edie, 86, 137
Mellors (gamekeeper, Bolsover), 318
Memoirs of a Midget (de la Mare), 329
Mendel (G. Cannan), 278, 431
Merrifield, Evelyn (OM's maid, Eva), 229, 284, 287, 366; has PM's child, 282–3, 285, 286; and Brett, 313n
Methuen, Algernon, 246
Mew, Charlotte, 402
Meynell, Viola, 216
Military Service Act (1916), 251
Mill on the Floss, The (G. Eliot), 122
Mirrlees, Hope, 7n, 405
Mirsky, Prince Dimitry Denovich Svyatopolk, 388, 389
"Mistral" (W. Faulkner), 396
Monet, Claude, 351
Monro, Alida, 300, 388
Monro, Harold, 300, 388n
Monroe, Harriet, 243
Montagu, Edwin, 195
Moore, G. E., 7, 75, 130; *Principia Ethica*; and Wittgenstein, 157
Moore, Thomas Sturge, 7, 375
Moravia, Alberto, 369, 390
Morgan, Charles, 411–12
Morrell, Frederica (later Peel) (PM's sister), 43, 176, 189, 338
Morrell, Frederick Parker (PM's father), 42; disapproves of PM's politics, 57, 65; death of, 82
Morrell, Harriette (PM's mother), 40, 43, 82, 93, 171, 247, 358n; OM's initial liking for, 44, 46; converted to Catholicism, 85; opens OM's letter from BR, 142–3; OM and, 153, 168, 169, 175, 197; death of, 338–9
Morrell, Herbert, 57
Morrell, Hugh St John (PM's brother), 43, 44, 284
Morrell, Hugh (son), birth and death of, 66, 67
Morrell, Julian Ottoline (daughter), 67, 68, 69, 82, 86, 102, 103, 104, 154, 160, 169, 185, 226, 229, 268, 311–12, 324–5, 348, 352–3, 370, 375; birth of, 66; relationship with OM, 67–8, 188–9; and BR, 128, 296; ill-health of, 174–5, 179, 316; in Leysin clinic, 179,

445

Morrell, Julian Ottoline – *cont.*
180, 186, 187, 188–9; at school, 290, 327; and Frank Prewett, 309; Brett's escape plan for, 312–13; two tours of Europe with OM, 318–20, 351–2; debutante seasons of, 335–8, 340–1; and Black Hall, 339; and OM's memoirs, 347; engagement to Igor Vinogradoff, 350–1; marries Victor Goodman, 357; disappointment at legacy, 372

Morrell, Lady Ottoline Violet Anne: birth and family, 11–13; childhood, 13–14; death of father, 15; at Welbeck Abbey, 18–19, 22–3, 29–31, 34; and Bolsover Castle, 20–1; in Italy, 26–7, 36, 38–9, 51–3; death of mother, 27; as young woman, 29–47; holds Bible classes, 30, 31; Continental tours, 33–4, 41; studies at St Andrews University, 34, and at Oxford, 39–40; nervous breakdown of, 41; engagement and marriage, 46–7; honeymoon, 51–3; two homes in Grosvenor Road, 53–4; early married life, 53–6; and PM's political career, 55–8, 65, 91, 95, 99–100, 104, 193; visits Spain, 64; at Bedford Square, 65–6, 75, 131, 166, 205–6, 313–14, 427–8; birth of children and death of son, 66; at Peppard, 68, 106–7, 150; and Contemporary Arts Society (CAS), 87–8, 139, 190; in Paris and Provence, 88–9; and Post-Impressionist exhibition, 89–91; 1910 visit to Continent, 100; at Studland, 126; at Marienbad, 150–1; in Lausanne, 160–3, 178–80; at Broughton Grange, 169–72; and Garsington, 176–7, 223–38, 263–75, 303, 330–2, 357–9; in Italy, 186–7; outbreak of war, 195–7; in Ireland, 310–11, 313; at Vale Avenue, 315–16; Continental tour with Julian, 318–20; in Freiburg, 332–5; Julian's coming-out season, 335–7, 340–1; at Black Hall, 338–9; works on memoirs, 7, 345–8, 408; problems with Julian, 348–53; Continental holiday, 350–2; at Gower Street, 355–7; cancer of the jaw, 360–1; Continental tour with PM, 369–70; in India, 370–1; final illness and death, 414–15
POSTHUMOUS TRIBUTES TO, 1–2, 416; influence of, 6, 416, 417; literary caricatures of, 3, 5, 246–7, 278–81, 317–18, 323–4, 431–2; portraits of, 69–70, 70–3, 106, 268–9, 385
CHARACTER AND ATTRIBUTES
appearance, 3, 31, 52, 69–70, 301, 306, 330, 386; passion for clothes, 12, 21, 70, 71–2, 168, 315; decoration, ideas on, 53–5, 74–5; desire for learning, 34, 39–40, 55, 61, 62–3, 88; emotional and intellectual insecurity, 6, 52, 94, 150; financial affairs, 4–5, 65, 176, 305–6, 313, 335, 338; generosity, 80, 83, 152, 213, 254, 274, 406; health, 5–6, 92, 100, 150–1, 160, 173–4, 179–80, 188, 219, 276, 306, 320, 332–3, 348, 356, 360, 385–6, 397, 403, 412–15, 429; pacifism, 202–4, 253, 257–8; religious beliefs, 25, 30, 122–4, 147–8, 163–4; sex, attitude towards, 4, 5, 120, 127, 149, 317; shyness, 21, 30; social problems, attitude towards, 55, 185–6
RELATIONSHIPS AND FRIENDSHIPS
artists and writers, OM's assistance to, 15, 86, 87, 91, 100, 293, 303, 313, 406, 416; circle of friends, 75–6, 80, 82; late friendships, 403–6; Herbert Asquith, 35, 40–1, 191–3, 257–9, 260–1, 359; Vanessa Bell, 133, 177–8; Arthur Bentinck, 6th Duke of Portland (half-brother), 373–5; Augusta Bentinck, Lady Bolsover (mother), 15, 25, 26–7; Lord Henry Bentinck (brother), 149–50, 372; Bloomsbury Group, 2–3, 76–8, 293–4; Elizabeth Bowen, 402; Dorothy Brett, 208–10, 268–9, 311–13; Gilbert Cannan, 178; Dora Carrington, 208, 210; Marion Colomb, 320; Joseph Conrad, 183–4; John Cramb, 61–3; Walter Cresswell, 406–7; Hilda Douglas-Pennant, 33–4, 35–6; T. S. Eliot, 314–15, 388–91; Vivien(ne) Eliot, 243, 256, 307, 313; Roger Fry, 60–1, 87, 90–1, 113–14, 131–2; David Garnett, 204–7; Robert Gathorne-Hardy, 334–5, 393; Mark Gertler, 190, 208; Lionel Gomme ('Tiger'), 316–18, 321, 356; Maxim Gorky, 333–4; Aldous Huxley, 247–8, 254, 323–4, 387–8; Maria Huxley (née Nys), 204, 219, 245; Henry James, 59–60, 183–4; Augustus John,

INDEX

80–6, 89, 385–6; Mother Julian, 32; Charles Kingsley, 14; Samuel Koteliansky ('Kot'), 381–2; Henry Lamb, 95–106, 129–31, 143–4, 165–6, 384–5; D. H. Lawrence, 211–19, 246–7, 248–9, 278–81, 361–3; Frieda Lawrence, 382–3; Vernon Lee, 38–9; Wyndham Lewis, 410–11; Desmond and Molly MacCarthy, 254–6; George MacDonald, 32; Katherine Mansfield, 269–70; Charles Morgan, 411–12; Julian Morrell (daughter), 67–8, 174–5, 179, 188–9, 316, 348; Philip Morrell (husband), 39–40, 42–7, 51–2, 74, 98, 111–12, 127, 161–2, 165, 277, 282–5, 286, 316, 326, 364–71; Axel Munthe, 35–7, 383–4; Middleton Murry, 275, 289–90; Vaslav Nijinsky, 167–8; Edith Olivier, 400–1; Logan Pearsall Smith, 133–6, 393; Dilys Powell, 402–3; Frank Prewett ('Toronto'), 309–10, 328; Bertrand Russell, 3–4, 93–5, 108–13, 114–15, 119–30, 132–3, 138–282, 288, 314, 322, 375–8, 414; Siegfried Sassoon, 271–5, 288, 291–2, 302–3, 328–9; Gilbert and Stanley Spencer, 190, 321; James Stephens, 380–1; Lytton Strachey, 101–4, 128–9, 137–8, 160–1, 170–2, 240–2, 253–4, 298–9, 378–80; Walter Turner, 329–30, 353–4; Ludwig Wittgenstein, 157–8; Virginia Woolf, 2–3, 69, 78–9, 287, 292, 295, 299–300, 322, 324–5, 331, 346, 355, 360–1, 391–8; Henry Yorke (Henry Green), 408–9, 416–17

Morrell, Philip Edward, 5, 46–7, 64, 71, 74, 79, 85, 86, 89, 126, 205, 230, 231, 233, 316, 327–8; and OM's memoirs, 7, 346, 347, 364–7; character of, 42, 43; first meetings with OM, 42, 43; OM visits family, 43–4; proposes to OM, 45; marries OM, 47; physical relationship with OM, 51–2, 111–12, 127, 316; on honeymoon, 51–3; political career, 55–8, 65, 91, 93–4, 95, 99–100, 102, 104, 108, 140, 152, 185, 195, 283*n*; birth of twins and death of son, 66; relationship with Julian, 67, 169; affairs of, 68, 80, 98, 232, 282–6, 366; death of father, 82, 84; and OM's affair with BR, 109, 110, 111–12, 119, 127, 134, 135, 138, 146, 261; and Lamb, 101, 104, 144, 161, 165–6; in Europe, 151, 179, 186, 319–20, 368–70; as portrayed in OM's journals, 165; and Garsington, 176, 224, 229, 236, 237–8, 306, 313, 318, 327–8, 357–8; nervous collapses of, 192–3, 283–4, 286, 287, 309, 366; pacifism of, 195–6, 235, 251, 252, 253; campaigns against *Rainbow* ban, 246, 247; seeks pardon for Casement, 260; increasing remoteness of, 277, 278; caricatured in *Women in Love*, 279; Sassoon describes, 288; financial difficulties of, 305–6, 313; and Virginia Woolf, 309, 325, 355, 397–8; and death of Tiger, 326; closer relationship with OM, 327; death of mother, 338–9; and Julian's engagement, 350; works on Greville's diaries, 367–8; in India, 370–1; and OM's last days, 414–15; after OM's death, 395, 416, 417

Morton, Cavendish, 71
Mrs Dalloway (V. Woolf), 232, 432
Munthe, Axel, 46, 347; OM's affair with, 35–7, 45, 51, 310; visits OM in 1929, 383–4
Murder in the Cathedral (T. S. Eliot), 390
Murray, Gilbert, 76, 101*n*
Murry, Arthur, 289
Murry, John Middleton, 383; D. H. Lawrence and, 211, 215, 264–5; BR and, 218; at Garsington, 249–50, 263, 270, 278, 288; OM and, 275–6, 290, 329, 354; at The Ark, 276; Katherine Mansfield and, 289–90; review of *Counter-Attack*, 299
Mussolini, Benito, 369
Mysticism and Logic (B. Russell), 124

Nation, The, 282, 299, 367
National Art Collections Fund (NACF), 87
National Portrait Gallery, 87
Needham, Francis, 368
Neville, Agnes, 71–2
Nevinson, H. W., 263
Newcastle, 1st Duchess of (Margaret Lucas), 301, 393; OM influenced by, 3, 21, 70, 76, 220
Newington, Oxfordshire, 59, 61, 69, 75
Nightwood (D. Barnes), 402

Nijinsky, Romola, 189, 373
Nijinsky, Vaslav, 6, 67, 137, 151, 165, 166, 301; and OM, 163, 167–8, 189; compares OM to giraffe, 182
Nijinsky Foundation, 167
Noble, Cynthia, 329–30
No-Conscription Fellowship (NCF), 251, 262, 264
Noel, Irene, 255
Norton, Harry, 113, 186, 267, 319
Nys, Maria (later Huxley), 209, 248, 257, 308, 361, 362, 387; and OM, 204, 245, 277; suicide attempt of, 219; at Garsington, 227, 229, 233, 261; and Huxley, 265; and Anrep, 276; and PM, 281, 284; marriage of, 307; in Italy, 319, 320, 328; OM blames for *Crome Yellow*, 323, 354; and OM's death, 416

O'Faolain, Sean, 406
Olivier, Edith, 400–1
Omega Workshops, 133, 410n
One-Way Song (W. Lewis), 410
Ottoline at Garsington 1915–18 (ed. R. Gathorne-Hardy), 7, 109n, 113, 219n, 221, 346–7
Owen, Wilfred, 405

Paris: OM's early visits to, 22; (1892), 26; (1909), 88; (1910), 90, 101; (1911), 130; (1920), 319; (1926), 351
Partridge, Ralph, 208, 332n
Paul, Humphrey, 195
Peacock, Thomas Love, 232–3
Pearsall Smith, Alys, *see* Russell, Alys
Pearsall Smith, Hannah, 56, 93, 94, 133
Pearsall Smith, Logan, 52, 59, 60, 72, 78, 126–7, 339, 354, 393; PM's friendship with, 42, 44; OM attends lectures with, 55, 57; and OM, 74–5; introduces BR to PM, 93–4; and affair between OM and BR, 133, 134–6, 141, 194
Pears, Mr, 58
Peppard Cottage, Henley, 91, 104; Morrells rent, 68; Julian at, 82, 144; Lamb and OM at, 97, 98, 100; Lamb moves to studio, 100–3; Strachey joins Lamb at, 101–2, 103; OM's dissatisfaction with, 107; BR and OM at, 136, 138, 143; sale of, 150
Perplexities of John Forstice, The (B. Russell), 124, 163–4

Petrushka, 168
Peverel of the Peak, 17n
Phèdre (Racine), 23
Picasso, Pablo, 88, 308, 319
Plomer, William, 1, 397, 402, 407, 409; 'The Planes of Bedford Square', 427–8
Poetry Bookshop, 300
Poetry Review, 388n
Point Counter Point (A. Huxley), 324n, 387, 431
Ponsonby, Arthur, 196
Ponsonby, Dolly, 285
Portland, 6th Duchess of (née Winifred Dallas-Yorke), 373; marries Duke of Portland, 24; supervises OM's season, 25; and OM's Bible classes, 30; introduces OM to Axel Munthe, 35; and OM's marriage, 46–7
Portland, 6th Duke of, *see* Bentinck, Arthur
Post-Impressionist exhibition (1910), 6, 89–91
Pound, Dorothy, 315
Pound, Ezra, 243, 315
Powell, Anthony, 408
Powell, Dilys, 405; and OM, 402–3
Powell, Nanny Jane ('Powie'), 15, 16, 17; guest at Garsington, 233, 288
Powys, Theodore (T. F.), 368
Prewett, Frank ('Toronto'), 302, 354; OM and, 308–10; Brett and, 312; and Garsington farm, 321; swindles PM, 327–8; and Julian, 349n
Principia Ethica (G. E. Moore), 77
Principia Mathematica (B. Russell and A. N. Whitehead), 112, 159
Principles of Mathematics, The (B. Russell), 156, 159
Problems of Philosophy, The (B. Russell), 141, 147–8
Prussian Officer, The (D. H. Lawrence), 211
Pryde, James, portrait of OM, 70–1
Pugs and Peacocks (G. Cannan), 323, 431

Rainbow, The (D. H. Lawrence), 219, 407; banning of, 246, 247
Rananim, D. H. Lawrence's plan to establish, 215–16, 246, 247, 248
Rau, Dr, 360
Ravagli, Angelo, 383
Raverat, Jacques, 205

INDEX

Read, Herbert, 405
Renan, Ernest, 31
Reymond, Jean, 320n
Ripon, Lady, 166, 182, 190, 300
Ritchie, Professor, 34
Rome, 37, 41, 51, 186–7, 320–1, 369
Rootes, Miss, 33, 34
Rosebery, Lord, 56
Ross, Robert, 259, 263, 271, 272, 302; Lord Alfred Douglas and, 245–6
Rothenstein, William, 190, 278
Rowse, A. L., 332
Runciman, Steven, 374
Russell, Alys, 56, 93, 94, 125, 171, 199, 213, 339; BR's wish to leave, 109; and BR's affair with OM, 111, 112, 113, 114–15; and Evelyn Whitehead, 125, 141; threatens divorce, 133–4, 135; agrees to parting, 136, 152
Russell, Bertrand Arthur William (3rd Earl), 1, 3–4, 61, 107; and OM's memoirs, 7, 347, 377; takes OM to Bolsover, 20–1, 220; OM's letters to, 33–4, 63, 183, 191; blindness to the effect of colour, 54; OM admires eloquence of, 57; egotism of, 92; introduced to PM, 93–4; attracted to OM, 94–5; love-letters to OM, 108, 109–10, 115, 142; start of the affair, 108–10; tries to persuade OM to leave PM, 109, 110; and OM's relationship with PM, 111–12; 'last' meeting with OM, 113, 114; affair continues, 114–15, 119–25, 131, 214-15; physical relations with OM, 120–1, 127, 128, 149, 155–6, 185, 187; and OM's religious beliefs, 121, 122–4, 147, 154, 170; with OM at Cliff End, 126, 127–8; news of affair spreads, 129–30, 139; OM visits in Cambridge, 130; Alys threatens divorce, 133–6; Evelyn Whitehead negotiates to end affair, 140–1; and PM, 138, 161–2, 261; work on Spinoza, 141, 142; at Peppard, 143; jealous of Lamb, 144; wants child by OM, 66n, 144–6, 187–8; and Julian, 144, 187; depressions of, 145, 180; quarrel at Ipsden, 146; and *The Problems of Philosophy*, 147–8; in Marienbad with OM, 151; settles at Bury Place, 152; quarrels with OM, 152–3; and Wittgenstein, 156–60, 174; reconciliation and further quarrel, 162; in Lausanne with OM, 162–3; and *The Perplexities of John Forstice*, 163–4; at Broughton, 169–70; OM analyses feelings for, 173; criticises OM as mother, 175, 179; feels OM's growing coldness, 180–1, 261–2; OM reviews affair with, 182, 339–40; in Rome, 186–7; and Liese von Hattingberg, 187; lecturing at Harvard University, 188, 193; and Helen Dudley, 193–4, 197–9; pacifism of, 196–7, 203, 251–2; and Irene Cooper-Willis, 200–1, 225n; at OM's Thursdays, 206; D. H. Lawrence and, 217–19, 249–50, 254; at Garsington, 229, 235, 242–3; and Vivien(ne) Eliot, 243–5, 261, 271; trial of, 262; and Katherine Mansfield, 277, 278, 281; wishes to form new relationships, 281–2, 285; no longer in love with OM, 288–9; in Brixton Prison, 295–6; intimacy with OM renewed, 296–7; second marriage and birth of son, 314, 316, 322, 333; in China, 320–1; false report of death of, 321; in *Crome Yellow*, 323; and OM's illness, 360; and OM's attitude to marriage, 375–6; and Peter Spence, 376, 378, 409; memoirs of, 377; OM seeks financial help for, 414
Russell, Dora (née Black), 297, 327, 332, 362; BR and, 314, 316, 320; marriage and birth of son, 322; influence on BR, 333; and Peter Spence, 376, 378, 409
Russell, Elizabeth, 295
Russell, George (Æ), 310, 405
Russell, John Francis Stanley (2nd Earl) (Frank), 295, 320
Russell, Lady John, 121–2, 323
Russell, Lord John, 93
Russell, John, 322, 376
Russell, Kate, 376
Russian Ballet, 166, 300–1, 319

Sackville, Lady Margaret, 263, 264
Sackville-West, Edward (Eddy), 204, 309, 388, 416; at Garsington, 330, 331, 332
Sackville-West, Vita, 355, 391, 393
Sands, Ethel, 61, 75, 108, 133, 140, 151, 184, 277, 341, 348, 355, 357, 370, 396, 408; OM's friendship with, 59–60; dinner-parties of, 80, 81; and OM's affair with BR, 134, 135; and sale of

Sands, Ethel – *cont.*
  Bedford Square, 313–14; lends Chelsea house to OM, 315, 340, 341
Sanger, Charles, 75, 181, 203, 263
Sanger, Dora, 79–80, 203, 263
Santayana, George, 249, 406, 414
Sargent, John Singer, 46, 75
Sassoon, Siegfried, 301, 308, 324, 327, 331, 339, 354, 360, 390; describes Garsington, 229, 273–4; first visit to, 271–2; OM and, 272–3, 274–5, 277, 285, 294, 309–10; growing pacifism of, 288; OM visits in Edinburgh, 291–2; and *Counter-Attack* review, 299; accuses OM of artificiality, 292, 302; OM introduces poets to, 303; loyalty to OM, 328–9, 350; on holiday with Morrells, 351–2; and Stephen Tennant, 399–400
Schepeler, Alick, 82
Schweitzer, Albert, 387
Scott, Henry Warren ('Chéri'), 26n
Scott, Louise Warren (Aunt Louise Bentinck), 26–7, 31, 33, 34, 38, 224
Selected Letters (D. H. Lawrence), 387
Sen, Boshi and Gertrude, 371
Shaw, George Bernard, 200, 245, 404
Shaw, Glen Byam, 351
Shearman, Montague, 302
Shelley, Percy Bysshe, 115
Sheppard, Sir John, 288, 324, 374
Sherwood Park Clinic, Tunbridge Wells, 412, 414, 415
Shove, Fredegond, 232, 235, 264, 278, 283, 303–4, 325
Shove, Gerald, 232, 235, 278, 283, 303–4, 325
Shrewsbury, Gilbert, Earl of, 17n
Sickert, Walter, 1, 80, 315, 318, 409
Siegfried's Journey (S. Sassoon), 272, 288
Silcox, Lucy, 154, 288, 290, 316
Simpson, Mrs Wallis, 365
Sinn Fein movement, 260; OM's support for, 313, 315
Sitwell, Edith, 315, 360, 393, 402
Sitwell, Osbert, 301, 302, 352, 360; *Triple Fugue*, 323, 354, 432
Skidelsky, Robert, 2
Slade School of Art, 60, 190, 207
Smith, Billy and Jimmie, 340, 353
Smith, Miss Nelson, 66
Smyth, Dame Ethel, 38, 396, 398, 405; and OM, 394–5
Snowden, Philip, 259

Somerville College, Oxford, 271; OM studies at, 39, 41
Sound and the Fury, The (W. Faulkner), 404
South Oxfordshire, PM as Liberal candidate for, 57; canvassing in, 58–9, 94, 95; PM wins seat, 65, and loses it, 91, 96
Spain, OM visits (1904), 64
Spanish Civil War, 397
Sparrow, John, 405
Spence, Patricia (Peter), and BR, 376, 377–8, 409, 414
Spencer, Gilbert, 88, 331, 341, 349, 359, 368; OM and, 190, 321
Spencer, Hilda, 386
Spencer, Stanley, 190, 202, 207, 331, 386
Spender, Stephen, 397, 405, 409; OM and, 407–8
Spinoza, Benedict, 141, 142
Spoils of Poynton, The (H. James), 44
Sprott, Sebastian, 331, 409
St Andrews University, Scotland, OM studies at, 34, 40
St Anne's Hill, Chertsey, 24, 25, 27, 29, 37
Stamfordham, Lord, 260
Stanley, Venetia, 192
Stawell, Melian, 55, 62
Stein, Gertrude, 88, 406
Stein, Leo, 88
Stephen, Adrian, 167
Stephen, Sir Leslie, 66
Stephen, Thoby, 76, 77
Stephen, Vanessa, *see* Bell, Vanessa
Stephen, Virginia, *see* Woolf, Virginia
Stephens, James, 311, 359, 404; at Gower Street, 380–1
Story of San Michele, The (A. Munthe), 383
Strachey, James, 76, 102, 103, 192, 206, 347n
Strachey, Lytton, 2, 72, 75, 79, 80, 121, 126, 130n, 151, 160–1, 163, 178, 179, 283, 354, 369, 373; biography of, 1, 417; friendship with OM, 2–3, 6, 102, 137–8, 170–3, 378–9; and Bloomsbury Group, 76–7; Lamb and, 96–7, 99, 101–4, 105, 153, 165, 166, 168; *Landmarks in French Literature*, 104, 141n, 160; illness of, 128–9; gossips about OM, 137–8, 199, 378–9, 391–2; suspected of being OM's lover,

INDEX

142–3; and Nijinsky, 167; and BR, 173, 174, 262, 298; depression of, 175, 186; and Asquith, 192, 258, 259, 298; conscription tribunal of, 252, 253, 287; attitude to war, 195, 197; and Dora Carrington, 208, 252–3, 265, 266–7, 293; and Garsington, 227–8, 232, 234, 236, 240–2, 249, 263, 265–6, 278, 332, 359; *Eminent Victorians*, 297–8; growing estrangement from OM, 298–9, 378; OM visits, 308; and OM's memoirs, 347, 348; visits Gower Street, 356, 378–9; and OM's illness, 360; and Greville's diaries, 367–8; death of, 379
Strachey, Marjorie, 206, 209
Strachey, Philippa, 338
Strong, Arthur, 31, 41, 42, 394; disapproves of PM, 44; death of, 62
Strong, Eugenie (née Sellers), 31, 41, 42, 62, 184, 394; disapproves of PM, 44, 45
Strong, L. A. G., 223, 331
Stuart, Arabella, 20
Studland, *see* Cliff End, Studland
Sturgis, George, 414
Sturgis, Howard, 60
Suhrawardy, Hussein, 248
Sullivan, J. W. N., 294, 295, 410, 412
Sullivan, Sylvia, 294
Sykes, Christopher, 353
Symons, Arthur, 72
Synge, John Millington, 115

Tate Gallery, 87
Taylor, Gordon, 360
Taylor, Walter, 315, 324, 331
Taylour, Lady Olivia, *see* Bentinck, Lady Olivia
Tennant, David, 353
Tennant, Stephen, 233, 253, 401; and Sassoon, 399–400
Tessier, Valentine, 203–4
Theory of Knowledge, The (B. Russell), 180
Those Barren Leaves (A. Huxley), 324n, 431
Three-Cornered Hat, The (de Falla), 308
Tiger, *see* Gomme, Lionel
Tilden, Philip, 341
Times, The 13, 166, 367
Titchfield, Ivy, 340, 378
Titchfield, Marquis of (William Arthur Bentinck, later 7th Duke of Portland) (Sonnie), 197, 337, 340, 365, 378

Tomalin, Claire, 2
Toronto, *see* Prewett, Frank
Townshend, Mildred (Billy) (Julian Morrell's nanny), 175, 185; in Switzerland, 179, 188, 189
Tree, Iris, 271
Tree, Viola, 340n
Trefusis, Violet, 259n
Trevelyan, Mrs Hilda, 167
Triple Fugue (O. Sitwell), 323, 354, 432
Turner, Delphine, 329–30, 349
Turner, Walter, 329–30, 346, 349, 405; and *The Aesthetes*, 330, 353–4, 432

Union for Democratic Control (UDC), 203

Van Gogh, Vincent, 88, 90
Venice, 90, 100
Victoria, Queen, 17, 341
Villa Capponi, Fiesole; OM visits, 26–7, 28, 37, 51; and Garsington, 224
Vinogradoff, Igor, 349; engagement to Julian, 350–1
Vinogradoff, Sir Paul, 349
Vittoz, Dr Roger, 158–9, 307, 328; treats OM, 179–80, 181, 182, 184
Vollard, Ambrose, 88
von Hattingberg, Liese, BR and, 181, 185, 187
von Richthofen, Baron, 212

Wainwright, Dr (OM's physician), 150
Walter family, 13, 15
Walton, William, 315
Warren, Dorothy (niece), 169, 175, 247, 306, 307; holds exhibition of Lawrence paintings, 362–3
Warren, Edward, 53
Warren, Margaret (née Morrell) (PM's sister), 43, 174, 176, 338
Waste Land, The (T. S. Eliot), 334
Water Babies, The (C. Kingsley), 14
Waterlow, Sidney, 132, 323
Waugh, Evelyn, 330, 401
Webb, Beatrice and Sydney, 56, 67
Weekley, Ernest, 214, 215
Welbeck Abbey, 17, 18–19, 22, 24, 25, 29–30, 45, 78, 236, 239–40, 337, 391, 415
Wells, H. G., 32, 245, 375; OM at party of, 322–3; at Gower Street, 404–5
Wertheimer, Ashley, 72n
Wharton, Edith, 53–4, 59, 224
Whistler, Rex, 401

Whitehead, Alfred North, 147, 197
Whitehead, Evelyn, 147, 148, 151, 153, 197, 200; and OM's affair with BR, 112–13, 125, 135
Wilde, Oscar, 23, 245, 399
Wilder, Thornton, 404
Wilhelm II, Kaiser, abdication of, 303; OM meets, 341, 369
Wilkins, Percy, 229
Witcomb, Mollie, 237, 238
Witcomb, Philip, 237
Wittgenstein, Ludwig, 153, 154, 218; and 'The Essence of Religion', 148; and BR, 156–9, 244, 376; and the Apostles, 173, 174; joins Austrian army, 197
Wolff, Charlotte, 387, 390
Women in Love (D. H. Lawrence), 361, 407; OM caricatured in, 3, 217, 251, 278–81, 431, 432; quarrel following, 318
Woolf, Leonard, 78, 213, 398–9; engagement to Virginia, 163; and Garsington, 232–3; and OM, 307, 369n
Woolf, Virginia, 75, 76, 104, 105, 132n, 177, 213, 241, 287, 290, 292, 301, 302, 367n, 369n, 378, 379–80, 388, 390; describes OM's beauty, 2, 69; conflicting attitude to OM, 2–3, 79; and start of Bloomsbury Group, 76–7, 78; charmed by OM's title, 78–9; at Bedford Square Thursdays, 131; and Fry and OM, 132, 133; announces engagement, 163; describes life at Garsington, 232; and OM's literary style, 264; PM and, 286, 309, 325, 355, 398; describes OM and villagers, 295; and OM's expectations of her friends, 299–300; approves of OM's generosity, 307; and OM's alleged attempt to meet Chaplin, 322–3; at Garsington, 324–5, 331; and OM's memoirs, 346, 347–8; and Julian's engagement, 350; and *The Aesthetes*, 354; and OM's move to Gower Street, 356; and OM's illness, 360–1; and abdication crisis, 365–6; friendship with OM flowers, 391–8; writes OM's obituary, 416; letters and diaries concerning OM, 417
Wreckers, The (E. Smyth), 394

Yeates (OM's coachman), 234
Yeats, W. B., 67, 308, 395, 408; at Garsington, 313, 324, 332; and OM's affair with Tiger, 317; at Gower Street, 359, 361, 392; end of friendship with OM, 405
Yorke, Henry (Henry Green), OM and, 408–9; tribute to OM, 2, 416–17
Young Visiters, The (Daisy Ashford), 307
Youth of Parnassus, The (L. Pearsall Smith), 44